Westbound No. 1 crosses Little Auglaize River near Melrose, O., in 1910. American 120 was one of three O's rebuilt with slide-valve cylinders. — *Collection of E. F. Wolf.*

THE NICKEL PLATE

STORY

BY JOHN A. REHOR

A KALMBACH  PUBLICATION

Library of Congress Catalog Card Number:
65-27730

To my wife Shirley

First printing, 1965. Second printing, 1967. Third printing, 1971.

Contents

Foreword

IN the 1880's it was common to point to the Nickel Plate Road as a prime example of the "unnecessary railroad," built parallel to an existing carrier to gain entry into a freight pool, or in hopes of sale for its nuisance value. Unlike many such railroads (notably the narrow gauge that became the Nickel Plate's Clover Leaf District), the Nickel Plate was an excellent piece of engineering. Direct, flat, straight, its main line was one of the glories of Eastern railroading, an asset that was to serve it well throughout its history.

Indeed, the Nickel Plate's origins and history were to suit it better for the railroading of our own day than for that of its early years. Its lack of branches proved an unmitigated blessing. The neglect of its passenger service during the long period of New York Central control prevented it from having a large volume of redundant passenger facilities, or from needing a re-engineering away from passenger orientation of the sort the Central itself has had in recent years. The Central's long neglect of the Nickel Plate's motive power led to rapid replacement in the 1920's and 1930's. By 1940 the Nickel Plate had an admirable fleet of modern steam locomotives that few Eastern roads could match. The financial problems which prevented double-tracking most of the line left it ideal for C.T.C. installation. Finally, the road's failure to build east of Buffalo, often a handicap in the past, had helped make the Nickel Plate the strongest Eastern railroad by the 1950's. The Lackawanna was left to climb the mountains, haul the commuters, pay the New Jersey taxes, and run the ferryboats.

Only in the poor physical plant of the Clover Leaf was history unkind to the Nickel Plate. The undulating right of way of the converted narrow gauge was the curse of Nickel Plate operating men for years. Whatever its weaknesses, the Clover Leaf did bring the Nickel Plate into St. Louis, just as the old Lake Erie & Western brought it into Peoria. The Nickel Plate by the 1920's had a lean system of main lines fanning from Buffalo and Cleveland to the three major Midwestern rail centers. The road became so attractive by modern standards that it was a prime merger candidate from the middle 1920's to the present.

In reading these pages, one understands much of the motivation for the Nickel Plate's merger with the Wabash into the Norfolk & Western system. Jay Gould's failure to secure control of the Nickel Plate while it was abuilding forced him to arrange an entry into Buffalo for his Wabash by trackage rights through Ontario on the Grand Trunk. This has never been an entirely satisfactory arrangement, partly because it involves an expensive ferry operation on the Detroit River. Similarly, the Clover Leaf, built as a cheap effort to parallel the Wabash main line from Toledo to St. Louis, has always been an expensive line to operate. The union of the Nickel Plate and Wabash in 1964 gave promise of solving both problems by diverting Buffalo freight to the Nickel Plate and St. Louis freight to the Wabash.

Particularly in railroading, where investment is so largely irrecoverable, the past and present are integral. It is folly to separate the industry's history from its economics. Happily, John Rehor is not an author who sets up such a dichotomy. His book appears almost simultaneously with the disappearance of the Nickel Plate from the *Official Guide* as an independent entity, but this volume is no obituary. In it we learn what made one of our strongest railroads great. Even though the name "Nickel Plate Road" has joined the line's handsome Berkshires and Hudsons in its history, this is a book to help us understand its future.

George W. Hilton.

Washington, D. C.
1965

Introduction

THROUGHOUT its tumultuous 83-year career the late Nickel Plate Road was never really regarded as an enduring institution. It was born without ceremony on a Thursday afternoon in February 1881, sired by a banker, an investment broker, an importer of tea, a fur dealer, and a merchant who had made a fortune selling supplies to the Union army. George Seney and the other incorporators of the New York, Chicago & St. Louis were not developers or builders in the true sense but neither were they of the breed of plunderers typified by Jubilee Jim Fisk and Jay Gould. They were ordinary opportunists living in a masculine era of uninhibited individual enterprise, monopoly, and financial manipulation. This was a time also when it cost more to ship a barrel of flour to New York from Columbus than from Minneapolis, and a railway was often a community's only tie with the rest of civilization.

A bitter reprisal for a breach of faith, a shrewd speculation, and an instrument of self-preservation, the new Seney road ended the most jealously guarded rail monopoly in America. Thus conceived, the nickel-plated railroad was fated to be the perennial orphan child of the East. Even before it ran a train, the road became a pawn in a spectacular power struggle between the two titans of finance, Gould and Vanderbilt. Three days after opening the Nickel Plate, the promoters sold out to the Vanderbilt-controlled Lake Shore & Michigan Southern which subtly restrained the road for many years. Subsequent masters often seemed more concerned with their personal ambitions than with the Nickel Plate's development as a permanent institution. All the same, this Spartan of railroading evolved from a frail and transitory enterprise to one of the strongest and most highly regarded railway systems in America.

Constructed in a matter of 500 days, the Nickel Plate connected Chicago and Buffalo with a 513-mile road characterized by long tangents, mild grades, and impressive bridges. It was built at great cost through a well-developed region already tapped by many railroads. There was, in fact, no town of consequence on the line not already touched by a railway, and the five states served ranked from first to sixth in terms of railroad mileage. Unlike most American roads, this was a private enterprise in the strictest sense, for no public assistance was sought or received. The company did not even offer its stocks on the open market. Records indicate that the Nickel Plate bought virtually all of its right of way, often at prices greatly inflated above normal market value.

The Nickel Plate was never heavily industrialized, a circumstance largely attributable to its late advent and the government of its affairs for 34 years by the competing Lake Shore. Prior to 1949 the road originated less than a fourth of its freight business and was extraordinarily dependent on bridge or overhead traffic. Lacking even a modest reservoir of captive business, the railroad grubbed out a living in an intensely competitive transportation arena purely on the strength of the service it rendered. Hence this became a proposition dedicated to the science of moving high-grade freight with dependability and dispatch. Indeed, the Nickel Plate was so adroit at its calling that it came to be synonymous with the fast manifest freight train.

From the beginning, the single-track Nickel Plate specialized in forwarding livestock, dressed meat, and other perishable foodstuffs requiring fast transit from Chicago to connecting lines at Buffalo. The congested LS&MS encouraged the diversion of such time freight to its vassal, and before long the Nickel Plate was famous as the "Meat Express Line." The development of passenger service in competition with the parent road was greatly retarded, however. Nickel Plate express trains running through between Buffalo and Chicago did not make their appearance until the tenth anniversary of the road's opening. Thereafter only a modest schedule of passenger trains was offered, and these became noted more for comfort and convenience than for speed.

Expansion of the Nickel Plate and its development as a powerful force in Eastern railroading followed the road's 1916 sale to the brothers Van Sweringen. Guided by the New York Central's Alfred H. Smith, the Cleveland realtors by 1924 were proposing the Nickel Plate as the fourth major Eastern system — a 13,000-mile giant equal in rank to the NYC, Pennsylvania, and Baltimore & Ohio. Although the I.C.C. thwarted this bid, the Nickel Plate was allowed to absorb two lesser roads which grossly enhanced its competitive position. The Lake Erie & Western afforded access to Indianapolis and Peoria; and the Clover Leaf, principal successor to the largest narrow-gauge system east of the Mississippi, gave the Nickel Plate railheads at St. Louis and Toledo.

Overcapitalization during the late 1920's nearly capsized the Nickel Plate during the great depression, but austerity and renewed dedication to the manifest freight train got the road past the 1930's and armed it for unprecedented responsibilities during World War II. Centralized traffic control, mile-a-minute freight schedules, and incomparable Berkshire steam locomotives underwrote a brilliant postwar record and put the Nickel Plate a decade ahead of its competition. After severing ties with the Chesapeake & Ohio in 1947, the road turned to expansion as a means of strengthening its future traffic position.

Acquisition of the Wheeling & Lake Erie in 1949 enlarged the Nickel Plate to a well-knit 2200-mile network of high-density trunk lines originating almost as much traffic as it received from connections. Manufactured goods and minerals now accounted for a whopping 86 per cent of tonnage, but the road continued to win an increasing share of perishable overhead traffic. Profits soared to 21 million dollars in 1950, and *Business Week* portrayed the Nickel Plate's president on its cover and cited his road as "proof that railroading can pay." Indeed, the Nickel Plate will be best remembered for its sensational performance during the last two decades — a showing in utter contrast with the dismal experience of its Eastern contemporaries. Between the end of World War II and Nickel Plate's October 16, 1964, merger with the Norfolk & Western, NKP grossed 2.8 billion dollars, turned in profits of 250

million, and paid its delighted stockholders some 144 million dollars in cash dividends.

Much of the Nickel Plate's latter-day success could be attributed to its light passenger schedules, productive long-haul bridge traffic, and strategic location. With or without passenger trains, however, a railroad netting nearly $10,000 per mile in the face of high fixed charges and a paucity of captive accounts was in a class by itself. Overhead business is the hardest to win and even harder to hold. A high-speed bridge operation demanded the most rigid (and costly) standards of track and motive power maintenance. Some measure of the Nickel Plate's strategic posture (as well as its competition) can be gauged by the fact that three premier passenger trains of the East — PRR's *Broadway*, Central's *20th Century Limited*, and B&O's *National Limited* — once ran over the road's main line within the span of a few months.

Above all, the Nickel Plate owed its triumphs to top-caliber manpower. By necessity the road demanded alert and dedicated management, and most of the time that is what it got. The determined Darius Caldwell molded the road's personality and engendered the tradition of excellence. Paddy Canniff added pride and organizational harmony and made the road a family institution. The dedicated Bernet and Ayers forged the Nickel Plate into a lean and hungry citadel of efficiency, gave it an unexcelled freight locomotive, and produced a proficient corps of enginemen. Optimistic John Davin restored financial integrity, increased capacity, and opened the door to expansion. The last president, the effervescent and tireless Myron Phipps, held the line against competition with piggyback, unit trains, and interline service.

A railroad so beset by competition and so completely reliant on exemplary performance as the Nickel Plate could ill afford the luxury of complacency. Keenly aware that survival was a day-to-day affair, high officials kept fingers on the road's pulse and wary eyes on competitors. Line supervisors fancied they could hear the thunder from the Terminal Tower on those rare mornings when CB-12 failed to make its 4 o'clock Buffalo cutoff.

And with good reason — for as CB-12 went, so went the Nickel Plate. Top brass could be expected to show up at the scene of any major derailment, for as long as the main track was blocked the road was out of business. A dozen Nickel Plate trainmasters supervised 2200 miles of railroad moving as much as 30 per cent of the ton-miles handled by the 11,000-mile NYC with its 91 trainmasters. Still, after 1956 the Nickel Plate was consistently judged the safest of the largest American railroads.

The proud Nickel Plate could boast dedicated career men at every level of the organization. In the early days there were Cantlins, Cherrys, Blairs, Wolfs, Forans, Mahoneys, Sliters, and Millers in the ranks. With the LE&W and Clover Leaf, the Nickel Plate adopted whole clans including Yetmans, Brimberrys, and Fraileys. One recalls that Tracy Culligan's case-hardened Buffalo yardmen needed only 6 hours to put together seven outbound freights in their tiny Abbott Road yard. But Buffalo had no monopoly on Nickel Platers who could switch box cars with skill; they were found in abundance at Fort Wayne, Madison, Calumet, Cleveland, and a dozen other yards. And what of the conductors who spent most of their lives setting hand brakes and riding bouncing seat boxes, yet had the ability to make a passenger feel welcome when they finally had whiskers enough to hold down a place on varnish. Then there was the legion of runners who built and preserved the golden reputation for speed — Archie Alfred, Frank Curtiss, "Dollie" Gray, Ed Chavanne, "Pokey" Vogt, Patrick McGushin, "Becky" Swift, Jack English, Ed Cloud, "Nick" Crosby, Ivan Albright, Jim Furlong, "Dutch" Mowery, Jack Lyon, "Stogie" Starr, Joe Hornic, "Bat-'em-High" Sanders, Sam Hawk, "Tilly" Palmer, Morgan Muir, and many others.

The development and application of the locomotive was the most fundamental aspect of any railroad's affairs, particularly in the days of steam. Even so, few railroads were so critically at the mercy of their engines, enginemen, and machinists as the Nickel Plate. The road was hardly what you could call a proving ground for motive power. It didn't have to be. For a long time reliance was placed on sturdy and conventional Brooks designs which were well suited for fast water-level operation. At first the fast freights rolled behind all-purpose 4-4-0's with 61-inch drivers. Then during the early years of this century Brooks Ten-Wheelers and Consolidations powered 30-car Nickel Plate manifests on 31-hour schedules. These had the maximum 18-ton axle loading dictated by the east end viaducts and were short enough to use the original 65-foot turntables. Once freed of Vanderbilt domination, the Nickel Plate turned to the Mikado. The first 2-8-2's were duplicates of an NYC design and later models were patterned after the outstanding USRA machine.

In 1934 the Nickel Plate developed the only freight locomotive that was tailored to its specific needs. Schenectady-built 2-8-4's were bought after bad times stepped up the competitive tempo and forced the road to upgrade its manifest schedules. The Nickel Plate Berkshire was a well-designed tonnage glutton that accelerated with amazing rapidity and produced maximum power at speeds in excess of 40 mph. A new eight-coupled standard, the 700's kept pace with mile-a-minute schedules and unbelievable traffic loads. Their performance was so outstanding that the road resisted total dieselization until 1958, when a recession and inflated maintenance costs finally prevailed. Thereafter the manifests were entrusted to 1500 to 2500 h.p. production-model hood units built by Alco and EMD.

At one time in its history the Nickel Plate scheduled more daily passenger trains than it owned passenger locomotives. A handful of 4-4-0 and 4-6-0 speedsters powered the varnish until 1922-1923, when 10 handsome Pacifics were added to the roster. During the late 1920's the road asked Alco and Lima to build eight home-designed 4-6-4's for new limited trains NKP operated jointly with the Lackawanna. The first L-1's came from Dunkirk a few weeks after Alco had delivered the original Hudson to the NYC. After 20 years of highly creditable performance, the 4-6-4's yielded their varnish assignments to 2000 h.p. Alco diesels. Nonetheless, there were L-1's on the active roster to the very end of steam operation. Their 74-inch drivers made them suitable for utility work, and they could turn in an excellent performance on fast freight when the occasion demanded.

Influenced first by the Central and later by the C&O, the Nickel Plate was quick to try out and adopt devices intended to increase locomotive performance and efficiency. NKP was one of the first users of the Baker-Pilliod valve gear and, like other Vanderbilt roads, embraced the superheater at an early date. The road was enthusiastic about the feedwater heater, booster, firebox syphons, and exhaust steam injectors. Although the Nickel Plate ultimately elected to educate its enginemen with a dynamometer car, it was the first railroad to test an automatic cutoff device. The Berkshires boasted such appliances as steam chest pressure gauges, radios, oscillating headlights, low water alarms, rail washers, and Firebar grates.

For a long time the most ardent Nickel Plate admirers were the shippers who patronized the line. The road seemed too austere and coldly purposeful to outbid four tracks of New York Central with their endless parade of trains. Even as steam was nearing extinction in the mid-1950's some members of the train-watching fraternity preferred a hunt for a lame 4-6-4 or for slogging PRR and B&O freights at Attica Junction to the challenge of committing elusive 2-8-4's to film. Many, however, discovered belatedly that the Nickel Plate was "The Right Place," as Eric Treacy would put it. The road was not without its attractions other than steam, and — if one knew where to look — some real surprises. There were the impressive mainline viaducts and the lovely Amish valleys traversed by the Zanesville locals. Roadmaster Joe Julio's 78-mile Fort Wayne Division tangent with its superb track, C.T.C., and running tracks was about as fine a railroad as there was under the sun. At the other end of the scale one found gantleted drawbridges and a timber-lined narrow-gauge tunnel, a line with 3 per cent uncompensated and 22-degree curves, an honest-to-gosh switchback.

The Nickel Plate offered all the storied romance of the high iron, yet possessed a distinctive flavor all its own. The need to excel, the tradition of reliability, the reputation for speed; the inordinate reliance on Super-Power, square valves, and skilled practitioners were intangible elements that gave the road an aura of nobility. The writer can only sympathize with those who never witnessed Berkshires assaulting Kimball Hill at dusk; who cannot recall the high-pitched cadence of empty reefers crashing over Painesville diamond at a mile a minute; who were never in the Black Swamp on an August evening so still that CB-12's smoke trail hung in the air for hours after the train's awesome passing; who could not ride with 7000 diesel horsepower taking ore up to Rexford Summit; who cannot savor even now the blend of a 700's coal smoke, hot oil, and superheated steam. When it came to classic good looks, how much less than a Southern Ps4 or Pennsy K-4 was a Nickel Plate K-1b on No. 9 at sundown? And was there ever an exhaust so sharp and quick as that of an L-1 leaving Rocky River at midnight? The promise of a pair of 2-8-4's doing battle with Adena Railroad's 2 per cent was reason enough to ignore the prospect of a B&O EM-1 in the same neighborhood. There was a sense of urgency about the business of servicing Berkshires at Bellevue after dark that was lacking at Altoona, Saint Luc, Willard, and other lairs of the steam locomotive. Yes, for those who looked and perceived, this was The Right Place.

This book is intended as a tribute to a notable business enterprise and to the men and machines that made it great. In all ways the Nickel Plate Road was a credit to the American railroad industry, and that it be remembered as such is only fitting and proper. As a competitive pace-setter, the road was a powerful and beneficial influence on the quality of transport service within and beyond the territory it served. Through taxes, payrolls, and outstanding service it contributed mightily to the advancement and betterment of the communities it served. This was an institution that never failed to cover its debts, and in our time it helped greatly to maintain the railroads' good name with the investing public. Above all else, the Nickel Plate was a symbol of success — a success achieved one day at a time in the face of formidable obstacles.

Eastbound local freight crosses Old Woman Creek near Shin Rock, O., en route from Bellevue to Conneaut. Class A 4-4-0's diamond stack dates photo as pre-1890. Timber trestle was replaced by fill and culvert in 1911. — *Collection of R. E. Lyon.*

The nickel-plated air line

COINCIDENT with the rapid colonization of the West and the industrial metamorphosis of the lower Great Lakes basin, the 25 years subsequent to the end of the Civil War saw the construction of more than half the steam railroad mileage in the United States. During the 1880-1883 boom alone, nearly as many miles of railroad were opened to traffic as existed at the end of 1865. By 1881 one out of every 32 persons in the nation was either gainfully employed by a railroad or was engaged in railroad construction. Industrial production was expanding in direct ratio to the ever-growing demand for rails, locomotives, and other railway supplies. In this era of unregulated, free-wheeling capitalism the railroad provided the American entrepreneur with his main chance to amass great wealth overnight. This was truly the Railway Age.

JAY GOULD ASSAULTS THE HOUSE OF VANDERBILT

Throughout the lower Great Lakes basin and especially along the south shore of Lake Erie, the early 1880's were years of dynamic growth. Here the proximity to much of the nation's mineral wealth, its markets, and principal trade routes had led to the establishment and rapid expansion of the iron and steel industry and related manufacturing activity. The region was served by a single east-west railroad, the owners of which were concerned only with the continued accumulation of great

13

wealth and the preservation of their monopoly. Local facilities for handling the growing volume of travelers and goods were inadequate, service was poor, and rates were based on what the traffic would bear. Discrimination against shippers and commodities, connecting railroads, and even against entire communities was not uncommon. The situation was not unique. It existed, more or less, wherever railroads enjoyed a monopoly in those times.

The railroad industry between 1880 and 1883 was dominated by Jay Gould and William H. Vanderbilt and this period was one of almost continuous conflict between them. Vanderbilt, by virtue of his birthright, possessed proprietary control of the New York Central & Hudson River Railroad and the Lake Shore & Michigan Southern Railway. Together the two lines formed a through route from New York City to Buffalo and Chicago. The Lake Shore road, 540 miles long, extended west from Buffalo along the south shore of Lake Erie and served the port cities of Cleveland and Toledo. After the Gold Conspiracy Panic of 1869, control of the Lake Shore had been acquired by Commodore Cornelius Vanderbilt

who already held virtual ownership of the New York Central & Hudson River. Upon his death in 1877, control of the two railroads and a fortune of nearly 100 million dollars passed to the Commodore's 56-year-old son William. No stranger to the railroad game, the son quickly added a second Buffalo-Chicago route to his holdings in 1878 by quietly buying up the stock of the Michigan Central and Canada Southern roads. At this particular moment in history Vanderbilt possessed a virtual monopoly on rail traffic moving between Buffalo, Cleveland, Detroit, and Chicago. He was to spend the remainder of his business career trying to preserve it.

Jay Gould by 1881 had reached the pinnacle of a remarkable career as an entrepreneur. Of humble origin, he ruled an empire embracing some 15,000 miles of railroads, about 15 per cent of the total U. S. mileage. West of the Mississippi Gould's holdings included the Union Pacific; Missouri, Kansas & Texas; International & Great Northern; Missouri Pacific; St. Louis, Iron Mountain & Southern; and Texas & Pacific. These roads fed an enormous volume of eastbound traffic to Gould's 3348-mile Wa-

Tiffin & Fort Wayne Rail Road $1000 first-mortgage 7 per cent bond, dated April 1, 1857. The company went under during the panic of 1857, after paying one semi-annual interest coupon. — *Collection of Allen County-Fort Wayne Historical Society.*

William H. Vanderbilt (1821-1885), heir of Cornelius Vanderbilt, was the richest man in America in his time. — *Collection of Allen County Historical Society.*

Jayson Gould (1836-1892), master speculator and opportunist, was the arch-rival of the Vanderbilts. — *Collection of Allen County Historical Society.*

bash, St. Louis & Pacific which in turn delivered much of it to Vanderbilt's Lake Shore at Toledo, O. In the East, Gould was firmly entrenched in the management of the Central Railroad of New Jersey and the Delaware, Lackawanna & Western. The Lackawanna extended from the Jersey tidewater to Binghamton, N. Y., and served the anthracite coal region of northeastern Pennsylvania. Largely at Gould's insistence, a subsidiary company was building a 207-mile extension to Buffalo. When this was completed, there would be only a gap of 300 miles separating the Lackawanna and the Wabash.

Gould's ruthless manipulations and the unsavory associations of the early years of his career had made him the most hated man in America. To the public he was the Robber Baron — a symbol of organized rapacity and greed. To the railroad world he was the father of all financial catastrophes and his every move was suspect. More recently, Gould had amassed considerable wealth and headed a clique of wealthy and enterprising men. His faithful ally, Russell Sage, had a fortune estimated at 12 million dollars. Still, Gould did not command anything approaching the Vanderbilt resources. He was endowed, however, with a shrewd and complex mind and his most devastating weapons were singleness of purpose, tenacity, and aggressiveness.

In the great conflict that ensued between these two titans of railroading, Gould relentlessly attacked the Vanderbilt citadel. The latter had little of his brilliant father's propensity for battle and ap-

pears to have been motivated by an overpowering instinct for self-preservation. He habitually compromised only to have his hopes for peace shattered by fresh Gould aggressions. In 1880, to appease Gould, Vanderbilt agreed to turn over the bulk of his westbound traffic to the Wabash and so deserted in the process his own friendly connections. Such abject surrender only served to encourage Gould to step up the attack.

SENEY AND COMPANY

During 1879 and 1880 the so-called Seney Syndicate linked together several short railroads in Ohio and Indiana to form the Lake Erie & Western Railway. The road extended 353 miles westward from the LS&MS at Fremont, O., to Bloomington, Ill., and invaded territory dominated by the Wabash. Although the Lake Erie presented Vanderbilt with an excellent avenue of retaliation against Gould, his traffic concessions of 1880 cut off most of the road's westbound receipts and alienated its owners. During the LE&W's first full year of operation, income had been high enough to meet fixed charges with a little to spare. The times were good, however, and unless the road could secure adequate westbound business there was little chance it could survive the next economic upheaval.

The group that controlled the Lake Erie was headed by George I. Seney, a New York banker, and included several other New Yorkers and a group of Midwestern men of varied backgrounds. The East-

15

CALVIN STEWART BRICE GEN. SAMUEL R. THOMAS GEORGE I. SENEY

erners included John T. Martin, Edward H. R. Lyman, Alexander M. White, and Walston H. Brown, all successful speculators. The western contingent appears to have been dominated by Calvin S. Brice, a 35-year-old Lima (O.) attorney who had been instrumental in the formation of the LE&W. Also from Ohio were Charles Foster, then Governor of the state and a close friend of Brice; Dan P. Eells of Cleveland; and Gen. Samuel R. Thomas of Columbus. Thomas, a relative newcomer to railroading, was allied with Brice in several rail ventures and ran a rolling mill which specialized in light rails for narrow-gauge roads. Columbus R. Cummings and William B. Howard of Illinois rounded out the syndicate. Their calling was railroad construction, although Cummings also ran a carbuilding firm and managed several syndicate rail properties.

Aside from the Lake Erie & Western, the Seney Syndicate controlled several widely separated railroads including the 2500-mile East Tennessee, Virginia & Georgia system; the Peoria, Decatur & Evansville; and the Ohio Central. The latter road extended from Toledo to the Hocking Valley coal fields and crossed the Lake Erie at Fostoria. There is no evidence to establish that the syndicate had any ties with Gould or Vanderbilt. If anything, Brice and some of the others maintained a cool disdain for both. The group was of little consequence in the railroad world of 1880, but in one audacious stroke these minor-league promoters stepped into the arena and took on both the great gladiators.

A SETBACK FOR GOULD

It was obvious to the Seney Syndicate that in order to protect their substantial LE&W invest-

ment it would be necessary to tap new sources of revenue. Toward the end of 1880 several extensions were planned which would carry the road to Cleveland, St. Louis, and Chicago. In the process the Lake Erie proposed to invade territory dominated by Gould, Vanderbilt, and the Pennsylvania system. Possibly the syndicate was counting on an alliance with one of the three, in which event the proposed incursion into the ally's territory would be dropped. At any rate, the St. Louis branch was projected from the LE&W at Frankfort, Ind., to East St. Louis, Ill., a distance of 250 miles. The route was similar to that later built by narrow-gauge Toledo, Cincinnati & St. Louis and paralleled Gould's Wabash. The Cleveland branch was to run from Frankfort northeast to Fort Wayne and then east to Cleveland, a distance of about 280 miles. From a point near Huntington, Ind., on the Cleveland branch, a line was projected to Chicago, 150 miles.

While it is doubtful that anyone took the proposals very seriously, it happened that the Frankfort-Fort Wayne-Cleveland line could be built quickly and at relatively low cost. In September 1880 the syndicate gained control of the 25-mile standard-gauge Frankfort & Kokomo Railroad connecting the cities named. For the 32 miles from Kokomo to Lagro the road would have to be built from scratch, but arrangements had been made to purchase 56 miles of the defunct Wabash & Erie Canal* from Lagro to Fort Wayne and the Ohio border. The canal towpath constituted a ready-made

*The canal was built by the State of Indiana and required a decade to complete between Toledo and Lafayette, Ind. Later an extension was built to Evansville. By 1881 most of the canal had been abandoned for a number of years.

CHARLES FOSTER   **COLUMBUS R. CUMMINGS**

Calvin S. Brice (1845-1898), able Ohio lawyer and a prolific railroad promoter. — *Allen County Historical Society.*

Gen. Samuel R. Thomas (1840-1903) was closely associated with Brice and Foster in the Seney Syndicate.

George I. Seney (1826-1893), New York banker, headed the syndicate that built the Nickel Plate. — *NKP photo.*

Charles Foster (1828-1904), known to his political foes as "Calico Charlie," was Governor of Ohio 1880-1884. His father's interest in the LE&W prompted his activity in railroad promotion and participation in the syndicate.

Columbus R. Cummings (1834-1897), first NKP president. — *NKP photo.*

roadbed and the deal included a right of way 250 feet wide through the city of Fort Wayne. East of that place the towpath was to be used as far as New Haven, 6 miles, and from that point there was a completed grade extending 100 miles eastward to Tiffin, O., 80 miles west of Cleveland.

The grade from Tiffin to New Haven was a perfect tangent, save for a 1-minute deflection in course. East of Tiffin there was a partly graded right of way across northern Ohio which reached a point near Youngstown. Seventy miles east of that city a straight line would strike the town of Red Bank, Pa. From this point the New York area was reached by a combination of the Allegheny Valley road's Low Grade Division over the Allegheny Mountains, the Philadelphia & Erie, Catawissa Railroad, and the Central Railroad of New Jersey. This entire route had been projected in the 1850's as part of the Clinton Air Line between New York and Omaha. Shortly after the completion of the Union Pacific the project was revived as the Continental Railway, a 1200-mile New York-Omaha "air-line." Most of the grade between Tiffin and New Haven had been cut through a primeval swamp forest during the mid-1850's by the Tiffin & Fort Wayne Rail Road, one of the old Clinton companies. The company failed to survive the 1857 panic and in 1871 the grade was acquired by the Continental. Villages were platted along the route, warehouses were built, and the grade was once again prepared for track. However, the panic of 1873 forced a suspension of construction work. Despite repeated attempts to secure Federal financial grants, the project remained dormant during the long depression of the 1870's.

In 1880 Gen. William H. Gibson owned the Tif-

fin-New Haven grade as well as most of the right of way between Tiffin and Youngstown and he had the whole business up for sale. In order to secure his own route to the East Coast, Jay Gould was reviving the Continental route as a means of connecting the Wabash and the Jersey Central. Having no reason to suspect that anyone else might be interested in the grade, Gould tried to drive Gibson's price down by demonstrating a total lack of interest in his wares. In January 1881 George Seney agreed to buy Gibson's grade for $85,000 and took the General into his syndicate. Later the same month, W. B. Howard negotiated the purchase of the Wabash & Erie Canal from Lagro to the Ohio border for $137,000. For a very nominal sum the syndicate had quickly acquired nearly 150 miles of grade which was for all practical purposes ready for the iron. Gould, who now controlled the Jersey Central and was negotiating with the Pennsylvania Railroad for rights over the Allegheny Valley and Philadelphia & Erie, had been caught flat-footed in his own back yard.

THE BIRTH OF A NEW RAILROAD

On February 3, 1881, the syndicate met in Seney's Metropolitan Bank in New York and organized the New York, Chicago & St. Louis Railway Company. Within minutes members of the syndicate subscribed to $14,666,666.66 of the proposed capital stock of 16 million dollars. A pact was made whereby each man deposited 80 per cent of his stock in trust. Before any of this stock could be sold there had to be majority approval and each man had to be given the opportunity to join the selling pool. The new road was to extend from Cleveland to

Gen. J. S. Casement, Painesville (O.) contractor and Nickel Plate builder. — *Collection of John H. Keller.*

Chicago, about 340 miles, with a 325-mile branch from Fort Wayne Junction to St. Louis. It was also proposed to complete the low-grade route over the Alleghenies. The contract for the construction of the road was awarded to Brown, Howard & Company, a firm formed by the syndicate. On February 18, 1882, the company was formally incorporated in Ohio as the New York & Chicago Railway and subsequently it was similarly incorporated in Indiana and Illinois.

The Buffalo, Cleveland & Chicago Railway was incorporated in the states of New York and Pennsylvania in October 1880 by Clark, Post and Martin, New York bankers. This road was to parallel the line of the Lake Shore & Michigan Southern between Buffalo and Cleveland, a distance of 185 miles. Surveyors located the route during January and February 1881 and in March the company was acquired by the Seney Syndicate. On April 13, 1881, the Buffalo, Cleveland & Chicago was consolidated with the New York & Chicago companies to form the New York, Chicago & St. Louis Railway Company. The consolidated company had authorized capitalization of 35 million dollars of which 24 million was in $100 par common stock and the balance in $100 par preferred stock. None of this stock was sold on the open market and virtually all of it was taken by the syndicate at 10 per cent of par on the common and 16⅔ per cent of par on the preferred.

In March 1881 headquarters were established at Cleveland and Maj. Henry L. Morrill was placed in charge of construction. By this time, surveyors had been in the field for a month locating those sections not already graded. The road between Buffalo and Chicago was given priority, but the St. Louis and Youngstown branches would be built "later." On April 12 Brown, Howard & Company announced the award of subcontracts for the construction of three sections of the road. Gen. J. S. "Jack" Casement, the celebrated Union Pacific tracklayer, got the biggest and toughest job — the 185 miles between Cleveland and Buffalo. R. G. Huston & Company of Cincinnati was to build the 80-mile Cleveland-Tiffin segment while the 150-mile Fort Wayne-Chicago Division was awarded to LM&D Construction Company of Chicago. The general contractors were to complete the 107 miles of grade between Fort Wayne and Tiffin, nearly all of which was essentially ready for the iron.

According to preliminary estimates, a single main track between Buffalo and Chicago would require about 90,000 long tons of steel rails weighing 60 pounds to the yard and more than 1.5 million oak crossties laid 3000 to the mile. There were to be 291 trestles and 49 bridges, including 12 major wrought-iron viaducts on the east end with a total length of nearly 2½ miles. These required more than 6500 tons of iron and 50,000 cubic feet of masonry. During April 1881 an order covering one half the rails required was awarded to the Cambria Iron Company of Johnstown, Pa., at $65 per long ton. The 60-pound steel rails were rolled in 30-foot lengths and were of a design developed in 1879 for the Pennsylvania Railroad. Also ordered were 30 4-4-0 type locomotives from the Brooks Locomotive Works of Dunkirk, N. Y., and 1000 flat cars from Cummings' La Fayette Car Works.

RAILROAD FEVER IN THE FIRELANDS

When surveyors began locating the Tiffin-Cleveland section in February 1881, a spirited contest developed between three Ohio towns seeking to be located on the new east-west trunk line. The towns were Norwalk, Bellevue, and New London — all located in the Firelands, a region granted to Connecticut Revolutionary War veterans whose homes had been burned by the British. A keen rivalry developed between Bellevue and Norwalk, both of which had a rich railroad heritage. Bellevue in 1838 had become the first southern terminus of the pioneer Mad River & Lake Erie Rail Road while Norwalk had been instrumental in the building of the Toledo, Norwalk & Cleveland Rail Road. This road, completed in 1853, was the last link in the first New York-Chicago rail route and for many years its shops were Norwalk's principal industry.

Since the formation of the Lake Shore & Michigan Southern, however, the use of the shops had been all but abandoned.

For its part, the company did all that it could to add fuel to the contest, since the town that was ultimately selected would be a division point with a yard, roundhouse, and other facilities. These would require a considerable amount of land which the promoters hoped would be donated to the road. Out of deference to Governor Foster it was decided to run the Buffalo-Chicago line through Fostoria, his home town, rather than Tiffin. This eliminated New London as a contender. During March 1881, at the height of the Bellevue-Norwalk competition, the Norwalk *Chronicle* several times referred to the road as "the great New York and St. Louis double-track nickel-plated railroad." Before a rail had been laid the company adopted the nickname, and from that time to the present the New York, Chicago & St. Louis has been better known as the Nickel Plate Road.

Norwalk lost the fight, Bellevue got the railroad, and by June 1, 1881, the entire 523-mile Buffalo-Chicago line had been located and construction was well under way. Use of the Wabash & Erie Canal southwest of Fort Wayne was abandoned in favor of a shorter and more direct route west from that city. From time to time it was asserted that the St. Louis branch would be built, but the plan was scrapped with the sale of the Frankfort & Kokomo

in April 1881 to the narrow-gauge Toledo, Delphos & Burlington.

VANDERBILT'S REACTION

William H. Vanderbilt evidently adopted at first a wait-and-see attitude toward his would-be south-shore competitor. The celerity with which the construction of the Nickel Plate was progressed during the spring of 1881, however, stirred him to indignantly denounce the Seney Syndicate and to belittle their new road. Even as the first rails were being spiked down, Vanderbilt was publicly describing the Nickel Plate as poorly built and discounting it as a menace to his "magnificent" Lake Shore. Elsewhere, the Wabash had opened an extension to Detroit and Gould was authoring a traffic agreement between that road, the Great Western of Canada, and the Lackawanna. Vanderbilt, showing some of his father's fire, turned on Gould, the Grand Trunk, and his other tormentors by instituting a savage rate war. In his anger he might also have made life miserable for the syndicate, but aside from derisive talk he did nothing.

Ever since the locomotive *Columbia* had collapsed the Lake Shore's Ashtabula bridge with its catastrophic toll of life in December 1876, no name was less popular in Ohio than Vanderbilt. In the northern part of the state where the Lake Shore enjoyed a virtual east-west monopoly, the Nickel Plate was receiving considerable popular support. Concerned

Class A 4-4-0 No. 28 built by Brooks in 1882 was used in building the NKP. She was patterned after standard LS&MS and LE&W freight haulers. — *Collection of John A. Rehor.*

First Nickel Plate steel (curving to the west) was laid at LE&W crossing, Arcadia, O., on May 28, 1881. Towerman operated stub-type crossover.—*Collection of Willis A. McCaleb.*

that a few absentee entrepreneurs might eventually control all of the state's major railroads, Ohio had served notice on Vanderbilt that it would oppose any move to expand his Buckeye holdings. Already the state had successfully gone to the Supreme Court to thwart his attempt to acquire the Cincinnati, Hamilton & Dayton. To take any overt action against "Calico Charlie" Foster's new road would practically guarantee his re-election as Governor and invite wholesale reprisals. Ohio was then a power in national politics and Foster's fellow Buckeye Republican, James A. Garfield,* occupied the White House. No one was more justifiably sensitive than Vanderbilt to the growing public pressure for Governmental regulation if not outright ownership of the railroads.

Construction During 1881

By June 1, 1881, Brown, Howard & Company and the three subcontractors had over 10,000 men and 5000 teams in the field at 40 points between Buffalo and Chicago. After clearing and resurfacing the Continental grade, the general contractor prepared to lay track westward from Arcadia, O., a station on the Lake Erie & Western 5 miles southwest of Fostoria. During the first week of May a wye and water tanks were completed at Arcadia and the first flat cars arrived there in an LE&W train. Later

*The Nickel Plate crossed a corner of Garfield's Lawnfield estate at Mentor, O. In July 1881, before a deed could be executed and conveyed to the railroad, the President was shot by a disappointed office seeker. He died two months later, but the matter was resolved without difficulty.

that month large shipments of rail and the first Brooks locomotives arrived at the junction. Crossties were being cut by the thousands from the Black Swamp's great virgin oaks at sawmills set up at McComb, Kiefersville, Hector, and other hamlets on the Continental grade. The first rails were laid at Arcadia on May 28 and on June 22 the construction train reached McComb, 15 miles to the west. In the grandest tradition a complimentary excursion train was run between Arcadia and McComb on July 4. The train carried mail and passengers in cars borrowed from the Lake Erie and was pulled by one of the new Brooks 4-4-0's.

On July 10 the track reached the Dayton & Michigan Railroad (CH&D) at Leipsic, 10 miles west of McComb. The track was being laid westward at the rate of a mile a day despite the fact that many of the Italian laborers were overcome by the Black Swamp's malarial fevers. Still others lost all interest in the premium wage of $1.50 per day the first night they heard the hair-raising screams of the swamp's wildcats. Observers at McComb reported that each day saw the passage through the town of many trains headed west with rails and laborers. By August 1 the tracklayers had reached the Auglaize River at Oakwood, 47 miles west of Arcadia. Early in September they crossed into Indiana and by October 1 had reached New Haven. On November 3, 1881, the first train ran through from Fostoria to Fort Wayne, 91 miles.

LM&D Construction Company, charged with the task of building the Fort Wayne-Chicago section,

NYC&StL and W&LE surveying parties reached Bellevue almost simultaneously in March 1881, igniting verbal war with nearby Norwalk. Here, camera's lens peers down Bellevue's main street toward NKP crossing. — *Collection of John A. Rehor.*

had begun heavy grading work at Knox in northwestern Indiana on April 15, 1881. By the end of that summer virtually all the 144-mile section was graded and ready for the track. In mid-August a gang began laying rail east from Wanatah, a station on the Louisville, New Albany & Chicago (Monon). By the end of September the track was down for 22 miles to Knox and beyond. On December 1 the tracklayers crossed the Indianapolis, Peru & Chicago road at Argos, 47 miles east of Wanatah. By this time a second force was already at work laying track eastward from Hobart toward Wanatah and a third party began spiking down steel at Hadley, a few miles west of Fort Wayne. By the end of the year this gang had laid 12 miles of track while the other two groups had completed a total of 71.57 miles of track between Tippecanoe and the Michigan Central's Joliet branch, 6 miles west of Hobart.

R. G. Huston & Company, working under a revised contract between Fostoria and Cleveland, began laying track eastward from Fostoria during the

first week of October 1881. A few miles out the work was halted by difficulty in securing a right of way across four acres of farmland. The company had offered the owner $5000 for the parcel, an amount about 25 times the going price. The crafty farmer, realizing the contractor was anxious to lay as much track as possible before the onset of winter, held out for $10,000. Finally, the frustrated contractor laid the track across the land on a Sunday, the one day the owner was powerless to obtain an injunction. Later the dispute was resolved in court. In November Huston's men reached Fort Seneca (Old Fort), 16 miles east of Fostoria. Here construction was again delayed — this time by a long spell of wet weather and the necessity of bridging the Sandusky River. It required the rest of 1881 to complete the 17 miles of road between Fort Seneca and Bellevue.

By mid-September 1881, Jack Casement had 100 miles of grade completed east from Cleveland and had track-laying gangs working west from both

Painesville and Ashtabula. East of Cleveland the Nickel Plate was built on the relatively narrow and level shelf of land between Lake Erie and the Appalachian foothills. For the entire distance the road was located south of the Lake Shore & Michigan Southern, often running directly alongside it. The road crossed the deep gorges of many streams and consequently most of the permanent bridges on the Nickel Plate were on Casement's Cleveland-Buffalo section. The bridgework was contracted for separately and this forced the subcontractor to lay track in sections, slowing his progress. Nevertheless, his Painesville party reached Willoughby, 10 miles to the west, on October 1 and by the end of that month had finished laying the remaining 12 miles of track to a junction with the Cleveland, Painesville & Ashtabula Railroad at Euclid. On October 29, 1881, Casement operated a seven-car excursion train from Cleveland to Painesville, a distance of 27 miles. The Ashtabula force reached Madison, 15 miles out, by December 1 and by Christmas had completed the remaining 10 miles to the Grand River at Painesville.

During 1881 nearly all of the 514-mile route had been graded, much of the bridgework erected, and 270 miles of track had been laid. On December 1 the Nickel Plate had issued 15 million dollars' worth of 6 per cent first-mortgage bonds with the Central Trust Company of New York taking 11 million dollars of the issue at par and the syndicate taking the balance at 80 per cent of par. An additional 15 million dollars in stock was also issued. In order to finance the purchase of 6 million dollars' worth of locomotives and cars, the road also issued 4 million dollars in 7 per cent 10-year equipment trust bonds, selling these as needed at 90 per cent of par. At the end of 1881 the contractors had 30 locomotives, 1051 flat cars, and 12 cabooses in construction service.

Suburban Railroads at Cleveland

In order to traverse the city of Cleveland, the Nickel Plate acquired control of two short suburban companies, the Rocky River Rail Road and the Cleveland, Painesville & Ashtabula Railroad. The latter, popularly called the "dummy line," started out as the Lake View & Collamer Railroad. Opened on May 1, 1875, the LV&C extended from Becker Avenue in Cleveland to Euclid Village, a distance of 6.86 miles. About 2½ miles of the road was located inside the city and ran parallel to and a short distance north of Superior Street. The westerly terminus was located in the neighborhood of the present intersection of Superior, East 71st Street, and Addison Road. At first the trains were run with "dummies," steam locomotives with boiler entirely

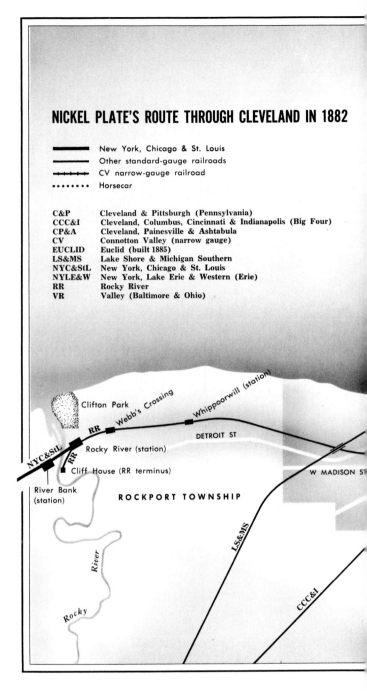

enclosed by a carbody. These were built locally at the Globe Iron Works. In August 1879 the LV&C was sold at foreclosure sale and thereafter operated as the Cleveland, Painesville & Ashtabula Railroad.* During 1880-1881 the CP&A partially graded a 4-mile branch from East Cleveland to the Cleveland & Pittsburgh Railroad (now Pennsylvania). When acquired by the Nickel Plate Road, the CP&A owned three locomotives — one of the dummies and two Baldwin Forneys — eight coaches, two baggage

*This was the second of three companies to bear the name Cleveland, Painesville & Ashtabula Railroad. The first was the predecessor of the LS&MS between Cleveland and Erie, Pa. The third was an interurban railway connecting Painesville and Ashtabula.

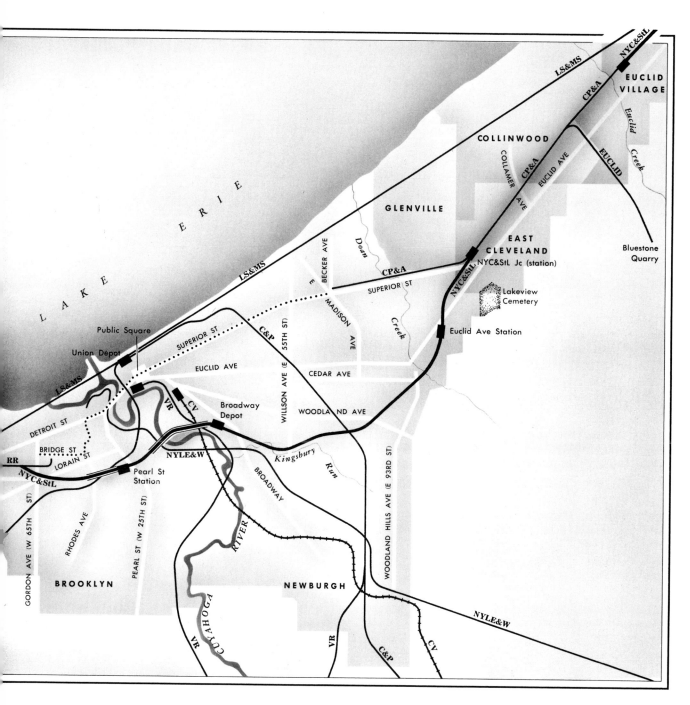

cars, and 12 freight cars. The little road boasted a number of long trestles, 25- to 27-pound iron rail, and a contract for hauling the U. S. Mail from Cleveland to Euclid.

The Nickel Plate secured access across most of Cleveland's west side through the acquisition of the Rocky River Rail Road on September 9, 1881. This road extended 5.53 miles from the end of a city horsecar line near Bridge Street and Waverly Avenue (now West 58th Street) in Cleveland to the east bank of the Rocky River in Rockport Township. The Rocky River terminated at the Cliff House, a popular inn located at what is today the intersection of Sloane and Edanola avenues in Lakewood. About a half a mile north of the Cliff House* the road operated an amusement park (Clifton Park) and a fine bathing beach. The company was organized on February 20, 1867, and commenced running trains on September 1, 1868. With three Baldwin 7-ton coal-burning tank engines, three coaches, and four open excursion cars, the Rocky River did a heavy summer business hauling picnickers, anglers, and bathers to the river. The normal weekday schedule called for 10 trains in each direction, but on summer Sundays there were 17 scheduled trains, with extras run on "pleasant days." The

---

*The Cliff House burned to the ground in 1882, not long after the sensational murder of its proprietor.

Baldwin 4-2-0 *Elias Sims* with one of Rocky River's closed coaches, 1881. — *NKP photo.*

fare was a dime, regardless of where one got on or off the train.

The owner of the Rocky River road, Elias Sims, had long had it on the block, and for a very nominal investment Vanderbilt could have deprived the Nickel Plate of a westerly entrance into Cleveland, then a booming city of 160,000. Similarly, the timely purchase of the Cleveland, Painesville & Ashtabula would have served to keep the Nickel Plate out of the Forest City altogether. Both the little roads retained their identity until 1887, although neither operated trains after 1882.

CONSTRUCTION DURING 1882

During January 1882 General Casement's men, now working eastward from Ashtabula, reached Conneaut near the Pennsylvania border. Following the completion of viaducts at Ashtabula and Paines-

Rockport poses at Baldwin's Philadelphia works in 1868. Seven-ton tanker, later renamed *Hannah*, had 17 x 24-inch cylinders, 42-inch drivers. — *Collection of H. L. Broadbelt.*

Major wrought-iron viaducts on the Nickel Plate in 1882

Over	At	Length (Feet)	Max. Height (Feet)
18-Mile Creek	Lakeview, N. Y.	690	100
Chautauqua Creek	Westfield, N. Y.	592	63
20-Mile Creek	N. Y.-Pa. line	712	113
Walnut Creek	Swanville, Pa.	870	99
Elk Creek	Girard, Pa.	1470	100
Crooked Creek	E. Springfield, Pa.	690	83
Conneaut Creek	Conneaut, O.	1320	76
Ashtabula Creek	Ashtabula, O.	822	109
Grand River	Painesville, O.	1310	106
Chagrin River	Willoughby, O.	730	50
Cuyahoga River	Cleveland, O.	3049*	68
Cleveland, Columbus, Cincinnati & Indianapolis	Cleveland, O.	726	63
Rocky River	Rockport Township, O.	673	88

*Double track with 225-foot swinging draw span.

Source: Report of the Commissioner of Railroads and Telegraphs to the Governor of the State of Ohio, 1882 and 1883.

Rocky River Rail Road,
Earnings and Expenses
September-October 1881
RECEIPTS

Collected by Conductors	$1173.21
Round Trip Tickets sold by Agent	595.47
Commutation Tickets sold by Supt.	297.00
Excursion Tickets	13.40
TOTAL RECEIPTS	**$2079.08**

EXPENDITURES

Payroll	$ 788.18
Rhodes & Co., coal	166.23
Geo. A. Stanley, lard oil	28.42
Cleveland Spring Co., repairs	8.56
Excelsior Iron Works, grate bars	12.99
Donation, Garfield funeral	100.00
A. F. Mulhern, hand smashed	40.00
Short & Foreman, printing	6.00
TOTAL EXPENDITURES	**$1150.38**
NET EARNINGS	**928.70**

Income account of the Rocky River Rail Road reflects few of the complexities that beset present-day railroading.

ville, a locomotive pulling the private car of Dan Eells ran over the 65 miles of track between Cleveland and Conneaut on February 17. The 28-mile section from Conneaut to Erie was built during February and March as fast as the four major bridges between the towns could be erected. At Erie nearly 2 miles of track was laid on 19th Street but not before considerable difficulty was encountered in securing a city franchise. In March Case-

STATEMENT OF EARNINGS.
ROCKY RIVER RAILROAD.

For Month of	Gross Earnings.	Operating Expenses. *Int. & taxes estimated $209 per month*	Net Earnings.
1882 January	644.18	805.33	
February,	530.47	671.07	
March,	627.17	709.70	
April,	891.27	741.32	
May,	1173.30	829.90	
June,	2032.05	1150.29	
July,	4195.77	969.69	
August,			
1881 September,	1161.04	777.19	
October,	918.04	773.71	
November,	751.99	634.86	
December,	771.41	631.88	
Total,	13696.99	8694.84	5002.15

Auditor.

Operating results of Rocky River during the 11 months the road was operated by Nickel Plate reveal dependence on summer traffic.

ment began laying track westward from Brocton, N. Y., and early in May his two forces met near the New York-Pennsylvania border. This left only the 50 miles between Brocton and Buffalo which was to be built, more or less simultaneously, with an extension of the Buffalo, Pittsburgh & Western Railroad (now part of the Pennsylvania) between the same points. The Nickel Plate track was located north of and adjacent to the BP&W track and it was contemplated that the two would be jointly operated as double track.* Construction gangs working east from Brocton spiked down the steel rails through Dunkirk and Silver Creek to Irving during May. In June, 10 more miles were completed to Angola and Derby and the last 15.6 miles from Derby to a junction with the New York, Lake Erie & Western (Erie) at Buffalo were finished during July and August of 1882.

Between Fort Wayne and Chicago, the two main construction parties met at Sidney, Ind., on April 5, 1882. By this time a third force had completed the road as far west as Hammond, near the Illinois border. During May and June the track was laid through the Lake Calumet swamps from Hammond to a junction with the Illinois Central at what is today East 83rd Street on Chicago's south side. From this point the track was laid next to the IC for about 1 mile to Grand Crossing — the junction of the IC, LS&MS, and the Pittsburgh, Fort Wayne &

*This arrangement is still in existence. The Pennsylvania track is used as the eastbound main while the Nickel Plate is the westbound track.

Cleveland skyline of 1882 was dominated by 3049-foot viaduct across Cuyahoga Valley. Bridge was renewed in 1907, 1944. Swinging draw over river was swept away by flash flood in 1904 and replaced by a jackknife span. — *Collection of John A. Rehor.*

July 1882 test run over original Rocky River viaduct is made by Brooks 4-4-0 and caboose. Dan Eells' west-bank estate, Oakwood, is visible at upper right. — *NKP photo.*

Chicago (Pennsylvania). The last rails were spiked down at Grand Crossing on August 24, 1882.

Huston & Company's forces, working east from Fostoria, reached Bellevue on January 3, 1882, a day the 2700 citizens of the town would long remember. Although six weeks of rain in the fall had slowed construction, the winter of 1881-1882 was so uncommonly mild that the work of laying track progressed without serious interruption. By the end of March Huston's men had reached Vermilion, 27 miles east of Bellevue. Here the Nickel Plate passed under the LS&MS main line and headed 28 miles east to the west bank of the Rocky. This section followed the Lake Erie shore line closely over a route that had been surveyed a few years before by the LS&MS. As a cutoff it shortened the distance between Cleveland and Vermilion by about 2 miles and eliminated the 8 miles of 1-per-cent-plus westbound grade out of Cleveland and a long eastbound grade near Amherst. However, the LS&MS had deferred the project owing to the high cost of bridging the Rocky River gorge.

In the latter part of May 1882 Huston's construction train arrived at the west bank of the Rocky and, upon the completion of the iron viaduct in June, connection was made with the Rocky River Rail Road. Operation of the suburban road was suspended in July and its old 30-pound iron rails were then replaced with 60-pound steel. This left only a 6-mile gap between Gordon Avenue and the Cleveland & Pittsburgh crossing. The right of way between those points cost the Nickel Plate 1.5 million dollars, roughly three times the normal market

value and $300,000 more than the cost of the entire 183-mile right of way between Cleveland and Buffalo. Between the C&P and the Rocky River road, the Nickel Plate had to cross the wide valley of the Cuyahoga River. It was first planned to span the river on a short low-level bridge and to bore a 1600-foot tunnel through the west bluff of the valley. However, this idea was dropped in favor of a double-track iron bridge, 3049 feet long and 68 feet high, spanning the entire valley. Work on the 100-odd masonry piers for the bridge was completed in May 1882 and it required most of the summer to erect the iron towers and girder spans. On August 25 the 225-foot swinging draw span was swung into place over the river and three days later Engineer Wallace W. Farley tested the great bridge by running 4-4-0 No. 20 across it. The event marked the completion of the Nickel Plate between Buffalo and Chicago.

OPENING OF THE NICKEL PLATE

The general contractor had steam excavators working in seven gravel pits along the line and by September 1, 1882, the work of ballasting the Nickel Plate was well advanced. Much of the telegraph line was already up and in operation. The road had purchased a large tract of land at Stony Island Avenue and 93rd Street in south Chicago and was erecting its main repair shops and a 16-stall roundhouse there at a cost of $500,000. A smaller shop, 22-stall roundhouse, and a large yard were close to completion at Conneaut. Other roundhouses were finished or well under way at Buffalo, Cleveland, Fort Wayne, and Bellevue. All had 65-foot turn-

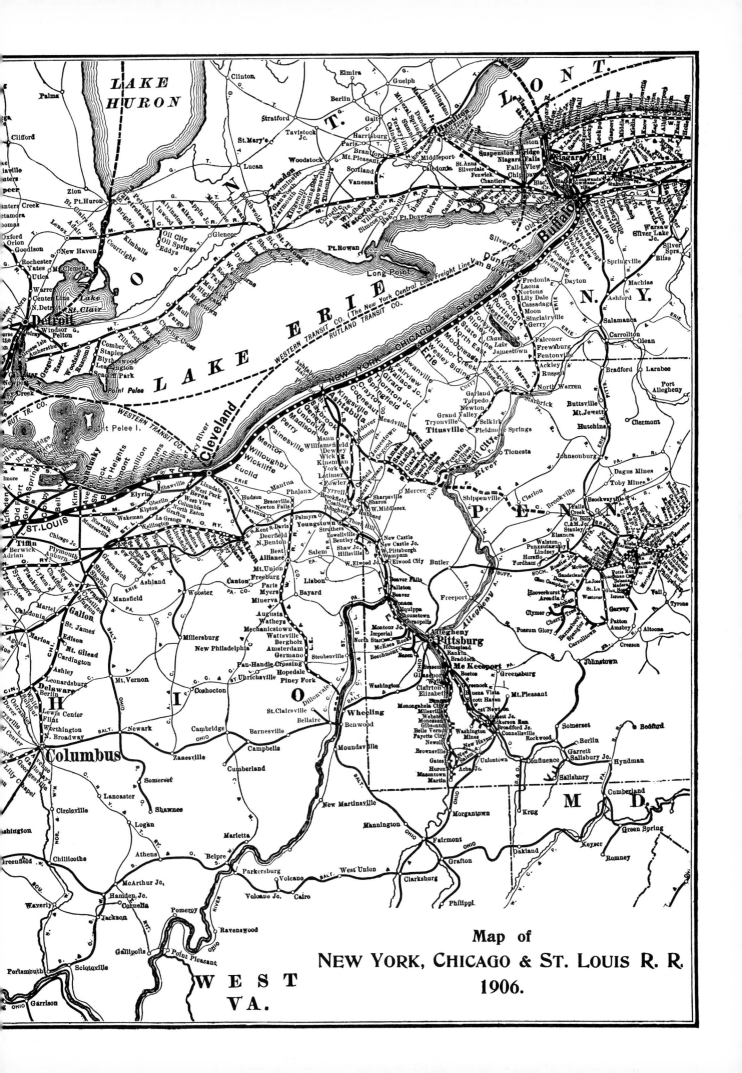

Map of
NEW YORK, CHICAGO & ST. LOUIS R. R.
1906.

Nickel Plate's brick and cut-stone Cleveland depot on Broadway is shown in this early engraving. Eastern Division superintendent maintained offices on second floor.

tables and collectively provided a stall for each of the road's locomotives. Of the 108 locomotives on order, 74 had been delivered; but like the freight cars, a goodly number had been leased to other railroads.*

An agreement had been made with the Illinois Central for the use of the joint IC-Michigan Central Great Central Depot located at the foot of Lake Street in Chicago. The agreement also afforded the Nickel Plate operating rights over 9 miles of the IC between Grand Crossing and Great Central Depot. A similar arrangement had been made with the New York, Lake Erie & Western (Erie) for use of that road's Exchange Street depot and 1.6 miles of track in Buffalo. At Cleveland the Nickel Plate planned to build a large permanent station on

*Most of the leased engines went to other Seney roads — the LE&W; Peoria, Decatur & Evansville; and Ohio Central. Curiously, Vanderbilt's New York Central and Big Four rented 15 Nickel Plate engines between them. All were returned to the road early in 1883.

Broadway, a little less than 1 mile southeast of the Public Square. Smaller depots at Pearl Street (now West 25th Street) and Euclid Avenue would temporarily serve the city.

Originally the Nickel Plate was divided into two divisions with a superintendent presiding over each. Each division, in turn, was composed of two operating districts as follows:

Eastern Division
1st District: Buffalo to Conneaut, 115.7 miles
2nd District: Conneaut to Bellevue, 132.3 miles
Western Division
3rd District: Bellevue to Fort Wayne, 122.9 miles
4th District: Fort Wayne to Chicago, 152 miles

Later the Eastern and Western divisions were renamed Cleveland and Fort Wayne divisions, respectively. In 1910 the four districts were renamed Buffalo, Cleveland, Fort Wayne, and Chicago, in that order, and in 1913 the term division was substituted for district.

The Nickel Plate's operating officials were all experienced men and came for the most part from the Pennsylvania system. The chief operating executive was Gen. Darius W. Caldwell, 52, a veteran of 29 years of PRR service. Prior to joining the Nickel Plate he had been the general manager of all Pennsylvania lines west of Pittsburgh. Chief Engineer Jacob A. Latcha had been the principal assistant engineer engaged in locating the projected Kansas Pacific line to California along the 32nd parallel and had spent the past decade with the Vandalia and other Pennsylvania properties. Henry Monett, the general passenger agent, had left the same post on PRR lines west of Pittsburgh. His assistant at Chicago, Benjamin F. Horner, had been the Pennsy's passenger agent in the same city. The superintendent of the Eastern Division, George H. Kimball, had held a variety of posts on the Pennsylvania including lines west bridge and building superintendent.

Before taking possession of the railroad on September 1, 1882, President Columbus R. Cummings made an inspection trip over it with the intention of going on to New York City to make his report to George Seney and other members of the syndicate. The inspection train left the Great Central Depot at Chicago at 7:10 a.m., August 30, 1882. The train was made up of Cummings' private car, an IC coach, and engine 152, a speedy Brooks 4-4-0 in the charge of Engineer Dennis McCarthy. On board were Cummings, W. B. Howard, and Lewis Williams, the general manager. En route to Fort Wayne the 152 dispatched a considerable number of cows that had wandered onto the yet unfenced right of way. All the same, the 152-mile run was made in 3 hours 45 minutes. Upon arriving at Fort Wayne roundhouse the 152 was such a gory sight that it was replaced by a sister, the 151, in the hands of Engineer John Wolf. Wolf made the 91-mile run from Fort Wayne to Fostoria in the amazing time of 2 hours 15 minutes, including stops, and he reported making several sustained runs at 70 mph on the long tangent through the Black Swamp. The special arrived at Cleveland at 5 p.m., having required less than 10 hours to cover the 340 miles from Chicago. It was a noteworthy run.

After an overnight stay at Cleveland the party resumed the journey to Buffalo. Jack Casement, anxious to at least match the previous day's performance, insisted on having engine 151 pull the train over the section he had built. However, he replaced the able Wolf with one of his own men, a hapless fellow who promptly ran into difficulty.

Hardly had the train left Cleveland when it ran through an open switch at Euclid and was derailed. Fortunately, no great damage was done and no one was hurt. After more than 2 hours of back-breaking toil the train was put back on the track and continued east.

The special had been expected at Conneaut at 9 or 10 o'clock in the morning. The depot there was decorated with flags and bunting and a cornet band was on hand along with most of the population. The telegraph line was not yet in service between Cleveland and Conneaut, and by noon almost everyone had given up and gone home for lunch. When the train finally arrived the depot was deserted. While the engine took on coal and water, Cummings sent word to the engineman that the track was too rough for the speeds he had been making. When the train made its next stop at Erie General Casement boarded the engine and, using language more forceful than elegant, chided the poor fellow for making such poor time over his section. Now the engineer sent the train over the road at lightning speed and in the vicinity of Dunkirk the speeding 4-4-0 rammed a handcar loaded with telegraph wire. Miraculously, no one was injured, but the front end of the celebrated 151 was completely caved in.

At the nearby Brooks works, workmen were just putting the finishing touches to 4-4-0 No. 168 and had her steamed up and otherwise ready for delivery. The new engine was hastily pressed into service, relieving the crippled 151, and took the special into Buffalo. Aside from the destruction of some four dozen sheep there were no further mishaps. At Buffalo, however, the New York Central refused to handle Cummings' private car and he was forced to leave it behind.

Shortly after accepting the road from the contractors, the Nickel Plate announced it would open for business on October 16, 1882. However, a shortage of experienced enginemen forced a postponement of one week. Trains were placed on the road on Monday, October 23, 1882. There were no through passenger runs; the only trains were daily-except-Sunday accommodations between Buffalo and Bellevue and between Cleveland and Chicago. Trains 3 and 4 were scheduled to cover the 340-mile Cleveland-Chicago run in 14 hours while Bellevue-Buffalo trains 1 and 2 required 10 hours 25 minutes to get over the road. Local freight trains, one in each direction over each district, carried passengers in the caboose. With experienced men in charge, the first day's operation went off without a hitch and all departures and arrivals were "on time."

Elegant dining car No. 102 was built by
Barney & Smith at Dayton in 1901.
– *Collection of Willis A. McCaleb.*

Vanderbilt's white elephant

IT is said that early in the summer of 1881 William H. Vanderbilt offered to pay George Seney and his friends a million dollars if they would abandon the building of the Nickel Plate. The road might never have been built if instead he had taken the Lake Erie & Western into the westbound freight pool on equitable terms and engineered an alliance with the syndicate. Vanderbilt was helping finance the Texas & St. Louis, then being built for the express purpose of breaking Jay Gould's Gulf Southwest monopoly. The LE&W and the Chicago & Alton formed a through route from the LS&MS to St. Louis and provided Vanderbilt with an excellent avenue of counterattack against his antagonist. To embrace such allies would have been strategy worthy of Gould himself, but Vanderbilt was avoiding any open maneuvers which might incur his enemy's wrath. Instead, he persisted in his verbal attack on the syndicate, assuming the risk of forcing it into Gould's camp and thereby inviting upon himself the ultimate catastrophe.

GOULD GOES AFTER THE NICKEL PLATE

The Nickel Plate perfectly complemented Gould's holdings east of the Mississippi, giving him the Chicago outlet he sought and diagonally crossing his Wabash lines to Detroit and Toledo. More important, with it he could deliver his heavy volume of eastbound traffic to the Lackawanna at Buffalo, forwarding it to eastern tidewater entirely over his own rails. Control of the Nickel Plate would enable Gould to wage his vendetta against Vanderbilt with renewed fury, and he began as early as the summer of 1881 to make friendly overtures to the Seney Syndicate.

A company of Ohio promoters had been trying for a decade to build a railroad from Toledo southeast to the Ohio River at Wheeling, W. Va. In all this time their Wheeling & Lake Erie had managed to build 12 miles of narrow-gauge road which by the end of 1879 had ceased operation. The economic upturn during 1879-1880 had revived the project, and a line of standard-gauge road was completed in November 1881 from the Lake Erie port of Huron south to Norwalk and east to the Massillon coal fields. Several months previous to this a group of Gould's lieutenants, including Sidney Dillon and Com. C. K. Garrison, bought control of the W&LE and dusted off the road's chartered right to build to Toledo. Almost overnight the track was laid from Norwalk to the Nickel Plate at Bellevue. Thoughtfully, Gould's men then had the charter amended to permit this deviation from the original route and continued to press construction westward to Toledo and the Wabash. A unified Wabash-Nickel Plate-W&LE operation would have given Gould a route from Chicago to Buffalo by way of Toledo as well as a high-speed cutoff around the latter city.

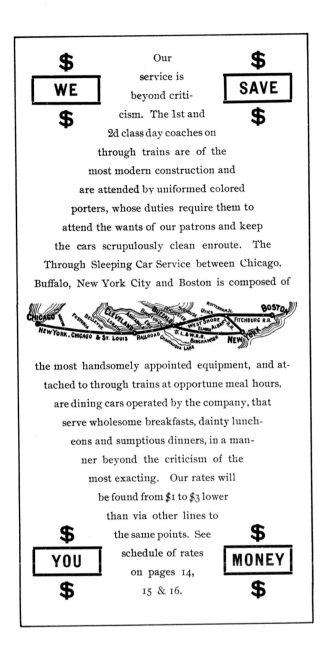

$ WE $

$ SAVE $

Our service is beyond criticism. The 1st and 2d class day coaches on through trains are of the most modern construction and are attended by uniformed colored porters, whose duties require them to attend the wants of our patrons and keep the cars scrupulously clean enroute. The Through Sleeping Car Service between Chicago, Buffalo, New York City and Boston is composed of the most handsomely appointed equipment, and attached to through trains at opportune meal hours, are dining cars operated by the company, that serve wholesome breakfasts, dainty luncheons and sumptious dinners, in a manner beyond the criticism of the most exacting. Our rates will be found from $1 to $3 lower than via other lines to the same points. See schedule of rates on pages 14, 15 & 16.

$ YOU $

$ MONEY $

Hebrides was one of the Wagner sleepers assigned to NKP expresses in the '90's. — *Collection of John A. Rehor.*

VANDERBILT MAKES HIS PLAY

The crisis that now confronted Vanderbilt was the most severe of his career. However, he had one ace in the hole — the greatest fortune in the land. Knowing he could outbid Gould or anyone else, Vanderbilt began an all-out campaign to panic the Seney Syndicate into selling out. In the spring of 1882 he stepped up his verbal barrage, promising that if the Nickel Plate was completed it would promptly be starved to death by the Lake Shore. This bare-faced threat of an all-out rate war was augmented by "research" circulars produced by a firm of Wall Street brokers. These described the Nickel Plate as being cheaply built with wooden bridges and secondhand iron rail. The road was

Further evidence of a Gould-Seney alliance was the announcement that the Nickel Plate and Wabash intended to run trains into Youngstown and Pittsburgh over the narrow-gauge Painesville & Youngstown and Pittsburgh & Western. Members of the syndicate joined forces with Solon Humphreys, president of the Wabash, and James Callery, president of the P&W, to acquire control of the P&Y. A third rail was to be laid on the narrow-gauge road to accommodate standard-gauge equipment.

In November 1881 a Nickel Plate official announced that the road had decided not to build the St. Louis line and was closing a contract with the Wabash for the joint pooling of through St. Louis-Buffalo traffic. Furthermore, it was openly admitted that the plan to build the Jersey Central low-grade connection had been dropped out of deference to Gould.

Well-staffed Barney & Smith diners assigned to *Nickel Plate Express* were instrumental in establishing the train's fine name. — *Collection of John A. Rehor.*

also reported as being without terminals and rolling stock and otherwise ill equipped to do business. Furthermore, the promotion was seriously embarrassed financially and might collapse at any moment. The spurious reports were so effectively distributed that the fables have persisted ever since.

The panic that Vanderbilt sought to stimulate failed to materialize, for the stock trust agreement of February 1881 was still in force and not more than 20 per cent of the Nickel Plate's stock could have been in outside hands. However, the road was proving more costly to complete than originally estimated and the syndicate had already sold its Ohio Central holdings to raise capital. Some of the men, such as Brice and Thomas, had very modest resources and it largely fell upon Seney, the largest

shareholder, to raise additional money. He is reputed to have sold most of his East Tennessee stock and to have negotiated a 7-million-dollar loan from New York banker Jesse Seligman.

LAKE SHORE VS. NICKEL PLATE

Actually, the new road was in many respects superior to its well-established neighbor. The Lake Shore of 1882 was suffering from many years of deferred maintenance and extreme traffic overload — this was neither the great LS&MS of 1872 nor the superb four-track steel highway of later years. Ignoring the fact that his roads were staffed by competent subordinates with proven executive ability, Vanderbilt had insisted on retaining ultimate authority over all his roads. Frugality ran in his

The morning after No. 5, behind 4-4-0 125, ran into rear of standing freight at Millers City, O., in October 1912. — *Collection of William S. Brown.*

family, and he was wont to veto even the most pressing expenditures for improvements. While earnings had held up well enough during the long depression to cover fixed charges and substantial dividends, the Lake Shore's expenditures for improvements and new equipment had been drastically curtailed after 1873 — this in the face of the rapid growth and industrialization of the area it served. Even the vital program of replacing the old iron rails with new 60-pound steel had slowed to a crawl. In 1882 fully a third of the road's tracks were still laid with iron rails.

Physically, the Nickel Plate compared most favorably with the LS&MS. Including trackage rights at Chicago and Buffalo, the road was 523.8 miles long. Poor's 1882 *Manual of the Railroads of the United States* gives the distance of the Lake Shore's main line between Buffalo and Chicago as 540.49 miles. For rate purposes the road listed its old roads between Toledo and Elkhart via Adrian and between Millbury Junction and Elyria via Norwalk as parts of its main line. In reality these were secondary to low-grade cutoff routes, which reduced the actual distance to 522.2 miles. From any station common between the two roads, Buffalo or Chicago was virtually equidistant on either line. As for track, the entire Nickel Plate main line was laid with new ties and new steel rails averaging 60 pounds to the yard. The Lake Shore's main tracks were also laid with 60-pound steel, but a good percentage of this was as much as 10 years old. For about half its route between Buffalo and Chicago the LS&MS was double track, the remainder single track. While there was only 56 miles of double-track operation on the Nickel Plate, the 4000-foot passing tracks were spaced but 8 miles apart and could be joined together as warranted.

The Ohio Railroad Commission made a detailed survey of the Nickel Plate in December 1882 and found the road to be in "excellent condition with smooth riding track and good gravel ballast." No less a personage than George Roberts, president of the Pennsylvania and an outstanding civil engineer, expressed great admiration for the design and construction of the Nickel Plate's iron bridges. These were engineered to withstand 10 to 15 per cent greater stresses than the bridges on the Cincinnati Southern, reported to be the best-built road in America.

The Cuyahoga viaduct avoided the long 55-foot-to-the-mile grade which hampered LS&MS operations at Cleveland. Nickel Plate reported that its worst grades in Ohio were 21 feet to the mile eastbound and 31 feet to the mile westbound. Both roads had severe ruling grades east of Dunkirk, although in later years the Lake Shore was partially relocated to eliminate the worst of these. The *Railroad Gazette* reported that the 78-mile Arcadia-New Haven tangent was then the longest in the country and the Nickel Plate boasted several other tangents as long as 30 miles.

At a rate of about $44,800 per mile of main track, the cost of building and equipping the Nickel Plate amounted to nearly 23 million dollars. Annual fixed charges including interest on the equipment notes came to 1.18 million dollars, or $2266 per mile of

Class G Mogul pauses for water at Rocky River in 1906. Brooks product of 1888 was assigned to westbound local freight between Cleveland and Bellevue. She was dismantled in 1914. — *Albert Loomis.*

main track. This compared well with the Lake Shore's charges of $2316 per mile. *Bradstreet's* described the Nickel Plate's interest charges as light and flatly predicted that the road would earn enough to cover them and pay substantial dividends.

Of the 533 locomotives owned by the LS&MS in 1882 only 156 were less than 10 years old and many had long been in use when the Lake Shore was formed in 1869. Most mainline freight and passenger trains were powered by 4-4-0's with 17 x 24-inch cylinders, 60-inch driving wheels, and a total weight of 31 to 35 tons. There were 205 such engines in service in 1882, including 70 bought in 1881 from the Grant and Schenectady firms. Most of the remainder had been acquired between 1871 and 1873. The fastest passenger engines, 26 in all, were similar to the others except that they had 66-inch drivers. Most of these were also predepression models. There were 24 Mogul freight engines assigned to the Buffalo Division and 25 others of the same pattern were working other sections with heavy grades. The bulk of these 2-6-0's were 30-to-33-ton Baldwin and Rhode Island models of 1873-1874 with 16 x 24-inch cylinders and 54-inch drivers. A handful of heavier

and more powerful Moguls had been built in the Lake Shore's shops during 1880-1881.

The Nickel Plate purchased 108 new locomotives from the Brooks Works at Dunkirk and the Hinkley Locomotive Works of Boston.* The 42 class A 4-4-0's, numbered 1-32 and 40-49, were intended for local passenger and fast freight service. These had 17 x 24-inch cylinders, 60½-inch drivers, and weighed 35 tons. The A's were patterned after the latest Lake Erie & Western engines and were virtually identical to the LS&MS Grant and Schenectady 4-4-0's of 1881. For fast passenger service Brooks furnished 18 class B 4-4-0's, numbered 150-167, with 66½-inch drivers but otherwise resembling class A, and eight class C 4-4-0's numbered 168-175. The latter — with 18 x 24-inch cylinders, 66½-inch drivers, and a weight of 44 tons — were bigger, faster, and more powerful than any LS&MS passenger engine. All 26 Nickel Plate passenger locomotives were equipped with Westinghouse automatic air brake equipment. The C's were also distinctive in that they sported cap-type smokestacks and smokebox extensions, while all other Nickel Plate engines were delivered with diamond stacks.

In November 1881 the Nickel Plate called for bids on 26 heavy-duty freight engines. The Rhode Island works submitted a bid covering Mogul engines similar to those it had built for the Lake Shore. Grant, Rogers, and Baldwin all proposed to furnish heavy Consolidation types. Brooks' successful bid covered a heavy 4-6-0 design which it subsequently demonstrated could move a heavier train faster than even the newest LS&MS Moguls. These class F Ten-Wheelers had a long-barreled wagon-top boiler, air brake equipment, 19 x 24-inch cylinders, 55¾-inch drivers, and a weight of 48 tons in working order. They were assigned numbers 33-39 and 50-68.

For switching service Brooks furnished the road 10 class D 0-4-0's with 16 x 22-inch cylinders and four class E 0-6-0's with 17 x 24-inch cylinders. These were numbered 200-209 and 210-213, respectively. The 0-4-0's had a straight-top boiler with central dome and two sandboxes while the E's came with the class A's wagon-top boiler. Like all Nickel Plate engines, these were painted Holland green with red trim and lettering.

The Nickel Plate started out with more than 6000 freight cars including 1500 box cars assigned to the Nickel Plate Line, the Lackawanna Line, and Trader's Despatch Fast Freight Line. The latter freight forwarder was organized jointly by the Nickel Plate, Erie, Lehigh Valley, LE&W, and the Cincinnati, Hamilton & Dayton. The road's pas-

---

COMPARISON OF MOTIVE POWER — 1882
Lake Shore & Michigan Southern-Nickel Plate

PASSENGER AND FREIGHT

	Type	Cyl. (in.)	Driv. (in.)	Wt. (tons)	Year built	No. built
LS&MS		17 x 24	60	35	1881	70
NYC&StL (a)	4-4-0	17 x 24	60½	35	1881-1882	42

FAST PASSENGER

	Type	Cyl. (in.)	Driv. (in.)	Wt. (tons)	Year built	No. built
LS&MS	4-4-0	17 x 24	66	33.5-35	1871-1879	26
NYC&StL (b)	4-4-0	17 x 24	66½	35	1882	18
NYC&StL (c)	4-4-0	18 x 24	66½	44	1882	8

HEAVY FREIGHT

	Type	Cyl. (in.)	Driv. (in.)	Wt. (tons)	Year built	No. built
LS&MS	2-6-0	16 x 24	54	30-33	1873-1874	38
LS&MS	2-6-0	18 x 24	54	40	1880	3
LS&MS	2-6-0	19 x 24	54	42	1880-1881	6
NYC&StL (f)	4-6-0	19 x 24	55¾	48	1882	26

SWITCHING

	Type	Cyl. (in.)	Driv. (in.)	Wt. (tons)	Year built	No. built
LS&MS	0-6-0	16 x 22	48	32.5	1873	4
LS&MS	0-6-0	16 x 24	48	27	1882	1
NYC&StL (e)	0-6-0	17 x 24	48	35	1882	4

The above table describes the newest and most powerful locomotives owned by the two railroads and used in the various types of service. Source: Railway & Locomotive Historical Society records, including LS&MS roster of July 1, 1882.

---

*Nickel Plate 4-4-0 engines 40-49 were purchased from Hinkley to overcome that builder's reluctance to furnish a relatively large number of narrow-gauge engines to Calvin Brice's Toledo, Delphos & Burlington.

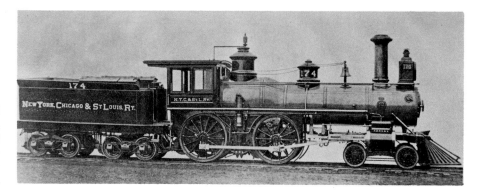

Cap stacked and equipped with air brakes, 44-ton No. 174 was one of eight class C 4-4-0's built by Brooks for express passenger train duty. — *Collection of Gerald M. Best.*

Heavy-duty freight hauler 35 was one of 26 class F Ten-Wheelers built at Dunkirk for the Nickel Plate. — *Collection of John H. Keller.*

senger cars were all built by the Pullman Palace Car Company and included 24 first-class coaches, 10 second-class coaches, 10 baggage cars, four combination mail-and-baggage cars. Painted Tuscan red with gold lettering and trim, the coaches seated 60 persons, weighed 25 tons, and were 59 feet long. All were equipped with Westinghouse air brakes, steam heat, and 42-inch-diameter Allen paper car wheels. The first-class cars had cherry woodwork and high-backed seats upholstered in crimson. The second-class cars or smokers were fitted with rattan seats. The Nickel Plate announced that its fast express trains would initially be made up of a baggage car, one smoker, one first-class coach, a diner, and two sleepers. Pullman was to furnish parlor-cafe and sleeping cars as required, under an arrangement similar to that made with other railroads. As it developed, however, a decade would pass before through express trains would be put on the road.

VANDERBILT BUYS OUT THE SYNDICATE

Despite his frequent jibes, William H. Vanderbilt had doubtless been kept well posted as to how the Nickel Plate was being built and equipped. He knew that the road had tremendous potential, perhaps more as an independent than as a member of the Gould household. The Burlington, Illinois Central, and other independent Western roads terminating at Chicago might discriminate in Vanderbilt's favor were the Nickel Plate a Gould property but would have no ax to grind against it as an independent. Their willingness to do business with

the Grand Trunk, Vanderbilt's aggressive Canadian competitor, had amply demonstrated this. Also, the Nickel Plate might easily form the nucleus of a powerful independent freight pool by entering into traffic agreements with the Chicago & Alton; Lake Erie & Western; Cincinnati, Hamilton & Dayton; Columbus, Hocking Valley & Toledo; and a number of other roads. In the spring of 1882 Nickel Plate and the Erie jointly acquired control of the CH&D and it was rumored that the new trunk line was also after the Valley Railway of Ohio, connecting Cleveland and Canton. As for westbound traffic, the Nickel Plate stood to receive a heavy volume at Buffalo from the Erie, Lehigh Valley, Lackawanna, and the New York, West Shore & Buffalo, then being built parallel to the New York Central. Despite his threats Vanderbilt had no real taste for a resumption of rate warfare. The revenue losses to his own roads during the 1881 fracas had been severe. Plainly, his only course was to buy the Nickel Plate before it fell into the hands of Gould.

As the summer of 1882 drew to a close, the Seney Syndicate publicly betrayed no desire to sell the Nickel Plate. Cummings confidently estimated 1883 earnings at $8500 per mile and predicted the road would show a 55 per cent operating ratio. In September it was announced that fast passenger trains would be run between Cleveland and Toledo in conjunction with the Wheeling & Lake Erie and in competition with the LS&MS. However, matters were not going as smoothly as appearances might indicate. Submitting to pressure from Vanderbilt, the

Illinois Central was backing away from the agreement which afforded the Nickel Plate access to the Great Central Depot at Chicago. The ornate Broadway passenger station at Cleveland would not be opened for business until October 1, 1883, and elsewhere many permanent structures were far from complete. Financial obligations in excess of 2 million dollars were due before the end of 1882.

As Calvin Brice later admitted, the Seney Syndicate and Jay Gould had been secretly negotiating the sale of the road throughout September and early October. The newspapers, however, had a good idea of what was happening. The Chicago *Tribune* of September 18, 1882, reported:

> The opinion is generally gaining ground that the road is for sale, and no one would be surprised to learn at any moment that Jay Gould has secured control of it. As stated in the *Tribune* a day or two ago, Gould wants the road to give the Wabash an eastern outlet from this city both to Toledo and Detroit, and also from Toledo to Buffalo, as from that point a connecting link between the Wabash and the Nickel Plate could readily be built without much expense. In connection with the rumor that Gould is trying to get control of the "Nickel Plate," it is also stated he will have a large interest in the Delaware, Lackawanna & Western, which is to form the eastern outlet from Buffalo for the "Nickel Plate."

More than likely Gould simply didn't have the money it took to buy control of the Nickel Plate. Unable to drive the syndicate's price down, he finally broke off negotiations and took a trip to the Far West. Gould was having his troubles on other fronts. There was a bear on Wall Street, and his antics with Wabash securities were about to catch up with him.

Upon learning that Gould had left for the West, Vanderbilt's friends urged him to buy the Nickel Plate at once on the syndicate's terms. On October 25, 1882, two days after the road had been opened for business, Brice was approached by John H. Devereaux, acting on behalf of Vanderbilt. According to Brice, he told Devereaux, "I will sell on these terms this week but next week we have 2½ million dollars to pay, and if we pay that the road cannot be bought on any terms." Another Vanderbilt agent, Stevenson Burke, called on Brice the next day, agreed to the terms of sale, and made a down payment to bind the transaction. Involved was the sale of 135,000 shares of preferred stock at $37 a share and 130,000 shares of common at $17 a share. This represented a 53 per cent controlling interest and cost Vanderbilt $7,205,000, an amount about 10 per cent greater than what had actually been paid into the entire capital stock of the Nickel Plate.

The purchase was a stunning victory for Vanderbilt and the turning point in his long war with Jay Gould. As for Gould, he had stood at the zenith of his career, ready to administer the *coup de grace* to the one man who stood between him and his dreams of a transcontinental dynasty. After October 1882 it was all downhill for Gould.

Wall Street concluded that the Nickel Plate had been built as a bold speculation by shrewd men who intended all the while to sell it to the highest bidder. While this may have been the case, the fall of 1882 found most of the syndicate members treading on the brink of financial chaos. For several weeks prior to the sale, the prices of Nickel Plate stocks had been dropping due to widespread fear that the road's opening would set off a rate war. Most of the promoters had so overextended themselves financially that they could afford no further risk. Certainly the syndicate could not hope to match Vanderbilt's losses in a rate war.

Brice estimated the profit realized by the syndicate members at 75 per cent. In this day and age such a return seems spectacular, but in a time when fortunes were made and lost overnight it was really quite modest considering the risks undertaken. Whatever their motives, the Seney group had built and opened the Nickel Plate and, ironically, by selling out to Vanderbilt had assured its survival.

The public did not learn the identity of the Nickel Plate's new owner until January 5, 1883, when William K. Vanderbilt succeeded Columbus R. Cummings as the road's president and most of the old Seney directors resigned. With Gould checked, a tired Vanderbilt was passing the active management of his railroads to his sons. William K. was to head the Lake Shore in addition to the Nickel Plate, while brother Cornelius II was to take over the Michigan Central and the New York Central. The LS&MS had possession of the Nickel Plate stock, having traded Vanderbilt 6.5 million dollars in second-mortgage bonds for the securities. The arrangement was in open violation of laws of all five states the Nickel Plate served, but no attempt was made at enforcement. Since Governor Foster of Ohio had undoubtedly countenanced the sale of the road, the anticipated opposition of that state failed to materialize. However, the bondholders and minority stockholders soon expressed their displeasure and as early as 1883 made a futile bid to wrest control from the LS&MS.

Expediency had forced Vanderbilt to purchase the Nickel Plate stock. He would have preferred to drive the road into bankruptcy and then acquire it at foreclosure, as his sons subsequently did in the case of the West Shore. Having triumphed over Gould, Vanderbilt nevertheless found himself confronted with a unique dilemma. If he permitted the Nickel Plate a free hand, it would be to the detriment of his own roads and to the convenience of

Buffalo accommodation trundles east over original Conneaut viaduct behind class C 4-4-0 in the 1880's before advent of through passenger trains and construction of Pittsburgh, Shenango & Lake Erie, B&LE predecessor. — *Collection of John A. Tyler.*

Buffalo Express, No. 2, leaves Conneaut in summer of 1893. PS&LE Conneaut branch (foreground) had been in operation about a year. — *Collection of John A. Tyler.*

41

Gen. Darius W. Caldwell, father of the fast freight, supervised NKP operation 1882-1895. — *NKP photo.*

his competitors. On the other hand, his investment in the Nickel Plate was substantial and if he restricted the road too severely he would have to either make restitution for its deficits or surrender control to the bondholders.

After Vanderbilt had purchased control of the Nickel Plate, General Caldwell remained in charge of the road's operations, such as they were. The passenger train schedule consisted of the Buffalo-Bellevue and Cleveland-Chicago trains which had opened the road and Nos. 5 and 6, accommodation trains put on between Cleveland and Conneaut early in 1883. Trains were so scheduled that the traveler arriving in Cleveland from either direction had a 15-hour layover if he wished to continue his journey on the Nickel Plate. On October 6, 1884, the Conneaut accommodations were dropped but trains 1 and 2, the Bellevue-Buffalo runs, were extended west to Fostoria in order to make connection with trains of the Indiana, Bloomington & Western* at Green Springs. Westbound No. 1 also made a fair connection at Fostoria with a Baltimore & Ohio train for Chicago.

From the time it was opened, the Nickel Plate had access to the Union Stock Yards at Chicago. Under a pool arrangement the road was allocated 10 per cent of all eastbound livestock shipments from the stockyards and operated a daily stock train from

---

*The IB&W extended from Sandusky, O., to Indianapolis and Peoria, was subsequently absorbed by the Big Four, and is now operated as part of the New York Central.

Chicago to Buffalo. An eastbound dairy train was also regularly originated at Chicago, and the Nickel Plate received a good volume of fruit and berries from the Illinois Central. The road's predominantly eastbound traffic also included Cincinnati beer received from the CH&D at Leipsic, O., and a regular through Indianapolis-Buffalo stock train was operated in conjunction with the IB&W. However, from the very beginning the Nickel Plate's meat trains were its stock in trade. Shipments of refrigerated dressed meat from Armour, Swift, and other Chicago packing houses reached New York via Nickel Plate and its Buffalo connections 10 to 20 hours in advance of any other route. By 1888 the road had been dubbed "The Meat Express Line." Observers at Fort Wayne reported that the Nickel Plate was running six long meat trains through that city every night.

The sawmills and stave factories of the Black Swamp, a handful of grain elevators west of Bellevue, and the fall grape harvest east of Cleveland accounted for most of the freight tonnage originated on the Nickel Plate. In slack times such business was routed to the nearest interchange with the LS&MS, with the Nickel Plate receiving the shortest haul possible. Similarly, the volume of through traffic fluctuated with the parent road's traffic load. Extensive interchange with non-Vanderbilt connections was discouraged. Repeated attempts on the part of the Lehigh Valley and the Lackawanna to establish through freight trains were ignored. Such a controlled economy, coupled with the recession of 1883-1886, soon led to bankruptcy. In 1883 and 1884 Nickel Plate's earnings fell short of its fixed charges by $661,776 and $608,770 respectively.

THE GREAT NICKEL PLATE FORECLOSURE SUIT

For two years after taking over the Nickel Plate Vanderbilt and the LS&MS met its deficits by issuing second-mortgage bonds and advancing the road cash. By January 1885 the Nickel Plate's financial embarrassment had become so acute that the LS&MS was in grave danger of losing control of the road. The semi-annual first-mortgage interest coupons totaling $450,000 were due June 1 and the road was also obliged to pay $140,000 in interest on the equipment bonds on April 1. The times were bad, earnings were poorer than ever, there was no working capital on hand, and the Lake Shore could no longer afford to advance large amounts of cash. In order to protect its investment of more than 10 million dollars, the LS&MS was faced with the prospect of having to retire the Nickel Plate's bonded and floating debt of nearly 25 million dollars. This appeared to be the only alternative to surrendering the railroad to the first-mortgage bondholders. In the process of effecting this,

Lake Shore's interest could be virtually obliterated.

In the face of the Lake Shore's seemingly insoluble dilemma Vanderbilt's legal wizards came up with a brilliant scheme. Without any great expenditure the Lake Shore's equity would be preserved and Vanderbilt would secure unchallenged control of the Nickel Plate. Beyond this the Nickel Plate's interest burden would be reduced to a tolerable level. The strategy, successful beyond the most sanguine expectations, brought about an amazing episode in the history of railroad finance. It very nearly precipitated a catastrophic panic as well.

The New York, Chicago & St. Louis was a consolidation of five separate companies chartered in five states. At the time of the consolidation none of the companies possessed completed track and no construction had as yet been undertaken. Under Ohio law railroad companies could be consolidated only when their tracks met. The LS&MS attorneys reasoned that under the law the Nickel Plate was not a legal corporation. In violation of another Ohio statute, the first-mortgage bonds had been sold before the road was completed and the road's directors had purchased some of them at less than par. On the other hand, the slightly more than 1 million dollars in second-mortgage bonds had been purchased by the LS&MS at par in 1883 after the Nickel Plate had been completed. Inasmuch as the state of Ohio had never opposed the 1881 consolidation, the Nickel Plate constituted a corporation *de facto* in 1883 and possessed at that time the power to execute a mortgage. In Ohio, at least, the second mortgage legally constituted a prior lien on the property.

Vanderbilt's strategy called for a foreclosure suit filed in Ohio in advance of any similar action on the part of the first-mortgage bondholders elsewhere. Not bound by the unique Ohio laws, a court outside that state would doubtless uphold the sanctity of the first mortgage. Thus it was imperative that the Nickel Plate default on the $30,000 interest due March 1, 1885, on the second mortgage. This accomplished, the trustee for the mortgage filed a foreclosure suit in the Cuyahoga County common pleas court at Cleveland, and General Caldwell was subsequently named receiver on March 28. The Nickel Plate then defaulted on the equipment bond and first-mortgage interest as they came due. The Central Trust Company subsequently declared the first-mortgage principal due and cross-petitioned for foreclosure. This action, if confirmed by the court, would have liquidated the road's capital stock and ended Lake Shore control.

The trial of the "great three-cornered Nickel Plate foreclosure suit" commenced at Cleveland in September 1886. It was followed with intense interest in Wall Street and in railroad circles throughout the land. The stakes were enormous and the trustees of the mortgages and equipment trust were represented by impressive batteries of distinguished legal talent. The allegation that the Nickel Plate was an unlawful corporation and that the first mortgage was fraudulent fell like a bombshell on an unsuspecting Central Trust. Yet few doubted the ultimate outcome. After all, whatever the legal quirks involved, the Seney Syndicate had built and equipped the road in good faith with money raised through

First run of No. 2 out of Bellevue on October 23, 1882, was pulled by No. 165, shown here some years later with straight stack. — *Collection of John A. Rehor.*

the sale of bonds now in the hands of thousands of innocent persons. No court had ever before upset a railroad's first mortgage.

On January 3, 1887, the court ruled that the Nickel Plate consolidation was indeed in violation of the law and that the first mortgage was null and void. The equity of the equipment bondholders and other creditors was specifically protected. The decision caused consternation in Wall Street and a wave of panic selling followed. Speculators and investors alike were cursing William K. Vanderbilt as another Gould. Central Trust's James A. Roosevelt promised an immediate appeal and a fight to the Supreme Court if necessary. Railroad men everywhere were badly shaken. One prominent Eastern railroad official stated, "The decision virtually gives the Nickel Plate to the Lake Shore for nothing." Even in the Vanderbilt camp jubilation was short lived.

The judges who had presided over the trial had no doubt of what would follow. Privately they pre-

Main Basin of the World's Columbian Exposition of 1893. Backed by Chicago's railroads, including NKP, the fair attracted more than 27 million visitors in six months. — *Courtesy Chicago Historical Society.*

forces and formed a purchasing committee. On February 4, 1887, they announced a plan of re-organization that was equitable to all concerned. Holders of the old 6 per cent mortgages would receive 18 million dollars in new 4 per cent bonds at par and accrued interest. Stockholders received 50 per cent of their former holdings in new shares and were assessed $10 per old share. The money raised through the assessment and the proceeds of the sale of 2 million dollars' worth of bonds was used to retire the equipment bonds and floating debt.

After buying the road at foreclosure sale on May 19, 1887, the purchasing committee incorporated the New York, Chicago & St. Louis Railroad Company in New York on June 22. On the same date companies were incorporated in Ohio, Indiana, and Pennsylvania to acquire the sections of the Nickel Plate in those states. That part of the road in Illinois, 9.96 miles, was conveyed to the Chicago & State Line Railroad on July 2. On September 22 the New York company absorbed the Ohio, Indiana, and Pennsylvania companies. Finally, the Chicago & State Line was leased in perpetuity and the new Nickel Plate formally took possession of the entire railroad on October 1, 1887.

The new company's capitalization amounted to 40 million dollars. Stock and floating debt totaling 33 million dollars had been wiped out. Annual fixed charges had been reduced by nearly 40 per cent. There was about $600,000 in cash for improvements and the new company owned 108 locomotives and 7244 cars outright. The LS&MS retained stock control by paying its share of the stock assessment, about 2.5 million dollars.

While William K. Vanderbilt was named chairman of the board, Roosevelt and other representatives of the bondholders were elected directors. As a further concession Darius Caldwell was elected president and was given a reasonably free hand in running the road. No longer would he be encumbered with the restrictions that had carried the Nickel Plate to bankruptcy.

The new status of the Nickel Plate was due in part to a pair of new laws enacted by Congress. The Interstate Commerce Act of 1887 prohibited the pooling of freight traffic between common points on competing roads and outlawed rate discrimination against persons, commodities, and localities. The Sherman Act of 1890 strictly forbade the restraint or destruction of competition through ownership or control of competing railroads.

Taking full advantage of the autonomy granted

dicted that there would be no appeal. Such action, they claimed, would eventually invalidate large financial obligations of a number of large railroad systems and cause grave panic among investors. Certainly this was not in the interest of any of the parties involved. Both Vanderbilt and Roosevelt would be anxious to avoid such an outcome and would quickly compromise. The result would be a speedy recovery of the stricken Nickel Plate.

Within a fortnight the antagonists had joined

the Nickel Plate, Caldwell quickly put the road on a paying basis. During 1890 operations netted a surplus of $250,000 and the next year the Nickel Plate paid its first dividend, 3½ per cent on the preferred stock. In 1891 Caldwell engineered an operating alliance with the West Shore, acquired by the Vanderbilts at foreclosure in 1885. The two roads formed a through New York-Chicago route 952 miles long. The aggressive Caldwell even managed to increase the Nickel Plate's volume of business after the panic of 1893, a feat which earned him the presidency of the LS&MS in 1895.

Growth of the Nickel Plate's business after the reorganization required the acquisition of 50 new freight engines between 1888 and 1896. In 1888 the road purchased 15 class G 2-6-0's which were comparable to the Lake Shore's standard freight haulers. Built by Brooks, they carried numbers 69-83. These were followed in 1890 by five Brooks class H Moguls numbered 84-88 which were intended for local freight service. The LS&MS went to the 4-6-0 for its freight trains in 1890, and Nickel Plate followed suit the next year when Brooks built 10 class I Ten-Wheelers. Assigned numbers 89-98, these had 18 x 24-inch cylinders, 50-inch drivers, and a total engine weight of 50 tons. In 1892 the road bought its first Baldwin engines, 10 class J 4-6-0's numbered 99-108. These were essentially identical to the I's, save for No. 100 which was a Vauclain compound

with 12 and 20 x 24-inch cylinders.* The Baldwins were followed by the class K 4-6-0's of 1896. The 109-113 were built by Brooks and the 114-118 were turned out by Schenectady. Although somewhat heavier, the K's were otherwise identical to the 4-6-0's of 1891-1892.

THE PEERLESS TRIO

On October 23, 1892, the 10th anniversary of the opening of the Nickel Plate, the road put on the first of its through Buffalo-Chicago passenger trains. No. 1, the *Chicago Express*, left the Erie's Buffalo depot at Exchange and Michigan streets at noon and got into Chicago at 8:10 the next morning. No. 2, the eastbound express, ran on a schedule calling for a 10:15 p.m. Chicago departure and 6 p.m. Buffalo arrival. Trains 3 and 4 were retained as accommodations between Cleveland and Chicago.

From May to November 1893, the World's Columbian Exposition was held at Chicago commemorating the 400th anniversary of the discovery of America. The fair was held on the present site of Jackson Park on Chicago's south side. On May 28, 1893, shortly after the fair opened, the Nickel Plate in conjunction with the West Shore began running through New York-Chicago passenger trains. At the time, the latter ran its trains into the LS&MS depot

*The only compound ever bought by the Nickel Plate, the 100 failed to measure up to her conventional sisters' performance and was converted to a simple engine in 1907.

Pre-Canniff class K No. 112 was assigned to fast merchandise in 1900. Brooks built in 1896, 4-6-0 had 18 x 24-inch cylinders, Fox tender trucks. — *Collection of C. E. Helms.*

on Buffalo's Exchange Street, practically next door to the Erie depot. Transfer of trains between the West Shore and Nickel Plate was effected by construction of about 500 feet of track between the two stations. At this time westbound No. 3 was upgraded to Buffalo-Chicago express status and the Nickel Plate's Peerless Trio was rounded out by a new westbound train, No. 5, the *Western Express*. The new flyer and its eastbound counterpart, No. 6, were put on a 16-hour schedule and assigned new Ohio Falls coaches and a pair of new Wagner dining cars. Through Wagner sleeping cars were assigned to all three westbound express trains, but Nos. 1 and 3 made meal stops at appropriate times of the day at company dining stations at Conneaut, Cleveland, Bellevue, and Fort Wayne. Train No. 4, the *Cleveland Mail*, still ran only as far east as Cleveland, but a new train, No. 8, was put on between Cleveland and Buffalo.

Prior to prohibition Berghoff Peerless beer was served on Nickel Plate passenger trains.

With dull times upon the country once again the Nickel Plate reduced its passenger schedule after the World's Fair closed. No. 3 reverted to a Cleveland-Chicago accommodation and No. 8 was taken off. Subsequently, however, the road began running through cars between New York and Chicago in conjunction with the Lackawanna as well as the West Shore and through sleepers between Boston and Chicago via the West Shore and Fitchburg Railroad (now Boston & Maine). The new service was well received, and in June 1897 trains 3 and 4 were changed to through express runs. New No. 4 carried both through coaches and sleepers for New York via the Lackawanna. Trains 2 and 3, now known as the *Nickel Plate Express*, were put on 15-hour schedules and assigned through New York and Boston sleeping cars. Nos. 5 and 6, the *Standard Express*, carried West Shore New York-Chicago sleeping cars.

The basic schedule of June 1897, save for minor time changes, was used until the end of New York Central control in 1916. In the face of the sternest sort of competition, the Peerless Trio enjoyed a high degree of popularity with the traveling public. Aside from excess-fare all-Pullman luxury trains like the 20-hour *20th Century Limited* and 23-hour *Pennsylvania Limited*, the *Nickel Plate Express* was the equal of any through express run between New York and Chicago in the early 1900's. In addition to a 28-hour schedule, the trains offered convenient departures and arrivals and a savings of as much as 3 dollars on a first-class fare.

For about 10 years after it was opened the Nickel Plate operated suburban trains at Cleveland in lieu of the service formerly rendered by the CP&A and Rocky River roads. Engine 199, an ex-CP&A Baldwin Forney, and a pair of CP&A coaches shuttled back and forth over the 19.3 miles between Euclid

---

WESTBOUND NICKEL PLATE EXPRESS
PASSENGER TRAINS — 1902
NO. 1 — ERIE, CLEVELAND, FT. WAYNE & CHICAGO EXPRESS

Vestibuled buffet-sleeper . . . New York-Chicago via DL&W

First-class day coach . . . New York-Chicago via DL&W

Vestibuled sleeper . . . Buffalo-Chicago

Dining car . . . Bellevue-Chicago

Transcontinental tourist car . . . Boston to west coast via Fitchburg, West Shore, and connecting railroads at Chicago

First- and second-class day coaches . . . Buffalo-Chicago

Baggage car . . . Buffalo-Chicago
NO. 3 — NICKEL PLATE EXPRESS

Vestibuled sleepers . . . Boston-Chicago via Fitchburg and West Shore railroads
New York-Chicago via West Shore
New York-Chicago via DL&W

Dining car . . . Buffalo-Chicago

First- and second-class day coaches . . . Buffalo-Chicago

Baggage cars . . . Buffalo-Chicago
NO. 5 — STANDARD EXPRESS

Vestibuled sleepers . . . New York-Chicago via DL&W
Buffalo-Chicago

First- and second-class day coaches . . . Buffalo-Chicago

Baggage and mail cars . . . Buffalo-Chicago

No. 3 ran on old No. 5's time, approximately. Note that trains have more or less followed the original 1893 schedule.

			FT.	
YEAR	BUFFALO	CLEVELAND	WAYNE	CHICAGO
No. 5 1893	5:50 a.m.	11:20 a.m.	4:44 p.m.	9:50 p.m.
No. 3 1899-				
1902	6:10 a.m.	11:19 a.m.	4:30 p.m.	9:15 p.m.
No. 3 1916	6:30 a.m.	11:25 a.m.	4:45 p.m.	9:20 p.m.
No. 3 1922	6:40 a.m.	11:30 a.m.	4:52 p.m.	9:20 p.m.
No. 3 1928	6:40 a.m.	11:30 a.m.	5:05 p.m.	9:50 p.m.

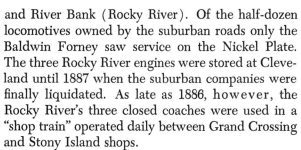

Westbound *Standard Express* crosses Vermilion River behind 4-4-0 No. 169. — *Collection of Willis A. McCaleb.*

and River Bank (Rocky River). Of the half-dozen locomotives owned by the suburban roads only the Baldwin Forney saw service on the Nickel Plate. The three Rocky River engines were stored at Cleveland until 1887 when the suburban companies were finally liquidated. As late as 1886, however, the Rocky River's three closed coaches were used in a "shop train" operated daily between Grand Crossing and Stony Island shops.

About 1892 the Cleveland short runs were discontinued, and a pair of commuter trains were put on between Lorain and Cleveland. No. 18 left Lorain in the early morning and returned in the evening as No. 21. During the day the equipment was used on a short turn to Dover (now Bay Village) to accommodate bathers headed for the fine beach at Dover Bay Park. Shortly before the turn of the century the commuter runs were discontinued and the Dover turn was extended to Vermilion, 11 miles west of Lorain. Operated daily, No. 19 left Cleveland in the early morning and returned in the evening as No. 20. These trains afforded pleasure-seekers a full day at popular resorts such as Lake Breeze, Oak Point, and Linwood Park.

Prior to the first World War the Nickel Plate did a heavy summertime excursion business, not only to the Lake Erie playgrounds west of Cleveland but to stellar attractions such as Lake Chautauqua and Niagara Falls. Beginning in 1883 the road ran an annual Niagara Falls excursion which featured solid trains of sleeping cars, bargain rates, and personally conducted tours. The first section originated at Valparaiso, Ind, and ran nonstop east of Fort Wayne. A second section followed out of Fort Wayne to handle fares east of that point.

DEPOTS AT CHICAGO

After October 23, 1882, the Nickel Plate ran its passenger trains into Chicago over the Illinois Central using a temporary station at 14th Street instead of the Great Central Depot. On May 1, 1883, the road moved into the joint Rock Island-LS&MS Van Buren Street Union Station, located on the present site of La Salle Street Station. In order to reach this facility, trackage rights were secured over the Lake Shore from Grand Crossing to 61st Street (Englewood), 2.4 miles, and over the Rock Island to Van Buren Street, 6.5 miles. In 1892 the road built its own passenger and freight facilities along the west side of Clark Street between 12th and Taylor streets. The passenger depot fronted on 12th and the freight-house faced Taylor. These quarters were a little less than 1 mile south of Van Buren Street but were

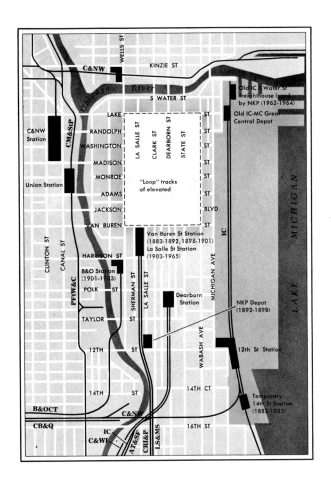

50

Van Buren Street Union Station of the Rock Island and LS&MS was located between La Salle and Pacific streets. Above photo was taken in 1883, when the Nickel Plate began running its passenger trains into the station. Above left: interior of station's trainshed some years after 1872 rebuilding following Fire of 1871. — *All photos, courtesy Chicago Historical Society.*

La Salle Street Station, opened in 1903, was located on site of old Van Buren Street Station and still serves trains of the Nickel Plate, Rock Island, and New York Central.

Engraving shows Van Buren Street Station after being renovated and enlarged about 1886.

William Henry Canniff, president of the Nickel Plate from 1898 to 1916. — *NKP photo.*

practically adjacent to the Polk Street or Dearborn station used by the Santa Fe, Wabash, and a number of other roads.

The opening of the "Loop" elevated railway in 1896 gave the Van Buren Street depot the most convenient location of any Chicago railroad station. Consequently, the Nickel Plate quit its 12th Street depot and moved back into Van Buren Street on March 6, 1898. When the latter was razed in 1901 to make way for the new La Salle Street Station, Nickel Plate ran its passenger trains into B&O's Grand Central Station at 5th Avenue and Harrison Street. The road has used La Salle Street since its opening in 1903.

WILLIAM HENRY CANNIFF

In May 1898 the Lake Shore's general manager William H. Canniff succeeded Samuel R. Callaway as president of the Nickel Plate. Canniff's long railroad career began in 1863 when he hired out as a night watchman on the Michigan Southern & Northern Indiana. One of the Nickel Plate's most popular presidents, Canniff was at the road's helm until July 1916 when the New York Central sold its controlling interest. His broad experience gave him a close familiarity with the workings of the various departments and he enjoyed intimate relationships with employees at all levels. His tenure as president was marked by a continuation of the Nickel Plate's modest prosperity, and 5 per cent dividends were paid on the preferred stock from 1901 through 1916 and on the common stock from 1910 through 1913.

Under Canniff there was consistent improvement in operational efficiency. Between 1898 and 1915

the operating ratio was reduced from 85.26 per cent to 74.36 per cent. More noteworthy, perhaps, was the harmony and loyalty engendered by this man. Canniff's Nickel Plate became a proud, closely knit family institution. No haven for boomers, the road was a place where men spent their entire working careers and watched their sons follow them into the organization.

Canniff's influence largely brought about the organization of the Veteran Association of the Nickel Plate Railroad on October 23, 1907. That day 115 men who were on the roster the day the road opened met at Cleveland to organize the Vets, the first such railroad organization in America. Among them were Wallace Farley, the engineer who made the first run across the Cuyahoga viaduct; Dr. James M. Dinnen, chief surgeon for the road for more than a half century; and Henry Hammersly, who as paymaster had driven a team deep into the Black Swamp in the spring of 1881 to pay the gangs resurfacing the old Continental grade.

THE SECOND GENERATION OF MOTIVE POWER

With the advent of the express passenger trains all of the class C and many class B passenger engines were returned to Dunkirk where they were reboilered and modernized. By 1904 the express trains had outgrown the capacity of the rebuilt 4-4-0's and that year Brooks built six class O 4-4-0's with 68-inch drivers, 18 x 24-inch piston valve cylinders, and a total engine weight of 62 tons. Originally numbered 176-181, these became Nos. 120-125 in 1910. All were equipped with firetube superheaters at Stony Island and Conneaut shops during 1911-1913.

The O's were followed by six Baldwin class R Ten-Wheelers with 72-inch driving wheels, slide valves, and Walschaerts valve gear. The R's, delivered in 1907, first carried numbers 182-187 but during the general renumbering of motive power in 1910 were assigned numbers 150-155. During 1912-1913 these engines were rebuilt with 20 x 26-inch piston valve cylinders and superheaters. In 1913 Brooks turned out three more R's, 156-158, which were practically identical to the rebuilt Baldwins. The R's were excellent steaming engines and quite fast. However, they had a severe lateral rolling motion at high speed and their shallow, narrow furnaces were tricky to fire. The 151 was probably the worst of the lot in these respects. She became notorious among Buffalo Division firemen who dubbed her "Cat-eye Annie."

"Paddy" Canniff's manifest freight trains ran on fast 31-hour schedules in four or more 30-to-35-car sections behind two types of locomotives. These were the class N 2-8-0 of 1902 and the class P 4-6-0 of 1905. Both types had 63-inch drivers and an overall length of slightly more than 61 feet, short enough

Class O 4-4-0 rolls westbound No. 3, the *Nickel Plate Express*, across 730-foot Chagrin River viaduct at Willoughby in 1906. Varnish includes dining car and through sleepers out of Boston and New York. — *Collection of Richard J. Cook.*

Patriotic Conneaut yardmen did their bit in helping arouse war fervor in 1898 when they decked out 0-4-0 No. 206 in red, white and blue and byword of the day. — *NKP photo.*

Consol 131 was outshopped at Brooks' Dunkirk works in 1903. N-1 weighed 80 tons, had 19 x 28-inch cylinders, 62-inch drivers. — *Collection of Paul W. Prescott.*

During June 1909 overhaul, class P Ten-Wheeler 42 got early design Baker-Pilliod valve gear. She became 302 in 1910; was dismantled in 1922. — *Collection of John H. Keller.*

Brooks-built Third 12, shown at Euclid about 1920, was one of 46 class M switchers bought between 1900 and 1910. — *Collection of John H. Keller.*

Baldwin outshopped 72-inch-drivered No. 186 in June 1907 for NKP expresses. Class R 4-6-0 became Third 154 in 1910; was rebuilt in 1913 with piston valves, superheater. — *Collection of H. L. Broadbelt.* Same engine (below) pauses at Celina, O., in November 1935 with lengthened tender, electric headlight, running-board ladders, modified Walschaerts. Steel cab and pilot beam were added before 1948 retirement. — *C. E. Helms.*

to fit the road's 65-foot turntables and roundhouse stalls. There were 60 Consolidations in all, numbered 400-459 after 1910, and the last group, the N-6's of 1913, differed from the 1902 models only in that they sported Schmidt superheaters and Walschaerts valve gear. Similarly, such improvements were all that separated the class P of 1905 and the P-3 of 1913. The 4-6-0's, numbered 300-366 after 1910, were used on the Second and Third districts (Conneaut to Fort Wayne) where they were rated at 1045 tons. The 2-8-0's worked the First and Fourth districts (later the Buffalo and Chicago divi-

sions) where they had a 1410-ton rating on eastbound manifest trains under normal conditions. Both types were wonderful steamers — fast and well liked by enginemen. Although new locomotives were bought each year from 1900 through 1911 and in 1913, only these two designs were ordered for freight service. Both were obsolete long before 1910 but were bought again and again, apparently instead of modifying the engine facilities.

Between 1900 and 1910 Brooks and other builders turned out 46 class M switch engines. Built to an 1896 design and numbered in the 200 series, these

Class P Ten-Wheeler moves empty reefers on Second District about 1908. By 1909 Chicago-Buffalo merchandise and stock trains were on 31-to-34-hour schedules. — *NKP photo.*

had 18 x 24-inch slide valve cylinders and 50-inch drivers. Finally in 1913 the Nickel Plate quit the obsolete design and purchased six class S 0-6-0's with 20 x 26-inch piston valve cylinders, superheaters, Walschaerts gear, and total weight of 75.5 tons.

Under Canniff, the old green-and-red paint job went out and engines were painted black with 5-inch gold leaf letters and numerals. The road's initials were painted on long wooden boards which were bolted to each side of the tank collar. The engine number was applied to the cab sides, a small board mounted on the smokebox door, and the back of the tank. After 1903 most new engines came from the builders with the initials simply painted on the tank collars rather than on the unique boards.

BRANCH LINES AND DOUBLE TRACK

That part of the old Cleveland, Painesville & Ashtabula along Cleveland's Superior Street between Becker Avenue and NYC&StL Junction (East Cleveland), 2.4 miles, was for many years the Nickel Plate's only branch line. Operation over the branch was suspended in December 1882 but the track remained intact until June 1894 when citizens re-

moved rails crossing several streets. A month later the Nickel Plate relaid its track over the streets only to again have it removed, this time by city authorities. Finally in March 1895 the Ohio Supreme Court ruled that the road no longer possessed the right to cross the streets and the Nickel Plate than removed the remaining track on the CP&A branch.

The Euclid Railroad — a 2.49-mile spur extending from Euclid Junction to the Bluestone quarries in what is today South Euclid, O. — was built and opened during the summer of 1885. Independently owned, the branch has always been operated by the Nickel Plate under contract. Originally the Euclid Railroad transported a steady flow of carloads of sandstone sidewalk slabs. The quarries have been defunct for many years and in modern times tonnage has consisted of inbound carloads of limestone, for the most part.

In 1895 Tom Johnson, later one of Cleveland's most celebrated mayors, moved a rolling mill from Johnstown, Pa., to a large tract of forest on the Black River near Lorain, O. By 1904 Johnson's mill was known as the National Tube Works and was in the process of being vastly expanded. That year the

Fourth District Engineer E. F. Wolf poses with his engine, new N-4 2-8-0 162, at West Wayne roundhouse in 1908. Wolf helped build the Nickel Plate, went braking on it in 1882, later transferred to engine service. His son and grandson became Fort Wayne Division engineers. At his right is Fireman "Haystack" Reesner. — *Collection of E. F. Wolf.*

Nickel Plate built a 3-mile branch south from Sheffield Junction to the Tube Works and shared its output with the Baltimore & Ohio.

Before long other railroads were projecting branch lines to booming Lorain. The Pennsylvania and Erie joined forces to build the ill-starred Lorain, Ashland & Southern. The Wheeling & Lake Erie built a subsidiary, the Lorain & West Virginia. The Lake Erie & Pittsburgh was partly built by the New York Central and Pennsylvania. The Pennsy, as it developed, never got to Lorain. However, that road hauled much coal as far as Cleveland where it turned it over to the Nickel Plate for movement to South Lorain. There was a substantial return haul of iron ore from the Tube Works ore docks over the same route.

The heavy traffic between Cleveland and Lorain necessitated extending the original 6.24 miles of double track at Cleveland to Lorain. Completed in 1907, the project also involved building a new double-track steel viaduct across the Rocky River gorge. Also in 1907 a second track was laid between Stony Island and Osborn Avenue at Hammond, 11.1 miles. At Osborn the Nickel Plate maintained an important

connection with the Indiana Harbor Railroad (IHB), another LS&MS property. Not only did the IH deliver much eastbound meat and perishable traffic to the Nickel Plate at this point, but both roads jointly operated a fleet of 12 daily suburban trains between Indiana Harbor and Chicago. These ran over the Nickel Plate from Osborn to La Salle Street, 22.8 miles. By 1912 a second track had also been installed between Stony Island and Grand Crossing and to Vanloon, 3 miles east of Osborn.

Between 1907 and 1912 the Nickel Plate was double tracked between Conneaut and Thornton Junction, Pa., 9.28 miles; Conneaut and Kingsville, O., 7.24 miles; and Colby and Kimball, O., 12.51 miles. Construction of the Cleveland Short Line Railway — the Lake Shore's cutoff around Cleveland — involved realigning much of the Nickel Plate's line through Cleveland's far east side. At the same time a second track was laid between East 55th Street and Euclid, 10 miles. Completed in 1913, the improvement gave the road a 38-mile stretch of double track between Lorain and Euclid.

In 1892 the LS&MS relocated a section of its main line east of Dunkirk, N. Y., and a 7.84-mile segment

Overhead coal dock at Euclid was built in 1906, retired in 1951. Locomotive crane X-003 supplied dock from hoppers on adjacent track. — *Collection of Willis A. McCaleb.*

Bellevue, long the hub of NKP operations, had a bustling engine terminal to judge from this 1903 photo. Locomotive crane coals engine while line of 4-6-0's await calls to duty. In foreground is a class M 0-6-0. — *Collection of Willis A. McCaleb.*

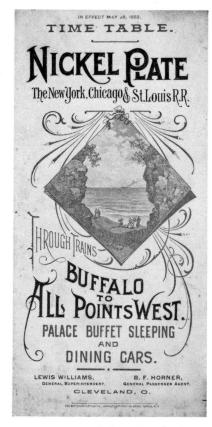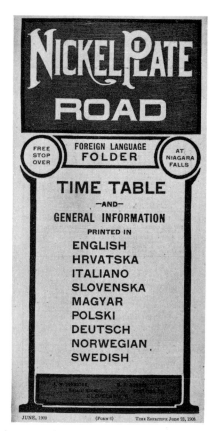

Idyllic scene beckons travelers on brochure published shortly after road came under LS&MS control. Center timetable features joint operations with West Shore and Fitchburg in 1898. NKP foreign language folder (right) accommodated flux of immigrants swelling industrial centers such as Cleveland, Lorain, and Gary after turn of the century.

of the original double-track main between Dunkirk and Silver Creek was leased to the Nickel Plate early in 1893. The original Nickel Plate track over this same distance was subsequently abandoned. In 1923 the road purchased this track and today operates a part of the original New York-Chicago road.

Between 1902 and 1910 practically all the viaducts were renewed or rebuilt. However, most of the new bridges had about the same strength rating as the old, a fact that gave the Nickel Plate much trouble in later years. In 1913 automatic block signals spaced 1 mile apart were installed between Stony Island and Edgerton, Ind., 157 miles. By 1916 all of the original 60-pound main track rails had been replaced by 75- and 80-pound steel. Only the Conneaut engine facility was upgraded during the period of New York Central control. A new roundhouse with 28 90-foot stalls and an 85-foot turntable were built here in 1911. New boiler and machine shops were also erected at Conneaut in 1912. The 22-stall roundhouse and hand-powered turntable built in 1882 were used as a tank shop.

Originally the engine terminals had low timber trestles called coal docks. Gondola cars were run up on the trestles and their contents shoveled by coal heavers into small four-wheel trams or "bug-gies." Locomotives were spotted alongside the coal docks and the buggies were tilted forward, dumping coal into the tenders. In the early 1900's the coal docks were replaced by locomotive cranes equipped with clamshells. By 1916 this was the method employed in coaling locomotives at all terminals.

During the 34 years the Nickel Plate languished under New York Central control, great pains were taken to create the impression that the road was independently operated and to a large degree it actually was. Considerable sums had been spent for improvements and for new equipment, but the road's growth and capacity had been subtly restricted through continued use of obsolete facilities and standards. By contrast, the capacity of the Lake Shore had been greatly expanded over the years and it was as fine a railroad as existed anywhere. The industrial growth of the territory the two roads served had continued unabated, but this benefit had accrued almost entirely to the Lake Shore. Little or no attempt had been made to locate new industries on the Nickel Plate and prime industrial sites were allowed to become residential neighborhoods. As a result the road was almost totally dependent on traffic received from its connections. By 1916 the Nickel Plate had fallen into almost total obscurity.

Rugged H-6f 662 debuts at Lima in June 1924. In her last days she toiled without the big Elesco feedwater heater. NKP's last 2-8-2 in service, 662 made her final run April 30, 1958. — *Collection of Willis A. McCaleb.*

Birth of an empire

A PAIR of daring young Cleveland real estate promoters broke into the lethargic railroad world of 1916 by buying out the New York Central's interest in the Nickel Plate Road. It would take 37-year-old Oris Paxton Van Sweringen and his 35-year-old brother, Mantis James, less than a decade to author one of the most breath-taking interludes in railroad history. With not much more than enthusiasm and Dutch tenacity, the soft-spoken bachelors rose from relative obscurity to become masters of an economic empire embracing nearly 23,000 miles of railway lines and assets of more than 3 billion dollars. They would literally make over to their own fancy the face of the nation's fifth largest city and would gain and lose a combined personal fortune far in excess of 100 million dollars.

Of humble origin, the Van Sweringens burst upon the American financial scene in the best rags-to-riches tradition. Forced to go forth with only grammar school credentials, the brothers seemed fated to follow mundane careers as clerks in a Cleveland chemical concern. However, in 1905 they ventured into the real estate business. In short order they had undertaken the imaginative promotion of an outstanding suburban development. The Van Sweringens platted a 4000-acre tract of farmland adjacent to Cleveland's southeast side and by 1915 were transforming it into the highly restricted community they called Shaker Heights. The heart of the suburb was 8 miles southeast of downtown Cleveland and the place was deliberately remote to the railroads serving the city. However, fast access to and from the downtown commercial district was to be afforded by a high-speed traction line, the Cleveland & Youngstown Railroad.*

Essential as it was to the successful development of Shaker Heights, the Cleveland & Youngstown was only a part of a radial network of rapid-transit lines envisioned by the Vans as serving the entire metropolitan area. One of the primary functions of the rapid-transit system was to provide private right-of-way access for the six electric interurban railways serving Cleveland. As early as 1909 the ambitious brothers had proposed to build a centrally located stub-end terminal for use by rapid-transit and interurban trains. The site of the terminal was one of the worst downtown eyesores in the country — the crowded and dilapidated loft district located between Cleveland's Public Square and the east bluff of the Cuyahoga River.

The Van Sweringen rapid-transit traction terminal proposals were supported by a group of local entrepreneurs headed by Henry A. Everett and Edward W. Moore. The Everett-Moore Syndicate, backed by every prominent Cleveland banker, controlled a large number of Midwestern traction properties, including three of the interurban lines that served Cleveland. Perhaps the best known of these was the perennially profitable Lake Shore Electric Railway. Having pioneered fast, limited-stop train operation

---

*Organized by the Van Sweringens in July 1911, the C&Y was opened on April 11, 1920, by a successor company, the Cleveland Interurban Railroad. Since 1943 the line has been owned and operated by the city of Shaker Heights.

MANTIS JAMES VAN SWERINGEN (1881-1935)

ORIS PAXTON VAN SWERINGEN (1879-1936)

The meteoric rise of the fortunes of the Van Sweringen brothers followed their 1916 acquisition of the Nickel Plate which they forged into the nucleus of a railroad empire within a decade. — *Collection of J. J. Anzalone.*

in the early 1900's, the LSE successfully competed with the New York Central for through Cleveland-Toledo-Detroit passenger business. The line did a good commuter business and scheduled 65 weekday trains over its 27 miles of double track between Cleveland and Lorain. During the summer months the LSE's rolling stock was taxed to the limit by

tremendous crowds headed for the many Lake Erie beaches and cottage groves west of Cleveland.

Like all the interurbans, the Lake Shore Electric reached downtown Cleveland over the tracks of the city's streetcar system. The big orange limiteds required 1 hour to make the trip to Lorain and fully half that time was expended in reaching the LSE's own tracks at Rocky River, 8 miles out. Inasmuch as the fares for those 8 miles went into the street railway's coffers, the commuter and week-end business was not lucrative. The LSE's need for private right-of-way access to a centrally located terminal was shared by Cleveland's other interurbans and it is not surprising that the Van Sweringens readily obtained the backing of the traction magnates.

The youthful opportunists realized that the only practical routes for their rapid-transit lines were the existing rights of way of the steam railroads serving Cleveland. Of these the Nickel Plate was the key road in their plans since it traversed the city from east to west, had a high-level crossing of the Cuyahoga Valley, and was strategically located to the proposed traction terminal. The Nickel Plate also provided natural routes to the terminal for the Cleveland & Youngstown and the three Everett-Moore lines. The Vans and their friends had watched with interest the progress of the Nickel Plate's 1909-1913 East Side grade separation project. They were also fully aware that Cleveland voters had approved a $725,000 bond issue in 1910 to cover much of the cost of depressing the road's line through the most congested part of the West Side.

THE STRATEGY OF THE NEW YORK CENTRAL

Between 1890 and 1913 the city of Cleveland experienced a fourfold increase in population and gained considerable prominence as a center of industry and commerce. During this period Cleveland also began to develop its celebrated civic consciousness about its appearance to the outside world, a trend which focused an increasing amount of attention on the city's railroad stations. The Erie, B&O, Nickel Plate, and Wheeling & Lake Erie occupied separate facilities scattered along the southerly perimeter of the downtown area. The LS&MS, Pennsylvania, and Big Four shared the Union Station located on the Lake Erie waterfront northwest of the Public Square. Built in 1865, the Union Station had become a decrepit bottleneck which began to get under Cleveland's skin around the turn of the century. In 1912 Mayor Newton D. Baker revived the idea of building a new union passenger station complementary to the Mall, the 104-acre tract east of the Public Square which the city was transforming into an attractive grouping of parks and public buildings. Designed primarily to accommodate the New York Central lines and the Pennsylvania, the

The Vans chose the unsightly loft district (foreground) on the southwest quadrant of Cleveland's Public Square for their Union Terminal site. Superior Avenue bisected the square, provided access for streetcars and interurbans. — *Collection of Willis A. McCaleb.*

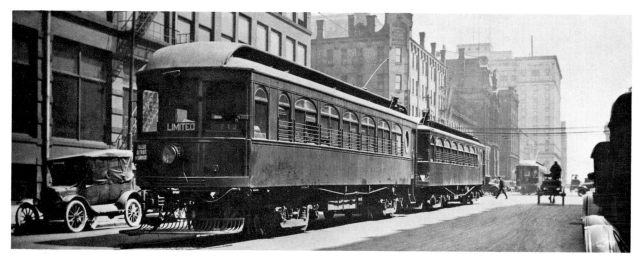

Cleveland's traffic slowed Lake Shore Electric's 177-mile Cleveland-Detroit run. On April 23, 1924, LSE Niles 157·and Detroit, Monroe & Toledo Short Line 7528, a Kuhlman, work M.U. on outbound limited on West 3rd Street. — *Corman E. Moore.*

Cleveland's Union Depot at the foot of Pegleg Hill jointly served trains of Lake Shore, Pennsy, and Big Four in 1890. — *Collection of Cleveland Public Library.*

The venerable lakefront Union Depot on a frosty January morning in 1930. NYC was still using the 65-year-old facility. — *Collection of John A. Rehor.*

proposed facility was to have been built on the lakefront a short distance east of the old depot.

Publicly, the New York Central endorsed the lakefront plan, but privately it was unhappy with what it was getting out of its 8-million-dollar share of the cost. Alfred H. Smith, the Central's senior vice-president and a native Clevelander, was unalterably opposed to a new lakefront depot. He pointed out to his colleagues that the new station would mean locating the NYC freight-handling facilities at the foot of a 7 per cent grade while the Pennsylvania and Nickel Plate were on the high level. Envisioning continued expansion of business, Smith didn't like the way the Central was hemmed in on the lakefront by land owned by the PRR and the city. Moreover, he appears to have been intrigued by the Van Sweringens' idea of building a terminal on the Public Square.* The Central, however, was in an extremely awkward position. Opposition to the lakefront site was certain to be interpreted as obstructionism and would earn the road Cleveland's wrath.

Committed as it was to the lakefront terminal, the NYC set about to at least secure a favorable high-level site for its Cleveland freighthouse. In 1913 it was decided to build on Orange Avenue, adjacent to the Nickel Plate's Broadway facilities. A branch was projected from the Cleveland Short Line near East 92nd Street through Kingsbury Run to the Nickel Plate and thence to Orange Avenue. In August 1913 the Central and the Vans entered into an agreement covering the joint construction of the Orange Avenue branch and the Cleveland & Youngstown. The project was palmed off on Cleveland as a Van Sweringen enterprise. However, the Central not only financed the Orange Avenue branch but ultimately underwrote virtually the entire cost of building the Shaker Heights rapid-transit line. This was probably the real beginning of the intimate but carefully concealed relationship that came to exist between Alfred H. Smith and the Van Sweringens. The latter became increasingly dependent upon Smith for counsel and financial assistance while the older man artfully cultivated a parental interest in their affairs. In this manner the New York Central managed to solve its dilemma at Cleveland. Years later the 77th Congress concluded that "The Central was, evidently, not popular in Cleveland, and part of the game may have required that the Van Sweringens give the appearance of being an independent and local phenomenon." There was another and far more significant result of the alliance. Smith was about to open the doors of the railroad world to the brothers.

Although the quasi-independent status of the Nickel Plate survived the trust-busting regime of Theodore Roosevelt, the passage of the Clayton Antitrust Act in 1914 and the antagonism of Wilson's attorney general, Thomas Gregory, heralded the end of New York Central domination. Before the end of 1914 Alfred Smith, now the Central's president, concluded that separation was inevitable and he began to prepare accordingly. Smith harbored no serious qualms about the Nickel Plate as a competitor as long as the road terminated at Buffalo and remained in friendly hands. He did not relish the idea of control passing to the Lackawanna which not only coveted the Nickel Plate but had the wherewithal to acquire it. Neither could he overlook the menace of the Pennsylvania Railroad. The old Central-Pennsylvania "community of interest" prescribed by the elder J. Pierpont Morgan as a means of effecting the peaceful coexistence of the two railroad giants had long ago passed into limbo.

In his ambitious but somewhat naive protégés, Smith saw the potential means of circumventing Federal interference and retaining practical control of the Nickel Plate. The Van Sweringens, in the light of their already announced intention to electrify the Nickel Plate at Cleveland as part of their master rapid-transit plan, had at least a reasonably plausible motive for acquiring the road. Beyond this, Smith may have been grooming the Vans as early as 1914 as a new and "independent" buffer force in Eastern railroading. Unwittingly, they could be the means of extending the Central's sphere of influence and precluding any aggression on the part of the Pennsylvania. Deliberately or otherwise, the Central was about to steal a march on its arrogantly powerful adversary.

By the time 1914 ended Smith apparently had managed to interest the Vans in the idea of buying the Central's controlling interest in the Nickel Plate. The brothers were supposedly negotiating with Nickel Plate President W. H. Canniff for a means of traversing the Nickel Plate's Broadway Yard which was crammed along the east bluff of the Cuyahoga Valley in such a manner as to effectively block the course of the Cleveland & Youngstown between Kingsbury Run and the Public Square. It is possible that Smith deliberately caused a bogging down of the negotiations in order to stimulate the Vans' interest in buying the Nickel Plate. It is also possible that this story was concocted by the promoters themselves as a means of gaining financial commitments from the interurban men and their bankers.

At the end of 1915 Attorney General Gregory advised the New York Central that the Justice Department considered the control of the Lake Shore, Michigan Central, and Nickel Plate lines between Buffalo and Chicago to be in violation of the Fed-

---

*Smith was well acquainted with the brothers, having met them sometime prior to 1912 through their purchase of his family's Shaker Heights farm.

This 1914 view of Broadway Yard in Cleveland shows location of Nickel Plate facilities on reverse curve starting in Kingsbury Run (upper left). Broadway is to the left; steel mill is at upper right, Broadway depot at lower right. — *Cleveland Union Terminals Company.*

eral antitrust laws. The NYC had already decided to dispose of its Nickel Plate stock to the Van Sweringens in the event of such a development. On February 1, 1916, Smith wired the Vans, "Will you please let me have any information you can by the 6th or 7th as to the possibilities of taking over the railroad that you were considering?" The equally well-prepared Vans, having invented a plan for raising the money, submitted an offer of 7.5 million dollars on February 4. This was quickly rejected and on the 17th they offered to buy the Nickel Plate stock for 8.5 million dollars, almost precisely the asking market price. The Vans proposed to pay 2 million dollars down, giving the NYC notes for the balance and putting up the Nickel Plate stock as collateral. For five years they would pay only interest on the notes at the rate of 4 per cent and the 6.5-million-dollar principal would be retired between 1921 and 1930. The NYC accepted the offer

and granted the extraordinarily liberal terms on April 13, 1916. For their part the Vans guaranteed the Central operating concessions over the Nickel Plate at Cleveland and one-third of the total capacity of the proposed Public Square station.

As they later candidly admitted, the Vans bought the Nickel Plate on a shoestring, borrowing the 2-million-dollar down payment from Cleveland's Guardian Savings & Trust on July 3, 1916. The formal transfer of ownership of the stock came two days later. In order to refinance the down payment the Van Sweringens formally organized a holding company, Nickel Plate Securities Corporation, on December 4, 1916. The nonvoting preferred stock of the holding company was taken by the circle of traction men and bankers who had backed the purchase offer. Notable among these were Joseph R. Nutt and C. L. Bradley, officers of the Union Trust Company; E. W. Moore, president of Lake Shore Electric; and Francis E. Myers, the Ashland (O.) pump baron.

The Van Sweringens personally invested $520,000 in Nickel Plate Securities common stock which gave them 75 per cent of the holding company's voting

power. The young entrepreneurs did not have this kind of money but were able to borrow it from Guardian Savings & Trust using their real estate holdings as collateral. In order for the Vans to meet the first semi-annual interest note given to the New York Central, it was necessary for the Nickel Plate to resume the payment of dividends in January 1917.

JOHN JOSEPH BERNET

Legend has it that one day in 1915 A. H. Smith and a party of his subordinate New York Central officials were riding in the president's private car near Cleveland. Smith pointed out a train moving on a nearby track and remarked, "There comes the poor old Nickel Plate." Most of his companions laughed but not the Central's 47-year-old Chicago resident vice-president, J. J. Bernet.

"That isn't such a bad road," he protested, "I wouldn't mind being president of it. I'd show you fellows that it's a good road."

Smith looked at Bernet in astonishment. "Do you mean that you would rather be president of the Nickel Plate than a vice-president of the New York Central?"

"Just that," replied the outspoken Bernet, "provided I had a free hand."

Whatever his personal motives or ambitions, John Bernet was destined to take over the reins of the Nickel Plate and serve for the rest of his life as the chief operating executive of the Van Sweringen railroad empire. In July 1916 he was probably the brightest star in the Central's galaxy of gifted operating men. Indeed, he was widely considered to be Smith's handpicked successor to the NYC helm. The gift of Bernet and other top-caliber talent to the Van Sweringens was tantamount to staking an opponent in a poker game. However, it was absolutely essential to the Central's purposes that the Nickel Plate make an outstanding showing. For one thing, Smith was anxious to allay any suspicion that the Vans were NYC puppets. Then, too, the Nickel Plate was going to have to earn the money needed to retire the notes the Vans had given to the Central.

John Bernet was born on February 9, 1868, the son of a Swiss blacksmith, and spent most of his youth at Farnham, N.Y., a station on the LS&MS and the Nickel Plate. After putting in a day at his father's smithy, Bernet was wont to spend his eve-

JOHN J. BERNET (1868-1935)   CHARLES E. DENNEY (1879-1965)   AUGUSTINE R. AYERS (1878-1958)

Among top-caliber talent responsible for establishing national prominence for the Nickel Plate were John Bernet, president 1916-1927; Charles Denney, who joined the railroad in 1916 and served as vice-president and general manager 1920-1927; "Gus" Ayers, who became motive power superintendent in 1916 and was general manager 1927-1948. — *Center photo, Northern Pacific; right photo, Nickel Plate.*

nings down at the Lake Shore's telegraph office. He soon learned to send a message "dry" with an idle key, and when the telegrapher was promoted Bernet got his job. That was in 1889 and six years later he was promoted to train dispatcher at Buffalo. Bernet advanced steadily along the familiar line of promotion — trainmaster in 1901, assistant division superintendent in 1903, division superintendent in 1905. He held the latter job but eight months before being sent to Cleveland as assistant general superintendent of the LS&MS. Finally in 1915 Bernet was appointed resident vice-president of the New York Central and Michigan Central at Chicago.

Bernet was endowed with an analytical mind and had a striking ability to take timely and decisive action. A born leader of men, he became renowned for his blunt honesty and his propensity for hard work. He had spent most of his career within earshot of the Nickel Plate and was unquestionably well acquainted with it. The challenge the road presented was one Bernet was constitutionally unable to resist. For their part the Vans had no intention of attempting to run the Nickel Plate themselves and were no doubt only too happy to secure Bernet's services. It was agreed that he was to take hold of the railroad and have a completely free hand in running it. When the new Van Sweringen directors took over the Nickel Plate board on July 15, 1916, Bernet was elected president and general manager.

Bernet understood that the Vans' financial needs would siphon off most of the Nickel Plate's surplus earnings and that the extensive physical improvements the road needed would have to wait. Entertaining no illusions about competing with his late

employer for the passenger trade, Bernet's plans were built around the Nickel Plate's freight business. The road's freight traffic density, measured in terms of revenue ton-miles per mile of line, was one of the highest in the country. On the other hand, the 1915 average revenue trainload of 355 tons was hardly impressive. The limiting factor of course was the Nickel Plate's motive power.

By doubling the length of its freight trains Bernet figured he could handle the Nickel Plate's ordinary volume of business at vastly reduced cost. Since almost 80 per cent of the 523-mile road's operation was still single track, fewer but longer trains meant less congestion, expedited train movement, and more dependable service. To give profits a mighty boost, Bernet had only to lengthen a few passing tracks, strengthen a bridge here and there, and replace the Nickel Plate's Lilliputian locomotive stock with modern high-capacity power.

For his second in command Bernet chose the brilliant Charles E. Denney, assistant to the president of the Union Switch & Signal Company. As Bernet's special engineer, Denney was charged with the task of upgrading the road's physical facilities. The 37-year-old signal engineer had started out in 1899 with US&S and moved to the LS&MS in 1905 as assistant signal engineer. During Denney's eight-year career with the Lake Shore, Bernet had a firsthand opportunity to assess his ability. In 1914 Denney had returned to the Switch but he now readily accepted Bernet's call.

It was only natural that Bernet should seek out another of his Lake Shore cronies for the all-important job of motive power superintendent. At that time the New York Central possessed what was perhaps the most enlightened mechanical corps in American railroading. The man Bernet tapped was Augustine R. Ayers, not yet 38 but the Central's principal assistant equipment engineer, lines east of Buffalo. Ayers had joined the LS&MS after graduating from Cornell in 1900 and by 1905 held the position of night roundhouse foreman at Elkhart, Ind. In seven short years he was the road's general mechanical engineer. In the meantime he had served as assistant superintendent of Collinwood shops, assistant master mechanic at Elkhart, and mechanical engineer headquartered at Cleveland.

The Third Generation of Motive Power

For years locomotive designers had been striving to increase the efficient use of a given amount of steam. By reducing cylinder condensation and heat loss, the superheater increased the capacity of a locomotive by as much as 20 per cent. The compound use of steam represented a less effective effort in the same direction. It was pointless to increase a locomotive's cylinder proportions, working steam pressure, or the number of driving wheels if the firebox grate was not large enough to burn the coal necessary to satisfy the increased demand for steam. Before 1916 the Central's mechanical engineers had recognized the value of the two-wheel trailing truck. They found it removed the restriction to firebox design so inherent in the 2-8-0 and permitted vastly increased combustion volume. The trailing truck allowed an elasticity in boiler design never before realized with consequent freedom to increase steaming capacity in direct ratio to increased cyl-

inder capacity. By 1916 the 2-8-2 or Mikado type was in extensive use throughout the New York Central system and was rapidly supplanting the Consolidation as the road's standard freight locomotive.

It was not surprising that Nickel Plate motive power began to take on a real Central flavor under Gus Ayers or that he turned to the latest NYC Mikado, the H-5, for the Nickel Plate's new freight locomotive. His specifications called for 35 engines to be built to the Central's drawings with only minor modifications. In the spring of 1917 Lima Locomotive Works built the first 10, numbered 500-509 and assigned class H-5a. The remaining 25, classed H-5b and numbered 510-534, were turned out by Alco's Brooks Works the following August.

The H-5's had 25 x 32-inch cylinders, 63-inch drivers, and weighed 287,000 pounds in working order. With 216,500 pounds carried on the driving wheels these 2-8-2's had an excellent 4.46 factor of adhesion. The straight-top, radial-stay boiler had a working pressure of 180 pounds and the engine boasted a rated tractive effort of 48,550 pounds. Like their sisters on the Central, the 500's came from the factory with Schmidt firetube superheaters, Baker valve gear, Ragonnet power reverse, Cole outside-bearing type trailing truck, and a single 8½-inch cross-compound air compressor.

Although later equipped with mechanical stokers, the new 2-8-2's were hand fired and their firemen doubtless were kept busy feeding the 56.5 square feet of grate area. The water-bottom tender had a Commonwealth cast-steel frame and carried 8000 gallons of water and 12 tons of coal. The Lima en-

The first H-5 is about to leave Conneaut on her maiden run March 10, 1917. Brand-new Lima-built Mike moved 2367-ton freight to Tifft Yard, Buffalo, in 7 hours 35 minutes. — *NKP photo.*

Last of the hard-to-fire "submarines," T class 473 gets set for a run over Minster branch October 5, 1933, scarcely six months before scrapping. — *Clyde E. Helms.*

gines came with the conventional N.Y.C. & St. L. lettering on the tank collars, but the H-5b's from Dunkirk sported NICKEL PLATE ROAD in bold gold leaf letters across the tank sides. These fine engines were the workhorses of the road. In their 41 years on NKP they saw nearly every type of service.

Shortly after joining the Nickel Plate, Ayers picked up 15 surplus NYC class G-43e 2-8-0's at bargain prices. As part of the transaction NYC put the engines through its Collinwood shops, adding Baker valve gear and superheaters. Built by Brooks in 1903, these became Nickel Plate 460-474, class T, and were dubbed "submarines" by their crews. The only secondhand locomotives ever bought by the Nickel Plate, the T's represented a considerable increase in hauling capacity over the road's own 2-8-0's and were short enough to be accommodated by the 65-foot turntables and roundhouse stalls at Fort Wayne and Chicago. When the new H-5's went into service east of Conneaut the T's and superheated N's bumped the last saturated engines off the Nickel Plate's manifest freight runs.

Of the 67 class P 4-6-0's holding down manifest schedules on the Fort Wayne and Cleveland divisions, only the eight P-3's of 1913 were equipped with superheaters. Like the 31 pre-1900 engines still on the roster in 1916, the rest were expendable. Only the N-6 Consolidations, 454-459, had come from the builder with superheaters, but the 30 oldest 2-8-0's, fitted with inside admission piston valves, were being equipped with superheaters as fast as they could be put through the shops.* Ayers decided to rebuild the remaining 24 slide-valve N's with Economy piston valve steam chests and superheaters.

*Engines 400-429 were all converted to 0-6-0 switch engines between 1920 and 1925.

Of the 55 yard engines on the roster only the six class S 0-6-0's were superheated. The rest were obsolete six-coupled L's and M's slated for retirement at the earliest possible date. For their replacements Ayers turned to the Central's fine B-11k 0-6-0 and U-2 0-8-0. The former had 21 x 28-inch piston valve cylinders, Walschaerts valve gear, 24-element superheaters, and a rated tractive effort of 33,150 pounds. The Nickel Plate bought three sets of 10 B-11's in 1916, 1917, and 1918. Engines 50-59, class B-11a, were turned out by Brooks in October 1916; the remaining 20 were built by Lima. The 1917 Limas, 60-69, were the first engines to carry NICKEL PLATE ROAD lettering on the tender. These were followed by the 1918 B-11c's numbered 70-79. The same year, Lima also delivered five U-2 eight-coupled switchers numbered 200-204. These had 23½ x 30-inch cylinders, Baker valve gear, 57-inch drivers, and a rated tractive effort of 45,700 pounds.

On December 28, 1917, less than 18 months after John Bernet had taken over the road, the Nickel Plate and the rest of the country's railroads were confiscated by the Federal government. A classic example of bureaucracy in action, the United States Railroad Administration ran up a 551-million-dollar deficit during the 26 months it operated the railroads. Bernet, as the Nickel Plate's Federal manager, was forced to accept some severe setbacks in operational efficiency. Many of the road's own locomotives were shipped off to other lines while the Nickel Plate was forced to rent in their place Delaware & Hudson Camelbacks and the notorious Government-owned 2-10-0's, the so-called Russian Decapods. Nevertheless, Bernet could look back with justifiable pride on the USRA experiment. The road had hauled more troops per mile of road than any

Bernet's pre-USRA additions to Nickel Plate roster were copies of successful Central designs. H-5 Mikes could handle more than double the capacity of the 2-8-0's they replaced. Lima built the 505 in April 1917. — *Collection of Clyde E. Helms.*

B-11 switchers 60-69 turned out by Lima in 1917 were first engines to carry Nickel Plate lettering on tender. — *Collection of George Sennhauser.*

Eight-coupled U-2's developed 45,700 pounds tractive effort, half again as much as any pre-Bernet switch engine. Lima built 200 in 1918. — *Allen County Historical Society.*

other line and was one of the select handful of properties that had made money for the Government.

One fortunate aspect of the USRA debacle was the development of several highly successful locomotive designs. In all, 1856 locomotives were built to 12 patterns and allocated to 72 railroads, at their expense, of course. Despite loud outcries throughout the industry that the varying needs of individual roads could not be met by standardized motive power, the USRA designs proved quite successful and they were reordered many times in the years that followed. The outstanding USRA standard freight engine was the light Mikado, 10 of which were assigned to the Nickel Plate. The new 2-8-2's were built by Alco at its Schenectady Works and delivered to the road at Buffalo in October 1918. Assigned numbers 601-610 and class H-6a, these were the first engines on the Nickel Plate equipped with mechanical stokers and electric headlights. They joined the H-5's on the Buffalo Division and were found capable of handling more than half again as much tonnage as the older 2-8-2's.

The H-6a had 26 x 30-inch cylinders, 63-inch drivers, and weighed 290,800 pounds in working order. The conical wagon-top boiler had a combustion chamber, a 40-element Type A firetube superheater, and brick arch with four steel tubes. At a working pressure of 200 pounds, the engine developed rated tractive effort of 54,700 pounds. The new 2-8-2 was equipped with Walschaerts valve gear, Ragonnet reverse, mechanical fire door, and a single cross-compound pump. The tender held 10,000 gallons of water and 16 tons of coal and rode on a pair of Andrews four-wheel trucks. The performance of the H-6a was so outstanding that the Nickel Plate bought 61 Lima-built engines of the same basic design between 1920 and 1924.

The first Lima 600's, the H-6b's, were turned out in December 1920 and had most of the USRA dimensions. However, these five engines were about 5 tons heavier and had a goodly number of refinements in their arrangements and appliances. Due to small ashpan openings the H-6a had a very drafty cab, no minor detail during a Buffalo Division winter. One engineer described a trip in one as being akin to a ride in a corn crib. This deficiency was corrected in the H-6b. The new Limas also came with rocking grates with much larger openings than those of the USRA box-type drop grates. Developed for the NYC, the new design permitted faster and easier dumping of the fire and was equipped with a steam-operated shaker. The H-6b cab arrangement was handier than that of the USRA and was designed to conform with standard Nickel Plate practice. Other changes included the Woodard outside-connected dome throttle in place of the USRA inside-connected Chambers design, and the H-6a's Hodge trailing truck was replaced by the new Commonwealth cast-steel Delta type designed to accommodate a booster engine.

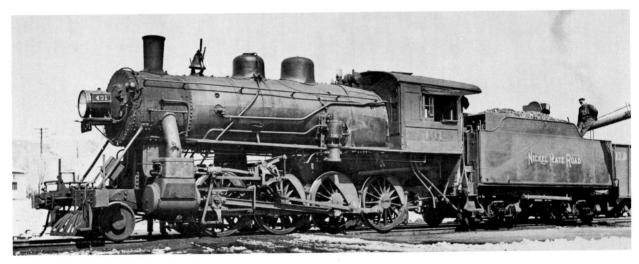

Ayers' disdain for saturated steam resulted in installation of superheaters in all N class 2-8-0's after 1916. B-9b 121 (below), formerly N-1 421, was one of 30 converted to 57-inch-drivered 0-6-0's with stubby, recess-collared tanks. Slide-valved N-2's, including 431 (above), were given Universal piston valves, Economy steam chests. — *Clyde E. Helms.*

A sixth Lima 2-8-2 was delivered in January 1921. It was identical to the 611-615 except that it carried the Franklin Railway Supply Company's Ingersoll-designed C-1 trailing truck booster engine, first used by the Central in 1919. Utilizing saturated steam from the boiler, the booster transformed No. 616's 43-inch trailing truck wheels into auxiliary drivers. The booster provided 9400 pounds of added tractive effort to overcome inertia in starting and to help get tonnage over grades. The value of the device was well demonstrated during the course of the 616's first run.* After being set up at Conneaut the engine was put on the head end of 3848 tons of freight train, roughly 22 per cent more tonnage than the H-6a's rating over the rugged eastbound Buffalo Division grades.

The 616 required somewhat less than 8 hours to cover the 115 miles from Conneaut to Tifft Yard at

*Literally speaking, the 616 was in a class by itself. Not only was this the only engine assigned to class H-6c, but it was the road's perennial guinea pig. Before being sold to the Akron, Canton & Youngstown in 1946, the 616 was subjected to 47 separate modifications.

Buffalo — a good run in those days. The booster was used in leaving Conneaut Yard and in three instances where the train was forced to take a siding. A few miles out of Conneaut the speed of the train dropped to 7 mph while ascending Springfield Hill. The booster was cut in and got the train over the crest at 10 mph. Good results also were had while working Big Delaware Hill, 3 miles of 1-per-cent-plus grade between Farnham and Angola. The acid test, however, came at Dunkirk where the 616 failed to get the target at a grade crossing. Although the train was stopped on a heavy ascending grade and a curve, the 616 got the tonnage rolling with the aid of the booster on the first try. At all times while the booster was in operation, maximum steam pressure was maintained and it was not necessary to lower the engine's water level. All of the 2-8-2's ordered after the 616 came from the factory with boosters and the H-6b's got them the first time they went through the back shop.

In October 1922 Lima delivered 15 duplicates of the 616, numbered 617-631 and assigned class H-6d.

Experimental H-6c 616 (above), built at Lima in January 1921, was first NKP engine with trailer booster. The 2-8-2 pauses for water 12 years later at Celina (below). Air pumps have been moved to pilot deck; shielded headlight, bar-type pilot, BL feedwater heater added. — *Upper photo, Allen County Historical Society; lower, Clyde E. Helms.*

Backhead view of Duplex-stokered class H-6e No. 660 turned out by Lima in January 1924. In 1946 this Mikado was sold to National Railways of Mexico where she was still racking up miles as late as 1962. — *Collection of Allen County Historical Society.*

Most of these went into service on the Chicago Division, and the roundhouses at West Wayne and Stony Island got new 90-foot turntables and extended stalls to accommodate them. The 30 Lima H-6e's of 1923-1924 were widely dubbed the "sports models." Although built to the same basic design as the earlier Limas, the H-6e's weighed 318,000 pounds in working order, had Baker valve gear, and were the first to come from the builder with two cross-compound pumps, a feedwater heater, and Precision reverse. Engines 632-646 came with the Worthington type BL feedwater heater and were meant for use in hard-water territory west of Bellevue. The 647-661 were delivered equipped with Elesco feedwater heaters mounted on top of the smokebox. Of the two designs the Elesco was more easily plugged with boiler scale, and engines with these heaters were assigned to divisions east of Bellevue where soft Lake Erie water was generally avail-

able. The last order of 2-8-2's, the H-6f's of 1924 numbered 662-671, also came with the Elesco feedwater heater. The 10 per cent or so savings in coal obtained through preheating of boiler feedwater quickly dictated the application of BL heaters to all pre-H-6e 600's.

BERNET'S OPERATING RESULTS

Despite retrogression during the USRA period John Bernet's program was paying off handsomely by the end of 1920. Resumed in 1919, dividends were being paid at the rate of 5 per cent on both classes of Nickel Plate stock. While there had been no spectacular increase in freight tonnage handled, operating revenues were 2½ times those of 1915, the last full year of NYC control. During the first two months of 1920, while the road was still under the USRA, there had been an operating deficit of more than $94,000. Nevertheless, Bernet managed to finish

Fifteen Lima "sports models" of 1923-1924, such as H-6e No. 645 (above), originally had Elesco feedwater heaters. Fifteen other H-6e's, including 660 (below), were fitted with Worthington BL feedwater heaters. — *Collection of George Sennhauser.*

the year with a net income of $3,740,737.11. A post-war depression combined with strikes in the coal fields and railroad shops made 1921 the worst year in the histories of many Eastern roads. By contrast, Nickel Plate held its own and due to a sharp cut in operating expenses managed a 25 per cent increase in net income. That year the Nickel Plate moved its cars at the average rate of 49.4 miles per car day — more than any other road and more than twice the national average. This was accomplished in the face of the congestion naturally inherent in the combination of a single-track railroad and heavy traffic density. As badly needed physical improvements were still being deferred, the road's facilities lagged far behind those of its competitors. As *Railway Age* for February 3, 1923, put it:

> The Nickel Plate is not favored with anything particularly noteworthy in the way of facilities of various sorts. It is the general impression that its unusually favorable operating results have been secured in spite of, rather than because of, the character of its physical plant.

One of the primary reasons for the marked improvement in earnings was the increasing amount of manufactured goods and other high-grade freight being hauled by the Nickel Plate. The road was building up a fine reputation for the dependability of its service and apparent ability to promptly handle almost any volume of business. For an operating man, Bernet was proving to be an exceptionally capable traffic solicitor. He insisted on maintaining close personal liaison with shippers. This reverence

for the customer had doubled the number of on-line industries by 1922. One striking example of his common-sense approach was the decision to buy 1000 automobile cars in 1922 after the auto industry had predicted a banner year in 1923. When the expected sales boom materialized, the Nickel Plate was well prepared for it. Time-honored railroad tradition dictated that repair programs and new equipment purchases be undertaken only when traffic volume outstripped capacity. Bernet's unorthodox policy kept back shops humming year in and year out and in slack times shopped locomotives were placed in storage. Steady work was good for morale, said Bernet, and when business boomed the road had an adequate reservoir of first-class motive power to fall back upon.

In 1923 A. R. Ayers was promoted to the post of assistant general manager, a move indicative of the increasing importance of motive power in the Nickel Plate scheme of things. Like Bernet, Ayers was an apostle of perfection and he sought it from both men and machines. Toward this end he assigned two traveling firemen to each division along with a steel-underframe, speedometer-equipped caboose. These officials rode the test cabooses behind Nickel Plate 2-8-2's day in and day out, measuring the performance of men and locomotives. They compiled a "book" on every engine, carefully noting any defects in valve gear, packing, front-end appliances, and general mechanical condition. Enginemen were invited to ride the cabooses and the dynamometer car bought in 1924. They were shown analyses of their own performance as compared with that of their co-workers. This constant education on the individual level was conducted year after year and eventually produced one of the most proficient corps of enginemen any railroad ever possessed. As early as 1925 it was possible to assess the notable advances that had been made in efficiency. Since 1916 average freight train speed and tonnage had been doubled, while fuel consumption per 1000 gross tonmiles had been reduced by nearly 50 per cent.

PASSENGER SERVICE AFTER 1916

During the early years of the Bernet regime there were marked reductions in passenger service. This was primarily due to the fact that what money was available was earmarked for freight equipment and physical improvements. In March 1917 the road quit the Erie's Buffalo depot and moved into the Lackawanna's new passenger terminal at the foot of Main Street. At the same time, the last joint operation with the West Shore — the Boston-Chicago sleeper service — was discontinued. On January 12, 1918, by USRA edict, trains 3 and 4 made their "last" runs. On the same date most of the through-car operation with Lackawanna was also discontinued. Through New York-Chicago sleepers were left only on trains 1 and 2, operated in conjuction with DL&W trains 4 and 5.

On June 6, 1920, trains 3 and 4 were restored to the schedule but, as during the first decade of operation, they were run only between Cleveland and Chicago. On that same date commuter trains were put on between Cleveland and Wickliffe, one in each direction. The Buffalo-Chicago trains were

handled by the nine R class 4-6-0's and four class O 4-4-0's were assigned to trains 3 and 4. Also available for passenger service were 20 class N 2-8-0's and eight P-3 4-6-0's. Trains 3 and 4 were restored to their prewar express schedules on April 30, 1922, and assigned through New York-Chicago day-coach and sleeper equipment. Some of the through arrangements with the DL&W were restored on the other trains at this time, including the Scranton-Cleveland sleeper on trains 1 and 2.

In December 1922 the Nickel Plate received its first new passenger locomotives since 1913 — four class K-1a Pacifics numbered 160-163. Built by Lima, these 4-6-2's boasted 22½ x 26-inch cylinder dimensions, 73-inch driving wheels, and a total engine weight of 245,000 pounds. Hand fired, the K's had Walschaerts valve gear, Type A superheater, Woodard throttle, and a single cross-compound pump. The tenders of these engines carried 10,800 gallons of water, 16 tons of coal, and rode on Commonwealth equalized high-speed trucks. The 4-6-2's also had the Delta trailing truck but were never equipped with booster engines.

The Limas were followed in August 1923 by six K-1b's, 164-169, built at the Brooks plant at Dunkirk. Although somewhat heavier than K-1a's they were otherwise essentially identical to them. When the new Pacifics were put on the road, they proved to be poor steamers. The installation of additional tubes and flues and Nicholson thermic syphons during 1924 and 1925 not only corrected the deficiency but gave the K's the reputation of being outstanding performers. Smooth riders, they could easily hold 70 mph with seven or eight 65-ton steel cars. They

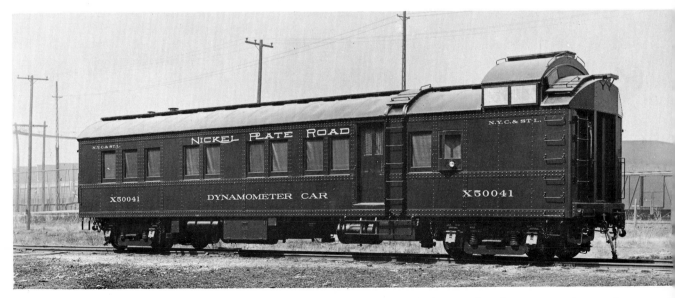

Dynamometer car built by Standard Steel Car at Hammond, Ind., in May 1924, was key to Nickel Plate's efficiency. X-50041 was equipped with kitchen and berths, accommodated crew of six and porter. Instruments in head end (right) recorded speed, back pressure, boiler steam pressure, and pounds of drawbar pull. — *NKP photos*.

76

Notable among industries Bernet attracted to the road was Glenn L. Martin's aerodrome and factory on Cleveland's east side. First transcontinental air-mail flight landed here in 1921, about the time of this photo. — *Collection of John A. Rehor.*

could also do a good job on freight and it was not unusual to see one of them making a good run with 40 to 50 loads of meat. A Worthington BL feed-water heater was installed on the 161 and this engine was widely held to be the best of the 4-6-2's.

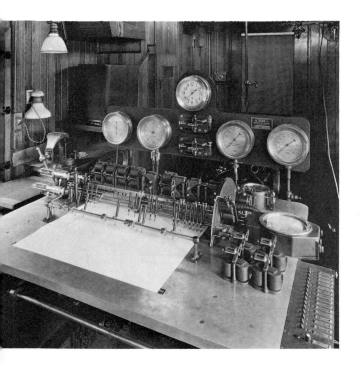

For years its regular assignment was trains 5 and 6 on the Buffalo Division. Also assigned to this tough division were the 160 and 164, equipped in 1926 with Elesco exhaust steam injectors.

EARLY VAN SWERINGEN EXPANSION

Although the Van Sweringens demonstrated an uncanny knack for turning to their own profitable account the needs and resources of others, they were constantly flirting with financial disaster. The first of their many crises was precipitated by the Federal seizure of the railroads at the end of 1917. The Vans had been using Nickel Plate dividends to meet the semi-annual interest notes held by the New York Central. However, with the road in the hands of the USRA, this income was cut off and they were unable to cover the $130,000 payment due in July 1918. The Vans still did not have the money at the end of the three-month grace period and they were faced with the prospect of having to surrender the Nickel Plate stock. At this time the Central was advancing the cash needed to complete the Shaker Heights rapid transit and was otherwise becoming increasingly involved in Van Sweringen enterprises. After suffering considerable anxiety, the Vans were granted enough time to negotiate the first of many rescue loans. In 1919 the USRA permitted a resump-

Double track at East 75th Street was later depressed as part of Union Terminal project.
Class M 0-6-0 20 is on spur in this 1925 photo. — *Collection of John A. Rehor.*

tion of Nickel Plate dividend payments. Still more dividends were used to retire the rescue loan in 1920.

Despite the fact that the people of Cleveland had overwhelmingly supported the lakefront terminal plan in a 1915 referendum, the Vans continued to promote their Public Square edifice. In 1918 they gained the blessing of Secretary of War Newton D. Baker, the former mayor who had backed the lakefront scheme. Still, the Vans were faced with formidable opposition led by the Pennsylvania Railroad and the energetic and outspoken Peter Witt, the street railway commissioner who is best remembered for having patented the front-entrance, center-exit streetcar. The Vans' champion, Councilman James McGinty, proved to be more than equal to the occasion. His battle cry, "The Pennsylvania Railroad cannot bulldoze the citizens of Cleveland," quickly rallied the city's press to the Van Sweringen cause. The Pennsy, always a handy target for Ohio newspapers, quickly became fodder for Cleveland's editorial cannon. The lakefront depot had met a sudden death. McGinty attempted to force the Pennsylvania into line by threatening it with ordinances requiring the elimination of all grade crossings and imposing a 5 mph speed limit on its trains. While the sudden change in fortune must have confounded the men in far-off Philadelphia, they nevertheless stuck to their guns and the Pennsylvania never did go into the Union Terminal. This skirmish marked the beginning of a long and bitter feud between the Pennsy and the upstarts from Cleveland.

At the end of World War I the American railroad community found itself caught in a drumfire of national criticism. For almost two decades there had been no significant improvement in the level of railroad service or efficiency. Indeed, the railroads had barely been able to cope with the nation's ever-growing volume of commerce. Technological advancement was painfully slow and then seldom universally accepted. Many of the smaller roads were in serious financial trouble. Government ownership had proved no panacea. During the monumental episode of confusion, the USRA had only intensified many of the railroads' problems.

Since 1890 the provisions of the Sherman Act had been widely interpreted as constituting a prohibition of railroad mergers. Now a desperate Congress began to consider wholesale unification as a possible means of moving the railroads off dead center. The Congressional change of heart was reflected in the Transportation Act passed on February 28, 1920. In effect, the new law exempted the railroads from Justice Department prosecution under the antitrust laws and empowered the Interstate Commerce Commission to rule upon matters of railroad control and consolidation. Further, the I.C.C. was obliged to prepare a tentative plan for the unification of the railroads into a limited number of systems of more or less equal size and strength. Subsequently, the I.C.C. commissioned William Zebina Ripley, professor of political economy at Harvard University, to prepare a preliminary grouping of lines.

The year 1920 found the Van Sweringens ready and willing to expand the scope of their activities. Construction of the Cleveland Union Terminal was assured. More than 8000 parcels in Shaker Heights had been sold, and the rapid-transit line was in operation. Largely as a result of the Nickel Plate's profound progress under Bernet, the Vans had been projected into national prominence. Not only was Cleveland solidly behind them but they suddenly possessed the backing of such New York banking houses as J. P. Morgan & Company, Chase National, and George Baker's First National Bank. Of course, the influence of the New York Central was largely responsible for such powerful support. Nevertheless, the Vans were beginning to pick up impetus on their own account. As builders they possessed a good public image and already there were those who saw in them the touch of Midas and an aura of invincibility.

Guided by Alfred Smith, the Vans were quick to capitalize on the dismal railroad situation and the new role of the I.C.C. Indeed, they appear to have interpreted the Transportation Act as their own personal mandate. In the fall of 1920 Professor Ripley wrote to O. P. Van Sweringen soliciting his opinions as to the manner in which the Nickel Plate should be treated in the unification study. O. P. turned to Smith for advice and was told, "You might merely say to him that the Nickel Plate's future, you believe, would best be provided for by having a connection with all lines diverging from Buffalo on the east . . . that you have opinions reaching into the coal districts and have made some studies in regard to such alliances and that you also believe there are other possibilities for the Nickel Plate extending into Michigan."

At the end of November 1920 O. P. met with Ripley at the Harvard Club in New York. With the aid of a detailed map he outlined what he envisioned as a new and expanded Nickel Plate system. Included were both the Lehigh Valley and the Lackawanna, the Pere Marquette, Clover Leaf, Lake Erie & Western, Reading, Wheeling & Lake Erie, Pittsburgh & West Virginia, Western Maryland, Bessemer & Lake Erie, and the NYC-controlled Cincinnati Northern. In Ripley's 1921 plan he forged 180 railroads into 22 systems including an expanded Nickel Plate that embraced many of the roads O. P. had asked for. The notable exceptions were the Lehigh Valley, Reading, and the Pere Marquette.

The I.C.C. published a tentative unification plan based on Ripley's report on August 3, 1921. The Commission allocated most of the railroads in the Eastern District to nine proposed systems built around the New York Central, Pennsylvania, Baltimore & Ohio, Erie, Nickel Plate, Pere Marquette, New Haven, Chesapeake & Ohio, and Norfolk & Western. System 5, the Nickel Plate-Lehigh Valley, was assigned the Clover Leaf, Lake Erie & Western, Wheeling & Lake Erie, Pittsburgh & West Virginia, and a half interest in the Bessemer & Lake Erie.

Early in 1921, prior to the publication of the I.C.C. tentative plan, the Vans had explored the possibilities of a Nickel Plate-Pere Marquette merger. Through circusman John Ringling they also arranged tentative terms for the acquisition of control of the Lehigh Valley. After the I.C.C. plan was revealed, the Vans dropped the PM idea and did not again attempt to acquire that road until 1924. Taking their cue from the I.C.C., they approached Ringling with an eye toward consummating the Lehigh Valley deal only to learn that his principals had already sold their stock or were no longer interested in selling. Undaunted, the Vans turned their attention to the Clover Leaf and the Lake Erie & Western. These roads perfectly complemented the Nickel Plate and afforded it trunk-line access to the Peoria and St. Louis gateways. Both railroads had fallen on bad times and their acquisition

Work of depressing 2½ miles of Nickel Plate line across Cleveland's West Side began in 1915, was completed in 1922. Cut was wide enough to accommodate the Vans' proposed West Side rapid transit, but its construction was delayed for 32 years. — NKP photo.

Hauling a transfer run, H-5 huffs steam into the thick industrial haze surrounding Broadway Yard in this smoky view from Vinegar Hill in the early 1920's. A long trestle connects first high-level freighthouse (left) with yard level. — *NKP photo*.

Old Cleveland enginehouse overlooked murky Cuyahoga valley, known locally as the "flats." On the ready track a 500 helps cloud the air. Also shown in this panoramic 1924 view are Broadway depot and yard, trestle to freighthouse (right). — *NKP photo*.

This building across the street from the Lorain (O.) depot housed the Nickel Plate Hotel, restaurant, and barbershop, and Railway Express office. The photo was made in 1924, the year Lorain was devastated by a tornado. — *NKP photo*.

might be readily accomplished on easy terms.

The Toledo, St. Louis & Western Railroad, commonly referred to as the Clover Leaf, consisted of a single-track line 450 miles long between Toledo and East St. Louis, Ill. It possessed stock control of the Chicago & Alton and shared ownership of the Detroit & Toledo Shore Line with the Grand Trunk Western. The Clover Leaf had issued collateral trust bonds to capitalize the purchase of the Alton stock and it defaulted on the bonds in 1914. Since then the road had been in receivership and there had been a general deterioration of the property. However, it was still regarded as a preferred route for fast freight. In December 1921 the Alton stock was surrendered in order to retire the troublesome bonds and accrued interest. The way had been cleared for lifting the receivership.

In 1918 the principal Clover Leaf shareholders had offered to pay the receiver, Walter L. Ross, half the proceeds if he could find a buyer for their stock. The Van Sweringens approached Ross, and after more than a month of negotiations, including several all-night sessions, they announced early in March 1922 that they had secured control of the road. The remarkable Clevelanders acquired the entire Ross block without laying out a cent. To cover the pur-

chase price of $2,744,000, they gave Ross and his principals notes payable in semi-annual installments over a period of 20 years. To secure such favorable terms the Vans gave Ross a contract whereby they agreed to permit operation of the Clover Leaf as a separate entity for five years. Ross was to manage the property during this period at an annual salary of $50,000. Additional purchases of Clover Leaf stock on the open market cost the Vans $778,000 and gave them 60 per cent of the preferred and 40 per cent of the common stock.

Since 1900 the 718-mile Lake Erie & Western had been operated as an integral part of the New York Central system. The main line extended 416 miles from Sandusky, O., to Peoria, Ill., and crossed the Nickel Plate at Arcadia, O., and the Clover Leaf at Frankfort, Ind. There were two long lateral branches, both in Indiana. The LE&W had paid the last dividend on its preferred stock in 1907 and had never paid one on its common. During 1920 and 1921 the road lost money and the Vans found their mentor Smith only too willing to give it up. Control of the LE&W proved to be a costly affair for the NYC as the stock acquired in 1899 for $5,760,000 was sold to the Vans for 3 million dollars. The terms reached on January 11, 1922, called for a $500,000 down payment with the balance payable over a period of five years. As in the case of the Nickel Plate, the Vans put up the LE&W stock as collateral.

Formal acquisition of the Lake Erie & Western came on April 26, 1922. Thus, within the space of nine months following the release of the tentative I.C.C. plan, the Vans had acquired two of the companies assigned to System 5. Some 1168 miles of railroad had been acquired for a total cash outlay of $1,278,000 and the brothers had once again demonstrated their amazing ability to use circumstances and credit to good advantage.

With I.C.C. approval the Nickel Plate began operating the LE&W on July 1, 1922, under a contract providing for a division of receipts. The Ross contract of course prevented a similar arrangement in the case of the Clover Leaf. The next step was unification. This would not only give Bernet the opportunity to achieve increased operational efficiency but would provide the Vans a new source of capital — a resource they were habitually short on. To strengthen their position of control, they borrowed 6 million dollars from J. P. Morgan & Company and used it to buy up more of the stocks of their three roads. Then on December 28, 1922, the directors of the several companies approved a plan of consolidation. A new New York, Chicago & St. Louis Railroad Company would absorb the old Nickel Plate and its subsidiary, the Chicago & State Line; the Clover Leaf; the LE&W and its subsidiary, the Fort Wayne, Cincinnati & Louisville. Stock of the existing companies was to be exchanged for that of the new company at varying ratios. Only the new common stock would carry voting rights, although preferred shareholders could exercise voting power in the event the dividend was not paid. Holders of the old Nickel Plate 5 per cent noncumulative received new 6 per cent cumulative preferred on a share-for-share basis. Although there was some grumbling, no organized minority opposition developed. The Clover Leaf and LE&W minority preferred shareholders were evidently so stunned by the prospect of getting a regular dividend that they offered no resistance to the plan.

After approval was secured from the several states involved, application was filed with the Interstate Commerce Commission on April 28, 1923. This was the first major consolidation plan since passage of the Transportation Act and was regarded as a test case throughout the industry. During the hearings the I.C.C. appeared to harbor more misgivings about its authority to rule on the petition than about the merger itself. There was no opposition and the I.C.C. failed to take exception to the new company's nonvoting stock. On June 18, by a majority of one, the I.C.C. authorized the unification and new stock issues, effective July 1, 1923.

The Van Sweringens had acquired the Nickel Plate through a holding company, Nickel Plate Securities, renamed Vaness Company in 1922. Except for token holding in the hands of J. R. Nutt and C. L. Bradley, officials of the Union Trust Company, the Vans held all the voting stock of Vaness which in turn held 188,286 shares of the new Nickel Plate's preferred and 191,700 shares of its common. Inasmuch as it needed to hold only a bare majority of the common stock to retain absolute control, Vaness sold all of the preferred and 27,000 shares of the common at rising market prices after the consolidation. From this sale the Vans realized $17,225,300. The 1916 investment of $520,000 in borrowed money had in seven short years brought this fantastic return and the Van Sweringens still had 54.17 per cent of the voting stock of a 1695-mile railroad system.

The daily Peoria fast freight gets rolling a few miles out of Sandusky. G-44 No. 5517 will handle SP-1 as far west as Lima. The 2-8-0 was built for LE&W in 1904, remained on NKP roster until 1950.—TRAINS *collection.*

The Natural Gas Route

THE Lake Erie & Western was formed by the Seney Syndicate in 1879 through the consolidation of the La Fayette, Bloomington & Muncie and Lake Erie & Louisville roads, and the construction of a connecting line between them. This 353-mile railroad linked the Lake Shore & Michigan Southern at Fremont, O., with the Chicago & Alton at Bloomington, Ill., and actively competed for trunk-line traffic moving to and from St. Louis and Kansas City. The Lake Erie & Western, however, was critically handicapped by its dependence on the Lake Shore for westbound traffic and it was largely this weakness which brought about the building of the Nickel Plate. William H. Vanderbilt's acquisition of the latter precluded the complementary relationship of the two railroads and placed the future of the Lake Erie as an independent in grave jeopardy. The complete collapse of the enterprise was barely averted in the late 1880's by the discovery of natural gas and oil along the road. A period of prosperity followed during which the LE&W more than doubled the mileage it operated. Nevertheless, the road eventually passed under Vanderbilt control and its status became essentially that of a feeder to the Lake Shore and the Big Four.

La Quinio Rawson's Railroad

The Lake Erie & Western was the direct corporate descendant of the Fremont & Indiana Rail Road, incorporated in Ohio on April 25, 1853, for the purpose of building a 120-mile railroad extending from Fremont, O., to the Indiana border at Union City. Fremont, located at the head of navigation on the Sandusky River, was a port of some consequence and a station on the Toledo, Norwalk & Cleveland Railroad, the completion of which — a little more than two months previous — forged together the first line of railroads connecting New York and Chicago. Ultimately, the Fremont & Indiana was intended to connect with the Jeffersonville Railroad, forming a 278-mile "grand trunk" between Fremont and Louisville, Ky. Its more practical and immediate role, however, was that of a replacement for a worn-out plank road between Fremont and Rome (Fostoria).

A Fremont physician, La Quinio Rawson, conceived the idea of building the Fremont & Indiana and devoted nearly a quarter of a century to its promotion. A native of Massachusetts, he emigrated to Ohio in 1826 to practice medicine among the Wyandot Indians. About 1834 he left the reservation at Tymochtee and took up residence at Fremont, then known as Lower Sandusky. Rawson's heroic exertions during the course of a devastating cholera epidemic gained him prominence in the community and promised him a very comfortable if prosaic career. But, like many professional men of his day, Rawson soon became involved in ventures unrelated to his chosen field. The doctor

successfully organized and built a plank road through the Black Swamp to Rome, and he was one of the incorporators of the Toledo, Norwalk & Cleveland. Shortly after that railroad opened in 1853, Rawson sold his stock at a handsome profit and set about to promote a railroad to replace the plank road, most of which had rotted away and was a source of constant irritation to the people of Rome. The new railroad was also intended to link Fremont with the Tiffin & Fort Wayne Rail Road,* the ill-fated Clinton road then under construction a few miles beyond Rome.

During the summer of 1853 the F&I's surveyors projected a route across the level swamp forest southwest of Fremont. Aside from clearing and grubbing the right of way, the work of construction promised to be relatively easy. The route selected consisted of six tangents, ranging in length from 9 to 30 miles, connecting the principal towns between Fremont and Union City. The only curves on the line were at those towns and served to connect the tangents. There were only six bridges and no cuts or fills of consequence.

Construction of the F&I was undertaken at Fremont in September 1853, but the financial revulsions of the mid-1850's made it extremely difficult for the company to raise money. Many subscribers to the stock paid the company in then-worthless swamplands, while still others satisfied their obligation by furnishing crossties at the rate of 25 cents each. But for the dogged perseverance of Rawson and Charles W. Foster, the leading merchant of Rome, the enterprise surely would have failed. During most of 1856-1857 all construction work was suspended. With the enterprise all but doomed, the intrepid doctor managed to gain the support of two prominent citizens of Findlay — Squire Carlin and David Cory. Through their efforts Hancock County was induced to advance the road $150,000. By the end of 1857 the 37-mile grade between Fremont and Findlay was ready for the iron. Beyond Findlay the grade was nearly finished to Shannon (Bluffton) and in an advanced stage of construction between Lima and St. Marys.

On June 14, 1858, the steamer *Mat McNary* arrived at Fremont with 300 tons of 54-pound iron rails from Oswego, N. Y., enough to lay a little more than 3 miles of track. Workmen began spiking down the iron to a track gauge of 4 feet 9¼ inches† at the Sandusky River landing on July 4. The track was

---

*The Fremont & Indiana charter betrays no designs in the direction of Fort Wayne, but an 1855 map reveals several large unimproved parcels in that city owned by the "Fremont & Indiana RR."

†A compromise between standard and 4 feet 10 inches, the gauge prescribed by Ohio law, was chosen because it could safely accommodate equipment of either gauge.

La Quinio Rawson (1804-1889)

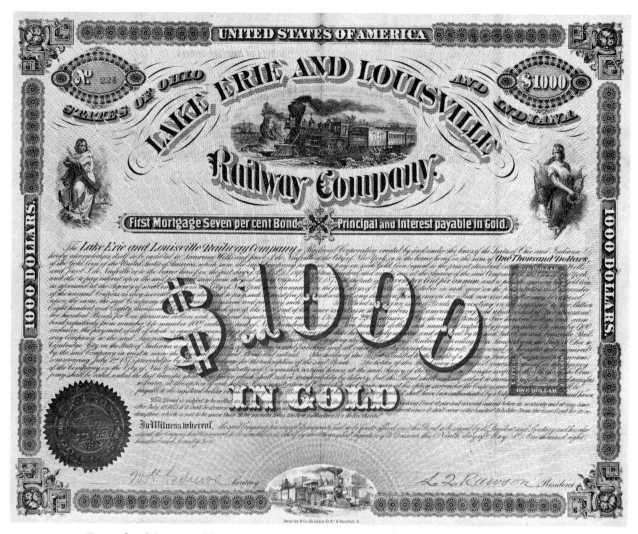

Proceeds of $1000 gold bond signed by L. Q. Rawson in 1872 helped complete Lake Erie & Louisville extension west of Findlay. — *Allen County Historical Society.*

completed to Foster's store at Fostoria on January 22, 1859, and the following February 1 the F&I began operating regular trains. The daily-save-Sunday mixed train ran on a leisurely 100-minute schedule, and was made up of a locomotive and cars rented from the Cleveland & Toledo, successor to the TN&C. With the opening of navigation in the spring the steamer *Island Queen* began making daily trips to and from Sandusky, connecting with F&I trains.

West of Fostoria the track was laid through Arcadia early in the spring of 1859 and by summer's end had reached a point 1 mile east of Findlay. Here all work stopped, for the company had utterly exhausted its resources and was once again forced to prevail upon its friends at Findlay for assistance. In the fall Judge Cory journeyed to New York where on his own credit he purchased enough iron to lay the track into Findlay. Operation extended to that place on December 26, 1859. A stage met the train at Findlay and ran to Lima, an arduous journey that consumed almost 24 hours.

The track of the embryonic Fremont & Indiana was unballasted and there were no stations, fences, or cattle guards. The first locomotive on the road was the woodburning *Fremont*, a 4-4-0 with 15 x 20-inch cylinders and 66-inch driving wheels. Built by the Boston Locomotive Works (Hinkley) in 1853, it was one of several engines rented from the Cleveland & Toledo. On April 5, 1861, *Fremont* turned out to greet the propeller *Equinox*, the first ship to come up the Sandusky that season. On board was the 24-ton *L. Q. Rawson*, a 4-4-0 built by R. Norris & Son of Philadelphia. The first locomotive owned by the F&I, the *Rawson* sported 5-foot drivers and 15 x 22-inch cylinders. About the same time, the road bought a pair of "first-class" coaches, a baggage car, and 25 freight cars.

Lima and the towns to the west of it treated the Fremont & Indiana with utter indifference and early in 1860 all work west of Findlay was suspended for want of money. A town named in honor of Rawson was platted in 1855 on the grade 9 miles west of

Woodburner *Fremont* of the Cleveland & Toledo reportedly opened Fremont & Indiana in 1859. Boston Locomotive Works built the 4-4-0 in 1853. — Fostoria *Review-Times*.

Findlay. Seventeen years passed and trees grew again on the grade before Rawson saw a rail, much less a train.

TWENTY YEARS OF FRUSTRATION

The F&I passed into receivership on October 14, 1861, and was subsequently ordered sold by the Sandusky County common pleas court at Fremont. This was the first of three forced sales ordered by this court over a period of 17 years. Rawson, Cory, Carlin, and Foster organized the Fremont, Lima & Union Railroad on January 21, 1862, managed to raise enough money to retire the old debts, and again took possession of the road. After selling about $300,000 worth of new bonds, they contracted to have the road completed between Findlay and St. Marys, a distance of 50 miles. The contractor completed the grade and placed 160,000 crossties but cash again ran out before rails could be purchased.

Rawson was instrumental in the organization of the Lake Erie & Pacific Rail Road, incorporated in Indiana on October 6, 1860. This company proposed to build 55 miles of road connecting the Fremont road at Union City with the Jeffersonville at Rushville, Ind. Most of the grade of the LE&P was completed by the summer of 1864 when the contractor died and all work was suspended. Unable to finance its completion, Rawson made a contract with the Jeffersonville under which the latter built 21 miles of the LE&P. This section, between Rushville and Cambridge City, was opened to traffic on July 4, 1868. It was operated by the Jeffersonville under a lease which could be terminated at the LE&P's option provided the Jeffersonville was refunded the

money it spent finishing the road. Actually, the LE&P had passed out of existence on February 4, 1865, when along with the Fremont, Lima & Union it was absorbed by a new company, the Lake Erie & Louisville Railroad.

Increased business following the outbreak of the Civil War prompted the addition of a second daily train between Fremont and Findlay, but the war did little to improve the lot of Rawson's road. Earnings in 1862 amounted to $7656 of which $6107 was paid out against the purchase price of the locomotive *Rawson*. Grain accounted for most of the road's freight business, and the failure of the 1863 wheat crop dealt it a crushing deficit. From that time to 1871 the company was in an extremely embarrassed condition, but Rawson managed to collect enough money on unpaid stock subscriptions to forestall bankruptcy. No construction work was started during this period, and most of the oak crossties that had been laid between Findlay and St. Marys rotted away. Finally, on April 4, 1871, Rawson was appointed receiver, and the following July 27 the property was sold to the bondholders. On April 12, 1872, the company was reorganized as the Lake Erie & Louisville Rail*way*.

With the nation in the midst of an economic revival, the new company was able to sell a considerable number of bonds. Rawson managed to survive the reorganization, but the active management of the road passed to Calvin S. Brice, an ambitious 27-year-old Lima attorney, and Charles Foster, son of one of the original promoters. The work of completing the St. Marys extension was undertaken at once. About $300,000 was expended for rail and three new locomotives were purchased, giving the road a total of five.

During the late summer and fall of 1872 31 miles of track was laid between Findlay and Lima, and regular trains began running to Lima on December 5. During the spring of 1873 tracklayers advanced to within a mile of St. Marys when once again the road ran out of rail and money. However, the people of St. Marys voted a $20,000 subsidy, payable when the trains began running into the town. On the strength of the grant, the LE&L was able to borrow $4000 — enough to buy the necessary rails — and the track was laid into St. Marys on July 24, 1873. On September 3 the town celebrated the opening of the railroad with a grand jubilee highlighted by a complimentary excursion to Lima and back. Five days later a regular freight train was put on west of Lima, but the passenger train did not run to St. Marys until May 26, 1874.

The panic of 1873 made short shrift of the affairs of the Lake Erie & Louisville and on April 25, 1874, it went into the hands of a receiver. La Quinio Rawson, disillusioned and all but bankrupt, was ultimately ousted from the organization. Brice and the younger Foster were now firmly in control and after the road was foreclosed on February 17, 1877, they reorganized it as Lake Erie & Louisville Rail*road*.

During the summer of 1877 work was started on a 10-mile extension south from St. Marys along the Miami & Erie Canal to New Bremen and Minster. A turntable and engine shed were built at Minster and on January 28, 1878, operation of the mail and mixed trains was extended to that point. The next month work was started on a 9.91-mile branch from St. Marys westward along the north shore of Grand Lake to Celina, a center of lumbering and woodworking activity. The last rails were laid at Celina on June 25, 1878. An excursion train ran through to the town on July 4, and regular trains were put on four days later. Both the Minster and Celina extensions were built to standard gauge and the rest of the railroad was changed to that gauge during the summer of 1878.

The return of prosperity early in 1879 found the imaginative Brice promoting an alliance with an Eastern syndicate that controlled the La Fayette, Bloomington & Muncie, a 201-mile road extending from Muncie, Ind., to Bloomington, Ill. He envisioned a combination of that road and the Lake Erie & Louisville forming a new east-west trunk line which would be the nucleus of a through route from Boston to Kansas City. The first order of business was the building of a 53.78-mile connecting link between Celina and Muncie by a subsidiary company, the Indianapolis & Sandusky Railroad. Construction of this line was started early in the summer of 1879, and by October track had already been laid between Celina and Fort Recovery, 15 miles. Tracklayers had by this time started working east from Muncie and just before Christmas the two parties met at Portland, Ind., 11 miles west of Fort Recovery. Regular trains were not put on between Muncie and Celina, however, until the latter part of May 1880.

THE BLOOMINGTON ROAD

The railroad which ultimately became the western half of the Lake Erie & Western was originally promoted as a feeder to the pre-Gould Toledo, Wabash & Western Railway. Its primary purpose was to give the granaries of central Illinois, particularly those at Bloomington, a more direct rail connection with their Eastern markets. The Wabash, which terminated at Toledo, bypassed congested Chicago and gave Bloomington's competitors at Decatur and Springfield a considerably shorter and cheaper route to the East.

Azariah Boody, president of the Wabash, employed an ingenious method to promote the building of the 117-mile feeder road between Lafayette, Ind., and Bloomington and a similar enterprise at Peoria. He encouraged locally influential people to organize a company and secure public grants sufficient to cover the cost of acquiring a right of way and constructing the grade. Bankers friendly to the Wabash then were given the opportunity to take mortgage bonds, the proceeds of which were used to pay for the track and necessary structures. Once built the railroad was operated by Wabash under a long-term lease.

The La Fayette, Bloomington & Mississippi Railway was incorporated in Illinois on February 28, 1867, by Gen. A. Gridley, James H. Cheney, W. A. Rankin, and other prominent men of Bloomington. The company's charter provided for the building of an 80-mile line eastward from Bloomington to Gibson, Paxton, and the state line near the Indiana village of Ambia. A complementary company was to be organized in Indiana to build about 37 miles of road between Ambia and a junction with the Wabash at Lafayette. Following the appearance of General Gridley at Lafayette in 1867 the La Fayette, Oxford & Bloomington Railroad was organized by Adams Earl, Moses Fowler, and Hiram Chase.

The citizenry of Ford, McLean, and Vermilion counties authorized the investment of $467,000 in public funds in the capital stock of the Illinois company. Since the railroad offered few tangible benefits to the Indiana counties, officials there were apathetic to it. As a result the La Fayette, Oxford & Bloomington quietly passed out of existence but its promoters had not given up. On July 13, 1869, they chartered the La Fayette, Muncie & Bloomington

Rail Road as a means of building the link between the Illinois company and the Wabash as well as an 85-mile line connecting Lafayette with the Cleveland, Columbus, Cincinnati & Indianapolis Railroad (Bee Line) at Muncie. By placing Lafayette on a new east-west trunk line and promising the city the road's main repair shops, the new company secured a $373,000 commitment from the Tippecanoe County commissioners. During the summer of 1869 the electorates of Benton, Tipton, and Delaware counties voted to take a total of $250,000 of the LM&B's capital stock. The ingenuity of the Lafayette promoters brought no joy to Azariah Boody for — innocent of the role of his road — they were proposing to give the Bee Line access to Wabash territory.

The La Fayette, Bloomington & Mississippi broke ground on October 11, 1869, at a point 2 miles southeast of Bloomington. In March 1870 work was similarly started on the Indiana road at Lafayette, and by the end of that year the entire road between Bloomington and Lafayette was graded and ready for the track.

In June 1871 the Illinois company leased its road to the Wabash for 999 years and in July the Indiana men were invited to Saratoga, N. Y., to attend a conference with Boody and the Wabash bankers. When they refused to follow the LB&M into the Wabash fold, Adams Earl and his associates were bluntly informed that if they did not fall into line the Wabash would build a short-line connection between the Illinois road and its own line at Williamsport, Ind. Unable to collect more than a fraction of the public money subscribed to their stock, the promoters were finally forced to lease their road to the Wabash in September 1871.

Mortgages were executed before the end of 1871 on the Illinois and Indiana roads, the proceeds of which were immediately used to effect their completion. The Wabash agreed to guarantee the bonds and furnish the locomotives and cars needed to operate the roads. In August 1871 the first carloads of 56-pound iron rails were delivered by the Illinois Central at Bloomington and the work of laying track eastward from that point began before the end of the month. By mid-October the track had reached Saybrook, 26 miles east of Bloomington. A month later the rails were down as far east as Gibson. By this time other gangs had begun laying track at Paxton, Ill.

During the first week of November 1871, 19 miles of the Indiana road between Lafayette and Templeton were completed and an inspection train carried Wabash officials over this section. Intense cold delayed completion of the track between Gibson and Paxton until the last week of 1871, by which time the Indiana portion was finished west of Lafayette. Construction gangs working east from Paxton reached Hoopeston on February 28 and drove the last spike at the Indiana border on March 22, 1872.

Prior to leasing the LM&B to the Wabash the Lafayette entrepreneurs had organized another company, the Cincinnati, La Fayette & Chicago Railroad. The purpose of the new enterprise was to connect the Illinois Central at Kankakee, Ill., with the Indianapolis, Cincinnati & La Fayette Railroad at Lafayette, forming a through route between Chicago and Cincinnati. This company actually built about 56 miles of road between Kankakee and Templeton and ran into Lafayette over the track of the LM&B, paying $5000 per annum for the 18.7 miles of trackage rights. The fee amounted to something less than 1 per cent of the estimated cost

Black Wolf, Toledo, Wabash & Western 9, worked the La Fayette-Bloomington line in the early 1870's. Rogers 4-4-0 was built in 1856. — *Collection of John H. Keller.*

of building another line over the same distance.

As it developed the CL&C operated the first regular trains over the LM&B, establishing service out of Lafayette on May 1, 1872. The Wabash inaugurated service to Bloomington exactly two months later, at first operating a mixed train in each direction daily. On July 15, 1872, these were augmented by a daily passenger train each way, scheduled to make the 117-mile run in 6 hours 40 minutes.

Helper engines were needed to start trains at both ends of the Bloomington Division, as the Wabash called the line. Leaving the South Street depot in Lafayette, trains had to negotiate a 21-degree, 45-minute curve, cross the Wabash River on a 660-foot bridge, and then do battle with more than 4 miles of stiff ascending grades and reverse curves. The task of leaving Bloomington was no less difficult and involved an assault on 1½ miles of 1.3 per cent grade, practically all of which was curved track. In the rolling hills between Bloomington and Saybrook there were 26 curves in as many miles, but farther east there were several long tangents including one 28 miles long east of Paxton.

The Wabash assigned about 15 of its oldest locomotives, 4-4-0's built by Rogers and Mason between 1855 and 1857, to the Bloomington Division. All had 15- or 16-inch cylinders, 5-foot drivers, and a total weight of 27 to 29 tons. The Masons, numbered 24 through 27 and 29, originally had 66- and 72-inch drivers and were altered out of respect for the Bloomington's tough grades. The Rogers engines were numbered from 1 to 10. The principal engine facility on the branch was the eight-stall Bloomington roundhouse. There was a two-stall shed at Paxton, and Bloomington Division engines were also serviced at the Wabash roundhouse at Lafayette.

The La Fayette, Muncie & Bloomington put the 84.6-mile section east of Lafayette under contract prior to leasing the westerly part of its road to the Wabash. The contractor started work in June 1871 and by the end of 1872 had the entire grade completed, bridges in place, and ties on the ground. In order to pay the contractor, the railroad was forced to sue Tippecanoe County for the more than $237,000 still due against the public stock subscription. The county commissioners claimed that the Wabash lease invalidated their obligation but ultimately lost their case in the courts.

Completion of the Muncie extension was authorized by the LM&B directors on May 28, 1874, and a contract was made with Stillman Witt of Cleveland under which he agreed to do the work in exchange for stock and mortgage bonds at the rate of $40,000 per mile. Witt died before he could begin work, but the obligation was assumed by his son-in-law Daniel P. Eells. By mid-October 1875 Eells had

35 miles of track down between Tipton and Muncie, and a month later completed 25 more miles of track between Tipton and Frankfort. At the end of the year Eells' forces had reached the line of the Indianapolis, Cincinnati & La Fayette at 3-Mile Switch (Altamont), a little more than 2 miles southeast of the junction of the Bloomington Division and Wabash at Lafayette Junction. Eells operated a six-car stockholders' special from Muncie to Lafayette on February 1, 1876, and 10 days later put on a daily accommodation train between Muncie and Tipton. On February 24 the accommodation was extended to Frankfort. Just as Eells was about to begin running regular trains into Lafayette early in March, his workmen discovered that the frogs in the crossing at 3-Mile Switch were missing. The IC&L had removed the frogs and had dumped them in a country wood lot near Lebanon. They were quickly located and retrieved by a LM&B "posse," hauled in wagons over 16 miles of muddy roads to Frankfort, and subsequently restored in the crossing. Eells posted an armed guard at 3-Mile Switch with orders to shoot anyone who might attempt to molest it, only to have the IC&L counter the move by obtaining a court injunction against use of the crossing. Freight trains ran as far as the crossing where goods were transferred to wagons for the last 3 miles to Lafayette.

To operate the East Division the LM&B purchased 10 33-ton 4-4-0 locomotives from Brooks during 1876. Engine No. 1, the *La Fayette*, was received at Muncie on May 8, followed in short order by the *Muncie*

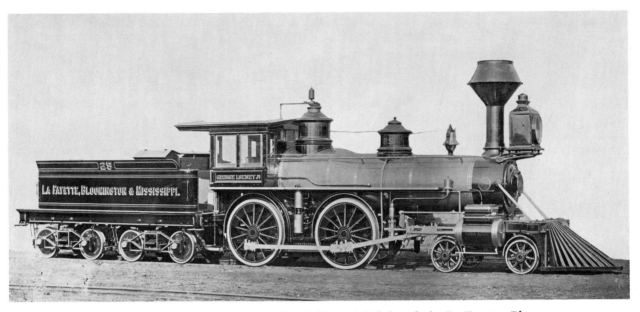

George I. Seney Jr., No. 25, was one of six Baldwin 4-4-0's bought by La Fayette, Bloomington & Mississippi in 1878. They were identical to Brooks engines purchased in 1876 by La Fayette, Muncie & Bloomington. — *Collection of John A. Rehor.*

and *Frankfort*, Nos. 2 and 3. The Barney & Smith works at Dayton furnished the road six coaches, two baggage cars, and eight cabooses, while a large number of freight cars were leased from the United States Rolling Stock Company.

After three months of wrangling and litigation, the IC&L and LM&B finally ironed out their dispute and the latter began running regular trains between South Street station and the Bee Line depot at Muncie on June 19, 1876. The trains were operated more or less in conjunction with Bee Line and Cincinnati, La Fayette & Chicago trains, forming a rather circuitous route between Cleveland and Chicago. Ironically, there was no coordination of operation with the West Division, which was still being operated by the Wabash.

Several of the Indiana counties which were major stockholders of the La Fayette, Muncie & Bloomington attempted to upset the Wabash lease in the courts and they finally succeeded in obtaining a decree setting it aside in May 1875. By this time, however, the Wabash had defaulted on the Bloomington Division bonds as well as its own and the road west of Lafayette had been in the hands of a receiver since February 22, 1875. The mortgage on the Illinois section was foreclosed and the property was sold on May 16, 1876, to its bondholders, represented by George I. Seney, John T. Martin, and others. The Illinois road was reorganized on September 27, 1876, as the La Fayette, Bloomington & Mississippi Rail Road, and on October 2 the Wabash lease was abrogated by mutual agreement. The road was leased the same day to the La Fayette, Muncie & Bloomington. For a short time Wabash equipment

continued to be used west of Lafayette because of a fear that the LM&B engines were too heavy to safely operate there. However, within a month, schedules were coordinated and through cars were operated between Muncie and Bloomington.

Eventually, the LM&B put on a through daily express train in each direction. The westbound covered the 201 miles in 7½ hours and made an excellent connection with a fast Chicago & Alton train for St. Louis. This train also connected with a Bee Line train out of Cleveland, and the combined Cleveland-St. Louis run consumed 25 hours. In addition to its express trains, the LM&B ran a daily accommodation between Frankfort and Bloomington connecting with trains of the Frankfort & Kokomo.

THE MIDLAND LINE

The first development in the formation of the Lake Erie & Western came on April 3, 1879, when the La Fayette, Muncie & Bloomington was sold under foreclosure to Dan Eells. Later the same month Eells reorganized the road as the Muncie & State Line Railroad, and on April 30 the property was consolidated with George Seney's La Fayette, Bloomington & Missssippi to form a new company known as the La Fayette, Bloomington & Muncie Railway. By this time the alliance of the Seney-Eells group with Calvin Brice and his Lake Erie & Louisville associates had been perfected and a merger of the several properties had been outlined. The Lake Erie & Western Railway was formed on August 4, 1879, by consolidating the LE&L and its subsidiary, the Indianapolis & Sandusky. Finally, on December 11, 1879, the new Lake Erie & Western formally

Intended for both fast freight and passenger duty, No. 41 was the last of 10 Brooks 4-4-0's furnished the new Lake Erie & Western in 1880. — *Collection of John H. Keller.*

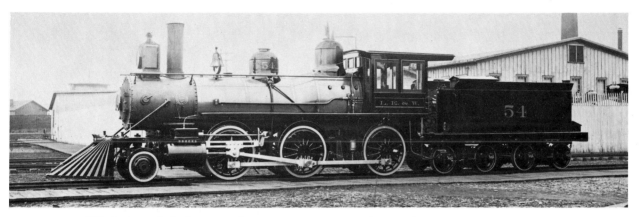

LE&W Moguls had oversized wood pilot and headlight on smokebox. No. 54 was out-shopped in March 1889, the first of 40 such Brooks engines. She was renumbered 5330 in 1905, was reboiled in 1908, dismantled in 1925. — *Schenectady History Center.*

absorbed the La Fayette, Bloomington & Muncie.

As early as 1877 Brice and Foster had planned to extend the LE&L eastward from Fremont to Sandusky, a distance of 23 miles. Every spring since 1865 the company had been obliged to dredge a channel through the bars of Black Swamp silt that continuously built up at the mouth of the Sandusky River. By 1877 navigation of the river was no longer practical although the stern-wheeler *Reindeer* was still making tri-weekly runs between Fremont and Sandusky. Then, when the Lake Shore & Michigan Southern reopened the long-abandoned northern line between Sandusky and Oak Harbor in 1872, the number of trains operated over the former main line through Fremont was drastically curtailed.

Early in 1880 the LE&W announced that it had allied itself with the Vanderbilt roads and the Chicago & Alton to form the Midland Line, a fast freight route between Boston and Kansas City. Work on the Sandusky extension was begun at once and upon its completion, it was stated, the road would run fast express passenger trains between Cleveland and Kansas City. These were to be operated in connec-tion with LS&MS trains from the East and would run over the Lake Shore's line between Cleveland and Sandusky. A subsidiary company, the Sandusky & Fremont Railway, was organized on April 23, 1880. The construction work, partly financed by Sandusky's $60,000 public grant, was essentially finished by the end of that year.

On February 20, 1881, the Lake Erie & Western began running trains into the Lake Shore depot at Sandusky, 376.8 miles east of Bloomington. By this time William H. Vanderbilt had made his futile bid to appease Jay Gould by making a traffic alliance with the Wabash. The Midland Line was dead and in bitter retaliation the Seney Syndicate had already begun the building of the Nickel Plate. However, the LE&W did put on a pair of express trains in each direction. No. 1, the *Kansas City Express*, left Sandusky at 8:55 a.m., 10 minutes after the arrival of a fast LS&MS train out of Buffalo. No. 1 ran to Bloomington in 16 hours and made an excellent connection with an Alton train for St. Louis and Kansas City. The evening departure from Sandusky, the *Denver Express*, ran on a schedule of 17 hours and carried

"Dr. Horton's patented reclining chair palace car."

During the summer of 1881 the Lake Erie began running well-patronized week-end excursions to Sandusky in connection with the steamer *Jay Cooke*. The sidewheeler touched at the Marblehead peninsula; at Johnson's Island, site of a Confederate prison; and the Bass Islands, celebrated for good fishing and superlative wines. The Grape Excursion, an annual pilgrimage to the vintage festival at Put-in-Bay on South Bass Island, was a highlight of the summer season. Another annual outing of note was the Emancipation Day special, chartered by the colored folk of Findlay and Lima for a gala day at Grand Lake.

Although the Lake Erie's offices were situated at Lafayette and that city had ardently sought the road's main repair shops, Calvin Brice saw to it that they were located at his home town of Lima. For its part, Lima donated $85,000 to the railroad as well as a tract of land. Here, during 1880-1881 the LE&W built a yard, 25-stall roundhouse and a turntable, a boiler shop, machine shop, and blacksmith shop. A complete carbuilding and repair facility with 175-foot transfer table was also built adjacent to the locomotive shops. For several years Brice operated the car shops as a private enterprise under the name of Lima Car Works.

NATURAL GAS

During 1881-1882 the LE&W managed to show a modest profit, but its fortunes began to run down-

LE&W excursions connected with *Jay Cooke* after 1881. — *Rev. Edward J. Dowling, S.J.*

hill with the national economy in 1883. The road was in deplorable condition, being almost entirely unballasted and laid mostly with battered 56-pound iron. The return of equipment rented from the Nickel Plate in 1883 aggravated an already acute

Straight stack and smokebox extension were post-delivery alterations to LE&W 52, one of 10 dual-service engines outshopped by Brooks in 1883. — *Collection of John H. Keller.*

Findlay's derricks were busy during natural gas boom. Drilling rigs were operated on steam from stationary boilers. — *Allen County Historical & Archaeological Society.*

shortage of locomotives and cars. The Seney Syndicate forestalled bankruptcy by advancing the LE&W $320,000 in June 1883, but the inevitable overtook the road in the spring of 1885. The management voluntarily instituted receivership when it found itself unable to meet the interest coupons on the La Fayette, Bloomington & Muncie mortgage. Ultimately, the LE&W defaulted on all its bonds, and in June 1886 the Central Trust Company acted to foreclose the several mortgages.

With ample justification the LB&M bondholders charged that the road west of Muncie accounted for most of the Lake Erie's freight traffic. Hoping to merge with the Bee Line, the bondholders demanded that their railroad be separated from the burdensome portion east of Muncie. It is entirely conceivable that the LE&W would have been dismembered in the courts but for an extraordinary event that literally shattered the mundane life of the village of Findlay on January 20, 1886. The Karg well, being drilled into the Trenton limestone at a site between the Blanchard River and the LE&W, vented 20 million cubic feet of natural gas with a deafening roar. A 100-foot tower of flame, the Karg

burned for months and was seen 50 miles away.

By the spring of 1887 the Karg and 30 other test wells were producing 60 million cubic feet of gas daily, enough to "supply a city twice the size of Chicago with all the light, fuel, and power it required." Projected overnight into national prominence, Findlay proclaimed itself "the Brilliant City" and offered industry free land, fuel, and light. Within two years Findlay became a booming city of more than 20,000 sprawled out over 24 square miles of what once had been worthless swamp. Real estate values skyrocketed as 4000 new buildings went up and derricks loomed everywhere.

In June 1887 Findlay staged a three-day natural gas festival and invited all America to come and see the town where "women split no wood" and the drudgery of the wood stove was only a memory. Three railroads hauled upwards of 70,000 people to the city and the LE&W ran free shuttle trains back and forth across town so that visitors might witness cornerstone layings. Gas also brought to Findlay 15 new glass factories, three more railroads, a pair of rolling mills, the world's largest brick works and its first seamless tube mill, and an oil refinery.

LE&W emblem during 1890's and early 1900's depicted train passing Karg well.

A nitro shot brings in another oil gusher in the Lima field. — *Allen County Historical Society.*

The events at Findlay brought recollections of foul-smelling vapors encountered by well drillers all over northwestern Ohio and east central Indiana. As it developed the LE&W traversed a gas field extending for 200 miles between Fremont and Tipton. Muncie enjoyed a spectacular boom and dozens of new factories went up at Fostoria, St. Marys, Portland, Elwood, Alexandria, and Albany.

In the spring of 1885 Ben Faurot brought in an oil producing well at Lima. At first the high sulphur content of Lima crude delayed its exploitation but the discovery of a successful refining process in 1886 triggered an oil boom in the Ohio-Indiana gas belt. Some 60,000 derricks came to be "strung out in ghostly procession across the landscape where before there had been only fields of waving green and gold." Lima became the center of the oil industry

and the Solar refinery located on the LE&W was for years the biggest such establishment in the world. As the demand for oil field machinery and supplies boomed, Lima became a manufacturing center as well. At the height of the boom, Lima boasted 17 hotels and an 800-seat opera house.

The oil and gas boom put down the uprising of the LB&M bondholders and Calvin Brice and Samuel Thomas bought out many of the erstwhile rebels. After the failure of his bank in 1884, George Seney had fallen into obscurity and, like most of the other members of the old syndicate, he no longer was connected with the LE&W. Brice assumed the dominant role in the road's management and on February 9, 1887, he incorporated the Lake Erie & Western Rail*road* as the successor to the old company. The decade that followed proved to be the most pros-

Brakeless LE&W No. 79 was outshopped by Pittsburgh in 1875 for Indianapolis, Peru & Chicago. Posing (at left) beside 35-ton 4-4-0 at Peru, Ind., in 1893 is R. E. Blick. — *Collection of Willis A. McCaleb.*

perous period in the entire history of the railroad.

The old management had sought to extend the road 40 miles from Bloomington to Peoria and toward this end had organized the Lake Erie & Mississippi Railroad on January 7, 1884. Very little work was done prior to the receivership, but after the reorganization Brice revived the extension. Construction workers broke ground at Bloomington on March 22, 1887, and the first rails were laid at that point the following July 28. By the end of 1887 most of the track was laid.

Arrangements were made to operate into Peoria over 2.42 miles of the Peoria & Pekin Union Railway. Leaving the tracks of that road, the LE&W headed east along the Illinois River for about 4 miles and then climbed out of the valley through 6 miles of ravines at the rate of 50 feet to the mile. In this distance there were 12 curves and a goodly number of deep cuts and fills. One cut, through a ridge called Hog Back, was 890 feet long, 59 feet deep, and 222 feet wide at the top.

Expecting to cut through Hog Back in three to four months at the most, the excavators ran into hardpan which defied scrapers and ruined plows. Wet weather transformed it into gumbo which would not support a team. The track was finally laid through the big cut on April 24, 1888, and the next day a special train — made up of 4-4-0 No. 24, a pair

of coaches, a sleeper, and General Manager Bradbury's private car — ran through to Peoria. Operation of the express trains to that point began on May 27, 1888.

INDIANAPOLIS & MICHIGAN CITY DIVISION

Shortly after reorganization, the Lake Erie & Western absorbed the first of two Indiana railroads which laterally intersected it and traversed the gas belt. By paying its bondholders some 3 million dollars the LE&W acquired the Indianapolis Division of the Wabash, St. Louis & Pacific on March 15, 1887. Formerly the Indianapolis, Peru & Chicago Railway, this 161-mile road connecting Indianapolis with Michigan City had been operated by the Wabash since 1881.

The IP&C was the descendant of the Peru & Indianapolis Rail Road, chartered on January 19, 1846, under a special act of the Indiana legislature. Financed almost entirely by local tax money, the P&I was built in the interest of the pioneer Madison & Indianapolis Rail Road, opened in 1847 between Indianapolis and the Ohio River at Madison, Ind. The P&I formed a 73-mile northerly extension of the Madison road to the Wabash & Erie Canal at Peru. The work of building the road was started in 1849 and the first section, 21.42 miles between Indianapolis and Noblesville, was opened to traffic on

97

Pile driver repairs west trestle approach to Sandusky River bridge at Fremont about 1898. Up front is ex-IP&C 4-4-0 No. 73. — *Collection of Walter Kundert.*

March 12, 1851. The next year the P&I was extended to Tipton and in 1853 the track reached Kokomo, 32 miles north of Noblesville. Between Kokomo and Peru the road was built through what was then the Miami Indian reservation. This last portion was completed in 1854.

Typical of the rudimentary pioneer railways, the Peru road was built with timber rails or planking crowned with a thin iron strap. In common with all strap-rail roads, the P&I was plagued with "snake-heads," the upward curling of the straps as they expanded under the heat of the summer sun. A horse could trot about as fast as the speed made by the Peru's trains, and it was a rare trip when the passengers were not called upon to assist the crew in re-railing the engine with jackscrews. As a concession to the merchants of Noblesville and Kokomo the track was laid down the middle of the main commercial streets of those towns. Not only did this accommodate the farm trade, but it afforded store-keepers a substantial savings in drayage.

At first the Peru road owned no locomotives or cars and its daily mixed train was operated by the Madison & Indianapolis. This arrangement was terminated in 1856 and the road was closed so that the troublesome strap rails could be replaced with 50-pound iron T rails. The P&I also acquired three locomotives, one of which appears to have been a 4-4-0 manufactured by William Mason in September 1856. The rails and equipment were paid for with money raised through the sale of bonds, most of which were taken by the Cuttings of New York.

Reopened on September 16, 1856, the Peru & Indianapolis failed to weather the financial storm of 1857 and was forced into a protracted receivership. It was reorganized on March 11, 1864, by Francis B. Cutting, Volney T. Malott, David Macy, and other bondholders as the Indianapolis, Peru & Chicago Railway which operated until September 1881.

The 88-mile portion of the IP&C north of Peru started out as the Cincinnati, Peru & Chicago Railway, incorporated in Indiana on June 23, 1853. This company proposed to build a 220-mile road extending across Indiana from a point on the Illinois border southeast of Chicago to Cambridge City where connection was to have been made with a projected line to Cincinnati and the Fremont & Indiana-Jeffersonville grand trunk. In 1855 the CP&C opened 28 miles of 4-foot 10-inch gauge track connecting the Michigan Southern & Northern Indiana (LS&MS) at La Porte with the Fort Wayne & Chicago Railroad (Pennsylvania Company) at Plymouth.

E-42 5367 was built for Northern Ohio in 1896 but spent most of her days on the Peoria Division, location of this scene. Brooks 2-6-0 went to AC&Y when that road took over the NO in 1920. — *Collection of John H. Keller.*

Further construction was suspended during the stringent money market of the late 1850's, but on June 11, 1863, a subsidiary was formed to complete a 74-mile extension from Plymouth to Peru and Marion. This company, the Indianapolis, Rochester & Chicago Railroad, purchased some right of way but did no actual work of construction. Finally, the CP&C was sold to its bondholders who reorganized it as the Chicago, Cincinnati & Louisville Railroad* on October 12, 1866.

During November 1866 the new company converted the old road to standard gauge and late in 1867 acquired the rights of the Indianapolis, Rochester & Chicago. Work on the extension to Peru and Marion was started the same year and in 1868 the first section, 21 miles between Plymouth and Rochester, was opened to traffic. The track reached Peru in July 1869 and regular trains began running between that town and La Porte, 73 miles, the following September 4.

The line between Peru and Marion was partly

graded before the project was dropped in favor of a 12.75-mile extension from La Porte to Michigan City on Lake Michigan. This line was built in the name of the Michigan City & Indianapolis Railroad, incorporated on June 4, 1870, and was completed in December of the same year. On April 9, 1871, the CC&L began operating regular trains into the Michigan Central depot at Michigan City. Shortly afterward, on May 12, 1871, the road was taken over by the Indianapolis, Peru & Chicago.

After taking over the CC&L, the IP&C did a very heavy freight business, the bulk of which was grain and lumber moving to the road's 1500-foot dock at Michigan City. For many years the principal engine facility had been the eight-stall roundhouse built at Indianapolis in 1850. However, in 1872 a large locomotive repair shop, a carshop, and a 15-stall roundhouse were built at Peru. On September 1, 1881, the IP&C was leased to the Wabash, St. Louis & Pacific, a contract which was abrogated during the latter's collapse in 1886. Subsequently, the bondholders sold the road in March 1887 to the Lake Erie & Western.

At the time it was leased to the Wabash the IP&C

*The CC&L is often confused with a company with the same name which in 1907 completed the present Chesapeake & Ohio line between Cincinnati and Chicago.

owned 28 locomotives—including four Rogers 4-4-0's of Civil War vintage; at least four Danforth & Cooke engines; four former CC&L steamers, including a pair of 30-ton Mason 4-4-0's built in 1868-1869; and nine Grant and Pittsburgh 4-4-0's acquired between 1870 and 1877. Numbered 1-12 and 14-29 on the IP&C, these locomotives received corresponding numbers in the 500 series of the Wabash roster. Several were subsequently retired and replaced by old Wabash engines — including six Rogers and Mason 4-4-0's that had seen duty on the Bloomington road in the 1870's, two Grant 4-4-0's of 1873, and a pair of 1871 Schenectady eight-wheelers. All told, the LE&W acquired 30 engines with the Indianapolis & Michigan City Division and renumbered these 61-90.

THE MUNCIE ROAD

On May 28, 1890, the Lake Erie & Western gained control of the Fort Wayne, Cincinnati & Louisville Railroad, commonly referred to as "the Muncie road." This 133-mile independent connected Fort Wayne, Connersville, and Rushville in eastern Indiana and crossed the LE&W at Muncie. Together with the White Water Railroad, the Muncie road formed a through route from Fort Wayne to Cincinnati, and its operation also was closely geared to that of the LS&MS branch line connecting Fort Wayne with Jackson, Mich.

The Muncie was a relatively prosperous road and its future had been considerably enhanced by the discovery of gas and oil along its route in the late 1880's. Even so, the group of Boston capitalists that owned the Muncie and the White Water had them both up for sale. The asking price for the FWC&L was 2 million dollars, an amount considered exorbitant by the Cincinnati, Hamilton & Day-ton and the Big Four, both of which coveted the road. Although the Big Four did buy the White Water, the Vanderbilts hesitated long enough to permit C. S. Brice to take the Muncie out of circulation for 1.8 million dollars.

The idea of building a railroad from the Wabash & Erie Canal at Fort Wayne south to Muncie and Louisville, Ky., was first espoused by John Studabaker of Bluffton, Ind., and David Haines of Muncie. These men chartered the Fort Wayne & Southern Rail Road on January 15, 1849, but were forced to abandon the enterprise in 1854 or 1855. Another unrelated company, the Cincinnati, Cambridge & Chicago Short Line Railway, was formed on February 12, 1853, with the intent of building a 40-mile road from Cambridge City southeast to the Ohio border in the general direction of Cincinnati. An affiliate, the Cincinnati, New Castle & Michigan Railroad, was later organized to build a complementary line through New Castle and Muncie to Fort Wayne and the Michigan border. As in the case of the Fort Wayne & Southern, both of these roads were partly surveyed and acquired some right of way before failing in the 1857 panic.

The plan to build a line through Cambridge City and New Castle to Muncie and beyond was revived by the Cincinnati & Indianapolis Junction Railroad, a 98-mile road connecting Indianapolis and Connersville with the Cincinnati, Hamilton & Dayton at Hamilton, O. A subsidiary, the Connersville & New Castle Junction Railroad, was incorporated on October 23, 1863, and opened 12 miles of road between Connersville and Cambridge City in April 1865. Early in 1867 the branch was extended to New Castle, 13.2 miles. Known as the Cincinnati, Connersville & Muncie Rail Road after January 2, 1868, the branch-line company opened still another

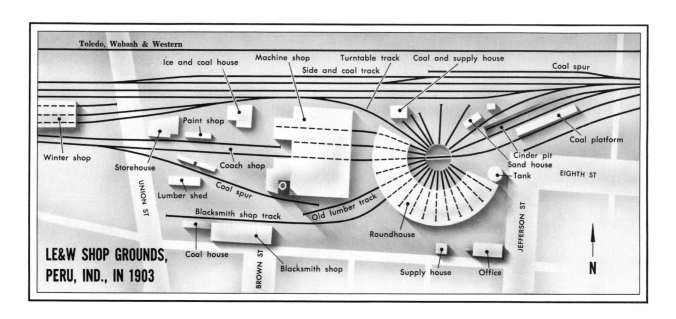

First Grant 92 is shown at Fort Wayne depot in mid-1890's. As Fort Wayne, Muncie & Cincinnati No. 2 it helped open that road in September 1870. It was later rebuilt in Fort Wayne shop and retired about 1900. — *Collection of Clyde E. Helms.*

LE&W No. 90 poses on Armstrong turntable at Peru in the 1890's. Grant built the locomotive in 1873 for Wabash. Lake Erie obtained it in 1887 with the Indianapolis & Michigan City Division. — *Collection of Roy W. Carlson.*

extension, to Muncie, in February 1869. Operated by the Cincinnati & Indianapolis Junction, the Connersville-Muncie branch was 43.31 miles long, including 2.4 miles of trackage rights at New Castle over the Columbus & Indiana Central (PRR).

The Junction management organized another subsidiary, the Fort Wayne, Muncie & Cincinnati Railway, on October 3, 1868, for the purpose of extending the Muncie branch to Fort Wayne. By forming a tenuous alliance with Studabaker and Haines, the Junction secured the rights of the long-defunct Fort Wayne & Southern. About 22 miles of road, between Bluffton and a junction with the Wabash 3 miles southwest of Fort Wayne, was completed on November 10, 1869. During 1870 the remaining 40 miles of road to Muncie was completed and regular trains began running over the entire 109-mile branch from Connersville to Fort Wayne on September 12, 1870.

The Fort Wayne, Muncie & Cincinnati and the Cincinnati, Connersville & Muncie were consolidated on June 8, 1869, to form the Fort Wayne, Muncie & Cincinnati Rail Road. The Junction road leased and operated this company until January 4, 1871, shortly before it succumbed to financial difficulties and passed under the control of the Cincinnati, Hamilton & Dayton.

About 1873 the Muncie road discontinued running into Fort Wayne over the Wabash and built a 2-mile extension from its junction with that road (now known as Hugo) to a connection with the Fort Wayne, Jackson & Saginaw. FWM&C trains ran into the Jackson road's Fort Wayne depot, using 1.75 miles of the latter's track. In 1874 the Muncie road built a frame enginehouse and a large brick machine shop near the FWJ&S depot.

Although the FWM&C passed into the hands of a receiver on November 12, 1874, a subsidiary company was formed in 1880 to build a 23.1-mile branch from New Castle south to Rushville. The New Castle & Rushville Railroad was built more or less simultaneously with the line of the Vernon, Greensburg & Rushville Railroad between Rushville and a connection with the Ohio & Mississippi Railway's Louisville branch at North Vernon. Completed during the latter part of 1881, the Rushville branch and the VG&R linked together a 206-mile route between Fort Wayne and Louisville.

On December 6, 1881, the Muncie road was reorganized as the Fort Wayne, Cincinnati & Louisville Railroad. From 1881 to 1890 the road operated the White Water line and ran its trains into Cincinnati. After the LS&MS took over the Jackson road in 1882, it was widely believed that the FWC&L would soon follow it into the Vanderbilt fold. However, natural gas and the unpredictable Calvin Brice delayed the inevitable for well nigh two decades.

The Muncie road's first locomotives were six 4-4-0's acquired under a rental contract from the Grant Locomotive Works during 1870-1871. Engines 7 and 8 were Manchester-built eight-wheelers purchased in 1873. The next year the road picked up a secondhand Rhode Island 4-4-0. These nine engines made up the roster until 1882 when another Manchester 4-4-0 was acquired. Engines 11 and 12 were husky 42-ton 4-4-0's turned out by Baldwin in 1889 for the Fort Wayne-Cincinnati trains. All 12 locomotives were in service in 1890 at which time they became LE&W 91-102.

Until 1889 all LE&W trains were powered by the American Standard 4-4-0. There were 50 such engines on the roster prior to the acquisition of the Michigan City and Fort Wayne lines, including the six original Lake Erie & Louisville engines and 16 that came with the La Fayette, Bloomington & Muncie. The newest 4-4-0's had 17 x 24-inch cylinders, 61-inch drivers, and weighed 35 tons. These Brooks-built locomotives were patterned after the standard Lake Shore & Michigan Southern eight-wheeler, the LE&W having adopted the design during the brief Midland alliance. There were 20 such engines, Nos. 32-41 built in 1880 and Nos. 44-53 built in 1883.

Practically all helper and yard assignments were held down by 4-4-0's, but the LE&W did have three engines built expressly for such duty. Engine 17, the *Leviathan*, was a 35-ton Baldwin 0-6-0 bought by the LB&M for helper service at Lafayette in 1879. There were also a pair of 26-ton 0-4-0's, the 42 and 43, built by Brooks in 1880.

In 1889 the Lake Erie went to the Mogul for its freight trains, purchasing eight 49-ton engines of this type from Brooks. Numbered 54-60 and 2, these had 18 x 24-inch cylinders and 56-inch drivers. Except when leaving Lafayette, Bloomington, and Peoria where tough grades cut their ratings in half, the 2-6-0's were good for 1050 tons on freight. Well liked by the LE&W, the 1889 engines were followed by 22 similar models built by Brooks in 1891 and 1893. These were numbered 103-124.

THE LOW-GRADE ROUTE REVIVED

In 1892 Findlay's supposedly inexhaustible supply of natural gas suddenly gave out. After several unsuccessful attempts to convert the kilns to oil, most of the glass factories were closed. Some of the firms chartered solid trains to move machinery and employees west to Muncie, Elwood, and other Indiana towns where the gas boom was still going strong. Despite a gradual decline in the gas and oil fields, the LE&W continued to enjoy a high degree of prosperity. The road was becoming less and less dependent upon the success of the grain crops and by

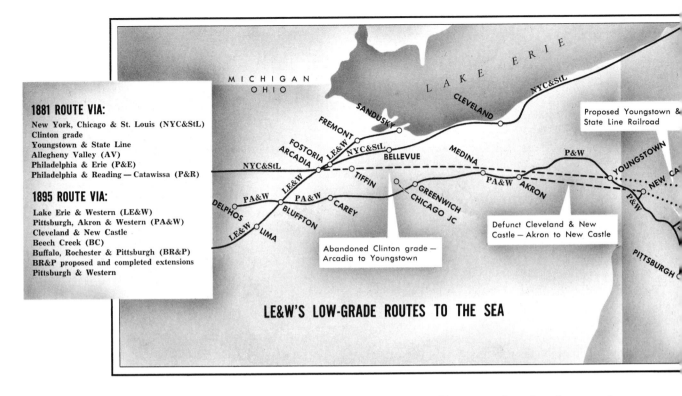

Proposed Youngstown &
State Line Railroad

Abandoned Clinton grade —
Arcadia to Youngstown

Defunct Cleveland & New
Castle — Akron to New Castle

LE&W'S LOW-GRADE ROUTES TO THE SEA

1895 merchandise and manufactured goods accounted for more than 40 per cent of freight tonnage. Under the judicious management of George Bradbury the LE&W enjoyed the distinction of being the most economically operated road in the central west. Throughout the 1890's the road consistently showed an operating ratio of less than 55 per cent. During the depression that followed the panic of 1893 the

Being midway between Tipton and Peoria, Rankin was selected as a division point in 1892, but it lost this status in 1933, eight years after this picture was taken. Local crews still lay over here, but roundhouse has been razed. — *NKP photo.*

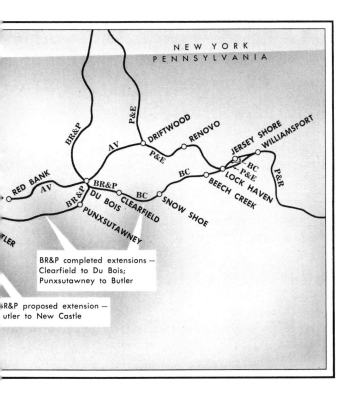

Here You Are!

DON'T MISS THE OPPORTUNITY!

GRAND CHEAP
EXCURSION
—TO—
MICHIGAN CITY
INDIANA,
—VIA—
L. E. & W. R. R.

Thursday, July 21, 1898

BELOW IS SCHEDULE OF SPECIAL TRAIN AND RATES.

LEAVES.	TIME.	RATE.	LEAVES.	TIME.	RATE.
	A. M.			A. M.	
Indianapolis	6.00	$1.50	Bunker Hill	8.20	$1.00
Malott Park	6.23	1.50	Peru	8.37	1.00
Castleton	6.32	1.50	Denver	8.55	1.00
Fishers	6.40	1.50	Deeds	9.02	1.00
New Britton	6.42	1.50	Macy	9.09	1.00
Noblesville	6.51	1.50	Wagoners	9.14	1.00
Cicero	7.04	1.50	Rochester	9.28	1.00
Arcadia	7.09	1.50	Tiosa	9.41	1.00
Atlanta	7.14	1.50	Walnut	9.44	1.00
Tipton	7.26	1.25	Argos	9.55	1.00
Jacksons	7.32	1.25	Plymouth	10.12	1.00
Sharpsville	7.38	1.25	Tyner	10.27	.75
Fairfield	7.42	1.25	Walkerton	10.39	.75
Kokomo	7.54	1.00	Stillwell	10.58	.50
Cassville	8.05	1.00	LaPorte	11.15	.40
Bennetts	8.07	1.00	Belfast	11.23	.30
Miami	8.13	1.00	Ar. Michigan City	11.45	

Returning, Train Leaves Michigan City, 6:00 P. M.

Here is a chance to spend an enjoyable day on the shores of
LAKE MICHIGAN.

The Attractions at this Point are Numerous and Entertaining.
BOATING, BATHING, BASE BALL, FISHING!
Strolling in the Beautiful Shady Park on the Lake Shore.

MAKE A VISIT TO THE
PENITENTIARY
and see hundreds of convicts at their daily toil.

Don't Fail to Scale the Famous Hoosier Sand Slide!!

After dinner take a ride on Lake Michigan, one of the largest lakes in the world, on the elegant new
Steamer, "America"
Capacity 1000 passengers.

TAKE YOUR WHEEL!
AND A BASKET OF LUNCH.

Have a Picnic and a General GOOD TIME.

There will be Ample Room

LET EVERYBODY GO!!

FOR FURTHER PARTICULARS, SEE TICKET AGENTS L. E. & W. R. R.
GEO. L. BRADBURY,   **C. F. DALY,**
Vice-President and General Manager,   General Passenger Agent
INDIANAPOLIS.

Wm. B. Burford, Printer, Indianapolis.   20m.

Lake Erie managed to maintain a 5 per cent dividend rate at a time when most of its contemporaries were unable to meet fixed charges.

Including trackage rights, the LE&W main line was 416 miles long and prior to 1892 it was split into five rather uneven operating divisions. Thereafter it was divided into two divisions, each comprising two operating districts. The Sandusky Division embraced the First and Second districts extending from Sandusky to Lima, 89 miles, and Lima to Tipton, 120 miles, respectively. The Peoria Division's Third and Fourth districts extended from Tipton to Rankin, Ill., 105 miles, and from Rankin to Peoria, 102 miles. Coincident with this change Muncie, Bloomington, and Lafayette ceased to be division points. Completely new facilities were built at the new division points and at Sandusky in 1892. At Rankin, a granger hamlet, the road erected a 11-stall roundhouse, turntable, coal chute, and a small shop. A 12-stall roundhouse, turntable, and an icing station were also installed at Tipton while Sandusky got a seven-stall roundhouse and a new turntable. At Peoria the LE&W always used the facilities of the Peoria & Pekin Union.

Calvin S. Brice, the colorful manipulator and self-made man of affluence, was elected by the people of Ohio to the United States Senate in 1890. During his six years in Washington Brice not only remained president of the Lake Erie & Western but embarked upon an ambitious plan to give that road a seaboard outlet.

In his second attempt to revive the old Clinton low-grade line across central Pennsylvania, Brice

Indianapolis & Michigan City Division of LE&W did a heavy excursion business. This 1898 flyer detailing the attractions of Michigan City was nailed to every depot door along the line. Bicycles were handled in the baggage car. — *Collection of H. J. Ulery.*

joined forces with Adrian Iselin, a New York banker with substantial interests in the LE&W and the Buffalo, Rochester & Pittsburgh. The 452-mile Brice-Iselin route extended from the LE&W at Bluffton, O., to a connection with the Philadelphia & Reading system at Williamsport, Pa. The proposed combination was parallel to and south of the 1881 Nickel Plate and Gould routes that would have used the Allegheny Valley and Philadelphia & Erie to reach the western railheads of the Central of New Jersey. Aside from giving the LE&W its long-sought access to tidewater, the route was to provide a western outlet for the coal and coke production of Pennsylvania's Clearfield District, "conservatively" estimated by the promoters as amounting to 9.5 million tons annually.

In addition to using part of the BR&P, the new low grade was built around a pair of existing railroads — the Beech Creek in Pennsylvania and the Pittsburgh, Akron & Western in Ohio. The latter was in operation between Akron and Delphos, 162 miles, and crossed the LE&W at Bluffton. The Beech Creek formed a westerly extension of the Reading and tapped the Clearfield District. The BR&P was to secure rights over the Beech Creek and build a 24-mile branch between Clearfield and a point on its own line near Dubois. Also, the BR&P was to extend its line 100 miles west from Punxsutawney to New Castle, Pa. For its part, the LE&W acquired the PA&W and backed the construction of the Cleveland & New Castle Railway, formed to bridge the 70-mile gap between New Castle and Akron.

The Unfortunate Northern Ohio

With the possible exception of the American Midland (the so-called Tangent Line between Findlay and Fort Wayne), the Pittsburgh, Akron & Western was probably the most superfluous addition to Ohio's steam railroad network during the latter part of the 19th century. In its meandering course across northern Ohio (149 curves in 162 miles), the road touched no community of any consequence not already served by a railroad. The history of this unfortunate enterprise dates back to 1881 when the notion that the nation needed a network of narrow-gauge trunk lines was still in vogue. Organized as the Cleveland, Delphos & St. Louis Railroad on March 7, 1881, the road was originally intended to link together the Pittsburgh & Western and Toledo, Delphos & Burlington narrow-gauge roads.

The organizers of the CD&StL included William Semple and James Callery of the Pittsburgh & Western and a pair of seasoned narrow-gauge promoters at Delphos. Joseph Boehmer, a bank cashier, and Carey Evans, a surgeon, had been instrumental in the creation of the Toledo, Delphos & Burlington

system. By 1881 they were no longer associated with the TD&B but emerged from "retirement" when that road announced its intention to build a 160-mile division from a point near Delphos to Cleveland.

In August 1881 the CD&StL received 20 carloads of 35-pound iron rails from the Rough and Ready Iron Works and began laying track westward from Columbus Grove, a station on the Dayton & Michigan (CH&D), 17 miles northeast of Delphos. The following November 26, the arrival of the construction train at Delphos was heralded by the shrill whistle of the One-Spot, a trim little Pittsburgh-built 4-4-0. The track of the new narrow gauge reached the city limits at the TD&B's shops and from that point the CD&StL was granted the right to lay its track on Washington Street to the Pittsburgh, Fort Wayne & Chicago depot, 1 mile to the south. Nevertheless, this franchise was complicated by the fact that the narrow-gauge main of the TD&B already occupied the street between those points.

The protests of the TD&B notwithstanding, the CD&StL began laying its track alongside that of the older road in January 1882. In an attempt to block the further infringement on what it considered to be its sole rights, the TD&B laid a sidetrack across the path of the newcomer's laborers, two blocks north of the Fort Wayne depot. Gondola cars filled with burly shop hands were spotted on the track and a classic donnybrook was just about to get under way when the town's harassed mayor finally ironed out the dispute.

The Cleveland, Delphos & St. Louis began running a daily mixed train between Delphos and Columbus Grove on January 25, 1882. Operations were progressively extended eastward to Pendleton (Pandora) on February 1, 1882, to Bluffton on May 22, 1882, and to Mount Blanchard on January 1, 1883. Finally, on October 1, 1883, the narrow gauge was opened to Carey, 56 miles east of Delphos but more than 100 miles short of Cleveland. For several years the road operated two mixed trains daily in each direction with a train laying over nightly at each end of the line.

Built across level country, the track of the Cleveland, Delphos & St. Louis was laid to contemporary narrow-gauge standards. In some places there was no subgrade at all and the oak ties were simply laid on the native sod. There were no fences or station buildings and the only structure on the property was a 36 x 108-foot frame building located adjacent to the TD&B shops on the north side of Delphos. This served as a combination shop and enginehouse. The CD&StL owned three locomotives including a pair of Pittsburgh 4-4-0's, two coaches, two baggage cars, and 32 freight cars.

On June 17, 1884, the CD&StL passed into the

LE&W 4160-series 4-4-0 trundles Northern Ohio's daily westbound mixed, No. 1, across Rocky River viaduct near Medina, O., in 1908. — *Collection of Willis A. McCaleb.*

hands of a receiver and on November 1, 1885, it was reorganized as the Eastern & Western Air Line Railway. The name was again changed on August 1, 1886, to the less pretentious title of Cleveland & Western Railroad. By this time operations had been reduced to a single mixed train daily. The road limped along on a very light granger business and an occasional excursion train.

By the middle of 1883 the theory that a narrow-gauge trunk system could compete with standard-gauge roads had been thoroughly discredited and the Pittsburgh & Western promoters turned to greener and more practical pastures. Once they had shaken off the narrow-gauge trance, Semple and Callery set about to complete their road as a standard-gauge bridge between Pittsburgh and the Baltimore & Ohio's Chicago Division. In this they were strongly influenced by Andrew Carnegie, the steel king, who was patently anxious to end the Pennsylvania Railroad's westbound monopoly at Pittsburgh. In 1883 the P&W organized the Ohio Railway as a westward extension of its line to be built on the abandoned Clinton grade as far west as Tiffin where it would intersect with the B&O.

The Ohio Railway did not get beyond the paper stage before the P&W went into receivership, but it was reorganized on July 1, 1887, as the Pittsburgh, Akron & Western Railway, following the parent road's recovery. The route was altered somewhat so as to touch the B&O at Chicago Junction (Willard), the eastern terminus of the Chicago Division. Provision was also made for building an appendage to Carey to connect with the Cleveland & Western. The recent conversion of the Toledo, St. Louis &

Kansas City to standard gauge had suddenly enhanced the value of the C&W.

The building of the PA&W was seriously delayed by the deaths of James Callery and William Semple, but in 1889 their sons determined to progress the project to its completion. In January 1890 orders were placed with the Edgar Thomson works at Braddock, Pa., for 60-pound steel rail and with the Pittsburgh Locomotive Works for two standard-gauge 4-4-0 locomotives. Initially, the C&W was to be converted to standard gauge and already the work of installing 130,000 new ties on that road had been started. On March 11 the C&W and PA&W were consolidated to form the Pittsburgh, Akron & Western Rail*road*.

The first new rails were laid at Delphos shop on April 15, 1890, and eight days later the road received engine No. 21, first of the new 35-ton 4-4-0's. With this engine shoving a string of flat cars, the work of laying the new rails was pressed eastward from Delphos at the rate of about 2 miles a day. On May 6 the tracklayers were in Columbus Grove. They reached Bluffton 15 days later, and on July 1 the last rails were spiked down at Carey.* The new rails were laid outside the old narrow-gauge iron and the narrow-gauge equipment continued to hold down the daily mixed run until August 4.

Working eastward from Carey, the 100-man steel gang passed through Sycamore in mid-July. The construction train appeared at Spencer on October

*Due to a taxpayer's suit, the gauge of the track on Washington Street in Delphos was not altered until March 21, 1891. In the interim PA&W trains ran into downtown Delphos over the Toledo, St. Louis & Kansas City, successor to the Toledo, Delphos & Burlington.

Northern Ohio 4216 was holding down helper and yard assignments at Bloomington around 1908. C-46 4-4-0 was built in 1890, retired in 1910.—*Collection of John H. Keller.*

11 and reached Medina on November 19, 1890. Three days later the tracklayers were at the west branch of the Rocky River, about 2 miles east of Medina. Here work was suspended temporarily pending the completion of a 23-span, 880-foot iron viaduct. After testing the bridge on December 16 the construction train continued working east toward Akron.

On January 1, 1891, the PA&W inaugurated service east of Carey by putting on a pair of mixed trains, one in each direction between Medina and Delphos, 140 miles. Engines 23 and 24, Pittsburgh 4-4-0's, powered the first eastbound and westbound trains. On February 16 operation of the trains was extended to Walnut Street at Akron. There remained one last major item of construction, the erection of a 22-span viaduct, 893 feet long and 105 feet high, spanning the Ohio Canal at Akron. This bridge was placed in service and the first trains ran into the Main Street station at Akron on May 28, 1891.

In February 1890, shortly after the PA&W had placed orders for new rails and locomotives, the Baltimore & Ohio chartered the Akron & Chicago Junction Railroad for the purpose of building its own 76-mile connection between the Pittsburgh & Western and Chicago Junction. This road was opened to traffic on August 1, 1891, by which time the B&O had laid out more than 2 million dollars to acquire a controlling block of P&W stock. These developments gave the B&O a main stem between Pittsburgh and Chicago and rudely left the Pitts-

burgh, Akron & Western stranded without prospects of traffic from any source.

The PA&W's first locomotives were Pittsburgh 4-4-0's, numbered 21-25, acquired in 1890. These were followed by six Brooks and Pittsburgh engines in 1891-1892. Details and origin of these locomotives are lacking, but they were apparently removed from the road shortly after it passed into receivership in 1893. After the road came under the influence of the LE&W, 10 Moguls were purchased from Brooks. Numbered 26-35, these were identical to the 2-6-0's on the Lake Erie.

The only engine facility on the PA&W was the old C&W shed at Delphos. Although a turntable was installed at Akron, there was no engine shed or other servicing facility at that point. Water was obtained from a city pipe and engines were coaled by hand. The Akron depot was an old residence on Main Street purchased for the sum of $450. A dwelling was also used to house the agent and accommodate the public at Delphos.

A single train operated in each direction daily was sufficient to handle the light traffic that passed over the PA&W. In desperation the promoters of the road proposed an extension to New Castle and it was this plan that caught the fancy of C. S. Brice. He reorganized the PA&W as the Northern Ohio Railway on August 14, 1895, and the new company issued 2.5 million dollars' worth of bonds, the proceeds of which were used to retire the old company's securities. On October 1, 1895, the Northern Ohio

Mogul 5365 derailed running in reverse on Minster branch.—*Collection of John H. Keller.*

was leased for 999 years to the Lake Erie & Western, that road having already endorsed as guarantor the Northern Ohio bonds.

THE NEW YORK CENTRAL ERA

The untimely death of Calvin Brice on December 15, 1898, brought a sudden end to his plans for expanding the scope of the Lake Erie & Western's operations. At the time, Brice was in the midst of a concerted attempt to wrest the P&W from the B&O. He had lately acquired control of the Cleveland, Akron & Columbus Railway and was talking about taking over the Cincinnati Northern. After Brice's passing, the Vanderbilts lost little time in neutralizing his railroad. In 1899 the Lake Shore & Michigan Southern purchased a bare majority of the LE&W's stock and on February 20, 1900, took over the active supervision of its operations.

There was a marked decrease in the Lake Erie's earnings after it passed under LS&MS control and this decline, in general, persisted throughout the 22 years the relationship existed. The LE&W and the Vanderbilt-controlled Big Four were competitors, but there were several other contributory factors including the tailing off of gas and oil production in the Lima-Indiana field. Brice's last bid to reach the sea also proved to be a debilitating drain on the Lake Erie's resources. Advances to the defunct Cleveland & New Castle and the sale of Cleveland, Akron & Columbus stock to the Pennsylvania resulted in a loss of more than $700,000. In addition,

the consistently unprofitable Northern Ohio cost the LE&W 3.5 million dollars over a period of 25 years.

The LS&MS answered criticism of the Lake Erie's operating results after 1900 by claiming that the road's vaunted level of efficiency had been attained only by deferring maintenance for years. To be sure, there was some merit to this charge and for several years after taking over the road the Lake Shore spent a great deal of money upgrading the track and other physical structures. Nonetheless, most of the LE&W's obsolete locomotives and cars were replaced with some equally obsolete Lake Shore hand-me-downs. Between 1900 and 1903 54 old 4-4-0's were retired and were replaced, in part, by LS&MS eight-wheelers built between 1877 and 1881 to the same pattern.

In 1902 the LS&MS thoroughly overhauled the LE&W's passenger train operation. Cafe-parlor cars were added to the consists of trains 1 and 2, the daily Sandusky-Peoria express runs. Even though 3 hours were trimmed off No. 1's time, its departure from Sandusky was timed hours between LS&MS arrivals from the East. Westbound No. 5 did make an excellent connection with LS&MS No. 3, the *Fast Mail Limited*, but this train operated only as far west as Lafayette. Eastbound No. 2 was scheduled to meet Lake Shore No. 16, the crack *New England Express*, at Sandusky. However, No. 2's schedule called for a 7 a.m. Peoria departure, 30 minutes ahead of Big Four No. 16 which also ran in connection with LS&MS 16.

One of the more convenient features of the new mainline passenger schedules were the four-way meets at Tipton. Three times a day, at 8:40 a.m., 1:50 p.m., and 8:50 p.m., east and westbound mainline trains met north and southbound Indianapolis & Michigan City Division trains. At Muncie, Fort Wayne Division trains were scheduled to connect with Big Four rather than LE&W mainline trains. In fact, the entire Fort Wayne Division operation was coordinated with the Big Four. Two new daily trains with vestibuled parlor cars were oper-

ated through between Fort Wayne and Indianapolis via Muncie and the Big Four. The new trains made their 119-mile runs in 4 hours.

The new timetable also showed a restoration of through service between Fort Wayne and Cincinnati via the White Water Valley line with a pair of trains operated each way. No. 19, the *Cincinnati Fast Mail*, left Fort Wayne at 11:35 a.m., 10 minutes after the arrival of a LS&MS train from Jackson, and made the 166-mile run in 6 hours 10 minutes. Like its northbound counterpart, No. 19 was assigned a buf-

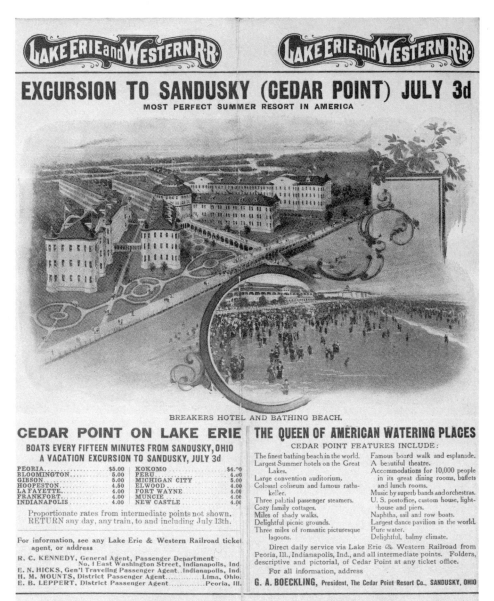

Advertisement for Cedar Point excursion on 1909 timetable listing the many attractions of Ohio's summer resort appealed co rural Midwesterners.

LE&W excursion trains ran over Big Four tracks to reach the Sandusky waterfront where passengers boarded sidewheel steamers embarking for Cedar Point, Lakeside, and the Lake Erie islands. Horse-drawn hack, parasols, the *Arrow*, steamcars, and Lake Shore Electric recall a bygone era. — *Collection of Willis A. McCaleb.*

fet-parlor car serving à la carte meals to passengers.

To power its improved passenger trains, the LE&W acquired 10 "new" locomotives in 1902. Of these, six were 53-ton Baldwin 4-4-0's outshopped in July 1902 for another Lake Shore vassal, the Lake Erie, Alliance & Wheeling. At first these locomotives bore LE&W numbers 75-80, but in 1905 they were renumbered 4244-4249 and assigned class C-49. Also purchased in 1902 were 12 ex-LS&MS 4-6-0's, the first engines of this type on the LE&W roster. Four had 63-inch drivers and were assigned to passenger

duty. Built by Brooks in 1892-1893, the Ten-Wheelers carried Nos. 5200-5203 and class F-47 after 1905.

IMPACT OF THE INTERURBANS

On June 26, 1899, the Elwood & Alexandria Railway opened a 9-mile traction line alongside the main stem of the LE&W in Indiana. Interurban roads paralleled fully 150 miles of LE&W lines by 1903 and half the 884-mile system by 1913. Nowhere did the interurban flourish as it did in Ohio and Indiana and probably no steam railroad anywhere was as

Sunrise at South Lima yard around 1903-1904 finds a 12-car special ready to leave for Sandusky, apparently on the occasion of a lodge outing. Immaculate E-1 4-6-0 192 is decked out with flags and bunting. Boiler explosion in August 1916 demolished this locomotive while it was pulling a South Bend-Indianapolis passenger train on the Kankakee Belt. — *Collection of John H. Keller.*

Outbound No. 3 rolls through Bay Junction on Sandusky outskirts about 1915. C-75 4158 had conventional wagon-top boiler, slide valves. Schenectady 4-4-0 was rebuilt at Collinwood in 1918 and junked five years later. — *Collection of Richard J. Cook.*

hard hit, comparatively, as the Lake Erie. Its losses of local passenger and express business were enormous. As was the case with most steam roads, the LE&W's efforts to combat the popular interurbans were feeble and ineffective. In 1904, shortly after the Indianapolis & Northwestern opened its line between Indianapolis, Frankfort and Lafayette, the Lake Erie proposed to electrify its lines between those points and motorize some of its passenger cars. This idea apparently never got past the Lake Shore & Michigan Southern front office.

In one last futile bid to best the electrics, the LE&W again upgraded its passenger train operation in 1906. Running times of trains 1 and 2 were trimmed to 13 hours 45 minutes on the Sandusky-Peoria run. Lateral division schedules were also improved. Pullman and the Lake Shore's Collinwood shops turned out a fleet of new cars, including 84-passenger vestibuled coaches with six-wheel trucks. The road also bought 20 rebuilt 4-4-0's with 69-inch drivers and Belpaire fireboxes from the Big Four. They were built by Schenectady between 1892 and 1895 and numbered 4150-4169.

Despite new equipment and improved schedules, the LE&W was caught in the grip of a competitive vise. Restrained from going after the long-haul passenger, the road was no match for the interurban when it came to the local trade. Operated almost solely for the benefit of the passenger, the traction cars offered low fares, fast and frequent service, and very often better access to the commercial district of a community. The first to forsake the steamcars were the drummers who peddled their wares across Indiana and were forever deriding the road they called the "Leave Early and Walk."

The plight of the passenger department became progressively worse as the interurbans extended the scope of their operations. The joint operation between Fort Wayne, Muncie, and Indianapolis was dropped not long after the completion in 1908 of the last link in the interurban chain between those cities. Through service between Peoria and Sandusky and much of the LE&W's excursion business was finished off by the 1911 advent of fast, limited-stop interurban trains between Lima, Sandusky, and Cleveland. Train No. 1 was cut back to Bloomington and No. 2 ran only as far east as Lima. The Fort Wayne Division passenger schedule was reduced to a single round trip between Fort Wayne and Connersville after interurbans began running beyond Muncie to New Castle in 1913.

Passenger revenues held up best on the Indianapolis & Michigan City Division despite heavy interurban operation between Indianapolis and Peru. About 1915 through trains were put on between Indianapolis and South Bend. These operated over the I&MC Division as far as Walkerton and then used 19.6 miles of the Chicago, Indiana & Southern (Kankakee Belt) to reach South Bend. Train 24 left Indianapolis in the late afternoon, laid over at South Bend at night, and returned the next morning as No. 23. Pullman cafe-parlor cars formerly used

Drummers and farmers mingle at an interurban way station in rural Indiana. Most traction lines in Ohio and Indiana were built parallel to steam roads, engendering an early passenger service withdrawal on many branch lines. — *Walter Neuman.*

on the Fort Wayne-Cincinnati trains were assigned to the South Bend run along with the four F-47 4-6-0's (5200-5203). In addition, the road ran two daily trains to Michigan City. On occasion, the prison car — a coach with barred windows — was added to the rear of one of these trains to transport felons to the penitentiary at Michigan City. The I&MC did a fair summertime excursion business, too, with as many as three or four specials operated out of Indianapolis on almost any summer Saturday. Some ran through to Michigan City. Others, with pleasure seekers on their way to Lake Manitou, turned at Rochester.

The volume of freight traffic on the LE&W held up well during the early 1900's and the road handled a lot of high-grade tonnage moving east from connections at Bloomington and Peoria. The daily handle of livestock and dressed meat moving out of Indianapolis often exceeded 30 loads. At Muncie, manifest consists were filled out with carloads of Mason jars and other glass goods. The road also did a heavy interchange business with the CH&D at Lima. No. 66, the manifest freight out of Peoria, was always built around eastbound shipments from that city's distilleries and was popularly dubbed the Whiskey Special. The westbound manifest, No. 65, carried the symbol SP-1 as early as 1908.

Although some of the Moguls were still hauling freight as late as 1922, the manifest trains were powered by 2-8-0's after 1903. The first Consolidations were 78-ton slide-valve Brooks models of 1899, purchased from the parent road in 1903. Classed G-41, they were numbered 5500-5514 after 1905. Disliked by their crews, G-41's were called "long barrels" in reference to the fact that the boiler back head was located practically at the rear of the cab. It was necessary for the engineman to stand up when backing one of these engines due to the position of the reverse lever along the side of the firebox.

In June 1904 Brooks delivered 10 new 2-8-0's to the LE&W and 15 engines of the same design to the Lake Erie, Alliance & Wheeling. The LE&W engines (400-409) were renumbered 5515-5524 and assigned class G-44 in 1905. The next year the 15 LEA&W engines were sold to the LE&W where they were numbered 5525-5539. Big power in their day, the G-44's weighed more than 101 tons, had 21 x 30-inch piston valve cylinders, 57-inch drivers, and developed a whopping 39,460 pounds of tractive effort, more than twice that of the Moguls. During 1912-1913 the G-44's were equipped with 30-element

Schmidt superheaters, the work being done at South Lima shops, Collinwood and Elkhart shops of the LS&MS, and the Big Four's Beech Grove shops at Indianapolis. All around good performers, they were easy on water and coal and could whale it across the main stem with 30- to 35-car manifests at speeds up to 50 mph.

The LE&W bought five heavy 2-8-0's from Schenectady in 1912 and numbered them 5395-5399. These superheated G-16w's had 25 x 32-inch piston valve cylinders, 63-inch drivers, an engine weight of 123 tons, and developed a tractive effort rating of 48,600 pounds. They were the last word in Consolidations. In 1915 they were joined by 10 G-16v's of almost identical dimensions built by Brooks for the LS&MS in 1911. Originally numbered 5300-5309, they were the 5385-5394 on the LE&W. Ten more ex-Lake Shore 2-8-0's came to the road in 1917. Also Brooks-built in 1911, these G-6v's were somewhat smaller and lighter and had 23-inch cylinders. The G-6 and G-16 engines were called "two-door sedans," the result of having a pair of fire doors through which their firemen worked feverishly to keep 56.47 square feet of grate area covered with coal.

The biggest and most powerful Lake Erie & Western freight power were the 15 USRA light Mikados assigned to the road in 1918. These Baldwin-built

Crews of G-41 5505 and four-wheel bobtail pose at Rankin, Ill., in 1909. Brooks 2-8-0 was rebuilt at Beech Grove in 1919, went to the torch in 1933 as Nickel Plate 403. — *Collection of Willis A. McCaleb.*

Three-car No. 4 takes on express while 4-4-0 4167 cools her 69-inch drivers. For more than 50 years an eastbound passenger train called at St. Marys station at midday. C-76 was built by Schenectady in 1892, was scrapped in 1922. — *Clyde E. Helms.*

The setting: Belt Junction at Indianapolis in December 1897. Left to right: William Ashinger, brakeman; Harry Bolser, conductor; Harry Young, fireman; John Beplay, engineman. Four-wheel-pony 61 was built in 1870. — *Collection of Paul Siess.*

H-6a's were numbered 5540-5554. After 1924 they carried Nickel Plate numbers 586-600.

The depressed state of the LE&W's passenger business justified only minimal investment in new equipment after 1906. The ex-Big Four 4100's held down most passenger runs as late as 1922. New York Central's disdain for saturated steam put 11 of these veteran engines through the back shops between 1918 and 1920 where they were rebuilt with piston valve cylinders and superheaters. A pair of famous LS&MS 81-inch-drivered Ten-Wheelers ran out their last miles on the LE&W. The 5002 and 5010 were the heaviest express passenger locomotives in the world when Brooks turned them out in 1899 as LS&MS 602 and 610. Transferred to the Lake Erie in 1914, they served on mainline passenger runs until retirement in 1918 and 1919. For a brief period during the early 1920's the main stem was graced by 10 NYC 4-4-2's, members of the famous Gibson Girl

clan. Schenectady-built between 1901 and 1904, these saturated I-class speedsters had 79-inch drivers and weighed 88 to 98 tons. LE&W records indicate that the road rented the 896, 911, 915, 935, 936, 967, 980, 985, 988, and 992 for about a year.

As a chattel of the New York Central, the LE&W managed to earn enough to pay dividends at a reduced rate on its preferred stock until 1907. Although the LE&W enjoyed several good years thereafter, the general decline of this railroad continued to the end of NYC control in 1922. Government ownership seems only to have intensified its misfortunes. In 1920 the moribund Northern Ohio was unloaded on the Akron, Canton & Youngstown, a 7.7-mile switching road at Akron. Nevertheless, operations during 1921 resulted in a $588,000 deficit. Revivified by the Van Sweringens, the LE&W became a vital part of the expanded Nickel Plate. Few railroad marriages have been so successful.

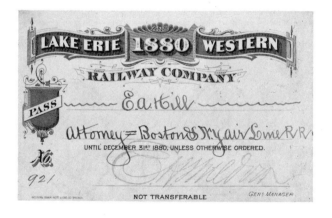

The Little Giant

THE Nickel Plate consolidation of 1923 brought to a close the colorful and impoverished history of the 450-mile Toledo, St. Louis & Western Railroad, better known as the Clover Leaf Route. Noted for its fast manifest freight trains, the Clover Leaf was endowed with a fair amount of bridge traffic moving eastward from St. Louis and Kansas City. Nevertheless, the road was in financial hot water during most of the 34 years it operated standard-gauge trains between East St. Louis, Ill., and Toledo, O. The Clover Leaf's perennial insolvency was largely attributable to the fact that it represented the principal remnant of that splendid narrow-gauge house of cards, the Toledo, Cincinnati & St. Louis. The TC&StL's imaginative promoters billed it as the "Little Giant Line — the Narrow Gauge System, which aims to gather and consolidate all the roads built upon the 3-foot gauge into one great and connecting chain which shall reach from the Atlan-

Joseph W. Hunt (1834-1879) was a druggist, narrow-gauge promoter. — *Collection of Walter T. Remlinger.*

tic to the Pacific." During its brief hour of glory, the Little Giant actually embraced more than 780 miles of narrow-gauge lines.

The era of narrow-gauge construction began in 1871 when the Denver & Rio Grande in Colorado and the Painesville & Youngstown in Ohio opened portions of road built to a gauge of 3 feet. Despite the economic doldrums of the 1870's, there were more than 8000 miles of narrow-gauge railways in operation in the United States by the end of 1881. Nearly one-third were in the states of Colorado, Ohio, and Texas. The typical narrow gauge was a flimsy affair with only the most superficial grading and unballasted track laid with 20- to 40-pound iron rails. Even the shallowest gullies were crossed on pile trestles — fills and iron bridges were luxuries few narrow-gauge roads enjoyed. Fences and cattle guards were equally rare. In general narrow-gauge practice, speeds of 15 to 20 mph were absolutely unsafe and derailments were part of the daily routine. Locomotives in use on these roads were both too heavy for the track and too light to overcome friction on the tortuous curves and grades. While some savings may have been realized in building a road to 3-foot gauge, the standards of construction precluded any possibility of economy in operation.

It is not difficult to find some logic in the building of narrow-gauge lines into the more remote regions of the West. These were seldom intended as permanent institutions and the amount of potential traffic hardly justified the expense of standard-gauge con-

struction. Narrow-gauge roads serving the mining camps of Colorado and Nevada enjoyed at least a degree of prosperity by charging exorbitant rates in the total absence of competition. The construction of more than 1200 miles of 3-foot gauge lines across the easy terrain of Ohio between 1871 and 1885 is another matter. At the end of 1881 there were 6664 miles of railroad lines in that state, about 1 mile to every 500 residents and 6 square miles of land area. Built for the most part to feed coal and wheat to navigable streams and Lake Erie ports, Ohio's early narrow-gauge roads failed to enjoy conspicuous success. Nonetheless, by 1880 there was growing support for the absurd notion that a narrow-gauge trunk system could successfully compete with established standard-gauge railways. The Toledo, Cincinnati & St. Louis was the manifestation of this concept, and its complete collapse in 1883 sounded the death knell of the narrow-gauge era.

DELPHOS

To the student of the narrow-gauge railway there are certain names irrevocably associated with it. Ophir, Alpine Tunnel, Orbisonia, Otto Mears—these and many more he knows and regards with veneration. In all likelihood he has never heard of Delphos, O., nor of Joseph W. Hunt, proprietor of "The Old Reliable Drug Store." Even in Delphos itself there is precious little to commemorate the narrow-gauge era or Joe Hunt. Both passed into oblivion many decades ago. All the same, when the narrow-gauge fever was everywhere in the land, the pharmacist of Delphos was concocting the prescription which would end the epidemic once and for all.

It would be difficult to conceive a more unlikely setting for narrow-gauge history than solid, Germanic Delphos. Located in the flat farmland of northwestern Ohio, it is one of those conservative and perpetually prosperous Buckeye towns that seem to pass unchanged from one generation to the next. In 1872 Delphos was a thriving community of 2000, comfortably situated on the Pittsburgh, Fort Wayne & Chicago Railway (Pennsylvania) and the Miami & Erie Canal, then in operation between Toledo and Cincinnati. To the north and southwest there lay almost a thousand square miles of virgin timber in the upper Maumee River basin, then known as the Black Swamp. One of the last great stands of the Central Hardwood Forest, the swamp was full of oak, hickory, black walnut, and chestnut — highly prized in the manufacture of furniture, wagon wheels, barrel hoops and staves, and tool handles. Delphos not only exported much milled lumber but became an important woodworking center in its own right.

Joseph Hunt, proprietor of the "Old Reliable,"

agent for the Adams Express Company, and manufacturer of a popular tonic called Slippery Elm, owned a modest interest in one of the four large woodworking factories in Delphos. Hunt and Dr. Carey A. Evans, the town's erstwhile mayor and sometime surgeon, realized the new factories would soon require a means of tapping the vast reserves of the forest wilderness. Allied with Joseph Boehmer, cashier of the First National Bank, and George Lang, editor of the *Weekly Herald*, they organized the Toledo, Delphos & Indianapolis Railway on March 14, 1872. A line of road was projected north from the Fort Wayne depot at Delphos to Holgate, a station on the Baltimore, Pittsburgh & Chicago Railroad (B&O). The 32-mile route also crossed the abandoned grade owned by the Continental Railway and was intended to give the factories of Delphos two new east-west rail outlets as well as access to the heart of the forest.

Following the panic of 1873, the TD&I's promoters were forced to defer the project for lack of capital. For several years there was sufficient timber in close proximity to the canal to satisfy local needs. By 1876, however, this source of hardwood was virtually exhausted and the railway project was revived. Despite the hard times, local people subscribed to $40,000 of the company's capital stock

in amounts ranging from $25 to $2500. A contract was let for 15 miles of grade extending from Delphos to Dupont, a hamlet on the Auglaize River, and on April 21, 1877, ground was broken at Delphos. About the same time, enough 30-pound iron rails to lay 5 miles of track were purchased from a Newport (Ky.) rolling mill. These were transported to Delphos on canal boats. The company bought a 12-ton locomotive named *Dupont* from Porter, Bell & Company of Pittsburgh and acquired eight double-truck flat cars elsewhere.

On June 20, 1877, laborers completed 5 miles of unballasted 3-foot gauge track connecting Delphos with the village of Fort Jennings. The latter was the site of one of William Henry Harrison's outer line of forts on the Auglaize River which, during the dark days of 1812-1813, was the practical western frontier of the United States and the only barrier preventing the British and their Indian allies from overrunning Ohio. The ingenious TD&I promoters decided to open their road on July 4 and succeeded in having Delphos' annual celebration held at Fort Jennings in commemoration of the town's historic past. The event was well advertised and attracted pioneer settlers from all over western Ohio. Nearly 6000 people wanted to go to Fort Jennings that day and the little woodburning *Dupont* had to make nine

Delphos' Main Street in 1879, looking south. Mushroomed by lumber boom, town then boasted 35 sawmills, 7 woodworking mills, 6 hotels, 36 saloons. Old Reliable drug store and express agency were on right side of street. — *Collection of Walter T. Remlinger.*

trips with the flat cars to get them there. Although thunderstorms thwarted a battery of orators, professors Pangle and Cordell managed several balloon ascensions, and the fireworks display rivaled that of the centennial celebration. A heroic parade was led by the Germania Band after which the crowd quickly disposed of a monumental supply of beer. Undaunted, the amiable folk of Fort Jennings then treated their visitors to a formidable cache of the town's principal export, corn whiskey. All in all, it was a memorable Fourth.

The TD&I opened the remaining 10 miles of track to Dupont on October 6, 1877. The event called for another pioneer excursion, and despite the lateness of the season the road was again blessed with a deluge of patrons. The next day, the TD&I inaugurated regular operation in the form of two daily mixed trains each way. At the time, Dupont was little more than a postal station and riverside picnic grove. Elias Dimmock, the postmaster and the TD&I's chief engineer, platted a townsite and before long the place boasted two hotels, two sawmills, a pair of stave mills, an axe-handle factory, and a population of 700. Business was so brisk on the narrow gauge that before the end of 1877 contracts were let to complete the remaining 16½ miles of line to Holgate. This was financed by placing a $30,000 mortgage on the completed section.

JOE HUNT'S RAILROAD

In addition to extending the road to Holgate, the TD&I decided to build a line into the big woods southwest of Delphos. Joseph Hunt, the road's president, took the contract to construct 26 miles of track from Delphos to Shane's Crossing (now Rockford). Hunt completed 9 miles of track between Delphos and Spencerville on June 25, 1878, and opened this section with four excursion runs on July 4 using the familiar flat cars and a second Porter woodburner, the *J. W. Hunt*. During the week the little engine was employed on the construction train, but each week end Hunt reaped an abundant harvest of excursion fares. The high-water mark of such outings was the Saturday night moonlight excursion, a sort of iron horse hayride. On September 15 the track reached Mendon, 9 miles beyond Spencerville, and on December 14, 1878, the *Hunt* steamed into Shane's Crossing, an isolated hamlet on the St. Marys River. A small enginehouse was built at this point, and on January 1, 1879, the TD&I put on a daily mixed train to Delphos.

North of Dupont, the extension to Holgate was completed in mid-November 1878. A new 4-4-0 passenger engine, the *Delphos*, was purchased from the Pittsburgh Locomotive Works and made the first run to Holgate on November 28. With the opening of the line to Shane's Crossing, the TD&I had a total of 58 miles of road in operation and owned three locomotives, three coaches, and a large number of flat cars. The *Delphos* worked a mixed run from Delphos to Holgate and back, covering the 32 miles between terminals in 3½ hours. The *Hunt* was assigned to the mixed train out of Shane's Crossing while the *Dupont* was employed on a pair of short

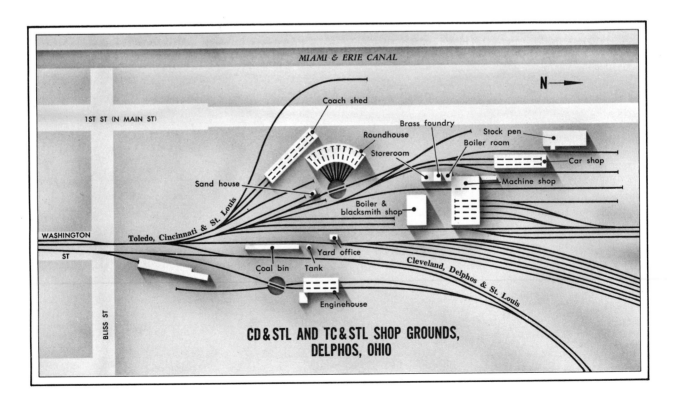

CD&STL AND TC&STL SHOP GROUNDS,
DELPHOS, OHIO

turns north of Delphos. In the morning it went as far as Dupont and back and in the afternoon ran beyond Dupont to Continental Switch.

THE MISSISSIPPI RIVER EXTENSION

While Joe Hunt was busy extending the TD&I, Carey Evans and Joseph Boehmer were promoting a branch to connect Delphos with the Mississippi River at Burlington, Ia. They called their line the Toledo, Delphos & Burlington and planned to build about 175 miles of 3-foot gauge track from Delphos to a connection with the Havana, Rantoul & Eastern Railway near the Indiana-Illinois border. The HR&E had been organized to build about 130 miles of narrow-gauge road from Havana, Ill., to the Indiana line.* The Mississippi at Burlington was about 65 miles northwest of Havana. The TD&B was projected through Willshire, O., and the Indiana towns of Decatur, Bluffton, Marion, Kokomo, and Frankfort. These latter two cities were then connected by the standard-gauge Frankfort & Kokomo which was to be acquired and converted to 3-foot gauge. At other points along the route, the promoters worked hard to generate local interest. They were well received at Bluffton and Willshire.

To connect Delphos with the F&K at Kokomo, Evans and Boehmer organized two companies, the Delphos, Bluffton & Frankfort Railroad and the Delphos & Kokomo Railway. The latter was chartered in Ohio on July 18, 1877, and subsequently Elias Dimmock located a route 25.7 miles long connecting Delphos with Willshire, an old settlement on the St. Marys near the Indiana border. The entire line traversed a dense stand of prime timber and touched but one community along the way. This was Venedocia, then a remote logging camp 8 miles west of Delphos. The D&K was built almost entirely with Willshire money, the 500 citizens of that town subscribing to $68,000 of the road's stock. Contractor Gen. Hugh McKee began grading work on July 17, 1878, and by late summer had 30-pound iron rails laid as far as Venedocia. The D&K's solitary locomotive, a Baldwin 0-4-0 named *Hugh McKee*, opened this section with an excursion train on November 9, 1878. More than 200 riders were packed on the road's three flat cars, and an even greater number had to be turned away for lack of space. Much of the available room was taken up by the Germania Band which by now was a regular fixture on excursions out of Delphos.

During November McKee received 800 tons of rails and pushed the track toward Willshire, day and

*The HR&E opened 40 miles of road between Alvan and Fisher, Ill., in 1876; was extended to West Lebanon, Ind., in 1878 and Leroy, Ill., in 1879. A portion of this 75-mile road between Leroy and Potomac, Ill., is now a standard-gauge branch of the Illinois Central.

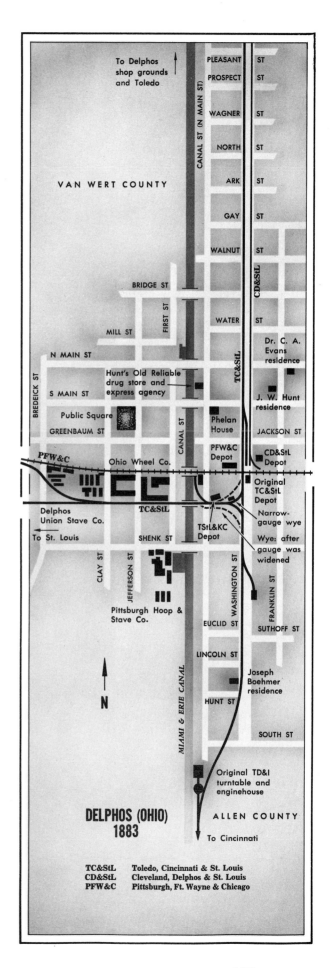

Coe Adams, first locomotive on standard-gauge Frankfort & Kokomo, was built by Danforth & Cooke in March 1874. — *Collection of John A. Rehor.*

night. Although the D&K's subscriptions stipulated that the road was to be completed by the end of 1878, it was not until January 24, 1879, that the last rails were spiked down at Willshire. The inaugural run was made three days later. A small enginehouse was built at Willshire, a coach purchased, and a mixed train put on a daily-except-Sunday schedule. Though the schedule required an average speed of only 7 mph, the D&K's Baldwin seldom got over the road without jumping the track at least once. Still, little Willshire was highly pleased with its new railroad as evidenced by this dispatch from the town.

> Old Willshire has thrown off her lethargy, and is up and doing, striving for the main chance; everything is activity . . . and all this is due to the Delphos & Kokomo Railway which now affords us the boon so long denied us — communication with the civilized world.

To bridge the 82 miles between Willshire and Kokomo, Evans and Boehmer incorporated the Delphos, Bluffton & Frankfort Railroad in Indiana on October 17, 1877. The clerk of the Wells County common pleas court at Bluffton, William J. Craig, became interested in the road and induced the county commissioners to take $30,000 of the DB&F's capital stock. This was nearly all the money needed to build 13.8 miles of unballasted track between Bluffton and Warren. James Crosbie took the con-

tract to build the road and broke ground at Bluffton on July 8, 1878. DB&F's 30-pound rails were rolled at Indianapolis and its solitary locomotive was a handsome 14-ton Pittsburgh 4-4-0 named *Bluffton.* The road was opened on October 11, 1878, by an excursion to Warren where a capacity load of patrons were treated to an ox roast, a band concert, and many stirring speeches. The train was made up of the *Bluffton* and every car the road owned — a coach, a box car, and six flat cars.

Standard-gauge Frankfort & Kokomo Railroad, organized on December 27, 1870, bridged the 25 miles separating the towns in its corporate name. Construction began in 1873, and when bad weather forced a suspension of work late in December of that year, most of the grade was completed and 56-pound iron rails had been laid 3 miles out of Frankfort. Track laying was resumed on March 20, 1874, and eight days later the first train ran into Michigantown, 7 miles northeast of Frankfort. On May 27 the track reached Kokomo and a regular mixed train was put on the road on August 10, 1874. Prior to that date, the contractors Adams and Wells had operated week-end excursion trains. There were 20 freight cars, a coach, and a pair of 4-4-0 locomotives on the road. The 1873 panic wiped out the promoters of the F&K, and the contractors retained possession of the road providing service as business

Pride of the Delphos roundhouse, Little Giant's One-Spot was built in 1879 by Porter & Bell for Frankfort & State Line. It usually pulled the pay car, but is assigned to work train in this scene at Bluffton. — *Collection of John A. Rehor.*

warranted. After July 1876 the F&K's daily train was operated in conjunction with trains of the La Fayette, Muncie & Bloomington between Frankfort and Bloomington, Ill. The F&K was never ballasted or fenced and was up for sale from the time it opened. As early as the summer of 1879 C. A. Evans had made arrangements to lay a third rail on the road to accommodate the narrow-gauge trains of his proposed Toledo, Delphos & Burlington.

The Frankfort & State Line Railroad was the last link in the chain connecting TD&I and the Havana, Rantoul & Eastern. Promoted by Doctor Evans, the F&SL was to extend about 50 miles from Frankfort to a junction with the HR&E at the Wabash River near Attica, Ind. During the summer and fall of 1879 the F&SL constructed about 11 miles of 3-foot gauge track from Frankfort to Clark's Hill. The road owned one 18-ton Porter 2-4-0 and a caboose.

THE TOLEDO, DELPHOS & BURLINGTON RAILROAD

On May 23, 1879, the Toledo, Delphos & Indianapolis; Delphos & Kokomo; Delphos, Bluffton & Frankfort; and the Toledo & Maumee Narrow Gauge Railroad were consolidated to form the Toledo, Delphos & Burlington Railroad. The new company had a total of 112 miles of narrow-gauge lines in Ohio and Indiana including two short segments

which had no physical connection with the rest of the system. These were the former DB&F, which had yet to complete the 24 miles of line between Bluffton and Willshire, and the 14.8-mile Toledo & Maumee. The latter road antedated the rest of the system and extended from Toledo to Waterville, 27 miles north of the TD&I at Holgate. Organized on May 16, 1873, by Toledo parties, the T&M was opened on August 12, 1874, between Toledo and South Toledo, 7½ miles. Even by narrow-gauge standards the T&M was a crude affair with its 25-pound rail, 24-degree curves, and no ballast. A regular mixed train was operated on weekdays but the road was heavily dependent on week-end excursion traffic. The T&M opened with a 9½-ton Porter woodburner, a coach, box car, and two flat cars which it classed as observation cars. A second Porter engine and two more flat cars were added to the roster in 1875. An extension of the T&M, the Toledo & Grand Rapids Railroad, was organized by Gen. D. W. H. Howard and others of the town of Grand Rapids on March 28, 1874. This company completed a 5.67-mile grade between Waterville and Maumee City in 1876 and leased it to the T&M. On July 1, 1877, the road was opened simultaneously with an extension of the T&M into Maumee City.

During the summer of 1879 traffic on the TD&B's Delphos lines increased to the point where it far

125

outstripped the road's capacity in terms of cars and locomotives. With every flat car needed in the lumber camps, the TD&B had to sharply curtail the operation of the profitable excursion trains. There were only four locomotives and three coaches available for operations out of Delphos, and construction work plus frequent accidents kept some of the equipment out of revenue service much of the time. Manufacturers were highly reluctant to extend credit to narrow-gauge roads and the TD&B was pouring its earnings into the 24-mile Willshire-Bluffton connection. The situation was eased slightly when Calvin S. Brice and James Irvine, Lima (O.) attorneys, bought into the road and engineered an arrangement with Clark, Post & Martin, New York equipment dealers, for the rental of cars and engines. A pair of Baldwin 4-4-0 passenger engines were purchased from the Springfield, Jackson & Pomeroy, a southern Ohio narrow gauge, and shipped to the TD&B in August 1879. At that time, the road's motive power was renumbered as follows: T&M 1-2 became TD&B 1-2; SJ&P 3 became TD&B 3; D&K 1 became TD&B 4; SJ&P 5 became TD&B 5; TD&I 1-3 became TD&B 6-8; DB&F 1 became TD&B 9.

The end of local management of the TD&B commenced with tragic suddenness on September 2, 1879. That day Joseph Hunt was killed as he stepped between two box cars "standing" on a PFW&C sidetrack at Delphos. By the end of the year, Carey Evans and Joseph Boehmer had sold out to New York and Boston speculators associated with Brice and Irvine. Evans' last official act was the supervision of the first run from Warren through to Delphos on December 16. One of the newly acquired Baldwins, No. 3, left Warren with four coaches at 7 a.m. and arrived at Delphos at 1:30 p.m., whereupon Evans led 120 thirsty passengers to Ben Hoerstman's Narrow Gauge Saloon to toast the event. Evans and Boehmer had realized a substantial profit on their investment, and along with all of Delphos they were certain the TD&B's new owners would extend the road to the Mississippi while keeping Delphos the focal point of its operations. In addition to mixed trains, regular mail and express trains were put on between Delphos and Warren on January 5, 1880. These were powered by the ex-SJ&P Baldwins which required 5 hours to make the 63½-mile run. A pair of "express" trains on the 57.6-mile Holgate-Shane's Crossing line ran on 6-hour schedules behind engines 8 and 9, the Pittsburgh 4-4-0's.

The TD&B's new owners included Gen. John M. Corse, postmaster of Boston; George W. Ballou, a New York banker; Charles R. Batt and George W. T. Riley of Boston; and Samuel Thomas of Columbus. At Brice's suggestion, the experienced

Isadore H. Burgoon was named general superintendent of the TD&B, a post he had previously held on the Lake Erie & Louisville. On January 17, 1880, a meeting was held at the Lima office of Brice and Irvine during which the owners voted to place a $1,250,000 mortgage on the Holgate-Warren line in order to finance the building of extensions to Waterville and Kokomo.

The 27-mile link between Holgate and Waterville was relatively well built with 40-pound iron rail, 6½-foot crossties, and sand ballast. At Grand Rapids the line crossed the Maumee River and the Miami & Erie Canal on an eight-span wooden bridge 1556 feet long including trestle approaches. The former Toledo & Maumee line between Toledo and Waterville was closed on July 20, 1880, so that it could be completely rebuilt. Between Toledo and Maumee much of the line was relocated and all of the badly worn 25-pound rail was replaced with new 50-pound steel. Track work between Toledo and Holgate was completed at Grand Rapids on October 3, 1880, and regular trains were put on the following December 2 between Toledo and Shane's Crossing, 100 miles.

In August 1880 the TD&B began laying track west from Warren on a 44-mile extension to Marion and Kokomo. Those two cities granted the narrow gauge $100,000 in subsidies which covered a good share of the cost of construction. The tracklayers reached Marion on October 1, Greentown a few days before Christmas, and the city limits of Kokomo by the end of 1880. Access through Marion was gained by laying a third rail on 1½ miles of the track of the Cincinnati, Wabash & Michigan (later Big Four). Through trains were put on between Delphos and Marion, 80 miles, on December 2 — the same day through service to Toledo was inaugurated. Regular operation to Kokomo, however, did not begin until July 24, 1881.

LINES SOUTH OF DELPHOS

On December 6, 1877, the Dayton, Covington & Toledo Railroad was incorporated in Ohio to construct a narrow-gauge railway between Dayton and Delphos. The incorporators were mostly Dayton men led by J. O. Arnold and George W. Kneisley. During the summer of 1878 the DC&T completed a 25.3-mile grade which extended south from Covington through the Stillwater Valley to a junction with the Pittsburgh, Cincinnati & St. Louis (Pennsylvania), 6 miles northwest of Dayton. The first section of track was laid in July 1879 from the Panhandle (PC&StL) at Stillwater Junction to Harrisburgh (Englewood), a distance of 7½ miles. On September 1, 1879, regular operation commenced to West Milton, 6½ miles beyond Harrisburgh, and by the end of 1879 the track had been laid to Ludlow Falls and Covington. During the spring of 1880 a 10-mile extension was completed between Covington and Versailles, and 6 miles of track was laid from Stillwater Junction to the line of the Cincinnati, Hamilton & Dayton at Dayton. The DC&T ran into the Union Depot at 3rd Street, paying the CH&D an annual fee of $5000 for the privilege of maintaining a third rail in its track.

Compared with the TD&B the 41-mile DC&T was a well-built road. The entire line was laid with 40-pound rail and was well ballasted with gravel. The road owned two locomotives, a Baldwin 4-4-0 named *Stillwater* and a Porter 0-6-0. Rolling stock included a coach, a combination car, eight box cars, and eight flat cars. At Stillwater Junction there was a unique device for placing narrow-gauge trucks under standard-gauge cars. Called the Ramsey Car Transfer,* it consisted of a long pit with a standard-gauge track entering at one end and a narrow-gauge track at the other. Supported by dollies at the side sills, a car was drawn across the pit so that its standard-gauge trucks rolled free of the carbody and into the pit. At the other end, narrow-gauge trucks with spe-

*The first Ramsey transfer was installed in 1878 on the Ligonier Valley at Latrobe, Pa. The DC&T also ordered installations for Versailles and Covington, but these ended up on the TD&B at Holgate and Toledo.

cial center plates and heavy-duty journals were pulled up out of the pit and attached to the car. The entire job took less than 2 minutes.

On June 21, 1880, the DC&T was absorbed by the TD&B and the latter immediately began surveying a connection between Versailles and Mercer, a station on the TD&B 22 miles southwest of Delphos. The connecting line was financed by placing a million-dollar mortgage on the DC&T and the TD&B's line between Delphos and Shane's Crossing. The first section, 8 miles between Mercer and Celina, was completed early in November 1880. Initial freight shipments from Celina were made on December 11, and regular mixed operation was started on January 10, 1881. A delegation of Findlay businessmen inspected the Celina extension shortly after it was opened and reported that "the part of the road from Celina to Delphos was very poorly constructed with but little grading, poorly ditched, and no ballast at all, and is altogether in a very bad shape although daily trains are run over it with more or less irregularity."

The 25 miles of line from Celina to Versailles, around the west end of Grand Lake was completed in May 1881. Later the same month, *Stillwater* made a trial run between Dayton and Monticello, covering the 81 miles in 3 hours 5 minutes, including

Ramsey car transfers were used by TC&StL at five Ohio points to install and remove special narrow-gauge trucks under standard-gauge cars. Trucks could be changed in less than 2 minutes and were often shipped along with the car on a special flat car.

five stops. The Baldwin attained speeds of 35 to 40 mph and covered one 11-mile stretch in 17 minutes. Regular operation between Delphos and Dayton, 96½ miles, began on June 22, 1881. The TD&B's Dayton Division embraced this line, the 4.3-mile Mercer-Shane's Crossing Branch, and the 1.11-mile Soldiers Home Branch. The latter, built during the summer of 1880, left the old DC&T 2 miles out of Dayton and ran south to the grounds of the National Asylum for Disabled Soldiers.

THE SOUTHEASTERN AND IRON DIVISIONS

By absorbing the Dayton & South-Eastern Railroad on March 17, 1881, the TD&B acquired a 115-mile narrow-gauge road extending from Dayton to Chillicothe and the Jackson County coal fields at Wellston. The D&SE was organized on December 16, 1871, and its charter provided for the building of a line across southern Ohio from Dayton to the Ohio River at Gallipolis. Surveys were completed in October 1875 and the next month the road's president, S. N. Yeomans, contracted to build the road as far as Wellston for $6716 per mile. On November 28, 1876, the contractor opened 29½ miles of road between Xenia and Washington Court House, and on June 1, 1877, operations were extended from Xenia to Dayton's 3rd Street depot. A 21-mile extension from Washington Court House to Musselmans station on the Marietta & Cincinnati Railway (B&O) was opened on October 29, 1877. At Musselmans the D&SE installed a Ramsey transfer and forwarded a considerable amount of ore and coal from this point to Dayton. This tonnage was handled in standard-gauge cars received from the M&C and was turned over to the Big Four at Dayton by means of another Ramsey transfer. Completion of the 108-mile Springfield, Jackson & Pomeroy narrow gauge in July 1878 provided the Dayton & South-Eastern another source of freight traffic. The SJ&P delivered a considerable amount of westbound Jackson County coal to the D&SE at Washington Court House.

Despite heavy freight tonnage and a good passenger business, the D&SE was unable to sell its mortgage bonds and had great difficulty in collecting on subscriptions to its capital stock. As a result, the road's general manager, J. E. Gimperling, was named receiver on August 9, 1878. Gimperling was allowed to raise money to extend the road to Wellston by selling securities to the Baltimore & Ohio which sought the D&SE as an entrance to Dayton. An 11-mile extension to Chillicothe, including a 1001-foot bridge over the Scioto River, was opened in October 1879. Before the end of that year the track was laid as far as Richmond Dale, 93 miles east of Dayton. The D&SE connected with the Marietta & Cincinnati at what came to be known as Baker's

Junction, 3½ miles east of Richmond Dale. Since the terrain in this section was quite rugged, the narrow-gauge road arranged to lay a third rail on the M&C for a distance of 7.515 miles. On March 1, 1880, the D&SE opened to Coalton, 6 miles beyond the end of the dual-gauge track at Byer's Junction. The remaining 5 miles to Wellston was completed the following May.

Prior to the receivership, the D&SE owned three Baldwin 18-ton 4-4-0's and a 12-ton 2-4-0 built by the National Locomotive Works of Connellsville, Pa. Car stock included four coaches, one baggage car, 30 box cars, and 50 flat cars. While receiver, Gimperling purchased in his own name three 18-ton Brooks Moguls, one from the builder and two from the SJ&P when that road was about to widen its gauge in 1879. However, the 50 miles of ascending grade west of the Scioto proved too much for the little 2-6-0's to negotiate with coal tonnage out of Wellston. In 1880 and 1881 the D&SE bought a pair of 28-ton Baldwin 2-8-0's and had two more on order when taken over by the TD&B. By that time, the road owned 267 freight cars, mostly gondolas.

The Baltimore & Ohio was about to assume control of the D&SE and lift its receivership when the TD&B purchased $400,000 of the railroad's preferred stock in February 1881. The move gave the TD&B control of the D&SE and the two were consolidated on March 17, 1881. During the winter of 1881-1882 the TD&B extended the Southeastern Division, as it called the D&SE, to Buckeye Furnace, 8.3 miles beyond Wellston. Work was also started on a connecting line between the Southeastern and the Iron Railroad.

For many years the principal internal improvement of the extreme southern part of Ohio was the Iron Railroad. The primary function of this enterprise was the haulage of Lawrence County ore and coal to the many blast furnaces in and around the Ohio River town of Ironton. Since the Iron Railroad had no connection with any other railroad, the river served as the only outlet for Ironton's heavy production of steel rails and pig iron.

The Iron Railroad was chartered on March 7, 1849, and opened to traffic in December 1852. It was built to the old legal Ohio gauge of 4 feet 10 inches and extended 14 miles from Ironton north to Centre Station. A short distance north of Ironton, near Vesuvius station, the road passed through a ridge of solid rock by means of a 1020-foot tunnel. As Ironton's furnace industry expanded during the 1870's, several short branches were built, including a 1.25-mile spur from Bartles to Deans.

The first locomotive on the Iron road was the venerable 4-2-0 *Essex*, built in 1837 by Seth Boyden for the Morris & Essex, pioneer New Jersey railroad. In the 1850's the road acquired at least one other secondhand locomotive. By 1881 the Iron road owned five engines, including a pair of Baldwin 0-6-0's named *Mt. Vernon* and *Olive* built in 1863 and 1867, and three Pittsburgh engines. These were No. 7 an 0-4-0 built in 1870, and the 8 and 9, 4-4-0's built in 1873 and 1879. The road also owned 218 gondola cars and a pair of coaches.

On October 21, 1881, the Iron Railroad was absorbed by the Toledo, Delphos & Burlington which had earlier secured the right to lay a third rail over the road between Ironton and Deans, 13 miles. The TD&B laid a $2,250,000 mortgage on the Southeastern Division in order to pay for the cost of constructing a 38.66-mile line between the Iron road at Deans and the Southeastern near Wellston. Work on this connection had already started when the TD&B acquired the Iron Railroad.

THE CINCINNATI NORTHERN

The concept of the narrow-gauge trunk system was born during the memorable Narrow Gauge Convention held at Cincinnati's Grand Hotel during July 1878. For several years afterward the Queen City was looked upon as the capital of the narrow-gauge world, and it is not surprising that it boasted no fewer than five 3-foot gauge roads. Not the least of these was the Cincinnati Northern,* successor to the

---

*Not to be confused with the standard-gauge road with the same name extending from Cincinnati to Jackson, Mich., and which is now part of the New York Central system.

Miami Valley Narrow Gauge Railway. The latter was organized on November 9, 1874, and projected northeast 55 miles from Cincinnati to Lebanon and Xenia. Ground was broken at Avondale, a Cincinnati suburb, on August 31, 1876, and by the end of 1878 36 miles of grade and bridges had been completed between Waynesfield and the Marietta & Cincinnati Railway at Norwood. By that time, MV promoters had run out of money, and the general contractor had filed a suit to enforce a mechanic's lien on the property. Very little, if any, track had been laid, but the Miami Valley owned a pair of handsome Baldwin 4-4-0's named *Warren County* and *Leila*.

The project lay dormant until March 1880 when the road was sold at sheriff's sale for $61,000 to Gov. Charles Foster, C. S. Brice, and Samuel Thomas. In league with Corse and Ballou of the TD&B, the purchasers and a group of Cincinnati speculators headed by Ozro J. Dodds and Albert Netter organized the Cincinnati Northern Railway on June 8, 1880. The new company quickly undertook the completion of the road and on May 30, 1881, began running mixed trains over 24.2 miles of track between Norwood and Lebanon.

Between Norwood and the basin of Cincinnati, there is a rather formidable ridge known as Walnut Hills. Early railroads entering Cincinnati from the north skirted the ridge by way of the valleys of the Little Miami and Mill Creek. Their termini were separated and ill situated to the central part of the

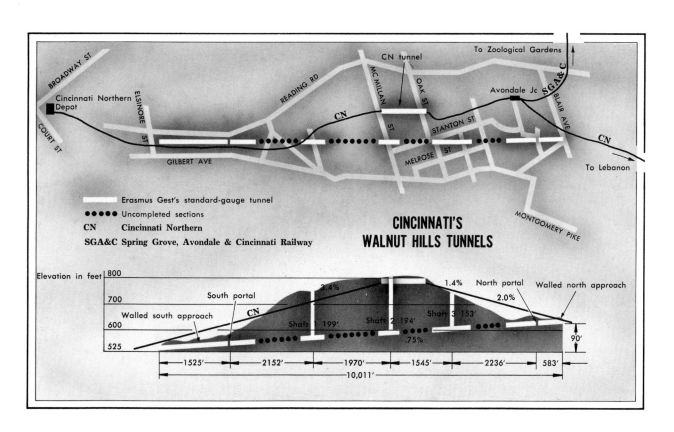

CINCINNATI'S
WALNUT HILLS TUNNELS

Gravesend, a 2-4-6T equipped with Walschaerts, poses at Mason Machine Works before its initiation on New York & Manhattan Beach in 1881. It was one of four 37-ton Fairlies acquired by E. B. Phillips for TC&StL and numbered 83-86. Successor TStL&KC converted them to standard-gauge passenger engines in 1888-1889. — *Collection of Thomas Norrell.*

Four of the 12 Forney 0-6-4T's which Hinkley built for Toledo, Delphos & Burlington during 1881-1882 ended up on Manistee & Luther, a Michigan logging road. Here, M&L No. 1 teams up with No. 5, a Baldwin 2-8-0. — *Collection of Albert J. Schimpke.*

city. The Miami Valley, however, had planned to locate its depot in the heart of the city. Its promoters came into possession of a 15-acre site on Court Street east of Broadway, a partly completed tunnel through Walnut Hills, and a right of way connecting them.

Walnut Hills or Deer Creek tunnel was originally engineered and partly built by Erasmus Gest as part of a proposed short line between Cincinnati and Dayton. Including walled and covered approaches, the tunnel was to have been 10,011 feet long, by far the longest tunnel project ever undertaken in Ohio. Between 1852 and 1855, 3336 feet of the tunnel was bored at the two portals and from

three deep shafts sunk from the top of Walnut Hills. Work on the project was abandoned in 1855 with the failure of Gest's Dayton & Cincinnati Railroad, but in 1871 a group of local promoters revived it as the Cincinnati Railway Tunnel Company. The new company hoped to complete the tunnel and interest the city's railroads in using it and the Court Street depot site. Very little work was accomplished before the enterprise collapsed in the 1873 panic.

The Cincinnati Northern came into possession of the Court Street property and finally fulfilled the long-cherished dream of building a depot there. Unlike the Miami Valley company, the Cincinnati Northern ignored the abandoned tunnel and settled for a shallow 1500-foot bore through the top of Walnut Hills. In place of Gest's sustained .75 per cent northbound grade, the CN climbed the south face of the ridge at the fierce rate of 3.4 per cent. There was also a long 2 per cent ascent to the tunnel from the north. Despite several proposals to complete the old Gest tunnel, no further work was ever done on it.

During the summer of 1881 the TD&B began work on a connecting line between the Southeastern Division and the Cincinnati Northern. The line left the TD&B at a point 5 miles east of Dayton known as Lebanon Junction. At about the same time, the CN began extending its road north from Lebanon and on December 20, 1881, the tracks of the two roads met at Utica (Dodds), 6.55 miles north of Lebanon and 16.82 miles south of Lebanon Junction. The first TD&B train over the Cincinnati Division ran into Dodds on January 12, 1882, and on the following February 20 the CN ran a train of 10 loaded freight cars from Cincinnati to Dayton. About two weeks later the CN put on a regular Cincinnati-Dayton passenger train.

The Cincinnati Northern did a fair suburban commuter business between downtown Cincinnati and Montgomery, reached by a 1.4-mile branch from the main line at Blue Ash. At Idlewild Junction between Avondale and Norwood, the CN connected with the Cincinnati & Eastern (now Norfolk & Western) and the latter ran its trains over the CN to the Court Street station. By February 1882 the CN owned seven locomotives, 12 coaches, one baggage car, 47 flats, and 10 box cars. Aside from the two ex-Miami Valley Baldwins, the roster included a Porter 2-4-0, two Mason Bogies, and a pair of Brooks Moguls.

LOCOMOTIVES OF TOLEDO, DELPHOS & BURLINGTON

After absorbing the Dayton, Covington & Toledo, the TD&B owned 11 locomotives, two first-class coaches, five excursion coaches, and about 100 freight cars. In order to ease the very critical shortage of equipment, George Ballou agreed to purchase cars and locomotives and rent them to the road under what came to be known as the Boston Car Trust. During 1880-1881 Ballou delivered 16 engines, 280 flat cars, 250 box cars, 124 coal cars, 13 coaches, two baggage cars, and 200 narrow-gauge trucks for the Ramsey transfers. The first set of engines, numbered 12-17 and named after TD&B stockholders, was built by William Mason during the fall of 1880. They were Mason's double-truck Bogie or Improved Fairlie pattern, a type used extensively on the Denver, South Park & Pacific; New York & Manhattan Beach; and other narrow-gauge roads. The TD&B's Bogies were of the 0-6-6T type with tank and boiler attached to a rigid frame. The six-coupled 36-inch drivers and 13 x 16-inch cylinders were attached to an independent truck frame which turned on a kingpin like any ordinary car truck.

Nos. 39 and 40 were 22-ton passenger engines turned out by Mount Savage shops of the Cumberland & Pennsylvania for the TD&B in January 1882. They were built to the order of Thomas H. Paul & Son. — *Collection of Thomas Norrell.*

Cincinnati's Grand Hotel was a mecca for promoters during the fever years of the narrow-gauge craze. Here, on January 7, 1881, the Cotton Belt and Little Giant announced their determination to complete the Grand Narrow Gauge Trunk between Ohio and the Rio Grande River. — *Collection of Cornelius W. Hauck.*

Steam admission and exhaust pipes were connected to boiler and cylinders by means of flexible joints. These permitted the driving truck to move independently of the boiler and adjust to track curvature. The Bogie thus required no engine truck and had the benefit of all 23 tons of boiler weight for adhesion. The design also permitted unrestricted firebox design and size. Bogies could be run equally well backward or forward.

Other Ballou-owned engines were six-coupled and four-coupled Forneys. Like the Bogie these had no engine truck and carried the tank behind the cab on an extension of the main frame. Though the Forney

had all the boiler weight for adhesion, it lacked the Bogie's flexibility and was intended to be run backward with the four-wheel truck under the tank serving as an engine truck. TD&B 18-23 were built by the Hinkley Locomotive Works, were the 0-6-4T type, and weighed 33 tons. These were employed with the Bogies on Southeastern Division coal trains. Engines 24-27, 24-ton 0-4-4T Forneys for passenger service, were turned out by H. K. Porter at Pittsburgh in the spring of 1881.

The Dayton & Southeastern engines were assigned TD&B numbers 28-36 and were followed by two Baldwin 2-8-0's, the 37-38, ordered by the D&SE

prior to the consolidation. In June 1881 the TD&B ordered six 22-ton 4-4-0 passenger engines from Thomas H. Paul & Son of Frostburg, Md. Two of these, the 39 and 40, were built in January 1882 by the Cumberland & Pennsylvania's Mount Savage (Md.) shop to Paul's order. A third engine, the 47, was built by Paul at Frostburg a few months later. The balance of the order was evidently canceled. TD&B's 47-engine roster was rounded out by the 41-46, Hinkley 0-6-4T Forneys built early in 1882.

TD&B 4, the D&K's diminutive 0-4-0, was relegated to yard duty at Delphos in 1880. Even there the little woodburner had a propensity for jumping the track, and on one occasion ended up on its back in a creek bed. On another unhappy day, a Delphos factory burned to the ground after the Baldwin showered it with sparks. Finally, a careless engineer launched the Four-Spot through an open draw into the Miami & Erie Canal where it effectively tied up both the narrow gauge and the canal for several days. Once retrieved, the engine was taken to Delphos shop and dismantled. The boiler was installed in the Dayton roundhouse in 1884, but the machinery was kept at Delphos for years afterward.

When the TD&B moved its general offices to Toledo in November 1880, Delphos began a determined campaign to secure the road's main repair

shops. William J. Craig, however, was just as determined to see them built at Bluffton, his home town. All Bluffton had to do was raise $40,000 and the issue was settled. When Bluffton's bond issue failed to get past the voters, the Delphos city fathers got the shops by granting the TD&B 12 acres of land and $30,000 cash. In August 1881 the TD&B completed a new 10-stall roundhouse and a 60 x 90-foot blacksmith shop about 1 mile north of the Fort Wayne depot. During the summer of 1882 a 130 x 80-foot machine shop with six pits was added.* By late 1882 the shops were employing more than 200 men.

THE GRAND NARROW GAUGE TRUNK

The Evans-Boehmer plan to extend the TD&B to the Mississippi was frustrated when Jay Gould's Wabash, St. Louis & Pacific acquired the Havana, Rantoul & Eastern narrow gauge in 1880. Although the move was a mortal blow to the Burlington extension, it served to turn TD&B's attention to St. Louis and the Gulf Southwest. Control of St. Louis, Iron Mountain & Southern and other roads gave Gould a virtual monopoly on rail traffic moving east from the cotton districts of Arkansas and Texas through the St. Louis gateway. The situation so alarmed planters and politicians of the cotton states that they openly offered to support the construction of a competing railroad. In 1879 a powerful combine headed by Col. James W. Paramore of St. Louis and Logan H. Roots of Little Rock, Ark., chartered the Texas & St. Louis Railway with the intent of building a 1000-mile narrow-gauge road from the Rio Grande at Laredo, Tex., to the confluence of the Mississippi and Ohio rivers at Bird's Point, Mo. The narrow-gauge Cairo & St. Louis† was then in operation between Cairo and East St. Louis, Ill., 146 miles. To bridge the Mississippi and reach the tracks of the C&StL, the Texas & St. Louis arranged to use Illinois Central transfer boats.

The Texas & St. Louis absorbed the 22-mile Tyler Tap Railroad of Texas, and by the end of 1880 had 203 miles of narrow-gauge road extending from Corsicana to Texarkana, Tex. There remained 411 miles of road to be built from Corsicana to Laredo and 418 miles from Texarkana to Bird's Point.

In the spring of 1880 W. J. Craig had conceived the idea of extending the TD&B to East St. Louis, forming with the Cairo & St. Louis and the Texas & St. Louis a narrow-gauge trunk line from Toledo to Laredo. The proposed 1628-mile-long route was

THE GRAND NARROW GAUGE TRUNK—1883

TC&StL	Toledo, Cincinnati & St. Louis	TT&RG	Toledo, Texas & Rio Grande
T&StL	Texas & St. Louis	TM	Texas-Mexican
StL&C	St. Louis & Cairo	TW	Texas Western
CD&StL	Cleveland, Delphos & St. Louis	K&G	Kansas & Gulf Short Line
HE&WT	Houston, East & West Texas		

---

*The shop buildings are still standing and are leased to the Krey Packing Company. The brick roundhouse was torn down in 1954.

†Reorganized in February 1882 as the St. Louis & Cairo Railroad, the line is now part of the Gulf, Mobile & Ohio's main line.

Ornate Mogul 32 was the first Little Giant engine in Illinois and opened the Charleston-Oakland section on June 26, 1881. Brooks 12 x 18 was built as Dayton & South-Eastern 5 in 1879. TC&StL at first used only locomotives owned outright in Illinois for fear that the state would seize rented equipment. — *Collection of John A. Rehor.*

to parallel Gould's 1512-mile Wabash-Iron Mountain-Texas & Pacific-International & Great Northern standard-gauge combination between the same points. After several preliminary meetings, the alliance of the narrow-gauge moguls was publicly announced at Cincinnati's Grand Hotel on January 7, 1881. Paramore and Roots of the Cotton Belt* and Craig and Corse of the TD&B declared their two roads would ultimately be consolidated to form the Toledo, Texas & Rio Grande Railroad. Moreover, the Grand Narrow Gauge Trunk would eventually be extended 600 miles beyond Laredo to Mexico City to compete with Gould's proposed road between those points.

In June 1880 Craig formed the Western Construction Company for the purpose of building the St. Louis Extension. Two months later he leased Carey Evans' Frankfort & State Line and revived the long-defunct Tuscola, Charleston & Vincennes Railroad. The latter had been chartered in Illinois on March 7, 1867, to build about 45 miles of standard-gauge road connecting Charleston, Ill., with a point on the Paris & Danville Railroad near the Indiana border. Two short segments of grade were completed before the enterprise folded in 1874. The principal of these

extended north from Charleston to Fair Grange and then northeast to Oakland, a total of 15 miles. In September 1880 Craig's surveyors laid out a route 26 miles long from Oakland to Ridge Farm, a station on the Paris & Danville 7 miles west of the Indiana line. That same month a contractor began resurfacing the old grade at Charleston. The first rails were laid at that point during the last week of 1880 and on June 26, 1881, an excursion train opened the TC&V between Charleston and Oakland. The next day the road began running a pair of mixed trains each way between those points using a locomotive and cars belonging to the TD&B. By November the track was laid as far as Brocton, 6 miles east of Oakland, and the entire 41-mile road to Ridge Farm was completed by the end of 1881.

Craig's Western Construction Company began laying rail at Ridge Farm and Clark's Hill on the 60-mile gap between those towns in June 1881. The Frankfort & State Line charter was used to bridge the 53 miles between Clark's Hill and the Illinois line. The remaining 7 miles of road to Ridge Farm was built under the charter of the Vermilion & State Line Railroad, a "paper" company organized in Illinois on July 18, 1881. Prior to this, on February 12, 1881, TD&B chartered the Toledo, Cincinnati & St. Louis Railroad as the extension of its road west of Kokomo. The new company assumed Craig's

---

*The Cotton Belt nickname applied to the Texas & St. Louis was retained by the St. Louis Southwestern Railway, ultimate successor to the T&StL.

TC&StL 9 pauses at Coffeen's, Ill., about 1884. Pittsburgh built the 4-4-0 in 1878 as *Bluffton* of the Delphos, Bluffton & Frankfort. — *Collection of John A. Rehor.*

lease of the F&SL and on May 20, 1881, absorbed the Frankfort & Kokomo.

The TD&B began running trains between Toledo and Kokomo on July 24, 1881, and the same week began the work of changing the gauge of the F&K. Regular operations to Frankfort commenced on October 3, 1881. Trains began running to Veedersburg, 43 miles beyond Frankfort, on May 28, 1882. By January 1882 there was a continuous line of narrow-gauge track from Toledo to Charleston, 319 miles, broken only by the Wabash River 2 miles east of Eugene Junction (Cayuga), Ind. The Wabash bridge, including trestle approaches, was more than a half mile long and consisted of five 160-foot Howe truss spans supported by masonry piers. An engine pulling two loads of wheat bound from Ridge Farm to Toledo made a trial run over the bridge during the first week of August 1882. On August 25 a daily Charleston-Frankfort mixed train began operating.

On September 14, 1880, Craig chartered the Charleston, Neoga & St. Louis Railroad to build that part of the St. Louis Extension between Charleston and East St. Louis, 132 miles. The following May the contractor began clearing and grading a right of way east and west from Neoga, a station on the Illinois Central's Chicago-Cairo main line 20 miles southwest of Charleston. A month later 30 carloads of iron rails were delivered at Neoga, and by mid-July track had been laid from that place 3 miles west to the Little Wabash River and to a point 2 miles east of Neoga. Thereafter, the contractor worked sporadically on the remaining 18 miles of road to Charleston, and it was not until March 11, 1882, that a train was run through from Neoga to Charleston. Work west of Neoga had been suspended owing to lack of capital.

The Toledo, Cincinnati & St. Louis absorbed the three Illinois companies in July 1881 and on Feb-

ruary 23, 1882, the TD&B directors voted to consolidate the TD&B and the TC&StL, retaining the name of the subsidiary. The new Toledo, Cincinnati & St. Louis had capital stock of 15 million dollars, a substantial increase over the sum of the stock of the old companies. In order to raise the money needed to complete the Ironton and St. Louis extensions, the New England capitalists who controlled the road engineered a unique arrangement with the American Loan & Trust Company of Boston. The bank, acting as trustee of what came to be known as the Toledo & Delphos Trust, furnished the road 1.5 million dollars and took up all the miscellaneous assets that the TC&StL possessed. These were, for the most part, uncollected subscriptions to the capital stock against which the bank called for periodic payments.

With fresh capital in hand the Little Giant resumed work on its extensions with the arrival of spring in 1882. In April the road gave J. H. Beeson, of Atchison, Kan., a contract to build 73 miles of line from East St. Louis to Ramsey, a station on the Illinois Central's Northern Division 40 miles west of Neoga. About the same time, Craig's Western Construction Company again undertook the task of completing the 36 miles of road between Ramsey and the end of track at the east branch of the Little Wabash River, west of Neoga. Although most of this section traversed a plateau known as the Bowling Green Prairie, 35 bridges had to be built to carry the narrow-gauge track across the broad hollows cut by the Kaskaskia or Okaw River and its tributaries. In June a St. Louis firm began work on these timber bridges and an even greater number west of Ramsey.

On July 26, 1882, Craig began laying track at the Wabash, St. Louis & Pacific crossing at Stewardson, 10 miles west of Neoga and 349 miles west of

Rome Moguls served briefly on TC&StL before being repossessed. Delivered as Cincinnati Northern 9 in 1883, this 32-ton hog was successively TC&StL 49, Portland & Willamette Valley 3, South Pacific Coast 25, and Nevada County Narrow Gauge 6. Here, she reposes in storage at Alameda, Calif., in 1907 as SPC 25. — *Collection of Gerald M. Best.*

1882 Grant Consols worked Dayton & Ironton after 1884 when the courts dismembered the Little Giant. No. 63 was sold in September 1887 to Oregon Improvement Company and finally became Columbia & Puget Sound 9. She is shown in Seattle in 1895. From 1898-1918 she was on White Pass & Yukon. — *Williamson's Marine Photo Shop, Seattle.*

Toledo. Slowed by the construction of a dozen bridges, Craig's men managed to lay only 10 miles of track during the next month. On August 28 they reached the east end of the nearly-completed 2400-foot bridge spanning the Okaw. The construction train tested the bridge on September 18 and the next day the rails were laid to the Ohio & Mississippi (B&O) crossing at Cowden, a little more than a mile to the west.

Aided by dry weather, the contractor laid track at an accelerated rate west of Cowden. Gandy dancers spiked down 2 miles of track on September 22 to reach Bridge 366.3, the 1140-foot trestle across Mitchell Creek. On the 28th they laid more than 3 miles of iron, and by the end of September the track was done to Beck's Creek trestle just beyond Milepost 372. In September another gang had closed the 6-mile gap between the Little Wabash and Stewardson. Still another force had begun laying track at Ramsey on August 25 and by September 5 had completed 6 miles of track to Beck's Creek. The 1300-foot trestle was completed and the two sections joined together on October 1.

Beeson had also begun laying track at Ramsey on August 25 and on September 12 his men reached Hurricane Creek, 6 miles to the west. The construction train appeared at Coffeen's farm near Milepost 394 on October 3, and beyond this point the tracklayers advanced to Sorento on October 24, to New Douglas on October 31, and to Alhambra on No-

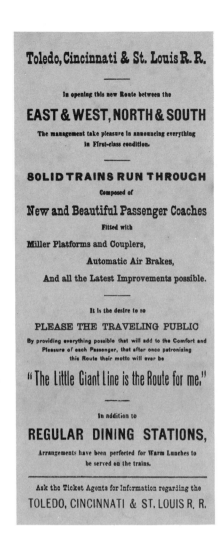
vember 7. Inclement weather and a sudden shortage of money and materials slowed progress on the remaining 32 miles to East St. Louis. There were several extended delays caused by a lack of rails and the refusal of the contractor's men to continue working without pay. Beeson's men did not reach Edwardsville, 14 miles beyond Alhambra, until December 13. However, by Christmas 1882 the tracklayers were advancing across the American Bottom, the Mississippi River flood plain, and at the end of the year they were working in the outskirts of East St. Louis.

Construction of the connecting link between Ironton Junction and Deans had been suspended by the TD&B at the end of 1881. At that time, about 2 miles of track had been completed between Ironton Junction and Berlin Crossroads. Work was resumed in the spring of 1882, and by September of that year the entire grade had been completed and an additional 15 miles of track had been laid. There were 51 trestles, three tunnels, and some very heavy grades on this line which ran through one of the most rugged and sparsely populated regions of Ohio. Tunnel No. 1, 400 feet long, was located 29 miles south of Ironton Junction. Farther south near Mount Vernon there were two 700-foot tunnels.

COLLAPSE

The Toledo, Cincinnati & St. Louis was constantly teetering on the brink of financial disaster, and the economic slide which began in the fall of 1882 placed it in grave jeopardy. In order to complete the extensions, the Toledo & Delphos Trust assessed the stockholders on November 15 to the tune of $225,000. The stockholders failed to respond and on December 7 it was necessary to cease work on the Ironton line with only 5 miles of track left to lay. The contractor had run out of rails, and rolling mills which heretofore had been extending credit, were demanding cash payment before making any more shipments. About the same time, the contractors stopped all work in Illinois. Their men had not been paid for weeks and were threatening to burn the road's trestles. In an effort to spur the stockholders into paying the assessment, the management wired them, "We are helpless. Will you act at once or shall the reaching of St. Louis and Ironton this winter be abandoned?"

First 90 was one of a dozen Brooks Moguls ordered by E. B. Phillips early in 1883. Never used on TC&StL, the 2-6-0 became Cincinnati & Eastern 7. She was one of six representative locomotives displayed by Brooks at the National Exposition of Railway Appliances at Chicago during the summer of 1883. — *Schenectady History Center.*

Before the end of 1882 a desperate TC&StL board elected Elijah B. Phillips to the road's presidency. A veteran of 43 years of railroading, Phillips was the president of the Eastern Railroad and a former president of the Lake Shore & Michigan Southern. He headed a wealthy clique of New England capitalists and it was largely his influence that had brought about the establishment of the Toledo & Delphos Trust. His timely ascendency to the TC&StL helm again saved the day, for his name alone was enough to stir stockholders to action and soothe worried contractors. Work was resumed on the Ironton line at once and the tracklayers reached Deans in mid-January 1883. On March 1 a trial run was made between Charleston and East St. Louis and on Monday, May 14, 1883,* regular mixed trains were put on between those points.

Beyond the task of completing the extensions, Phillips was faced with the Little Giant's never-ending shortage of serviceable locomotives and cars. At the time of the March 1882 consolidation, the road possessed the 47 TD&B engines plus four acquired in its own name. Subsequently, contracts were made with the Grant Locomotive Works of Paterson, N. J., under which the builder furnished

the road 10 30-ton Consolidations and 10 24-ton 4-4-0's. These were numbered 57-66 and 67-76. However, until Phillips took over the TC&StL, Grant had refused to release the last five 4-4-0's because of the shaky financial condition of the road. In February 1883 the board authorized Phillips to acquire 25 additional engines which he was forced to purchase in his own name as a result of the Little Giant's embarrassment.

Five of Phillips' engines were 26-ton Hinkley 2-6-0's numbered 78-82 and delivered in March 1883. Four were secondhand Mason 2-4-6T Bogies numbered 83-86 which were purchased on the advice of the new master mechanic Lewis H. James. These engines had been badly damaged in a car shed fire on the New York & Manhattan Beach in December 1882 and were subsequently repaired by Mason. Phillips also ordered four 32-ton Moguls from the New York Locomotive Works at Rome. Originally assigned numbers 87-90, these were actually delivered as Cincinnati Northern-Avondale Branch 8-11. Finally, Phillips contracted with Brooks for 12 2-6-0's with 15 x 18-inch cylinders, 37-inch drivers, and an engine weight of 47,500 pounds. The first of this group, the 87, was received in January 1883.

The TC&StL had sought to absorb the Cincinnati Northern as early as February 1882 but had been thwarted by the opposition of Albert Netter and other Cincinnati stockholders. It also fell upon Phil-

*May 1883 proved to be the high-water mark of the narrow-gauge era. Except for the bridging of the Arkansas River, the narrow-gauge trunk between Ohio and Texas was completed. In the West the Denver & Rio Grande opened its 756-mile trunk line between Denver and Ogden.

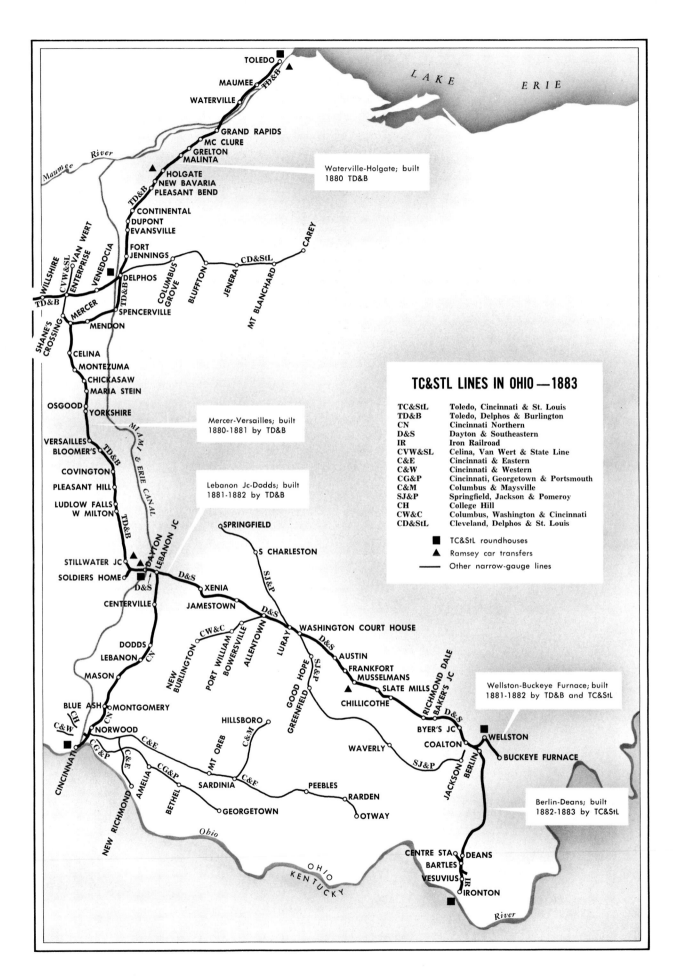

LAKE ERIE

TOLEDO
MAUMEE
WATERVILLE
GRAND RAPIDS
MC CLURE
GRELTON
MALINTA
HOLGATE
NEW BAVARIA
PLEASANT BEND
CONTINENTAL
DUPONT
EVANSVILLE
FORT JENNINGS
CAREY
CD&StL
VAN WERT
CVW&SL
ENTERPRISE
VENEDOCIA
DELPHOS
COLUMBUS GROVE
BLUFFTON
JENERA
MT BLANCHARD
WILLSHIRE
SPENCERVILLE
SHANE'S CROSSING
TD&B
MERCER
MENDON
CELINA
MONTEZUMA
CHICKASAW
MARIA STEIN
OSGOOD
YORKSHIRE
VERSAILLES
BLOOMER'S
TD&B
MIAMI & ERIE CANAL
COVINGTON
PLEASANT HILL
LUDLOW FALLS
W MILTON
TD&B
STILLWATER JC
SOLDIERS HOME
DAYTON
LEBANON JC
D&S
CENTERVILLE
XENIA
JAMESTOWN
D&S
SPRINGFIELD
S CHARLESTON
SJ&P
WASHINGTON COURT HOUSE
CW&C
NEW BURLINGTON
PORT WILLIAM
BOWERSVILLE
ALLENTOWN
LURAY
AUSTIN
FRANKFORT
MUSSELMANS
SLATE MILLS
D&S
DODDS
LEBANON
CN
MASON
GOOD HOPE
GREENFIELD
SJ&P
CHILLICOTHE
RICHMOND DALE
BAKER'S JC
D&S
Wellston-Buckeye Furnace; built 1881-1882 by TD&B and TC&StL
BLUE ASH
MONTGOMERY
CH
C&W
NORWOOD
CN
BYER'S JC
WELLSTON
COALTON
BUCKEYE FURNACE
HILLSBORO
MT OREB
C&M
WAVERLY
SJ&P
JACKSON
BERLIN
CINCINNATI
CG&P
C&E
AMELIA
CG&P
BETHEL
SARDINIA
C&F
PEEBLES
RARDEN
Berlin-Deans; built 1882-1883 by TC&StL
NEW RICHMOND
GEORGETOWN
OTWAY
CENTRE STA
DEANS
BARTLES
VESUVIUS
IR
IRONTON
Ohio
OHIO
KENTUCKY
River

Maumee River

Waterville-Holgate; built 1880 TD&B

Mercer-Versailles; built 1880-1881 by TD&B

Lebanon Jc-Dodds; built 1881-1882 by TD&B

TC&STL LINES IN OHIO —1883

TC&StL	Toledo, Cincinnati & St. Louis
TD&B	Toledo, Delphos & Burlington
CN	Cincinnati Northern
D&S	Dayton & Southeastern
IR	Iron Railroad
CVW&SL	Celina, Van Wert & State Line
C&E	Cincinnati & Eastern
C&W	Cincinnati & Western
CG&P	Cincinnati, Georgetown & Portsmouth
C&M	Columbus & Maysville
SJ&P	Springfield, Jackson & Pomeroy
CH	College Hill
CW&C	Columbus, Washington & Cincinnati
CD&StL	Cleveland, Delphos & St. Louis

■ TC&StL roundhouses
▲ Ramsey car transfers
— Other narrow-gauge lines

lips to consummate this important affair, and he succeeded in forcing through the merger during a CN stockholders' meeting on May 5, 1883. Netter and the Cincinnati faction bitterly charged that while they had been notified of the meeting, they had not been informed as to where and when it would take place. Nevertheless, consolidation of the TC&StL, CN, and the Spring Grove, Avondale & Cincinnati Railway was effected on May 30, 1883.

The SGA&C was a spur line projected west from the Cincinnati Northern at Avondale Junction to the Zoological Gardens, Clifton, and the Spring Grove Cemetery, about 3 miles. The road was graded as far as Clifton, but track was laid only to the "Zoo," 1.2 miles. Operation of the Zoo Line commenced on July 1, 1882. During weekdays a shuttle train made 15 trips from Court Street depot over Walnut Hills to the Zoo, mostly for the convenience of commuters. The 3½-mile run consumed 18 minutes. Since it then required more than an hour to reach the Zoo by any other route, the CN did a heavy business, especially on Sunday afternoons. Sunday trains ran every hour until 1 p.m. when the headway was reduced to 20 minutes. From 1 to 6:30 p.m., three sets of equipment were needed to hold down the schedule. Light Mason Bogies and Porter Forneys were used on the Zoo run. Designed for operation in either direction, it was not necessary to turn them at the termini.

Equipment purchased in the name of the SGA&C included the four heavy Rome 2-6-0's, 45 box cars, 15 stock cars, and two coaches. Quaintly, the 11 CN locomotives were assigned TC&StL numbers 2, 4, 96, 54, 55, 56, 77, 48, 49, 50, and 90.

In the summer of 1883 the Little Giant inaugurated its long-awaited Toledo-Cincinnati and Toledo-East St. Louis express passenger trains. Powered by one of the Grant 4-4-0's, the *Cincinnati Express* left Toledo at 7 a.m. and required 12 hours to cover the 229 miles to Court Street depot. Train No. 2, the *St. Louis Express*, was scheduled to make its 450-mile journey between Toledo and East St. Louis in less than 24 hours. The narrow-gauge flyers maintained a respectable 19 mph average and carried Pullman Palace coaches equipped with Miller cou-

plers and Westinghouse air brakes. The Cincinnati trains were a sharp improvement over express packets which required four days and five nights to negotiate the 242-mile Miami & Erie Canal. Nonetheless, they were no match for the Cincinnati, Hamilton & Dayton's 8-hour schedule between Cincinnati and Toledo.

In addition to the express trains, the Little Giant operated accommodation runs between Delphos and Cincinnati, Toledo and Frankfort, Delphos and Frankfort, and Ramsey and East St. Louis. No. 26, the *Wellston Mail*, was timed to connect with the daily train out of Ironton but arrived at Dayton too late to connect with trains for Toledo and Cincinnati. However, No. 28, the accommodation out of Chillicothe, made good connections with both north and southbound express trains at Dayton.

Despite the gaudily advertised express trains, the dream of the Narrow Gauge Trunk had just about run its course. The beginning of the end came on July 31, 1883, when a minor creditor petitioned the United States Circuit Court at Chicago for the appointment of a receiver. The TC&StL board of directors made no effort to ward off the inevitable. There were no terminal facilities whatsoever at either Toledo or East St. Louis. In June the Mississippi had gone over its banks and washed away most of the road across the American Bottom. Less than a third of the road was ballasted and hardly as much was fenced. Along the older parts of the system many trestles were already rotted out and unsafe to run trains across. The 1500-odd employees had not been paid since May, and in July the 200 shopmen at Delphos had refused to continue working without pay. The Little Giant's 784 miles of track, valuated at a little more than 1.5 million dollars, was mortgaged for more than 22 million dollars. Outstanding, in addition, were more than 15 million dollars in stock, 2 million dollars in equipment bonds, $400,000 in unpaid vouchers, and a floating debt of $964,000. Payment of two interest coupons on the first-mortgage bonds was delinquent and the Central Trust Company was about to foreclose the mortgage.

Wabash River bridge at Bluffton gave way under weight of westbound narrow-gauge freight on July 30, 1886. TStL&KC had Baldwin 2-8-0 24 working sans cab in Delphos yard within a week. — *Collection of John A. Rehor.*

The Clover Leaf

THE completion of the Cotton Belt on August 12, 1883, marked the opening of a 1581-mile combination of narrow-gauge railways extending from Ironton, O., to the Brazos River, west of Houston, Tex.* The dream of a narrow-gauge trunk line connecting Lake Erie with the Rio Grande at Laredo was at the threshold of fulfillment. All that remained to be built was a mere 150 miles of track

*Composed of the 3-foot gauge lines of the Toledo, Cincinnati & St. Louis; St. Louis & Cairo; Texas & St. Louis; Kansas & Gulf Short Line; Houston, East & West Texas; and the Texas Western Narrow Gauge.

between the Brazos and Corpus Christi, eastern terminus of the narrow-gauge Texas Mexican Railway. This development, however, brought little joy to the credulous Bay State backers of the Toledo, Cincinnati & St. Louis. General Manager Edwin E. Dwight had been named receiver the previous week.

About to step down from the Little Giant's helm, Elijah Phillips told the press that "I have had and still entertain great faith in the outcome of the enterprise which has been forced to succumb to the inevitable for want of money and lack of faith among its friends." As for the bondholders, they had run out of patience not only with the TC&StL management but with the narrow-gauge concept itself. James M. Quigley, representing a majority of the bondholders, was quoted by a Toledo newspaper as stating:

> There has been a long series of blunders which have finally resulted in a crippled and halting apology for what should have been a profitable railroad property. The first and most serious mistake of all was, of course, in the adoption of the narrow-gauge system through a country completely gridironed with great standard-gauge systems.

DEATH THROES OF THE NARROW GAUGE

During October 1883 the Central Trust Company filed foreclosure bills on eight separate TC&StL mortgages in the United States Circuit Courts at Toledo, Cincinnati, Indianapolis, and Springfield (Ill.). Dwight was replaced as receiver by William J. Craig, still an outspoken exponent of the narrow-gauge theory. In opposition to the Quigley faction, he was actively promoting the Toledo, Texas & Rio Grande alliance and attempting in the name of that company to raise money to build a 190-mile cutoff line between Charleston and Cairo.

It took the courts more than 15 years to unravel the Little Giant's complex corporate structure, its mortgages, liens, and sundry debts. On June 28, 1884, the divisions south of Delphos were removed from Craig's jurisdiction and all but the Cincinnati Northern were sold to parties representing their respective bondholders. The Southeastern Division, which accounted for more than 40 per cent of the system's freight tonnage, was reorganized as the Dayton & Ironton Railroad and converted to standard gauge in April 1887. Two months later the D&I was consolidated with the old Dayton Division to form the Dayton, Fort Wayne & Chicago Railway. In 1891 this company was absorbed by the Cincinnati, Hamilton & Dayton which promptly set about to widen the gauge of the Dayton-Delphos line. The first standard-gauge trains ran over that section on July 13, 1891. Most of the old Ironton extension was abandoned about 1916 by the CH&D. The line between Stillwater Junction and Delphos was operated as the Dayton, Toledo & Chicago Railroad from about 1916 to 1922 when it was abandoned.* The Dayton-Buckeye Furnace line ultimately became the Baltimore & Ohio's Wellston subdivision.

The Iron Division was reorganized as the Iron Railway in July 1884. Most of this old road is now operated by the Detroit, Toledo & Ironton. The Cin-

cinnati Northern was succeeded by the Cincinnati, Lebanon & Northern Railway on August 1, 1885. As late as 1887, this company ran its trains into Dayton over the TC&StL's Cincinnati Division and the D&I. The 16.82-mile Cincinnati Division connecting Lebanon Junction with Dodds was turned over to its bondholders in 1884. It owned no equipment, provided no service, and had no formal corporate organization after the TC&StL passed out of existence in 1886. When the Dayton & Ironton was converted to standard gauge, the CL&N discontinued all operations north of Lebanon and the former Cincinnati Division was "abandoned." On January 29, 1889, the bondholders organized the Dayton, Lebanon & Cincinnati Railroad and began to rebuild the line between Lebanon and Lebanon Junction as a standard gauge. Operations between those points were restored in January 1893. Both the DL&C and CL&N eventually passed under the control of the Pennsylvania Railroad.

After June 1884 the receiver continued to operate the TC&StL main line between Toledo and East St. Louis. Freight traffic on this line was highly seasonal, predominantly eastbound, and consisted mainly of wheat, lumber, and cotton. Most of this tonnage was forwarded to Toledo, but a fair amount of grain moved in standard-gauge cars to the Ramsey transfer at Holgate. During 1884 expenses exceeded revenues by more than 15 per cent and the receiver ran up an operating deficit of almost 1 million dollars. One of the prime factors behind this melancholy showing was the operation of many unprofitable excursion trains during the presidential election campaign that year. For example, when the Republican candidate, James G. Blaine, appeared at Toledo late in September, the road ran a special from Delphos to Toledo charging only a 50-cent fare for the 146-mile round trip. The train carried 309 revenue passengers and grossed the Little Giant a little more than 1 dollar per mile.

It seemed to the Federal judges that the turning of each wheel only served to intensify the plight of the narrow gauge. In the absence of any feasible plan of reorganization, they ordered a drastic curtailment of operations. On January 6, 1885, all trains were discontinued save for a single mixed run in each direction. The courts restrained the road from interchanging cars with its narrow-gauge connections, ordered the immediate return of all foreign cars, and closed the Ramsey transfers. Practically all way stations were closed and all but 20 shopmen at Delphos were furloughed. Most of the equipment acquired through car trusts was surrendered to the owners.

At the time it passed into receivership the Toledo, Cincinnati & St. Louis possessed 3410 freight cars,

---

*The Nickel Plate acquired 3664 feet of DT&C main track and a small yard at Delphos and shared ownership of about a mile of DT&C track at Celina with the New York Central. The narrow-gauge Shane's Crossing Branch was abandoned in 1887.

69 coaches, 13 baggage and mail cars, 11 cabooses, and 260 special narrow-gauge trucks for application to standard-gauge freight cars. There were 101 locomotives on the roster, including five broad-gauge Iron Railroad engines. Phillips' contract with Brooks had been expanded to cover 16 Moguls but only eight, the 87-89 and 91-95, were actually delivered. The 90 had been sent by the builder to Chicago to be displayed at the National Exposition of Railway Appliances. Its replacement and seven other engines, numbered 96-102, were at Dunkirk in various stages of construction. During Dwight's short term as receiver he arranged to lease the 91-95, but the other engines were sold by Brooks to different roads. Dwight also thwarted the attempt of the Grant Locomotive Works to repossess the 20 locomotives it had leased to the TC&StL. Most of these engines were laid up with broken frames, burned-out fireboxes, and boilers full of mud. The relatively heavy Grants had literally battered their machinery into ruin on the Little Giant's light rail. Dwight refused to surrender the engines and was sustained by the courts when Grant charged unlawful conversion of property. However, when the Dayton & Ironton was organized, the 2-8-0's were transferred to that property, and toward the end of 1885 Grant was permitted to take back the 4-4-0's. Most of these were repaired by the Cleveland, Delphos & St. Louis before being sent to narrow-gauge roads in Florida.

In addition to the Grant 2-8-0's, the D&I obtained the TC&StL engines that had originally belonged to the Dayton & Southeastern and the Dayton, Covington & Toledo. The Cincinnati Northern also got back its engines, except for a Mason Bogie that had been demolished in a collision. The Iron Railroad's equipment had never left that property and always bore the original initials and numbers.

The judicial decree of January 1885 stipulated that the Little Giant could keep in service no more than 16 locomotives, 450 freight cars, 11 passenger cars, and the 11 cabooses. In compliance the receiver turned over 12 engines and more than 650 cars to George Ballou the same month. Ballou leased the 4.3-mile Shane's Crossing Branch and stored his cars there. A group of 14 locomotives and several hundred cars owned by the American Loan & Trust Company were laid up at Delphos pending their resale. This left the receiver with the five engines he had personally leased from Brooks, two owned outright by the TC&StL, five leased from Clark, Post & Martin, and nine Mason and Hinkley engines rented from Elijah Phillips.

The depression winter of 1884-1885 found most of the narrow-gauge railroaders of Delphos leading a wretched hand-to-mouth existence. Many headed south when word came that the Florida Southern narrow gauge was hiring men. Those who stayed behind and were fortunate enough to stand for jobs were paid in receiver's certificates in lieu of cash. At best these could be redeemed at the rate of 35 to 50 cents on the dollar. Delphos merchants were forced to "carry" the railroad men for months at a time. The Little Giant was all but defunct and in such a sorry state of deterioration that men who accepted a call assumed a terrible risk. The timbers of the Auglaize River bridge at Dupont were so badly rotted out that the road did not dare to run even the lightest engines across it. Mixed trains out of Delphos and Toledo exchanged loaded cars at the bridge one at a time, using empty cars as idlers.

At the insistence of the bondholders, Gen. John McNulta replaced Craig as receiver in July 1885, and the affairs of the TC&StL quickly took a turn for the better. For the first time in more than two years the employees were paid in cash. Repairs were made to the Dupont bridge and the road began moving wheat to Toledo at the rate of 30 to 40 carloads a day. On August 9 McNulta was permitted

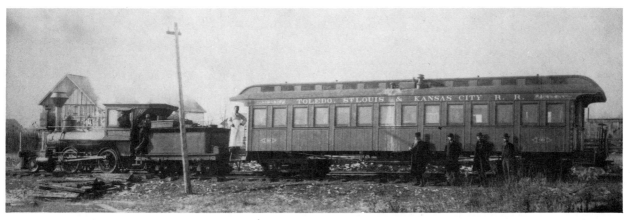

Pay car 99 pauses at Dupont, O., March 30, 1887. TStL&KC 2-4-0 No. 1 was built by Porter in 1879 for Frankfort & State Line. Some standard-gauge ties are in place but narrow-gauge iron has yet to be replaced. — *Collection of Sylvan R. Wood.*

to restore the Toledo-Delphos accommodation trains and later the same month a passenger run was also put on between Frankfort and Bluffton.

In October 1885 James Quigley announced that the bondholders had perfected a plan of reorganization and intended to start reconstructing the road east of Frankfort in the spring of 1886. He estimated that the cost of converting the easterly 206 miles of road to standard gauge would amount to more than 3 million dollars. While 87 miles of existing 50-pound steel rails could support standard-gauge locomotives and ladings, 119 miles of light iron would have to be replaced with new steel rail. More than 600,000 new ties were needed and nearly every bridge would have to be completely rebuilt. The width of the right of way was to be increased from as little as 30 feet to as much as 100 feet. The worst curves would have to be ironed out, sags had to be filled in, and the grade substantially built up and ballasted.

RESCUED FROM THE WRECKERS

Despite their optimistic facade, Quigley and the other bondholders were in no position to raise the money needed to pay off the judgment creditors, much less rebuild the narrow gauge. They had little hope of gaining the support of Eastern capitalists and bankers, especially in the light of the notoriety that had attended the Little Giant's collapse and its consistent inability to earn expenses. Even as Quigley talked about reconstruction, the TC&StL bonds were commanding as little as 3 per cent of par on the market. Bad times and the seemingly endless parade of lawsuits arising out of old obligations foiled several attempts to unload the property on some other railroad. Elsewhere, the Denver & Rio Grande and the Texas & St. Louis had also slipped into receivership, and trade journals were writing the obituary of the narrow-gauge era.

On December 30, 1885, the Toledo-East St. Louis line was sold under foreclosure at Indianapolis for $1,501,000 — $135,000 in cash and the balance in the par value of bonds held by the Quigley faction. The cash outlay was required to pay court costs and certain obligations of the receiver. Quigley's financial position was so desperate that he was personally unable to raise even a fraction of the amount. For weeks prior to the forced sale he had been making futile attempts to borrow the money from New York bankers. At the eleventh hour, with the spectre of abandonment hanging over the narrow gauge, Quigley managed to enlist the aid of Sylvester H. Kneeland, an adroit New York speculator. Kneeland had gained prominence, if not success, as Jay Gould's resourceful arch-opponent during the latter's 1881-1884 campaign to gain control of New York's elevated railways.

Kneeland came to Quigley's rescue with the understanding that the junior securities of the TC&StL would be wiped out and the bondholders would forfeit their prior lien and accept preferred stock in the reorganized company. For his part Kneeland agreed to pay off the creditors and reconstruct the road. He was to raise the necessary money by selling the new company's bonds and was to realize a commission based on the amount he could secure for them. As a further consideration for his services, Kneeland was to receive 1 million dollars' worth of preferred stock and all of the new company's common stock at the rate of $25,000 per mile. Unknown to the TC&StL bondholders, the two men made a clandestine contract under which Quigley was to receive half of Kneeland's profits.

After the bondholders consented to take stock in exchange for the all but worthless bonds, there still remained the paramount task of raising several million dollars to pay off the Little Giant's legion of creditors and the more than 9 million needed to rebuild the road. Without having anticipated it,

Boiler explosion demolished Rhode Island 4-6-0 No. 58 while it was switching Nickel Plate interchange at Continental on July 17, 1902. — *Collection of John H. Keller.*

Rhode Island 4-4-0 12 poses on 18-degree 50-minute curve at Delphos depot sometime after June 27, 1887, date she worked first standard-gauge passenger train between Delphos and Toledo. — *Collection of Willis A. McCaleb.*

Kneeland and Quigley were suddenly blessed with an incredibly well-timed stroke of good fortune. Just as it had saved Brice's Lake Erie & Western, the Karg well completely altered the destiny of the moribund TC&StL. In February 1886, a few weeks after the great gas well was brought in at Findlay, gas was also discovered near Delphos. By the end of that year gas and oil had been found in vast quantities at many points between Toledo and Frankfort. Toledo soon became "the glass capital of the world," while booming Marion portrayed itself as "the queen city of the gas belt." Kokomo also enjoyed spectacular growth as a manufacturing center. As far as Kneeland and Quigley were concerned, the most important effect of the gas boom was the receptive market it created for the securities they had to sell.

The formal reorganization of the Toledo, Cincinnati & St. Louis was affected in two steps. First, the portions of the road in Ohio, Indiana, and Illinois were conveyed to three new companies, the Toledo, Dupont & Western; Bluffton, Kokomo & Southwestern; and the Toledo, Charleston & St. Louis, respectively. Then, on June 12, 1886, these

companies were consolidated to form the Toledo, St. Louis & Kansas City Railroad. In recognition of its extraordinary good luck, the new company adopted as its emblem a white clover with three leaves, each bearing the name of one of the states the road served. First called the Kansas City Route or simply the KC, the TStL&KC came to be known universally as the Clover Leaf Route.

WIDENING THE GAUGE

Within a year after the reorganization Kneeland had been able to sell more than 3 million dollars' worth of first-mortgage bonds at 95. The bulk of these were taken by Phil Armour, the Chicago meat packer, and his brother Herman, a New York capitalist. By October 1886 six construction trains were in service between Frankfort and Toledo, and more than 600 men were employed spiking 61.5-pound steel to new white oak crossties. There was still a distance of only 3 feet separating the rails, but spikes were driven at the outer ends of the ties so that one set of rails could be quickly moved when the time came to widen the gauge.

Priority was given to rebuilding the many trestles

147

Second No. 1 of TStL&KC was one of two six-coupled switchers purchased in 1891 from South Chicago Dock Company. Engine's builder and vintage are unknown, but domes resemble handiwork of Pennsy's Altoona shop. One-Spot was assigned to Toledo yard duty and retired in 1898. — *Collection of Roy W. Carlson.*

and the work of erecting new iron bridges spanning the Maumee at Grand Rapids, Wildcat Creek near Kokomo, the Wabash River at Bluffton, and the Auglaize at Dupont. However, the new bridges came too late to avoid a pair of tragic accidents. In July 1886 the condemned bridge at Bluffton collapsed under the weight of engine 24, a Baldwin 2-8-0, killing the engineer, head brakeman, fireman, and a student fireman. Five months later, two more enginemen died when the 94, a Brooks Mogul, went through a bridge near Frankfort.

The last regular Clover Leaf narrow-gauge trains east of Frankfort were operated on June 25, 1887. At 5 a.m. the daily mail left Delphos for Frankfort and shortly thereafter the Toledo accommodation went east. The latter left Erie Street, Toledo, on its return run at 4 p.m. and got back to Delphos 4 hours later. The other train turned at Frankfort and arrived at Delphos at 9:30 p.m. At dawn on Sunday, June 26, construction trains steamed out of Delphos, Toledo, and Frankfort. More than 2000 men working in gangs of 40 undertook the work of changing the gauge to standard. Blessed with perfect weather, they had the entire job done by night-

fall. Test trains left Delphos at 4 p.m. and Frankfort at 7 p.m. and ran through to Toledo and Delphos respectively without incident. The next morning, the operation of the regular schedule was resumed.

The first standard-gauge engines on the Clover Leaf were cap-stacked 4-4-0's built by the Rhode Island Locomotive Works. These had 17 x 24-inch cylinders and a total engine weight of 47.5 tons. Engines 11 and 12, delivered with 68-inch drivers, were purchased to hold down the passenger schedule. The others, numbered 13-23, had 62-inch drivers and were assigned to freight and mixed trains. Jackson & Sharp's Delaware Car Works furnished the Clover Leaf its first standard-gauge passenger cars — five 62-passenger coaches, five baggage cars.

The first scheduled standard-gauge passenger train left Delphos for Frankfort at 5 a.m. on June 27, 1887. Engineer Sam Hersey at the throttle of engine 11 and Conductor Volney Rhines drew the coveted assignment. Thirty minutes later engine No. 12 steamed out of Delphos for Toledo in the charge of Tom Campbell, engineer, and Jake Henry, conductor. The old narrow-gauge schedule was used until late 1887 when through Frankfort-Toledo trains

Hinkley built this 26-ton 2-6-0 in 1883 for the TC&StL. She is shown here as TStL&KC 16 at Charleston, Ill., around 1889. For a brief period there was some overlapping of narrow-gauge and standard-gauge engine numbers. This engine and her four sisters ended their days as standard-gauge yard goats. — *Collection of John A. Rehor.*

were added. New No. 1 left Toledo at 7 a.m. and arrived in Frankfort 8½ hours later. The eastbound, No. 2, was scheduled out of Frankfort at 12:15 p.m. and into Toledo at 8:30 p.m. Upon arriving at Frankfort, Clover Leaf passengers could take the Vandalia Line to Terre Haute and St. Louis or the LE&W to Bloomington. The traveler wishing to ride the narrow-gauge mixed train to Charleston had 16 hours to see the sights of Frankfort. The entire 245-mile trip to East St. Louis consumed more than 36 hours including a 12-hour layover at Charleston.

The work of rebuilding the Clover Leaf west of Frankfort was started in 1887 with the goal of run-

ning standard-gauge trains into St. Louis by the end of 1888. However, this was a far more difficult and expensive proposition than the reconstruction of the eastern half of the road. West of Charleston the narrow gauge could be best described as a succession of hogbacks, sags, and trestles. In fact, there were 11 miles of timber bridges between Frankfort and East St. Louis.

Toward the end of June 1888, the gauge of the 61 miles of track between Frankfort and Eugene Junction (Cayuga) was changed to standard. Two months later the remaining 52 miles to Charleston was similarly altered. Severe weather during the

Converted narrow-gauge Mogul 91 toiled in Delphos yard for several years after rebuilding in 1889. Sister engines replaced mules used in Toledo yard after end of narrow-gauge operations. Brooks goat apparently ended up in some type of stationary service. — *Collection of John H. Keller.*

winter of 1888-1889 hampered work on the 132-mile Charleston-East St. Louis section and it was not until May 31, 1889, that the Clover Leaf operated its last narrow-gauge train. At 7 o'clock the next evening the work of widening the gauge was completed, and on June 2 mixed train service was restored between Charleston and East St. Louis.

In July 1888 the Delphos shop began rebuilding the first of about 20 narrow-gauge locomotives, and in the fall turned out a pair of Mason 2-4-6T Bogies for passenger service and a Baldwin 2-8-0 for freight duty. Before the end of 1888 the shops started converting the five Brooks Moguls to 0-6-0 yard engines. During 1889 and 1890 11 Hinkley 2-6-0's and Forneys were rebuilt as yard goats and renumbered 100-110. Judging by contemporary accounts, some of these were rather ridiculous-looking machines. One of the rebuilds that labored in Delphos yard was rudely described by the local newspaper as "old flint-lock, not a sweet bird at all."

Samuel R. Callaway, president of the Clover Leaf since September 1887, announced that the road would begin running its trains into the Union Station at St. Louis on July 4, 1889, using the Eads Bridge and tracks of the Terminal Railroad Association. Since May 13 the TStL&KC had been running into Toledo's union depot, reached by rights over about 2000 feet of the Lake Shore & Michigan Southern main line. Callaway also talked about putting on through Pullman trains between Detroit and Kansas City, but more than a year elapsed before the Clover Leaf began running through trains between Toledo and St. Louis, much less beyond those cities. Despite the fact that Kneeland had sold bonds worth 9 million dollars, he had run out of money and the last 15 miles of track between Glen Carbon and East St. Louis was still laid with badly worn 40-pound iron. Substantial portions of the road west of Frankfort were still unballasted and hardly safe to run fast passenger trains over.

In May 1890 Callaway went to New York and arranged the purchase of 1500 tons of steel rails, enough to relay the track into East St. Louis. Although ballasting and other heavy work still remained to be done, the new rails were all in place by August. On the 14th of that month Engineer P. A. Eich made a high-speed test run from Delphos to East St. Louis with engine No. 3, one of the con-

Clover Leaf freights were ruled by Rhode Island hogs prior to 1905. Class E 4-6-0 No. 38 and crew pose at Delphos in 1893. — *Collection of John H. Keller.*

Package steamers chartered by Clover Leaf Steamboat Line plied waters of Lake Erie between April and December. Propeller *Roanoke* was damaged by fire on first Clover Leaf trip. Steamers provided direct connection at Buffalo with Lackawanna, Lehigh Valley, and other Eastern roads. — *Collection of Rev. Edward J. Dowling, S.J.*

verted Mason Bogies. Finally, on August 31 the Clover Leaf extended the runs of its express passenger trains beyond Frankfort to St. Louis. These left St. Louis and Toledo in the early morning and arrived at the opposite termini in the early evening. On May 3, 1891, the day trains were augmented by a pair of overnight express runs equipped with Wagner combination buffet-sleeping cars.

Freight revenues were practically doubled after the standard-gauge operation was extended to East St. Louis. The tonnage of grain and cotton moving east was so heavy that at times the road ran as many as nine or ten eastbound freight trains a day. The preponderance of this traffic was routed to the Nickel Plate at Continental, and by January 1890 the volume of interchange at that point had outstripped the Nickel Plate's capacity to handle it. At times, for miles on each side of Continental every Clover Leaf siding was jammed with loaded eastbound cars.

About 1891 the Clover Leaf began running scheduled livestock and meat trains out of East St. Louis. Limited to from 20 to 25 loaded cars, these trains were powered by 54-ton Rhode Island 4-6-0's, the standard Clover Leaf freight locomotive prior to 1905. The first of these 18 x 24-inch cylindered, 54-inch drivered Ten-Wheelers, numbered 27-29, were acquired in October 1888. By the spring of 1890 the road had added 13 similar engines, numbered 35-50, to its roster. Between 1891 and 1893 Rhode

Island built 25 more 4-6-0's for the Clover Leaf. Engines 51-61 and 66-70 were identical to the earlier models, but the 62-65 and 71-75 had 19 x 24-inch cylinders and 56-inch drivers.

In order to compete with the Wabash the early Clover Leaf manifest schedules had to be fast. With all opposing trains headed into the sidings, the Ten-Wheelers could make surprisingly good time across the roller-coaster profile of the erstwhile narrow gauge. One of the fastest runners in Clover Leaf history, Charley Waldo, set the pace for the manifests in 1892. In a test run with 4-6-0 No. 56, Waldo rolled 25 livestock loads over the 132 miles between Frankfort and Delphos in 5 hours 25 minutes.

The Clover Leaf Steamboat Line was organized on April 11, 1890, as a means of giving the TStL&KC direct access to Eastern railroads terminating at Buffalo. Two propeller-driven package steamers were chartered each season from 1890 to 1901. The first vessels used were the *Dean Richmond** and *Roanoke*, the latter replaced by the *Osceola* after it was damaged by fire on its first trip. In later years the Clover Leaf line also used the *John Pridgeon, Jr.*, *B. W. Blanchard*, *A. A. Parker*, *Norwalk*, *J. S. Richards*, and the *Flint & Pere Marquette No. 5.*

---

*The *Dean Richmond* sank off Barcelona, N. Y., during a wild Lake Erie gale on the night of October 14-15, 1893. Her master and all 18 hands were lost. At the time the ship was hauling Clover Leaf cargo from Toledo to Buffalo.

Much to the chagrin of Delphos the Clover Leaf tried mightily to forsake its birthplace. In the interval of January 24, 1886, to January 23, 1887, the road used Decatur (Ind.) as a division point instead of Delphos. Decatur was practically midway between Frankfort and Toledo, whereas Delphos was 133 miles east of Frankfort and only 73 miles west of Toledo. In 1886 the TStL&KC surveyed a 36-mile cutoff line between Dupont and Decatur which would have reduced the distance between those points by 13 miles and eliminated 48 curves. Since Delphos was the home of most of the operating employees on the east end and the location of the only engine terminal east of Charleston, the cutoff was never built.

The Clover Leaf sought a more centralized location for a new set of repair shops. The cities of Marion and Frankfort voted in May 1889 to subsidize their construction. The road was still trying to collect much of the money that Marion had pledged to the old Toledo, Delphos & Burlington and chose Frankfort as the site of its new facilities. Frankfort had promised to donate $57,000, free land, and free natural gas to the railroad. However, the Clover Leaf ran into a lot of difficulty trying to collect the municipal grant and its subsidy ultimately came from a private enterprise. The Frankfort Improvement Company — formed by 29 citizens of the town — purchased 100 acres of land, 20 of which were leased to the railroad and the rest platted as a real estate addition. From the sale of parcels in the addition the Improvement Company was able to raise an $80,000 contribution that assured the construction of the shops.

Four brick locomotive shop buildings, a 231 x 30-foot car repair shop, and a 12-stall roundhouse were completed at Frankfort in June 1892. Elsewhere, a six-stall roundhouse had been built in 1889 at MC Junction, the Michigan Central connection 2 miles southwest of the Erie Street terminus at Toledo. New roundhouses were also built at Charleston and Madison in 1890 and 1893. The Madison terminal was located near the connection with the Terminal Railroad Association's new Merchant's Bridge line, 3½ miles east of the Front Street freighthouse in East St. Louis.

The loss of the locomotive shops to Frankfort was a bitter pill for Delphos to swallow. With the supply of hardwood timber nearly exhausted, most of the woodworking factories had been closed, and the loss of the Delphos shop payroll would have been a calamity. In addition to making all repairs to the standard-gauge engines, Delphos shop had been busy altering narrow-gauge locomotives. However, in 1890 the Clover Leaf mollified the vexed city fathers by making a contract with the New York Equipment Company to repair second-hand locomotives it had sold to Western roads. In October of that year the first large group of such engines arrived at Delphos. These were 23 New York Central engines en route to the Mexican government. At times during the 1890's there were as many as 30 foreign locomotives awaiting overhaul at the shops.

THE SECOND BANKRUPTCY

One of the first railroads to go under during the financial storm of 1893 was the Clover Leaf. Despite a growing volume of business the road had been in trouble for several years. Sylvester Kneeland had failed to pay off many of the old TC&StL debts, and the number of judgment creditors increased with each passing year. During the summer of 1891 they nearly succeeded in throwing the Clover Leaf into receivership. The road was unable to pay its Illinois taxes in 1892, and on May 19, 1893, President Callaway was appointed receiver by the circuit court at Cleveland.*

The Clover Leaf receivership quickly developed into a four-cornered free-for-all between Kneeland, who held all the common stock and was, in effect, the management; the preferred stockholders led by Quigley; the judgment creditors; and the Armour brothers and other bondholders. Quigley and Kneeland had broken up their illicit partnership in 1887 and had been at odds ever since. Kneeland had wanted the road to issue a second mortgage as a means of retiring the old debts, while Quigley was outspokenly unhappy with the high cost and slow progress of the reconstruction. Creditors wanted the road sold to satisfy the judgments they held, whereas the bondholders wanted only to wipe out everyone's equity but their own.

One of the more celebrated railroad bankruptcies of the 1890's, the case was tried before the United States District Court at Toledo. The trial judge was William Howard Taft, who later became 27th President of the United States and Chief Justice of the Supreme Court. In a desperate bid to upset the validity of the first mortgage, the preferred stockholders retained ex-President Benjamin Harrison as their trial counsel. Citing the 1887 Nickel Plate case, Harrison charged that the Quigley-Kneeland relationship violated the Ohio law that forbade the sale of bonds to directors at less than par.

The battle dragged on through the mid-1890's. In September 1897 Taft condemned the "vicious and corrupt" arrangement between Quigley and Kneeland but refused to throw out the mortgage.

*Callaway held this post until January 1895. Subsequently he served as the president of the Nickel Plate, LS&MS, New York Central, and the American Locomotive Company.

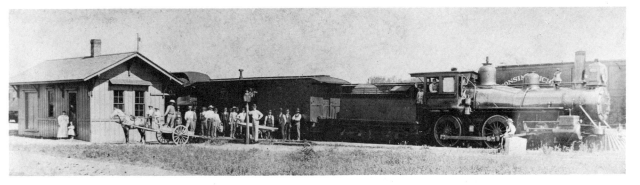

Most of the population of Fillmore, Ill., is present to greet late-afternoon arrival of westbound day train on September 23, 1892. On the head end is 4-4-0 No. 20, one of the original Rhode Islands of 1887. Depot is still in use. — TRAINS *collection.*

Seven months later the jurist ordered the Clover Leaf sold under foreclosure. In other courts the company was fighting creditors, trying to collect old grants from Indiana cities and the insurance carried on the ill-fated *Dean Richmond* and its cargo. The road had refused to join the railroad rate associations and had undercut the rates of its competitors. As a result the Clover Leaf was regularly boycotted by its connections.

Rumors concerning the fate of the Clover Leaf were as prevalent as ever. In the early 1890's it had been alternately the Michigan Central, Missouri Pacific, and the Grand Trunk that were to have absorbed the hapless TStL&KC. In 1897 J. Pierpont Morgan was reputedly manipulating a deal to add the road to the Vanderbilt holdings. Toward the end of that same year, Collis P. Huntington of the Southern Pacific publicly denied that he was attempting to buy the Clover Leaf. In the spring of 1899 John D. Rockefeller was supposed to have been after the road on behalf of the Missouri, Kansas & Texas. A few months later the weary Clover Leaf bondholders let it be known that they wished the Erie or some other road would buy them out.

Original Clover Leaf depots were plain and well built, and contained a special fascination for small-town boys. Local agent tends depot at Glen Carbon, mining town 13 miles east of East St. Louis. — *Collection of C. L. Eyrse.*

153

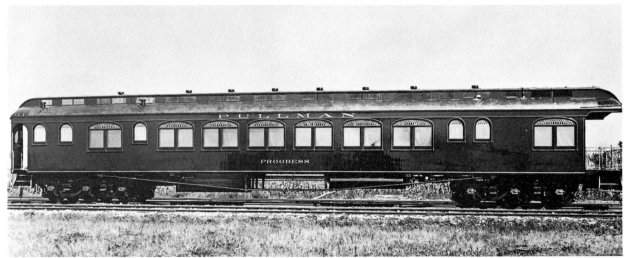

Pullman built 12-section observation–drawing room car *Progress* and a twin, the *Advance*, for the *Commercial Travelers* in 1901. Unique sleepers were still assigned to those trains as late as 1931. — *Collection of Arthur D. Dubin.*

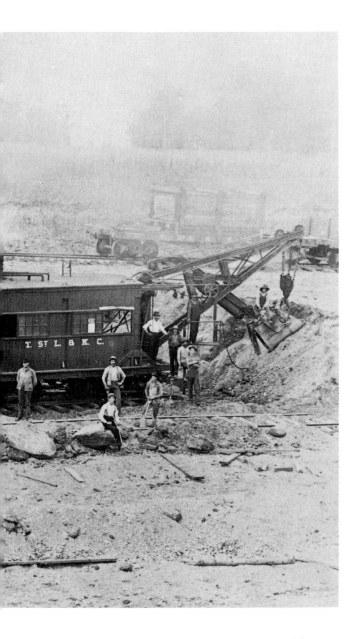

On March 27, 1900, the TStL&KC was sold to its bondholders for 12.2 million dollars. A new company, the Toledo, St. Louis & Western Railroad, was incorporated on July 9, 1900, and formally took over the property on the 31st of that month. Under the reorganization, holders of the old bonds received new 4 per cent bonds, and a syndicate of conservative New York bankers took a new 6.5-million-dollar issue of prior lien bonds. These men assumed control of the road and placed it in the hands of Benjamin Norton, former general manager of the Long Island Rail Road. Provision was made for the TStL&KC stockholders, but they were heavily assessed. The preferred holders (the old TC&StL bondholders) were forced to pay a 20 per cent assessment to save their equity. Assuming that Sylvester Kneeland still held all of the common stock, his share of the assessment amounted to $1,320,000.

The money raised through the sale of the new

bonds and the stock assessment was used in part to pay off the creditors, court costs, back wages, and obligations incurred by the three receivers. The surplus was used to buy new equipment and to renovate the railroad, which had suffered badly during the seven-year receivership. The Clover Leaf reorganization was unique in that the new company had considerably higher fixed charges than its insolvent predecessor. However, it was generally conceded by financial observers that the TStL&W would make a better showing than the old company, especially since times were good.

The Norton management lost little time in upgrading the Clover Leaf. During the first year they had the road, more than 55 miles of track were relaid with new 70-pound steel, and 60 miles of road were ballasted with gravel from the company's pits at Silverwood, Ind. New brick depots were built at Frankfort, Charleston, Kokomo, and Clark's Hill, and all the frame stations on the road received repair and paint. Seven new coaling stations, a like number of water tanks, and five interlocking plants were installed. The roundhouse and shops at Frankfort were extensively enlarged. As for trestles, 133 were rebuilt, strengthened, or filled. Although the Clover Leaf's earnings did not measure up to expectations, the new management did end up the first year with a small surplus.

THE COMMERCIAL TRAVELERS

In anticipation of the opening of the Pan-American Exposition at Buffalo on May 1, 1901, Norton decided to upgrade the overnight trains, 5 and 6, and give them names. In December 1900 American Car & Foundry's St. Charles works turned out three new vestibuled cars for each train — combination mail-and-smoker cars; 78-foot, 46-chair buffet cars; and standard 72-passenger coaches. Pullman also furnished a pair of new 12-section observation-drawing room sleepers, named *Advance* and *Progress*, for the trains. The five-car consist of each train was filled out by one of the road's older chair cars. In January 1901 Clover Leaf adopted the name *Commercial Traveler* for its refurbished night trains.

On April 28, 1901, new schedules were published which cut the running time of the eastbound *Commercial Traveler* to 12 hours 39 minutes, while No. 5's time was trimmed to just under 13 hours. The improved schedules were made possible by cutting out five regular and six flag stops between Ramsey and St. Louis through the addition of a pair of new

Commercial Travelers were first powered by Baldwin Ten-Wheelers 40-43 built in 1901. They were first Clover Leaf engines with carbon-arc headlights. After 1904, high-stepping saturated Atlantics handled *Commercial Travelers* east of Frankfort. Clover Leaf adopted the Pennsy system of locomotive classification about 1908, and thereafter the Brooks-built Nos. 44 and 45 (below) bore classification E-3. — *Upper photo, collection of H. L. Broadbelt; lower photo, Schenectady History Center.*

accommodation trains between those points. To power the *Commercial Travelers*, the Clover Leaf purchased four new class E-3 Ten-Wheelers from Baldwin which were delivered in March and May 1901. The new 61-ton passenger engines came from the builder with carbon-arc headlights, 68-inch drivers, and 19 x 24-inch cylinders. Trains 3 and 4, the daytime express runs, were also upgraded and were assigned a trio of 4-6-0's purchased from the Richmond (Va.) Locomotive Works in February 1901 and numbered 109-111. The Richmonds had 19 x 24-inch cylinders and 62-inch drivers.

The *Commercial Traveler* departed from St. Louis within an hour after the arrival of fast Missouri Pacific and Burlington trains out of Kansas City. The westbound run also made excellent connections with these roads as well as the Frisco, Cotton Belt, and the MK&T. During the Pan-American, however, Clover Leaf trains were timed to provide the best possible accommodations at Toledo. Train No. 4,

the daytime *Exposition Special*, arrived at that city shortly before the departure of LS&MS 22, the eastbound *Lake Shore Limited*, while the Frankfort-Toledo mail, No. 2, connected with Lake Shore 6, the *Fast Mail Limited*. The eastbound *Commercial Traveler* reached Toledo in time to make an excellent connection with the LS&MS, but more than likely its Buffalo-bound passengers elected to take the less-expensive combination steamship trip. A Detroit & Cleveland Navigation side-wheeler left Toledo 40 minutes after the arrival of No. 6, made a dinner stop at Put-in-Bay, and arrived in Cleveland in time for supper. A Cleveland & Buffalo Transit steamer made a connecting overnight run to Buffalo.

The *Commercial Travelers* were well patronized and soon became famous throughout the Midwest. In the spring of 1904, just before the World's Fair opened in St. Louis, the trains got another face lifting. Barney & Smith sold the Clover Leaf two new smokers, a pair of 86-passenger day coaches, and another buffet-chair car for the trains. With the *Commercial Travelers* expanded to six or more cars, the Clover Leaf also bought a pair of handsome 4-4-2's to handle them east of Frankfort. These Atlantics were built by Brooks in March 1904 and numbered 44 and 45. The 75-ton class C's were heavier than any other locomotives then on the Clover Leaf roster, and with their 73-inch drivers and 19 x 26-inch piston valve cylinders they could easily outperform the 1901 Baldwins in level country. Nevertheless, the 4-6-0's continued to power the *Commercial Travelers* west of Frankfort.

The Clover Leaf's arch-competitor, the Wabash, went all-out for the St. Louis Fair and operated its trains directly to the fairgrounds. Wabash No. 3, the overnight train from Toledo to St. Louis, was charted to cover its 449-mile run by way of Montpelier in 14 hours. The westbound *Commercial Traveler* left Toledo at 5:50 p.m., 20 minutes after the Wabash train, and made its 454-mile journey in 13 hours 50 minutes. However, the Clover Leaf never seriously attempted to compete against the Wabash fleet of daylight trains. During the Pan-American and the Ohio Centennial Exposition at Toledo in 1902, trains 3 and 4 operated on 14- and 15-hour schedules, but in later years they reverted to long-haul local passenger runs. During several slack periods these trains were not operated east of Delphos, and in April 1918 they were permanently cut back from St. Louis to Charleston. This left only the *Commercial Travelers* running the full length of the railroad. For a half century these nocturnal Clover Leaf flyers plied their trade between Toledo and St. Louis, meeting in the dead of night somewhere be-

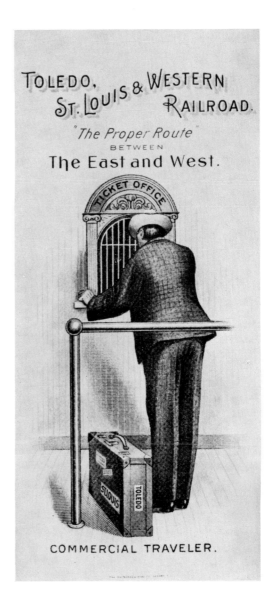

Souvenirs advertised Clover Leaf's popular night trains, the *Commercial Travelers*.

tween Frankfort and the Wabash River crossing.

In contrast with the Lake Erie & Western and most of the other steam railroads in Ohio and Indiana, the maverick Clover Leaf got along famously with the interurbans. Lacking branch-line feeders of its own, the TStL&W filed joint passenger tariffs with a number of traction lines and capitalized on their low fares. Shortly after the Lake Shore Electric opened through service between Cleveland and Toledo, it began selling interline tickets to points on the Clover Leaf. During the summer of 1904 this interurban sold more than 2000 round trip fares to St. Louis from Cleveland alone. The Indianapolis & Northwestern also fed a horde of fair-bound passengers to the Clover Leaf. The I&NW maintained a station at Frankfort directly across the tracks from the TStL&W depot.

In January 1905 the Dayton & Troy Electric inaugurated its *Clover Leaf Special*, a daily run between Dayton and Delphos by way of Troy, Piqua, Wapakoneta, and Lima. The *Clover Leaf Special* left Dayton each afternoon at 5:18 and covered the 95 miles to Delphos in 2 hours 34 minutes. This was then the fastest long-distance interurban run in the United States. Connection was made with Clover Leaf trains 4 and 5. Reservations for Pullman space on the latter could be secured in advance at any station on the interurban route. One of the attractions was the savings of 1 dollar on all-steam coach rate between Dayton and St. Louis.

In competition with the *Clover Leaf Special*, the *Interstate Limited* of the Dayton & Western Traction left Dayton at 5:55 p.m. for Indianapolis, where connection was made with an I&NW car due into Frankfort at 11:10 p.m., ahead of the *Commercial Traveler*. Three hours after the departure of the *Interstate Limited*, the Pennsylvania ran a train out of Dayton which arrived at St. Louis 1 hour ahead of the *Commercial Traveler*. However, the 390-mile Clover Leaf-interurban combination saved the traveler the sum of $1.40 on a first-class fare.

One of the memorable Midwestern institutions of the early 1900's was the Clover Leaf's interline excursion to Niagara Falls. The "Honeymoon Special" was an inexpensive and deliberately leisurely interlude in the harsh and lackluster life of rural and small-town folk. It was a popular accommodation in a day when 100 miles was still a long way from home and newlyweds were expected to send off a bundle of picture post cards at every stopoff. Sold anytime between April 1 and mid-November, the Niagara Falls excursion was a combination steamcar, steamboat, and traction adventure for two. Upon arriving at Toledo on the *Commercial Traveler* honeymooning couples rode the Summit & Broadway streetcar downtown and had several mid-

day hours to window-shop and dine before boarding a Lake Shore Electric limited for Cleveland. The 4½-hour interurban ride left ample time for an evening meal and sight-seeing at Cleveland as well as a streetcar ride to the Cuyahoga River berth of the *Seeandbee*. The great four-stack flagship of the Cleveland & Buffalo line departed at 8 p.m. on its overnight run to Buffalo. The last leg of the romantic journey was made in the cars of the International Railway Company.

THE GREEN YEARS

Like the Nickel Plate, the Clover Leaf originated a relatively small amount of freight tonnage and depended on overhead perishable and merchandise traffic to make ends meet. Despite gross physical deficiencies and the fact that it was up against the Wabash, one of the fastest freight haulers in the business, the road managed to gain a good share of the high-grade traffic moving through the St. Louis gateway.

By the mid-1890's the Clover Leaf was running two daily manifest freight trains to Toledo on 25- to 26-hour schedules. No. 40, the *Meat Special*, left Madison Yard about 8 or 9 in the morning, while No. 42, the livestock train, was called for a late afternoon departure. Seven miles out of Madison these trains hit Glen Carbon hill, the ruling eastbound grade. Here the 5-mile, .77 per cent climb out of the American Bottom limited the Rhode Island 4-6-0's to 700 tons. Farther east at Donnellson, 2½ miles of 1.55 per cent coupled with 10 curves could be negotiated without "doubling" only if the hogger had been able to get a fast roll down Sorento Hill. East of Charleston the Rhode Islands were rated at 850 tons, but required a helper engine to climb out of the Wabash valley at Silverwood.

The lone westbound manifest, No. 43, was probably one of the fastest freight trains of the 1890's. Designed to compete for redball tonnage coming off the LS&MS, Nickel Plate, and Erie, the *Merchandise Special* was scheduled to cover the serpentine 444-mile run from MC Junction to Madison in 20 hours 30 minutes. In this distance, the train had to traverse 323 curves and 496 ascending grades, cross more than 350 bridges, and change crews and engines three times. In addition, No. 43 had to make three intermediate stops for coal, replenish its engine's 4000-gallon water tank on as many as 16 or 17 other occasions, and make a score or more of positive stops at railroad grade crossings. In the interest of safety, Clover Leaf rules required that a train stopped to receive a 31 train order could not proceed until the conductor had first read and signed the order. When this rule was lived up to, the train was delayed for as long as it took the

Frankfort depots of Clover Leaf (right) and Indianapolis & Northwestern (left) were practically next door. The two companies worked hand in hand for years. The interurban was later operated as part of THI&E. — *Collection of C. L. Eyrse.*

Barney & Smith combination cars were standard Dayton & Troy Electric equipment on *Clover Leaf Special* of 1905. Dayton-Delphos limited service ended about 1906 when Lima Route interurbans put on through cars to Toledo. — *Collection of John H. Keller.*

LSE Brill combine crosses line of competitor LS&MS at Slate Cut between Huron and Sandusky in early 1900's. Interurban required 2 hours longer than steam road to get from Toledo to Cleveland but offered fare savings of almost 50 per cent. — *Collection of Willis A. McCaleb.*

Overnight run from Cleveland to Buffalo was specialty of 500-foot *See-andbee*, flagship of the Cleveland & Buffalo line. In this circa 1913 scene, she is in the process of clearing the Cuyahoga River at dusk. The 6381-ton liner accommodated 1500 passengers. — *Albert E. McCaleb.*

Open-side, bench-type trolleys traversed the Niagara Gorge in the days of the "Honeymoon Special." — *William L. Bennett.*

Multiple-unit International Railway trains connected Niagara Falls with Lake Erie steamers at Buffalo. Train heads east on Buffalo Avenue in Niagara Falls in August 1924. — *Corman E. Moore.*

Maid of the Mist is framed by Falls View International Bridge at Niagara Falls at the time of the Pan-American Exposition. Steel arch was destroyed by an ice jam in 1938. — *William L. Bennett.*

Coaling station at Van Buren was about midway between Delphos and Frankfort on second subdivision. Facility was built in 1906, retired in 1954. — *Collection of John H. Keller.*

conductor to walk from his caboose to the engine. Inferior trains had great difficulty in getting past any open office without having to stop for orders.

Since eastbound trains were superior by direction to westbound trains of the same class, No. 43 was carried in the timetable as a first-class train. This gave it right over all eastbound freight and mixed trains. Normally the train headed into sidings on only two instances — for passenger trains 4 and 6. West of Frankfort the *Merchandise Special* was restricted to about 600 tons due to two severe operational obstacles. Beginning at Cayuga where all freight trains stopped for coal and water, there was a 5.4-mile combination of ascending westbound grades up to 1.3 per cent and 13 curves. A helper engine coupled to the rear of westbound freights and pushed them up the hill, cutting off on the fly when they reached the summit just west of the Indiana-Illinois border. Much farther west there was the 1.57 per cent ascent out of The Hole to Sorento followed by the Devil's Eyebrow, 4 miles of reverse curves. Nonetheless, No. 43 had the railroad to itself all the way from Charleston to Madison, running just ahead of No. 5, the night express.

The amazing performance of the Clover Leaf fast freights was achieved by an elite corps of enginemen who surely must have had ice water in their veins. Men like Ed Eckenrode, Jack Bertolett, Sam Hawk,

Charley Waldo, and Morgan Muir built the Clover Leaf reputation for speed. Muir became a living legend after making a futile bid to save his mortally injured conductor by running an engine backward at breakneck speed all the way from Silverwood to Frankfort. At the throttle of the 107, one of the Rhode Island 19 x 24's, Muir made the tortuous 58-mile trip in 50 minutes. In this remarkable feat he set a speed record for that section that has never been equaled.

Following the 1900 reorganization, the growth of business dictated the purchase of heavier and more powerful freight locomotives. The first of these were the six class D-1 2-6-0's delivered by Baldwin in May 1901. These chunky 66-ton engines were bigger than the run-of-mine Mogul and with their 63-inch drivers they could do a creditable job of moving a fair-sized train over the road. East of Delphos the D-1's were rated at 1600 tons and on occasion they were known to horse as many as 75 cars across that relatively level part of the railroad. In February 1902 Baldwin shipped the Clover Leaf a pair of Consolidations, the 130 and 131. With 20 x 26-inch cylinders and 57-inch drivers, the 71-ton class F 2-8-0's developed 27,915 pounds rated tractive effort. Schenectady sold the road two similar engines in January 1904, the 132 and 133. These four 2-8-0's were the west end's maids of all work.

164

Old Maude, a 1901 Baldwin Mogul, held down Cayuga helper assignment for years. Here in 1916, No. 124 gets brief respite from hill wars by a stint on the Marion yard job. Engineer Herschel Johnson is under cab. — *Collection of Simon E. Herring.*

Consolidations were standard Clover Leaf freight power after 1905, the year Brooks turned out 30 models including the 180. Saturated H-6 had 21 x 28-inch cylinders, Stephenson link motion, 57-inch drivers. — *Schenectady History Center.*

G-10a 860 was one of five former Clover Leaf H-6 2-8-0's rebuilt at Frankfort in 1926 with superheaters, 22 x 28-inch piston valve cylinders, Baker valve gear, cast-steel pilot beams. The Brooks is shown at Bellevue on October 27, 1947. — *Clyde E. Helms.*

165

Heavier motive power required heavier rail. Thus, during the latter part of 1904 the TStL&W completed laying new 70-pound steel between Frankfort and MC Junction and began replacing the 61.5-pound rail west of Frankfort with new 75-pound section. During 1904 and 1905 the road purchased 40 new freight locomotives from Brooks and removed the last Rhode Islands from fast freight service. Ten of the new engines were class E-4 4-6-0's, Nos. 150-159, built in November 1904. Good for 1500 tons east of Frankfort, the 82-ton E-4's had 19½ x 30-inch cylinders and 63-inch drivers. The remaining 30 newcomers to the roster were 21 x 28-inch slide valve 2-8-0's delivered in 1905, 15 in February and 15 in December. The new Consolidations, Nos. 160-189, had 57-inch drivers. At 200 pounds boiler steam pressure they developed 36,800 pounds rated tractive effort and 1470 h.p. at the cylinders. The F-2's (later reclassed H-6) carried a west end hill tonnage rating of 1500, more than double that of the Rhode Islands. With a working order weight of 192,000 pounds, the Brooks hogs were 42 tons heavier than the Ten-Wheelers they displaced and more than treble the weight of the narrow-gauge Grant 2-8-0's of 1882. They had 7000-gallon tanks and could run as far as 40 to 45 miles in level country between water stops. With improved spacing of wayside tanks, as many as 8 to 10 water stops were eliminated on the through manifest runs.

In 1913 Baldwin outshopped five class H-7 Consolidations, Nos. 190-194, that were practically duplicates of the 1905 Brooks engines. They were followed by 15 Lima-built 2-8-0's, the 201-212 and 214-216.* Nos. 201-205, class H-8, were purchased in 1916; the others, classed H-9, were acquired in 1921 and 1922. The Limas were the only superheated engines on the Clover Leaf roster. They weighed slightly more than 100 tons, had 22 x 28-inch piston valve cylinders with Baker valve gear but were otherwise similar to the earlier 2-8-0's in dimension and appearance. In performance the Limas were excellent steamers, quite fast, and capable of handling about 300 tons more train than their "wetback" Brooks and Baldwin sisters.

Aggressive management between 1902 and 1907 more than doubled freight tonnage and revenues and produced a tidy surplus at the end of each year. For a brief period the Clover Leaf actually paid dividends on its preferred stock. More important, the road's reputation as a service route was firmly established. The eastbound manifests were built around shipments from the stockyards and packing

houses of the American Bottom and were filled out with overhead freight from the Missouri Pacific, Cotton Belt, and the Frisco. There were always four or five carloads of live poultry and a poultry caretaker's car bringing up the rear of No. 44 (old 42) as it left Madison. In the summer months it was common to have four or five solid trains of cantaloupe dispatched daily to the East. Most of this traffic and a good volume of citrus fruit tonnage came off the Missouri Pacific.

The Clover Leaf did a heavy interchange business at several points east of Madison. Two or three turns were operated daily from Charleston to the Chicago & Eastern Illinois connection at Mode, 37 miles to the west. A like number of runs were also dispatched daily to the Illinois Central at Neoga to gather up carloads of lumber, naval stores, sisal, and bananas. By 1908 1 million tons of bituminous coal accounted for one-third of the Clover Leaf's freight tonnage. Most of this was originated at mines at New Douglas, Coffeen, and Panama. Daily output of the deep-shaft Shoal Creek Mine at Panama in The Hole between Sorento and Donnellson ran as high as 90 carloads. About 40 per cent of the coal shipped from Panama was used to fire the Clover Leaf's locomotives.* One of the 1901 Baldwin 2-8-0's, the 130 or 131, was kept at Sorento to switch the Shoal Creek Mine. Each morning it would go to Panama with a coach loaded with 100 or more miners. From a dead stop at Panama depot in the bottom of The Hole, the Baldwins could fight their way to the top of Donnellson Hill with all of 16 loaded hoppers in dry weather. Double-heading with a Brooks 2-8-0 operated out of Charleston on a turn, they could manage 2200 tons up the hill.

The bulk of eastbound manifest traffic was delivered to the Erie at Ohio City, but most of the Clover Leaf's grain tonnage moved east over the Nickel Plate. The road's position with regard to traffic moving to and from Detroit and Canada was materially strengthened on September 8, 1903, with the opening of the Detroit & Toledo Shore Line Railroad. Owned jointly by the TStL&W and the Grand Trunk Western, the Shore Line extended 47 miles from Boulevard Junction on Toledo's north side to a junction with Wabash at Delray Tower near Detroit.

Incorporated on April 14, 1899, the D&TSL was the successor to the Pleasant Bay Railway of Michigan and the Toledo & Ottawa Beach Railway of Ohio. It was promoted by Henry A. Everett and Edward W. Moore as an interurban line intended to connect their Michigan traction lines with the

---

*Use of the number 13 was scrupulously avoided by the superstitious TStL&W management. After 1903 the road switched from the three-leaf to a four-leaf clover emblem and began calling itself "The Lucky Way."

*Shoal Creek "stone" burned hot but tended to clinker. Noted as the place where John L. Lewis got his start, this was the last active coal mine on the Clover Leaf. It was closed in the depression of the 1930's.

Prior to consolidation of 1923 Clover Leaf did a heavy interchange business with Erie at this point. Originally known as Enterprise, Ohio City grew around junction of TD&B and narrow-gauge predecessor of Cincinnati Northern (NYC). CN track crosses Clover Leaf at left, Erie at right. — *Clyde E. Helms.*

Lake Shore Electric. Construction of about 36 miles of road between Toledo and Trenton, Mich., was in an advanced stage in 1902 when Everett and Moore ran into acute financial difficulty. The Shore Line and other Everett-Moore properties were thrown into receivership. The promoters ultimately made a remarkable recovery, but not before they had unloaded the Shore Line on the TStL&W and the GTW. The steam roads guaranteed a new bond issue and completed the work of building the road.

Curiously, the D&TSL never had had a physical connection with either of the parent roads. The Grand Trunk was reached by trackage rights over 3.1 miles of the Wabash between Delray and West Detroit. Although the Shore Line and Clover Leaf were but 3 miles apart at Toledo, their tracks were separated by the downtown section, and it was necessary to use a long and circuitous route around Toledo to connect them. D&TSL trains reached MC Junction by means of 18.9 miles of trackage rights including 13.2 miles over the Toledo Railway & Terminal from Boulevard Junction to Copeland and the rest over TStL&W. From the time it was opened, the Shore Line was a freight-only operation.

THE ALTON FIASCO

In an ill-advised attempt to secure a larger share of overhead traffic moving through the Kansas City gateway, the Clover Leaf purchased a controlling 53.5 per cent interest in the 982-mile Chicago & Alton system on August 1, 1907. The price of the Alton stock, $11,527,000, was raised by issuing 10-year, 4 per cent collateral trust bonds. The interest on these bonds nearly doubled the Clover Leaf's fixed charges, a circumstance that ultimately brought about another long receivership.

Although there was a physical connection between the Alton and its new master at East St. Louis, the most direct routing for Kansas City traffic utilized 103 miles of the Cincinnati, Hamilton & Dayton (B&O) between the C&A at Springfield (Ill.) and the Clover Leaf at Metcalfe (Ill.). In 1910 the TStL&W secured trackage rights over this part of the CH&D but exercised them only briefly before the end of joint Clover Leaf-Alton operation in 1912. Normally about 35 to 40 carloads of meat moved daily to the Clover Leaf over this route.

Dividends on the Alton stock were paid at successively lower rates each year until after 1911 when

Westerly trestle approach to Wabash River bridge at Silverwood was swept away by floodwaters on several occasions, but in this 1913 photo Clover Leaf and borrowed C&EI pile drivers repair derailment damage. — *Collection of C. L. Eyrse.*

Saturated slide-valve switcher was outshopped by Baldwin in January 1921 but not delivered until December 1922 when the road emerged from receivership. Originally numbered 17, the B-12 was renumbered 717 in 1924. Old Clover Leaf number was restored in 1942. It became 317 at the time of this February 1947 photo in Kokomo.—*Malcolm D. McCarter.*

they were eliminated altogether. This resulted in a very serious drain on the Clover Leaf's earnings. During the fiscal year which ended June 30, 1915, the road ran up a deficit of more than $500,000. Apparently seeking some avenue of escape from the burden of the collateral bonds, the Clover Leaf refused to pay the interest due on them on August 1, 1914. At the time, the road had an unappropriated cash surplus of nearly 2.8 million dollars. Walter L. Ross, president of the company, was ap-

pointed receiver on October 22, 1914, and the stockholders immediately sued to have the bonds thrown out on the grounds that the Alton stock purchase was in violation of the Sherman Act. When the collateral bonds matured in 1917, the Clover Leaf denied liability for them but finally made an out-of-court settlement with their holders in December 1921. The Alton stock and cash were used to retire the bonds and more than 4 million dollars in accrued interest.

Daylight accommodation heads west a few miles out of Toledo. At the time of this photo, about 1921, No. 3 ran only as far west as Frankfort and was down to three cars. Rhode Island 4-4-0 on the point came to the road in 1887. — *Charles E. Fisher.*

The Toledo, St. Louis & Western receivership of more than eight years' duration was a strange episode, to say the least. Ross had followed a program of rigid economy and had abandoned the intensive program of upgrading the railroad embarked upon in 1900. A few major improvements were undertaken during the receivership, including the building of new steel bridges across the Wabash at Silverwood and the Maumee at Grand Rapids. However, there was an over-all deterioration of the physical plant which by 1918 had manifested itself in a slowing down of the train operation. Running time of the manifest freights had been increased to as much as 38 hours. New passenger cars had not been purchased since 1904 and the locomotive roster was hardly that of a first-class freight forwarder. On the other hand, the Clover Leaf's gross annual income had risen from 4.6 to 11.5 million dollars during the receivership. This remarkable showing was made in the face of a continuous decline in coal carloadings.

When the Van Sweringens approached Walter Ross in 1922 with an eye toward buying control of the Clover Leaf, the road's securities were not well thought of and were selling at depressed prices. However, the settlement with the collateral bondholders had brought the excellent financial condition of the Clover Leaf to light. There was no need for a reorganization since the company had continued to meet all of its financial obligations other than the collateral bond interest and had a corporate surplus of more than 7 million dollars. With the burdensome bonds retired, the road could prove to be a very lucrative property and the value of its stocks might be greatly inflated. This plus the fact that the Clover Leaf admirably complemented the Nickel Plate and Lake Erie & Western fast freight operation explains the willingness of the Van Sweringens to do business on Ross' terms.

The Terminal Tower is a tangible reminder of the Van Sweringen era. The Nickel Plate was the lofty skyscraper's first tenant. — *Collection of Terminal Tower Company.*

The Greater Nickel Plate

INSPIRED by Alfred H. Smith and the powerful coterie of bankers that had rallied behind them, the Van Sweringens continued to exploit the power vacuum that existed in Eastern railroading after the advent of the Transportation Act. Even before they had consummated the consolidation of the Nickel Plate, Lake Erie & Western, and the Clover Leaf, the brothers were hard at work attempting to expand their railroad holdings. Abnormal dependence on bridge traffic and a dearth of on-line sources of freight revenue were liabilities common to their three roads. The Vans sought to offset this weakness by acquiring complementary lines with an inverse ratio of originated tonnage. This desire for balance was characteristic of the Van Sweringen personality and was an important factor in the success the promoters had enjoyed.

The Chesapeake & Ohio

In 1920 Smith had suggested to O. P. that future Nickel Plate expansion ought to be aimed at the booming automotive centers of Michigan and the Pocahontas coal districts of West Virginia. The roads involved in Smith's thinking were the Pere Marquette and Chesapeake & Ohio, neither of which was affiliated with the three large Eastern systems. Despite the fact that the I.C.C.'s tentative plan had built consolidated systems around both the PM and C&O, the Vans had begun a campaign to gain control of both roads prior to the perfection of the 1923 Nickel Plate consolidation. A 1921 effort to gain a PM foothold was repulsed, but the determined Clevelanders had little difficulty in the case of the Chesapeake & Ohio.

The Chesapeake & Ohio in 1922 embraced 2558 miles of lines extending principally from the Virginia tidewater at Hampton Roads to Cincinnati and Chicago. The road was primarily a hauler of bituminous coal. This commodity accounted for more than 77 per cent of its total freight tonnage. A growing proportion of the C&O's coal traffic moved northward from West Virginia to the port of Toledo over the tracks of the Norfolk & Western and the Hocking Valley. The C&O held 80.35 per cent of the Hocking's stock and possessed restricted trackage rights over the N&W's Scioto Valley line between its own southern Ohio railhead and the HV near Columbus.

The C&O was not considered a particularly lucrative property in the early 1920's, even though its earnings had mushroomed as the union movement spread through the Pennsylvania and Ohio bituminous coal fields. The road's great dependence on coal and the lack of on-line markets for it were

171

Station at Celina, O., betrays NYC's influence over LE&W. A "two-door sedan" assigned to the local putters around layout of 30 years ago. Pleasant Grand Lake resort town was important stop on TC&StL narrow-gauge line between Toledo and Cincinnati. – *Clyde E. Helms.*

viewed as serious weaknesses. Many observers believed the C&O's prosperity was strictly a temporary condition. However, the westward migration of heavy industry to the Great Lakes basin augured well for the C&O's future. This, plus the fact that the road's common stock was selling for considerably less than par, created a situation made to order for the Van Sweringens and their bankers. In the face of an economic upturn and rising stock values, the C&O presented attractive speculative prospects.

Nominal control of the C&O was held by Henry E. Huntington and his wife through the ownership of about 12 per cent of the common stock. In November 1922 the Vans obtained an option on the Huntingtons' stock at par and the following January applied to the I.C.C. for permission to replace the Huntington directors with Nickel Plate men. In this instance the Van Sweringens were unable to secure their usual deferred payment terms, and they were too deeply in debt to borrow through another of their special-purpose corporations. Hence they turned to the Nickel Plate which had previously secured approval to raise more than 7 million dollars through the sale of 6 per cent second-mortgage bonds. During January 1923 the Vans' bankers sold most of the bonds, and on the 29th of that month the Nickel Plate purchased 70,000 Huntington shares for 5.6 million dollars. Vaness Company acquired the remaining 3000 shares at a cost of $1,700,600. Fearful of minority stockholder reaction if the road paid an amount greatly exceeding the current $72 bid price, the Vans had absorbed 20 per cent of the cost of the Nickel Plate's shares. The remainder of the bond proceeds was used to acquire 18,700 additional shares of C&O common on the open market shortly after the acquisition of the Huntington block.

THE FOUR-SYSTEM CONSOLIDATION PLAN

In permitting the Nickel Plate to control the C&O, the I.C.C. had indirectly rendered its own tentative consolidation plan obsolete. The significance of this development was not lost on the Van Sweringens, nor did they fail to capitalize on the opportunity it presented. Early in 1924 they advanced a plan under which the Nickel Plate, Pennsylvania, New York Central, and Baltimore & Ohio would acquire the bulk of the other railroads in Eastern territory, exclusive of New England. The four systems were to be more or less equals in terms of mileage operated,

net income, and coal tonnage hauled. The Van Sweringens' immediate objectives were to finish off the 1921 plan and clear the way for the prompt amalgamation of their properties, and at the same time, to gain greater stature within the railroad industry.

The timing of the Vans' big move was perfect and the four-system plan was well received by the I.C.C. The Commission as a body was seemingly pleased that someone within the railroad industry was taking the initiative in fulfilling the mandate of the Transportation Act. Surprisingly, there was a notable lack of opposition from the three large systems. Samuel Rea, the practical president of the Pennsylvania, actually endorsed the fundamental principle of the plan.

Prior to launching the four-system plan, the Van Sweringens secretly acquired large blocks of Pere Marquette and Erie Railroad stocks with money and credit realized through the 1923 consolidation. Through George F. Baker they picked up a 26 per cent interest in the 2500-mile Erie system, nu-

Reduced yard costs and round-the-clock utilization accompanied advent of heavy Lima 0-8-0's in mid-1920's. U-3b's 210-219 and U-3c's 220-229 were purchased in 1924 and 1925. C&O bought 20 similar engines during 1925-1926. — *John B. Allen.*

cleus of system No. 4 in the I.C.C.'s 1921 plan. As recently as 1920 the Erie had been on the brink of bankruptcy and was widely considered to be in need of reorganization. Since 1901 dividends had been passed, and the great bulk of earnings had been expended in an enormous improvement program. The Erie, however, was handicapped in that it had but one western terminus, Chicago, and its 998-mile main stem was the least direct rail route between that city and New York. West of Youngstown there was very little on-line industrial activity and a great deal of excess capacity.

Early in 1924 the Vans again turned their attention to the Pere Marquette, buying one-third of that company's common stock through the use of fictitiously named accounts. The PM had been another weak sister and its 2262-mile system embraced a number of unproductive Michigan branch lines. Like the Erie, the PM competed with the Nickel Plate, operating a 583-mile line between Chicago and the Niagara frontier by way of Detroit and southern Ontario. The road also reached Toledo and operated carferries across Lake Michigan to Milwaukee and other Wisconsin points. Since the World War the growth of the automobile industry had grossly improved the PM's fortunes. In 1923 the road had paid 5 per cent on all classes of its stock and had retired all of its preferred dividend arrearages.

Just as the Van Sweringens were preparing to launch their four-system offensive, they lost their valued advisor and patron, Alfred Smith. The Central's president died in March 1924 after being thrown from a horse in New York's Central Park. The loss of the author of much of their success at this critical hour may have been one of the underlying causes of the Vans' initial and ultimately fatal reverse of fortune. At the time, though, the Vans were too far committed to pause even momentarily in their drive to build a fourth Eastern system. With their scheme endorsed by the bankers, tacitly approved by the I.C.C., and literally unopposed from any quarter, they appear to have thrown all caution to the four winds. First they decided to bring their designs on the Pere Marquette out into the open by transferring ownership of the PM stock to the Nickel Plate. This served to release a considerable amount of money which Vaness urgently needed elsewhere.

In the spring of 1924 the Nickel Plate realized 24.7 million dollars through the sale of high interest rate refunding mortgage bonds. A large part of this money was used to acquire 120,000 of the 150,000 shares of Pere Marquette held by Vaness as well as 66,300 additional shares of C&O common. The Nickel Plate thus held 19.88 per cent of

all C&O stock in line with the 1923 I.C.C. stipulation that it acquire not more than 20 per cent. During July 1924, however, Vaness began buying large blocks of C&O common and within one month secretly held a total of 174,832 shares. Combined with Nickel Plate holdings, this gave the Van Sweringens an arithmetical majority of this class of C&O stock.

After securing the approval of their bankers, the Vans initiated a series of conferences designed to work out the ultimate allocation of the Eastern railroads under the four-system plan. The first meeting was held on May 8, 1924, at the Pennsylvania's New York offices and was attended by Patrick E. Crowley, John Bernet, Samuel Rea, and Daniel Willard — respective presidents of the Central, Nickel Plate, Pennsylvania, and Baltimore & Ohio. Eight similar conferences were held during the course of the following summer. By July it was evident that the PRR was fighting to hold its own against what the press styled the "Triple Alliance."

From the very beginning the Pennsylvania and the other roads conceded that the Nickel Plate should absorb the C&O, HV, PM, and Erie. This was probably more than the Vans had ever hoped to win without a hard fight — at least it satisfied their immediate speculative needs. However, they apparently were carried away by this easy victory and demanded more. Bernet insisted that the Greater Nickel Plate system would have to include the Lackawanna, Bessemer & Lake Erie, Wheeling & Lake Erie, Virginian, Pittsburgh & Shawmut, and the Pittsburgh, Shawmut & Northern. In addition, Nickel Plate and the Central were to jointly acquire the Chicago & Eastern Illinois. Bernet's road was to have a part interest in the Delaware & Hudson, Pittsburgh & West Virginia, and six smaller roads. The B&O was to get the Reading, Central of New Jersey, Monon, and some other properties. New York Central's principal acquisitions were the Lehigh Valley and New York, Ontario & Western. For its part, the Pennsylvania was assigned the Norfolk & Western, the Chicago & Alton lines east of the Mississippi, and the Grand Trunk Western. The four systems as proposed under the final plan compared as follows:

	1923 miles	Proposed mileage	Net operating income (millions)	Investment in property (millions)	Coal tonnage
PRR	11,561	16,237	$116	$2,726	100,778,396
NYC	11,785	15,745	145	2,396	67,177,362
B&O	5,397	13,405	95	1,843	77,828,554
NKP	1,690	13,056	88	1,806	86,157,679

At first the Pennsylvania was simply suing for better terms. Rea thought his road was entitled to at least a half interest in the Virginian, the Detroit & Toledo Shore Line, and the Reading. He also wanted a protective interest in the Lehigh Valley. Moreover, he asked for the C&EI instead of the Alton and was opposed to giving the Nickel Plate full ownership of the Lackawanna. In view of what Rea was ready to concede to the other roads, the objections were not unreasonable. Matters had been going badly enough for the Pennsylvania without its management forfeiting all the plums. In 1921 the I.C.C. had served notice that it thought the Pennsylvania was big enough and had proposed to build a new and independent system around its vassal, the Norfolk & Western. The changing coal picture made it imperative that the PRR maintain its relationship with the Pocahontas carrier. Broad Street had been fighting the proposed PRR-N&W divorce for more than two years. Then, in recent years, industry had been leaving the cramped valleys the Pennsy had long monopolized. At Chicago, Detroit, Cleveland, and other Great Lakes industrial centers, the Pennsylvania was just another railroad. Control of a tremendous volume of commerce was at stake and the four-system plan did nothing to strengthen the PRR's competitive position where it was weakest.

The Van Sweringens committed a grave blunder by attempting to further exploit the weak bargaining position of the Pennsylvania. In assigning it the N&W, Alton, and GTW, the Triple Alliance gave the PRR what it already had, what it did not want, and what it probably could not get. The humiliating terms roused the corporate giant from

its pacific disposition and a second set of meetings in the fall of 1924 failed to produce a compromise. Finally, on January 26, 1925, the Triple Alliance submitted the proposed four-system plan to the I.C.C. By this time the Vans were on the threshold of consolidating their railroads into a new Nickel Plate system.

THE NICKEL PLATE UNIFICATION CASE

Details of the Vans' latest scheme were disclosed to the public during August 1924. A new company, the New York, Chicago & St. Louis Rail*way*, was to lease and operate the Nickel Plate, C&O, Hocking, Erie, and Pere Marquette properties for a period of 999 years. At the time, through the holdings of Vaness Company and the Nickel Plate, the Vans controlled 32.85 per cent of the combined stocks of those companies. They had always held that they could effectively manage a company only when they held a majority of its voting stocks. Their activity in the stocks of the several companies had greatly appreciated their market values, and the Vans could not have pushed their equity to the 50 per cent level without spending prohibitive sums of money. Inasmuch as the great motivating factor behind the proposed unification was the speculative one, the Vans elected to attain their majority through a bold stock exchange plan. The shareholders of all the roads except the Nickel Plate were to exchange their stocks at varying ratios for securities of the new company. The old Nickel Plate was to remain in existence as a holding company and was to receive,

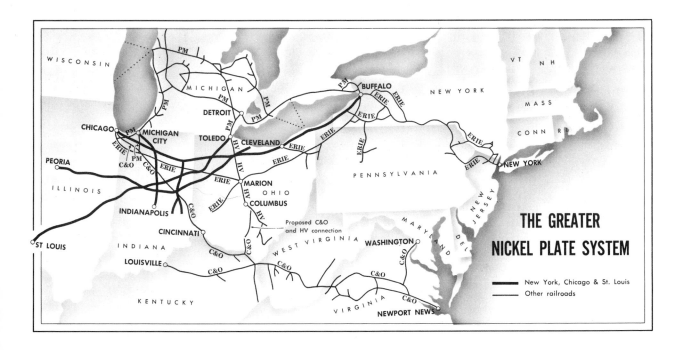

THE GREATER
NICKEL PLATE SYSTEM

━━━ New York, Chicago & St. Louis
──── Other railroads

in exchange for its physical properties, as many shares in the new company as there were outstanding shares of its own stock. This arrangement and the use of nonvoting preferred stock, as in 1916 and 1923, increased the Vans' equity in the unified company to 50.93 per cent of the voting securities.

In the case of the C&O, preferred stockholders surrendered their 6½ per cent $100 par shares for nonvoting 6 per cent $115 par preferred in the new company. The Vans figured that the average preferred holder would value the slightly increased annual yield more than the voting rights which he was giving up. As for the common, one C&O $100 par share was exchanged for .55 share each of new 6 per cent common and preferred. Inasmuch as C&O had been paying 4 per cent on its common, the yield jumped from $4 to $6.60. Of course the Vans' interest in C&O stock was confined to this class. Thus the exchange greatly reduced the voting equity in the new company accruing to the C&O's stock as a whole while increasing the Vans' share of that equity. It also greatly increased the rate of return on the Vans' C&O investment and provided them with a large block of preferred stock which could be sold at inflated values without disturbing their voting equity.

The formal announcement of the unification plan was released on August 20, 1924, the Nickel Plate board having approved the plan the previous day. On August 25 the C&O and Hocking directors met and similarly endorsed the plan at meetings convened just 20 minutes apart. Five of the men who had voted affirmatively at the August 19 meeting took the same action at the C&O and HV meetings. The Vans did not control the PM and Erie boards, however, and the directors of those roads negotiated for and got better terms than had been offered. The PM board approved the plan in December and the Erie directors formally endorsed it on January 23, 1925. Although the four-system plan had been in the news for months, the first revelation that the Vans had an interest in the PM and Erie came with the announcement of the unification plan. Trade journals were somewhat awe-struck, judging by this excerpt from the September 6, 1924, *Railway Age*:

> One is impressed first by the fact that it is the Nickel Plate that is acquiring a trunk-line connection and not a trunk line that is absorbing the Nickel Plate, as everybody at one time expected. It hardly seems possible that it can be true, but it nevertheless is the case that the 9145 miles of the new system have been assembled in a short space of but two years. . . . And then, Erie stockholders are finally to get a dividend — the seemingly impossible actually is about to happen.

On January 20, 1925, the New York, Chicago &

St. Louis Railway was formally incorporated, and on February 21 the Interstate Commerce Commission was petitioned for authority to perfect the union under Section 5 of the Transportation Act. Application was also made for a certificate of public convenience and necessity covering the construction of a 63-mile connection between the Hocking at Valley Crossing (O.) and the C&O near Waverly. To be built in the name of the Nickel Plate, the line was intended to replace trackage rights over the Norfolk & Western between the same points.[*] Including trackage rights, the Greater Nickel Plate embraced 9213 miles of road in the United States and 337 miles in Canada. The system would have been exceeded in size only by the New York Central and Pennsylvania in the East and represented an investment of more than 1.22 billion dollars. Out of projected annual operating revenues of 340 million dollars, the unified management was expected to carry nearly 60 million to net railway operating income. The system would have two widely separated trunk routes to the Atlantic seaboard at New York and Newport News while reaching all three major traffic gateways in the west. In many respects the Greater Nickel Plate promised to be one of the best balanced railroads in the land.

Hearings on the Nickel Plate Unification Case began on April 15, 1925, and continued intermittently throughout the rest of that year. The case not only put to trial the Transportation Act and the Interstate Commerce Commission's role in governing the affairs of the railroads, but it exposed to public scrutiny the lives of the Van Sweringens and the world of financial manipulation. The transcript ran to nearly 10,000 pages with 386 exhibits entered as evidence. The I.C.C. admitted a number of interveners, including short lines that wanted to be taken into the new system and several stockholder protective committees. During a special 26-hour C&O stockholders' meeting on March 30, 1925, the unification plan had polled more than a majority of the non-Van Sweringen shares. However, in dealing with the minority the Vans employed the rawest sort of steamroller tactics, a blunder that earned them the intransigent opposition of a group of Richmond (Va.) men led by George Cole Scott and John Stewart Bryan. Confident that the I.C.C. would quickly approve their scheme as it did in 1923, the Vans were ill prepared for the spirited fight provided by the hostile Scott faction's counsel, Henry W. Anderson.

Anderson hammered away at the Van Sweringens,

---

*The N&W had expressed unwillingness to renew the rights which expired on September 17, 1927. The arrangement restricted the C&O to move no more than 600 cars a day over the N&W, a fraction of the available tonnage.

labeling the unification as nothing more than a gigantic manipulation designed to yield huge profits to save the Vans' "failing" real estate ventures. He claimed the NYC was the real sponsor of the plan and foresaw it being forced through by unnamed men "high in the economic and political life of the land." The head of the Vans' legal corps, Newton D. Baker, dismissed Anderson's charges as so much "hocus-pocus" and called on the reticent O. P. to outline the aspirations that motivated his activities in the financial world. In a day when speculation was a way of life, it is doubtful that the cause of the unification was injured by the sensational revelations that followed. During his many hours on the stand, the elder Van Sweringen left no doubt that he and his brother "intended to be the owners of the companies they managed and managers of the companies they owned." He also imparted an impatience with dissident stockholders, betraying a get-in-line-or-get-out attitude towards them. Under cross-examination on a matter concerning the Hocking Valley, O. P. offered to sell 85 miles of that road east of Valley Crossing for 1 dollar to anyone who would assume its bonded indebtedness.

Unquestionably the most effective witness to testify in behalf of the unification was John Bernet. Although he insisted that he believed the plan was equitable and just to all concerned and was obviously well versed in its fine points, Bernet's forte was railroad operation. It was in this field that he was accepted as an expert witness. His Nickel Plate was still setting the performance pace, and Bernet went before the Commission with a golden reputation and an impressive blueprint for increasing the over-all efficiency of the roads which were to compose the Greater Nickel Plate.

Bernet pointed out how substantial economies could be realized through the joint use of facilities at Buffalo, Toledo, Lima, Chicago, and other cities. Preliminary studies at selected points, he related, had already shown where 8.5 million dollars in necessary capital expenditures and more than 6 million dollars in annual operating expenses could be eliminated. The Nickel Plate president cited the situation at Chicago, served by all four of the major roads in the unification plan. He related how the Nickel Plate had acquired a large tract of undeveloped land in the Lake Calumet district and built a 2200-car yard there in 1924. Already the C&O had abandoned its local facilities and was using the new yard, the Stony Island engine terminal, and 8 miles of the Nickel Plate between that place and Hammond. The PM and Erie would eventually use the Calumet facility and, like the C&O, would save the cost of badly needed new facilities. As an example of operational economy, Bernet con-

vincingly described how he would reduce the total number of daily yard engine assignments at Chicago from 53 to 42 and upgrade the over-all level of service at the same time.

Bernet's plans for through interline train runs were also of great interest to the I.C.C. In 1924 the Hocking and Nickel Plate had begun running coal trains from Parsons Yard at South Columbus through to Bellevue, 124 miles, eliminating the normal interchange at Fostoria.* Some momentous changes were planned once the unification was approved. Bernet intended to divert C&O coal traffic moving west from Russell (Ky.) to Chicago via Cincinnati to a joint C&O-Erie route through Marion, O. Between Marion and Chicago the double-track Erie had an excess daily capacity of 1500 cars and was physically better suited to the operation of heavy trains. The Nickel Plate's Chicago-Buffalo main stem was to be used almost exclusively for fast freight and the Erie's heavy eastbound perishable volume would be diverted to that route. A new 60-mile long double-track cutoff line was to be built between the Nickel Plate at Dunkirk and the Erie at Hornell, N. Y. Second tracks were to be built as soon as possible on all single-track sections of the Nickel Plate between Brocton, N. Y., and Lima, O. The alternative, according to Bernet, was the 55-million-dollar cost of rebuilding the C&O's Chicago Division and long segments of the Erie between Hornell, Meadville (Pa.), and Marion. Part of the great savings which the unified system would enjoy had already been earmarked for great new locomotive shops at Clifton Forge, Richmond, and Huntington on the C&O; and Fort Wayne on the Nickel Plate.

After Bernet's testimony was concluded, the industry conceded that the I.C.C. would find the unification to be in the public interest. It was widely held and publicly expressed by several members of the Commission itself that the minority suits were matters better decided by a court of equity than by the I.C.C. Wall Street had little doubt of the ultimate outcome — the price of Nickel Plate common was still soaring upward. The Scott committee, however, was not yet ready to concede defeat. Throughout the summer of 1925 Colonel Anderson relentlessly probed for the flaw in the Vans' armor.

By September the Vans were hurting financially. They had looked to the unification as a means of freeing themselves from the 35-million-dollar debt they were carrying. With the dogged resistance of the insurgent C&O stockholders all that stood be-

*These trains were powered by HV 2-6-6-2's and 2-10-2's, dubbed "Nightcrawlers" and "Lollipops" by Nickel Plate crews. These were not the first foreign runs into Bellevue. Prior to this time, the Big Four operated trains from Bellefontaine to Bellevue by way of Green Springs Junction.

tween them and Commission approval, Professor Ripley arranged a mid-September meeting between O. P. and Scott's brother in a vain attempt to gain some sort of compromise. It was not long afterward that the persistent Anderson hit pay dirt. Somehow he learned about a secret stock trust agreement between the four stockholders of the Vaness Company.

The Vaness stock trust agreement, described as the Vans' last will and testament, was dated January 11, 1924, but the actual arrangement or some prior version of it may have existed as early as 1916 when the brothers began to borrow heavily from Cleveland bankers. The Vans, Joseph R. Nutt, and C. L. Bradley deposited the entire common stock of Vaness with the Union Trust Company. Nutt and Bradley, it will be recalled, were both officers of this bank and held nominal amounts of Vaness stock. Through a provision for the appointment of successors, the agreement assured the existence of the trust for a period of 21 years after the death of the last of the original trustees (the Vans, Nutt, and Bradley). Thus the heirless Van Sweringens provided for continuity of control over Vaness, the cornerstone of their holding company empire, in the face of any contingency. Conceivably the Vans or their successors could divest their proprietary interest in Vaness and still retain voting control of the Greater Nickel Plate system.

The idea that such an arrangement existed had a profoundly adverse effect on the I.C.C., and the darkness and mystery enshrouding the trust agreement was heightened by the "inability" of attorneys to locate Nutt, reportedly traveling in the West in a Nickel Plate private car. Nutt finally made his appearance, but the prolonged delay was anything but a benefit to the cause of the unification. It suddenly appeared very unlikely that there would be a repetition of the coup of 1923.

On March 2, 1926, the I.C.C. rejected the Nickel Plate application by a 7-1 vote, approving the plan from a transportation standpoint but objecting to the financial arrangements. The petition to build the C&O-HV connection was also denied. The existence of the Vaness agreement as a means of perpetuating private domination of a major railroad system was the crux of the objection but the Commission had been influenced by other factors as well. For one thing, the I.C.C. had not been happy about the Vans' surreptitious stock purchases. The misgivings about nonvoting stock expressed in articles by Professor Ripley, and the tactics used against the C&O and HV minorities also had their effect. There had been some Congressional opposition, and in February Sen. Burton K. Wheeler of Montana introduced a resolution requesting that the I.C.C. hold up the merger pending the passage of a law which would subject it to certain protective restrictions.

The denial proved to be a fatal reverse for the Van Sweringens and was a harbinger of many bleak years for the Nickel Plate. Had the Vans been content to rely on their own prowess in managing and developing the unified system instead of insisting on majority control, the I.C.C. probably would have quickly given its assent. In fact, had they offered the C&O and HV shareholders the same treatment they gave the Erie and PM people, the Greater Nickel Plate would have been a reality. The Van Sweringens had lost their untarnished image of invincibility. Never again would they attain the status in the railroad industry that they had enjoyed in August 1924. Gone, too, was the *de facto* recognition the I.C.C. had granted them and the precious initiative that had accompanied it. The Pennsylvania Railroad had a new president, Gen. William Wallace Atterbury, and already this formidably aggressive and resourceful personality was changing the complexion of Eastern railroading.

Two weeks after the unification was denied, the Vans eased their financial squeeze by borrowing more than 31 million dollars through the House of Morgan. Having made peace with Scott and Bryan — leaders of the victorious C&O minority — they seated both on the C&O board on March 17. Subsequently a revised Nickel Plate Unification Plan was announced which offered improved terms for minority stockholders of the C&O, HV, and PM. The Vans reluctantly abolished the Vaness trust on the advice of their associates and decided to grant voting rights to all classes of the new company's stock. Nevertheless, they found that they were still confronted by C&O minority opposition, now led by Scott's brother. Overtures to members of the I.C.C. were met with indifference, and the Vans were given to understand that their best course lay in building the fourth system around the C&O. The decision to exclude the Nickel Plate altogether was made on September 29, 1926. The following February the C&O applied to the I.C.C. for authority to acquire the Hocking Valley, Pere Marquette, and Erie. This was ultimately denied in 1929.

The New Role of the Nickel Plate

Throughout the early years of the Van Sweringen-Nickel Plate association, the benefits of the relationship flowed generously in both directions. While it is true that they greatly enriched themselves through the 1923 consolidation, it is also true that the Nickel Plate's competitive position was grossly enhanced in the process. In many ways, too, the partnership was highly beneficial to the railroad industry and to the public. However, there was a pronounced change in the Nickel Plate's fortunes after the decision was made to exclude the road from the unified system. In contrast with their treatment of the other roads, the Vans thereafter used their proprietary control to exploit the Nickel Plate in whatever fashion suited their purpose. Holding less than 25 per cent of the outstanding capital stock and none of the bonds, the Vans ruled the road by virtue of the nonvoting feature they had incorporated in the preferred stock.

In 1926 the Nickel Plate organized a wholly-owned subsidiary, the Special Investment Corporation, to hold its PM and C&O stock and acquire additional securities of those roads. At the end of that year, the subsidiary transferred the PM stock to yet another holding company which in turn optioned it to the C&O. Then, in May 1927 the ownership of Special Investment was transferred from the Nickel Plate to the new Chesapeake Corporation. With the subsidiary went 345,000 shares of C&O common, then worth far more than 50 million dollars. In exchange the Nickel Plate treasury received 589 shares of Chesapeake Corporation stock which it carried on its books at a value of slightly more than $35,000. Chesapeake Corporation also distributed 516,911 shares of its stock to Nickel Plate common shareholders at the rate of 1.7 shares for each share of Nickel Plate held. The Nickel Plate sustained a loss of more than 30 million dollars in equity through this manipulation, while the Van Sweringens increased their own worth by about half that amount. The C&O and PM stocks — purchased with more than 18 million dollars raised through the sale of mortgage bonds — had a market value of more than 47 million dollars when disposed of by the Nickel Plate. This equity was reduced to an amount consisting of a little more than 1 million dollars' worth of stocks in a Van Sweringen holding company.

From the beginning of 1923 to the end of 1930, the Nickel Plate's total net income amounted to 51 million dollars. Dividends at the rate of 6 per cent were paid each year on both classes of stock except during 1926 and 1927 when 11 and 8½ per cent were paid on the common. During the same period, indebtedness of the consolidated company increased from less than 73 million to more than 158 million dollars, and preferred stocks were issued with a total par value of 13 million dollars. Still the road went into the year 1930 with a deficit in its working capital account.

Physical Improvements 1916-1933

Despite the tremendous increase in capitalization, the Nickel Plate would go into the great depression with light capacity bridges built by Paddy Canniff and Sylvester Kneeland, and portions of the main line east of Bellevue would remain the busiest single-track operations in the United States. Engines at most mainline terminals would continue to be coaled by clamshell and housed in the dark dirt-floored roundhouses of 1882. The Nickel Plate still did not own a repair shop worthy of a railroad a fraction of its size.

The bulk of money spent to upgrade the physical plant during the Van Sweringen era went into track and signaling. An intensive rail program was instituted in 1917 and faithfully progressed to a conclusion in 1933. Between 1922 and 1931 alone, 245,000 tons of new 90- and 110-pound rail was laid, this being roughly the equivalent of 1500 miles of track. By 1923 all the old 75- and 85-pound section in the Buffalo-Chicago main track had been replaced with 90-pound rail. Again, between 1925 and 1933 this part of the system was relaid with 110-pound steel. During the same period, light rails on the Clover Leaf and parts of the LE&W were replaced with new and relay 90-pound section.

In 1923 the Nickel Plate announced it intended to double-track the remainder of its main line between Buffalo and Chicago — the work to be done over a period of three to four years. During the unification hearings in 1925, John Bernet revealed that this program had been modified to cover the construction of 182 miles of second track between Lima, O., and Brocton, N. Y., at an estimated cost of 8 million dollars. On the 96-mile section between Cleveland and Fostoria, provision was to be made for eventual expansion to four-track operation. Selected sections of the main line west of Arcadia were also to receive priority attention. These included a 40-mile stretch between Knox and Claypool in Indiana. A little more than 70 miles of road was actually converted from single- to double-track operation between 1923 and 1927. The first section — 12.1 miles between Hadley, Fort Wayne, and New Haven — was opened to traffic in 1923. The 27-mile second-track extension from Colby to Fostoria was completed in 1924, as was the 8-mile length from Lorain to Kishmans near Vermilion. In the latter instance, most of the grading and a series of protective Lake Erie piling-type breakwalls had been completed prior to the World War.

In 1925 interlocking towers were built at the westerly yard limits at Fostoria and at Arcadia, and the parallel LE&W and Nickel Plate mains between them were converted to double-track operation. Finally, about 19 miles of second track was laid on the Cleveland Division between Kingsville and Madison during 1926-1927. In this distance, .9 mile at Ashtabula, including the viaduct, remained single track. Including trackage rights and joint operation, there was a total of 233 miles of double-track opera-

179

Legend has it that Bernet moved coal dock from Leipsic Junction (below) to remote Yellow Creek (above) to keep crews out of restaurant. Leipsic scene in 1931 shows B&O crossing, depot, XN tower. Until advent of C.T.C., operator controlled power switches at both ends of Yellow Creek running track from this tower. — *Clyde E. Helms.*

tion on the 523-mile Nickel Plate District. East of Arcadia there were still three long stretches of single track: from Brocton, N.Y., to Thornton Junction, Pa., 58.29 miles; Madison to UD Tower (Euclid), 28.2 miles; and Kimball to KM Tower (Kishmans), 21.5 miles. The last two bottlenecked the heavily trafficked Cleveland Division and slowed down its operation appreciably.

The Interstate Commerce Commission on June 13, 1922, ordered the installation of automatic train-stop and train-control devices on one division over which passenger trains of each of the 49 largest railway systems in the country were operated. In the Nickel Plate's case, installation of the apparatus on the Chicago Division — the one division that was fully equipped with automatic block signals between yard limits — was specifically required. Curiously, the I.C.C. denied the road's petition that it be allowed to install A.T.S. on the Buffalo Division rather than the Chicago Division, which had the lesser traffic density.

The 124-mile Union Switch & Signal intermittent inductive type installation, the first of its kind, was completed in 1926. In lieu of a second A.T.S. order, the Nickel Plate installed automatic signals during 1926 and 1927 between Arcadia and Conneaut, 170 miles. Similar protection had been placed in service between Conneaut and Thornton Junction in 1924, and finally in 1930 the 67-mile Arcadia-Edgerton and 58-mile Thornton-Brocton segments became automatic block territory. West of Arcadia on the Fort Wayne Division, several changes had been made during the 1920's to help speed up the operation. A second track, known as Yellow Creek running track, was laid between Leipsic and Townwood, a distance of more than 4 miles. All westbounds except scheduled passenger trains used the running track, and it was occasionally used by eastbounds being overtaken by faster trains. Dual-control power switches controlled from XN Tower at Leipsic Junction were installed at both ends of the running track in the 1920's. Similar switch machines were also employed in the turnouts of passing tracks at Payne, Latty, and Continental.

During the 1920's several major realignment and grade reduction programs were considered and a few minor improvements of this type were actually completed. Parts of the Clover Leaf became forests of surveyors' stakes. Near Sorento, Ill., the worst of the Devil's Eyebrow was eliminated by a 2-mile track relocation. However, plans to iron out severe operational obstacles at Cayuga and Bluffton and to bypass The Hole between Sorento and Donnellson were deferred.

As for yards, engine facilities, and shops, the Nickel Plate was woefully in need of wholesale at-

tention. A program attacking such deficiencies was undertaken in 1922 when the road acquired 431 acres of undeveloped swampland in the Lake Calumet District near Chicago. The tract was purchased from an old land company, control of which had lately passed to the Van Sweringens. It was intended as the site of an entirely new complex of facilities. A new yard was completed at Calumet in 1924, but 27 years passed before the engine terminal, car repair shop, and other facilities materialized. It was also proposed to develop a harbor basin connected to the Calumet River on an adjacent 2000-acre site. The Nickel Plate wanted a 100-foot-wide strip of right of way around the harbor for the tracks of a subsidiary, the Lake Calumet & Harbor Railroad. Endorsed by the aldermen of Chicago but opposed by the State, the plan was never fulfilled.

Between Fort Wayne and New Haven, 200 acres of land were purchased for a new yard, engine

Conneaut's 700-ton concrete dock erected in 1924 was first modern coaling plant at an NKP terminal. A 500-ton plant was built at Bellevue in 1925, but other terminal coal docks were deferred after I.C.C. denied unification plan. — *Paul W. Prescott.*

Intersection of Prospect Avenue and West 3rd Street (above) is a busy place on April 15, 1924. City streetcar passes Niles interurban of the Cleveland, Painesville & Eastern. Eight days later (below) steam shovel clears debris while workmen remove paving bricks and trolley rails. Photographer was standing at what became the heart of the Cleveland Union Terminal. — *Corman E. Moore.*

terminal, and a 2.5-million-dollar shop big enough to handle all heavy repairs to the road's locomotives. A yard with a capacity of 1085 cars and a water tank were all that graced the East Wayne landscape for almost three decades. The yard itself was used only for eastbound classification while the old 600-car West Wayne Yard was retained for handling west-bound tonnage. However, the shop was never built.

At Frankfort in the mid-1920's a new 27-stall roundhouse and adjoining machine shop were erected, but on March 9, 1926, a fire devastated the new buildings as well as some older shop structures. More than 600 men were thrown out of work, and it was necessary to reopen the old narrow-gauge shop at Delphos while the facility was being re-constructed. Reinforced concrete coal docks were built at Conneaut and Bellevue in 1924-1925 and some roundhouse stalls were extended elsewhere. Yet the roundhouses at Stony Island, Bellevue, West Wayne, and Buffalo remained cramped artifacts of the era of the American Standard 4-4-0.

THE CLEVELAND UNION TERMINAL

Most of the outstanding physical improvements undertaken by the Nickel Plate during the Van Sweringen era were directly related to the construction of the highly controversial Cleveland Union Terminal. This project, carried out over a period of eight years, involved far more than the building of a great new railway passenger station. Associated undertakings included the construction of a double-track electrified line 17.1 miles long, a carefully planned complex of commercial buildings, two suburban stations, and a rapid-transit line. According to the June 28, 1930, *Railway Age*, 179 million dollars had been spent as of that time on the CUT and collateral projects. The Cleveland Union Terminals Company had expended 88 million dollars on the station proper, approach lines, and electrification. Twenty million had gone into rapid-transit lines. The Cleveland Terminals Building Company's outlay for air rights buildings amounted to 31 million. Expenses of 40 million dollars had been incurred by the three proprietary railroads. Considering the relatively unimportant role of passenger trains in the Nickel Plate's operation, the road's share of the 40 million was inordinately high. Upwards of 10 million dollars were spent in relocating tracks and facilities in the Broadway-Kingsbury Run area alone, and the total expenditure may have exceeded 20 million dollars. To be certain, the Nickel Plate derived considerable benefit from the terminal project, particularly through the expansion of its yard and freight-handling facilities.

The Nickel Plate's interest in the Terminals Company was a modest 7 per cent of its capital stock. The New York Central and its subsidiary, the Big Four, held the rest. As owners of the CUT, the three roads were also guarantors of the 60 million dollars' worth of mortgage bonds which were sold to finance its construction. The relationship between the railroads and the Terminals Company was established in the fall of 1920, but it was not until December 6, 1921, that the I.C.C. approved the arrangement and the financing. The actual work of construction commenced on January 1, 1922, under the direction of Chief Engineer H. D. Jouett. Graham, Anderson, Probst & White of Chicago were the architects. The contract for grading the terminal site was given to

Cleveland Union Terminal steam concourse is 18 feet below Public Square level, 23 feet above track platforms. Baggage and waiting rooms, cab stand, and ticket counters flank concourse. — *Collection of Terminal Tower Company.*

the Walsh Construction Company of Davenport, Ia.

The terminal was built on a triangular tract of land on a bluff overlooking the Cuyahoga River bordered on the north by West Superior Avenue, on the east by Ontario Street, and on the south by Canal Road. The site was occupied by a large number of old and ramshackle buildings and by several streets which were to be vacated through enabling ordinances that had been ratified by popular referendum in January 1919. The location was an excellent one from the standpoint of commercial development, for it abutted on the very heart of the city, the hub of a system of radiating streets and trolley lines reaching the entire metropolitan area. Topographically, however, the site left much to be desired and the Central's engineers and others had opposed it from the beginning. The approaches to the terminal would necessarily be very costly to construct and would inherently create serious operational restrictions. The west approach required a very long viaduct with steep ascending grades from both directions to the point where the bridge crossed the Cuyahoga. The east approach had to be threaded through a

East Cleveland station under construction, looking east. NKP tracks and platforms are at right. Old Cleveland Short Line roadbed at left will soon support NYC catenary to CUT. Joint NYC-NKP facility opened June 22, 1930. — *Collection of Willis A. McCaleb.*

Euclid Avenue station built in 1910 was the Nickel Plate's finest passenger facility. It was closed on August 19, 1929, and razed to make way for New York Central's electrified tracks. — *Collection of John A. Rehor.*

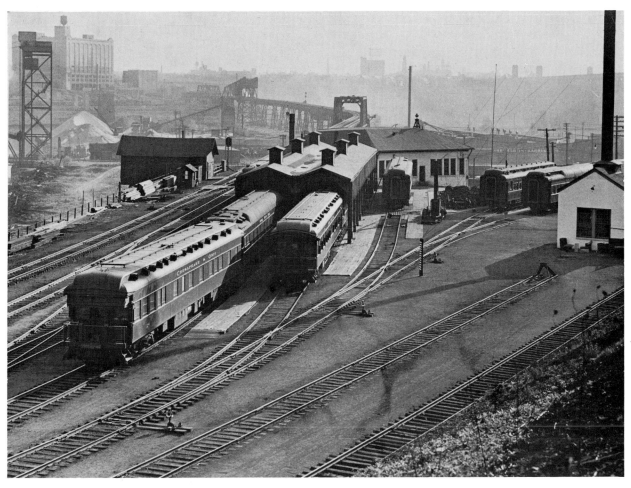

Demolition of Broadway facilities in 1929 led to building of sorely needed Commercial Road coach yard. Boilerhouse at right replaced the locomotives which had steam-heated cars for almost five decades. This yard has serviced NKP and C&O business cars for many years. Photo was made on May 24, 1945, prior to modernization. — *Richard J. Cook.*

narrow defile along the bluff of the river valley and then pass through a cut of formidable proportions.

The track level of the terminal was 40 feet below that of the Public Square and required the excavation of 775,000 cubic yards of material. From a large portico fronting on the Square, two large ramps descended to the main or steam concourse at an intermediate level. Flanking the main ramps were smaller passages leading to separate rapid-transit concourses. A total of 28 tracks were actually built, increasing in length from north to south. The six shortest tracks and adjacent platforms at the north end of the terminal were allocated for rapid-transit use, while the next 12 were for the use of steam-road trains. Track 23 was classed as a running track and the southerly nine tracks were utilized by the Central as a coach yard. The entire platform area was nearly covered; the station building itself covered most of this area.

Double-track approach lines built and owned by the Cleveland Union Terminal extended approximately 1.75 miles on each side of the terminal. The east approach ran southeast to a junction with the Nickel Plate at the old Broadway passenger station. The west approach extended practically due south from the terminal, crossing the Cuyahoga valley on a four-track viaduct 3450 feet long. Then a long cut carried the line into Walworth Run, where connection was made with the Nickel Plate and the Big Four. The entire CUT operation was electrified, employing a 3000-volt D.C. overhead catenary system. A pair of new electrified tracks 17.1 miles long extended from Collinwood, the huge NYC steam terminal in the northeastern part of the city, to the Big Four facilities at Linndale in the southwest.

Aside from the CUT's approach trackage, all of the Collinwood-Linndale line was built at the expense of the three proprietary railroads. From Collinwood to Coit Road, about 1 mile, the Central built new tracks adjacent to its main line. From Coit Road to the Nickel Plate at Superior Road, 2.4 miles, the tracks were built alongside the Cleveland Short Line, the NYC freight belt around the city. Then, between Superior and Fairmount Road (now Fair-

hill), 2.5 miles, the NYC built the new electrified tracks on the old Short Line alignment and added two new tracks to the north of them for its freight trains. The connecting 3.1 miles of double track between Fairmount Road and the CUT's own tracks at East 37th Street were built by the Nickel Plate and leased to the NYC. The Big Four built the 4.6 miles of electrified line from Walworth Run to Linndale and spent 6 million dollars for the new tracks and new facilities at Linndale including a passenger station, 12 added roundhouse stalls, a coal dock, and other structures.

All told, about 6.3 miles of the Nickel Plate's line through Cleveland's east side required extensive reconstruction at tremendous cost. Over much of this distance the road also financed the partial construction of the Vans' East Cleveland rapid-transit line.* Between East 15th and East 55th streets, 1.7 miles, the road had to be relocated, and at many points it was necessary to erect great concrete retaining walls. The 2 miles of roadway between East 55th and Quincy Avenue was depressed and widened to accommodate eight tracks. The construction of 10 street overpasses and the excavation of a million cubic yards of material was involved. East of Quincy, the 2.6 miles to Superior was extensively widened and rebuilt.

As a result of the terminal construction, the Nickel Plate lost two passenger stations, its principal yard and its roundhouse at Cleveland, its high-level freighthouse, and a smaller freight facility at East

*When work on the project was suspended in 1930, one unballasted track had been laid and catenary towers erected for 4.2 miles between East 65th Street and Superior Road. This and some right of way on the West Side, carried on the books at a value of 4.6 million, were sold to the City of Cleveland in 1951 for 2.75 million dollars.

75th Street. In place of cramped Broadway Yard which was built on a reverse curve, a new 630-car classification yard and office building were built at East 55th Street. The high-level Broadway freight facilities were bisected by the CUT's eastern approach, so a new 824 x 150-foot freighthouse, adjacent team tracks, and a 380-car concentration yard were built east of the old location. This required the vacation of part of Broadway itself and the expensive condemnation of adjoining property. In place of the 1882 roundhouse, a wooden shed was built at East 75th Street. As in the past, locomotives were coaled by a whirley, but it was now necessary to run them to the Erie's roundhouse whenever they had to be turned. The attractive Euclid Avenue passenger station built in 1910 was razed to make way for the electrified tracks; however, the Nickel Plate and NYC jointly built a new station farther east in East Cleveland. The convenient location of the old depot had gained the road a lot of business from the Heights area. As a result of the CUT project, it now had to finance its arch-competitor's incursion into that territory.

Most New York Central passenger trains, except for those which did not stop at Cleveland, were diverted to the combined CUT-Big Four line between Collinwood and Berea. Nickel Plate trains were powered by CUT box-cab electrics for the less than 5 miles between East 37th and West 38th streets. Steam locomotives simply ran light over the road's own tracks between those points. Only about 2000 feet of the Nickel Plate's main was actually electrified — this being between West 38th and the CUT connection.

The Nickel Plate also built a huge ultramodern produce terminal north of the new East 55th Street

High-level freighthouse, adjacent to Broadway, was built during World War I and utilized material excavated from West Side grade depression. Cleveland Union Terminal east approach was cut through here in 1929. — *Ernst-Eidman Company, Cleveland.*

Culbertson's cut through NKP's high-level freight layout was wide enough to accommodate four Union Terminal and two rapid-transit tracks. — *Collection of John A. Rehor.*

187

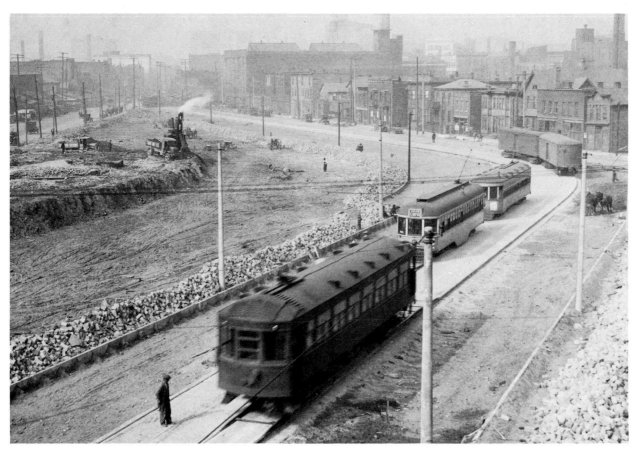

Traction traffic is heavy on Broadway (above) during street's December 1927 relocation to make room for NKP's new freighthouse facilities. Construction of CUT's east approach through old facility site forced relocation. Cleveland Railway cars pass Northern Ohio Power & Light freight train and passenger car. Completed layout of freight terminal and team tracks in May 1930 is shown below. — *Collection of John A. Rehor.*

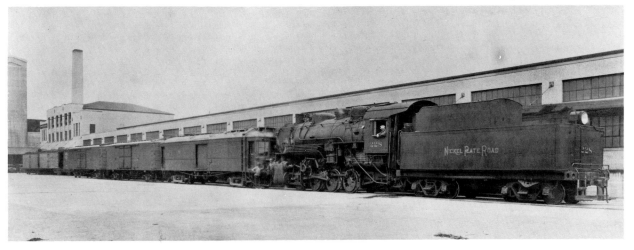

Nickel Plate yard goat spots Northern Ohio Power & Light freight at Northern Ohio Food Terminal. NKP and NO filed joint freight tariffs. This uncommon arrangement ended in June 1931 when the interurban quit freight service. — *Collection of John A. Rehor.*

classification yard. The 34-acre Northern Ohio Food Terminal opened in the summer of 1929 and was considered to be the finest facility of its kind in the U. S. for many years. Four large steel and concrete buildings provided space for 96 wholesale food outlets, and there were large fruit-auction and cold-storage buildings. An adjoining 320-car concentration yard served the food terminal and nearby warehouses. The food terminal proper embraced some 20 tracks with a capacity of 460 cars.

When the railroads agreed to build the Union Terminal in 1920, they forfeited the air rights to the Van Sweringens. The air rights, valued at 15 million dollars, were exploited in the form of an outstanding complex of commercial buildings. The central structure was erected over the northerly portion of the station and fronted on the Public Square. The Terminal Tower, a 52-story skyscraper

rising 708 feet above the street level, was a handsome building of unique design. The limestone-faced tower was the tallest edifice outside Manhattan Island and became Cleveland's great landmark. Flanking the Terminal Tower on the west was a 1000-room hotel built in 1918. On the east a 12-story department store was later built. Along the southerly portion of the terminal tract, three 18-story buildings were erected in the late 1920's. These were the Midland Bank Building, the Medical Arts Building, and the Builders' Exchange-Terminal Garage Building. Other foundations were completed farther west. The principal one was later used for the post office built during the depression.

Ground was broken for the Terminal Tower on September 28, 1923. In order to provide a safe foundation for the building, it was necessary to sink 87 concrete piers to bedrock, some of which ran as

GE and Alco turned out 22 double-ended 2-C-C-2 locomotives designed to start train of 15 85-ton cars on 1.56 ascent of CUT west approach. Six-wheel motor trucks gave these box cabs a 1-hour rating of 3030 h.p. and 75,000 pounds starting tractive effort. New 1051 poses on March 30, 1930. — *Collection of Willis A. McCaleb.*

The Terminal Tower Building
(New Union Station)
Public Square, Cleveland, Ohio

New Home
of the
General Offices
Nickel Plate Road

The New York, Chicago and St. Louis Railroad Co.

View from the southeast at Eagle and Ontario on October 5, 1927. Limestone facing is completed on most of building. — *Collection of Willis A. McCaleb.*

Front of skyscraper as seen from Public Square on August 2, 1927. — *Cleveland Union Terminals Company.*

Superstructure reaches 32-story level on June 27, 1927, 14 weeks after cornerstone laying. — *Cleveland Union Terminals Company.*

Terminal Tower is completed and partly occupied by 1928. — *Terminal Tower Company.*

August 22, 1928, vista from Terminal Tower shows progress of east approach construction. From bottom to top: Ontario Street subway, W&LE depot, Culbertson's cut, Nickel Plate's Broadway Yard. — *Collection of Willis A. McCaleb.*

W&LE Vinegar Hill depot blocked east approach of Cleveland Union Terminal. Its extended stay of execution was mute evidence of bitter predepression struggle between the Vans and the PRR. Depot fronted on Ontario Street and occupied site of 1883 station of Connotton Valley narrow gauge. Private car *Brewster* is shown in 1928 photo.

Ontario Street subway work was well advanced and, except for W&LE depot, all buildings on west side of street were razed by December 19, 1928. Taplin's suit to annul depot's sale went all the way to Supreme Court. — *Collection of Willis A. McCaleb.*

West approach catenary has reached terminal yard by February 14, 1930. Westbound Big Four and Nickel Plate sleepers have been using the terminal for more than three months, although it is not yet formally opened. — *Cleveland Union Terminals Company.*

On December 24, 1928, the Terminal Tower was completed and occupied, but the opening of the Cleveland Union Terminal was still 18 months away. Big Four switcher shuffles loads of construction material in the foreground.

deep as 250 feet below the street level. Great difficulty was encountered in the execution of this work, and the foundation was not completed until November 7, 1926. The cornerstone was laid in March 1927, and most of the superstructure was completed before the end of that year. Although not dedicated until 1930, parts of the tower were occupied much earlier. Its first tenant, the Nickel Plate, moved its general offices into the building on January 1, 1928.

THE WHEELING CLAYTON ACT CASE

During the winter of 1926-1927, as the Van Sweringens were reshuffling their corporate pawns and preparing to take the C&O unification plan before the I.C.C., a dramatic clash occurred between the great railroad powers of the East. The episode had a profound effect on the future of the Nickel Plate, and it nearly upset the Cleveland Union Terminal project.

About the time that the Nickel Plate Unification Case hearings began in Washington, the brilliant president of the Delaware & Hudson, Leonor F. Loree, had presented his proposal to the I.C.C. for

a fifth Eastern system built around the so-called Kuhn-Loeb lines and the Lehigh Valley. Kuhn, Loeb & Company, more or less in competition with J. P. Morgan & Company, acted as bankers for the Pennsylvania, Delaware & Hudson, Wabash, Ann Arbor, and some other railroads. Loree's D&H and the Wabash, in which he had an interest, began buying Lehigh Valley stock in 1925. By the end of 1926 their combined equity in that road amounted to 44 per cent of the outstanding capital stock.

Some time after taking over the reins of the Pennsylvania, General Atterbury apparently adopted a patronizing interest in Loree's ambitions, possibly finding them the means through which he could deal with the Van Sweringens' Greater Nickel Plate system. Although the NYC acquired a large block of Lehigh stock, the Triple Alliance made no overt attempt to head off Loree during 1925 and 1926. In this period, of course, the Vans had their hands full with the C&O minority and subsequently were preoccupied with mending their financial and corporate fences. At the end of 1926, though, O. P. apparently became apprehensive about the Wheeling & Lake

Evening rush-hour traffic flows past partly completed CUT Cuyahoga viaduct June 3, 1929. Tracks had not yet been laid in station yard. Erie depot is in center; B&O facilities are at right. Both roads eventually used the CUT. — *Collection of John A. Rehor.*

Erie, a road assigned to the Nickel Plate under the four-system plan, and he began to make heavy purchases of its common and preferred stocks. Loree's acquisition of the W&LE, Pittsburgh & West Virginia, and Western Maryland would have been a reincarnation of George Gould's plan to gain a seaboard outlet for the Wabash. The combination would have given Loree's fifth system separate trunk-line routes to tidewater at New York and Chesapeake Bay, precisely what the Vans were seeking in their unified system.

After Gould's aspirations collapsed in the panic of 1907, his properties went through bankruptcy and eventually passed under the control of Kuhn, Loeb & Company. The bankers quickly sold their interest in the W&LE to aging oil king John D. Rockefeller who also acquired control of the Western Maryland. Before the four-system era, about 1919, Rockefeller had made an unsuccessful bid to sell his Wheeling stock to the NYC. The idea was followed up by Patrick Crowley in January 1925 on the eve of the four-system plan submission to the I.C.C., but apparently nothing came of this contact. Rockefeller held nearly all of the Wheeling's prior lien stock — an issue that carried with it the sole right to name directors in the event the 7 per cent dividend was not paid. The W&LE owed Rockefeller more than 8 million dollars in unpaid dividends

at the end of 1926, and he thus possessed absolute control over the road.

Control of the Pittsburgh & West Virginia, successor to Gould's unfortunate Wabash Pittsburgh Terminal, had been in the hands of Frank E. Taplin, Cleveland coal magnate, since 1923. About the same time O. P. Van Sweringen decided that Loree was after the W&LE, Taplin and his brother Charles apparently arrived at the same conclusion. They, too, made a determined effort to corner the Wheeling's stocks. The brisk activity in these issues during January 1927 set off a wild speculative spree that shot W&LE common from 27½ in January to 130 on February 7. In the meantime, the Triple Alliance came to terms with Rockefeller on January 20 for the purchase of his W&LE and WM holdings. B&O took all of the latter while splitting the W&LE securities with the Nickel Plate and the Central. The three-way ownership was also extended to the stocks O. P. had picked up on the open market. The total cost of the Wheeling control to each road was roughly 10 million dollars. Combined holdings totaled more than 53 per cent of all W&LE stocks.

The Taplins reacted bitterly to the Van Sweringen stroke, and during a sensational three-year battle they did everything they could to frustrate it. At one time they claimed control of 231,000 shares of Wheeling common and preferred — a majority of

196

Tracklayers work on westerly throat of station yard July 30, 1929. Tracks ascend to and partly across Cuyahoga viaduct at a rate of 1.56 per cent. West approach separated B&O (left) and Erie (right) stations. — *Cleveland Union Terminals Company.*

General Railway Signal designed and built for CUT the world's largest power interlocking plant. This controlled approach tracks and terminal track layout.

Reconstructed Nickel Plate roadway through Cedar Glen in October 1930. At far left are freight-only Cleveland Short Line tracks, rising to cross over electrified CUT passenger tracks, NKP double-track main, and East Cleveland rapid transit. One unballasted traction track will be completed before economic slide forces suspension of work. — *Collection of John A. Rehor.*

those issues — but they held only a handful of prior lien shares. The dispute was quickly carried to the I.C.C. which had expressed displeasure over the unauthorized transfer of the Rockefeller holdings. Late in 1927 an examiner recommended that the Triple Alliance be restrained from electing directors. A 6-5 majority of the Commission in May 1928 held that the three roads had violated Section 7 of the Clayton Act.

In 1927 the I.C.C. had refused Loree the right to lease the Buffalo, Rochester & Pittsburgh, and subsequently the Van Sweringens took that property out of circulation. This reversal had the effect of driving Loree out of the consolidation wars and exposing General Atterbury's strategy. In 1928 it was necessary for the Pennsylvania to acquire Loree's Wabash and Lehigh Valley holdings at greatly appreciated values. Whether or not a relationship

actually existed at this time between the Pennsylvania and the Taplins has never been revealed. However, when the I.C.C. ordered the Triple Alliance to divest the W&LE stock within 90 days on March 14, 1929, it appeared that the Taplins and Atterbury had won the field.

There was another aspect to the Wheeling power play which jeopardized the great quasi-civic enterprise at Cleveland. The W&LE passenger depot straddled the narrow passage which had to accommodate the CUT east approach. Nestled on the steep bluff known as Vinegar Hill, the property took up all the space between Ontario Street on the high level and the floor of the Cuyahoga valley. It was, of course, immune to condemnation. The Taplins opposed the sale of the property, but on July 3, 1928, the W&LE executive committee agreed to sell the facility to the Terminals Company for 1.6

million dollars. The Wheeling also was to have the privilege of running its trains into the CUT for a nominal annual fee.

The day after the executive committee met, William McKinley Duncan, the board chairman, called the Cleveland Heights home of Frank Taplin in hopes of gaining his acquiescence to the terminal deal. The previous month, the Taplins had overcome massive trunk-line opposition to gain the I.C.C.'s blessing for the building of a 38-mile connection between the Pittsburgh & West Virginia and the Western Maryland. However, this success did little to improve their disposition toward their adversaries, and they insisted that Duncan hold out for at least 5 million dollars as the price for giving up the Vinegar Hill property. The directors ultimately approved the original terms and asked the I.C.C. for authority to abandon the depot on December 9, 1928. Pending the opening of the CUT, the Wheeling trains used the Erie's passenger station beginning on January 25, 1929.

Several weeks prior to the divestiture order of March 1929, the B&O and NYC had transferred their W&LE holdings to the Vans' new public holding company, Alleghany Corporation. The B&O traded its Wheeling stock for the Vans' interest in the BR&P and cash. Recalling the vigorous minority opinion that the Clayton Act had been violated only by the B&O and Central, the Vans countered the I.C.C. order on April 15 with a Nickel Plate petition asking for authority to acquire the Wheeling. This brought immediate reaction on the part of the Wabash and Pennsylvania, the former being allowed to intervene. About the same time, though, the I.C.C. ordered the Pennsylvania to show cause why it should not be made to divest its Wabash holdings. In the midst of the confusion, Frank Taplin convened a "rump" board which elected him president of the W&LE, but the Vans secured a last-minute injunction preventing him from taking over the road. They also managed to mollify the Commission by depositing the W&LE stock held by Nickel Plate and Alleghany with the Federal Reserve Bank at Cleveland under a trust agreement.

In June 1929 the I.C.C. allowed the W&LE to abandon its Cleveland depot. By this time the facility was already gone and CUT construction through Vinegar Hill was well advanced. On August 7, 1929, the P&WV filed a complaint in Federal Court at Cleveland asking that the I.C.C. certificate be annulled. Upon the dismissal of this suit, the Taplins futilely carried their case to the U. S. Supreme Court. Although delayed nearly six months, completion of the Cleveland Union Terminal was at last assured. The Vans had also successfully thwarted the fifth system, and before the end of 1929 the Taplins sold their P&WV holdings to Atterbury's Pennroad Corporation.

Just prior to the stock market crash of October 1929, the Nickel Plate proposed to acquire Alleghany's W&LE certificates of deposit at a net cost of $19,965,411 raised through the sale of 6 per cent promissory notes due October 1, 1932. Before the end of the year, the I.C.C. gave its assent to the plan. Already carrying an intolerable burden of debt, the Nickel Plate was now saddled with this heavy short-term obligation. With the treasury all but barren and business falling off at an alarming rate, it was obvious as early as mid-1930 that the Nickel Plate's day of reckoning was close at hand.

Kitchi Gammi Club brings up rear of No. 9 inside CUT. After April 1939 Pullman 8-section lounge-buffet car shared assignments with *Carleton Club* on trains 9 and 10. In 1953 it became business car 7. — *Richard J. Cook.*

The crucible

WHEN the Van Sweringens decided to leave the Nickel Plate out of their unified system, the Erie naturally assumed the role of the primary east-west trunk line in that system. At the end of 1926 John Bernet was moved to the helm of the Erie in the hope that his brand of operational magic would cure the road's traffic deficiencies. With Bernet went C. E. Denney as well as Bill Black, the superintendent of motive power, and some of the best mechanical men on his staff. A. R. Ayers succeeded Denney as general manager, and he in turn tapped Tom Coe for the post of superintendent of motive power. Lately the master mechanic at Conneaut, Coe was one of several motive power men Ayers had brought over from the NYC. The new president of the Nickel Plate was 62-year-old Walter L. Ross, the senior vice-president who had made his services part of the price of the Clover Leaf.

Before ascending to the Clover Leaf presidency in 1912, Ross had been that road's general passenger agent, and his new status augured well for the passenger department. In the gloomy offices on Cleveland's Prospect Street, they could only recall with nostalgia the Nickel Plate's gallant struggle to establish and maintain a noteworthy passenger service in the face of awesome competition. In recent years the road had made no pretense of competing with the Central's fleet of crack trains and had not even bothered to fill the post of general passenger agent. The depressed state of passenger business and lack of modern equipment on the Clover Leaf and Lake Erie & Western further complicated the Nickel Plate's dilemma. There had been no integration of service over the three districts and, in fact, practically no change in the schedules since 1922. The timetable showed three No. 5's and called for a daily meet at Fostoria between a pair of No. 2 trains. As for the main line, there was a remarkable similarity between the 1926 schedule and that of the late '90's.

As early as 1923, the swelling popularity of the private passenger automobile was having a cataclysmic effect on the local passenger revenues of both steam and electric rail carriers in the Great Lakes region. The interurbans were especially hard hit, and by the end of 1926 the lines connecting Cleveland with Erie, Pa., had been junked. Even the lordly Lake Shore Electric came up with a deficit in 1926, its first in more than 20 years. Between

Walter L. Ross, president of Nickel Plate 1927-1933, went after long-haul passenger business and produced sharp increases in passenger and freight revenues. He began railroading on the Wabash in 1887, spent almost 30 years with Clover Leaf and Nickel Plate.

1923 and 1927 the Nickel Plate sustained heavy losses of local traffic and the number of passengers carried annually dropped by more than 30 per cent. Acceding to an alarmed passenger department in 1925, Ayers had instituted a casual study of the potential value of using self-propelled gas-electric motor cars on local runs, particularly those serving the LE&W branch lines. The "doodlebugs" were also being considered as a low-cost means of speeding up mainline trains by relieving them of local responsibilities.

Ross was astute enough to write off the future of local and branch-line business and he quickly shelved the "doodlebug" study. Aware that growing long-haul traffic had held up the Nickel Plate's passenger revenues, he began to weigh the idea of making an all-out effort to compete with the New York Central. This meant sweeping improvements in service, a thorough overhaul of the joint operation with the Lackawanna, and the modernization of the aging varnish roster. In the first stages of his program, Ross would ignore the paucity of modern coaches and head-end cars while adding all-steel diners, sleepers, and club cars to the consists of his trains. But first of all he needed a new passenger locomotive brawny enough to master the weight of such cars and fast enough to lop hours from the schedules.

THE OTHER HUDSONS

On February 14, 1927, the main plant of the American Locomotive Company turned out a revo-lutionary new passenger locomotive for the New York Central. On that day the celebrated 5200, first of the famous 4-6-4 Hudsons, made her debut at Schenectady amidst a great deal of fanfare. In the erecting hall of one of Alco's lesser works, four other engines of the same wheel arrangement were beginning to take shape. The Brooks plant, nearing the end of its locomotive building days, was quietly producing the Nickel Plate's new passenger power. The L-1a's, as the railroad classed them, were ordered on January 28, 1927, four weeks after Walter Ross moved into the president's office and the same day the boiler of the Central's 4-6-4 appeared on the erecting floor at Schenectady. No record reveals what prompted the sudden ordering of the Nickel Plate 4-6-4's or the choice of this particular wheel arrangement. The rivalry between the two railroads, the friendship Gus Ayers shared with many high-ranking New York Central motive power men, and the unusually short time required to complete both orders add a touch of mystery to the whole business.

Outshopped during the first week of March 1927, the new engines bore the numbers 170-173, first applied to the original C class 4-4-0's delivered by the same builder in 1882. Just as the C's had been, the Hudsons were magnificent passenger locomotives for their day and were perhaps somewhat ostentatious power for a half-dozen very ordinary trains working a 523-mile run. They were the biggest locomotives on the roster of a railroad unabashedly dedicated to the science of moving freight tonnage. Even the heaviest Mikados, with feedwater heaters, boosters, and dual air pumps, outweighed the L-1a's by only 1000 pounds. Powerful enough to get a fast roll on heavy trains, the 4-6-4's had a boiler big enough to produce the steam needed to keep them moving at a mile a minute and then some. Although they had missed immortality by a mere two weeks and went unnoticed to their toil, the Hudsons ushered in a new era of passenger service on the Nickel Plate.

The apparently home-designed Nickel Plate 4-6-4 was a hybrid offspring of the proven H-6 Mikado and K-1 Pacific coupled with the latest auxiliaries and a boiler of great evaporative capacity. A 25-inch cylinder bore was selected, and the designers chose to retain the 26-inch stroke and 73-inch driver of the K-1 and R. Experience with this combination had shown it to be well suited to the frequent stops and 60 mph speed limit of the main line. Rated tractive effort at 215 pounds steam pressure was 40,680 pounds, a third greater than that of the Pacifics. The Hudson carried only 175,500 of its 316,500 pounds of working-order weight on the drivers, and it lacked the K-1's outstanding adhesion. Nevertheless, the 4-6-4's factor of 4.32 was highly respectable and was nearly the same as that of the Central's new 5200.

Horsepower thinking gave the L-1a a big boiler barrel 20 feet long between the tube sheets and 90 inches in diameter at the back sheet. This was the first Nickel Plate locomotive equipped with the E-type smokebox superheater combined with a multiple front-end throttle. The firebox was interchangeable with that of the H-6 2-8-2 and had a total area of 66.7 square feet. However, the four-wheel Delta trailing truck was designed to accommodate a furnace with considerably greater combustion volume. For example, the NYC 4-6-4 had the same truck and boasted a grate area of 81.5 square feet. Some of the difference may have been offset by the use of Nicholson thermic syphons and the Simplex stoker in the L-1a. Triangular water legs in the firebox, syphons afforded improved boiler water circulation. Their installation in the K-1's during 1924-1925 had amply demonstrated their value. In place of the Duplex stoker used to fire most of the Nickel Plate 2-8-2's and the 5200, the L-1a had the Standard Type B Simplex or Dupont model. Tried out in 1924 in several Mikados, the Simplex employed steam jets to distribute finely ground coal across the grates. Proper use of this stoker resulted in a uniformly thin fire, avoided banking, and afforded maximum combustion.

Externally, features adopted from the earlier locomotives were readily apparent. As with the H-6, the Hudson's bell was hung over the top of the smokebox door and the cabs of the two locomotives were interchangeable. The vertical bar pilot, running-board ladders, and Walschaerts valve gear were patterned after K-1 equipment. The tender carried 11,000 gallons of water and 16 tons of coal,

This Hudson could be bought for $71,551.62 in 1927. Four Brooks L-1a's performed well on 407-mile Chicago-Conneaut run. Builder's view of 173 below shows Elesco SF-205 exhaust steam injector (below firebox) and main air reservoirs. Outshopped two weeks after renowned NYC 5200, the 173 received precious little glory at her coming out at Dunkirk in March 1927. Location of shielded pump on pilot deck reduced intake of fly ash and dust; pump on right side was added 10 years later. — *Both photos, Collection of Willis A. McCaleb.*

Boiler of L-1b 176 heads for Lima's erecting floor. Hudson's firebox was interchangeable with that of H-6 Mikados. L's were first NKP locomotives with boiler which theoretically could produce more steam than cylinders could expend. — *NKP photo.*

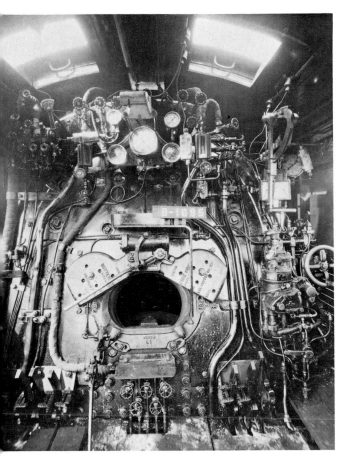

Brooks and Lima 4-6-4's were equipped with Standard single-screw stokers. Type B in L-1a (above) had firing pot inside firebox. BK type furnished with L-1b (left) used external gooseneck shaft and firing table. — *Collection of John A. Rehor.*

THE 1927 HUDSONS Original dimensions		
	NYC	**NYC&StL**
	J-1a	L-1a
Cylinders	25″ x 28″	25″ x 26″
Drivers	79″	73″
Valve gear	Walschaerts	Walschaerts
Weights, working order (lbs.)		
On drivers	182,000	175,500
Total engine	343,000	316,500
Tender	209,000	208,100
Wheel base, rigid (ft.)	14	13
Wheel base, total engine	40′ 4″	37′ 9″
Working steam pressure (lbs.)	225	215
Rated tractive effort		
(lbs.) at 85%	42,400	40,680
Rated tractive effort		
booster (lbs.)	10,900	- - - - -
Factor of adhesion	4.3	4.32
Grate area (sq. ft.)	81.5	66.7
Arch tubes	4	2
Nicholson syphons	0	2
Firebox length x width	130″ x 90¼″	114⅛″ x 84¼″
Heating surface (sq. ft.)		
Firebox, arch tubes, syphons	288	302
Tubes and flues	4203	3917
Superheater	1965	1055
Length over tube sheets (ft.)	20½	20
Tender capacity:		
Water (gal.)	10,000	11,000
Coal (tons)	18	16
Builder	Schenectady	Brooks

rode on Commonwealth equalized high-speed trucks, and was virtually identical to those furnished with the Pacifics. Unlike the K-1, though, the 4-6-4 had its single 8½-inch air pump mounted to the pilot deck casting on the left side. This arrangement, first tried out on the 616 in 1925, reduced the intake of fly ash and dust. In place of the conventional Worthington and Elesco feedwater heaters, the L-1a had the Elesco model SF-205 exhaust steam injector mounted on the left side. Three K-1's had been equipped with this device in 1926, and the mechanical department was enthusiastic about their performance. The exhaust steam injector used live steam to preheat boiler feedwater only in starting. When back pressure in the cylinder exhaust passages reached a given point, the device automatically switched over to exhaust steam. This reduced the drain on live steam at high speed, but the exhaust steam injector was actually better suited to freight practice where sudden changes in back pressure were less frequent.

Like the R's and K-1's, the Hudsons were reordered once and from another builder. In June 1929

the road awarded Lima a contract for four additional 4-6-4's, the 174-177. The L-1b's delivered in November of that year were practically identical to the Brooks engines except that they had cast locomotive beds and BK-type Simplex stokers. The L-1's could have used a little more firebox and superheater, and as a result they were more sensitive to poor coal than the Pacifics. They did not ride quite as smoothly as the K-1's, but they didn't get uncomfortable until they were hitting 80 or more. Dynamic augment, the centrifugal force of the driver counterbalances exerted upward, tended to literally raise the driving wheels off the rails thus causing a vertical pounding. Oddly enough, this action subsided after the speed climbed beyond 90.

The L-1a was about 13 tons lighter than the 5200, most of the weight differential resulting from the former's lack of a trailer booster and conventional feedwater heater. However, there was no great difference in the weight carried on the drivers, and in terms of adhesion the two locomotives were equals. In later years the L-1a's boiler pressure was boosted to 225 pounds and the driver diameter changed to 74 inches. This had the effect of changing the rated tractive effort to 42,000 pounds, nearly the same as that of the 5200. The longer firebox and much larger superheater of the Central's J-1a made it about 3½ feet longer than the 170's. Moreover, the Nickel Plate engine was taller and had greater boiler girth at the back sheet.

Albeit the L-1's never had the distinction of having powered the *Empire State Express*, the *Wolverine*, or the *Ohio State Limited*, they were nonetheless engine enough to last three decades on a railroad with mechanical and operational standards of the first order. They could go down through the country like the wind and do a workmanlike job on 15 to 20 heavy cars. Their melodious whistles and good looks attracted small boys like a swimming hole in August. Who, once having seen and heard them, could forget the midnight sight and sounds of an L-1 walking the *Nickel Plate Limited* up the tree-lined ruling grade at Rocky River?

THE COMFORTABLE ROUTE

Back in the early 1900's when the Clover Leaf was fighting to hold its own against the overwhelming competition of the Wabash, Walter Ross established his road's reputation for comfort, convenience, and courtesy. The "Comfortable Way," as Ross styled the Clover Leaf, could not outrun the Wabash flyers, but it could and did try harder to please. The overnight trains enjoyed many years of popularity simply because they offered convenient departures and arrivals and provided a pleasant, comfortable way to travel. In overhauling the Nickel Plate's passenger service, Ross relied on the same technique. If the Central had speed and frequency of operation out of reach, the Nickel Plate could score in many other areas. Cars could be cleaner and more comfortable, food could be prepared better and served faster, and employees could be more congenial and helpful. The Nickel Plate could afford to concentrate on the needs of Cleveland and lesser cities even more so than its competitors.

For many years the railroads operating trains between New York and Chicago had agreed to charge an excess fare on any train scheduled to run between those cities in less than 28 hours, and for each hour under that time the charge amounted to $1.20. It was stipulated that failure to meet the schedule entitled the passenger to a proportionate refund of the excess fare. This agreement tended to discourage improvement in the Nickel Plate-Lackawanna schedules, since the fare differential was an important attraction of the service offered by these roads. Hence the premier trains, Nos. 2 and 3, were still operated in 1927 in conjunction with the DL&W on the 28-hour schedules of 1897. No. 3 made the best time between Buffalo and Chicago, 14 hours 40 minutes, despite the fact that it made 28 sched-

uled and 12 conditional stops and could be halted anywhere else for passengers transferring from the Lackawanna.

The four new Hudsons went into service on the 407-mile Conneaut-Chicago run and were normally assigned to trains 1, 2, 5, and 6. While the last two had the poorest Buffalo connections and worked locally east of Cleveland, their overnight schedules between Cleveland and Chicago were growing in popularity. Nos. 1 and 2 offered convenient daytime service between Cleveland and Chicago as well as through New York and Scranton sleeping cars. In June 1927 the Nickel Plate bought a pair of new 30-chair dining cars and assigned them to these trains west of Cleveland. The Pullman-built cars featured fully carpeted floors and unusually spacious pantry and kitchen areas, the railroad having insisted on the latter feature as a means of expediting table service. The 84-ton diners were 81 feet long and rode on six-wheel Commonwealth cast-steel trucks. Both cars were equipped with roller bearings, the 104 with Timken and the 105 with Hyatt.

The scope of Ross' strategy was revealed by sweeping changes put into effect on Sunday, February 19, 1928. New York-Chicago and Cleveland-Chicago service was sharply improved, and a number of new trains were added to the timetable. New No. 8 left Cleveland's West 25th Street Station* at 6 p.m. and made a 4½-hour run to Buffalo where it connected with Lackawanna 14, the *Whitelight Limited*. The dining car assigned to No. 8 was dropped at Buffalo, but the coaches and a 12-section, drawing-room Pullman ran through to Hoboken, arriving there at 9:35 a.m. Connecting Hudson River ferries docked at Manhattan 17 minutes later. This excess-fare train was intended to compete with NYC No. 4, the all-Pullman *Cleveland Limited*, which also departed from Cleveland at 6 p.m. and was due into Grand Central Station at 8:05 a.m. No. 8 made regular stops only at Ashtabula, Conneaut, and Erie but could be flagged at Painesville and Dunkirk. Power used was generally a Brooks R class 4-6-0, the 156, 157, or 158. Coincident with the advent of this train, the operation of Nickel Plate No. 4 was discontinued east of Cleveland.

In competition with the westbound *Cleveland Limited*, NYC 21, the DL&W put on the new *Western Special*, No. 7, which left Hoboken at 6 p.m. and connected with Nickel Plate No. 1 at Buffalo. The latter was rescheduled to arrive at Cleveland at 8:55 a.m. and Chicago at 4:50 p.m. Over-all running time of less than 24 hours represented a 4-hour reduction over that of the old combination with DL&W 5. The schedule could have been cut

---

*Broadway station was permanently closed on February 1, 1928.

Lone steel cars on LE&W roster were three 68-ton Standard Steel Car-built R.P.O.-baggage cars. Numbered 230-232, they became NKP 830-832 in 1923. — *Clyde E. Helms.*

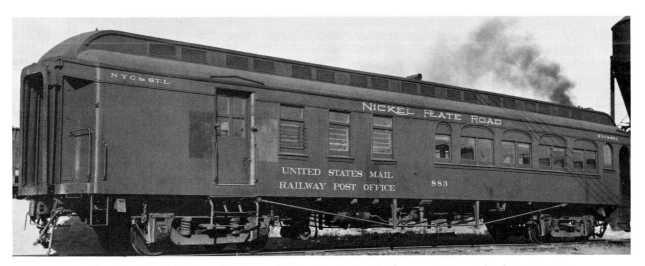

Combination R.P.O.-smoker was rebuilt with steel underframe at Stony Island in 1924. Pullman built the 36-passenger combine as LE&W 83 in 1906. — *Clyde E. Helms.*

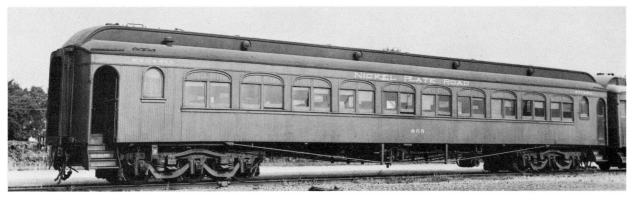

Pullman built 84-passenger coach 868 for LE&W in 1906. Car was rebuilt with steel underframe in 1920's and stayed on the revenue roster until 1951. — *Clyde E. Helms.*

Overnight Cleveland-New York flyer, No. 8, is about to depart from West 25th Street Station for last time on June 28, 1930. Next day NKP passenger trains commenced running into CUT. Coaches and sleeper ran through to Hoboken. — *Rev. James H. Dean.*

The R's feats with heavy passenger trains were legendary. Even when burning Shoal Creek "stone," Baldwins could hold down St. Louis Division schedules of trains 9 and 10 with 10 or more cars. Here 152 works train 21 across the Sandusky Division on March 3, 1937, before she received steel cab and running-board ladders. — *Clyde E. Helms.*

even more, but the Nickel Plate elected to hold back No. 1's Buffalo departure in order to utilize the engine that brought No. 2 into that city at 2:30 a.m. Refurbished 12-1 sleepers *St. Elmo, St. Cloud, St. Angele, St. Collins,* and *St. Leon* were assigned to these trains and the Cleveland-Hoboken runs. In addition to the sleepers and roller-bearing diners, Nos. 1 and 2 handled the plush parlor-observation cars *Mountainburg* and *Monte Carlo* between Chicago and Conneaut.

The Buffalo-Chicago schedules of trains 5 and 6 were also tightened up. No. 5 now made its run in 14½ hours and departed from Cleveland at 11:30 p.m., the same time as NYC 89, the all-Pullman *Forest City,* which stopped only at Toledo, Elkhart, and Englewood. The Nickel Plate train still pulled into La Salle Street at the convenient hour of 7:30 a.m., 15 minutes behind the *Forest City.* Eastbound, NYC 90 left Chicago at 11:30 p.m., 10 minutes after the departure of Nickel Plate 6, and arrived at Cleveland at 7:40 a.m. No. 6, running on a new 13-hour 50-minute schedule, had an 8:35 a.m. Cleveland arrival and carried Pullmans for that city, Buffalo, and New York.

February 19, 1928, also saw the inauguration of new Nos. 9 and 10, operated on overnight schedules over the 533.6 miles between West 25th Street, Lima, Muncie, Frankfort, and St. Louis Union Station.* No. 9 left Cleveland 5 minutes after No. 8 and arrived in St. Louis at 7:57 a.m. No. 10 started out at 5:15 p.m. and rolled into West 25th Street at 8:45 a.m., 10 minutes ahead of the departure of No. 6 for Buffalo. The two trains met at Frankfort at 12:40 a.m. and west of that point they carried the equipment of Nos. 15 and 16, the *Com-*

*Between Madison and St. Louis the new trains used 8 miles of Terminal Railroad Association track and the Merchants bridge. Trains 11, 12, 17, and 18 continued to use the Terminal Railroad Association's Eads Bridge line between East St. Louis and the Union Station.

Fishbelly all-steel 30-seat diners 104 and 105 were Pullman built for trains 1 and 2 in 1927. The 81-foot, 84.3-ton 105 (below) rode on Commonwealth cast-steel roller-bearing trucks. — *Collection of Arthur D. Dubin.* NKP insisted on large kitchen and pantry for roller-bearing diner 104 (left). This car was among seven Pullman diners purchased in 1927 and 1930. — *NKP photo.*

mercial Travelers. Initially, No. 9 left Cleveland with a baggage car, two 40- or 50-series steel underframe coaches, a 12-1 Pullman, and a steel underframe Barney & Smith parlor-cafe car which was dropped at Lima and picked up by No. 10 the next morning. Added at Frankfort were the mail car, chair car, coaches, and 12-1 sleeper brought out of Toledo by No. 15. West of Frankfort, trains 9 and 10 usually had eight or more cars plus a diner between Charleston and St. Louis. Occasionally the trains carried cars chartered by the St. Louis Browns baseball club. Often as not, the consists were fattened by carloads of spinach, bees, and strawberries. The schedules were so arranged that a single Pacific could hold down both trains east of Frankfort if necessary. At first the 162 and 163 were regulars on the trains, but west of Frankfort Baldwin R's 152, 153, 154, and 155 did the honors. Even with 10 or more cars, these seemingly dainty Ten-Wheelers could do a creditable job on the undulating profile of the St. Louis Division. The ex-Clover Leaf Atlantics 744 and 745 continued to hold down the *Commercial Travelers* between Frankfort and Toledo.

A pair of new daytime trains were also put on between Toledo Union Station and Indianapolis. Replacing Clover Leaf 3 and 4 between Kokomo and Toledo and LE&W 23 and 24 between Kokomo and Indianapolis, new trains 13 and 14 operated over the 235-mile interdistrict run on 8-hour schedules. These coach trains were usually powered by ex-Clover Leaf 2-8-0's, the 890-series Baldwins and 900-series Limas. Nos. 23 and 24 continued to run between Michigan City and Kokomo where they

connected with the new trains. No. 14 also connected with No. 22, the Bloomington-Sandusky plug at Tipton and No. 2 at Continental.

The Nickel Plate Limiteds

The success of the improved "Nickel Plate-Lackawanna Scenic Line" schedules helped bring about improved NYC service on both sides of Cleveland. On April 28, 1929, the *Cleveland Limiteds* and the *Ohio State Limited* were assigned new 8-section lounge-buffet cars and faster schedules between Cleveland and New York. Though the Nickel Plate and Lackawanna made no changes in their competing service between those cities, they did add a pair of crack new trains the same day between New York and Chicago. Nickel Plate No. 4 experienced a startling transition from a Chicago-Cleveland accommodation to a new excess-fare train, the *Nickel Plate Limited,* operated in connection with DL&W 6, the *Lackawanna Limited.* The westbound *Nickel Plate Limited,* No. 5, now ran between Buffalo and Chicago in 13 hours but still competed with NYC 89 west of Cleveland. This train with DL&W 3 offered a 9:37 a.m. New York departure and 23-hour service to Chicago. Four 12-1 Pullmans, the *Bijou, Anbury, Imola,* and *Planter,* were assigned to the through pool and the *Nickel Plate Limiteds* were also graced by a pair of Pullman club cars, the *Barnegat* and *Bellefontaine.* No. 5 continued to handle sleepers for Chicago originating at Buffalo and Cleveland as well as a new Pullman between Cleveland and Fort Wayne.

West of Fort Wayne No. 4 now stopped only at

N-6 Consolidations had 63-inch drivers, were used in passenger service after 1924. Here well-kept 458 heads No. 22 at St. Marys, O., on October 29, 1936. — *Clyde E. Helms.*

Adorning faultless double track at Kishmans in 1930 are L-1b and 10 cars of No. 1. Nickel Plate track standards ranked with the best, helped to establish popularity of overnight trains. — *Collection of John A. Rehor.*

Polished cylinder head covers gleam in morning sunlight as a Pacific highballs No. 10 on the double west of Cleveland. Hand-fired K-1b is nearing the end of 533-mile overnight run from St. Louis Union Station. — *Harold S. Ludlow.*

211

Englewood, Hammond, and Knox. The Chicago Division local chores formerly performed by this train were assigned to a new accommodation, No. 20. The local got into Fort Wayne just ahead of No. 4 and had a coach for through passengers which was added to the consist of the *Nickel Plate Limited.* No. 5's fast new schedule was made possible by the elimination of most of the stops it formerly made east of Cleveland. A new train, No. 7, did the local work and also provided a tight connection between DL&W 15 at Buffalo and No. 9 at Cleveland.

The timetable of April 28, 1929, was the high-water mark of Nickel Plate passenger service. A total of 28 passenger trains, the bulk of which were operated daily, and 11 daily-except-Sunday mixed trains provided varnish accommodations over all lines of the system. The road carried only 25 passenger locomotives on its roster — four Hudsons, two Atlantics, 10 Pacifics, and nine R class 4-6-0's.

However, 86 units classed as freight power were equipped for passenger duty. Included were 16 superheated P-1 and P-3 Ten-Wheelers, 48 Consolidations, and a trio of saturated Moguls. Car stock included 68 coaches and chair cars, six diners, 15 combines, 62 baggage and mail cars, and eight business cars.

During August 1929 passenger service was withdrawn from 175 miles of LE&W lines, most of which were paralleled by interurbans. On August 3 trains 27 and 28 made their last runs between Fort Wayne and Connersville,* and mixed service between New Castle and Rushville was dropped. Then, on August 31 the runs of trains 21 and 22 between Sandusky and Fostoria were discontinued. These trains con-

---

*Ultimately, the Indiana Railroad took over the mail contract between Fort Wayne, Muncie, and New Castle, operating its famed interurban R.P.O. cars between those cities until January 1941.

Last regular passenger train out of Sandusky arrives at Fostoria on August 31, 1929. Consist of Bloomington-bound No. 21 includes steel R.P.O. car and steel underframe coach. Rebuilt mill is superheated Brooks P-1. Fireman in cab is E. A. "Jumbo" Donovan. Others pictured are A. Stober, engineer; Darcey Stemen; Oscar Sullivan; and E. G. Bresson. — *Collection of Roy W. Carlson.*

tinued to operate between Fostoria and Bloomington in connection with Nos. 1 and 2.

Despite the continued decline of local business and the abandonment of service over more than 10 per cent of the system, the Nickel Plate's passenger receipts for 1929 were 17 per cent higher than in 1927. The popularity of the new trains had vindicated Ross' belief that the road could successfully compete with the New York Central, and the decision was made to again upgrade the operation coincident with the opening of the Cleveland Union Terminal. Neither Tom LeSueur, the aggressive general passenger agent, nor his assistant Frank O'Brien was satisfied with the equipment the Pullman Company was providing for their trains. After April 1929, when the NYC trains got combination lounge-buffet-sleeping cars, these men began clamoring for similar equipment for the *Nickel Plate Limiteds* and for single bedroom-lounge cars for trains 5 and 6 between Cleveland and Chicago. Late that summer the Central announced that its *Forest City* trains would be completely re-equipped by Pullman in time for the opening of the Cleveland Union Terminal. In the words of Frank O'Brien, it was "time for the Nickel Plate to get busy."

In June 1929 the Nickel Plate ordered the four Lima Hudsons and gave Pullman an order for 21

new all-steel cars. Among the equipment delivered during the winter of 1929-1930 were eight new 80-passenger coaches (90-97); three more heavy roller-bearing dining cars (106-108); a pair of 84-ton cafe-parlor cars (125-126); and eight baggage and mail cars. Pullman agreed to furnish 12 sleepers of the latest designs making a total of 34 assigned to the Nickel Plate. Two new cars with six single bedrooms, sun parlor-observation room, and lounge — *Summit Lake* and *Summit Grove* — were added to trains 5 and 6 on December 21, 1929. This was shortly after the Nickel Plate began using the Union Terminal to load Chicago and St. Louis sleepers originating at Cleveland.

The other new Pullmans included five 8-section sleepers with a lounge seating 16, buffet-soda fountain, and sun parlor-observation room. The lounges of these solarium cars were luxuriously carpeted and furnished with table lamps and deep-seated armchairs and settees upholstered in green, buff, gold, and black. The *Knickerbocker Club* and *Cleveland Club* were assigned to NKP 8/DL&W 14 and DL&W 7/NKP 1 operating between Cleveland and Hoboken. The *Baltusrol Club, Buffalo Club,* and *Chicago Club* were assigned to the *Nickel Plate Limited-Lackawanna Limited* trains. There were also five refurbished 10-section, 1-drawing room, 2-

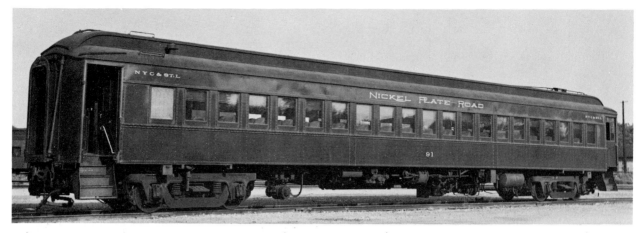

Lightweight Pullman coaches 90-97 seated 80 and weighed 62.5 tons. Addition of inside-duct mechanical air conditioning in 1937 increased weight by 8 tons. Cars were delivered early in 1930, measured 79 feet over the buffers. — *Clyde E. Helms*.

Radio-equipped and air-conditioned car 104 seated 10 in lounge and served 18 diners after rebuilding. On June 1, 1937, it went into service on trains 5 and 6 between Cleveland and Buffalo. — *NKP photo*.

Pompeian décor highlighted dining car 108 in regular service on No. 8, *Nickel Plate Limited*, and No. 7, *Westerner*. Pullman Company took over operation of company diners in April 1934. — *NKP photo*.

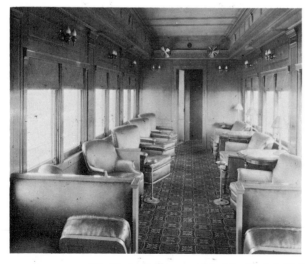

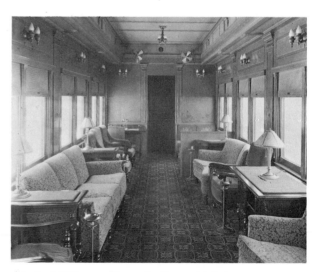

First new Pullmans added to Nickel Plate consists in 1930 were *Summit Grove* (right) and *Summit Lake*. Sister cars *Breeds Hill* and *Murray Hill* were operated by Pennsylvania and New Haven in the *Federal*, Washington-Boston flyer. *Commander* (left) and *Captain*, built in 1930 for C&EI, replaced *Summits* in 1934. — *Pullman-Standard*.

compartment sleepers furnished by Pullman to replace 12-1 cars assigned to these trains. *Lake James, Lake Harriet,* and *Lake Benton* went into the Chicago-Hoboken pool, while *Lake Louise* and *Lake Frederick* were placed in Cleveland-Hoboken service. Pullman was unable to furnish all the cars in time for the formal dedication of the CUT on June 28, 1930, or the start of full electrified operation the next day. However, *Baltusrol Club* was delivered on June 25 and was publicly displayed in the larger cities between Chicago and New York before going into service with the other cars in mid-July.

During 1930 the consists of trains 9 and 10 were also substantially upgraded. On March 30 10-1-2 Pullmans went into daily service between Cleveland and a pair of resort hotels, the Greenbrier at White Sulphur Springs, W. Va., and the Homestead at Virginia Hot Springs, Va. Nickel Plate 9 and 10 handled the cars as far as Fostoria, while the C&O's *Sportsman* took over for the balance of the 563-mile run. After the CUT opened, a St. Louis coach and No. 9's parlor-cafe car originated at Buffalo on No. 7. This train was renumbered 9 on September 28, 1930, making the latter's 720.8-mile Buffalo-St. Louis run the longest in the road's history. Briefly during the fall of 1930 the Hot Springs sleeper also originated in Buffalo. The use of 4-6-0's on 9 and 10 west of Frankfort was discontinued in 1930 and thereafter Pacifics pulled the trains the entire 536 miles from Cleveland to St. Louis without change. Finally, in December the standard 12-section sleepers were replaced by new 10-section observation-lounge cars, the *Mount Cory* and *Mount Summit.*

The ebbtide of prosperity soon brought about wholesale retrenchment of the passenger operation. On September 28, 1930, train No. 4 was discontinued and No. 8 became the premier eastbound. Like the *20th Century Limited,* the eastbound *Nickel Plate Limited* did not stop at Cleveland after the CUT was opened. No. 4 ran through from Rocky River to East Cleveland and crossed the Cuyahoga on the Nickel Plate's own viaduct. This affront to proud Cleveland lasted but three months. As the *Nickel Plate Limited,* No. 8 originated at Chicago at 9:25 a.m. and made a daylight run to the Cleveland Union Terminal. The old Cleveland departure and overnight service to New York were maintained and the over-all running time of the new *Nickel Plate Limited-Lackawanna Limited* combination was less than 23 hours. With the change, Chicago Division accommodations 19 and 20 were taken off and No. 2, which left Chicago 90 minutes behind No. 8, now did the local work west of Fort Wayne. The lounge-buffet sleeping cars, 10-1-2 Pullmans, and through coaches survived the change. In addition, No. 8 carried a 26-seat parlor car, one of the new diners, and Chicago-Buffalo coaches.

Baltusrol Club lounge seated 16. Eight-section lounge-buffet-observation car and two sisters went into service on *Nickel Plate Limited* in 1930. — *Pullman-Standard.*

Summit Grove was rebuilt by Pullman in 1939 before going to PRR. — *Pullman-Standard.*

215

Ready to leave East Peoria behind 519 in 1929 is train of Caterpillar tractors headed for East Coast and Russia. Automobile industry's growth during the 1920's fattened Nickel Plate freight revenues. — *Collection of John A. Rehor.*

OB-2 is hot on the tail of No. 6 west of Cleveland. The Mike on the point in this 1939 photo is Walschaerts-geared 628 with a 16,000-gallon tender. — *Harold S. Ludlow.*

Hudsons were seldom used on Buffalo Division varnish, but on April 23, 1932, 177 blasts out of Conneaut on the head end of No. 6. Sister 175 has been relieved after bringing the train in from Chicago. — *Paul W. Prescott.*

Expansion of the Manifest Fleet

The basic fast freight operation of the original Nickel Plate was established long before the turn of the century and was built around two eastbound manifest trains. The standard-bearers had always been No. 52, the meat express nearly as old as the railroad itself, and the stock train, No. 54. The road's fast westbound merchandise run, No. 55, and a number of through time freights — 35, 36, 37, 38, and 39 — also claimed seniority dating from the era of Darius Caldwell and the link-and-pin coupler. By 1910 No. 52 was running on a 29-hour schedule calling for a 4:30 p.m. Stony Island departure. The several sections of this train were followed east by the 30-hour stock train, for years carded out of Chicago at 7 p.m. In the early 1900's train 56 was added to the manifest fleet. Also, there was a No. 50 which originated at Continental, O., leaving that point about 7 p.m., after the arrival of Clover Leaf 44 from Madison. The westbound version, No. 51, was timed to make a close connection with the swift "KC" *Merchandise Special*.

During the first decade of Van Sweringen control, the growth of business made it necessary to expand the manifest fleet. A new meat run, No. 58, left Chicago around noon in advance of the 52 and filled out with loads coming off the Indiana Harbor Belt at Hammond. No. 52, usually assigned the symbol OB-2, still ran against a 10:30 p.m. Buffalo cutoff but had a somewhat later departure than previously. The midnight cleanup run, No. 56, was carried in the timecard as the CB-10. With as many as 80 carloads of livestock received daily from the Union Stock Yards, a special train, the *Chicago Stock*, was dispatched ahead of No. 54 which carried symbol CB-2 and left Chicago later in the evening.

Not long after the 1923 consolidation, through interdistrict freight runs were established between Lima and Bellevue. Trains were operated by both LE&W and Fort Wayne division crews under a mileage pool arrangement. Of the three daily manifest runs dispatched from Peoria, the KB-2 (No. 62) and the KB-4 (No. 68) ran through from Lima to Bellevue, 90 miles. The other through train, No. 66, continued to run to Sandusky as in the past. No. 64, which originated at Tipton and filled out as a rule at Muncie and Lima, also ran through to Bellevue. This eastbound forwarded the heavy volume of stock, meat, Marmon autos, and other redball freight brought out of Indianapolis each evening by No. 82.

A Clover Leaf-Fort Wayne division pool was also established, and trains were operated from Delphos to Bellevue via Continental, 96 miles. Eastbound manifests KC-44 and KC-48 ran through during the 1920's as well as the fast westbound merchandiser, No. 41. Mikados were used on the Bellevue-Lima trains but the Delphos runs were restricted to 2-8-0's by the old bridge at Dupont. On these trains Fort Wayne Division "submarines," the ex-NYC T's, were pooled with the Clover Leaf's superheated 800's and 900's. KC-44, the Clover Leaf stock train, was scheduled to leave Madison at 5 p.m. and arrive at Bellevue early the next evening behind the CB-10. During 1926-1927 the Bellevue arrival was moved up 5½ hours to mid-afternoon in order to coincide with that of KB-4 out of Peoria. The speedup was made possible by boosting the freight train speed limit from 30 to 40 mph west of Continental. Often combined with CB-10 and KB-4 east of Bellevue, the KC-44 offered 31- or 32-hour service over the long 715-mile run between Madison and Tifft Yard at Buffalo.

Early in 1930 another fast St. Louis-Buffalo train was added in the form of No. 46, the MB-98. Out of Madison at 10 a.m., this train ran on a 31-hour schedule with an early morning Bellevue arrival sandwiched between those of the OB-2 and KB-2. A new westbound St. Louis manifest was also added in 1930. No. 47 carried the symbol NS-1, left Buffalo at 9:30 p.m., and was due into Madison early on the second morning. In 1931 No. 66 became a through Peoria-Buffalo train, the PB-6, and its schedule was altered to replace that of the KB-4. Later the same year a new Cleveland-Madison hotshot, CS-7, went into service. Eventually carried as No. 49 in the timecard, this train left Cleveland at 6 p.m. and was due at Madison around noon the next day.

The initial crew and engine on the CS-7 came out of Conneaut in the morning and worked the west local into Cleveland. Eastbound, a train of perishable and other high-grade Cleveland freight was dispatched from Bellevue in the early morning, ahead of OB-2 and MB-98. Originally called Advance MB-98, this run was due at the high level yard at Broadway at 5:30 a.m. This crew then continued on to Conneaut working the east local. Another new eastbound, the *Cleveland Merchandise* (CD-54), left Cleveland at 7 p.m. and ran against a 3 a.m. Buffalo cutoff. Yet another Cleveland run was established in 1931 or 1932. The FS-2 came out of Lima each evening with hot freight off the B&O and Erie, and filled out at Bellevue with Cleveland cars brought in by the PB-6 and KC-44. Not only did these new trains enable the Nickel Plate to give its Cleveland customers outstanding service, but they permitted a speedup of through fast freights which formerly had set out and picked up at that city.

The Leanest Years

Capitalizing on the Van Sweringens' recurrent financial crises and impotence before the I.C.C.,

Narrow-gauge trains once crossed the Auglaize River over iron bridge at Dupont. This bridge and two others of similar 1886 vintage are still used by Clover Leaf trains. Dupont was named after an early American admiral. — *Willis A. McCaleb*.

Lack of yard capacity at Buffalo compelled Nickel Plate to block manifests for quick delivery to eastern connections. Final classification had to be done at Bellevue. This is how outmoded facilities there appeared in 1930's. — *Collection of John A. Rehor*.

Combine came off Minster Branch with end of mixed service in September 1930, but daily train's caboose continued handling express and l.c.l. Ex-Clover Leaf 263 poses in October 1932 after side door was added at Lima. — *Clyde E. Helms.*

General Atterbury had the Eastern consolidation game well in hand by the onset of the depression. In July 1929 the Pennsylvania-controlled Wabash proposed that it be permitted to form a fifth Eastern system through the acquisition of the Wheeling & Lake Erie-Pittsburgh & West Virginia-Western Maryland "Lakes to Sea" line as well as the Lehigh Valley, the Akron, Canton & Youngstown, and other roads. In its new consolidation plan of December 9, 1929, the I.C.C. not only agreed to most of what the Wabash had asked for but assigned it the Seaboard Air Line, Norfolk & Western, Ann Arbor, and Chesapeake & Ohio of Indiana as well. This huge system also included 40-odd short lines, a half-interest in the Detroit, Toledo & Ironton, and trackage rights over hundreds of miles of PRR lines. The I.C.C. also endorsed a consolidated Van Sweringen system embracing the C&O east of Cincinnati, the Erie, DL&W, Nickel Plate, Pere Marquette, and a number of shorter roads.

Just as Loree had been the foe in 1927, the Wabash represented an intolerable threat to the Van Sweringens in 1930. Aside from crushing the fifth system, the Vans sought to stop the Pennsylvania-controlled road's persistent pressure on the I.C.C. to enforce the Wheeling Clayton Act order. As usual the brothers were not lacking for strategy. In 1930 they purchased control of the Missouri Pacific system, which in turn controlled the Texas & Pacific and held a half-ownership of the Denver & Rio

Grande Western. It was widely believed that the acquisition of these properties was part of a bold, if impractical, revival of the old Gould dream of a transcontinental system. It seems more likely, though, that the move was intended to strengthen the Van Sweringen position in dealing with Atterbury by putting the skids on the suddenly aggressive Wabash. That road was heavily dependent on the

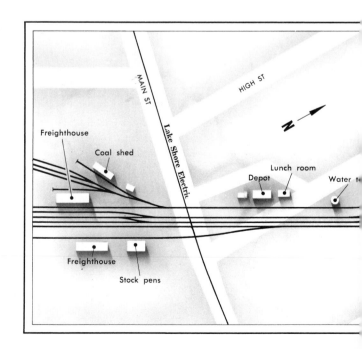

Missouri Pacific for eastbound traffic, traffic which could move just as easily over the Nickel Plate. Whatever the effect of the Missouri Pacific grab, the Wabash slipped into bankruptcy in 1931, thus ending the threat of the fifth system. Subsequently, General Atterbury extended the olive branch and offered the Vans the Lehigh Valley and other concessions for a free hand with the Virginian and trackage rights over the Nickel Plate main line, an idea first advanced by Samuel Rea in 1924. A new Four-System Plan was submitted to the I.C.C. in 1932, but the consolidation proposals passed into limbo with the end of the Hoover administration and the railroads' increasing preoccupation with the fight for survival.

The early stages of the Great Depression were viewed by the Van Sweringens and others as nothing worse than a mild economic adjustment similar to the postwar recession of 1921-1922. By the end of October 1930, however, the Vans were at the wall. They needed 40 million dollars to cover their debts and prevent the complete collapse of their empire. Once again the coalition of New York banks led by the House of Morgan came to their rescue. To secure the rescue loan, the bankers demanded every item of marketable collateral the promoters had. Four Cleveland banks, holders of a 14-million-dollar Van Sweringen note, released the collateral they held so that the Vans might save themselves as well as what remained of Cleveland's prosperity. It was soon obvious that the recovery they were banking on was not just around the corner.

After remaining at a relatively static level between 1924 and 1928, the Nickel Plate's operating revenues had increased appreciably in 1929. By driving the transportation ratio down to 34.52 per cent, Ross and Ayers managed to carry more than 7 million dollars to net income in the face of wildly inflated interest charges. However, November 1929 saw the onset of a decline in revenues that accelerated with each passing month and persisted for three and a half years. Despite the fact that the Nickel Plate's reputation was founded on its ability to handle meat and perishable traffic, the road depended on merchandise and manufactured goods for fully 40 per cent of its freight tonnage. As the economic paralysis of the early 1930's devastated America's prosperity, an eerie quiet enveloped the industrial cities of the Great Lakes basin. The effect on the Nickel Plate's traffic was catastrophic. Inside of three years the depression cost the road 84 per cent of its automotive business, 78 per cent of its iron and steel receipts, and more than half its total freight tonnage. Staggering under a terrible burden of debt, the company faced the most desperate challenge in its history.

After October 1930 the Nickel Plate's net earnings after expenses and taxes were no longer sufficient to meet the average of nearly 1 million dollars needed each month to pay fixed charges, dividends, and sinking fund installments. Unearned dividends on both classes of stock were paid at the quarterly rate of 1½ per cent through the first half of 1931. The Van Sweringens' financial needs and the desire to hold up the market value of the common dictated the delay in passing the dividend on that class. In the case of the preferred, the dividend was cumulative. If it was not

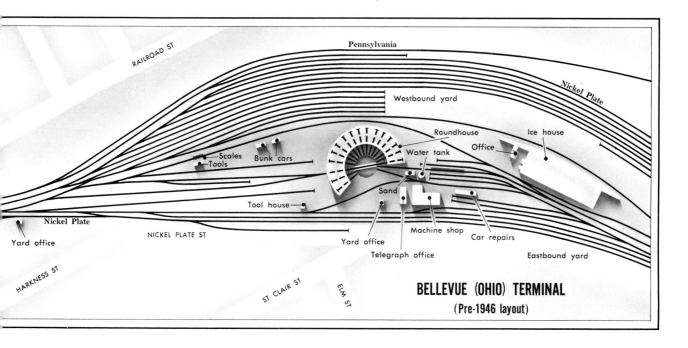

BELLEVUE (OHIO) TERMINAL
(Pre-1946 layout)

paid, the shareholders gained the right to vote. This had the immediate effect of reducing the Vans' voting interest then vested in the Alleghany Corporation to less than 25 per cent. While the Vans did not relish the idea of losing their majority interest, it was either this course or that of giving the Nickel Plate to its bondholders. Even with the more than

2 million dollars in paid dividends discounted, the road showed a deficit in 1931.

Gus Ayers made a determined bid to offset lost revenues with reduced expenses. Nonetheless, a decade of close attention to such matters had left precious little fat to trim. The passenger department's brief era of glory came to a rude end with sweeping

R 158 takes water from joint NKP-Big Four tank at Templeton in 1930's. CCC&StL (right) and predecessors have had Templeton-Lafayette trackage rights since 1872. — *Collection of John H. Keller.*

reductions in service during 1931-1932. On May 2, 1931, trains 13 and 14 made their last runs and the operation of No. 3 east of Cleveland was discontinued. The same date marked the end of the Toledo sleeper and through operation of coaches between Toledo and St. Louis. After February 1, 1932, trains 11 and 12 no longer crossed the Missis- sippi and terminated at the Front Street freight- house in East St. Louis. This was the end of regu- lar use of the Eads Bridge by Nickel Plate trains.

April 16, 1932, saw the final operation of Nos. 23 and 24, the Indianapolis-Michigan City runs and trains 2 and 3 were taken off the following June 18.[*] Shortly afterward, the *Commercial Travelers* quit the Union Station at Toledo on July 5 and subsequently tied up at the Erie Street freighthouse. Then, on October 1, 1932, these trains were relegated to mixed status east of Delphos. The wholesale reduction of passenger service on the Clover Leaf culminated in the withdrawal of trains 17 and 18 on July 11, 1932. Since November 1, 1930, these trains had been operated only between Charleston and Frankfort.

The year 1932 proved to be the worst in the history of the Nickel Plate. Gross revenues were 48.3 per cent less than those of 1929 and not much higher than in 1922 prior to the consolidation. The road ran $4,410,434 in the red, and its common stock which had peaked at 240½ in 1927 sank to a low of 1½. Even the preferred commanded as little as 2 dollars a share. Most observers wrote the Nickel Plate off, certain that the *coup de grace* would be delivered by the holders of the 20 million dollars' worth of unsecured promissory notes due on October 1, 1932. The company was utterly broke and was in no position to meet its fixed charges, much less so large a maturity.

The Federal government, through the Reconstruction Finance Corporation, advanced the Nickel Plate $18,111,587 without security during the course of 1932.[†] The first loan, made in February, was used to pay off 6 million dollars borrowed from a New York bank to meet 1931 obligations. Other loans late in the summer made it possible for the road to pay its taxes and first-mortgage interest. Unable to lend the Nickel Plate the 20 million needed to retire the three-year notes, the RFC offered instead to advance 5.6 million dollars, enough to pay 25 per cent of the notes and accrued interest. Consequently, on September 13 the management admitted that it could not refund the notes through normal banking channels and proposed to pay $250 against each $1000 note and issue new three-year notes for the balance. Since the Nickel Plate was so utterly top-heavy with mortgage bonds, the noteholders knew they had little or no chance of recovery in the event of bankruptcy. By the end of 1932 92 per cent of the notes had been deposited for exchange and the road had once again sidestepped calamity.

The joint management of the C&O and PM took over the reins of the Nickel Plate in February 1933, the month the road's revenues hit rock bottom. On February 8 Walter Ross resigned and was replaced as president by John Bernet who had headed the C&O and PM since 1930. Bernet knew that the Nickel Plate was going to have to fight its way out of the depression on its own. The prospect of more outside help was bleaker than ever after the bank panic of March. Even if the road could earn enough to meet its fixed charges, it would still be faced with the 1935 maturities of the promissory notes and RFC loans. As if the road did not have trouble enough, its burden was unexpectedly increased by the April 1933 failure of the Northern Ohio Railway and its lessor, the Akron, Canton & Youngstown. The LE&W had guaranteed the Northern Ohio first mortgage of 1895. While the AC&Y had agreed to assume this guaranty when it took over the NO on March 1, 1920, the bondholders were never parties to the agreement. Hence the Nickel Plate was obligated to pay the interest on the bonds.[*]

By the end of May 1933 Bernet had started the Nickel Plate down the road to recovery. For the first time since 1929 revenues were on the rise, a trend that continued for more than a year. Moreover, the operating ratio had been depressed from 75 to 59 per cent in less than four months. Paramount in Bernet's program was the drive to gain the largest possible share of freight still moving through Nickel Plate territory. Although Bernet slashed expenses to the marrow, he was willing to spend money where it would work to speed up the operation. Like all railroads, the Nickel Plate had to live with a level of efficiency that was bogged down by the use of obsolete locomotives on secondary lines. Light bridges and rail barred the operation of heavy and efficient power over the Clover Leaf and much of the LE&W. This slowed down operating schedules and undermined the over-all competitive position of the railroad. Bernet sought to relieve the light 2-8-0's on Clover Leaf manifests with Mikados, but first he had to find the cash needed to rebuild a large number of bridges and trestles. To raise funds he ordered the scrapping of every surplus locomotive and car on the Nickel Plate. Before the end of 1933, 7154 cars — more than a third of the roster — and 119 locomotives were reduced to scrap at Stony Island, Frankfort, Lima, and Conneaut. Of the 444 engines on hand at the beginning of 1933, a total of 156 were dismantled by the end of 1934. Most of the antiquated and worn-out power acquired with the Clover Leaf

---

[*]During the 1934 Century of Progress fair at Chicago, Nos. 3 and 4 were restored as excess-fare trains with through sleepers operated in conjunction with DL&W 6 and 9. They ran daily from June 17 to and including September 8.

[†]The Van Sweringen roads, excluding the C&O, borrowed a total of 75.6 million from the RFC. Only the Nickel Plate and the Pere Marquette, borrower of 3 million, repaid their loans. The other roads passed into bankruptcy.

[*]This liability was affirmed by the United States Supreme Court on December 8, 1941. The New York Supreme Court had previously ruled that the Nickel Plate was also liable for the principal of the bonds. Prior to the 1944 reorganization of the AC&Y, the Nickel Plate settled with most of the bondholders.

Atlantic 744 was laid up at Frankfort in 1931 and was stricken from roster in John Bernet's motive power purge of March 1933. Brooks 4-4-2 spent working career on Clover Leaf *Commercial Travelers.* — *Collection of Willis A. McCaleb.*

"Two-door sedan" 483 was one of 156 steam locomotives scrapped by Nickel Plate during 1933-1934. The big G-6v Consolidation was assigned to a westbound freight at Lima on June 23, 1933. — *Clyde E. Helms.*

and LE&W went to the torch. Only four saturated units, all switchers, survived the purge.

By rebuilding, filling, or strengthening 37 Clover Leaf bridges west of Frankfort, it was possible to extend the operation of 2-8-2's to Madison. Whereas the 2-8-0's working the St. Louis Division were rated at 1800-1900 tons, H-6's were good for 2700 tons westbound and 3000 tons eastbound. Use of the larger engines also cut out many water stops and permitted the elimination of helpers at Cayuga and Silverwood. To turn the Mikados at Madison the 65-foot turntable there was replaced by a 90-foot power table formerly used at Peru. In April 1933 the road moved into the C&O's Peru terminal

Competition was tough at the St. Louis gateway after the 1933 appearance of H-6 Mikados on west end of Clover Leaf. The 646, with a 22,000-gallon tender, relaxes briefly at Charleston's coal chute. — *Richard J. Cook.*

and abandoned its yard, six-stall roundhouse, and other facilities in the Circus City. Although Nickel Plate road engines continued to service the Indianapolis Division, Peru yard crews now used a C&O 0-8-0 rented at the rate of $2.25 per hour.

In order to further expedite the St. Louis-Buffalo operation, agreements were negotiated with the operating brotherhoods which brought an end to the practice of running manifests between Frankfort and Bellevue over two separate routes. The Clover Leaf bridge at Dupont, built in 1886, would accommodate no engine heavier than a class G-44 2-8-0. This restriction limited manifest freights to 2300 tons between Frankfort, Delphos, and Bellevue. By contrast, 2-8-2's could handle 3000 to 3500 tons over the LE&W-Fort Wayne division combination which was 6 miles shorter, had longer sidings, and fewer slow orders. Clover Leaf manifests KC-44, CS-7, MB-98, and NS-1 were diverted to the LE&W route on June 4, 1933. The same day Rankin and Tipton ceased to be Lake Erie division points. One operating division was eliminated by extending the Sandusky Division from Tipton to Frankfort, 25 miles to the west, with crews running through from Frankfort to Lima, 144.4 miles. The Peoria Division now constituted a single operating division, 181.2 miles long, from Frankfort to Peoria. These important changes permitted sharp improvement in St. Louis and Peoria service and put a good dent in operating expenses.

Also during 1933, the mainline freight speed limit was raised to 45 mph, and heavy repairs to several Cleveland and Buffalo division viaducts eliminated long-standing slow orders. Now consolidated with the KB-2 at Frankfort, MB-98 was running on a 29-hour schedule and followed the OB-2 into Buffalo.

Speeded up, too, were the CB-2, CB-10, PB-6, IB-64, and some of the westbounds. The BC-1, or "Bozo," was now due into Chicago 3 hours earlier than in the past.

A considerable amount of Bernet's scrap money was spent to increase the efficiency of the 288 locomotives left on the roster, especially the Mikados. In 1930 the 662 had been equipped with the new Waugh Firebar Unit grates and had subsequently made four consecutive runs, a total of 628 miles, before her fire needed cleaning. With the old grates it was usually necessary to dump the ashpan as often as coal was taken on. With Firebars and good coal it wasn't even necessary to shake the grates. The savings in fuel consumption and terminal delays were extraordinary. During 1933-1934 178 other Nickel Plate engines were equipped with Firebars and almost as many were also re-drafted for better economy. In an effort to cut down on coal and water stops, the road began boosting the capacity of the H-6 tenders in 1930. In most cases the collars or dashboards were built up with boards to increase coal capacity from 16 to 19 tons. A number of H-6 tanks were torn down and rebuilt with new frames and new Buckeye or Commonwealth six-wheel trucks in place of the lead Andrews four-wheel trucks. These rebuilt tanks carried 16,500 gallons of water and 19 tons of coal, enough to get a 2-8-2 across the 115-mile Buffalo Division without stopping. The road figured that under normal circumstances a 22,000-gallon tank would permit nonstop runs across all mainline divisions. Early in 1934 Lima was given an order for 25 such units for use with H-6e 2-8-2's.

However vital these efforts were to win back business and increase efficiency, the Nickel Plate's sorry

Booster-equipped Mikado 633 is ready to take MB-98 out of Madison on October 4, 1938. Buckeye tank assigned to H-6e weighed more than the engine. Braces were applied to 2-8-2's after rash of cylinder breaks in early 1930's. — *Robert J. Foster.*

Unusual 16RB tenders were rebuilds of 10,000-gallon H-6 units. Single six-wheel Buckeye truck helped support 19 tons of coal and 16,500 gallons of water. Nickel Plate 2-8-2's seemed to emerge from each shopping with a different tender. — *Paul Stringham.*

Extra tenders delivered by Lima in 1934 gave boost to nonstop range of 25 H-6e Mikados. Water-bottom 22RA's carried 22,000 gallons of water, 20 tons of coal on six-wheel Buckeye trucks. Note familiar diamond plate on tank. — *NKP photo.*

plight demanded a dynamic remedy that only a revolutionary new locomotive could promise. The H-6 Mikado, which could take high-grade tonnage away from competing lines at will in 1926, had become outmoded in the fast moving evolution of the freight locomotive. The Nickel Plate no longer enjoyed a monopoly on speed. Out of Chicago alone the road competed with eight other lines — all of which had improved their freight schedules. Bernet had dealt the cruelest blow by transforming the dawdling Erie into a high-speed freight hauler. Big 2-8-4's were rolling manifest trains across three divisions at a time. The Erie had the advantage of running all the way to tidewater, whereas the Nickel

Plate had to rely on Buffalo connections still steeped in drag era tradition. If the Nickel Plate was to survive, Bernet would have to come up with a new eight-coupled standard — a "Super-Power" engine which could eclipse not only the H-6 but the Erie S and the 4-8-2's of the Central and Wabash as well.

THE SUPER-POWER EVOLUTION

Between 1906 and 1925 the tremendously expanded volume of goods transported by the railroads was accommodated by running trains of ever-increasing length. During the same period there was only a minuscule gain in speed. In fact, in 1925 American freight trains averaged all of 11.8 mph in getting over the road. The railroads were still seeking the cheapest rather than the fastest method of hauling freight. Almost universally their mechanical men regarded tractive effort* as the standard of comparison between locomotives and the true measure of their power. To a few outspoken design engineers, such as Alco's A. W. Bruce and Lima's W. E. Woodard, tractive effort was an indefinite 2-foot rule where a precise yardstick was needed. The old standard, according to Bruce, made no allowance for the elements of time and distance.

As early as 1913 Francis J. Cole had given the industry formulae for rating locomotives on an indicated horsepower basis. Nevertheless, proportions continued to be based on the tractive effort standard with little heed paid to the horsepower potentials of cylinders, boiler, and furnace and their vital relationship to each other. Mechanical men were also loath to adopt changes and new devices designed to deliver increased locomotive performance and efficiency. The booster, mechanical stoker, firebox syphons, and other proven auxiliaries were often rejected as "unproductive jewelry." The not-

*The rated tractive effort of a steam locomotive was measured in pounds and based on the diameter of the cylinder bore, the length of piston stroke, the mean effective pressure of steam in the cylinders, and the diameter of the driving wheels. As an example, the computation for the Nickel Plate 4-6-4 was:

$$\frac{25^2 \times 26 \times 182.75}{73} = 40,680.7$$

able gap in this wall of apathy was the New York Central. This was the railroad which provided the impetus for the horsepower breakthrough that came in the 1920's.

In the so-called light Mikado, the United States Railroad Administration had given the industry a most versatile and universally successful freight locomotive. This was a truly dual-purpose design, dual in the sense that it was equally at home on drag tonnage or on a fast manifest. The 2-8-2's furnace was ample for its boiler which was liberal enough to produce nearly as much steam as its 26-inch cylinders could transform into pulling power. The combination of a 30-inch stroke and 63-inch driver was well suited to fast running. Sufficient weight rode on the drivers to give the locomotive excellent adhesion. Under the patronage of the NYC, the Lima Locomotive Works sought to produce an improved 2-8-2 which would provide substantially more horsepower at the drawbar than the USRA, without a corresponding increase in fuel consumption or driving axle load.

Michigan Central 8000, Lima's "Super-Mikado," went into service trials early in the summer of 1922. The engine had the USRA's firebox combined with a somewhat larger boiler, the new Type E smokebox superheater, a feedwater heater, and a trailer booster. With slightly higher boiler pressure and

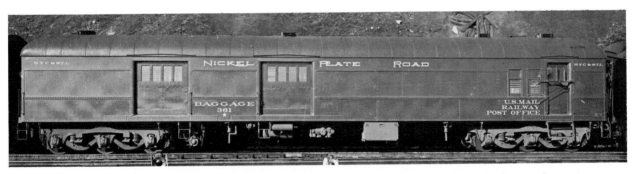

Turtleback-roofed 361 was only St. Louis Car Company product on Nickel Plate's varnish roster. R.P.O.-baggage car built in 1934 is 74 feet over buffers. — *NKP photo.*

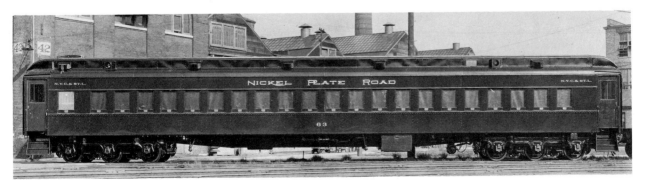

60-series coaches, bought from Pullman in 1934, seated 58 in main compartment, 14 in smoker, 6 in ladies' lounge. These seven cars weighed over 81 tons, were 83 feet 3¼ inches long over buffers. — *NKP photo.*

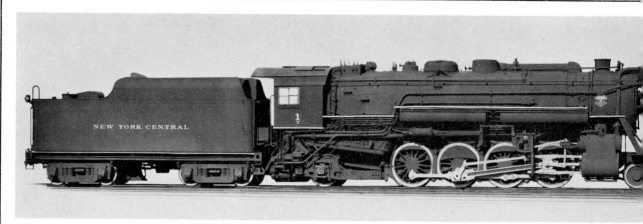

NYC H-10 (Lima 8000, Prototype)

Erie S-4

NKP S

2 more inches of cylinder bore, the 8000 developed considerably more drawbar horsepower with a given amount of coal than the USRA engine. The Super-Mikado reflected the increasing emphasis on fuel economy and the NYC was enthusiastic enough over its performance to buy 300 duplicate machines. There was one glaring weakness not present in the earlier 2-8-2's. The designers had violated the "25 per cent law" which dictated a ratio of not more than 1 pound of tractive effort to each 4 pounds of adhesive weight. The Super-Mikado's 3.72 factor of adhesion spelled chronic driver slippage, a characteristic which robbed the engine of power, promoted rapid tire wear, and played havoc with the fire. Wet rail and worn tires aggravated the problem. Heavy rail sanding helped adhesion, but often

	NYC H-10	LIMA A-1	ERIE S-4	C&O T-1	NKP S
			3385-3404	3000-3039	700-714
	2-8-2	2-8-4	2-8-4	2-10-4	2-8-4
Cylinders	28″ x 30″	28″ x 30″	28½″ x 32″	29″ x 34″	25″ x 34″
Drivers	63″	63″	70″	69″	69″
Working steam pressure (lbs.)	210	240	250	260	245
Rated tractive effort					
M.e.p. (lbs.) at:	85%	60%	60%	85%	85%
Main engine:	66,700	69,400	72,000	91,584	64,100
Booster	11,000	12,000	13,000	15,000	------
Total	77,700	81,400	85,000	106,584	64,100
Weight, working order (lbs.)					
On drivers	248,000	249,500	286,500	373,000	261,100
Total engine	335,000	389,000	468,800	566,000	428,900
Factor of adhesion	3.72	3.60	3.98	4.07	4.07
Engine wheelbase	37′	41′ 8″	44′	49′ 3″	42′
Boiler diameter at first ring	86″	88″	92″	99¾″	86″
Total evaporative surface (sq. ft.)	4578	5110	5697	6635	4818
Superheater surface (sq. ft.)	1780	2111	2545	3030	1932
Grate area (sq. ft.)	66.4	100	100	121.7	90.3
Builder	Lima	Lima	Lima	Lima	Alco
Year	1922	1925	1929	1930	1934

C&O T-1

LIMA A-1   *All photos, Allen County Historical Society.*

this also worked for increased train resistance.

If there was one deficiency common to all freight locomotives in the mid-1920's it was inadequate boiler capacity. The combination of the tractive effort standard and the railroads' quest for drag power that could single-handedly "clean out the yard" was producing one over-cylindered design after another. The designer of the Super-Mikado, Will Woodard, was keenly aware of the folly of enlarging cylinder proportions without a corresponding increase in furnace volume and the capacity to generate steam. Realizing that the 8000 represented the 2-8-2's maximum potential in these respects, Woodard and Lima set about to design an entirely new two-cylinder locomotive which would pierce the horsepower barrier and still satisfy the carriers'

231

obsession with both fuel economy and drag power.

In the famed A-1, Lima's Super-Power standard-bearer of 1925, Woodard came up with an eight-coupled engine with a big boiler and a firebox so large that a four-wheel trailing truck was needed to bear its weight. Hence the new machine was a 2-8-4. The grate area of 100 square feet was half again greater than that of the Super-Mikado, and by using cast-steel cylinders Lima was able to increase working steam pressure from 210 to 240 pounds. The 28 x 30-inch cylinder and 63-inch driver of the 2-8-2 were retained. To transform the increased steam pressure to drawbar horsepower while keeping tractive effort within reasonable limits, Woodard chose to limit maximum cutoff in full gear to 60 per cent — that is to say that steam admission to the cylinders was cut off when the piston had completed 60 per cent of its stroke. At very slow speeds limited cutoff permitted the greater expansive use of steam within the cylinders with resultant fuel economy. It was also felt that the "more even" starting torque with limited cutoff gave the designer greater liberty with adhesion than that of a full stroke engine. The A-1 had a factor of only 3.60.

In trials on the Boston & Albany, the A-1 easily outperformed the Super-Mikado, and that road subsequently bought 55 duplicates of the locomotive. The 2-8-4 was thereafter most generally referred to as the Berkshire type, after the hills the A-1 had conquered on the B&A. Between 1926 and 1930 a total of 282 Berkshires were built, including 75 Lima units of the A-1 design for the Illinois Central and Boston & Maine. Alco turned out a number of similar engines for the Missouri Pacific, Chicago & North Western, and the Toronto, Hamilton & Buffalo. A group of 2-8-4's built by Baldwin for the Santa Fe in 1927 were essentially a beefed-up USRA heavy Mikado and lacked the high boiler capacity and limited cutoff of the A-1.

The advent of the prototype 2-8-4 was a milestone in steam locomotive development which turned the attention of the industry to the free-steaming, high-capacity boiler. The A-1 locomotives, however, were generally used in drag service at low speeds where friction was minimal and the limited cutoff feature produced maximum economy. As a result they seldom fully utilized the high-speed horsepower their boilers were deliberately designed to deliver. These engines were also notably slippery and were troubled with dynamic augment at moderate speeds. The combination of high pressure and relatively large cylinder bore had resulted in excessively heavy piston thrusts with corresponding increases in reciprocating weights.

During John Bernet's 1927-1930 tenure as president of the Erie, that road bought 105 Berkshires from the three builders. The Erie S was as much as 40 tons heavier than its 2-8-4 predecessors, and in Bernet's zeal to speed up the Erie a 70-inch driver was adopted. Compared with the 2-10-2's they displaced in fast freight service between Marion, O., and Hornell, N. Y., the Berkshires moved 10 per cent more tonnage in 35 per cent less time and consumed 30 per cent less coal in the process. The designers had combined the A-1's firebox with a tremendous boiler, a monster 112-unit superheater, and a 28½-inch cylinder bore. With a potential boiler horsepower output far greater than that of the A-1, the Erie engines had a substantial reserve of steaming capacity which came in handy when working a manifest across an undulating profile.

There were significant differences in the Erie engines built by Lima and Alco. Inexplicably, Lima again went to 60 per cent limited cutoff to harness high boiler pressure while Alco, which always had reservations about limited cutoff, built an essentially full-stroke engine and held tractive effort down by cutting pressure back to 225 pounds. The adhesion of both engines was improved over that of the A-1, and the Alco's lighter piston thrusts spelled less trouble with dynamic augment. Both builders used a 32-inch stroke, the same as that of the Erie's 2-8-2's and 2-10-2's which had 63-inch drivers. The result was maximum power delivery at a much higher rate of speed, but the stroke proved a trifle short for the leverage needed to start heavy tonnage. Even at this late date the designers failed to fully appreciate the relationship of bore, stroke, and driver diameter to the speed range where the locomotive developed peak power output.

In 1929 the principal Van Sweringen roads—C&O, Nickel Plate, Erie, and Pere Marquette—pooled their mechanical talent and formed the Advisory Mechanical Committee. Almost at once the AMC began work on a new 10-coupled, two-cylinder design of heroic proportions intended for use on the C&O between Russell, Ky., and Toledo. The C&O wanted the speed and boiler capacity of the Erie 2-8-4 but had no desire to buy a new engine which required help starting the heavy coal tonnage it was intended to haul. After extensive tests, AMC chose the 69-inch driver, recommended for general freight service by A. W. Bruce in 1927, and a 34-inch stroke. With a half-inch of tire wear the crankpin would be midway between the axle and the outside tire rim. A tremendous boiler with working pressure of 260 pounds provided 15 per cent greater rated horsepower than the cylinders. Bore was held to 29 inches, and limited cutoff was discarded. The engine's rated tractive effort was 91,584 pounds. With 373,000 pounds riding on the drivers the factor of adhesion was an excellent 4.07.

Delivered by Lima in 1930, the C&O's new T-1 class 2-10-4's were the most powerful two-cylinder locomotives yet built and immediately began turning in sensational performances on 15,000-ton coal trains. The T-1 was precisely what the advocates of Super-Power had been seeking — compatibility of power both in starting and at high speed. For a long time the Advisory Mechanical Committee was to believe that it had hit the magic factor of adhesion and a perfect boiler-cylinder horsepower ratio.

ADVENT OF THE 700's

In 1933, when John Bernet was seeking a locomotive to restore the Nickel Plate's speed supremacy, he called upon the AMC to deliver a 2-8-4 design that would be nothing less than a scaled-down, eight-coupled T-1. The designers at Cleveland undertook their task, using as a basis four fundamental elements — the T-1's 69-inch driver, 34-inch stroke, 115 per cent boiler, and 4.07 adhesive factor. To arrive at the latter, AMC took 70 per cent of T-1's adhesive weight, 261,100 pounds, and married it to 70 per cent of T-1's rated tractive effort, 64,100 pounds, which happened to be exactly that of the H-6 Mikado with trailer booster cut in. The cylinder bore of 25 inches was unusually small and the required tractive effort rating was obtained by setting working steam pressure at 245 pounds. Nickel Plate considered streamlining its new freight hauler in order to dramatize its advent and the improved freight schedules. The preliminary design which came off the drawing boards in January 1934 called for bullet-nosed shrouding that covered the entire boiler and smokebox, leaving only the stack, feedwater heater, and bell exposed. The new 2-8-4 would have ranked as America's first streamlined steam locomotive, but the shrouding, like roller bearings, was ultimately ruled out in the interest of economy.

On December 23, 1933, the Nickel Plate mailed inquiries for the new 2-8-4's to the builders. Fifteen engines were to be bought, including 10 equipped with automatic train stop. Alco came up with the low bid, $89,909.43 each for the train stop models and $89,352.39 for the others. Lima got an order for five heavy 0-8-0 switchers in addition to the 25 extra tenders for 2-8-2's. To pay for the new engines, tenders, and 1200 freight and eight passenger cars, the Nickel Plate sold the Public Works Administration 4.8 million dollars' worth of equipment trust certificates in March 1934.

The new Berkshires were numbered 700-714 and assigned class S, requiring the renumbering of several ex-Clover Leaf engines and the reclassification of the Brooks 0-6-0's of 1913. The 700 rolled out of the erecting hall at Schenectady in September 1934 and the 714 followed in November. Believed too heavy to safely cross a high bridge at Westfield, N. Y., the 700's were hauled over the NYC as far west as Erie, Pa. From that point they were taken to Bellevue where they were set up and broken into service. The train stop engines, 705-714, went into operation on the 265-mile Bellevue-Chicago territory while the 700-704 were normally assigned to manifest trains between Frankfort, Lima, and Bellevue, 224 miles. On occasion a 700 worked the FS-2 from Lima to Cleveland, 145 miles. Because of bridge restrictions the Berkshires were not used east of Cleveland or west of Frankfort.

In physical appearance the 700 was a dead ringer for the T-1 except that it had one less pair of driving wheels, and wherever possible, parts were interchangeable with those of the C&O 2-10-4. Like the T-1, the 700 had a headlight centered on the smokebox door, Commonwealth outside-bearing engine truck and Delta trailer truck, spoked drivers, two shielded cross-compound pumps mounted on the pilot deck, and a Worthington Type 5-S feedwater heater mounted in a recess in the top of the smokebox ahead of the stack. Water from the tender was delivered to the heater by a centrifugal cold water pump mounted on the left side just ahead of the lead trailer truck wheel. Preheated by exhaust steam, the water was then fed to the boiler by a reciprocating hot water pump located on the left side of the boiler above the valve gear. Steam distribution was effected by Baker valve gear controlled by a Franklin Precision power reverse gear.

The 700's liberal boiler was of the conical type with three shell courses and a 116-inch smokebox. The outside diameter tapered from 98 inches at the back sheet to 89 1/16 inches at the smokebox, and the barrel was 19 feet long over the tube sheets. The steam dome was located on the first course ahead of the big rectangular 60-cubic-foot sandbox. The firebox boasted 90.3 square feet of grate area and contained Firebar grates and a brick arch with two arch tubes and two Nicholson syphons. A 42-inch combustion chamber separated the firebox from the back sheet. Total evaporative surface amounted to 4818 square feet, and the 700 had an E-type superheater with 1932 square feet of surface. The furnace was fired by a modified five-jet Type B Simplex stoker.

Innovations for Nickel Plate power included the Nathan Type B low-water alarm, a combination back pressure and steam chest gauge, multiple-bearing type crossheads, a floor pedal for operating the fire door, and Nathan and Detroit force-feed lubricators. The low-water alarm was located immediately behind the sandbox on the left side and had a steam-operated whistle in the cab. The whistle automatically began blowing when the boiler water level dropped to a point 4½ inches above the crown sheet. Virtually all Nickel Plate steam locomotives were eventually equipped with

The 703 awaits her tender at Alco. American multiple front-end throttle was integral with superheater header. Steam distribution was effected by Baker long-travel valve gear controlled by Franklin Precision-type reverse gear. — *NKP photo*.

Alco Berk's cab featured abundant headroom, minimum of congestion, and well-designed arrangement of fittings and appliances. Pipes along left side of backhead fed steam to jets of modified Type B Simplex stoker. Fireman regulated jets and coal distribution with valves located to the right of his seat. — *Collection of John A. Rehor.*

Erecting hall at Schenectady was a lonely place in 1934. Commonwealth locomotive bed already supports 700's boiler and cylinders, nickel-steel multiple-bearing type crosshead and guide, and Worthington feedwater heater. — *NKP photo.*

Black Ripolin finish set off appearance of S fresh from Alco's paint shop. Left-side view reveals Nathan Type B low-water alarm behind sandbox; centrifugal cold water pump ahead of forward trailing-truck wheel; and reciprocating hot feedwater pump above valve guides. — *Collection of Willis A. McCaleb.*

Moment of truth for a Ten-Wheeler. R class has a good roll on regular two-car consist of No. 26 and five steel Pullmans loaded with CCC boys on 1 per cent climb from Illinois River valley. The 156 is still faced with 6 miles of tough uphill running coupled with 12 curves. This October 14, 1938, event was recorded at Farmdale Junction, Ill. — *Paul Stringham.*

this safety device as were their sisters on the C&O.

Though not streamlined, the 700 was notably neat in appearance with the firebox sheathed and piping concealed by the jacket wherever possible. The cabs were large and had plenty of headroom, maximum visibility, and the least congested arrangement of fittings possible. The Berkshire carried a total of 428,900 pounds on its Commonwealth cradle and was 100 feet 8¾ inches long over the coupler faces. This was 13 feet greater than the total wheelbase, enabling the 700's to be turned on the Nickel Plate's 90-foot turntables. The 42-foot engine wheelbase permitted operation over 20-degree curves. The rectangular water-bottom tender carried 22,000 gallons of water and 22 tons of coal on its six-wheel Buckeye trucks and weighed 358,000 pounds when it was loaded.

Together with the New York Central 4-6-4 and C&O 2-10-4, the Nickel Plate 2-8-4 relegated to obsolescence most of the standards for estimating the potential performance of a steam locomotive, including Cole's formulae. According to Cole, the 700 had a maximum cylinder horsepower potential of 2754. Yet this engine was capable of developing more than 4000 horsepower at the drawbar and could maintain that sort of power output almost indefinitely. In computing tractive effort, the mean effective steam pressure was arbitrarily set at 85 per cent of working pressure. However, the 700's pressure drop was so low that m.e.p. was seldom less than 95 per cent. Even at 230 pounds m.e.p. the engine developed more than 72,000 pounds rated tractive effort compared with its conventional rating of 64,100 pounds.

The 700 proved that the relatively small bore, rather than limited cutoff, was the truly effective method of harnessing high boiler capacity for high-speed work. The locomotive's cylinder proportions were almost perfect. Peak power output was reached at about 40 mph, just under what was to be normal running speed. Moreover, the boiler's great capacity for overload enabled the 700 to sustain that output to speeds of 60 mph and beyond. Although the new 2-8-4 was in its element with a 4000-ton manifest, it was powerful enough to start and get a fast roll on the 10,000-ton coal trains that came off the C&O at Fostoria. When it came to tonnage, the Berkshire was such an all-round star performer that the Nickel Plate soon scrapped its complicated tonnage rating tables. The engine displayed an amazing ability to rapidly accelerate heavy trains, a priceless attribute on a heavy-trafficked single-track road like the Nickel Plate. Enginemen who at first babied their new charges soon learned they couldn't run them out of steam and found they used less coal and water than the H-6 under comparable conditions. Yet another advantage of the small bore was the lighter piston thrust and better counterbalancing conditions. Excessive dynamic augment which plagued earlier 2-8-4's was not present in the 700-series Berkshires.

In its new 2-8-4 the Nickel Plate had a flawless powerhouse that it would reorder, without basic modification, five times in the next 15 years. The 700 was indeed the new eight-coupled standard, and the vast majority of Berkshire locomotives built after 1934 were patterned after it. Not only was this new engine admirably suited to the task for which it

Although he still has upwards of 5000 gallons of water, 700's hogger has elected to take on more at St. Marys before moving the KC-44 into Lima. Alco Berks, noted for good looks as well as performance, were delivered with sheathed fireboxes and Viloco bell ringers. Photo was taken in 1935. — *Clyde E. Helms.*

Open switch at paper mill in St. Marys, O., on March 6, 1937, brought about this unhappy experience for a young Berkshire. The accident occurred while the 701 was working a Lima-Frankfort freight across the Sandusky Division. — *Clyde E. Helms.*

Eight-wheel ponies work Frankfort Yard and Monon transfer (upper left) while eight road engines await calls to duty. Flanked by an R (foreground) and a 2-8-4, steam whirley's clamshell takes a bite of coal for a locomotive's tender. — *NKP photo*.

George Ball's Mason jar plants fed as many as 100 carloads a day to the New Castle Division at Muncie during depression. A B-10 switcher crosses the White River on the former FtWC&L main on Muncie's north side. — *Collection of John A. Rehor.*

was designed, but as the years passed it demonstrated a remarkable capacity to keep pace with unprecedented traffic loads, mile-a-minute speed limits, and the most demanding freight schedules in America. On their record, if for no other reason, the Nickel Plate 2-8-4's must be ranked among the most successful steam locomotives ever built.

The End of an Era

Only one of the Cleveland banks that had made the 1930 Van Sweringen rescue loan possible managed to survive the bank panic of March 1933. With the banks had died the last vestiges of the city's prosperity and the popularity the Vans had formerly enjoyed there. The brothers were finished. Their fortune was gone, and they seldom ventured from their 54-room Daisy Hill mansion near Cleveland. A number of their properties were already in receivership, and it now fell on the practical railroad men led by Bernet to save what they could of the crumbling Van Sweringen rail empire.

In spite of the marked recovery of the national economy from the lows of 1932-1933, the Vans were

in no position to meet the 1935 maturity of the rescue loan. Faced with a loss of more than 40 million dollars, the New York banks prepared to salvage what they could through a forced sale of the securities the Clevelanders had put up as collateral. Involved was control of Alleghany Corporation and the Vans' real estate holding companies. In a desperate eleventh hour bid to save the empire, O.P. turned to George A. Tomlinson, Cleveland shipping magnate and long-time Van Sweringen associate. At Tomlinson's suggestion the two men motored to Muncie in August 1935 and obtained the backing of George A. Ball, the frail 74-year old Mason jar king and unabashed Van Sweringen admirer. On September 28, 1935, O. P., Ball, and Tomlinson formed the Mid-America Corporation and in its name purchased the Vans' "paper" from J. P. Morgan & Company at the auction held two days later in New York. The securities, which represented control over assets valued at 3 billion dollars, were bought for a little more than 3 million dollars. The bankers estimated their loss at 45 million dollars.

239

The 161 glides into Cascade, Pa., with 11 cars of No. 6. The best of the K's, the Lima spent most of her career on the Buffalo Division. Worthington BL-3 feedwater heater, this engine's secret of success, was mounted on left side. — *Paul W. Prescott.*

Eastbound 13-car No. 6 glides through Avon, O., at 70 mph on June 24, 1939. The Lima-built Hudson is carrying green, indicating a second section following. For many years this photo graced Nickel Plate dining-car menus. — *Harold S. Ludlow.*

Ball and Tomlinson had put up the purchase money and they had given the Vans a generous living allowance plus a 10-year option to buy control of Mid-America for a pittance. The strain of empire-building and fighting their creditors and enemies, however, was about to exact its toll. M. J.

died in December 1935, and O. P. was stricken in a private car in the Lackawanna's Hoboken yard on November 22, 1936. With his death the next day, the curtain came down on one of the more colorful episodes of American financial history. Inseparable in life, the brothers were buried side by side in Lakeview Cemetery above the glen where Nickel Plate eastbounds stormed the long grade through Cleveland's east side.

After O. P.'s death, Mid-America was virtually the outright possession of George Ball, who already had more money than he knew what to do with. Ball was not at all comfortable with the tyrant that had hounded the Vans into premature graves. In the spring of 1937 he placed the Mid-America stock in the hands of his family's philanthropic foundation. The Ball Foundation, in turn, sold the stock to a 40-year old stock broker, Robert R. Young, and his partner Frank F. Kolbe. About 75 per cent of the 4-million-dollar purchase price had been put up by Allan P. Kirby, scion of a very wealthy family.

Kirby had no interest in the management of Mid-America and Young eventually bought out Kolbe and dissolved his brokerage firm so that he could devote all of his time to the erstwhile Van Sweringen holdings. From the beginning Young sought to consolidate the C&O, PM, and Nickel Plate — all under a common management since 1933. The year before, Alleghany Corporation had optioned its 57 per cent block of Nickel Plate common to the C&O. On December 29, 1937, the I.C.C. authorized the exercise of that option and gave the C&O permission to control the Nickel Plate.

Unlike John Bernet, who died on July 5, 1935, the Nickel Plate managed to survive the depression. After three consecutive annual deficits, the road showed a very small profit in 1934 and went over a million in the black in 1935. Although the Nickel Plate was not out of the financial woods by any means, gross revenues climbed from 29 million dollars in 1932 to 42 million in 1936. The management was able to obtain another three-year extension of the promissory notes in 1935 and met the Reconstruction Finance Corporation maturities by issuing 16 million dollars' worth of collateral trust notes in 1936. The next year the Nickel Plate and LE&W first mortgages were extended for a decade at sharply reduced rates of interest. The 1938 relapse, nonetheless, dealt the road a million-dollar deficit and the third maturity of the 1929 notes nearly brought on a receivership. A sudden rise in revenues and the willingness of most of the noteholders to go along with yet another extension saved the day.

The Great Depression was the crucible that fused the Nickel Plate into a lean and hungry paragon of efficiency that effectively competed for every carload that moved through its territory. In as stunning a comeback as the railroad world has ever witnessed, the company made good on every dime of its debt, kept faith with its stockholders, and soared to a new plateau of prosperity. In contrast with its Eastern neighbors, the Nickel Plate had yet to see the Golden Years.

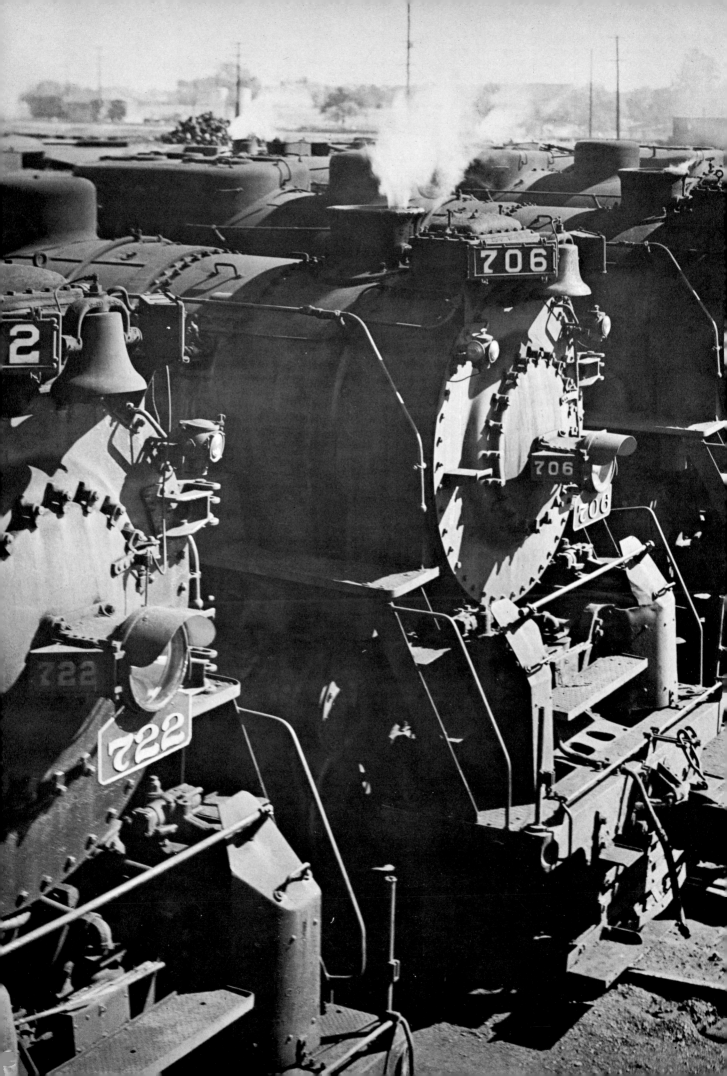

A place
in the sun

JOINT management of the Chesapeake & Ohio, Pere Marquette, and Nickel Plate — the only Van Sweringen roads able to ride out the depression — lasted from 1933 to the end of 1942. The correlative freight traffic position of the three Alleghany roads was greatly enhanced during this period, a development that was particularly beneficial to the Nickel Plate. Train after train of C&O coal rolled onto Nickel Plate rails at Fostoria destined for the great steel mills at Gary, South Lorain, Cleveland, and Buffalo. This steady stream of lucrative traffic involved little or no terminal handling, a minimum of loss and damage in transit, and practically no new investment in road or equipment. Kinship with the PM also helped impel the Nickel Plate down the road to recovery and stimulated an intensified competitive struggle with the Wabash.

William J. Harahan and George D. Brooke — John Bernet's successors at the common helm — wisely chose to place restoration of financial integrity above all other Nickel Plate considerations. This policy precluded any massive assault on the road's physical deficiencies and barred participation in the futile and costly last-ditch campaign to win back the passenger. The spartan course charted during the critical prewar years forced renewed reliance on freight-train speed and locomotive performance. The choice was one that admirably armed the Nickel Plate for an epic World War II role and underwrote its postwar brilliance.

243

With the wholesale 1930-1932 withdrawals of service, the passenger train reverted to its normal subordinate role in the Nickel Plate scheme of things. During the decade that followed there was little variation in the number of passengers carried, average passenger haul, and passenger train-miles. Economic tides appear to have had little effect on these statistics, although the Great Lakes Exposition at Cleveland during 1936-1937 did inflate them somewhat. Faster schedules and air-conditioned cars (1934), a one-third reduction in fares (1936), and abandonment of the road's last interurban competitor (1938) served only to offset the general passenger decline that had persisted in the East since the mid-1920's. The Nickel Plate's experience between 1932 and 1941 can be cited as a refutation of the oft-delivered charge that the railroad's passenger problem was one of their own making. The road operated a limited number of trains on schedules designed to win the most lucrative trade; cars were modern and comfortable; and potential was optimum. Furthermore, there were no branch-line runs or commuter trains* to muddy up the picture. Only in 1932 did the Nickel Plate's average passenger haul dip below 200 miles. By 1938 passenger-train receipts amounted to 1.43 million dollars, about 4 per cent of total operating revenues. That year passenger trains ran 1.5 million miles, roughly 22 per cent of total train-miles. Gross revenue per passenger train-mile, including income from mail, express, and dining cars, amounted to a meager 95 cents. The figure was even lower in 1939 and 1940 and only 2 mills higher in 1941.

After September 8, 1934, the Nickel Plate ran only two trains each way daily between Chicago and Buffalo. The westbounds were No. 5, the *Nickel*

*Trains 6, 9, and 10 provided attractive commutation schedules between Cleveland, Rocky River, and Lorain. After the 1938 abandonment of the Lake Shore Electric, 9 and 10 were also stopped at Vermilion for Cleveland passengers. Commuter patronage, however, was always light.

Plate Limited, and No. 7 (formerly No. 1). Originated at Chicago were No. 6 and the eastbound *Limited*, No. 8. Train No. 10 ran between St. Louis and Cleveland as in the past, while No. 9 was still originated at Buffalo. The Fort Wayne-Cleveland sleepers were dropped from trains 5 and 6 on July 19, 1936, and the following February 1 saw the demise of the White Sulphur Springs car. Lack of patronage prompted the September 24, 1939, removal of Pullmans operated between Cleveland and Hoboken in trains 7 and 8. Simultaneously, the 10-1-2 sleepers assigned to this line — *Devils Lake*, *Medicine Lake*, and *Bowman Lake* — replaced section-lounge-restaurant cars *Creek Club*, *Brook Club*, and *Saturn Club* operating in the same trains between Chicago and New York.

After May 1938 trains 5 and 6 were assigned through New York-Chicago coaches and 12-1 Pullmans, but the overnight service these trains provided between Cleveland and Chicago remained the most popular and lucrative facet of Nickel Plate passenger service. Regularly assigned to this service were the *Captain* and *Commander*, bedroom-lounge-restaurant cars; 14-section sleepers *Park Summit* and *Park Terrace*; and a pair of 12-1's. The latter were replaced on August 5, 1940, with Pullman's lightweight demonstrators *Roomette I* and *Roomette II*, which had 18 individual roomette compartments, picture windows, pressed-steel carlines, and four-wheel roller-bearing trucks. Since a roomette cost only $1.05 more than a lower berth in a standard sleeper, the cars proved very popular. They were bought by the Nickel Plate in 1945 and renamed *Moses Cleaveland* and *Robert de La Salle*.

In August 1939 the Nickel Plate petitioned the Public Utilities Commissions of Ohio and Indiana for permission to withdraw Clover Leaf District trains 15 and 16, neither of which was earning expenses. Despite their mixed status, the *Commercial Travelers* still connected with trains 9 and 10 at Frankfort and provided overnight service between Toledo and St. Louis. However, through patrons

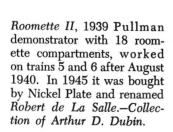

Roomette II, 1939 Pullman demonstrator with 18 roomette compartments, worked on trains 5 and 6 after August 1940. In 1945 it was bought by Nickel Plate and renamed *Robert de La Salle.—Collection of Arthur D. Dubin.*

Toward the end, road engines were cut off eastbound *Commercial Traveler* at MC Junction and a switcher pulled train remaining 1.6 miles to Erie Street. This 1939 consist of reefer, R.P.O. car, and arch-windowed coach has just arrived at Erie Street behind B-9a 0-6-0 107. Overnight service between St. Louis and Toledo was still offered, but NKP had already petitioned to withdraw mixeds east of Frankfort. — *Robert W. Richardson.*

were few and far between, and the R.P.O.-express cars probably produced more revenue than the arch-windowed coaches. As was the case with all subsequent passenger-train withdrawals, the Nickel Plate encountered considerable opposition to its petition. Ohio gave in first and the graveyard run left Toledo's Erie Street terminus on March 8, 1941.

Indiana compelled the Nickel Plate to provide daily mixed service over the 104 miles between Frankfort and Pleasant Mills, first station west of the Ohio border, until April 4, 1943. Freights 40 and 43 were assigned an old combination car and ran on a leisurely 7-hour daylight schedule. No. 40 terminated and No. 43 originated at Delphos but passengers were not allowed to ride the combine east of Pleasant Mills.

Lake Erie & Western District local trains 21 and 22 were cut back from Fostoria to Lima and the operation of No. 9 east of Cleveland was discontinued on May 9, 1942. Prior to these "temporary" wartime curtailments, the LE&W trains had made close connections with Nos. 7 and 8 at Fostoria. No. 22 left Frankfort mornings, except Sunday, at 8:30 a.m. and arrived in Fostoria at 3:20 p.m., 17 minutes ahead of the eastbound *Nickel Plate Limited.* The R class 4-6-0, R.P.O. car, and coach lay overnight at Fostoria and started back to Frankfort at 11:10 a.m., 11 minutes after the arrival of the *Westerner.* Trains 25 and 26 continued to serve the Peoria Division but neither connected with anything

at Frankfort. A single Ten-Wheeler, R.P.O. car, and coach were all that was needed to handle the 362-mile round trip. These trains were replaced on June 13, 1943, by extending the runs of 21 and 22 to Peoria. Both 327-mile runs consumed most of the daylight hours.

For all its economic worthlessness, the passenger train remained railroading's No. 1 status symbol long after it was obvious that the intercity passenger was irrevocably lost. Economic revival prior to Pearl Harbor spawned dozens of new diesel-powered streamliners, de luxe all-coach economy trains, and ultrafast schedules. In some eastern quarters it became popular to mock the freight-conscious Nickel Plate as a "wooden-axle" road. However, the only schedules over which Gus Ayers lost sleep were those of his manifest freights, and he would answer his detractors with statistical barometers buried in the back pages of the annual report — gross ton-miles per train-hour, car-miles per car-day, freight locomotive-miles, and gross ton-miles per pound of coal burned. Unencumbered by a repetition of the predepression overemphasis on passenger service, Ayers was free to hone his railroad's freight operation to a razor's edge. With one exception, his competitors were unable or unwilling to follow his lead.

WABASH VS. NICKEL PLATE

Probably no keener rivalry existed in American railroading than that between the Nickel Plate and

245

Early morning sunlight filters through a haze of coal smoke and steam at Frankfort coal dock as a pair of 600's are readied for the road. — *Richard J. Cook.*

ST-96 rolls into Delphos yard in 1946. Train competed with Wabash 96 for freight moving from St. Louis to Toledo and Detroit. USRA Mikes 587 and 599 were regulars on Clover Leaf manifests between Frankfort and Delphos. Too long for Delphos turntable, they were turned on AC&Y's wye for 1 dollar a ride. — *Richard J. Cook.*

the Wabash after 1933. Both were service routes heavily dependent on overhead freight traffic and they scrambled for every carload moving east through Chicago, St. Louis, and Kansas City. Nickel Plate 90, the KC-44, competed with a Wabash redball with the same number out of Kansas City, while the MB-98 ran against Wabash 98 dispatched daily from East St. Louis. Although the 725-mile St. Louis-Buffalo run of the Wabash was the longer of the two routes, physically it was far superior to most of its Nickel Plate counterpart. Wabash 70-inch-drivered 4-8-4's and 4-8-2's highballed over a line boasting long double-track tangents, automatic block signals, and even an early centralized traffic control installation. By contrast, automatic block signals were lacking on virtually all of the 426 miles of paralleling Nickel Plate single track between Arcadia, O., and Madison, Ill. Ironically, the 1931-1943 Wabash receivership produced many improvements to that road's physical plant.

Just as the 240 miles of Clover Leaf between Frankfort and Madison was the Nickel Plate's perennial headache, the 240-mile combination of ferryboat and trackage-rights operation east of Detroit was the weakest link in the Wabash chain. Buffalo-bound Wabash manifests crossed the southern extremity of Ontario between Windsor and Fort Erie over unsignaled Canadian National trackage. For 80 miles out of Windsor the route was double tracked, but east of Glencoe the 145 miles of single-track CN line was not unlike the Clover Leaf west of Frankfort. In terms of short sidings, bridges, curves, and terrain, there was little to separate the two railroads. Even the toughest operational obstacle of each — the ruling westbound tonnage grade

— was called Cayuga Hill. Though Wabash K-3 Mikados got across the CN in 5 to 6 hours, as much or more time was often spent crossing the Detroit and Niagara rivers.

The third major speedup of the manifest schedule in less than a decade was initiated in 1936. To set the stage, the freight-train speed limit on the Nickel Plate District and the Sandusky Division west of Frankfort was raised from 45 to 50 mph. Also about this time, maximum speed for Clover Leaf freights west of Frankfort was boosted to 45. Hotshots between Madison and Buffalo were now moving over the road at an average of 35 mph, excluding time spent in intermediate terminals. Because the Nickel Plate could ill afford to plug its tiny yards with through cars, terminal delays had to be held to an absolute minimum. Time required to change engines and cabooses, perform a terminal air test, and highball it out of Charleston, for example, seldom exceeded 15 to 20 minutes. Even when it was essential to set out hot cars for the Erie, manifests paused at South Lima less than 30 minutes. Six-hundreds now powered hot eastbounds all the way from Bellevue to Buffalo without change, and delays at Conneaut were not expected to exceed 15 minutes. Only at Bellevue, where final blocking was performed for Buffalo connections, was it normally necessary to tie up a manifest for more than an hour.

The 1936 speedup enabled the Nickel Plate to hold its own between St. Louis and Buffalo and led to the establishment of competitive St. Louis-Detroit and Chicago-Toledo schedules. A new Madison hotshot, ST-96, was inaugurated to compete with Wabash 96 for Detroit perishable traffic. This train was due out of Madison at 2 a.m. and ran on a 17-

Booster-equipped H-6f's 669 and 667 lead a long SD-2 up the 1.6 per cent grade carrying the Indianapolis Division out of the Wabash valley at Peru. Rider car indicates that this April 9, 1948, manifest had more than 69 cars, requiring a third brakeman under Indiana law. Helper on the point will drop off at Macy, 13 miles to the north. SD-2 offered fast service from St. Louis to Chicago as well as Detroit. — *Malcolm McCarter.*

Leaving Frankfort Yard, First PB-12 blasts across the Monon on August 13, 1945. Inaugurated in 1940, this crack manifest ran on a 24-hour 30-minute schedule between Peoria and Buffalo. The 712 was considered to be best of the 1934 Alcos. — *Richard J. Cook.*

hour schedule direct to the Pere Marquette's Ottawa Yard at Erie, Mich. To reach that facility, ST-96 and westbound 95 used 13.57 miles of Toledo Terminal and Pere Marquette trackage between Gould, Tower K, and Ottawa Yard. Assigned the symbol TS-7, No. 95 left the PM yard in the evening, picked up outbound Toledo cars at Gould, and made a 6-hour run to Frankfort. There it was consolidated with CS-7, the Cleveland-St. Louis hotshot.

Not long after the advent of ST-96 and TS-7 the Nickel Plate started overnight service between Chicago and Toledo in direct competition with the Wabash and NYC. New FT-98 left Frankfort about 30 minutes after the arrival of MB-98 from Madison and ran over the Clover Leaf as far as Bluffton. From this point the train ran over the New Castle Division to West Wayne Yard at Fort Wayne. After filling out with perishable brought out of Chicago by OB-2, this unique train ran over the Fort Wayne Division to Continental where it returned to the Clover Leaf. The scheduled 5 a.m. arrival at MC Junction permitted perishable carloads to be spotted at Toledo produce houses before they opened for the day's business. FT-98's crews were changed only at West Wayne, and assignments were split between the three districts on a mileage basis. Although it bypassed the Dupont bridge, FT-98 usually ran behind a stoker-fired G-8 or G-9 Consolidation. Occasionally an H-5 2-8-2 took the train into Toledo.

Operation of the Clover Leaf manifests into Ottawa Yard ended early in 1941 following the debut of a pair of symbol freights on the Indianapolis Division. After new bridges at Peru and Bunker Hill ended motive power restrictions in 1940, trains 86 and 87 were given expedited Indianapolis-Michigan City schedules designed to provide a bridge for hot Michigan traffic destined for St. Louis and beyond. New DS-1 (No. 87) left Michigan City each afternoon and was built around cars received from the Pere Marquette and Michigan Central. Automotive traffic from Flint and Pontiac was picked up from the Grand Trunk Western at Stillwell. DS-1 also made a tight connection at Argos with a setoff train from Chicago and turned over its westbound cars to Clover Leaf 43 at Kokomo. West of Frankfort, No. 45 carried the symbol DS-1 and had a scheduled 5:30 a.m. Madison arrival. The service was dependable enough for the Nickel Plate to offer first-morning delivery between Chicago and St. Louis in competition with the Alton, Wabash, and Illinois Central. SD-2 (No. 86) left Indianapolis about 5 a.m., picked up St. Louis cars from the KC-44 at Tipton, and got into Michigan City around noon.

At first H-5 Mikados were used on DS-1 and SD-2, but in later years 600's were regularly assigned to the trains. A single locomotive could hold down

both schedules, but severe grades on both sides of Peru required the use of helper engines. Northbound, the ascending grade out of the Wabash valley was 1.6 per cent for about a mile and there were long stretches of 1 per cent-plus all the way to Deedsville, 11 miles out. Under favorable conditions a pair of booster-equipped 600's could take 3500 tons up the hill. Helpers dropped off at Deedsville when pushing but stayed on the point to Macy, 3 miles beyond, when pulling. Southbounds leaving Peru fought 7 miles of .8 per cent uncompensated combined with 18 curves. Helpers were needed here, too, and these generally dropped back at Bunker Hill.

The Nickel Plate added yet another manifest to its expanding freight operation early in 1940. Originated at Peoria, new PB-12 (No. 68) was intended to complement the KC-44 in giving the road Buffalo arrivals timed to connect with Lehigh Valley and Lackawanna early-morning departures. Originally the train was scheduled to cover its 649-mile run in 24 hours 30 minutes with a 4 a.m. Buffalo arrival. Due out of Frankfort at 10:43 a.m., PB-12 filled out with cars brought from Madison by ST-96 about an hour earlier. In effect, this gave the Nickel Plate three fast Madison-Buffalo trains, with the ST-96/PB-12 combination actually the fastest of the lot.

The ST-96/PB-12 service was so well received that the Nickel Plate was prompted to complement it with a new train out of Chicago. For some time No. 56, the CB-10, had been running on a leisurely 12-hour schedule between Chicago and Bellevue, where it was consolidated with the KC-44. In 1941 the train's symbol was changed to CB-12 and its Osborn departure was set back from late evening to 8 a.m. The train now arrived at Bellevue in the late afternoon, well after KC-44 and about an hour ahead of PB-12. CB-12 also ran against a 4 a.m. Buffalo cutoff, and on slack days it was often combined with PB-12 east of Bellevue. About the time the "12" trains appeared on the scene, the Nickel Plate also added westbound symbol trains NS-5 and NC-5. Originated at Buffalo, these ran as extras and were dubbed "White Flyers" by east end crews. Quite often they were consolidated east of Bellevue as NCS-5.

PREWAR ENGINEERING PROGRESS

The Nickel Plate's stringent financial situation held capital outlay for physical improvements to a minimum during the depression and prewar years. However, the general level of maintenance was kept high, and what little money was available was spent wisely. Heavier motive power and faster schedules rendered many of the high bridges on the Cleveland and Buffalo divisions obsolete, and the Nickel Plate was confronted with the need to replace or rebuild

Interlocked lap sidings at North Findlay gave Fort Wayne Division dispatcher the equivalent of a running track more than 14,000 feet long. Track in foreground is the westward siding, and westbound freight is leaving the eastward passing track. Opposing turnouts and Ohio Central crossing were interlocked and operated from S Tower at left. Prior to 1947 this station was known as Mortimer. — *Clyde E. Helms.*

a dozen steel viaducts ranging from 600 to 3000 feet in length. This was an exceedingly costly program that promised to involve intolerable interruptions of service. In 1934 the 730-foot Chagrin River viaduct at Willoughby was dismantled and replaced with a long fill and a new 320-foot solid-floor deck girder bridge with concrete piers. The Nypenn or State Line viaduct, highest on the railroad, was renewed during 1935-1936. This new E-70 structure was 712 feet long and towered 113 feet above 20-mile Creek, a short distance east of the New York-Pennsylvania line. The long bridge at Silver Creek was replaced in 1937, and later the Nickel Plate and Pennsylvania jointly erected a new double-track concrete arch bridge in place of the old 18-Mile Creek viaduct at Lakeview, N. Y.

Timely development of a low-cost method of structural strengthening enabled the road to defer the reconstruction of its longest bridges for several years. The technique of welding additional plates and bracing to columns and towers was first employed in 1933 on the Walnut Creek viaduct, and the next year the 1470-foot Elk Creek viaduct and the Chautauqua Creek bridge at Westfield were beefed up in the same manner. In 1940 it was necessary to renew all the girders of the long viaduct spanning Conneaut Creek, but the Nickel Plate was able to satisfactorily brace the existing towers.

Inasmuch as westbound Nickel Plate trains were inferior by direction to eastbounds of the same class, the westbounds normally took the siding at meeting points. In a pre-C.T.C. drive to reduce delays to westbound manifests, the Nickel Plate installed spring switches in the westerly turnouts of many passing tracks east of Bellevue. These permitted a train to trail through the turnout at speeds up to 35 mph and eliminated the stops normally required to operate hand-thrown switches. At other Nickel Plate District points where passing track turnouts were located near a station or tower, the switches were interlocked in a further effort to speed movement. A pair of overlapping sidings a short distance west of Vermilion were equipped with interlocked switches in the opposing turnouts to permit running meets. By running a westbound through the eastward siding and an eastbound through the westward siding, or vice versa, the dispatcher had what was, in effect, a 2-mile running track and he could return both trains to the main track simultaneously at 35 mph. A similar interlocked lap-siding arrangement existed on the Fort Wayne Division at Mortimer (North Findlay).

Between Madison and Buffalo the Nickel Plate crossed 61 railroads at grade, and as late as 1937 25 of these intersections were protected only by tilting targets or gates. On the St. Louis Division all trains were required to stop at Linden and Lerna where track gates were still in use. East of Frank-

Sandusky Division operation was hampered by an abundance of slow orders and grade crossings with other railroads. Interlocking replaced tilting target at Grand Rapids & Indiana (PRR) crossing at Portland in 1932, but trains were still restricted to 25 mph through the plant. Eastbound No. 22 heads for Lima on July 4, 1946. Depot was demolished by April 28, 1962, derailment of manifest NS-1. — *Clyde E. Helms.*

fort an abundance of noninterlocked crossings and local speed ordinances helped make the Sandusky Division the slowest-running ground on the Madison-Buffalo run. Except for a 5-mile stretch of reverse curves at Fort Recovery, O., the division's 186 miles of single track west of Arcadia was unsignaled and operated strictly by timetable and train orders. Nonetheless, the capacity of a single-track railroad with or without automatic block signals and interlockers is governed largely by the length and spacing of its passing tracks. In this respect the Sandusky Division was particularly inadequate for the volume of traffic dispatched across it. There were a half-dozen 15- to-20-mile stretches between passing tracks, and on one 42-mile section east of Muncie it was impossible to operate simultaneously two opposing trains of more than 66 cars.

The 1933 diversion of the Clover Leaf manifests aggravated the Sandusky Division's shortcomings and a program attacking them was launched in the late 1930's. Between 1936 and 1943 all remaining 90-pound rail in the main track between Arcadia and Frankfort was replaced with control-cooled, end-hardened 112.28-pound section. During the same period interlockers replaced remaining targets at all but one crossing outside of yard limits. The work of adding new mile-long passing tracks at critical points and extending many existing sidings

to 135-car capacity was well under way by 1939. Starting with the 281-car Adgate Road siding west of Lima, a new Sandusky Division passing track was placed in service each year from 1941 through 1945.

Peoria Division was a locomotive proving ground in the days of steam. Engineer Jim Lugar coaxes 615 up Crandall Hill. Road Foreman of Engines W. G. Yetman uses telephone to relay changes in throttle position, cutoff, back pressure, and steam pressure to men in dynamometer car. "Winnie" Yetman's father and grandfather were LE&W enginemen and his son also worked for Nickel Plate. — *Collection of John A. Rehor.*

As traffic surged upward from the depressed levels of 1938, Gus Ayers kept dynamometer car X-50041 and Traveling Engineer Don Coon busy on the Sandusky Division and other operational bottlenecks. Aside from pinpointing locations where alignment and profile changes would be most effective in speeding up operation, the dynamometer car delivered some sensational improvements in locomotive performance. For example, Berkshires were moving freight at the rate of 70 to 75 pounds of coal consumed per 1000 gross ton-miles. This was 30 per cent less than the average for the years 1929-1933. It was shown that full-throttle operation coupled with moderate reductions in cutoff accelerated a 2-8-4 at a much faster rate than was formerly believed possible. On the undulating Sandusky Division with its many slow orders and stops this ability enabled enginemen to trim precious minutes from normal running time without circumventing the restrictions laid down by rulebook, timetable, and dispatcher.

The May 16, 1940, run of the then new PB-12 over the 145-mile Frankfort-Lima run graphically illustrates the stepped-up performance of 2-8-4's on the Sandusky Division. Working under normal conditions, S class 705 managed to get the 75-car, 3573-ton manifest and dynamometer car across this critical stretch of railroad in 4 hours 22 minutes. The 34.96 mph average speed was obtained despite the fact that the train was stopped three times en route — by an occupied crossing at Elwood, the need to take water at Liberty (East Muncie), and an air

hose separation. On 10 other occasions it was necessary to reduce from 50 mph to as low as 15 because of track gangs laying rail and timetable speed restrictions. After being stopped by a PRR train at Elwood, the engineer needed only a mile of fairly level track with one mild curve to get his charge moving at 30 mph. Six miles beyond he had to reduce from full to half throttle to keep from exceeding maximum authorized speed. Leaving Liberty, the 705 accelerated to 30 mph in 2 miles of .5 per cent ascending grade. Again, after only 7 miles of running, throttle reduction was needed to avoid violating the 50 mph limit.

The locomotive purge of 1933-1934 reduced the Nickel Plate roster to a bare 308 units, and the 1936 retirement of four engines cut the freight pool to 15 Berkshires, 121 Mikados, and 62 Consolidations. Except for a pair of 2-8-0's on stationary boiler duty, all were in active service in 1938. That year the road's freight engines individually averaged 2700 miles per month in handling some 3.9 billion ton-miles of revenue freight. Rearmament, improved service, and a general business revival made 1941 the best year in Nickel Plate history up to that time. Unlike most other roads, the Nickel Plate had no host of stored engines which could be pressed into service as traffic boomed, and no power would be bought until mid-1942. The same 196 engines had to run 4800 miles each month to forward the 6.8 billion revenue ton-miles of 1941. The monthly mileage figure soared to 5633 in 1942, highest of any American railroad.

Between 1940 and mid-1945 the Nickel Plate had

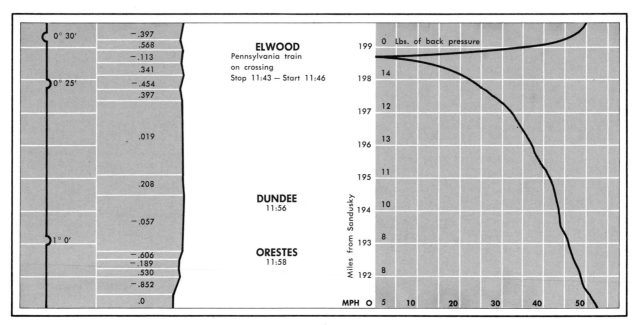

Dynamometer chart shows full-throttle acceleration of Alco 2-8-4 705 with 3573-ton PB-12 during Sandusky Division test run in May 1940.

Hudson and two 700's receive class repairs at Conneaut in 1945. During 1942-1943 this cramped little backshop and smaller facilities at Lima and Frankfort kept fleet of freight locomotives rolling at average rate of 5600 miles per month — highest of all American railroads. — *NKP photo*.

to turn its engines as fast as they came into the terminals. To accomplish this the road had to be getting superb running maintenance. Inasmuch as the Stony Island locomotive shop had been closed in 1932, there were only the cramped little backshops at Conneaut, Lima, and Frankfort to keep the fleet rolling. The fact that this was done, in the face of a critical shortage of skilled shopmen, was one of the real domestic miracles of the war years.

Whereas Gus Ayers' freight locomotives were setting the national mileage pace, his railroad was once again moving freight cars with record-breaking dispatch. Since 1929 the Nickel Plate had scored consistent gains in gross ton-miles moved per train-hour and in car-miles per car-day. The former was considered the industry's yardstick for measuring operational efficiency, but it was not a particularly accurate criterion of service. A railroad hauling trains of heavy tonnage (coal, for example) at moderate speeds might make every bit as good a gross ton-miles showing as a road moving light tonnage at high speeds. Furthermore, the statistic revealed nothing of how fast cars were expedited through yards and interchange points. Car-miles per car-day was a far superior indicator of the over-all level of service a railroad rendered its customers. While Eastern roads with their countless junctions and comparatively short hauls were seldom able to

match their Western cousins in car-mile performance, the Nickel Plate had led all U. S. roads in average car movement during the early 1920's. Though this advantage had been lost during the Van Sweringen-inspired preoccupation with consolidations, terminals, and passenger trains, Ayers had restored the Nickel Plate's car-miles supremacy by 1942. The 96-mile-per-day average scored the following year was almost double the road's 1929 performance.

From the time the Nickel Plate was opened to traffic its freight trains were scheduled, and their superiority by class and direction was therefore established by the operating timetables. As traffic soared to record-breaking levels in 1941, the road's yard and passing-track limitations forced dispatchers to greatly increase the number of trains operated rather than the length of regular trains. Instead of cluttering up the railroad with extra trains lacking timetable authority, they simply ran the scheduled freights in as many sections as necessary to keep traffic flowing smoothly. Time freight and manifest loads got pretty much the same treatment, a practice which kept the over-all level of service high and earned the Nickel Plate an ever-growing share of the traffic moving through its territory. Since little or no effort was made to switch out so-called "hot" cars for preferred movement,

After 1943 it was not necessary to stop a Nickel Plate District train when delivering form 19 train orders. Engineer Sam Plosila is about to take orders on the fly while rolling the west local through Painesville. Operator is hooping up a set to brakeman in rider car. Orders in lower hoop are for conductor. — *Richard J. Cook.*

yardmasters could keep their tracks fluid and their engines busy blocking outbound trains. Hence the Nickel Plate was able to expedite an unbelievable volume of wartime traffic through yards such as Bellevue's 1400-car eastbound facility and 510-car Abbott Road at Buffalo.

Although the operation of regular trains with the current of traffic across double-track A.B.S. territory was a relatively uncomplicated business, the matter of moving them through long, congested sections of single track was something else again. By virtue of its strategic location, the Nickel Plate's Chicago-Buffalo main stem was used as a detour route by all three major eastern trunk lines — the Pennsylvania west of Fort Wayne, the B&O east of Fostoria, and the New York Central east of Cleveland. Again and again during World War II the trains of the four-track Central were thrust

upon the east end which was already sagging under the burden of 50 to 60 trains a day. On one memorable occasion the Nickel Plate forwarded the Central's great fleet of passenger trains into the Cleveland Union Terminal without delaying one of them. By any contemporary standard this was a physical impossibility. In those days, however, Nickel Plate men were too intent upon doing what had to be done to worry much about whether or not it could be done.

Only a breed of brilliant and indefatigable men working in incredible unison could have wrought the wartime wonders of the east end, and perhaps it is absurd to say that one man deserves any more credit than the next. Still, it seems iniquitous that there is no monument on Big Delaware Hill, at Nypenn or Cascade, commemorating the deeds of Homer Jones, the steel-nerved chief train dispatcher at Conneaut. This almost legendary man ruled the Cleveland and Buffalo divisions for two decades prior to Pearl Harbor and possessed a consummate knowledge of his 245-mile railroad and the idiosyncrasies of two rosters of enginemen. Beyond this, he had the instincts of a gambler and an uncanny ability to improvise successfully. Jones was charged with far more than the task of moving an unprecedented volume of traffic across an inadequate piece of railroad. During the war he faced a complete motive power changeover, hordes of inexperienced employees, complications attending the rebuilding of seven major bridges, the advent of C.T.C., a new book of operating rules, and a change in train order forms.

Train Orders, Fixed Signals, and C.T.C.

Prior to about 1916 the Nickel Plate used only a form 19 train order which was normally addressed to both the conductor and engineer of a train. Rule 509 required that the delivering operator set the blade of his train-order semaphore at a 45-degree angle in the upper quadrant (green light by night), the *Stop for Orders* signal. The operator was further obliged to read the order to both conductor and engineer and obtain their signatures before restoring the semaphore to *Clear* (vertical). About 1916 a form 17 order was introduced which could be delivered without stopping a train. At first the new form could not be used to restrict the right of any train, but eventually Rule 509 was relaxed to allow the use of 17 orders when restricting freight-train rights on double track and on single-track A.B.S. territory except at meeting points. The diagonal day aspect and yellow night aspect were used to indicate 17 orders, while the semaphore blade in horizontal position and red light required a stop for 19 orders.

When the Nickel Plate issued a new book of rules in December 1943, it adopted the standard 19 and 31 order forms that had always been in use on the LE&W and Clover Leaf districts. The old form 17 gave way to the standard 19, and the old 19 was replaced with form 31. Whereas the 31 required that the train be stopped for delivery, the operator now needed only to obtain the signature of either the engineer or conductor. In the rare event that the conductor did the signing, he had to personally deliver copies to each engineman before the train could proceed.

With the advent of 17 train orders, the Nickel Plate changed the color-light aspects of its fixed signals. This move apparently was prompted by the switch to electric engine headlights from the old yellow-glowing oil burners. Formerly, white had signified safety, green called for caution, and red indicated danger. Train order boards, automatic

block signals, and the distant signals of interlocking plants were of the three-position, upper-quadrant semaphore type. A vertical blade by day and white light by night were proceed indications on all three. The blade of a block or distant signal in diagonal position by day and green light by night permitted a train to proceed prepared to stop at the next signal. The day aspects remained unchanged, but green was substituted for white as the *Clear* signal and yellow replaced green as the *Caution* or *Proceed* indication. A white banner and white light on a switchstand formerly indicated that the switch was in closed, or normal position. By 1924 green lights had supplanted the white, but the color of the banners was never changed.

After 1930 all automatic block signals on the Nickel Plate District were of the three-indication color-light type. A green aspect was a *Clear* signal; a yellow, *Approach;* and red, *Stop.* A red aspect on a block signal with a number plate was a *Stop and Proceed.* This signal permitted the engineer to proceed at restricted speed after bringing his train to a full stop. By 1940 certain interlocking home signals could give a *Restricting* signal — red over yellow, or red over red over yellow. Still another new signal, *Advance Approach,* made its appearance about this time. A yellow over yellow, this permitted the engineer to "proceed preparing to stop at second signal indication."

Medium speed (a speed not exceeding 35 mph) was introduced on the Nickel Plate in January 1942 along with centralized traffic control. First installed on the Ohio Central in 1927, C.T.C. was a system of power-controlled signals and switches remotely operated by a dispatcher or operator. Under C.T.C. operation, the superiority of all trains was superseded by the signal indications, and this ended the reliance on train orders which was such a fundamental part of single-track railroading. The use of dual-control power switches in passing-track turnouts practically eliminated the head-on collision and made it possible for two opposing trains to pass without stopping. C.T.C. also saved the time previously needed to transmit and receive train orders and did away with delays caused by operation of hand-thrown switches. The track diagram on the C.T.C. control console showed the dispatcher the precise location of all trains and enabled him to do a better job of running his railroad.

The development of C.T.C. made it possible for the Nickel Plate to live with its heavy density single-track operations, but conservative budgeting forced the deferment of planned installations until 1941. The improved two-wire system was adopted, with Union Switch & Signal apparatus used almost exclusively. Power transmission was at 440 volts A.C. stepped down to 110 volts for rectifier feed.

Low-voltage direct current from the rectifier was used to charge battery banks which, in turn, supplied the 26 volts D.C. needed to operate the switch machines. Signals normally were lighted by 10 volts A.C., but in the event of transmission failure they drew direct current from the battery banks.

Wherever conditions permitted, the Nickel Plate went to 7500-foot, 150-car passing tracks spaced 4 to 6 miles apart. Controlled sidings had 35 mph turnouts at both ends. When the dispatcher was arranging a meet between two trains, he set the distant signals at *Approach Medium* (yellow over green, or yellow over green over red) which required both engineers to proceed approaching their home signals at medium speed. Normally the home signal for the train being headed into the siding would be *Medium Approach* — red over yellow over red. This indication allowed movement through the turnout into the siding at medium speed with the engineer preparing to stop his train short of the next signal, usually located at the far end of the siding. This would remain red over red — *Stop* — until the opposing or overtaking train or trains had cleared. To move the train out of the siding, the dispatcher

Bracket-mast home signal at BM Tower, Brocton, N. Y., gave Nickel Plate color-light and Pennsylvania position-light indications. This marked east end of Buffalo Division C.T.C. and beginning of joint NKP-PRR double-track, manual-block operation. — *John A. Rehor.*

changed the aspect to red over green over red — *Medium Clear*. This indication restricted movement through the turnout to medium speed; but once clear of the interlocking limits, the engineer could proceed at maximum authorized. Depending on the length of the trains and siding involved and other factors, it was entirely possible to move a train through a passing track without stopping it. To a skilled DS such running meets were routine. In the case of a meet between freight and passenger trains, often delays to both could be best avoided by putting the varnish in the hole.

The first Nickel Plate C.T.C. installation was completed in January 1942 on a troublesome 16.7-mile section of the Buffalo Division between North East, Pa., and Westfield, N. Y. Existing passing tracks at Ripley and Whitehouse were connected to make a continuous siding more than 3 miles long with single-track gaps of slightly less than 6 miles at each end. Before the end of 1942 two more single-track bottlenecks were eased with C.T.C. — the 21.5 Cleveland Division miles between Kishmans and Kimball and 19.7 miles of the Chicago Division between South Whitley and Hadley. On the former there were five controlled sidings, and the longest stretch of single track between them was less than 4 miles. This installation was controlled from GC, the interlocking tower at the sidings west of Vermilion.

The Nickel Plate figured that its early C.T.C. installations boosted single-track capacity to about 75 per cent of double track with automatic signals. An all-out campaign to convert all remaining single-track main line to C.T.C. was slowed only by production limitations of suppliers and the shortage of skilled technicians. However, by the end of 1943 C.T.C. on the Buffalo Division had been extended 8 miles east from Westfield to the end of the joint double track at Brocton. This new section boasted a controlled running track more than 4 miles long with three controlled intermediate crossovers. If necessary, the dispatcher could have a train meet and/or overtake as many as three other trains here.

THE WAR

Notwithstanding the fact that the depression had driven 37 Class 1 railroads into bankruptcy and delivered a cruel economic mauling to many others, the industry responded magnificently to the uncompromising demands made upon it during World War II. There was no repetition of the madness of 1917 — Government control was imposed for but 23 days and then only to head off a general strike. The same railroads which had lost 2 million dollars a day under the USRA poured 3 million in taxes daily into the Federal coffers and moved nearly twice the volume of passengers and goods in the

Fifteen miles out of Peoria, the hogger and 615 have a good roll on an eastbound oil train. Paul Stringham recorded this scene at Deer Creek, Ill., on October 27, 1942.

Nazi submarines diverted wartime petroleum traffic from coastal tankers to railroads. Nickel Plate forwarded solid trains of gasoline from all three western railheads and dispatched a half-dozen or more trainloads of crude oil daily from Lima, a major pipeline terminal. In 1943 a westbound LE&W train of empty tanks clears FS Tower at Fostoria moving into the old Lake Erie main. — *NKP photo*.

Specialized all-steel equipment highlighted Nickel Plate's small but modern postdepression freight-car fleet. Low-side 100-ton container gondolas (top left) of 1939-1940 were assigned to Narlo (O.) refractories complex. Eleven removable containers held 88 tons of dead-burned dolomite. Original 70-ton covered hoppers for dry bulk were bought in 1937 (left); the road eventually acquired 1400 cars of this type. Nickel Plate's first 50-foot box cars were also built in 1937. Nos. 87000-87099 (top right) had staggered double doors and end door for auto body and furniture loads. Heavy-duty flat cars 2900-2901 (above) of 1936 had six-wheel Buckeye trucks.

bargain. In 1943 American railroads hauled 730 billion ton-miles of freight, three times the combined total of all the vessels on inland rivers and lakes, the pipelines, aircraft, and trucks. In this, their great hour of glory, the railways were entrusted with 90 per cent of the nation's war matériel and 97 per cent of its military and naval personnel.

During the first year of the war the Nickel Plate carried more than 10.4 billion ton-miles of revenue freight, a 54 per cent increase over 1941 and nearly double that of 1929, the peak predepression year. Passenger-miles also reached 84 per cent above the 1941 figure, a new high, and operating revenues soared to more than 88.7 million dollars. In this year, when the Nickel Plate led all U. S. roads in freight locomotives and car-mile performance, the road also registered operating and transportation ratios of 52.37 and 28.78 per cent respectively. Both would stand as all-time lows. In 1943 and 1944 revenue ton-miles would go well over the 11 billion mark and operating revenues would exceed 100 million dollars. All the same, 1942 would be remembered as the year the Nickel Plate did more with less than at any time in its history.

As during the first World War, the Nickel Plate was called upon to move a staggering volume of troops and munitions toward Eastern ports of embarkation. There was no letup in the usual traffic of foodstuffs and agricultural products, and the factories and mills of the Great Lakes basin poured forth manufactured goods in a never-ending stream. In 1942 the Nickel Plate hauled 15 million tons of jeeps, armored tanks, trucks, aircraft parts, guns, machinery, locomotives, steel, pipe, and other manufactured goods. Added to this was nearly 10 million tons of coal, plus ore, refractories, scrap, coke, and chemicals. The Nickel Plate's 1942 share of the gasoline and oil diverted to the rails because of German U-boats came to 5.3 million tons, nearly 10 times what the road handled in 1940. About 40 per cent was crude oil loaded on line at Lima, a major pipeline center, and forwarded to East Coast refineries. For three years it was commonplace to have five or six 80-car oil trains dispatched nightly from South Lima yard as sections of No. 66. Solid tank-car trains loaded with aviation gasoline came to the road at all three western termini as well.

Rearmament and war caught the Nickel Plate critically short of rolling stock, and shippers who only months before had been all but idle were suddenly clamoring for cars the road didn't have. At the end of 1939 the Nickel Plate owned only 10,763 freight cars, fewer than half of what it had had a decade before. Every wood- or steel-underframe car considered surplus or requiring heavy repairs had been retired to help pay for the 4000-plus steel cars bought since 1929. These gave the Nickel Plate a small but modern fleet of cars, most of which were

War baby 730 rolls the westbound Bozo (BC-1) down the hill between Valparaiso and Spriggsboro, Ind. This October 29, 1944, Chicago Division scene was used by Lima Locomotive Works in its postwar advertising. — *Robert A. LeMassena.*

Leased C&O, Lackawanna, and Pere Marquette engines helped ease NKP's acute motive power shortage during 1941-1943. C&O 2337, a 2-8-2 built at Richmond in 1926, teams up with a Nickel Plate H-6 to move a westbound Sandusky Division freight. Sister 2314 blew up at Red Key, Ind., in March 1942. — *Clyde E. Helms.*

assigned to specific shippers. After the outbreak of war the increasing demand for ordinary box cars, flats, and gondolas, as well as covered hoppers and other special cars, prompted management to buy 3450 cars during 1940-1941. The last 1600 of these were ordered a scant three months before Pearl Harbor and were not delivered until 1942. Two years would pass before the road could acquire any substantial number of additional cars.

Surging traffic forced the conservative Brooke management to approve the purchase of more road freight engines in the spring of 1941. An order was given to the Lima Locomotive Works in June for 15 new 2-8-4's to be essentially duplicates of the Alcos of 1934. Numbered 715-729 and assigned class S-1, these were delivered to the road during June and July 1942. All were equipped with automatic train stop and all went into service on the Fort Wayne and Chicago divisions. Ten almost identical S-1 engines with train stop — Nos. 730-739 — were ordered from Lima in March 1942, but a year elapsed before the first of these went into service.

Even before Pearl Harbor the Nickel Plate had been leasing locomotives from other roads. At least six Chesapeake & Ohio 2300-series heavy Mikados saw service between Frankfort, Lima, and Bellevue during 1941-1943. These 1926 Alcos developed 67,700 pounds tractive effort and outweighed the heaviest Nickel Plate 2-8-2's by 15 tons. They had all the C&O trademarks, including headlight mounted on the pilot beam, cylindrical Vanderbilt tank, and dual air pumps mounted on the smokebox door below an Elesco K-40a feedwater heater. For all their brawn, the K-3's failed to outperform 600's on Sandusky Division manifests. Vibration at high speed jarred their fires so badly that maintaining full-throttle operation often was impossible.

Lackawanna and Pere Marquette also sent the Nickel Plate some surplus Mikes. Most of the DL&W engines were 28 x 32-inch-cylindered heavies like the C&O K-3's, but their trailer boosters gave an added 11,500 pounds of tractive effort. Inasmuch as these engines had small tanks, most of their Nickel Plate mileage was accumulated on Bellevue-Lima runs and on turns from Bellevue to Fostoria, Lorain, and Cleveland. In addition to 1922 Alcos 2103, 2108, 2112, 2114, 2117, and 2118, the older and smaller 1227 and 1228 were also lent by the DL&W. A pair of PM USRA light 2-8-2's — MK-1's 1028 and 1037 — joined hard-pressed 600's on the east end, and a group of C&O 2-8-0's saw extended service in Bellevue Yard. Included were G-7's 965, 987, 993, and 994 — superheated 100-tonners which had served on the LE&W District at times during the depression.

When the Nickel Plate received the first S-1 2-8-4's, it also acquired its first diesel-electric loco-

motives — six 1000 h.p. Alco switchers numbered 1-6. These 115-ton model S-2 units each had a McIntosh-Seymour six-cylinder in-line, single-action 4-stroke-cycle diesel engine and a General Electric main generator. The four axles had 40-inch wheels and were driven by GE model 731-C traction motors. In the fall of 1942 Electro-Motive delivered four of its standard model NW-2 switchers bearing Nickel Plate numbers 7-10 and designated class DE-2. The 1000-h.p. EMD's were somewhat heavier than the Alcos and were powered by a 2-cycle V-12 engine, model D-4-D main generator, and four D-7-C traction motors with 62:15 gear ratio.

The Alco diesels went into service at Buffalo and the EMD's at Chicago, in the Nickel Plate yards closest to the plants where they were built. The road was happiest with the Alco units, for its first Electro-Motives were plagued with traction-motor pinion failures and injector trouble. Wheel-slip relays solved the pinion problem, and the injector difficulty was traced to incompatibility of fuel and lubricating oils being used. Although the Nickel Plate's experience with the EMD engines may have had some bearing on its later diesel purchases, it did little to diminish the road's enthusiasm for the diesel-electric switcher per se.

The second group of S-1 Berkshires delivered early in 1943 went into west end service, after which Nos. 715-719 were transferred to the Sandusky Division. This made a total of 20 2-8-4's in service between Bellevue and Frankfort. In March 1943 the Nickel Plate received War Production Board priority for the purchase of 15 additional Lima 2-8-4's and the steel needed to beef up its east end bridges. Later 15 more 2-8-4's were ordered and the 30 new engines were deemed adequate to replace most of the 600's which had been doing such an admirable job of handling the system's heaviest tonnage between Bellevue and Buffalo.

S-2's 740-754 made their debut on the Cleveland and Buffalo divisions during the first quarter of 1944 just as the Nickel Plate was deluged with men and matériel headed for Eisenhower's invasion armies in England. Nos. 755-769 came from Lima during August and September of the same year. With an average working-order weight of 220.4 tons, the S-2's outweighed the 1934 Alcos by a little less than 6 tons. All 30 were equipped with automatic train stop and had Timken roller-bearing journals on the driving and engine-truck axles, an improved feedwater heater, and other minor improvements.

Lima's feverish wartime production seemingly had no adverse effect on its quality control, for the S-2's were judged by Nickel Plate enginemen to be the best of the 700's in every respect. Ten of the class, along with 10 S-1's, were equipped for passenger service during 1944-1945 and they could handle

During peak of wartime traffic, Nickel Plate rebuilt a half-dozen east end viaducts so that 700's could operate all the way to Buffalo. This was an amazing accomplishment since more than 50 trains were normally dispatched daily across the Cleveland Division. In the summer of 1943 B&B forces rush a new span into place 109 feet above the Ashtabula River.

Timely advent of first group of S-2 Berkshires helped get Nickel Plate past European invasion buildup during winter of 1943-1944. Front and backhead views reveal that Lima's wartime workmanship was still exemplary.

20 to 30 Pullmans at speeds of 70 mph and more. The S engines had an alarming tendency to buck violently when drifting or slowing with light trains, a habit which often convinced novice firemen that they were riding on the crossties. This malady was cured with installation of Franklin radial buffers.

Contrary to popular opinion, the war years were anything but profitable to the nation's railroads. In their zeal to meet the demands of war, the carriers wholeheartedly put aside their normal concern with economy and efficiency of operation. Unprecedented traffic burdens quickly wore out depression-debilitated roadway and rolling stock, while the materials allocated by the Government were insufficient to meet even ordinary maintenance and renewal standards. In subjecting the railroads to a 95 per cent excess profits tax, Congress refused to permit them to retain tax-exempt reserves with which they could effect postwar physical rehabilitation. Just as the railroads would have to cope with postwar inflation and pork-barrel subsidies for all their nonrail competitors, they also would have to find the means of restoring their battered track to prewar standards and replacing worn-out equipment.

Selective service, depression-lean rosters, and all-time traffic peak spelled wartime manpower crisis for railroads. By mid-1944 nearly 3000 Nickel Platers were in the armed forces and the road had turned to wives and daughters of employees to fill jobs. Three of the 131 women on mechanical department roster swab down a tender at Frankfort. — *William M. Rittase.*

Albeit the Nickel Plate's wartime revenues were greatly inflated and its fixed charges were sharply reduced, profits for 1942-1945 never came close to the 1941 net income of 12.7 million dollars. Taxes paid in 1942 were seven times higher than for the previous year, and the 1943 tax bill of $26,564,020 was almost as much as the road had grossed in 1932. During 1942-1944 the Nickel Plate paid out more than 72.5 million dollars in taxes, an amount sufficient to retire all of its capital stock or more than 70 per cent of its mortgage bonds at par.

As far as obtaining new equipment and materiel was concerned, the Nickel Plate and a few other strategic roads with glaring physical shortcomings fared comparatively well during the war. In acquiring 55 new 2-8-4's, the road replaced more than 25 per cent of its prewar fleet of freight locomotives. The 3250 freight cars received during 1942-1945 represented 27 per cent of the number on the roster at the end of 1941. The Nickel Plate was generally able to secure 80 per cent or more of its rail needs and enough structural steel to renew three of its longest bridges and strengthen four others. During the war, yard capacity at Fostoria and Frankfort was doubled; 126 miles of C.T.C., some new interlockers, and a number of passing tracks were installed; several roundhouses and the Conneaut shop were enlarged; and a million dollars' worth of shop machinery and tools were purchased.

When it came to manpower, the Nickel Plate's wartime plight was probably as serious as that of any road. A railroad's forces were scattered across the land, with many men headquartered in small groups. They came under the jurisdiction of local draft boards which had little or no understanding and even less sympathy with the vital role such men played in the road's operation. Between 1929 and 1939 the number of men hired by the Nickel Plate had been practically nil and many employees furloughed during the depression went to work in defense plants. It was still customary to give preference to sons of employees when hiring, and men recruited after 1939 were prime draft material. Since every attempt to secure a deferment for a vital man had to be appealed to Washington on its own merit, the road was practically powerless to keep its forces from being decimated. By 1943 2433 Nickel Platers were in the armed forces and 42 per cent of the 12,000 employees on the rolls had less than three years' experience. In desperation, the Nickel Plate was hiring high school students, Mexicans, and even the wives and daughters of employees. The mechanical department alone had 131 women on its roster.

Green hands, traffic congestion, prolonged tours of duty, and the mental distraction so common in times of stress were instrumental factors in the wartime rash of train accidents on the Nickel Plate. In

Two men died in a head-on collision at Albany, Ind., on August 3, 1943. Crew of Second 68 failed to heed time order, and their train — headed by S-1 717 — met a westbound local on the main track at 35 mph. The local's engine, Consolidation 382, was junked after the accident. — *Collection of Willis A. McCaleb.*

NYC 4-8-2 burns at Alexandria, Ind., after ramming Nickel Plate's Second IB-64, an eastbound oil train, on June 3, 1944. Crew of southbound Big Four freight jumped before the collision and escaped serious injury. — *Collection of Paul Siess.*

Sabotage twice brought misadventure to CB-2 at Cleveland. Mikado 666 and 17 cars of eastbound manifest were spilled at Scranton Road overpass on September 27, 1941 (above). Engineer Walter Herbel and crew escaped injury, but when the same train derailed at the same spot on May 11, 1942, all head-end men were seriously hurt. H-6d 628 and 11 cars still block the double-track main the day after the mishap (below). — *Upper photo, Steve Lakosz; lower photo, Corman E. Moore.*

one nine-month period during 1943-1944 three head-on and six rear-end collisions took place on the system. On the Sandusky Division, where an average of 30 trains were being pushed daily across 186 miles of unsignaled railroad, it was inevitable that mental lapses and fatigue would bring tragedy. The first bad wartime wreck on that part of the system came on March 28, 1942, when the KC-44, powered by 2-8-4 703 and C&O 2-8-2 2345, plowed into the rear end of another eastbound at Coldwater. Three days later a C&O Mike, the 2314, was literally disintegrated by a boiler explosion as it was approaching Red Key with Second 49. Three men died in this second and last Nickel Plate boiler accident. In 1943 there were two serious Sandusky Division collisions. The first occurred on August 3 a little east of the town of Albany. A westbound way freight consisting of G-44 382 and 15 cars collided head-on

Hard-luck Mikado 636, shown at Madison in 1938, was thrice wrecked on St. Louis Division during World War II. The career of the H-6e was ended by a broken spring hanger at the foot of Cayuga Hill on November 23, 1944. — *Robert J. Foster*.

with Second 68, a 52-car eastbound pulled by S-1 717. The impact was so great that the 2-8-0 was driven back 155 feet and 12 of the cars it was pulling were destroyed. The accident was caused by the failure of the eastbound to heed a time order, and two men lost their lives.

For a while during the war it seemed that once an engine was involved in an accident it was almost certain to figure in another. The 717, for example, was pulling an oil train through Alexandria in June 1944 when a Big Four 4-8-2 cut the train in two. The 640 was twice wrecked in St. Louis Division derailments, and the 630 and 632 were both involved in two collisions. After running into the rear of a freight at Jonestown, O., on March 23, 1944, H-5 Mikado 521 was repaired and rushed back into service in time to meet the 636 on the main track at Fair Grange, Ill., on April 27. This was the second of three wrecks for the 636, all on the St. Louis Division. On February 21, 1942, the Mike was derailed at 40 mph while approaching the Illinois Terminal crossing at Edwardsville with Second 49, an incident that cost the engineer and head brakeman their lives. The career of the ill-starred H-6 was abruptly ended by a broken spring hanger at the foot of Cayuga Hill on November 23, 1944. Six months later a trainman was killed at Cayuga when the 646 collided with a Jordan spreader being pushed by 2-8-0 916. This was 646's second collision and the fourth wreck involving Second 49.

Two nonfatal rear-end collisions which could have been major catastrophes occurred on the Cleveland Division 10 days and 11 miles apart during the bitter winter of 1944. The first came shortly after midnight on February 2 while a mass meet was being staged in 10 below zero weather at Painesville. Three westbound freights had already arrived and were occupying the two paralleling sid-

ings. Third 53 with engines 655 and 602 and 100 cars was in the 140-car westward siding, north of the main track. Holding the main was an eastbound section of No. 66 with 80 tank cars of aviation gasoline. Behind it were two troop trains and another oil train. The fourth westbound, First 37, had to clear up before the eastbounds could proceed, and the only place this train could go was behind Third 53 in the westward passing track. However, before this train could pull ahead to make room, First 37 — 2-8-2 608 and 40 carloads of high explosives — entered the siding on a *Restricting* signal and rammed its rear end. Luckily, the Mike nosed into a ditch north of the siding, away from the oil train. Third 53's caboose burst into flames, but an old refrigerator car somehow had become wedged between it and the gasoline-laden tank cars standing on the adjacent main track. The fire was contained and Painesville slept on, oblivious of what might have been.

Ten days later three brand-new S-2's were involved in a rear-end collision at Madison, east end of a 28-mile section of single track. Shortly before this accident a New York Central express train and a light Pennsylvania engine had collided at Ashtabula and the Central's trains were running over the Nickel Plate between Conneaut and Willoughby. A host of westbounds, including the crack *Commodore Vanderbilt*, were stacked up on the westbound main just east of the end of double-track operation, waiting for four Nickel Plate eastbounds to pass. The first of these, No. 98, arrived behind the 742 and pulled into the eastward passing track to allow No. 6 to overtake it. Once the passenger train had cleared, No. 98 began to pull out of the siding into the eastbound main. Hard behind No. 6, though, were the second and third sections of No. 66 moving with dispatch behind 741 and 743. Although it was day-

Rainbow trout at Castalia, O., occasionally lured John Davin from his Terminal Tower office. Immaculate G-44 397, coach, and private car 30 wait on siding at the Sandusky Division village while the president indulges in a brief diversion. — *Richard J. Cook.*

light, falling snow curtailed vision. Running on a *Clear* signal, the engineer of Second 66 saw No. 98 leaving the siding ahead of him in time to stop his train short of the turnout. Third 66, also running at full speed on a *Clear* signal, was not so fortunate. The enginemen and head brakeman huddled against the backhead of the 743 as she ground her way through caboose 1160 and 16 or more flat cars loaded with armored tanks. The collision took place alongside the *Commodore*, which was sandwiched between the wreckage and a freight standing in the westward siding. All the elements necessary to produce a hideous accident were present, but the fast-running S-2 stayed on the rails, sparing the passenger train a mauling by cartwheeling freight cars. Providentially, the Conneaut wrecking crane was waiting at Madison for an NYC engine to take it to the Ashtabula wreck and was able to start clearing the debris at once. For a long time the appearance of the 741, 742, and 743 on the ready track at Bellevue at the same time was a bad omen to superstitious Cleveland Division enginemen.

A little more than a month after the Madison wreck, the Nickel Plate again was spared a major disaster, this time on the Fort Wayne Division. An eastbound troop train taking coal and water on the running track at Yellow Creek was struck in the rear by First 52, engine 726. Miraculously, there was but one fatality — the engineer of the manifest who jumped from his cab just before the collision.

John Wysor Davin (1892-1949), an affable and dedicated railroader, had but one credo — going ahead. His six-year term as Nickel Plate president was the most dynamic period in the road's history, and he left to his successors an expanding establishment fully a decade ahead of its competitors.

The end of common management of the Chesa-peake & Ohio lines came with the resignation of George Brooke on December 15, 1942. On that day each of the three roads elected a president of its own. The new head of the Nickel Plate was a 50-year-old West Virginian named John Davin. Mild-mannered and affable, this former C&O vice-presi-dent radiated optimism. He had no use for the philosophy of inevitable shrinkage that already permeated Eastern railroading. To Davin there was only one course — going ahead — and his confidence in the future spread to every level of the organiza-tion. Davin's Nickel Plate was not only a formidable competitor but a dynamic and expanding enterprise with morale and individual productivity at their highest. At the same time it was an institution as keenly conscious of its responsibilities to the public and the welfare of its employees as the interests of its stockholders.

John Wysor Davin was born at Montgomery, W. Va., on March 10, 1892, and at the age of 18 went to work for the C&O as a check clerk at Hand-ley, W. Va. In less than one year he was appointed chief clerk to the general yardmaster at Handley and later he became a car distributor. By 1923 Davin was the C&O's assistant superintendent of transpor-tation, and prior to joining the Nickel Plate also held the posts of assistant to the president and vice-president. Possessing outstanding executive ability, he knew how to lead and inspire men. Like Bernet, he placed great reliance on outstanding subordi-nates and enjoyed their unswerving loyalty. Dur-ing most of his six-year tenure as the Nickel Plate's chief executive, Davin suffered with cancer, but this malady seemingly did little to diminish his dedication to his task or change his philosophy.

When Davin came to the Nickel Plate at the end of 1942, the road's long-term debt stood at slightly more than 130 million dollars, down 33.8 million from the 1934 high. Moreover, the annual fixed charges had already been cut from 7.71 to 5.83 mil-lion. Although the road's credit was far from re-established, the preferred stockholders were already clamoring for the 24.9 million dollars of accrued dividends the road owed them. The paint was hard-ly dry on Davin's door when he bluntly declared that he would follow a strict policy of "debt reduc-tion before dividends." Iron-willed and sternly pur-poseful, he would not go back on his word.

The Nickel Plate was faced with the 1947 maturi-ties of the 6-million-dollar LE&W first mortgage and $15,188,000 of the original NYC&StL first mortgage bonds. These could not be extended again because of commitments made to holders of the junior re-funding bonds. The LE&W mortgage was retired in 1943 along with the last of the troublesome three-year notes of 1929, and the next year the Nickel Plate first mortgage was paid off. A favorable bond market during 1945-1946 enabled Davin to refund 86 million dollars of 4½ and 5½ per cent junior bonds, the 6.5-million-dollar Clover Leaf 4 per cent mortgage, and a 10-million collateral trust note at sharply reduced rates of interest. The new 3 and 3¼ per cent bonds mature in 1980 and 1986 and reduced the Nickel Plate's fixed charges from 5.4 to 3.4 million dollars. Debt, including short-term equipment notes, now stood at a low of 113 million.

At the end of 1945 unpaid preferred stock divi-dends amounted to $30,287,376, the equivalent of $84 per share. At that time the Nickel Plate declared its first dividend since mid-1931 — 6 dollars payable on the preferred during 1946. Davin also announced that the road was now financially sound enough to set aside 20 per cent of its net income to retire the dividend arrearages. Restoration of the preferred dividend followed what was, in effect, a parting of the ways with the C&O. Late in the summer of 1945 that road had proposed to absorb through merger the Nickel Plate, Pere Marquette, and Wheeling & Lake Erie. The Nickel Plate board of directors approved the C&O's stock exchange offer, but the preferred stockholders staunchly opposed the merger on the grounds that their dividend claims were not adequately provided for. As a result, the C&O withdrew its offer to the Nickel Plate on Octo-ber 30, 1945. The controversial and unpredictable chairman of the C&O, Robert R. Young, was sud-denly covetous of the New York Central, and as a prelude to his bitter fight to gain control of that road he gave the Nickel Plate its freedom. If the judi-cious Davin had not foreseen this development, he had surely prepared his charge well for its coming.

John Davin's concern for the Nickel Plate's finan-cial health was matched by his anxiety over the road's ability to cope with the economic aftermath of the war and the brutally intensified competition he was certain lay ahead. In launching an ambitious improvement program in 1944, Davin had declared that the Nickel Plate would have to elevate its en-gineering standards if it was to provide train service surpassing in excellence that which had prevailed before the war. Taxation, shortages of manpower and materials, and the drive to reduce debt pre-cluded an immediate and massive assault on physi-cal restrictions, but by the end of 1945 Davin's pro-gram was under way. C.T.C. was already installed on all single track east of Bellevue and was planned for the Fort Wayne, Chicago, and Sandusky divi-sions west of Arcadia. Automatic block signals were also approved for the St. Louis Division's worst bottlenecks. After upgrading the bridges on that division for a decade, the road was already running its 2-8-4's into Madison. Seven-hundreds would also

A 1947 face-lifting at Bellevue saw demise of dirt-floored roundhouse built in 1882 (above). Revamped engine terminal was built around a new 18-stall brick and glass enginehouse, machine shop, powerhouse, and 110-foot turntable (below). — *Both photos, Nickel Plate.*

go into Peoria Division service after the 1947 renewal of a long viaduct at Mackinaw Dells, Ill.

A considerable portion of the 21.3 million dollars expended in additions and betterments to plant between 1945 and 1949 was earmarked for the long-neglected mainline engine terminals. First in line was Bellevue, where the westbound yard was substantially revamped and enlarged to 1800-car capacity during 1945-1946. An ultramodern 18-stall roundhouse with concrete floors, rolling overhead doors, and a 110-foot turntable replaced the 1882 facility in 1946-1947. Completed in 1947 were a machine shop adjoining the roundhouse, a boiler-house, and a two-story office building. The advent of diesels at Cleveland brought the 1948 construction of a modern diesel-electric maintenance shop at East 75th Street, replacing the "temporary" wooden engine shed in use since 1929. A new 300-ton reinforced concrete coal dock was also completed at East 75th Street in 1949. Entirely new engine terminals at Calumet and Fort Wayne costing 5.1 million dollars were also designed and approved during the Davin era.

The Sandusky Division west of Arcadia also re-

After Broadway roundhouse was torn down in 1929, this one-stall shed at East 75th Street served as NKP's Cleveland facility. B-11 switchers and No. 9's Pacific shown in this 1947 photo were soon to be replaced by Alco diesels. Framework of new diesel shop can be seen beyond the 2-8-2 being coaled with a clamshell. — *Richard J. Cook.*

ceived priority attention after 1944. Grade and curve reductions and construction of the 145-car Ayers passing track near Albany in 1944 were prompted by the 1943 wreck. A new 163-car siding was built at Boyleston (east of Frankfort) in 1945 after a cut 19 feet deep was made to eliminate 1-per-cent-plus grades in both directions. Seven miles of relocations and cuts completed in 1947 at and approaching the summit at Oakland relieved the worst operational headache on the division. Extending east from the Wabash River at Fort Recovery, the road climbed 90 feet and traversed three sets of reverse curves in 3½ miles. The worst of the curves were ironed out by a relocation, and an 8000-foot cut lowered Oakland summit by 20 feet and eased the grades on both sides. The line was also relocated from Fort Recovery to a point 2 miles west. In all, seven curves were eliminated.

The first Sandusky Division C.T.C. installation was completed between Arcadia and Lima in 1947, and by 1950 the entire 186-mile stretch between Frankfort and Arcadia was controlled from the console at South Lima yard. There were 22 controlled sidings varying in capacity from 131 to 157 cars and spaced 3 to 10 miles apart. On the Clover Leaf west of Frankfort automatic block signals were installed in 1946 from Donnellson through The Hole to Sorento and beyond. Two years later the 30 miles from Mellott to the crest of Cayuga Hill was changed from manual block to A.B.S. territory and signals were also installed on the 16-mile stretch between Madison and Edwardsville.

Some important alignment changes were completed and a number of interlockers replaced crossing targets on the Nickel Plate District between

1944 and 1949. Automatic block signals were installed on 9.5 miles of joint double track between Brocton and Plate in 1947 and on the 5-mile Yellow Creek running track in 1945. C.T.C. was extended in 1946 from South Whitley to Claypool, making a total of 34 miles of the Chicago Division boasting both automatic train stop and C.T.C. The 80.4 miles of Fort Wayne Division single track between New Haven and Arcadia was put under centralized traffic control between 1947 and 1949. On this part of the railroad there were 11 controlled sidings including the Yellow Creek and Latty running tracks and the lap sidings at North Findlay. The east and west sidings at Continental were greatly lengthened and overlapped so that they now provided the equivalent of a 3-mile running track.

By 1947 Nickel Plate passenger revenues had fallen off to less than half the 1944 high of 5.35 million dollars and passenger-miles were hardly more than one-third of the 186.7 million tally of 1945. However, the road's passenger service took on a new look after Robert R. Young's 1946 pronouncement that his roads would lead the way in bringing about the comeback of the nation's passenger trains. Unlike the C&O, which ordered replacements for every passenger car on its roster, the Nickel Plate at first contented itself with simply modernizing some of its older cars. Ten 80-series coaches were put through Stony Island shop during 1946 and 1947 and were completely rebuilt with picture windows, reclining seats, flat ceilings, and air conditioning. All seven dining cars also were modernized, with the remaining straight diners converted to diner-lounge cars. In 1947 the road ordered 25 new stainless-steel lightweight cars — 10 coaches, 2 bedroom-lounge-

Concrete coal dock at East 75th Street was built to serve freight power two years after Cleveland yard operations were dieselized. Brand-new silos were already blackened by soot when this 1949 scene was recorded. An also new S-3 sets out Cleveland perishable from consist of IB-64. — *Nickel Plate photo.*

diners, and 13 roomette-bedroom cars. But they were not delivered by Pullman-Standard until 1950.

The wartime passenger boom had been accommodated by equipping 20 Berkshires and a number of USRA 2-8-2's for passenger duty. After the 1946 restoration of the Cleveland-Fort Wayne sleepers swelled the consists of trains 5 and 6 to 15 or more cars, the 700's regularly powered these trains between Conneaut and Chicago. This permitted the Nickel Plate in 1946 to rebuild the Alco Hudsons with cast integral beds and cylinders and to apply roller-bearing engine trucks to all eight 4-6-4's. Dur-

271

The 700's began running between Frankfort and Madison during the war. Lima-built 722 roars past the station at Brocton, Ill., with westbound 49 on an autumn afternoon. Since the westbound train order semaphore is set at *Clear*, the orders are for another train. — *Collection of Charles Gammell.*

ing 1946 the appearance of the L's was strikingly altered by the addition of illuminated number boards and large sheet-steel smoke lifters. When these engines were drifting at high speed or slowing for station stops, smoke would lie back along the boiler, blocking the view from both sides of the cab. After two unsuccessful 1945 experiments with small steel plates mounted vertically on each side of the 177's stack, the orthodox elephant ears were adopted in 1946. The 177 and 175 were equipped with 16,500-gallon tenders from 2-8-2's in an effort to extend their nonstop range, but this experiment ended after an equalizer failure spilled No. 7 on the Chicago Division.

EARLY DIESELIZATION

Even as the Nickel Plate was upgrading its fleet of passenger engines, the decision was made to completely dieselize the St. Louis and Chicago runs. With freight traffic booming after the 1945-1946 lull, the road could no longer afford to tie up its splendid S-2's on varnish; and the Hudsons simply didn't have the beef to cope with the expanded night trains and the new 70 mph mainline speed limit. Eleven sleek blue and gray 2000 h.p. A units were purchased

from Alco during the winter of 1947-1948. Eight were intended for operation in pairs on the Buffalo-Chicago trains, two were bought to replace stoker-fired 4-6-2's on 9 and 10, and one was a spare unit. "Bluebirds" 180-190 weighed 154 tons in working order and measured 65 feet 8 inches over the coupler pulling faces. Their prime mover was Alco's turbosupercharged Model 244 4-cycle V-16 engine driving a General Electric 600-volt main generator. Four GE traction motors drove the outer axles of the six-wheel trucks, and the 62:21 gear ratio afforded 90 mph maximum speed and 30,500 pounds continuous tractive effort at 20 mph. The DP-1's (later reclassed as AP-20a) had Timken roller bearings, a Clarkson steam generator, conventional and Mars oscillating headlights, and 24RL air-brake equipment with F-3-D feed valves and deadman control.

Two Bluebirds leaving Bellevue with a 15-car No. 5 could overcome the tough westbound grade easily enough to have their charge moving at 70 mph by the time they reached Colby, 6½ miles out. The 177, and perhaps the 175, with perfectly squared valves and good coal, might have matched this performance; but it would have taken the likes

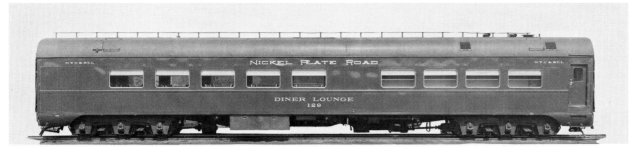

of Tilly Palmer, Ivan Albright, or Fred Hilker* to turn the trick.

By mid-1949 the Nickel Plate had 57 diesel-electric switchers which had largely supplanted steam power in the yards at Buffalo, Cleveland, Chicago, and Madison. There were, in fact, more diesels on system switching assignments than steamers. The first postwar diesels were Alcos 19-43, 1000 h.p. models of 1947 similar to Nos. 1-6 of 1942, most of which went into service at Cleveland. A pair of Baldwin 1000 h.p. switchers numbered 100-101 were also bought in 1947. Next came a dozen more Electro-Motive NW-2's, Nos. 11-22 of 1948, which increased the diesel force at Stony Island to 16 units. Early in 1949 the Nickel Plate acquired nine new Fairbanks-Morse 1000 h.p. units numbered 125-133. These six-cylinder, 2-cycle, opposed-piston diesels were bought for service at Muncie and Madison. Lima's first diesels, DS-8's 305-308, replaced 0-6-0's

*The taciturn Hilker and the 177 once covered the 125.5 miles between West Wayne yard office and Bellevue depot in 115 minutes flat with a troop train. This may have been the fastest run ever made across a Nickel Plate division.

Stony Island shop rebuilt 80-series coaches (below) in 1946-1947 adding flat ceilings, picture windows, and 52 reclining seats. Former 30-chair diner 106 was converted to a diner-lounge and modernized at Stony Island in 1948. Renumbered 129, it was still sheathed in Pullman green when outshopped (above).

on the Muncie yard jobs in 1949. The solitary DS-9, a 44-ton 380 h.p. General Electric shifter numbered 90, was purchased the same year to take over the yard assignment at Bloomington.

The Nickel Plate had retired more than a third

Wartime passenger boom coupled with holiday traffic made it necessary to run No. 10 in two sections on July 3, 1945. K-1b rattles across B&O leaving Fostoria with First 10. Red, white, and blue tender exhorted public to buy war bonds. — *Richard J. Cook.*

Leaving Fort Wayne with No. 8 (upper left), Hudson 177 had original ineffectual smoke lifters of 1945. Later version (upper right) extended a foot ahead of smokebox in another vain effort to scoop air upward. In September 1945 L-lb leaves Painesville with No. 6. L-1a 171 (above) blasts away from West 38th Street after relieving a CUT motor on No. 7. She has orthodox elephant ears applied to all 4-6-4's in 1946. — *Upper left, Richard E. Dill; upper right, Richard J. Cook; above, Nickel Plate photo.*

Displaced Pacifics worked trains 21 and 22 between Lima and Peoria after advent of passenger diesels. The 165 leads 21 into Carlock, Ill., near end of 327-mile run. Only agent awaits train in twilight of Peoria Division passenger service. — *Paul Stringham*.

Turbosupercharged Alco Bluebirds are set to leave Chicago's La Salle Street Station with No. 6, the eastbound *Nickel Plate Limited*, not long after Nickel Plate dieselized its principal passenger trains. — *Nickel Plate photo*.

Borrowed Burlington F3's, dynamometer car, and 79 cars of Buffalo-Chicago manifest NC-3 pause at West Wayne for crew change. The best Electro-Motive had, this 6000 h.p. diesel-electric combination failed to oust Berkshires from mainline jobs. The last S-2 headed west from Fort Wayne 10 years 2 days after this June 17, 1948, test run. — D. Allen Bauer.

Sylvan setting surrounds diesel-electric 27 as she climbs the rugged southbound grade of the Euclid Railroad. This was one of 19 Alco 1000 h.p. B-B switchers purchased for Cleveland Yard in 1947. — NKP photo.

of its prewar roster of steam locomotives by the end of 1949. A total of 107 engines were sold or scrapped during this period, including 29 surplus H-6 Mikados sold to the National Railways of Mexico and the Akron, Canton & Youngstown during 1945-1947. Consequently, when carloadings soared in 1948 the Nickel Plate once again found itself short on freight power. The diesel-electric that was already holding down the majority of the road's passenger and yard assignments seemed the logical choice. This was certainly the trend in the industry, and there were no longer any ties with the coal-conscious C&O to hinder a move in the direction of total dieselization. But the Nickel Plate was not at all certain that internal-combustion power was the equal of the 700's which were so ably filling its treasury. The magnificent 2-8-4's were piling up 7000 to 8000 miles a month and having no trouble living with the new mile-a-minute freight speed limit or with the increased train tonnages that C.T.C.-lengthened sidings permitted. Nevertheless, before placing a sixth order for 2-8-4's, management intended to take a long look at the freight diesel.

A VICTORY FOR STEAM

General Motors' Electro-Motive Division had introduced a successful multiple-unit diesel-electric freight locomotive in 1940, and its postwar all-purpose F3's were vanquishing steam freight power from the rails as fast as the builder could turn them out. Four 1500 h.p. F3's — two A and two B units owned by the Burlington — were brought by EMD to the Nickel Plate for trials in June 1948. The proposal was that diesels would relieve S-2 Berkshires then handling four crack manifests on the Chicago-Buffalo run, namely the CB-12, OB-2, BC-1, and NC-3. With the X-50041 in tow, the invincible F3's in 4500 h.p. and 6000 h.p. combinations would be pitted against S-2's — for better or for worse — handling the four trains over their entire 513-mile runs.

These were the only F3's ever to pull Nickel Plate manifests, and three years would pass before the road bought its first diesel-electric freight power. At the conclusion of the trials it was observed that the 4500 h.p. F3 combination developed over 1000 drawbar horsepower more than the S-2 at low speeds. Of far greater significance to the Nickel Plate, the opposite was true once the speed had advanced beyond 40 mph. The S-2 not only made better terminal-to-terminal running time than the diesels but did it at slightly lower fuel cost. The 6000 h.p. combination, however, developed more drawbar horsepower than the 2-8-4 at any speed, and four F3's were calculated to raise average train speed 5 to 7 mph.

	S-2 2-8-4	4500 h.p. diesel	6000 h.p. diesel
Average drawbar h.p. under 30 mph	2130	3338	4699
Average drawbar h.p over 30 mph	3915	3750	5001
Average tonnage handled	3945	3939	[1]
Average time over road (513 miles)	12H-45M	13H-30M	12H-11M
Fuel cost per 1000 gross ton-miles	.1795[2]	.1796	.2075

[1]Exact figure unknown, but stated as being approximately the same as in the S-2 and 4500 h.p. diesel test series.

[2]Computed to include fuel consumed in terminal standby operations, fire cleaning and dumping, boiler blowdown, and so forth.

The diesels afforded almost no savings in terminal delays since an hour or so was consumed at Bellevue in icing and reblocking. Intermediate delays at Conneaut and Fort Wayne were usually held to about 15 minutes, which was required for crew and caboose changes regardless of power used. Offsetting the performance of the 6000 h.p. combination was the increased operational cost; and although some savings would be realized in maintenance costs, the annual net cost of dieselizing the four trains was computed at over a quarter of a million dollars. With its frequency of operation, Nickel Plate had been able to reach a high degree of steam-power

GE's 4500 h.p. gas turbine-electric locomotive broke in on Nickel Plate freights before going to Union Pacific. Below, the orange and black 101 rolls a westbound — one of 16 runs it made between Bellevue and Buffalo during March 1949. Dynamometer car accompanied 101 on its NKP travels to assist designers in evaluating the turbine's performance. Above, Traveling Engineer Don Coon, long-time intimate of X-50041, pores over Buffalo Division profile. — *Both photos, General Electric.*

F7 demonstrators 801-802 roll tonnage across Peoria Division in the spring of 1949. Numbers and blue and silver paint job betrayed EMD's confidence that the 1500 h.p. freighters would end up on the Nickel Plate roster. This second attempt to vanquish the 700's failed to produce an order, however. After barnstorming across the U. S. and Canada, the units became Great Northern 272A-272B.

No. 90 lends its 380 h.p. to 711's battle against the 1.3 per cent uncompensated of Bloomington Hill. Peoria Division's tough grades made it a prime candidate for dieselization. General Electric's 44-tonner worked on and off at Bloomington for 15 years. — *Collection of Howard R. Watson.*

utilization, and the usual diesel superiority in this respect was not a factor here.

Less than two weeks after the F3's were sent back to the Burlington, the Nickel Plate gave Lima an order for 10 more 2-8-4's. This was the first time a road had tested the diesel in freight-train service and then reordered steam power in lieu of the diesel. It was to happen only once again, in the case of the Norfolk & Western. Even before the new engines were delivered, another series of tests were implemented using General Electric's brand-new 101, a 4500 h.p. B-B-B-B exhaust gas turbine-electric locomotive. The purpose was to develop the performance of this experimental machine and to compare this with the results of the steam-diesel tests.

During March 1949 the 101 made a series of 16 test runs over the two easterly mainline divisions. In a subsequent report Nickel Plate observers noted that the turbine had performed very well, especially in view of the fact that it was still an experimental machine. Unlike the F3, the turbine developed its full rated horsepower handling the usual 4000-ton train at 60 mph. The report also stated that 101 had an insatiable appetite for Bunker C fuel oil, consuming 4 gallons a minute while idling — roughly 60 to 70 per cent of consumption at full-capacity operation. Prophetically, it was noted that although fuel costs were too high for the 101 to compete with steam or diesel on the Nickel Plate, the turbine might find successful employment in territory where Bunker C was cheaper and where long sustained runs were involved.

Shortly after the 101's trials on the Nickel Plate, General Motors dispatched two of its new model F7 diesel-electric freighters for a Peoria Division demonstration. Numbered 801 and 802, these A units had the blue and gray colors of the Bluebirds and were considered a shoo-in to win a berth in the Peoria Division pool. The F7 was a beefed-up version of the F3 with redesigned injectors and higher compression ratio. EMD declared that the F7 could handle 25 per cent more tonnage on a 1 per cent grade than its predecessor, and the Peoria Division had some of the toughest grades on the Nickel Plate system. As predicted, the F7's outperformed the 700's on Crandall Hill and at Lafayette and Bloomington but couldn't match their speed elsewhere. The diesel's cab was so designed that it was almost impossible for the engineer to run the locomotive and look to the rear for signals at the same time. Since local work was an important part of Peoria Division operation, Electro-Motive again failed to make the sale.

S-3's 770-779 were delivered by Lima-Hamilton in the spring of 1949 at a unit cost of $226,315.10, 2½ times that of the 1934 Alcos. With an average weight of 446,250 pounds (814,167 with tender),

these were the heaviest Nickel Plate 2-8-4's. Originally a proposal was made to move the steam dome to the third boiler course, as in the case of C&O's 2-8-4's; but the S-3's came from the builder essentially identical in appearance to the previous group of S-2's. They had radial buffers, bronze bells, insulated cabs, valve pilot speed recorders, and valves arranged for Line & Line exhaust clearance — now a Nickel Plate standard.

The 779 was delivered on May 13, 1949, and proved to be the last steam locomotive built at Lima. Set up and broken in from South Lima yard, in the very shadow of the works where she was built, this engine brought down the curtain on the Super-Power era. The S-3's were not equipped with automatic train stop or passenger appliances and they were used strictly in freight service, generally east of Bellevue. In their nine years of operational life, the class compiled a remarkable mileage record considering that they were confined to less than 250 miles of railroad.

	Miles first full 10 mos. service	Total miles accumulated 1949-1958	Most miles accumulated in one month
770	78,108	697,441	9,059
771	82,148	712,731	9,313
772	80,241	710,822	8,927
773	80,689	703,243	9,342
774	81,950	685,697	9,513
775	81,978	706,531	9,388
776	80,903	708,601	8,893
777	79,304	697,605	8,937
778	77,564	721,517	8,756
779	79,146	677,095[1]	9,369

[1]The 779 spent most of the summer and fall of 1949 at the Chicago Railroad Fair and was one of the first S-3's to be laid up.

THE GOLDEN LEGACY OF JOHN DAVIN

John Davin's death on January 7, 1949, followed the most successful year in the history of the Nickel Plate. Operating revenues in 1948 totaled 109.4 million dollars, a new high. For the first time this amount was greater than the sum of the road's bonded debt. In the face of rampant inflation, the operating ratio had been held to a respectable 67.82 per cent, and $15,353,838 was carried to net income. After the 1948 payment of a $16.50 dividend, the Nickel Plate's obligation to its preferred stockholders was reduced to 26.5 million dollars. A totally independent entity since November 10, 1947, the Nickel Plate was now at the zenith of competitive strength and vitality. Thanks to Davin, the road had a gilt-edged reputation and it stood on the threshold of expansion.

During 1946 the Nickel Plate had acquired a large block of Wheeling & Lake Erie common stock from the C&O, and in 1947 NKP bought back the 115,000 shares of W&LE prior-lien stock it had sold to the C&O in 1941. These purchases cost the Nickel Plate more than 15 million dollars and gave it 80 per cent

of the Wheeling's stock. After May 28, 1947, Davin was the chairman of the W&LE board of directors, and on October 11, 1948, stockholders of the two railroads approved the lease of the Wheeling to the Nickel Plate. At the time of Davin's death the plan was before the Interstate Commerce Commission for approval.

Through acquisition of the freight-only Wheeling & Lake Erie, the Nickel Plate gained far more than a profitable 530-mile railroad with modern locomotives and cars, C.T.C., and spacious shops. In contrast with the Nickel Plate, the W&LE originated most of its traffic, and it was an important link in a service route to the East Coast. The long deferred union of the two railroads added traffic balance to the Nickel Plate's postwar gains and ended its abnormal dependence on its Buffalo connections.

S-3 779 was the last steam locomotive bought by the Nickel Plate and the last out-shopped by Lima Locomotive Works. Fifteen days before delivery, on April 28, 1949, the 2-8-4 was in an advanced stage of assembly in the builder's cavernous erecting hall (upper right). After running 12,000 miles during her first 1½ months of service, 779 was sent to Chicago Railroad Fair for a 3½-month public relations assignment. Below, 407-ton Berkshire shares limelight with Illinois Central 4-8-2 2602 on Windy City lakefront. No. 779 spent her active career in fast freight duty on main stem between Bellevue and Buffalo. S-3 ran the equivalent of that 245-mile run every day of her 92 months of active service. En route to Buffalo with KC-44 (far left), she pauses at Conneaut for coal, water, and a new crew. March 5, 1957, found 779 working NC-3 up 1.56 per cent westbound grade of Cleveland Union Terminal's Cuyahoga viaduct (upper left) while Nickel Plate's own bridge was closed to permit installation of new vertical-lift draw span. After more than five years of storage, the 2-8-4 made her second trip to Chicago to be prepared for permanent display at Lima. Shortly afterward, 779 arrived at her birthplace (lower left) sans diamond builder's plates. A new set has since been provided by the "Loco."—*Far left, Jim Shaughnessy; upper left, John A. Rehor; lower left, Willis A. McCaleb.*

Long Run tunnel, 9 miles west of the Ohio, was last major hurdle in the building of the Wheeling & Lake Erie main line. In this 1889 photo a construction train pulls excavated material from the 700-foot bore. No. 26, a 4-4-0 built by Rome in 1883, assists diamond-stacked Mason Fairlie No. 11. — *Collection of Charles Matt.*

The Connotton coal roads

UNLIKE the other railroads which made up the latter-day Nickel Plate, the Wheeling & Lake Erie was created to open up an undeveloped region and its mineral resources. Actually, the W&LE of 1949 represented two concurrent and unrelated attempts to exploit the coal fields of eastern Ohio, long ignored by the western stepchildren of the Pennsylvania system. Both the original W&LE and the predecessors of its 1899 acquisition, the Cleveland,

Canton & Southern, were doggedly promoted by obscure Ohioans with more imagination than money or influence. Both roads were notably weak enterprises that languished through long periods of insolvency. The Wheeling itself required nearly 20 years to build a 217-mile line from Toledo to the Ohio River and was reorganized four times in as many decades. But for the same Gould-inspired schemes that were so instrumental in bringing about

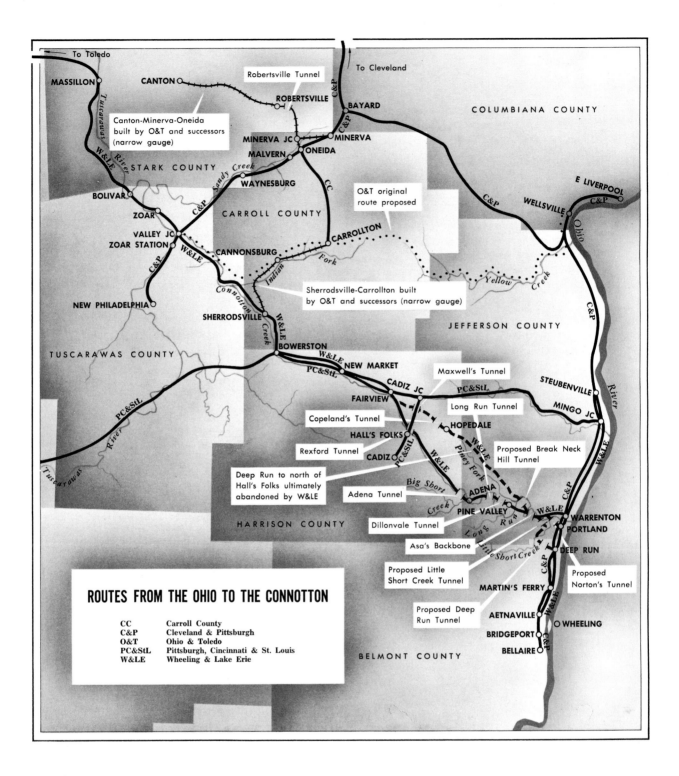

ROUTES FROM THE OHIO TO THE CONNOTTON

CC	Carroll County
C&P	Cleveland & Pittsburgh
O&T	Ohio & Toledo
PC&StL	Pittsburgh, Cincinnati & St. Louis
W&LE	Wheeling & Lake Erie

the launching of the Nickel Plate, the road more than likely would never have materialized.

After World War I the W&LE recovered from the ill-starred ambitions of two generations of Goulds and passed into a long era of robust health. This change in fortune was paced by the growth of a stable market for the steam coal mined along its lines. Blast furnaces, steel mills, oil refineries, and other heavy industry also contributed mightily to the road's belated prosperity. Finally, after the Taplins managed to build the connecting link be-

tween their Pittsburgh & West Virginia and the Western Maryland, the Wheeling became a vital link in a new trunk line to the East Coast.

THE WHEELING COAL ROAD

Ohio had yet to see a steam locomotive when the first plans were advanced to build coal roads from the Ohio River to Toledo. The southeastern portion of the state was then, as it is now, one seemingly endless coal field in which enormous veins of bituminous outcropped wherever streams cut through the ancient plateau. In the valley of Connotton Creek, a 30-mile trench feeding the Tuscarawas River, there were exposed to view as many as three or four horizontal seams 4 to 6 feet thick which could be easily mined with a pick and shovel. Between the Connotton and the Ohio River the great Pittsburgh, or No. 8, seam outcropped in almost every ravine and valley in Jefferson, Harrison, and Belmont counties. One early test boring indicated that the seam ran as much as 17 feet in thickness.

On March 12, 1836, Ohio gave a charter to the Bridgeport, Cadiz & Sandusky Rail Road, the first of several companies that would seek to connect the coal fields with the Ohio River and Lake Erie. As with most early Ohio railroads, this enterprise never advanced beyond the paper stage. In 1855 the Steubenville & Indiana Rail Road opened a line from Steubenville to central Ohio which traversed the upper Connotton valley, but this predecessor of the Panhandle (Pittsburgh, Cincinnati & St. Louis) soon came under the control of the Pennsylvania. For obvious reasons the latter saw no benefit in exploiting Ohio coal at the expense of the mines PRR served in western Pennsylvania. Thus the beds along Connotton Creek remained undisturbed in their primeval state.

Not long after the Civil War the challenge of the southeastern Ohio coal fields was taken up by Joel Wood of Martin's Ferry and Gen. E. R. Eckley of Carrollton. They were men of dissimilar backgrounds, but their common denominator would prove to be pathos and utter failure. Yet the Wheeling & Lake Erie as it ultimately came to exist was largely the product of what they started. Joel Wood was the ticket agent of the Cleveland & Pittsburgh (PRR) at Martin's Ferry, a river town a little upstream from Wheeling. A founder of the Free Soil Party and a Quaker, he was first an ardent abolitionist and later a champion of prohibition. Fate deprived Wood of formal education and wealth, but the man was endowed with native shrewdness and a talent for inspired oratory.

In 1871 Joel Wood quit the secure and tranquil life of a small-town agent and dedicated himself to the promotion of a railroad through the coal fields to Lake Erie. After opening an office in Wheeling and gaining the support of several moneyed men of that city, he formed the Wheeling & Lake Erie Rail Road Company. Articles of incorporation were drawn up on March 10, 1871, and on the following April 6 the company was chartered by the State of Ohio. The times were propitious and the aldermen of Wheeling quickly enacted an ordinance which granted $300,000 to help build the road. Wood had every reason to believe that substantial subsidies would also come from the ambitious lake ports of Sandusky and Toledo, and he was well aware that Massillon, a northern Ohio city of 6000 located in the heart of a field of the best grade of coking coal, was agitating for a new rail outlet.

The Pennsylvania-controlled Pittsburgh, Fort Wayne & Chicago ran through Massillon, but practically all the coal mined in the area had to be shipped by barge on the Ohio Canal. The situation was one which had the town fathers bristling with indignation. In January 1868 a delegation from Massillon met with the Toledo Board of Trade to urge the joint promotion of a new road connecting their cities with Wheeling. The next month representatives from Toledo, Massillon, and other towns on the proposed line met at Wellington, but this convention ended in failure over a dispute between Toledo and Sandusky. Despite this development, Wood was confident that northern Ohio would rally behind him when the time came to open his subscription books.

On February 7, 1872, the Wheeling & Lake Erie gave Hugh Bowlsby Willson of New York a contract to build and equip its railroad as a standard-gauge line for $35,000 per mile. Of this amount, $25,000 was to be paid in the face value of stocks and bonds and the rest in cash raised through local stock subscriptions. Almost at once Chief Engineer A. K. Robinson began a preliminary survey to locate the shortest route with gradients of 50 feet to the mile or less. From a starting point a half mile north of the C&P depot at Martin's Ferry, Robinson's line extended 160 miles through the coal fields to Massillon and Sandusky. The line ran north along the Ohio for 3 miles to the mouth of Deep Run and then west along that stream for 1.3 miles. A proposed 2650-foot tunnel was to carry the W&LE to Little Short Creek which was followed northeast for 1.2 miles. Tunnel No. 2, a 2800-foot bore, progressed the road due north to Big Short Creek which was to be followed west for 3 miles to its confluence with Piney Fork. In this distance there were 350-foot and 1100-foot tunnels.

Robinson ran his proposed line northwest along Piney Fork for 11 miles to Hopedale. Just west of that town a 950-foot tunnel was required to carry the W&LE through Copeland's Hill, and about 3 miles beyond another tunnel would have to be cut through Maxwell's Hill. This was to be about 1600 feet long and would cross under the Panhandle's Cadiz branch at a station called Hall's Folks. At an elevation of 1160 feet, Maxwell's Tunnel was the summit of the 23-mile-long, 415-foot climb out of the Ohio valley. Beyond this point the line continued northwest, descending sharply to the Connotton and the Panhandle main line at Fairview (Jewett). Robinson's route then followed Connotton Creek for 30 miles to Zoar Station, where the stream joined the Tuscarawas River. Still running on a north-

The 4000 persons who rode over W&LE's 4 miles of newly laid track during the First Grand Complimentary Stockholders' Excursion on May 31, 1877, crammed on three narrow-gauge flat cars. John Ray ran the little 4-4-0 *Milan*; subcontractor Hugh McKee served as conductor. — *C. H. Kellogg, the Milan Historical Museum Collection.*

westerly course, the W&LE would use the Tuscarawas valley to reach Zoar, Bolivar, Navarre, and Massillon. West of Massillon 6 miles of heavy ascending grades carried the line to Sippo Summit in the Pigeon Run coal field. Beginning at Dalton, a little west of Sippo, 7 miles of the abandoned Grafton, Medina & Tuscarawas Railroad grade was to be used to reach Orrville. The remaining 73 miles of route to Sandusky traversed rich rolling farmland and touched the towns of Lodi, New London, Norwalk, and Milan. In his survey report Robinson noted that good white oak for bridges and crossties was abundant all along the line and many large gravel beds for ballast were to be found between the Ohio and Massillon.

The Wheeling & Lake Erie was a promising venture in 1872 but the next year a series of blows threatened to add it to the growing list of defunct Ohio railroad projects. In March a Wheeling taxpayer obtained an injunction blocking the municipal grant, and the city's aldermen later were forced to repeal the ordinance of 1871. Later in 1873 the ruinous financial panic wiped out all hope of securing other subsidies and large-scale private investment. Joel Wood worked in vain to drum up support for his railroad in the towns along the proposed route. Toledo was preoccupied with coal roads to the Hocking valley and had joined forces with the Pennsylvania to build a connection with the Fort Wayne

road. The 1872 completion of a coal road to central Ohio had exhausted most of Sandusky's loose capital, and even that perennial suitor of railroads turned its back on the W&LE.

Shortly before the panic the Lake Shore & Tuscarawas Valley (now B&O) opened a line from Lake Erie, at the present site of Lorain, to Massillon. This event not only cooled Massillon's ardor for the W&LE but presaged a crueler stroke. The LS&TV awaited only an economic revival to begin laying track from Massillon to Wheeling. Several narrow-gauge companies and the standard-gauge Valley Railway were also seeking to reach the coal fields and Wheeling. The Valley already had completed a grade between Cleveland and Canton. All the same, the indomitable Wood kept riding the circuit, matching wits with skeptical Orrville one day and miserly Lodi the next. He was forever exhorting the contractor to resume work and attempting to wheedle grants of right of way from farmers too niggardly to part with anything more substantial than vague promises.

In 1873 Willson graded a few miles of road on each side of Navarre, and on March 3, 1874, he put several large forces to work between Maxwell's and the Ohio. The original route was altered somewhat by extending the line about 3 miles farther north along the Ohio to Portland. At this point the passage through the escarpment to Big Short Creek required a tunnel only 900 feet long. The change added a mile of road but eliminated the long Deep Run and Little Short Creek tunnels. During 1874-1876 about 11 miles of grade was completed from the head of Connotton Creek to a point on Piney Fork 7 miles southeast of Hopedale. Some work was done on all six tunnels and three were actually completed. These were Maxwell's, Copeland's, and Asa's Backbone (the 350-foot bore in the valley of Big Short Creek).

THE FIRELANDS NARROW GAUGE

By the end of 1875 the W&LE had managed to raise only $26,103.79 through the sale of its securities, and all of this money had been expended in construction. The company and the contractor had a bitter falling out and the directors were constantly at each other's throats. Wood's associates were forever plotting behind his back and he was, in his words, "exposed to a constant fire from the rear." A clique of directors clamored for a switch to 3-foot gauge, claiming that as such the W&LE would cost as little as $20,000 a mile to build. During the 1875 annual meeting Wood was barely able to muster enough support to defeat the narrow-gauge faction. His victory was short lived.

Those who favored narrow gauge were from towns at the north end of the proposed route — Norwalk, Milan, and Huron. Huron, suggested as the W&LE's principal Lake Erie terminus, was a sleepy fishing village at the mouth of the Huron River east of Sandusky. Milan, once one of the great wheat shipping ports of the world, was located 8 miles upriver from Huron. Lake Erie schooners had formerly called at Milan's warehouses by way of a short canal. Norwalk, a mere 4 miles south of Milan, had railroading in its blood. Prior to the formation of the LS&MS, the town's economy had been built around the main shops and terminal of the Cleveland & Toledo Railroad and its predecessor.

The first proposal to connect Norwalk, Milan, and Huron with a railroad had resulted in the March 7, 1835, organization of the Norwalk & Huron Rail Road. Although this road was never built, the Huron & Oxford Rail Road had materialized some years later as a feeder from Huron to the line of an early railroad running south from Sandusky. By 1875 the H&O had been torn up and the Milan Canal was filled with silt and rotting logs. The C&T shops at Norwalk were closed and the town was shopping for a new railroad—one which needed its skilled boilermakers and blacksmiths. The three Firelands towns, allied in a common cause, moved to assure the building of the W&LE.

The Firelands faction led by Frank Lockwood, a Milan merchant, managed to oust the weary Joel Wood and most of the original W&LE progenitors at the end of 1876. By this time the former group had already forced the change to a gauge of 3 feet and had acquired the towpath of the abandoned Milan Canal. In March 1877 Lockwood effected a reconciliation with contractor Willson who now agreed to build the road for $17,000 in securities and $3000 in cash per mile. Willson announced that he planned to use the cash to buy rails which, in turn, would serve as collateral to secure loans to pay for labor and other materials. With the end of winter, work was started on the line from Huron south.

On May 5, 1877, the LS&MS delivered a flat car bearing a small 4-4-0 locomotive to Willson at Norwalk. The 10-ton *Milan*, built by the National Locomotive Works* at Connellsville, Pa., had a peaked roof, diamond stack, and 3-foot drivers. The little engine sported the unique National tender which was fitted with a conventional four-wheel pivoting truck aft and a single rigid axle forward. By the time *Milan* arrived Willson had already begun spiking 35-pound iron to 6-foot, 7 x 5-inch section crossties at the Milan Street terminus in Norwalk, and by May 31, 1877, track was in as far as Milan. On that date the contractor staged what he called the First Grand Complimentary Stockholders' Excursion. With the *Milan* shuttling back and forth with three flat cars, more than 4000 passengers were given a ride over the 4-mile line. By the end of June 1877 a total of 12½ miles of track had been laid between Norwalk and the Government Pier at Huron. A second National engine, the *Norwalk*, was on the road along with a Barney & Smith combine, two box cars, and 19 flats. Although an occasional mixed train ventured over the road, the W&LE subsisted mainly on Sunday excursions patronized by curious Firelands folk. During the winter the little road was closed down altogether.

The contractor stopped all work at the end of the summer of 1877, at which time 9 miles of grade had been completed on both sides of New London. One mile of track had been laid in that town when the supply of iron ran out. In six frustrating years the W&LE had succeeded in laying 13½ miles of track and in addition had graded about 37 miles of road. Company and contractor were again at odds — this time over Willson's charge that without his consent the management had sold bonds to pay off old creditors and other contractors. In December 1877 Willson succeeded in taking over the company, but the next spring the hopelessly insolvent W&LE filed a petition of dissolution. In a desperate attempt to escape responsibility for the road's debts,

---

*One of the more obscure locomotive builders, National catered to the narrow-gauge trade and produced about 260 light engines. The firm, originally known as Dawson & Bailey, was called W. H. Bailey & Company after 1875 and was liquidated in 1878.

the stockholders appealed to the courts again and again during 1878-1879 for the right to go out of business. Finally, at the end of the 1879 season, the W&LE announced that it was abandoning operations and the equipment was laid up at Norwalk pending disposition. The stormy and inept career of the Wheeling & Lake Erie apparently had come to a close.

THE ELDERBERRY BRANCH

The luckless Joel Wood had not made the only abortive bid to build a coal road from the Ohio to Lake Erie in the 1870's. Carrollton's Gen. E. R. Eckley was similarly frustrated in his ill-timed venture. Eckley had once represented his district in Congress and had served in the Union Army during the Rebellion, but neither episode in his life had been particularly noteworthy. In 1871 he had a reasonably lucrative law practice in and about the bucolic seat of Carroll County and was the president of a bank in nearby Minerva. While Eckley was something of a plutocrat by Carrollton's standards, his resources were relatively meager. What Eckley lacked in the way of opulence, however, he more than made up for in imagination and ingenuity. Eager to have a hand in exploiting the mineral riches so close at hand, he brought about the formation of the Ohio & Toledo Rail Road on May 7, 1872.

Like the Wheeling & Lake Erie, the Ohio & Toledo sought to traverse the Connotton and Tuscarawas valleys; but the O&T's Ohio River terminus, Wellsville, was a considerable distance upriver from Wheeling. The road was projected from Massillon to Toledo on a line elastic enough to reach any of a large number of towns that might be anxious to aid in financing its construction. To breach the wall of hills separating the Ohio and the Connotton, the O&T was to be built over a route first surveyed in 1834 by the defunct Yellow Creek, Carrollton & Zoar. This ran west from the Ohio, scaling the escarpment along the winding banks of Yellow Creek to a summit in the neighborhood of Carrollton. West of that point the line descended to the Connotton by way of Indian Fork. Instead of employing the tunnels and moderate gradients used by the W&LE, Eckley settled for the cheaper gauge of 3 feet, hairpin curves, and 2 to 3 per cent ruling grades.

Before the General could seriously undertake the building of the O&T he was "blessed" with the gift of Carrollton's railroad — a primitive and totally unreliable strap-rail affair that connected the town with a branch of the Cleveland & Pittsburgh. For more than 20 years the "Elderberry Branch" had been a local joke and a financial burden for the men who had built it. Still, it was Carrollton's one all-weather connection with civilization, and its owners were anxious to unload it on someone who might

transform the line into a first-rate conveyance.

As were many early Ohio railroads, the Carrollton branch was conceived as a feeder to a canal. In 1827 the route of the Sandy & Beaver Canal* was projected through the valley of Sandy Creek 10 miles north of Carrollton. Upon completion it was to connect the Ohio Canal with the Ohio River. The former gave access to Cleveland, Lake Erie, and the lower Ohio; the latter to Pittsburgh, Wheeling, and the upper Ohio. It seemed essential to Carrollton that its iron furnaces and sawmills have a connection with the canal, so the enterprising folk of those parts obtained a charter on April 3, 1837, for the Carrollton & Lodi Rail Road. The charter stipulated that the proposed 10-mile road between Carrollton and Lodi (now Malvern) be completed within five years. Owing to the prolonged delay in completing the canal, the railroad charter was allowed to lapse. On February 20, 1846, two years before the Sandy & Beaver was opened, the charter was revived in the name of the Carroll County Rail Road. Once again, though, the railroad failed to materialize. Finally, on March 9, 1850, the charter was again amended — this time to authorize the building of the road in conjunction with a branch of the Cleveland & Pittsburgh.

The new Carroll County Rail Road was promoted by Isaac Atkinson, Gen. Henry A. Stidger, and others of Carrollton. About $30,000 was pledged to the stock, and construction work was started early in the summer of 1851. A superficial grade was formed by digging drainage ditches on each side of the right of way with the excavated soil banked up between them. No heavy cutting or filling was attempted. The superstructure consisted of timber sleepers imbedded in the soil to which were attached oak crossties spaced about 5 feet apart. The rails were 4 x 6-inch white oak stringers as long as 16 feet, crowned with iron straps 2 to 3 inches wide and $\frac{5}{8}$ to $\frac{7}{8}$ inch thick. Carroll County's track gauge was the same as that of the C&P — 4 feet 10 inches. The first iron was spiked down on May 24, 1852, and toward the end of that summer the road purchased 350 tons of used strap rail at $25 per ton. Practically every prominent man in Carrollton was needed to guarantee the purchase price.

The Cleveland & Pittsburgh branch left that road's main line at Bayard and extended 7 miles southwest to Minerva and to Oneida, the Carroll County's northern terminus. Service was inaugurated by the C&P between Carrollton and Bayard on May 25, 1853, under an agreement with the CC providing for a pro rata division of receipts. The daily train left Carrollton in the morning and re-

---

*The Sandy & Beaver Canal, famed for its tunnels and some other engineering wonders, required 20 years to build. It was opened in 1848 and abandoned four years later.

turned from Bayard in the afternoon. A turntable and a depot spacious enough to house the locomotive were built at Carrollton. More than likely the locomotive assigned by the C&P to the Carrollton train was a Lowell-built 2-2-0 "Whistler" of 1839 vintage purchased in 1851 or 1852 from the Western Railroad (Massachusetts). This 12 x 18, formerly named *Suffolk*, was probably the only C&P locomotive light enough to travel safely over the Carroll branch. It was so light, in fact, that a collision with a cow or other large animal usually was sufficient to throw it from the track. Since the road had neither fences nor cattle guards this happened with lamentable frequency.

In 1854 the C&P extended its branch 5 miles west from Oneida to Waynesburg, and for about a year the train ran from Carrollton to Waynesburg, then to Bayard, then back to Carrollton. The 44-mile round trip took all day. With the further extension of the C&P's Sandy Valley branch to New Philadelphia, the operating arrangement with the Carroll County was terminated. This rude development placed the owners of the strap-rail road in a most embarrassing position, for they had never intended to operate the road themselves.

Early in 1855 Isaac Atkinson and General Stidger went to New York and for $550 arranged to buy the old 4-2-0 *McNeill* — the first engine to run on the pioneer Paterson & Hudson River Railroad of New Jersey. This 58-inch-gauge predecessor of the Erie had bought the locomotive in 1835, and there appears to be little basis for doubt that it had been outshopped by Robert Stephenson & Company at Newcastle-upon-Tyne, England, on February 14, 1835. The *McNeill* had been dispatched from Liverpool eight days later on the packet *Tally Ho* and arrived at New York in mid-April. The 4-2-0 was taken to Paterson, N. J., where it was assembled in the shop of Thomas Rogers.* On June 17, 1835, it went into service on the P&HR.

McNeill originally had a pair of inside-connected 54-inch drivers and 10 x 15-inch cylinders mounted under the smokebox. The boiler was of the short and shallow wagon-top design with the dome well forward on the barrel. The front end was supported by a Jervis four-wheel engine truck, and there was a small tender with two rigid axles. The locomotive had been stored for several years and required considerable attention before it could be declared fit for service. Repairs cost nearly as much as the locomotive itself.

McNeill served Rogers as the pattern for his first locomotive, the *Sandusky* of the Mad River & Lake Erie. Built in 1837, this engine was similarly fitted to run on 58-inch-gauge track, and the MR&LE was subsequently built to that gauge. This remains the only plausible explanation for the origin of Ohio's "legal" gauge and the fact that it was peculiar to railroads in that state and New Jersey.

After the panic of 1857 the Carroll branch deteriorated to the point where its daily train required most of the day to run to Oneida and back. Wherever the railroad passed from one man's land to that of another, a gate had to be opened and closed before the train could proceed. This ritual was performed 30 to 40 times during a round trip. Since the only fences ran perpendicular to the railroad, there were the inevitable collisions with livestock to slow things up. Not infrequently nightfall arrived at Carrollton before the train, and service was so unreliable that riders were rare except in weather so inclement that stages could not run. Even so, the Carroll County continued to carry the mails and provided the local wits with all manner of funny stories. Elderberry bushes encroached upon the right of way and threatened to engulf the track. Small boys were fond of riding the flat car behind the *McNeill* and without overexertion they could fill a tub with elderberries in less time than it took to reach Oneida. In a particularly sarcastic moment, the editor of one Carrollton weekly wrote that "the track has a tendency on wet days to spread itself to a 12-foot gauge, the engines get the colic in the middle of a trip, or, worse yet, die of glanders or epizootic about the time of the starting of the train."

On February 9, 1859, the hopelessly insolvent strap-rail road was sold by the sheriff to its creditors. Isaac Atkinson held the principal interest in the venerable *McNeill*, and since he was no longer associated with the road, the 4-2-0 was laid up and stored inside the Carrollton depot. The old locomotive apparently was in urgent need of major repairs and the strap-rail superstructure could no longer be trusted to bear its weight. Operation of the crude unballasted road was resumed but transport in Carroll County had taken another giant step backward. The best the owners could provide was mule-powered operation from 1859 to 1867.

After reorganizing the company as the Carrollton & Oneida Railroad on February 26, 1866, the owners resolved to restore the road to good running order. During 1866-1867 the track was extensively repaired, some bridges were rebuilt, and three water tanks were erected. To replace the mules, the C&O ordered a new steam locomotive from Thomas Reeve, proprietor of the Novelty Iron Works at Cleveland. Reeve was in the frog and track specialty line and this was probably the first and only locomotive he built. The 0-4-0T was a unique machine in appearance, having a large rectangular water tank mounted on the top of the boiler barrel and a stack that must have been all of 6 feet high. The cylinders were located under the cab, behind the drivers, and there was no headlight or cowcatcher. Very likely the bell and some other parts came from *McNeill*, which was still stored at Carrollton at this late date. Named *Carroll*, the new locomotive made its maiden run from Oneida to Carrollton on September 4, 1867.

Carroll was personally handled by Mr. Reeve who found that it steamed well and had no trouble negotiating the crude track and the steep grade north of Carrollton. Virtually all the able-bodied citizenry of the town, perhaps some 600 strong, were on hand to greet the new engine. One of the local editors reported that "about 6 o'clock our town was thrown into quite an excitement by a very unnatural noise in the direction of Oneida. Shortly after the first alarm was given the object itself came dashing around the curve a short distance north of town. The new engine was halted in front of the station where it was carefully examined by the inquisitive crowd. It was then 'switched off' and run into the enginehouse and the crowd returned to their homes to deliberate during the remainder of the evening on the future destiny of Carrollton. Doubtless many arrived at the conclusion ere sleep closed their eyes that New York City was nowhere compared to our town now."

The Carrollton & Oneida acquired a commodious "first-class" four-wheel passenger car to augment the ancient dinkey and two very dilapidated flat cars the mules had drawn over the line. The operation was entrusted to Mark T. Wiggins who daily served as the locomotive engineer, fireman, conductor, and brakeman. He also held the titles of master mechanic, general superintendent, chief engineer, roadmaster, master of car repairs, and purchasing agent. In his spare time Wiggins ran a carriage and wagon shop in the village, conducted a school of voice, and led both the Presbyterian choir and the town's brass band. With the rejuvenated C&O in the hands of such a dynamo, the lot of travelers to and from Carrollton was vastly improved. Indeed, to cover the 10 miles to Oneida the *Carroll* required but 1 hour 15 minutes compared with the 3 to 6 hours which formerly had to be allowed for the mules. However, the owners realized no more return on their investment than they had in the past. During 1867 receipts came to $3555.62 whereas expenses amounted to $10,397.94.

THE OHIO & TOLEDO

The principal internal improvement of Carroll County continued to lose money year in and year out, even during the prosperous era preceding the 1873 panic. More of a liability than an asset, it was sold to General Eckley's Ohio & Toledo for 1 dollar on July 15, 1873. For his part Eckley agreed to replace the strap rails with iron T rails and have a train running by August 1, 1874. Title to the *Carroll*, cars, and strap rails was retained by the C&O al-

though Eckley was permitted to use the engine and cars in the reconstruction work.

Eckley lost interest in building the O&T to Toledo and he now proposed to extend his road from the Connotton through Carrollton to Youngstown, where it would connect with the narrow-gauge Painesville & Youngstown. Although the O&T was hard hit by the 1873 panic, it somehow managed to live up to its commitment to rebuild the Carrollton & Oneida. Iron rails weighing 32 pounds to the yard were bought from an Alliance (O.) rolling mill and were laid to 3-foot gauge on 8-foot crossties. All of the iron was down between Carrollton and Oneida by July 30, 1874, and the O&T by that time had taken delivery of a Dawson & Bailey 2-4-0 named *E. R. Eckley*.

The line to Youngstown was projected through Minerva, New Lisbon, and Columbiana using the abandoned Sandy & Beaver towpath over much of the distance. The first 3.8 miles of track, from Oneida to Minerva, was opened with an excursion run on October 20, 1874. No further effort was made to build beyond Minerva, but during 1875 the O&T was extended 9.5 miles southwest of Carrollton to Cannonsburgh (Dell Roy). This brought the narrow gauge to a point only 5 or 6 miles short of Connotton Creek. Tracklaying began at Carrollton on December 11, and on the last day of 1875 Eckley drove the final spike at Cannonsburgh. A second National engine, a 4-4-0, had already been put on the road along with a number of cars acquired from the Pittsburgh & McKeesport Car & Locomotive Works under a rental contract.

At the end of 1874 the O&T had suddenly abandoned the plan of connecting with the P&Y at Youngstown. Eckley was influenced in this decision by the 1874 formation of the Lake Erie, Alliance & Wheeling, a narrow gauge with ambitions similar to those of the O&T. The General now wanted to build a line from Minerva north to Kent, Chagrin Falls, and Painesville in the name of the Painesville, Canton & Bridgeport Narrow Gauge Rail Road incorporated on January 12, 1875. A 5.15-mile portion of this road was actually built between Chagrin Falls and Solon, a station on the Cleveland & Mahoning (Erie). Laid with 30-pound iron, the PC&B was opened in November 1877, shortly after the receipt of a 12-ton 2-4-0 from Connellsville. There were seven freight cars and a "fifth-class" passenger car described by the Ohio Railroad Commission as a "very old and rickety caboose."

The Chagrin Falls narrow gauge was operated by the contractors — local men who had financed and built the road — until August 13, 1880, when they brought about the appointment of a receiver. The following September 28 these men bought the road

Carrollton & Oneida's four-wheel dinkey was drawn across the strap-rail road by a pair of mules between 1859 and 1867. Passengers had to allow from 3 to 6 hours for the 10-mile trip. On this afternoon in September 1863, the "train" had made it back to Carrollton depot before nightfall (above). Most of Carrollton turned out to greet Thomas Reeve and new locomotive *Carroll* on September 4, 1867 (below). The crude saddletank 0-4-0 was light enough to traverse the Carrollton & Oneida's strap rails and brought an end to eight years of mule operation. Photo shows the "new" car built by Mark Wiggins in his Carrollton carriage shop. — *Both photos, Collection of John Wert Helfrich.*

A washout was the cause of this February 18, 1887, dilemma on the "Silver Plate." CF&S No. 2, a 33,000-pound Porter 9 x 14, hangs precariously over a collapsed bridge a short distance south of Chagrin Falls. The little narrow gauge required two weeks to extricate the engine, rebuild the bridge, and restore service. — *Collection of Leonard W. Siegel.*

Sandy Creek crossing at Oneida was the setting for this 1875 view of the Ohio & Toledo's narrow-gauge train out of Minerva. Engine No. 1, the 2-4-0 *E. R. Eckley,* was built by National Locomotive Works. The coach came from the York (Pa.) Car Works of Billmeyer & Small, specialists in narrow-gauge stock. — *Collection of John Wert Helfrich.*

from the Cuyahoga County sheriff for $16,672, and two days later they organized the Chagrin Falls & Southern Railroad. CF&S, known locally as the Silver Plate, operated a daily mixed train until 1890. In 1884 a first-class coach and a new Porter-built 2-4-0 were put on the road.

General Eckley's fortunes were on the decline on all fronts. The Ohio & Toledo was no more lucrative a proposition than its Carroll County predecessors and by 1877 the property was derelict. The impoverished Eckley succeeded in interesting Dr. Norman A. Smith in taking over the O&T management and making repairs needed to put it in safe operating condition. According to agreement, Eckley was to remain the road's president, but before long Smith was doing everything possible to unseat him and all the original promoters. A bitter controversy arose over Smith's insistence that the northern terminus be Youngstown, and on August 29, 1877, Smith and his Eastern friends incorporated the Youngstown & Connotton Valley Railroad. The dispute between Smith and Eckley finally culminated in the forced sale of the Ohio & Toledo to the Cleveland Iron Company, holder of a $5000 judgment note given by Eckley for the Cannonsburgh rails. On December 20, 1878, the Iron Company conveyed the deed to the Y&CV and the O&T was summarily liquidated along with Eckley's interest.

After taking over the O&T management, Smith improved the service and did much to rehabilitate the property. By the end of 1878 he had done an about-face and announced that the road would be extended to Painesville after all. The old Eckley route would be altered so as to touch Canton, then a city of 12,000. The first 16 miles of the Painesville extension, from a point between Oneida and Minerva to Canton, was put under contract in January 1879 and work was started at once on a 774-foot tunnel through a ridge called Hog's Back near Rob-

Scene looking west toward old narrow-gauge tunnel at Robertsville (top). Minerva Junction looking in direction of Canton (above). Branch to Minerva runs off to the right. Connotton Valley depot at Carrollton (below) later was razed by W&LE for new brick station which is still in use. First Carroll County depot burned in 1875.

293

ertsville. Tracklaying on the extension was completed on May 7, 1880, and eight days later an excursion ran through to Canton. Regular trains started operating on May 18. Since October 20, 1879, the company had been known simply as the Connotton Valley Railroad and on March 23, 1880, a subsidiary, the Connotton Northern Railway,* was incorporated to build the rest of the Lake Erie extension.

BLOOD'S NARROW GAUGE

Smith gained the backing of an experienced syndicate of Massachusetts entrepreneurs including Hiram A. Blood, William J. Rotch, and Nathaniel Thayer. These men put a 2.6-million-dollar mortgage on the Connotton Valley and placed one of their own men in charge of its management. By the end of 1880 the decision had been made to terminate the road at Cleveland rather than at Painesville, and a contract was let for a 7.7-mile extension from Dell Roy to Sherrodsville, a mining camp on Connotton Creek. Construction of the 60-mile Cleveland extension commenced on July 5, 1880, but the work of building a grade through mile after mile of swamp north of Canton went slowly. Rows of 60-foot pilings had to be driven into the bogs to provide a firm foundation for the roadbed. The first 20-mile section, to Mogadore, was not completed until January 1881; nearly four months more was re-

---

*The Connotton Northern and Connotton Valley were merged on October 25, 1880, to form the Connotton Valley Railway.

quired to reach Kent, 7½ miles beyond. However, by July 4, 1881, CV trains were running as far north as Bedford, only 11 miles southeast of the heart of Cleveland. A depot was erected on the village square practically next door to the Cleveland & Pittsburgh station. Passengers going on to Cleveland transferred to C&P trains at Bedford while the Connotton Valley completed its own line into the city.

Access to Cleveland was gained by way of the Cuyahoga valley, and beginning at Newburgh the CV descended 250 feet into the "flats" in 4 miles. At a point easily reached by lake ships the CV developed a 2200-foot riverfront wharf called Coal Docks, and track was laid to this point in November 1881. The completion of a drawbridge early in 1882 carried the narrow-gauge track across the Cuyahoga to a temporary depot at Commercial Street. Regular operation of passenger trains was extended from Bedford to this point on February 21, 1882. The Sherrodsville Extension and a 1-mile spur from that village to the New York & Ohio Mine had been opened on January 1, and at long last Connotton Valley coal was moving to Lake Erie by rail.

Two first-class passenger trains were operated daily except Sunday between Cleveland and Sherrodsville, 102 miles, and these made uncommonly good time for narrow gaugers. The schedule allowed only 2 hours 25 minutes running time over the 60 miles between Cleveland and Canton, and the CV trains were popular despite the fact that they

Porter built eight 4-4-0's for Connotton Valley including No. 9, *Mogadore*, shown here with Straitsville Division passenger train at Sugar Creek, O. Engine had 4-foot drivers, 13 x 18-inch cylinders. — *Collection of Uriah G. Reinhold.*

competed with the standard-gauge Valley road. On summer Sundays and holidays the narrow gauge used its passenger equipment to haul large crowds to the pavilion and picnic grounds which the CV operated at Congress Lake 13 miles north of Canton. The Connotton's passenger runs were powered by five 4-foot-drivered 21.5-ton 4-4-0's built by H. K. Porter during 1880-1882. These were numbered 9, 10, 11, 14, and 15, and were backed up by a trio of smaller and older Porter 4-4-0's. By 1883 the roster of varnish included 30 coaches and eight baggage and mail cars. Like the locomotives, these were equipped with Westinghouse air brakes.

In contrast with most of its narrow-gauge contemporaries, the Connotton was a well-built road with steel rails and liberally ballasted main tracks. The Ohio Railroad Commission called the CV "one of the best roads of recent construction in Ohio — absolutely well-built" and described its Canton station as "a model building of its kind for convenience, comfort, and adaptability to its intended purpose." The imposing two story brick structure with a clock tower 96 feet high housed the road's general offices as well as its passenger accommodations. It was located in the heart of the city at East Tuscarawas and Cherry streets. The Commercial Street depot was situated about 1 mile south of Cleveland's Public Square and could be reached by omnibus.

Coal accounted for 80 per cent of all CV freight tonnage, and during 1882 the road moved more than 100,000 tons of this commodity from mines at Sherrodsville, Dell Roy, and Osnaburg (East Canton) to the docks at Cleveland. The coal drags were drawn by six Baldwin 15 x 18 Consols with 3-foot drivers, straight-top boilers, straight stacks, and a grate area of 13.5 square feet. There were more than 700 freight cars on the Connotton by 1883, mostly gondolas and stake-pocket flats in coal service. Nearly all CV cars were built at Minerva in the Pennock Brothers shops. A 25-ton Baldwin 0-6-0T, *Wharf Rat*, shunted cars at Coal Docks and a little 0-4-0T named *Fido* was used in the yard at Canton. The six-stall roundhouse with adjoining machine shop at Canton was the principal CV engine facility. Smaller enginehouses were located at Cleveland, Dell Roy, and Sherrodsville.

Instead of extending the CV east along Connotton Creek toward Wheeling, the Blood Syndicate elected to build a 115-mile branch southwest from Canton. This line was projected through Coshocton and Zanesville to the Hocking valley coal fields in the vicinity of New Straitsville and Moxahala. The subsidiary Connotton Valley & Straitsville Railroad was formed on June 20, 1881, and started

Queen of Ohio narrow-gauge passenger trains, Connotton Valley No. 1, pauses at Hartville. Brooks 4-4-0 18 heads the southbound express on its 115-mile Cleveland-to-Coshocton run. The three men on the right (from right) are Martin U. Reinhold, fireman; Peter Reynolds, engineman; and Tom Javins, conductor. — *Collection of Uriah G. Reinhold.*

work at once on the first section — 55 miles between Canton and Coshocton. The route passed through the beautiful and untapped valleys of Sugar Creek and White Eyes Creek, known to hold valuable deposits of coal and black band iron ore. In 1881 the CV&S acquired the 35-mile grade built by the defunct Cleveland, Canton, Coshocton & Straitsville Railroad* between Coshocton and Barrs Mills. This property and construction of the remaining 20 miles between Barrs Mills and Canton cost the CV&S a cool 2.1 million dollars. The company laid no track and was on the verge of failure when it was hastily absorbed by the embarrassed parent company on May 24, 1882.

The Connotton raised 1.5 million dollars through the sale of bonds, then began laying steel at Canton at the end of June 1882. By mid-July 11 miles of track was laid to Navarre and the first train entered that town in time to save a $5000 subsidy. About September 1 the Straitsville Division was opened to Justus, 3½ miles southwest of Navarre. The contractor pushed the work day and night with 1200 men and 200 teams, and on December 18, 1882, a regular train was put on between Canton and Beach City, 19 miles. Tracklaying continued through the winter of 1882-1883 and on February 1, 18 miles of road was opened beyond Beach City to Buena Vista (Baltic). The daily train was extended to the latter place where a small shed and turntable were built to service the engine. Finally, on June 11, 1883, the first Connotton Valley train ran into Coshocton.

After the CV was opened to Coshocton, trains were operated through from that city to Cleveland, 114.7 miles. Two 5-hour express runs and a local train made the trip each way. The line from Canton to Sherrodsville was now operated as a branch and was served by two trains in each direction. No. 27 left Canton after the morning arrival of No. 1 from Cleveland and No. 5 connected with No. 4, the afternoon train out of Coshocton. Mail trains 1 and 4 operated every day but the only other Sunday runs were a pair of Cleveland turns originating at Kent. Last run out of Cleveland each evening was No. 9, a Kent accommodation which came to be known as the theater train. The timetable advised that this train would "wait, if necessary, until the theaters are out." Regular engine on this run was George Kingsbury's 17, a 42-inch-drivered 4-4-0 acquired from the Cotton Belt. The Brooks 12 x 16 was named *Oscar Wilde* after the young Irish "Apostle of Estheticism" who had lectured at Cleveland in 1882.

---

*Cleveland, Canton, Coshocton & Straitsville was incorporated August 25, 1877, as the successor to the Massillon & Coshocton Railway. The latter's corporate history dated from May 21, 1874.

Early in 1883 the Connotton bought eight new locomotives from Brooks: six 23.4-ton Mogul freight engines and two husky 4-foot-drivered 4-4-0 passenger engines, Nos. 18 and 19. The latter were assigned to enginemen John Sexton and Ed Pedlar on the daily mail trains. The CV now numbered 26 engines on its roster and had 941 freight cars, 38 passenger cars, and 13 cabooses. The roll of 534 employees included 26 engineers, 26 firemen, 26 station agents, 20 conductors, 39 brakemen, and seven telegraphers.

After deciding to extend the Straitsville Division to Zanesville, the CV prevailed upon its stockholders for the estimated $760,000 cost of the necessary rail. Less than half that amount was raised, so the company deferred the extension and used the money to build a permanent passenger station at Cleveland. The new two-story edifice overlooking the Cuyahoga from a bluff called Vinegar Hill was formally opened on August 29, 1883. The narrow-gauge facility fronted on the intersection of Ontario and Huron streets, less than 1000 feet south of the Public Square, and was Cleveland's most conveniently located passenger station. A half-mile-long trestle with a 1.6 per cent ascending grade carried the narrow-gauge track from the old Commercial Street terminus to the Vinegar Hill depot.

May 1882 saw the management of the Connotton's affairs pass to W. W. Hungerford, former superintendent of the Texas Mexican narrow gauge. In short order the new general manager fired many key supervisors and replaced them with his Texan cronies. As a result the CV operations went sour overnight. Four months of minor mishaps culminated in a pair of disastrous rear-end collisions in the territory between Cleveland and Canton. These accidents cost Hungerford and his "cowboys" their jobs. However, the appointment of the popular Sam Briggs to the post vacated by Hungerford failed to stem the run of ill fortune on the narrow gauge. On January 26, 1883, a broken axle spilled a freight at Bedford, and later the same day a dispatcher's error resulted in a head-on collision near Canton. Two enginemen were killed, two locomotives were destroyed, and a number of passengers were injured in the wreck. A washout at Brimfield the next month drowned a fireman and made it necessary to rebuild one of the Baldwin 2-8-0's. In the spring of 1883 a landslide piled up a passenger train as it approached Robertsville tunnel; still another passenger train failed to stop short of the rear end of a freight.

Although 1883 brought substantial increases in the Connotton's coal tonnage and passenger fares, the 161-mile narrow gauge was hardly a bonanza for its Massachusetts masters. Traffic originating on the Straitsville Division was disappointingly light

Original Vinegar Hill depot was built by Connotton Valley in 1883. Five horsecar lines ran past the station's front door on Cleveland's Ontario Street.

— only a fraction of that produced by the Sherrodsville line. The road was capitalized at the rate of $71,000 per mile — more than three times the actual cost of construction — and all of its engines and cars were leased under equipment trusts. With an operating ratio of 81.7 per cent, the CV simply could not meet its heavy fixed charges and defaulted on its bonds in June 1883. Its embarrassment was temporarily eased, but the Connotton was soon overtaken by insolvency. On January 19, 1884, Sam Briggs was named receiver.

GOULD REVIVES THE WHEELING

With the return of prosperity in 1879 the Wheeling & Lake Erie stockholders resolved to make one last bid to build their road. In September of that year C. Robinson Griggs of New York agreed to complete and equip the W&LE as a standard gauge for $30,000 per mile. The Huron-Norwalk narrow gauge was relinquished in June 1880 by Willson, the former contractor, and some land was subsequently bought for docks at Huron. However, no construction work was started during 1880. A fresh canvass for financial support ended in failure and Griggs found no enthusiasm for W&LE securities in the East. The winter of 1880-1881 nevertheless brought a providential turn in the fortunes of the ill-starred coal road. The latest episode in the Gould-Vanderbilt conflict would assure the building of the Wheeling & Lake Erie.

Jay Gould had suddenly decided to build a trunkline connection between the Wabash and the Central of New Jersey over the old Continental low-grade route. Projected from Toledo southeast to the abandoned Continental grade at New London, the W&LE represented about one-third of the road Gould needed to reach the western railhead of the Allegheny Valley. This was just one of the chain of Pennsylvania-controlled roads Gould intended to use in reaching the Central of New Jersey. Without exposing Gould's strategy, his agents began buying large blocks of W&LE securities that Griggs had put on the market. George J. Forrest, John P. Kennedy, and C. K. Garrison — all associated with Gould's New York elevated railways — together with Sidney Dillon were the buyers. Griggs lost no time in putting the capital to work. In February 1881 he ordered a dozen Bogie engines from William Mason and gave a large contract for 56-pound steel rail to the Edgar Thomson works.

The charter of the W&LE called for a branch extending northwest from Milan to Toledo on a line that skirted the south shore of Sandusky Bay. Following the formation of the Nickel Plate a new line was surveyed farther south. This paralleled the LS&MS from Norwalk to Bellevue and Fremont before turning north to meet the original route at Oak Harbor. W&LE surveyors locating the new route and their Nickel Plate counterparts passed through Bellevue less than a week apart in

297

Mason Bogies of 1881-1882, so popular with enginemen, carried tank syphons and could take on water from any trackside pond or stream. No. 11 was assigned to Elmer "Yank" Robinson, W&LE's one-eyed engineer. Here he poses with his fireman, Clarence Ransom (left), at Norwalk in 1890. — *Collection of John A. Rehor.*

March 1881. After the Nickel Plate decided to build through Bellevue or Norwalk, the Wheeling discarded its partly built line through New London and staked out a new route east of Norwalk. This crossed the New York, Pennsylvania & Ohio (Erie) at Creston. Gould decided to use the NYP&O between Creston and Youngstown, leaving him a scant 70 miles short of the Allegheny Valley at Red Bank.

The first Wheeling standard-gauge locomotives, Mason 2-4-6T Bogies 1 and 2, arrived at Creston with the first rail shipments in May 1881. Griggs' master mechanic, Lewis James, was particularly fond of the Bogie and had a justifiably high regard for the craftsmanship of William Mason. Before joining the W&LE, James had held a similar post on the narrow-gauge New York & Manhattan Beach and he had induced three veteran NY&MB enginemen to go to Ohio with him. Charles Jackson, Ira Cowen, and Henry "Deacon" Mills had had considerable experience running Mason's Bogies on the Long Island summer line. The former NY&MB *Manhattan* and *New York*, 0-4-4T Bogies, had been on the W&LE since the summer of 1879. These were returned to Mason and rebuilt as standard-gauge 2-4-4T's 6 and 7. The rebuilds arrived at Creston in October 1881, not long after Mason had delivered three splendid 0-6-6T's numbered 3, 4, and 5. Intended for heavy-duty freight service, the 0-6-6T's had 17 x 24-inch cylinders, 49-inch drivers, diamond

stacks, and were reputedly the first locomotives in the Midwest equipped with Walschaerts valve gear.

A roundhouse was built at Creston, and during the summer of 1881 tracklaying trains pushed east and west from that point. By mid-November 1881 the steel had been laid from Massillon to Huron, 81.3 miles, and workmen were busy building docks at Huron. The narrow-gauge line was taken up and only part of the 12-mile route was relaid as a standard gauge. The new line turned north toward Huron just east of Norwalk and the old line into that city was abandoned. Irregular operation of a mixed train between Huron and Massillon was inaugurated January 9, 1882.

The contractor began laying track toward Toledo at Huron Junction (just east of Norwalk) on December 8, 1881. W&LE tracklayers reached Bellevue during the first week of 1882, only a day or two after the Nickel Plate's steel gang had spiked that road's track into the town from the west. The 38 miles of road between Fremont and Toledo crossed the eastern portion of the Black Swamp which had yet to be cleared and drained. Although the swamp forest provided all the white oak needed for crossties to build the W&LE and a fair chunk of its early freight traffic, it slowed the progress of Griggs' tracklayers to a crawl. Not until July 10, 1882, did the Wheeling's steel reach the east bank of the Maumee (at what would come to be known as Iron-

Mason built this Fairlie for narrow-gauge New York & Manhattan Beach in 1877. After being rebuilt as a standard-gauge in 1881, the little mill carried number 6 on W&LE. For several years it was assigned to a passenger run between Norwalk and Toledo and gained fame for its ability to outrace the LS&MS *Fast Mail.* — *Collection of Richard J. Cook.*

ville) opposite the old community of Manhattan and a little downriver from Toledo proper. About a half mile of track was laid from the west bank to the long-abandoned bed of the Miami & Erie Canal's Manhattan Extension. This point, later known as Manhattan Junction, became the Wheeling's important junction with the Toledo, Ann Arbor & Grand Trunk Railway. The W&LE bought about 2 miles of the old canal bed extending southwest from Manhattan Junction to Cherry Street. This location near the heart of the city was the site of the Wheeling's Toledo depot. It was 64.72 miles west of Huron Junction and 136.66 miles west of Massillon. The 1311-foot Maumee River bridge was completed in mid-August 1882, about the same time that the Nickel Plate finished work on its Cuyahoga River span.

By July 1882 Mason had shipped 2-4-6T Bogies 8-18 to the W&LE and in August the road received four graceful 16 x 24 4-4-0's from the same firm. Said to be among the last locomotives personally designed by the brilliant William Mason, Nos. 19-22 had smokebox extensions, ornate cap stacks, and fancy bell hangers. The drivers were 68½ inches in diameter, and all engine and tender wheels were spoked. The 4-4-0's were bought for the express passenger runs to be jointly operated with the Nickel Plate between Cherry Street, Toledo, and Broadway depot at Cleveland. The proposed run was 117 miles long, about 4 miles more than that of the LS&MS between those cities via Norwalk.

August 1882 also saw the completion of an extension that carried the W&LE 20.1 miles east of Massillon to the confluence of the Tuscarawas River

and Connotton Creek. The extension ran along the Tusc and crossed the river seven times. The new eastern terminus was Valley Junction — formerly known as Zoar Station — on the Cleveland & Pittsburgh's Sandy Valley branch. The previous May W&LE stockholders had voted to merge with the Cleveland & Marietta Railroad, a 98-mile coal road extending from Marietta to Canal Dover. The C&M reached Valley Junction over 7 miles of the C&P branch and was operated as the W&LE's Marietta Division for some time.

The first regular trains were operated out of Toledo on August 25, 1882, the day after the Wheeling formally opened its road with a complimentary excursion to Massillon and back. The train was made up of five spanking-new Wason coaches and was pulled by No. 17, a Mason 2-4-6T in the charge of Frank Kuhn. Toledo's mayor, most of city council, and many other public officials — only too happy to forsake the late summer heat of the city — accepted the railroad's invitation. The special was out of Cherry Street at 7:07 a.m. and arrived at Massillon at 2 p.m. The mayor of that city and many local celebrities met the train and invited its riders to a banquet at the Park Hotel. After toasting the new link of steel between their cities, the Toledo party and their hosts attacked a feast of Lake Erie whitefish, turkey, venison, pigeon pot pie, Western Reserve cheese, whortleberry pies, Catawba wine, and many other delicacies from the Buckeye horn of plenty. Notably absent on this festive occasion were Joel Wood and most of the other early W&LE promoters.

Beginning on November 19, 1882, express passen-

ger trains were operated through between Toledo and Marietta, 261 miles. The eastbound left Cherry Street at 7:15 a.m. and arrived in the Ohio River town 12 hours 15 minutes later. The westbound cleared the C&M's Marietta depot at 7:20 a.m. and was scheduled into Toledo at 7:50 p.m. A second westbound express ran daily between Canal Dover and Toledo, and an eastbound accommodation was operated between Massillon and Cambridge. Other short hauls included a Toledo-Massillon accommodation and a daily Norwalk-Toledo turnaround run. Two round trips ran daily over the Huron branch, connecting at Norwalk with Toledo-Massillon trains.

At first the Wheeling waxed fat on a diet of Massillon and Cambridge coal and Black Swamp oak. A fair volume of Toledo-bound freight was received from the Erie at Creston, and beneficial traffic alliances were made with the Toledo, Ann Arbor & Grand Trunk and the Detroit, Lansing & Northern.

However, Vanderbilt's thwarting of the Wabash-W&LE-Nickel Plate confederation was a rude blow to the fledgling Wheeling, and the future soon looked as dim as ever. On November 20, 1882, two passenger trains collided head-on at Creston, and the following December 7 the roundhouse at that place burned to the ground. (A new enginehouse and shop at Norwalk were nearly completed so the Creston facility was not rebuilt.) One of the Mason 0-6-6T's was destroyed in the fire and its boiler was later installed in the new Norwalk shop. Another cornfield meet between passenger trains occurred at Sippo Summit on March 29, 1883. A third calamity at Creston — another head-on collision — was all that was needed to drive the W&LE to its knees financially. Shortly afterward, on July 7, 1884, General Manager M. DeWitt Woodford was appointed receiver.

When the Cleveland & Marietta was thrown into

Wabash at Toledo. This 4.55-mile double-track line extended generally southwest from Ironville to junctions with the Cincinnati, Hamilton & Dayton and the LS&MS near East Broadway and Fassett streets. Trackage rights over the LS&MS Maumee River bridge gave the W&LE direct access to the Walbridge Street yard of the Wabash. Construction of the Toledo Belt was deferred until after the 1886 reorganization. It was finally opened to traffic in April 1888.

Dunbar's Locomotives

Lewis James left the W&LE in February 1883 to join the staff of the Toledo, Cincinnati & St. Louis and was succeeded as master mechanic by Oliver P. Dunbar, a native of Norwalk and lately the master mechanic of the Canada Southern's U. S. Division. Dunbar had nearly 30 years of railway service and some inflexible ideas about what constituted a good locomotive. Like most of his contemporaries, he had no use for the Bogie and many of Mason's advanced design concepts. However, Dunbar was one of the few mechanical men of his time who saw merit in the Belpaire boiler, and he was a patron of the young New York Locomotive Works (Rome), a firm that became noted for its artistic craftsmanship and attention to detail.

During 1883 Dunbar sold two of the Bogies to the Cleveland & Marietta and rented a number of others to that road and to the Detroit, Lansing & Northern. No. 1, one of the participants in the 1882 Creston wreck, was sent to Rome and rebuilt there in July 1883 as a conventional 4-4-0. To replace the Masons that had been sold and rented, six smart-looking Rome 4-4-0's with wagon-top boilers, cap stacks, and 62-inch drivers were bought. Nos. 23-26 were 16 x 24's delivered in the fall of 1883; Nos. 27-28 had 17 x 24-inch cylinders and went into service early in 1884. The second Creston wreck took two more Bogies from service, but the loss of credit that came with the receivership precluded the purchase of more new locomotives. Short on power during the winter of 1884-1885, Dunbar recalled two Bogies from the C&M and purchased a pair of repossessed 4-4-0's built by Rome in 1884 for the Lackawanna & Pittsburgh.[*] Two similar 17 x 24's, L&P 201 and 202, were leased from Rome in March 1885.

During his Canada Southern and W&LE service Dunbar tried out a number of freak locomotives.

[*]Lackawanna & Pittsburgh was a predecessor of the Pittsburgh, Shawmut & Northern.

receivership early in 1883 its ties with the W&LE were severed. This development came hard on the heels of the completion of the Valley Railway's extension from Canton to Valley Junction. Despite pronouncements to the contrary, the Valley might decide to build to Wheeling after all and proceed to occupy the Connotton valley before the W&LE could take action. In the spring of 1883 the situation forced the hurried undertaking of an extension eastward from Valley Junction. The onset of receivership delayed the progress of the work, and the first 11 miles of track, to Sherrodsville, was not opened to traffic until December 1884. A full year was required to complete a 6-mile section beyond Sherrodsville to Bowerston. For the time being, construction of the remaining 43 miles of road to Martin's Ferry was deferred.

The Wheeling chartered the Toledo Belt Railway on November 6, 1883, to build a connection with the

Fontaine No. 2, 17 x 24 friction-drive model turned out by Grant in 1881, was purchased by W&LE's general manager after demonstrating its unfitness for serious work in trials on the Erie, New York Central, and other roads. It was rebuilt as a conventional 4-4-0 in 1885 and spent 14 years on the W&LE roster. — *Collection of Sylvan R. Wood.*

Symond's four-cylinder Ten-Wheeler equipped with the first Vanderbilt firebox, and the *America*, the Chicago Locomotive & Improvement Company's return-flue curiosity of 1884, were operated over the Wheeling. This bizarre engine had its stack next to the cab. Dunbar was also intrigued by the friction-drive locomotive patented by Eugene Fontaine in July 1880. Fontaine sought to materially increase the distance traveled per piston stroke without increasing the size of the driving wheels. This gearing up was accomplished through the use of a pair of 72-inch friction wheels which were driven by the cylinders. These were mounted above the single pair of 70-inch track drivers, each of which was fitted with a 56-inch friction wheel. The engine truck had four wheels, the trailer two.

First of Fontaine's 4-2-2 friction-drive engines was built by Grant in October 1880. The 31-ton 16 x 24 was tried out by Dunbar between Toledo and Detroit on the Canada Southern during the winter of

1880-1881. The 4-2-2 also spent some time on the Detroit & Bay City between Detroit and Oxford. While the friction gearing produced greater track speed per stroke, it sharply reduced the pulling power of the locomotive. A second Fontaine with 17 x 24-inch cylinders was turned out by Grant in September 1881. After brief trials on the Erie, Fontaine No. 2 was put to work early in 1882 on the New York Central between Syracuse and Buffalo. There it proved inadequate to handle 20 freight cars. After a stint on the Detroit, Lansing & Northern this engine became the property of M. D. Woodford. By 1884 Oliver Dunbar had bought Fontaine No. 1 which had languished for some time in the Canada Southern's Detroit roundhouse. In March 1885 the Fontaines were sent to Rome where they were rebuilt as conventional direct-connected 4-4-0's with 63-inch drivers. As such they were rented to the W&LE at the rate of $12 per day and carried the numbers 16-17. Dunbar and Woodford personally employed Ike Aldridge and Robert Cooper to run their engines. After its reorganization, the W&LE bought the erstwhile Fontaines and the men joined the enginemen's roster.

The active roster was enlarged by post-receivership repairs to the two Bogies wrecked at Creston in 1884. No. 14 was returned to service in January 1887 after being rebuilt at Norwalk as a 4-4-0 with new 16 x 24-inch cylinders and a slab-type frame. The Wheeling's first Ten-Wheelers, two 49-ton Romes with 56-inch drivers, made their appearance on the road in 1886. Three similar machines numbered 36, 37, and 38 were acquired from the same builder in 1888. Between these orders Dunbar bought a trio of 4-6-0's from Cooke — slack burners with Wootten boiler and central cab. Commonly called Camelback or Mother Hubbard, this type was relatively uncommon west of the Alleghenies. These 4-6-0's, originally numbered 33-35, suffered from leaky boiler seams and were soon rebuilt to conventional single-cab units with shallow Belpaire firebox and diamond stack. For years they ranked as the best steaming engines on the W&LE roster.

THROUGH TO THE RIVER

After reorganization as the Wheeling & Lake Erie Rail*way* on June 25, 1886, the company began work the following spring on the 43 miles of road still to be built from Bowerston to Martin's Ferry. A new issue of bonds was sold to raise 1.5 million dollars for building the extension. As previously noted, much of the original route from the Ohio to the head of Connotton Creek had been graded in the mid-

Second W&LE tunnel cut through Maxwell's or Rexford Hill was completed about 1888; was highest point on Toledo-Wheeling line. — *Collection of Sylvan R. Wood.*

1870's. Inexplicably, the W&LE now chose to abandon the 14-mile section from the summit at Maxwell's (Rexford) through Hopedale to the mouth of Piney Fork.* The tunnels at Maxwell's and Cope-

---

*The 3 miles of road from Maxwell's to Hopedale became part of the Pittsburgh & West Virginia; the 11 miles beyond Hopedale was ultimately completed by the **Lake Erie, Alliance & Wheeling.**

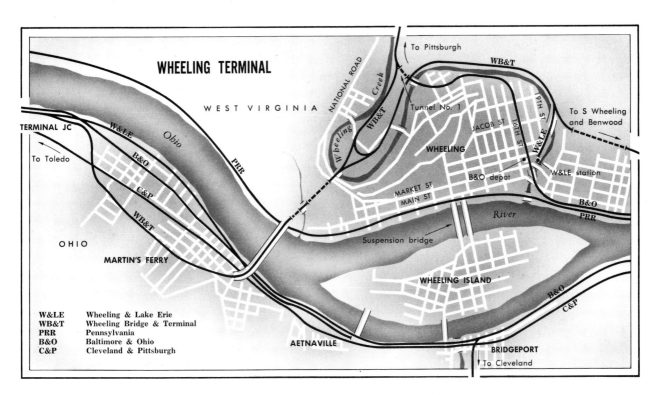

WHEELING TERMINAL

W&LE	Wheeling & Lake Erie
WB&T	Wheeling Bridge & Terminal
PRR	Pennsylvania
B&O	Baltimore & Ohio
C&P	Cleveland & Pittsburgh

Westbound W&LE trains had to battle 22 miles of unbroken 1-per-cent-plus ascending grade leaving Ohio valley. On way to Rexford Summit was this 500-foot bore through a ridge west of Adena. Cooke-built 4-6-0 No. 88 is backing down to Pine Valley after pushing a drag up to Rexford between 1896 and 1899. — *Collection of Richard J. Cook.*

land's were probably in ruinous condition after so many years, but it would not have taken any great sums to shore them up. Otherwise only 3 miles of grade and a short tunnel remained to be built. A new 15.7-mile route nevertheless was staked out from the summit to where Piney Fork joined Big Short Creek.

The new route followed Big Short Creek and a tributary most of the way. The first of four tunnels involved was at the summit itself, immediately west of the abandoned Maxwell's Tunnel. This 457-foot bore also crossed under the Panhandle's Cadiz branch. The second tunnel was 8.2 miles east, near Adena. Ten miles beyond, a 700-foot tunnel was required to carry the line through a ridge at Long Run. The fourth, a shorter bore, was located 2 miles

east of Long Run. On the original route east of Piney Fork the old Asa's Backbone tunnel was day-lighted and the proposed Norton's tunnel at Portland was abandoned in favor of a more circuitous route to the Ohio.

The tracklayers reached Martin's Ferry in October 1889, but for about a year regular service was provided only as far east as the W&LE coal mines at Lauralton, just east of Piney Fork. The valley of Big Short Creek was sparsely settled when the W&LE was built, but villages materialized as the mines were opened. An engine terminal was established at Piney Fork which eventually came to be known as Pine Valley. The town of Dillonvale, named in honor of Sidney Dillon, grew up next door to the terminal.

Depot at Adena, 23 miles west of Wheeling in the heart of the No. 8 coal district, is still in use. Before 1900, the agent passes time with a one-legged pensioner. Such casualties once were a common sight around railroad centers. — *Collection of Richard J. Cook.*

Warrenton, the junction of W&LE's main line and Ohio River Division, is periodically inundated by floodwaters. In modern times, the offices at Warrenton and Terminal Junction have been housed in rolling stock. About 1898, an ex-Ann Arbor Cooke is set to take the accommodation to Steubenville. — *Collection of Sylvan R. Wood.*

Masonry piers are nearly completed in this circa 1890 view of the Wheeling Bridge & Terminal bridge across the Ohio. Town of Martin's Ferry can be seen on west bank of river. The bridge was built to give W&LE trains access to Wheeling and was used by them from 1892 to 1938. — *Collection of John J. Young Jr.*

In the fall of 1890 the Wheeling completed a 13.64-mile branch along the Ohio River from the main line at Portland (Warrenton) north to Steubenville. This closely paralleled the C&P's Bellaire branch over the entire distance. A 2.3-mile extension of the main line from Martin's Ferry to Aetnaville was opened to freight traffic in 1891. Access to the city of Wheeling proper was gained over 4.77 miles of the Wheeling Bridge & Terminal Railway. The line of this company started at a connection with the W&LE on the north side of Martin's Ferry at what came to be known as Terminal Junction. From this point the WB&T ran south to the south end of Martin's Ferry and crossed the Ohio on a long steel bridge. Two tunnels carried the Terminal through the West Virginia escarpment into the valley of Wheeling Creek, and the line then followed that stream south to the heart of Wheeling. W&LE trains left the WB&T at Jacob Street and ran over 1300 feet of the road's own track to the depot on Market Street. This property was owned by the W&LE and was sandwiched between Wheeling

Creek and the B&O depot. Regular service into Wheeling was initiated on February 1, 1892.

During the 1890's the W&LE operated five trains out of Wheeling daily, including a pair of accommodation runs to Steubenville. Express No. 6 left Wheeling at 8:45 a.m. and required 9 hours to cover the 221 miles to Toledo. No. 12 left mornings for Massillon, and Express No. 8 departed at 2:15 p.m. for Creston where a connection was made with an Erie train due into Chicago at 7:25 the next morning. There were eastbound counterparts of all these trains, plus accommodations between Toledo and Massillon and between Toledo and Creston.

FEAST OR FAMINE

After the 1886 reorganization, the Wheeling prospered for several years and paid dividends on its preferred stock from 1888 to the mid-1890's. The rapid development of mines in the No. 8 district east of Bowerston swelled coal tonnage to such an extent that by 1892 there were 4000 coal cars on the property. After the Mesabi Range was opened about

Steam-powered coal dumper at Huron replaced dockside cranes as larger lake boats went into service; was superseded in 1902 with rotary dumper. — *Collection of John A. Rehor.*

Few masters could negotiate the currents of the Huron River channel unassisted. In the 1890's W&LE owned and operated its own steam tugboat, the *Oscar C. Stedman*, here seen towing a whaleback up the 18-foot-deep channel. — *Collection of John A. Rehor.*

1890 the W&LE began to haul ore in volume to mills in the Ohio valley. The tonnage of coal and ore handled at Huron soon rendered the dockside locomotive cranes inadequate and the W&LE was forced to put a tugboat in service. In mid-1890's a car dumper and four combination stiff-leg hoists and conveyors (designed by George Hulett and built by McMyler of Cleveland) were installed at Huron.

Camelback 33 is set to leave Massillon with solid train of steam tractors manufactured by the Russell company. During 1890's W&LE handled many such trains, including one operated each year to the West Coast. This was routed to Northern Ohio at Spencer and Clover Leaf at Delphos and was delivered by UP. — *Collection of Keith Buchanan.*

No. 70, one of the rebuilt Cooke Camelbacks, and her crew at Huron docks. In background are Hulett double-track conveyors used to unload ore. The man in the cab is mercurial Mike McGreevy. Fireman Marion Arlin is standing on running board and rugged brakemen on the pilot are Sherman North (left) and Slim Gilson. Dock Superintendent Oscar Stedman is at extreme left. — *Collection of Sylvan R. Wood.*

Early action photo shows Rome 4-4-0 No. 33 rolling through Navarre with a westbound inspection train. The date: September 26, 1897. — *William L. Bennett.*

Business was so brisk that between 1890 and 1896 the Wheeling was obliged to add 42 Ten-Wheeler freight engines to its roster. Included were the road's first Pittsburghs, 17 x 24's 39-41, bought early in 1890. Later that year Cooke shipped the W&LE three more 4-6-0's similar in dimension to the Pittsburghs. Numbered 42-44, they had straight-top Belpaire boilers and 50-inch drivers. Rome and Pittsburgh outshopped 18 more 17 x 24's in 1891. Romes 46-53 had wagon-top Belpaire boilers; Pittsburghs 54-63 had straight-top Belpaires. Next came Nos. 65-70, 52.5-tonners built by Pittsburgh in 1893. These had shallow Belpaire fireboxes, 18 x 24-inch cylinders, and 50-inch drivers. The majority were intended for mine runs out of Pine Valley and were delivered with tender pilots. A pair of 56-ton Cooke 18 x 24's came to the road from the Ann Arbor in 1894. They were originally assigned W&LE numbers 71 and 72. Cooke-built 91-100 rounded out the fleet of 4-6-0's in 1896. These 60-ton engines were the heaviest hogs on the roster and boasted 19 x 26-inch cylinders and a 25.3-square-foot grate. The little Romes continued to hold down most of the passenger assignments, and after 1886 most of the surviving Bogies were relegated to yard duty. They were largely supplanted by six-coupled switchers bought from Pittsburgh and Cooke in the early 1890's.

A depression and a prolonged coal-miners' strike brought about the third W&LE receivership on January 15, 1897. Like many early coal roads, the old Wheeling led a feast-or-famine existence. When the mines were busy there were never enough empties for the tipples and too many trains were trying to get over too little railroad. In good times or bad, crews worked to the point of physical exhaustion and the spectre of sudden death was no stranger to the men of the W&LE. In those days, of course, life insurance actuaries shunned any man in train or engine service, but mile for mile, the W&LE may have killed and maimed more men than any other American road. The life expectancy of brakemen was notably brief, and these two-fisted alumni of the school of staff brakes and link-and-pin couplers thought nothing of "cooning" a freight to tie down a dozen or more brakes coming into every town and passing track in any kind of weather. Enginemen never knew what awaited them on the other end of every curve — a headlight, slide, washed-out fill, or perhaps a bridge undermined or carried away altogether by a spring freshet. Hence the Wheeling was the kind of railroad that appealed only to the most colorful and fearless breed of men. Time has washed into oblivion the names of the old-time "shacks," but the fame of enginemen such as "Skip" Sherman, "Soapy" Jones, John Foster, "Daddy" Turner, one-eyed "Yank" Robinson, and "Baldy" Johnson spread far beyond the hills of southeastern Ohio and outlasted their generation.

In a letter written many years ago to S. R. Wood, the late Frederick Westcott recalled the tragic fate of one of the little Rome 4-4-0's and its crew on New Year's Day 1893. According to the veteran W&LE engineman, John Connell was running No. 25 light from Ironville to Norwalk. Westcott wrote:

For some reason they wanted her at the other end of the road and ran her out of Ironville as the second section of No. 1. We had a terrible blizzard that day, and while running at full speed she collided with the westbound local at a place

"Smoking" in southeastern Ohio hills sometimes had dire consequences. First 43, an 1890 Cooke 4-6-0, and an unidentified 1893 Pittsburgh 4-6-0 tried to hold the main in an unscheduled meet circa 1895. — *Collection of Charles Matt.*

Mason 4-4-0's of 1882, bought for proposed Cleveland-Toledo express trains, had an alarming tendency to roll at high speed. Second 28, the former 20, was assigned to Michael Donivan (center) when this 1897 photo was made at Columbia. Donivan came from LS&MS in 1883 and was never involved in an accident during a remarkable 30-year career as a W&LE engineer. — *Collection of Richard J. Cook.*

Cooke outshopped this deckless Ten-Wheeler in 1896. Her cylinders were 19 x 26 and she weighed 60 tons. Brand-new, the 4-6-0 posed on the "Armstrong" table at Columbia with Engineer Irving Mears (under cab). — *Collection of Harry L. Brown.*

Formal portraits were in vogue in Warrenton in mid-1890's. Dressed up for posterity are Engineer Harry "Daddy" Turner (right), Fireman Philo Comstock, and their Pittsburgh, No. 85. Originally numbered 70, the 4-6-0 was one of six purchased in 1893. — *Collection of Richard J. Cook.*

Rome 4-4-0's with 62-inch drivers replaced Masons on passenger trains during 1883-1885. Second 32 was one of two 17 x 24 machines acquired secondhand in 1885. They had been built the year before for Lackawanna & Pittsburgh. The man in the bowler is Ira Cowen, one of the original enginemen of 1881; Fireman Neil Isenhour is at the left. — *Collection of Richard J. Cook.*

First Ten-Wheeler on W&LE was 31 built by Rome in 1886. The 17 x 24 is shown a few years later ready to leave Columbia with a freight. Her regular engineer, Charley Horton, is at the left; Mark Tobin, Horton's fireboy, is in the gangway. — *Collection of Richard J. Cook.*

Third lot of Rome 4-6-0's, eight in all, was added to the W&LE roster in 1891. These had wagon-top Belpaire boilers, 17 x 24-inch cylinders, and 56-inch drivers. The 48 was assigned to Jean Miller (in cab) when this portrait was made at Columbia in 1896. — *Collection of Richard J. Cook.*

311

called Garrigan's Spur, a few miles west of Bellevue. A little mercurial red-headed Irishman named Mike McGreevy was on First 1. He was always tooting his whistle when he met a train and later claimed he whistled signals at the local, which was in the siding at Bellevue. The green flags were covered with snow and ice and had become wrapped around the staffs and in the storm were not noticed by Sam Stowell, the local's engineer. He was an old and careful engineer, but the fatal combination of McGreevy's whistling propensities and the obscured flags led to dire consequences as Stowell thought Mike was simply living up to form. To have two sections of a passenger train was almost unheard of on the W&LE. The 25 hit the local at such high speed that the tank was split in two parts on the boiler head. Connell and his fireman Bob McMullin were . . . thrown clear of the wreckage, but the terrible shock killed both of them. Stowell and his fireman were but slightly hurt but the head brakeman, Bruce Johnson, was instantly killed.

McGreevy was later killed on the River Division while racing a C&P passenger train with a light engine in reverse. Multifatality collisions were hardly rare on the Wheeling before or after the Garrigan's wreck. One of the worst head-ons occurred exactly 50 years later and also killed three men.

THE TIP-TOP ROUTE

After a relatively short receivership the Connotton Valley was reorganized by the Blood Syndicate on May 9, 1885. Known thereafter as the Cleveland & Canton Railroad, the company took immediate action to build a 29-mile extension from Coshocton to Zanesville. A subsidiary, the Coshocton & Southern Railway, started construction work on September 4, 1885. Although the fallacy of the narrow-gauge concept had been amply demonstrated by this time, the company indicated no intention of switching horses in midstream. At the insistence of the bondholders, the reorganization of the road had been effected with the understanding that the 3-foot gauge would be retained. The road's embarrassment had been mild and was largely the result of overcapitalization and the stringent money market of 1884-1885. These were maladies that plagued most railroads of the day and had little relation to the gauge of the track. The nature of the Connotton's traffic and its geographical posture rendered this the one Ohio narrow gauge that might have prospered as such. Though the Zanesville extension would leave the road still short of the Straitsville coal fields, it would provide connections with the head of navigation on the Muskingum River and the Bellaire, Zanesville & Cincinnati. The "Bent, Zigzag & Crooked" operated a circuitous narrow-gauge line from Zanesville to the Ohio River near Wheeling and traversed promising coal lands.

The question of gauge was far from settled, though, and it soon brought into the open a split between the principal security holders. Hiram Blood held the largest block of common stock and he advocated an early widening of the gauge. New Yorker Austin Corbin represented the preferred holders and bondholders who were apprehensive about increasing the fixed charges and favored staying with narrow gauge. In December 1885 the dispute brought both the suspension of work on the Zanesville extension and the deposition of Sam Briggs. Blood had replaced the capable general manager with one of his New England cronies in order to strengthen his position. Through the use of heavy-handed tactics he managed to prevent the Corbin faction from voting during the annual meeting in May 1886, despite the fact that the preferred stockholders possessed the sole voting rights. When Corbin appealed to the Ohio Supreme Court, Blood held on by buying out the insurgents. This end to the hostilities came in May 1887 and cleared the way for an early change of gauge. The work of widening cuts and fills, rebuilding trestles, and installing standard-gauge ties was in an advanced stage by the end of that year. Construction to Zanesville was resumed in the spring of 1888.

The cost of converting the Cleveland & Canton to standard gauge was estimated at 1.7 million dollars. The money was raised through the sale of bonds during the bullish winter of 1887-1888. About 15,000 tons of 60-pound steel rails were bought, along with a dozen new Brooks engines and a fleet of new cars. In April 1888 the C&C paid $155,000 for the standard-gauge Canton & Waynesburg Railroad,* a 6½-mile coal road extending southeast from Canton along Indian Run. At the time it was acquired by the C&C, the road owned a Pittsburgh 0-4-0 named *John Hadley*, 17 coal cars, and a caboose.

The new engines delivered by Brooks in November 1888 included 51-ton Mogul freighters 18-23 and 16 x 24 4-4-0's 44-46. The latter were intended for passenger duty and had 68-inch drivers. There also were three new 0-6-0's — the 2, 3, and 4. All the new standard-gauge engines came from the builder lettered C.C. & S. since the plan was to change the name of the road to Cleveland, Canton & Southern with the switch in gauge. The road also had on hand No. 1, the ex-C&W 0-4-0, and five secondhand 4-4-0's. Engine 50 came from one of the Pennsylvania lines, but not much is known about this 4-4-0 aside from the fact that it was quite old. The others were bought from the Old Colony Railroad probably more out of sentiment than for any other reason. The 41, 42, and 43 had once been named *Fitchburg*,

---

*The Canton & Waynesburg was organized by Canton men on January 22, 1884, and was opened for traffic in December 1885. Ultimately, it was extended to a length of 10.88 miles and reached a point 3 miles north of Waynesburg.

N. Thayer, and *H. A. Blood* during the period when Blood and his associates were connected with the Old Colony and a predecessor, the Boston, Clinton & Fitchburg. These had 16 x 22-inch cylinders while the other Old Colony engine, No. 40, had 15 x 22-inch cylinders. All four were built by Taunton between 1866 and 1870.

The work of re-laying the C&C with 60-pound steel was completed by the fall of 1888, and on Sunday, November 18, the gauge was changed to 4 feet 8¾ inches. Porter No. 3, the 4-4-0 that opened the Canton extension in 1880, pulled the last narrow-gauge train — No. 28, the Sherrodsville-Canton local. The first standard-gauge trains were operated the next day, and on the 20th the city of Canton celebrated the event with a Grand Industrial Parade with businessmen's procession, balloon ascension and parachute jump, and a meeting at Schaefer's Opera House. The New York Equipment Company acquired all of the narrow-gauge equipment, most of which was in excellent condition. The little engines were soon scattered across the country on other narrow-gauge roads.

The Coshocton & Southern was opened on June 12, 1889, by an excursion run from Zanesville to Cleveland, 144 miles. The maiden trip was made by Engineer Ed Pedlar in 5 hours and carried 150 members of the Zanesville Commercial Travelers.

By the time of the C&S's formal opening on June 17, the Cleveland & Canton had acquired two more Brooks 19 x 24 Moguls, the 16 and 17, and four more 4-4-0's. No. 47 came from the Lakeside & Marblehead, another Blood road in Ohio. This apparently was another expatriated Old Colony engine rebuilt by Brooks in 1887. No. 51 was a 17 x 24 bought new from Brooks, and the 52 and 53 were 1866-1867 Tauntons purchased from the Old Colony.

On May 17, 1890, the Blood Syndicate finally got around to formally organizing the Cleveland, Canton & Southern Railroad. The deed to the Coshocton & Southern was conveyed to the new company in February 1891 and that of the Cleveland & Canton was acquired in May 1892. The Cleveland, Chagrin Falls & Northern Railroad was organized to acquire and rebuild the Chagrin Falls & Southern narrow gauge as well as to build a 3-mile connection between the Silver Plate at Solon and a point on the CC&S main line between Bedford and Twinsburg. The 8.19-mile standard-gauge Chagrin Falls-Falls Junction branch was opened in July 1890.

In the early 1890's the CC&S operated two daily express trains each way between Cleveland and Zanesville plus a Cleveland-Canton turnaround. Two connecting trains ran each way between Canton and Sherrodsville and the timetable still carried a Kent accommodation. Six commuter trains were

C&C local passenger train in palmy days that followed the switch to standard gauge. The rebuilt Brooks 4-4-0 was originally No. 1 of Lakeside & Marblehead, another Blood road. A freight train pulls out of the siding at left. — *Collection of Uriah G. Reinhold.*

SPECIAL

Excursion Rates!

—TO—

TOLEDO

and RETURN

—OVER—

Wheeling and

* * Lake Erie

**** RAILWAY. ****

Sunday, Aug. 23, 1891

OCCASION:

ENCAMPMENT

—OF—

PATRIARCHS MILITANT

—AT—

Presque Isle.

Inquire of any Agent of the Wheeling & Lake
Erie for Full Information and
Excursion Tickets.

THE BEE JOB ROOMS, Printers, Toledo, Ohio.

W&LE excursion was operated for patriarchal branch of Independent Order of Odd Fellows.

with 16 new locomotives, including four 40-ton 4-4-0 passenger engines, six heavy 4-6-0's for the coal drags, and six yard engines. One of the 1893 4-4-0's, No. 49, was demolished by an 1896 derailment south of Carrollton. A young boy caused the accident by placing an object on the rail ahead of the locomotive. The engineer happened to be Joseph Kirk, the boy's uncle. He and his fireman were killed outright and the engine was so badly damaged that it was never repaired.

Three subsidiary companies were organized to construct CC&S branches during the 1890's. The Cleveland Belt & Terminal Railroad was chartered on May 13, 1891, as the successor to the Cleveland Belt Line Railroad. Originally the intention was to have the latter build a 6½-mile line from Newburgh to the Nickel Plate at Willson Avenue (East 55th Street), but the CB&T ended up connecting the CC&S with the Big Four. The Belt Line was opened in January 1893 and ran from the CC&S, in the "flats," west for 5.39 miles to the Big Four near Denison Avenue. The Massillon Railroad was chartered on January 6, 1892, and extended from the CC&S main line at Run Junction (near Navarre) west for 5½ miles. Opened on March 1, 1896, the Massillon Railroad served the Warwick company mines in the Pigeon Run coal fields. The Canton & Wooster Railroad was built in 1895 to the Nutwood coal mine near what later became the W&LE's Brewster terminal. The C&W was 3.93 miles long and extended west from the CC&S at Justus.

The CC&S proudly referred to itself as the Tip-Top Route, but the career of the Connotton Valley coal road as a standard gauge was unsuccessful. It had been overcapitalized as a narrow gauge and proved incapable of also carrying the indebtedness that came with its rebuilding. The 1886 discovery of a successful refining process for Lima crude oil caused many Cleveland industries to switch to this cheap fuel for firing their furnaces and boilers. Shipments of coal over the CC&S dropped off sharply as a result and the road lost its largest account — a Cleveland firm that had used 100,000 tons of Connotton coal annually. The Tip-Top Route succumbed shortly after the financial collapse of 1893 and General Manager J. W. Wardwell was appointed receiver on September 15 of that year. Thereafter the road's physical condition deteriorated rapidly and the equipment was permitted to go almost totally unattended. The condition of the Coshocton-Zanesville line was so bad that the courts ordered it closed in July 1898. By 1899 fewer than half of the 36 locomotives on the roster were serviceable by even the most liberal standards. No effort was made to draw up a plan of reorganization, and on August 5, 1899, the CC&S was purchased by the newly organized Wheeling & Lake Erie Railroad.

scheduled each way between Cleveland and Chagrin Falls, 24.5 miles. This schedule was reduced to a pair of round trips — one in the morning and one in the afternoon — after the 1895 advent of a competing interurban line. The "sub" runs were powered by the ex-Old Colony Tauntons. One Taunton, the 42, was disintegrated by a boiler explosion while she was leaving Newburgh with train 13 on February 3, 1891. Taunton 52 was reboilered by Brooks in 1890 and was a regular on the sub runs for years.

During 1891 and 1893 Brooks furnished the CC&S

Equipped with a tender pilot, CC&S 52 was assigned to suburban service between Cleveland and Chagrin Falls. Photo was made at Dunkirk in 1891 after Brooks had reboilered the ex-Old Colony Taunton.— *Schenectady History Center.*

Morgan Run Railway was short coal road that fed CC&S a few miles north of Coshocton. The Baldwin saddletanker ran into Coshocton with a trainload of miners each Saturday night until November 25, 1899, when it was demolished in a head-on collision with a CC&S freight in which 13 died and 76 were injured. Earlier in the day another head-on near Canton claimed the lives of two enginemen. — *Collection of Uriah G. Reinhold.*

This Brooks Mogul was the other engine in the Morgan Run disaster. Although Engineer John Reinhold (in cab) survived the collision, he very nearly perished in its aftermath. Belated arrival of relief train, delayed by wreck at Canton, saved Reinhold from being lynched by an angry mob of miners. This famous engineman was killed three years later in another wreck near Coshocton. — *Collection of Uriah G. Reinhold.*

Atlantic 2306 pulls into Zoar, O., with Wheeling-bound No. 32 in twilight years of W&LE passenger service. — *Collection of Dale Smith.*

ZOAR

The Iron Cross

DESPITE poor health and extraordinary reverses during the mid-1880's, Jay Gould remained a potent force on the American financial scene until his death in December 1892. Gould's railroad holdings were largely intact and he still controlled Western Union and the New York elevateds. Paradoxically, this most hated man of his generation commanded to the end of his days the steadfast loyalty of a small but powerful clique of kindred spirits. The other members of the so-called Wall Street Trinity—Sidney Dillon and Russell Sage — never deserted him. Dillon led the successful fight to regain control of the Union Pacific in 1890 while Sage maintained the hold on the Missouri Pacific lines and the Wabash. Banker Louis Fitzgerald was a resolute ally to the end, as was W. E. Connor, the brokerage partner who singlehandedly saved Gould from total disaster in the spring of 1884. Above all, though, Gould owed the preservation of his empire after 1885 to the energy and acumen of his eldest son George.

Unlike most offspring of wealthy men, George Jay Gould had an abbreviated formal education. During his formative years, however, he received an extensive entrepreneurial grooming for the role of his

317

George Jay Gould (1864-1923), heir to the ambitions of his father, failed to fulfill his dream of ruling a transcontinental system. — *Western Pacific photo.*

father's successor. At 16 George was being schooled in the fundamentals of finance by the able Connor, and in a few years he assumed the active management of much of his parent's affairs. At the age of only 32 he inherited control of the Gould corporate empire and fortune of more than 70 million dollars. With these great assets went the allegiance of Dillon, Sage, Fitzgerald, and Connor. In 1892 George won the eleventh-hour support of English capitalists in an unexpectedly successful bid to save his father's grip on the Union Pacific. The elder Gould treated this triumph with characteristic indifference, but the son had earned the legacy of leadership.

George Gould was particularly adept at turning a situation to his personal advantage and, like his father, was a sagacious opportunist and an expert manipulator. Although the Gould roads remained notoriously poor investments, their value to the public as common carriers was considerably enhanced. In fact, the younger Gould had an abiding interest in the routine affairs of his railroads — an inclination that was not particularly beneficial to them and often led to clashes with subordinates. More than anything else, George Gould's grandiose dream of a great transcontinental railway system was the key to his ultimate downfall. It was a scheme that also had a profound effect on the destiny of the Wheeling & Lake Erie.

Since 1888 the W&LE had paid dividends on its preferred stock, a practice ended by the long 1895 strike in the Ohio coal fields. In spite of record earnings in 1896, receivers were appointed on January 15, 1897. Strangely, the Wheeling had yet to default on its bonds, and during the first year of receivership an amount more than twice the annual fixed charges was spent on additions and betterments. Dillon and other Gould men had held a substantial interest in the road since the 1886 reorganization but had taken no active part in its management. It will be recalled that the W&LE materialized largely because it formed the eastward extension of the Wabash toward Jay Gould's proposed low-grade route across Pennsylvania. Although Gould's post-1883 embarrassments had forced abandonment of this plan, his son watched with keen interest the Brice-Iselin effort of the 1890's to link the Lake Erie & Western with the Buffalo, Rochester & Pittsburgh and the Reading. After opening its Punxsutawney-Butler extension and gaining trackage rights to New Castle, the independent BR&P was within a relatively short distance of the W&LE. Gould never admitted coveting the BR&P, but his subordinates claimed that the road played an important role in his early transcontinental plans.

Gould's interest in the Wheeling was well exposed by the 1897 receivership. Fitzgerald headed the reorganization committee and Connor presided over the board of directors after 1896. The reorganization plan put forth early in 1898 required foreclosure of the general mortgage bonds and their exchange for noncumulative preferred stock. This strategy was a favorite of both Goulds and had been used on the junior bondholders of the Wabash several times. It cleared the way for a new bond issue without material increase in fixed charges and was a good indication that expansion was in the wind. Earnings, incidentally, never got high enough to pay the preferred dividend.

Receiver of the W&LE from 1897 to 1899 was Myron T. Herrick (1854-1929), a dynamic and colorful force in the commercial life of Cleveland in the 1890's. Herrick, a banker, seemed to be on intimate terms with every prominent Cleveland industrialist and was one of the most politically powerful men of his day. He had personally saved McKinley from financial ruin in 1893 and had helped groom him for the presidency two years later. After his appointment as W&LE receiver, Herrick formed a syndicate with the idea of buying the all but defunct Cleveland, Canton & Southern. He was joined in the venture by William G. Mather and Earl W. Oglebay, Clevelanders prominent in the development of the Lake Superior iron ranges. Both now headed ship-

Gov. Theodore Roosevelt of New York addresses a 1900 crowd at Navarre from platform of a W&LE parlor car while he was a candidate for vice-president of the United States. Roosevelt's running mate, McKinley, hailed from nearby Canton. Last campaign train to run over the W&LE was chartered by Richard Nixon in 1952. — *William L. Bennett.*

ping and mining enterprises, and Oglebay was closely associated with John D. Rockefeller. He also had an avowed desire to establish first-class rail service between Cleveland and his native Wheeling.

Shortly before the April 28, 1899, reorganization of the W&LE, the Herrick syndicate bought out the bondholders who had purchased the CC&S at foreclosure the previous February. On August 5 the syndicate delivered the Tip-Top Route to the W&LE, accepting in payment that road's new $3,850,000 issue of consolidated mortgage bonds and preferred stocks. Gould retained nominal control of the expanded Wheeling but seated Herrick, Mather, and Oglebay on the board of directors. Early in 1900 Herrick was elected chairman of the W&LE board, a post he held until 1912. By joining forces with Herrick, Gould had gained valuable allies at Cleveland; through Oglebay he was to build a briefly amicable relationship with Rockefeller as well.

The east-west Toledo Division and north-south Cleveland Division, the two intersecting main lines of the new 470-mile Wheeling & Lake Erie Railroad, formed a crude cross on the map of Ohio and after 1899 the road was commonly referred to as the Iron Cross. The consolidation was of little immediate benefit to the W&LE, largely because great sums were needed to put the CC&S lines in good condition. Since the Wheeling itself needed heavier rail and bigger engines to cope with growing coal and ore traffic, it could ill afford the cost of rebuilding the CC&S. Possession of a through line from Cleveland to Wheeling was an important traffic advantage, but in this respect the W&LE got something it already had. In 1896 the road perfected a 99-year traffic alliance with the Cleveland Terminal & Valley Railroad (successor to the Valley Railway) providing for through train operation between Cleveland, Valley Junction, and Wheeling. The contract gave the W&LE operating rights over the CT&V and the right to construct whatever facilities W&LE required at Cleveland. Unlike the CC&S, the CT&V served Akron as well as Canton.

The 1898 demise of Calvin Brice and his proposed link with the BR&P stimulated George Gould's interest in the moribund CC&S. Less than 80 miles separated the Tip-Top Route at Minerva and the BR&P at Butler. Cheap access between Minerva and Lisbon, 17 miles, was offered by the abandoned Sandy & Beaver towpath. Beyond Lisbon, the Pittsburgh, Lisbon & Western Railway extended 25 miles east to New Galilee, Pa., a station on the Pennsylvania's Chicago main line. The PL&W charter called for an eastern terminus at Chewton, a hamlet in the Beaver River valley 5 miles east of New Galilee and 31 miles west of Butler. BR&P trains had the right to run over the Pittsburgh & Western (B&O) from Butler to Chewton and New Castle. Ultimately, Herrick gained control of the PL&W and placed Gould in an excellent position to quickly effect a cheap connection with the BR&P-Reading low-grade route.

THE PITTSBURGH-TOLEDO SYNDICATE

Before Gould and Herrick could progress the W&LE-PL&W-BR&P idea beyond the planning

319

stage, a change in the Pennsylvania Railroad's management diverted their attention to Pittsburgh. In June 1899 Alexander J. Cassatt was named president of the PRR, and he immediately set into motion that road's greatest era of expansion and improvement. Ostensibly motivated by a desire to abolish kickbacks, or rebates, to major shippers such as Rockefeller and Carnegie, Cassatt allied the Pennsylvania with the Vanderbilt lines and moved to end the independent status of their Eastern competitors. New York Central joined PRR in neutralizing the Chesapeake & Ohio in 1899 and subsequently bought outright control of the Big Four and Lake Erie & Western. By 1900, in calculated defiance of the Sherman Act, the Pennsy had bought 40 per cent of the Baltimore & Ohio's stock and installed L. F. Loree as its president. Under Cassatt the PRR also added Norfolk & Western, Long Island, and a number of lesser systems to its holdings and gained control of Reading through the B&O.

The Cassatt-Vanderbilt assault on rebates and competition was particularly offensive to Andrew Carnegie. Long a foe of the Pennsylvania, he had built railroads to combat PRR's Pittsburgh monopoly and had encouraged the B&O to link its Chicago Division and Pittsburgh & Western in the 1890's. Carnegie was adept at playing one road against the other in order to command freight rates lower than those charged his competitors. His steel mills were concentrated at Pittsburgh, which in 1900 accounted for more than 20 per cent of American pig iron production and annually shipped 80 million tons of freight by rail. The city had a metropolitan population of more than 800,000 and was surrounded by 14,000 square miles of coal lands, then considered the richest bituminous district in the world. Pittsburgh's furnaces and collieries lay but 40 miles west of the Wheeling & Lake Erie's Ohio River line, and the Wheeling connected with Gould's 11,700-mile network of rails to the west and southwest. These were circumstances readily appreciated by Carnegie, Gould, and the Herrick syndicate.

Joseph Ramsey Jr., the 50-year-old vice-president and general manager of the Wabash in 1900, generally has been credited with the idea of building a low-grade connection between the W&LE and Carnegie's Union Railroad at Pittsburgh. A civil engineer, Ramsey went railroading in 1869 and spent many years in the service of the Pennsylvania and its subsidiaries. In 1882 he personally surveyed a route extending west from Pittsburgh to the Ohio River at Mingo Junction which was parallel to and south of the Panhandle's line between the same points. Early in 1901 Ramsey was promoted to the Wabash presidency and elected to the same post on the W&LE. He was also made active manager of the Pittsburgh-Toledo Syndicate at its formation

on February 1, 1901, and together with Gould, Herrick, and Fitzgerald pledged 20 million dollars to build the Pittsburgh Extension. Three days later the syndicate made a 20-year contract with Carnegie Steel and the Union Railroad which obliged the syndicate to provide a rail connection between the Union and the Wabash at Toledo. For his part, Carnegie guaranteed the syndicate 25 per cent of all the tonnage he controlled moving from Pittsburgh to points within and beyond Central Traffic Association territory. Another suddenly aggrieved PRR customer, the Pittsburgh Coal Company, later agreed to ship at least 4 million tons of coal annually over the proposed Gould line.

PARLOR CARS AND THE PAN-AMERICAN

Formal operation of the former CC&S lines was assumed by the W&LE on August 14, 1899, and by the following October through passenger service had been initiated between Cleveland and Wheeling. Train 101 left Cleveland at 9:20 a.m. and arrived at Navarre 2 hours 26 minutes later with through coaches for Wheeling. These were added to the consist of No. 1,* the *Wheeling Express*, due into Navarre from Toledo at noon. No. 1 had a scheduled Wheeling arrival of 3 p.m. The afternoon Cleveland-Coshocton accommodation, No. 103, also left through cars at Navarre for eastbound express No. 3. Six hours was required for this combined 152-mile Cleveland-Wheeling run.

By the spring of 1901 the Wheeling had restored through passenger service to Zanesville and had expanded its Cleveland-Wheeling service to three trains in each direction. Hopeful of doing a heavy business during the Pan-American Exposition at Buffalo, the road purchased three sets of new passenger cars from American Car & Foundry's Ohio Falls works in 1900. Included were three 66-foot combination baggage-smoker cars, six 70-foot 72-passenger coaches, and a trio of plush six-wheel-truck 34-chair parlor-cafe cars with buffet.

Boat train 2/102 of 1901, the *Pan-American Express*, was normally assigned one of the parlor cars, a baggage-smoker, and two of the new coaches. This train was due out of Wheeling at 1:20 p.m., and its scheduled 7:10 p.m. Cleveland arrival permitted a connection with the Cleveland & Buffalo line's overnight steamer to Buffalo. For travelers preferring an all-rail journey to Buffalo, the W&LE ran the *Cleveland Special* out of Wheeling at 3:55 p.m. with the same equipment assigned the boat train. The *Special's* 5-hour 40-minute schedule allowed an hour at Cleveland for passengers to board an over-

---

*In contrast with practice on most east-west railroads, **W&LE** westbounds still carried even numbers. On the Wheeling, westbounds were always superior to eastbound trains of the same class.

Fresh from Dunkirk, E-1 2003 poses at Toledo Union Station early on a morning in 1905. The 4-4-2 is set to leave for Pittsburgh with limited No. 2. Like their Wabash sisters, W&LE Atlantics had carbon-arc headlights. — *Collection of Robert V. Hubbard.*

H-3 Pittsburghs were first W&LE Consols. Engineer Bob Smith (left) posed with new 192 at original Ironville roundhouse in 1900. — *Collection of Harry L. Brown.*

Zanesville Belt passed Mill Run shops of narrow-gauge Bellaire, Zanesville & Cincinnati (later Ohio River & Western) at Hall Avenue. Shops and west end of OR&W were abandoned in 1928. — *Wheeling & Lake Erie photo.*

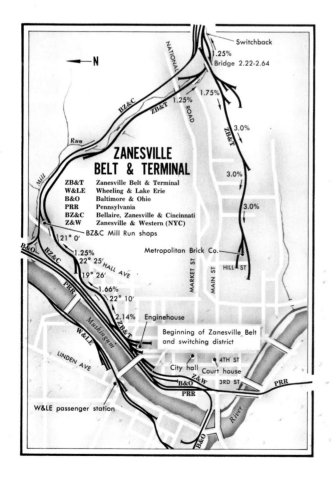

ZANESVILLE
BELT & TERMINAL

ZB&T	Zanesville Belt & Terminal
W&LE	Wheeling & Lake Erie
B&O	Baltimore & Ohio
PRR	Pennsylvania
BZ&C	Bellaire, Zanesville & Cincinnati
Z&W	Zanesville & Western (NYC)

night Lake Shore sleeper train to Buffalo.

Master carbuilder C. S. Morse built the Wheeling's first parlor car, the 71-foot *Zanesville*, at Ironville in 1899. Each morning, train 104 brought the car to Cleveland and each afternoon No. 103 took it back to Zanesville. À la carte meals were served on *Zanesville*, which seated 31 patrons and had an observation platform. One of the ex-CC&S coaches was converted to a parlor car at Ironville in 1901 and as such was assigned to trains 2 and 3 between Toledo and Creston.

COAL MINES AND TONNAGE GRADES

Prosperity following the Spanish-American War substantially raised the volume of freight moving over the Wheeling & Lake Erie lines. New steel mills in the Ohio valley and increased capacity at Huron doubled the tonnage of iron ore handled between 1901 and 1902. Coal was still the W&LE's bread and butter and was accounting for an ever-increasing share of its traffic. Between 1901 and 1904 the amount of bituminous moved over the Iron Cross jumped from 1.8 to 3 million tons, 51 per cent of all freight hauled. Output of the small Pigeon Run field at Massillon and mines in the Connotton valley remained almost constant during this period and soon lagged far behind production in the

No. 8 district around Dillonvale. Particularly popular as a locomotive fuel, this coal was used extensively by the Erie, DL&W, Pere Marquette, and railroads in the Northwest and Canada. The Nickel Plate and many Great Lakes steamship lines were virtually exclusive users of No. 8.

By mid-1903 there were 39 active deep-shaft, slope, and drift mines on the W&LE with potential daily production of 23,000 tons. More than half this capacity was represented by 10 mines in the No. 8 district, four of which were newly opened. The biggest was the 3000-ton Bradley Mine at Crow Hollow, 2½ miles north of Pine Valley. Coal from this mine moved to Pine Valley over the Dillonvale & Smithfield Railroad built in 1902 by the United States Coal Company and operated under contract by the W&LE. Two other short branches feeding the Toledo Division near Dillonvale were opened in 1903. The 2-mile Mount Pleasant Branch connected Dunglen with the Wheeling & Lake Erie Coal Mining Company's Dillon No. 2 mine, and the Long Run Branch extended 3 miles southwest from Long Run tunnel's east portal to the big Roby No. 2 mine.

On March 5, 1901, the Wheeling chartered the subsidiary Adena Railroad to build a 25-mile road south from Adena to St. Clairsville and Bellaire. This branch, which actually terminated at Neffs, a station on the B&O's Central Ohio line 4 miles west of Bellaire and 20.94 miles south of Adena, required more than five years to build mainly because it ran over the hills from valley to valley rather than along the courses of streams as did most railroads in southeastern Ohio. As a result there were 75 curves and 2 per cent ruling grades in both directions. From one end to the other, however, the Adena Railroad traversed the richest coal veins in Ohio and virtually doubled the output of the No. 8 district. Within three years the branch served five major mines — Black Diamond, Lorena, Trolls, Provident, and Roby No. 1.

Work on the Adena Railroad started in December 1900, and by the end of 1902 about 1½ miles of track had been laid from Adena to the Roby mine. In June 1903 irregular operations were begun to Maynard, a station on the Cleveland, Lorain & Wheeling 9 miles south of Adena. Full operation over the remaining 12 miles to Neffs was not initiated until December 1905. The entire Adena Railroad was laid with 56-pound rail rolled in 1882 and used until 1901 in the Toledo-Norwalk main line.

Leaving the valley of Short Creek at Adena, the Adena Railroad climbed from elevation 871 to 1131 feet at the summit near Harrisville. In this 3-mile stretch there were 13 curves, and the sustained opposing gradient southbound varied from 1.2 to 2 per cent. At Harrisville the branch passed through a 1129-foot tunnel, then descended 5½ miles to the valley of Wheeling Creek at Maynard. After about a mile of fairly level running, the line began a 3½-mile ascent from elevation 834 to a second summit at St. Clairsville. A 532-foot tunnel under part of the town and the National Road marked the beginning of a 7-mile descent to Neffs. In this distance the elevation dropped from 1151 to 732 feet at a rate up to 105 feet to the mile (2 per cent).

Considering the tonnage hauled, the Adena Railroad's grades were the toughest operational restrictions on the W&LE. A number of steeper grades were to be found on the road however. Newburgh and Baltic hills on the Cleveland Division had grades of 2.63 and 2.15 per cent compensated for curvature, and the Cleveland Belt offered a 2.45 per cent climb. Sub runs out of Chagrin Falls battled a stretch of 2.1 compensated, and there was a 2.9 per cent grade at Steubenville.

Prior to the building of the Adena Railroad the four Toledo Division helper districts between Dillonville and Huron were the Wheeling's worst headaches. The most powerful Ten-Wheelers — the 19 x 26 Cookes of 1896 — were rated at no better than 600 tons on the 10-mile eastward pull from Milan to Hartland. Working westbound coal over the 15 miles between Pine Valley and Rexford Summit, these engines were restricted to 700 tons. They were good for 750 tons on the 7-mile westward climb from Columbia to Sippo Summit, and could horse 18 40-ton gondola loads of ore from Jewett to Rexford. With relatively long distances involved, doubling these hills was impractical and helper engines were used to get tonnage trains over them.

On a warm, dry day two of the most powerful 4-6-0's in good condition could take no more than 25 ore-laden gondolas up Hartland Hill even if the hoggers ran on low water all the way. Always a foolhardy practice, this was suicidal with the Cookes which had an unusually small water space. In a move to boost hill tonnage ratings, the Wheeling went to the Consolidation in 1900. Pittsburghs 191-200 had straight-top Belpaire boilers and weighed 74 tons compared with 60 tons for the Cookes. These 20 x 28's had 57-inch drivers and were rated at 30,064 pounds tractive effort, nearly half again as much as the W&LE's most powerful 4-6-0's. Working solo, the Pittsburghs could take 1000 to 1100 tons of coal up to Rexford and Sippo. Westbound on the Adena Railroad they were good for all of 600 tons.

THE ZANESVILLE BELT

Shortly after the turn of the century the Wheeling acquired a 3.76-mile terminal road at Zanesville which had steeper grades and sharper curves than any line on the system. This little road started out on January 4, 1886, as the Zanesville, Mount Vernon & Marion Railway and was promoted by Col. Albert E. Boone, a flamboyant speculator who appeared in Zanesville about 1883 and kept things lively there for years afterward. Boone was fond of trooping around town in shoulder-length hair and a high silk hat, fancied himself the benefactor of the "oppressed" workingmen of Zanesville, and once claimed to be the "only man in America not afraid of the Pennsylvania and B&O railroads." When certain businessmen opposed his petition for a city franchise in 1887, Boone suggested that Zanesville needed "a few first-class funerals" if it expected to catch up with the rest of the world.

Construction of the ZM&M got under way in November 1887 in the face of determined opposition from the B&O. The latter road bought up many dwellings blocking the path of Boone's tracklayers, but the promoter brazenly ordered his workmen to evict the tenants and raze the buildings. This was accomplished before the B&O could secure an injunction. Completed in 1888, the ZM&M followed a meandering course from the Muskingum River, between Third and Fourth streets in downtown Zanesville, to a hilltop brickworks overlooking the city. For about a mile the line ran northeast along the east bank of the Muskingum and then turned abruptly southeast following Mill Run and the narrow-gauge Bellaire, Zanesville & Cincinnati to the National Road 2 miles east of Zanesville. In one stretch the ascending grade was 2.14 uncompensated and there was a reverse curve 22 degrees 10 minutes to the left and 19 degrees 26 minutes to the right. A short tangent separated this and curves 22 degrees 25 minutes to the left and 21 degrees to the right.

Just beyond the National Road the ZM&M connected with the BZ&C, then changed course from east to due west by means of a switchback. At Milepost 2.64 the road crossed over its own line on a bridge and then headed west for Zanesville, ascending at the rate of 3 per cent uncompensated. Elevation at Hill Street, the end of track, was about 175 feet higher than at the starting point, and the termini were separated by a distance of less than three-quarter mile. The W&LE chartered the Zanesville Belt & Terminal Railway on March 1, 1901, and this company bought the bankrupt ZM&M, complete with its old Pittsburgh 0-6-0 and caboose, at foreclosure two weeks later. Although the W&LE's Linden Avenue depot was directly across the Muskingum from the ZB&T's Third Street terminus, it was necessary to use 1.24 miles of the B&O to connect them.

THE HIGH AND DRY

Shortly after making the traffic contract with the Pittsburgh-Toledo Syndicate in 1901, Andrew Carnegie sold his steel mills to J. P. Morgan's newly created United States Steel Corporation. Fearful that Morgan was seeking a monopoly in steel and intended to fix the price of rail, the Pennsylvania Railroad countered by buying steel mills at Johnstown and Harrisburg, Pa. As a result Morgan at first did not abrogate the Gould contract but used it as a weapon against the PRR. When the two were finally reconciled, the Pennsy agreed to withdraw from the steel business and Morgan tore up Carnegie's contract. The tonnage commitments made to Gould were scrapped, but he was allowed to connect his Pittsburgh Extension with the Union Railroad.

For a time it seemed that the PRR had delivered a mortal rebuff to the Pittsburgh Extension, but Gould was not that easily repulsed. In 1902 he turned the tables on Cassatt by buying control of the Western Maryland Railroad from the city of Baltimore and promising to link it with his other roads. Not content with combating the giants of the East, Gould now menaced those in the West. Through the Missouri Pacific he gained control of the Denver & Rio Grande and Rio Grande Western in 1901, and two years later he organized the Western Pacific to build a 924-mile road from the Rio Grande at Salt Lake City to San Francisco Bay. This move engendered a long and bitter struggle with E. H. Harriman, ruler of the Union Pacific and Southern Pacific.

Gould's mélange of allies was shrinking about as fast as he was picking up powerful adversaries. Carnegie was now intent only on giving away his fortune, and Sage would soon be gone. Rockefeller and Gould had a falling out, and Herrick finally answered the call of politics. After turning down McKinley's 1901 offer of a cabinet post, Herrick ran for governor of Ohio against Tom L. Johnson in the famous 1903 campaign of the Three H's. Herrick's running mates on the Buckeye Republican ticket were Mark Hanna and Warren G. Harding, and he whipped Johnson by the largest plurality in the state's history. Nonetheless, Herrick remained chairman of the W&LE board until 1912 and a manager of the Pittsburgh-Toledo Syndicate until its 1904 liquidation.

Joseph Ramsey and his chief engineer, James W. Patterson, needed nearly four years to build Gould's road to Pittsburgh. Before starting construction Ramsey gained what appeared to be the right of access to Pittsburgh itself. In 1900 Congress approved the Pittsburgh & Mansfield Street Railway's petition for the right to bridge the Monongahela River at Pittsburgh. Franchises and rights of the proposed trolley line later passed to the Pittsburgh, Carnegie & Western Railroad, Ramsey's connection between Pittsburgh and the West Virginia pan-

handle. The remainder of the Pittsburgh Extension was to be built by the Cross Creek Railroad in West Virginia and the Pittsburgh, Toledo & Western Railroad in Ohio.

Gould spent a million dollars for a terminal site four blocks long in the Lower Triangle or Point District of downtown Pittsburgh. This was hardly more than a block north of the Monongahela, and since the War Department had insisted on 70 feet of clearance between the bridge and the river, the station's tracks would be 35 feet above street level. The elevation had to cross block-long sections of four streets, obliging the PC&W to petition the city for an enabling ordinance. By the fall of 1902 the ordinance had been buried in councilmanic committee for almost two years and the PC&W's Patterson ordered his workmen to proceed without it. Acting on the plea of the city, the Pennsylvania Supreme Court issued an injunction against the road on January 1, 1903. After suspending work, Patterson asked for and got an expression of public support and the ordinance was passed on February 4, 1903. More instrumental in this Gould victory, perhaps, was the fact that the PC&W had made "contributions" totaling $87,500 to three Pittsburgh politicians.

The 59.9-mile Pittsburgh Extension was one of the boldest and most interesting railroad construction projects ever undertaken and completed in the eastern United States. The line traversed extremely difficult terrain, but moderate grades made it superior as a tonnage carrier to the paralleling St. Louis main line of the PRR. At the time the extension was built, it possessed not a single crossing of highway or railroad at grade and the two great cantilever bridges spanning the Ohio and Monongahela rivers were the engineering wonders of their day. There were 18 double-track tunnels with an

Balloon-style WPT trainshed at Pittsburgh (above) covered six tracks 35 feet above street level. The structure was gutted by fire on March 21, 1946. Wabash station (below) fronted on Liberty Avenue, one of Pittsburgh's principal commercial streets. The 185-foot-high building was home of W&LE general offices 1904 to 1909.—*Both photos, collection of D. W. McLaughlin.*

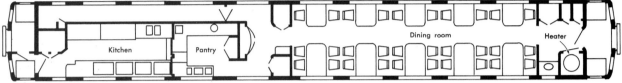

Dining car 05 built by AC&F in 1904 for W&LE limiteds seated 30 people. It was converted to parlor car *Kent* in 1907 and after 1938 retirement served as Warrenton's portable depot. — *Collection of Robert V. Hubbard.*

aggregate length of almost 4 miles. New 90-pound steel was used throughout, tie plates anchored rails on all curves, and the entire road was ballasted with gravel and stone.

Ramsey's Pittsburgh, Toledo & Western left the W&LE main line just west of Rexford Summit at what came to be known as Pittsburgh Junction. For the first 3 miles to Hopedale the road utilized the abandoned grade and tunnels built by the original W&LE in the 1870's. From a 1160-foot summit at Hopedale, the PT&W descended 465 feet in the 17.3 miles to the Ohio River at Mingo Junction. Opposing westbound gradient for almost the entire distance was .7 per cent. Built through a virtually uninhabited region between Hopedale and Mingo, the PT&W had six tunnels, three viaducts, and some

imposing fills supported by 50-foot concrete arches. One fill was 188 feet high. The high-level crossing of the Ohio valley was one of the more spectacular engineering achievements of the Pittsburgh Extension and explains why W&LE men called the road the "High and Dry." After passing through the Ohio escarpment by way of 845-foot Coens Tunnel, the PT&W crossed the Mingo Bottoms on a 3500-foot combination of trestle, truss bridges, and fills. The Ohio River bridge was a through pin-connected cantilever type with a 700-foot channel span and two 298-foot anchor spans. At the West Virginia end the road plunged through a 300-foot tunnel into the valley of Cross Creek. Less than 5 miles of the Pittsburgh Extension was in West Virginia, since the road crossed the narrowest neck of that state's north-south panhandle.

At the west portal of 1430-foot Klein tunnel the Pittsburgh Extension passed into Pennsylvania. Hickory Tunnel, 13 miles east, marked the summit of the long climb away from the Ohio. Near Carnegie, the PC&W built a yard and engine terminal called Rook. The 4.8 miles of road from Rook to Pittsburgh was double-tracked and had a sustained descending 1 per cent grade eastbound. In this section were the longest tunnels — 4718-foot Greentree and 3342-foot Mount Washington. The latter carried the PC&W through a rock-bound ridge to the great bridge spanning the Monongahela. The double-track steel superstructure was supported by pneumatic caissons sunk to bedrock 42 feet below the river surface, weighed 7000 tons, and was 1504 feet long. It was the longest cantilever in America and took nearly three years to build. Twenty men died erecting the 812-foot channel span.

For many years Gould's elevated stub-end station was one of the most imposing structures in downtown Pittsburgh. The flat-iron-style station building, which faced northeast, was nine stories and 185 feet high. It was located on a triangular parcel fronting on Liberty Avenue 10 blocks west of the PRR depot and was bordered by Ferry Street on the east and Fourth Street on the south. The building was faced with granite and embellished with many fancy moldings and columns. Offices occupied the upper six stories while the first floor housed ticket offices and waiting rooms with tile floors, marble walls, and stained-glass windows. A winding staircase and elevators reached the second-floor concourse which opened on the trainshed. The 415-foot balloon-type trainshed abutted the station building on the south and covered six tracks above freighthouse buildings occupying three city squares between First and Fourth streets.

Ramsey had hoped to complete the Pittsburgh Extension by the April 30, 1904, opening of the Louisiana Purchase Exposition at St. Louis which was served exclusively by the Wabash. He estimated that fair-bound travelers would pour 2.5 million dollars into the PC&W's coffers and even more into those of the W&LE and Wabash. However, the severe winter of 1903-1904 stopped the contractors for weeks at a time, and the following spring two vicious storms washed away fills and grade from one end of the extension to the other. Strikes, smallpox, and the cave-in of an old mine under Greentree Tunnel delivered other delays. The same storms that visited the extension did so much damage to the W&LE that it was closed east of Massillon for some time. Since the Wheeling was doing much of the work on the PT&W, construction work west of Mingo was almost suspended.

By May 1, 1904, the Pittsburgh-Toledo Syndicate had advanced Ramsey $15,873,000, most of which had been used to build the extension. According to the original agreement, the syndicate would accept mortgage bonds in exchange for its 20-million-dollar subscription. After Morgan had emasculated Carnegie's pledge, the syndicate wanted the W&LE or the Wabash to guarantee the bonds. Gould then invented an ingenious plan which not only transferred the syndicate's risk to the Wabash but enabled its managers to dispose of their W&LE stock at a fat profit. On May 9, 1904, PC&W, PT&W, and Cross Creek were consolidated to form the Wabash-

Pittsburgh Terminal Railway. The Wabash had already consented to take all of the new company's stock and 6.6 million of its first mortgage bonds. All the Terminal's securities — 10 million dollars in stock and 40 million in bonds — were delivered to the syndicate in consideration of its 20-million-dollar subscription. After the Wabash had bought the agreed amount of stock and bonds, the WPT paid the syndicate about 6 million dollars for 51.73 per cent of the Wheeling's stocks. Managers of the syndicate evidently retained enough WPT bonds to assure their hold on the road in the event it was forced through bankruptcy. Connor picked up fat commissions selling the 10-million-dollar second-mortgage and many first-mortgage bonds to savings banks and insurance companies. Syndicate managers realized a profit of at least 15 million dollars through the sale of the bonds alone. Those who bought the second mortgage bonds never received a dime of interest and ultimately lost their entire investment.

In October 1902 the syndicate had moved to protect its interest in the Pittsburgh Extension by authoring a 20-year traffic contract between the PC&W, W&LE, and Wabash. This provided for reciprocal trackage rights, through train service, and rate divisions which allowed the 60-mile extension arbitrary mileage of 100. As a further means of protecting the syndicate, the contract was amended the day after the WPT was formed, obliging the Wabash and Wheeling to pay the Terminal 25 per cent of their gross revenues on traffic to and from the road in the event WPT was unable to meet its fixed charges. The remaining 75 per cent was deemed sufficient to cover the larger roads' costs in handling the traffic.

On top of 3.5 million dollars received from the syndicate after May 9, 1904, about 8 million dollars was raised by the Terminal through the sale of more bonds. Most of this money apparently was used to complete the road. Total capital obligations of the WPT now amounted to $60,229,000, whereas about 25 million had actually been spent in construction. Something less than 10 million was also expended buying control of the W&LE and the Pittsburgh Terminal Railroad & Coal Company, owner of the

By 1906 W&LE had 12,000 freight cars, including more than 11,600 gondolas for hauling coal and ore. Car No. 43357 with a capacity of 40 tons was turned out by AC&F in 1905. — *Wheeling & Lake Erie photo.*

High noon in Navarre finds the W&LE staging a four-way meet in the summer of 1904. Pittsburgh-bound No. 2 (left) has through cars from Chicago and St. Louis. Parlor-cafe car holds down rear of No. 3 (right) while No. 33 from Zanesville pulls by the depot. Not shown but on hand is No. 32 from Cleveland. — *William L. Bennett.*

West Side Belt Railroad and coal lands south of Pittsburgh.

The West Side Belt connected with the WPT near the south portal of Mount Washington Tunnel. For a long time this road and the W&LE were the Terminal's only connections. The West Side Belt was the July 25, 1895, successor to the Little Saw Mill Run Railroad, an old 3-mile link between the village of Banksville and a junction with the Pittsburgh & Lake Erie at West End (about 1 mile west of downtown Pittsburgh on the south bank of the Ohio). In September 1902 the WSB opened a 5.6-mile line from Castle Shannon west to the former Little Saw Mill Run 1.4 miles east of West End. This was extended during 1903 to Clairton, a Monongahela River mill town 20.7 miles southeast of West End. Here Gould made his connection with the Union Railroad. In 1904 the WSB owned five locomotives — a pair of husky Pittsburgh 2-8-0's, an old 4-6-0, and two venerable switch engines.

Work on the 39.4 miles of track between Pittsburgh and the Ohio River was finished by the WPT contractors about June 1, 1904, and five days later a test run was made across the Mingo bridge. A special carrying Ramsey and Pittsburgh dignitaries to St. Louis opened the road to Mingo the following July 2. Three passenger trains were put on the next

day between Pittsburgh and Toledo (via Warrenton) which carried through cars for St. Louis and Chicago. After arrival at Mingo station, WPT westbounds backed down to the Wheeling's River Division on a long ramp. Eastbound trains had to back up the ramp, which had an ascending 2 per cent grade. This switchback arrangement ended with the opening of the Mingo-Pittsburgh Junction section of the WPT in November 1904.

From 1904 to 1909 the Wabash-Pittsburgh Terminal and West Side Belt were operated as an integral part of the Wheeling & Lake Erie. There were a dozen large mines on the two roads near Pittsburgh, and as late as 1915 coal and iron ore moving to Monongahela Valley mills accounted for 85 per cent of WPT tonnage. A modest amount of merchandise and perishable business was handled at the elevated terminal in Pittsburgh which could accommodate about 40 cars spotted.

Aside from six old engines bought by the PC&W for construction service, no equipment was owned by the WPT prior to 1909. The W&LE was obliged to furnish both cars and locomotives needed to operate the new railroad. Between 1902 and 1905 the Iron Cross bought 6600 freight cars, 25 passenger cars, and 96 locomotives at a cost in excess of 5.5 million dollars. Most of the freight cars were 40-ton wood gondolas, but in 1904 the W&LE bought its first all-steel cars — 500 self-clearing 50-ton hoppers — at a unit cost of $800. Built at the Wilmington works of AC&F, the passenger cars were delivered in time for the advent of Toledo-Pittsburgh service. All had vestibules and six-wheel trucks. The order included 15 coaches which seated 82 and weighed 50 tons, two 78-foot dining cars with service for 30, another parlor car, four combination baggage-smokers, and three baggage cars.

THE PITTSBURGH LIMITEDS

With the opening of the Wabash-Pittsburgh Terminal, the W&LE again quit its Cherry Street depot and ran its varnish into Toledo's Union Station in order to connect with Wabash trains. Three daily trains were operated each way between Toledo and Pittsburgh, a distance of 261 miles by way of Warrenton. The fastest eastbound was limited No. 16, scheduled to cover the 710-mile St. Louis-Pittsburgh run in 18 hours — an average speed of just under 40 mph. Both No. 16 and the Pennsylvania's *New York Limited* left St. Louis at 12:30 p.m., but the latter was due into Pittsburgh at 5:55 a.m., 35 minutes ahead of the Wabash-W&LE train. The Panhandle's train actually averaged only 35.5 mph but traveled 89 fewer miles than its new competitor. Leaving St. Louis, No. 16 had through coaches and sleepers for Pittsburgh; it picked up Pullmans at Montpelier brought from Chicago by Wabash 6. Stops were made to discharge Wabash fares west of Massillon, but after changing crews at Columbia, No. 16 ran nonstop over the 84 miles to Mingo.

Wabash-W&LE 6/16 vied with both PRR and B&O service for the overnight Chicago-Pittsburgh Pullman trade. Out of Dearborn Street station at 3 p.m., Wabash 6 offered 15½-hour service to Pittsburgh. B&O 6 left Chicago at 3:30 and stopped at Pittsburgh at 6:40 a.m., 10 minutes after No. 16. PRR's *Atlantic Express* also departed the Windy City at 3 p.m. and, having 26 fewer miles to run,

arrived in Pittsburgh some 40 minutes ahead of the Wabash flyer. The time saved, however, was of little consequence to a Pullman passenger. For those who were willing to pay an excess fare, the *Pennsylvania Limited* offered a 6 p.m. Chicago departure.

Complementing nocturnal No. 16, daylight limited No. 2 was operated by the W&LE from Toledo to Pittsburgh. This train cleared Union Station at 8:20 a.m. with chair cars and Pullmans brought out of St. Louis by Wabash 2 for Pittsburgh and Wheeling, and a dining car which was dropped at Dillonvale. No. 2's schedule called for a noonday stop at Navarre where connection was made with No. 32 out of Cleveland and No. 33, a Zanesville-Cleveland train. Pittsburgh-Toledo local No. 3 was supposed to clear Navarre ahead of No. 2's time, but more than once the quiet village was the scene of a four-way meet. St. Louis-Wheeling cars carried by No. 2 were transferred to an accommodation run at Warrenton. The other through eastbound was local No. 28, operated on a leisurely 9½-hour schedule between Toledo and Pittsburgh.

The fastest westbound limited, No. 19, left Pittsburgh at 7:30 p.m. and arrived at St. Louis at 1:44 the next afternoon. Assigned a chair car and Pullman for St. Louis and a Chicago sleeper, this train gave the Panhandle's *St. Louis Limited* a real run for its money but was no match for the Chicago-bound *Pennsylvania Limited* or the B&O's *Chicago Limited*. Train 15 handled the Wheeling-St. Louis sleeper, through St. Louis coach and Pullman from Pittsburgh, and diner from Dillonvale to Toledo. The W&LE offered parlor-car service between Cleveland and Wheeling but operated no through Cleveland-Pittsburgh equipment and made no effort to compete with the PRR between those cities.

LOCOMOTIVES OF THE WABASH ERA

The Wheeling's fleet of little Rome and Brooks 4-4-0's were hardly capable of coping with the con-

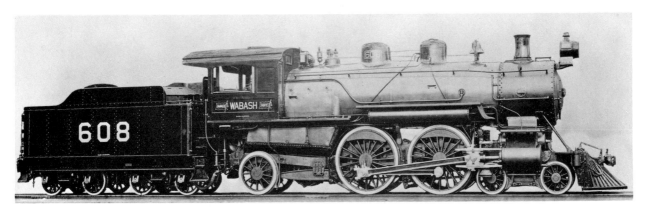

Wabash Atlantics with 80-inch drivers worked W&LE-WPT limiteds during 1904-1905 and served as pattern for Wheeling's 4-4-2's. — TRAINS *collection.*

During summer of 1903 contractors worked on masonry piers of **PT&W** Ohio River bridge at Mingo Junction. Completed Wellsburg or Ohio River tunnel through West Virginia escarpment is also shown. — *Wheeling & Lake Erie photo.*

sists and schedules of the Wabash limiteds, and in 1903 the road bought six husky 70-ton Baldwin Americans for them. Engines 63-68 (later 350-355 and 2201-2206) had 19½ x 26-inch cylinders, 72-inch drivers, and surprisingly big boilers. In theory, two of the D-4's could hold down all four limited schedules while the balance could handle the Pittsburgh-Toledo locals and connecting Cleveland trains. During 1904-1905, however, it was necessary to augment the Baldwins with Wabash 80-inch-drivered 4-4-2's then working the limiteds between Toledo and St. Louis. Six Atlantics similar in appearance to the Wabash engines were delivered to the WPT by Brooks in April 1905. These were numbered 2001-2006 and were transferred to the W&LE roster in the fall of 1905. The 95-ton E-1's boasted 79-inch drivers, 21 x 26-inch piston valve cylinders with Stephenson gear, carbon-arc headlights, and sheathed fireboxes.

Master Mechanic J. E. O'Hearne's familiarity with the compound Consolidation in his days on the Union Pacific brought the W&LE two such Pitts-

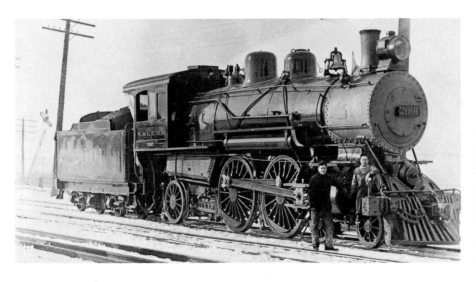

E-1 Atlantics were well designed, free steaming, and fast. Saturated 4-4-2's hauled Wheeling varnish for 33 years, were never radically modified. No. 2001 posed at Fremont shortly after 1909 return from 14-month tour on the Wabash. — *Collection of Robert H. Lorenz.*

Towering 104 feet above a Columbiana County meadow, PL&W's curved Elkton viaduct was one of Ohio's railroad wonders. Cost of rebuilding the frail structure ultimately doomed west end of the erstwhile W&LE subsidiary. — *Wheeling & Lake Erie photo.*

burgh-built engines in 1902. Two-cylinder cross-compounds 203-204 had a 22-inch high-pressure cylinder on the right side and a 33-inch low-pressure cylinder on the left. When the engines were working compound, exhaust steam from the high-pressure cylinder passed to a receiver pipe and was then supplied at the proper instant in the stroke to the steam chest of the low-pressure cylinder. Consequently, the cross-compounds had but two exhausts per revolution instead of the usual four. An inter-

Over-and-under four-cylinder Vauclain compounds 250-264 came from Baldwin in 1903. They were later renumbered in 700 and 3500 series and rebuilt as single-expansion engines. — *Collection of Robert V. Hubbard.*

cepting valve permitted single-expansion operation through admission of live steam to the LP cylinder in starting and any other time maximum tractive effort was needed. The H-4's failed to deliver the performance O'Hearne had hoped for largely because of insufficient LP cylinder volume resulting in unequal distribution of power and a brutal racking to machinery. They were converted to simple 20 x 28 machines in 1909.

In 1903 the W&LE bought 15 Baldwin-built Vauclain four-cylinder compounds, a design claimed superior to the cross-compound in terms of efficiency and uniformity of power output. The H-5 2-8-0's, numbered 250-264, weighed 95.5 tons, had a grate area of 47 square feet (more than half again that of the Pittsburghs), and developed 35,512 pounds tractive effort. One 15½-inch HP and one 26-inch LP cylinder cast integral with saddle were mounted on each side of the locomotive. The LP cylinder was located directly above the HP, and the piston-type valve was located in a cylindrical chamber in the saddle. Piston rods of both high- and low-pressure cylinders were coupled to a single heavy-duty crosshead. These "over-and-under" compounds were rated at 1000 tons on Hartland Hill and 700 tons on the Adena Railroad. Considered unsatisfactory performers, they were all rebuilt to single-expansion engines by the end of 1909.

The engines ordered by the WPT and bought by the W&LE in 1905 included 50 Consolidations built at Dunkirk and six Rogers 0-6-0's. Advent of the H-6 engines eased the motive power shortage that followed completion of the WPT and Adena Railroad. Rated at 41,360 pounds tractive effort, hogs 2101-2150 originally had 21 x 30-inch cylinders and 57-inch drivers. For a long time the H-6's were restricted by their 104-ton weight to Dillonvale-Huron employment where they were rated at 2850 tons in pairs on westbound coal.

THE LORAIN AND YOUNGSTOWN EXTENSIONS

Prior to his election as Ohio governor Myron Herrick had promoted an extension of the W&LE to Youngstown. This involved building a connection between Minerva and the Pittsburgh, Lisbon & Western at Lisbon in the name of the Lake Erie, Youngstown & Southern Railroad. Also planned was the purchase of the PL&W and the Youngstown & Southern Railway. When the Pittsburgh-Toledo Syndicate transferred its financial risk in the Pittsburgh road to the Wabash, the decision was made that the W&LE would finance and complete the Youngstown line.

A 25-mile east-west affair between Lisbon, O., and New Galilee, Pa., the Pittsburgh, Lisbon & Western was the 1896 successor to the Pittsburgh, Marion & Chicago Railway which in turn succeeded the

New York, Pittsburgh & Chicago Railway of 1881. In October 1902 the PL&W absorbed the Salem Railroad which connected Depot Street in Salem with the Erie's Lisbon branch at Washingtonville. Built by the Salem town council under a special act of the Ohio General Assembly, the 6.92-mile Salem Railroad owned one locomotive and seven cars. It was opened in September 1892 and ran four trains daily to Washingtonville. A receiver took over the Salem road's affairs in 1897, and four years later Herrick bought the road at foreclosure and delivered it to the PL&W.

The Youngstown & Southern Railway opened a 16-mile road from Youngstown to Columbiana in 1903 (electrified in 1907) and planned to eventually extend this south to the PL&W and East Liverpool. A branch was also to be built from Columbiana to the Salem branch at Washingtonville. The W&LE bought control of the PL&W for 1 million dollars in May 1904 and ultimately spent $570,000 on the Minerva-Lisbon connection. An apparent inability to buy out the Y&S stockholders caused the W&LE to scrap the Youngstown idea in 1906. That year the Salem branch was leased for 99 years to the Youngstown & Ohio River Railroad which later electrified it.*

Attracted by the National Tube complex at South Lorain, the Wheeling chartered the Lorain & West Virginia Railway on January 15, 1906. Two months later contractors began work on a 25.25-mile line extending generally north from Wellington to connections with the Nickel Plate and Lake Terminal at South Lorain. At Quarry Junction, 10 miles north of Wellington, a 2½-mile branch ran due west from the L&WV to stone quarries at Kipton. From a point midway between Kipton and Quarry Junction, a 7-mile line ran north to the huge sandstone quarries at South Amherst and a connection with the LS&MS main line 2 miles west of Amherst. The Quarry Branch terminated only a few rods west of the north-south roadbed of the long-abandoned gravity railroad connecting South Amherst with Oak Point.

Opened in September 1907, the L&WV main line was laid with 90-pound steel and had three 3800-foot passing tracks spaced 6 miles apart. At South Lorain were a wye, five-stall roundhouse, coal dock, and small yard. No passenger service was ever offered, and the W&LE operated the L&WV under a contract which provided for fixed rate divisions. As usual the Wheeling did not fare very well in the arrangement. On traffic moving from Lorain to the Wabash at Toledo, W&LE's share of the revenue

---

*The W&LE acquired the deed to the Salem Railroad in 1916 in exchange for giving up its PL&W stock. However, the Y&OR continued to use the road until its own demise in 1931. The Wheeling never operated its Salem branch and abandoned it in 1932.

Hulett steam-hydraulic machines with 15-ton buckets joined W&LE's conveyor-type rapid unloaders at Huron in 1914. Self-propelled Wellman ore bridge (left) was built in 1906 and served million-ton ore storage dock. — *Wheeling & Lake Erie photo.*

was only slightly higher than the L&WV's. At times a large amount of ore was unloaded at the Tube Works' Black River dock and hauled to mills in the Pittsburgh district. Although W&LE tracks were used for 103 of the 188 miles from South Lorain to Pittsburgh, the W&LE received only 41 per cent of the revenue. Under the 100-mile guarantee of 1904, the WPT got nearly the same slice. Since the Terminal was not earning its mortgage interest, it also claimed 25 per cent of the Wheeling's share.

From an operational standpoint, the L&WV was superior to the W&LE line between Huron and Wellington. With the South Lorain yard goat pushing as far as Seaman siding, an H-6 could handle 3300 tons of ore train on the L&WV, whereas two 2100's out of Huron were hard pressed to get 2300 tons past Hartland Hill. Since the Kipton and South Amherst quarries were already served by other rail-

roads, they produced very little traffic for the L&WV. At one time the W&LE considered extending the Quarry Branch over the 4-mile gravity grade to the mole at Oak Point, but the branch was abandoned and taken up about 1916.

COLLAPSE OF THE GOULD LINES

Financial panic in November 1907 brought an abrupt end to the long postwar era of prosperity and triggered the collapse of George Gould's empire. One by one the Gould lines went under; the first and most complete failure was the Wabash-Pittsburgh Terminal. From the beginning it had been obvious that a radical adjustment of that road's capitalization was inevitable. Since 1904 the WPT had barely covered expenses even though it had been spared the cost of equipment and had received healthy subsidies from the W&LE and Wabash. By 1908 the road

From 1902 to 1906 W&LE's Huron facilities consisted of a single slip with a rotary car dumper (left) and four Hulett-designed combination stiff-leg hoists and conveyors (right) for unloading ore. Photo was made in 1903. — *Wheeling & Lake Erie photo.*

This is how Brewster shops and terminal looked about 1912. From left to right: locomotive shop, storehouse, roundhouse, and ready tracks. — *Wheeling & Lake Erie photo.*

was some 3 million dollars in arrears in its first mortgage coupons. More than likely the Wabash never received a cent of interest on the Terminal bonds it held. Certain that bankruptcy could no longer be forestalled, the parent road brought about the appointment of receivers on May 28, 1908. This action canceled the traffic and rate contracts between the WPT, W&LE, and Wabash and made it necessary for each company to stand on its own legs.

Although its revenues had more than doubled between 1901 and 1907, the Wheeling was not long following the Terminal into receivership. Fixed charges had been inflated to the point where they accounted for more than 25 per cent of income and left precious little corporate surplus to get the road through traffic lulls. The most painful of the new capital obligations was an 8-million-dollar issue of 5 per cent gold notes maturing in August 1908. These had been sold in the fall of 1905 to pay for the 62 locomotives and 2000 cars built for the WPT and to provide funds for urgent physical improvements. Principal due was almost twice the W&LE's 1904 revenues, and the $400,000 annual interest was an amount equal to the deficit for fiscal 1908. Then the depression following the 1907 panic wiped out all hope that the notes could be refunded at their maturity. This certainty and a barren treasury forced the Wheeling to submit to receivership on June 8, 1908.

The fourth Wheeling & Lake Erie receivership was the longest and the least necessary — a paradox created by the road's growing traffic strength and an inability to design a reorganization plan acceptable to the bankers holding the matured three-year notes and the WPT security holders. Faced with ruinous losses through the overhaul of their own company, the latter were naturally opposed to any plan which diminished the value of W&LE stock — still one of the Terminal's prime assets. And they were not in a mood to accept assessments against the stock as a means of retiring the three-year notes. Thus, the 1905 notes and the interlocking relationship with the Wabash kept the Wheeling in receivership long after it was obvious that the road could live comfortably with its capitalization.

George Gould's chronic inability to give his operating men freedom of action brought a parting of company with Joseph Ramsey in 1905. Gould then installed Frederick A. Delano at the head of the Wabash and Wheeling, and Delano tapped B. A. Worthington to manage the W&LE and affiliated lines. This move proved beneficial to the Iron Cross both before and after the onset of receivership, for Worthington was a practical railroad man who recognized the road's basic weaknesses and worked effectively to overcome them. During his seven years as W&LE manager and receiver, Worthington carried out many improvement programs that increased the road's traffic capacity.

Shortly after Worthington joined the W&LE in June 1905, surveying parties set out to locate a new low-grade line to eliminate the long 1 per cent grades on both sides of Sippo Summit. A 22-mile cutoff line was projected south of the Toledo Division between Orrville and Bolivar bypassing Massillon and Navarre by way of the Sugar Creek valley. The distance between Orrville and Bolivar was 6.6 miles shorter via the cutoff, and the new line had no grade heavier than .4 per cent compensated. One other problem partially solved by the cutoff was the unpredictable Tuscarawas River. The old main line crossed the Tusc many times between Massillon and Bolivar and was periodically subjected to closure and heavy damage by floodwaters.

A resolution was made to build the new line without delay, and the Sugar Creek & Northern Railroad was formed for that purpose on December 28, 1905. Part of the SC&N project included the building of a new 1500-car hump yard to replace and augment crowded Columbia Yard at Massillon and Canton

W&LE depot-office building at Brewster, built in 1914. — *Wheeling & Lake Erie photo.*

Yard, neither of which could be expanded. The site chosen was a 625-acre tract of level farmland on a 4-mile tangent west of the Cleveland Division crossing at Harmon. Here the W&LE would also locate its permanent locomotive shops, principal engine terminal, and operational headquarters. By the end of 1906 the yard had been graded and a land company had platted an adjoining townsite called Brewster. About 1.2 million dollars had been spent on the Brewster cutoff and yard by December 1907, when all work was suspended owing to the stringent money market.

Prior to the panic Worthington had also undertaken an ambitious program of grade reduction and realignment on the Toledo Division west of Orrville and east of Bolivar. Opposing grades were to be no heavier than .4 per cent westbound and .5 per cent eastbound between Hartland and Jewett. This work was completed by 1912, along with major reductions to the worst grades west of Norwalk and east of Rexford. Going up to Rexford, westbound hogs now overcame .7 instead of 1.6 per cent. Also by 1912, all the badly worn 70-pound rail in the main track between Huron Junction and Warrenton was replaced with new 90-pound steel permitting the use of the heaviest classes of locomotives across that territory.

Dock facilities at Huron were expanded and the new South Huron supporting yard was built during 1906-1907. Four steam-operated Hulett conveyor-type "rapid-unloaders" were installed at the ore dock and a second McMyler car dumper was built adjacent to the coal slip. Dock area between the two slips was now utilized for ore storage, and a 10-ton Wellman ore bridge 72 feet high, 396 feet long, and with a 1300-foot runway was installed there in 1906. In 1907 a new car dumper was also set up on the riverfront dock at Cleveland.

On August 19, 1908, the locomotive shops at Norwalk were destroyed by fire, prompting Worthington to sell $3,359,000 in receiver's certificates to finance the rapid completion of the SC&N and Brewster facilities. Work was resumed at the end of 1908, and the cutoff and yard were opened on August 1, 1909. About two weeks later the first locomotives were serviced at Brewster. At the time, the 26-stall roundhouse, powerhouse, and locomotive backshop were still under construction. Temporarily, power was obtained from an old stationary engine, and locomotives were coaled with a clamshell.

Pending completion of Brewster shop, the 20-stall Norwalk roundhouse was converted to an erecting shop. This and the Canton shop could handle routine repairs to about 60 per cent of the Wheeling's 206 locomotives. The others, at the rate of three to five per month, were sent to the Lima Locomotive & Machine Works for shopping. After the Brewster roundhouse was finished, the 10-staller at Columbia was closed and the 6.56 miles of former main line between Bolivar and Navarre was abandoned. To accommodate train and engine crews and other employees, the W&LE ran 11 daily trains between Massillon and Brewster. Usually made up of an engine and two coaches, the trains were dubbed "hoodle-

Warrenton depot was so vulnerable to high water that agent was furnished a rowboat for emergencies. Ohio River and West Virginia escarpment form backdrop for the deserted depot. — *Collection of Robert V. Hubbard.*

bugs." A shop train also operated between Canton and Brewster.

The Brewster locomotive shop was formally opened by an elaborate ceremony on July 4, 1910. One 530 x 229-foot steel and brick building contained erecting, boiler, machine, blacksmith, and other shop departments. A showpiece in its day, the backshop had 18 bays, 38 erecting pits, a 150-ton overhead crane, electric lighting and power, and forced air heating. Nearby was a three-story storehouse and a powerhouse with stoker-fired boilers. A car shop was added to the complex in 1912, and two years later W&LE built a large depot and office building on Wabash Avenue, Brewster's main street.

EARLY YEARS OF THE DUNCAN REGIME

After four years as the Wheeling's receiver, B. A. Worthington yielded the role to William McKinley Duncan in June 1912. The nephew and namesake of the slain president had been a member of a prominent Cleveland law firm before joining the W&LE as its general attorney. Until his death in 1945 he ruled the Iron Cross in much the same implacably conservative manner that he would have managed a bank or a client's estate. Duncan's approach to railroading tolerated additions and betterments only when they guaranteed a healthy return on investment. Hence the Wheeling became an increasingly profitable institution. Indeed, the little road managed to pay earned dividends even during the depression of the 1930's. On the other side of the coin were the W&LE's unpainted buildings, one of the busiest unsignaled main lines in America, and an employee casualty rate that belonged in the 19th century. Under Duncan there were many contrasting facets to the Wheeling personality. Here was a railroad that offered saturated Atlantics and hostess-staffed wood-underframe parlor cars on the one hand and the last word in roller-bearing switch engines on the other.

During Duncan's first year as receiver, the W&LE's revenues soared to more than 7.8 million dollars, and for the fifth consecutive year the road showed a net profit. Traffic density between Brewster and Pittsburgh Junction reached 8 million tons per mile, "greatest of any single-track railroad in operation." The combined volume of coal, ore, and steel carried reached a new high of 7.5 million tons. With more Hulett unloading machines installed at Huron during 1913-1914, ore tonnage nearly matched the amount of coal dumped at the port, permitting virtually a 100 per cent backhaul. After clearing nearly a million dollars in 1912, however, the W&LE could do no better than post a net deficit of $503,141.39 between January 1913 and April 1915. This showing resulted from a series of natural and man-made calamities and served to obscure the Wheeling's improving status.

Throughout its early history, the Iron Cross was plagued with fires, floods, washouts, slides, and even tornados. Few springs passed without the Ohio submerging much of the River Division and the Tuscarawas visiting havoc upon the Toledo Division between Massillon and Valley Junction. Ice gorges recurrently disrupted west end operation by taking spans out of the Maumee bridge and forcing the

Muskingum River swept away most of the Wheeling's facilities at Zanesville in March 1913. Officials survey remnants of the yard after the water has receded. — *W&LE photo.*

Sandusky over its banks at Fremont. Before flood control dams were built in the 1930's the rivers and creeks of eastern Ohio delivered unbelievable destruction to railroads whenever heavy rains came before the frost was out of the ground. The most memorable of such disasters occurred during the last week of March 1913, barely 60 days after what may have been the worst blizzard in Ohio history.

Floods beginning on March 24, 1913, forced the W&LE to suspend service over much of its system for as long as a month. Full operations were not restored until April 29. Eighteen permanent bridges were destroyed, scores of culverts and trestles were washed away, and washouts cut the road in hundreds of other places. Sugar Creek carried off four

almost new steel bridges on the "flood-proof" Brewster cutoff. The Tuscarawas destroyed two major spans at Bolivar and cut the Cleveland Division in two by taking out a bridge at Navarre. Short Creek's raging torrent left no trace of eight bridges in a 10-mile stretch between Rexford and Warrenton. The Muskingum did the most complete job of destruction, leaving little of the Wheeling's yard, depot, coal dock, and roundhouse at Zanesville. Only the three-year-old freighthouse was left standing, and this had to be completely rebuilt. There was heavy damage even on the comparatively level west end. Weakened by the flooded Black River, bridge 83-B at Wellington collapsed under Consol 2140 on March 25. Three men drowned and the engine was

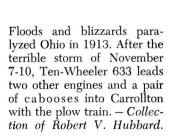

Floods and blizzards paralyzed Ohio in 1913. After the terrible storm of November 7-10, Ten-Wheeler 633 leads two other engines and a pair of cabooses into Carrollton with the plow train. — *Collection of Robert V. Hubbard.*

nearly demolished. Later it was rebuilt at Brewster.

Before the natural devastation of 1913 could be repaired, a strike closed all the mines on the Iron Cross on April 1, 1914. This lasted until May 11, 1915, and brought about generally depressed business conditions. Coal hauled over the W&LE during fiscal 1915 amounted to less than half the 1913 tonnage, and ore traffic was off 30 per cent. In an effort to avoid defaulting on the first mortgage, Duncan closed the W&LE's shops in September 1914. Subsequently the courts ordered the shops reopened and the receiver had to borrow the money to pay the mortgage coupons.

The first radical changes in the Wheeling's passenger schedules after the WPT opened came in 1906. Cleveland trains 32 and 35 were terminated at Wheeling instead of Zanesville, and Pittsburgh-St. Louis limited No. 19 and Toledo-Pittsburgh local No. 28 were permanently withdrawn. Limiteds 5 and 6 (formerly 15 and 16) were still operated in connection with Wabash trains but now carried only Chicago Pullmans and chair cars. Sleepers between St. Louis and Pittsburgh were handled by W&LE trains 2 and 3, but the latter's 25½-hour through schedule was a good indication that the Wabash was losing the competitive struggle with the Panhandle. By 1909 No. 6 terminated at Wheeling instead of Pittsburgh.

During the 1913-1915 ordeal, remaining through service to Pittsburgh was discontinued and the daily schedule between Harmon and Toledo was reduced to one train each way. Nos. 3 and 6 now ran between Cherry Street and Wheeling via the Brewster cutoff and covered their 216.4-mile daylight runs in 8 hours. WPT No. 3 was scheduled out of Pittsburgh at 6:25 a.m. and was due to reach Jewett at 8:47, 8 minutes ahead of W&LE No. 3 out of Wheeling. The latter's 3:40 p.m. Toledo arrival offered connecting 9-hour 15-minute service — less than a half hour longer than No. 3's time in the days when it originated at Pittsburgh — but there was no through car operation and no corresponding eastbound service.

Despite strong competition from the B&O and the Northern Ohio interurban line, the Wheeling's most lucrative passenger trains were the four running each way between Cleveland and Canton. One regular run left Cleveland in December 1915 with 1021 fare-paying passengers, and the conductor had to stop the train outside Canton to collect all the tickets. As late as 1916 three trains still ran from Chagrin Falls to meet Cleveland-Canton flyers at Falls Junction. Since 1910 the W&LE had operated morning and afternoon trains each way over the Adena Railroad connecting with mainline trains for Toledo, Wheeling, Cleveland, and Steubenville. The branch runs carried the mails to St. Clairsville and stopped at the mines, most of which were remote to anything resembling a good road.

Beginning about 1909 the W&LE provided through service between Sherrodsville, Canton, and Cleveland via Carrollton. Northbound No. 31 made a 4½-hour early morning run to Cleveland and returned to Sherrodsville in the early evening as No. 30. Usually these trains were powered by old Rome and Brooks 4-4-0's that owed their extended lon-

Mahoning Street engine terminal in Cleveland as it appeared in 1916. Elevated rail line behind roundhouse belongs to Erie. Slide-valve yard goat heads for Ontario Street depot with abundance of riders. — *Wheeling & Lake Erie photo.*

gevity to light rails and Robertsville tunnel's narrow-gauge clearances. Occasionally the D-2's and D-3's were spelled by the 2751, a Ten-Wheeler with light axle loading built by Brooks in 1899 for the LS&MS. The solitary G-5 came to the W&LE in 1917 with the Coshocton, Otsego & Eastern.*

By the time Duncan relieved Worthington, some 15 to 20 plans of reorganization had been proposed and the courts had unsuccessfully tried to sell the W&LE four times. WPT bondholders dominated the reorganization committee and wanted to levy huge assessments against the W&LE stocks in hopes of squeezing out the minority shareholders. This strategy created two stockholders protective committees — one headed by W. G. Mather and the other by Joseph Ramsey, the long-deposed Gould lieutenant. Both groups tried desperately to lift the receivership, but it was soon obvious that reorganization of the W&LE and WPT would have to be simultaneous events effected on terms acceptable to everyone involved.

Ironically, the 1914-1915 Ohio coal strike promoted the ultimate recovery of the Wheeling by creating increased demand for coal mined on the Terminal. With improved earnings, the prospect of successfully operating that road brightened. Purchased at foreclosure by the reorganization committee, the WPT was turned over to the newly created Pittsburgh & West Virginia Railway in January 1917. The reorganization was unusually drastic, with the equity of the sole stockholder (Wabash) and the second-mortgage bondholders wiped out completely. Those investors willing to pay a $300 assessment for each $1000 first mortgage bond held received $1300 in P&WV stocks plus $628 in W&LE stocks that had reposed in the WPT treasury. Once the WPT plan was in motion, the reorganization of the W&LE proved a simple business. At midnight on December 31, 1916, Duncan turned over the Iron Cross to the new Wheeling & Lake Erie Railway. None of the road's securities were disturbed and a new 11.5-million-dollar issue of 7 per cent prior-lien stock was given to the bankers holding the long-matured gold notes of 1905.

Kuhn, Loeb & Company held the bulk of the new prior-lien shares which conferred the right to control the W&LE for five years and thereafter if the dividend was in arrears. Leonor F. Loree headed the new board and looked after Kuhn-Loeb's interests, and Duncan was elected the W&LE's president. Directors included Ohio industrialists Frank Seiberling, John Willys, and Thomas Grasselli. In May 1917 Kuhn-Loeb sold its proprietary interest to

John D. Rockefeller who replaced Loree with Carl R. Gray.

STEEL, HIGHBALLS, AND STRIP MINES

A phenomenal change in the Wheeling's personality came with post-receivership expansion of the time freight service introduced during the Wabash era. The automotive industry's rapid growth and concentration at Detroit and other Michigan cities transformed the Iron Cross from a ne'er-do-well coal road to a notably proficient mover of manufactured goods. By 1924 manufactures had replaced coal as the road's leading tonnage commodity and four years later exceeded coal and ore combined. Steel tonnage alone jumped from 573,000 to 2.3 million during the first decade following reorganization. The Wheeling during this period feasted on an incredible flow of goods moving from steel mills, foundries, rubber plants, and machine shops of eastern Ohio to the insatiable assembly lines of Ford, Packard, Dodge Brothers, and other auto manufacturers.

Development of neighboring Canton and Massillon as centers of alloy steel production spurred the metamorphosis of the Wheeling & Lake Erie. In 1902 the Timken brothers had established a plant at Canton to produce their patented tapered roller bearings for carriage and wagon axles. By 1916 the Timken firm had added a steel and tube mill with electric furnaces and was the world's premier producer of roller bearings and seamless alloy tubing. A large steel mill was built adjacent to the Wheeling's Columbia Yard at Massillon by a predecessor of Republic Steel. United Furnace, another forerunner of Republic, erected a huge steel-making plant on Canton's east side in 1916. United, served by a new 3-mile W&LE belt line, was long the largest producer of vanadium-alloy steel in the U.S. The firm had developed this extra-strength lightweight metal for Henry Ford, and much of its production moved toward the Rouge complex over W&LE rails.

After World War I Canton's shipments of steel, roller bearings, street-lighting poles, and paving bricks surpassed the capacity of local W&LE facilities. During 1920-1921 the road built two new yards and an engine terminal with 10-stall roundhouse at Gambrinus, on Canton's southwest side. Adjoining tracts of farmland were bought for industrial development. Timken subsequently built another steel mill on one 177-acre parcel, and a large oil refinery ultimately graced the Gambrinus landscape.

Michigan-bound steel rolled west behind W&LE locomotives from the Pittsburgh, Cleveland, Youngstown, and Steubenville-Wheeling districts as well as from Canton-Massillon. At Cleveland the Wheel-

*The Coshocton, Otsego & Eastern Railroad was a 2.63-mile coal road opened about 1909 and purchased by the W&LE in July 1917. It connected the Cleveland Division south of Coshocton with the Warwick Mine at Coal Valley.

Blast furnaces of Republic Steel's Cleveland Furnace works form a backdrop for a transfer run at Belt Line Junction. This was one of 15 iron and steel plants served by the Wheeling & Lake Erie.

ing served three major steel plants — Corrigan-McKinney, Otis, and Cleveland Furnace. By allowing the Big Four to use its tracks to reach these mills, the W&LE gained operating rights over that road from the Cleveland Belt to Wellington, 32.14 miles. The distance between Cleveland and Homestead Yard at Toledo via the Big Four was only 117 miles compared with 205 by way of Canton and Brewster. Now able to offer Cleveland shippers expedited schedules to the west, the W&LE ran daily time freights in both directions over the new route. The first Toledo highball was operated on February 16, 1914, and left Cleveland behind Consol 2143.

Virtually all rail traffic moving from Ohio and western Pennsylvania to Detroit, Flint, and Pontiac had to pass through Toledo, a circumstance that was immensely beneficial to the Wheeling. Only the New York Central ran through Toledo and its huge Air Line Junction yards were a classic bottleneck. Most of the railroads terminating at Toledo relied heavily on the belt line around the city to transfer through cars to connections. Congestion at Toledo became so serious that delays there of 12 to 20 hours in transit were routine. As the automotive market boomed, Detroit demanded faster and more dependable handling of traffic to and from its plants. Failure of a shipment to arrive on schedule could close down an assembly line with heavy losses of production and sales.

One of the Wheeling's prime assets was an ability to expedite shipments through the Toledo bottleneck faster than its competitors. Direct connections were maintained with the Wabash, NYC, and B&O by way of the Toledo Belt and with the Ann Arbor and Detroit & Toledo Shore Line at Manhattan Junction. Wheeling pullers ran directly to the Detroit, Toledo & Ironton's Temperance Yard over 5 miles of the AA and Toledo Terminal. Ann Arbor tracks were also used to reach the Michigan Central's North Toledo Yard and the Pere Marquette's Ottawa Yard.

By 1926 the W&LE was operating seven daily time freights into Toledo. Three were overnight runs originated at Cleveland, Youngstown, and Canton. Train 186/99, the *Knickerbocker West*, departed Gambrinus Yard at 9 p.m., filled out at Brewster with cars brought out of Zanesville by time freight 185, and was due into Homestead at 5 a.m. The *Overland West*, No. 87, left Cleveland about 10 p.m. and followed No. 99 into Toledo. As suggested by its name, this fast freight was built around

Westbound Pittsburgh-Toledo time freight hurries toward P&WV's Ohio River crossing behind W&LE 2-8-2 6020. Wheeling's development as bridge line was spurred by growth of auto industry and extension of P&WV to Connellsville. — *John J. Young Jr.*

carloads headed for the Willys plant at Toledo. Behind the *Overland* came No. 77, scheduled to leave Youngstown at 10:30 p.m. This highball used Erie tracks from Youngstown to Creston, 78 miles, and W&LE rails from Creston to Toledo, 102 miles. Erie and Wheeling engines were pooled and operated all the way through, but crews were changed at Creston. Loads from the three overnight fast freights consigned to Packard, Chrysler, and Hupp were delivered by puller to the Michigan Central in time to make manifest MC-10 which had an advertised 6:30 p.m. arrival at Palmer Yard in Detroit. Ford loads forwarded to Temperance Yard by 3 p.m. were in Dearborn by 7:30 p.m.; traffic routed to Detroit, Flint, and Pontiac via Shore Line and Grand Trunk Western was moving out of Toledo by mid-afternoon.

Westbound fast freight 95 was operated in three sections and connected with a Wabash manifest with the same number. Pittsburgh departures for the 95's were at 10 p.m., 1 a.m., and 2:45 a.m. and advertised schedules allowed 14 hours for the 232 mile runs. W&LE and P&WV crews and equipment were pooled and ran through from Rook to Brewster, 102.7 miles. Second 95 filled out with westbound freight brought from Mingo and Terminal Junction by First and Second 85. Upon arrival at Homestead the 95's were broken up and dispatched

by pullers to the Wabash, MC, DT&I, PM, and D&TSL. Wabash 95, due to leave Toledo at 11 p.m., offered Chicago delivery at 8 p.m. the next day. Michigan Central MC-8, out of North Toledo at 11 p.m., arrived at Detroit's Davison Yard by 5 a.m. with cars consigned to Chrysler, Hudson, Paige, Maxwell, Liberty, and other auto plants. The PM had an 11:30 p.m. departure with 30-hour service to Milwaukee and morning deliveries at Flint. Both Shore Line and DT&I ran trains off the Wheeling 95's which arrived at Detroit before dawn.

The premier eastbound freight was No. 92 which ran off Wabash 92 and afforded 36-hour service between Chicago and Pittsburgh. Perishable loads for Akron were set off for the AC&Y at Spencer, and cars bound for Mingo were switched out for No. 88 at Brewster. Fast freight 84, scheduled to leave Toledo at 4 p.m. (2 hours behind No. 92), ran through to Terminal Junction with hot traffic for the Wheeling area and Baltimore. Both 84 and 92 were due at their respective termini at 6:15 a.m. Canton loads and Pittsburgh cars received at Toledo too late to make No. 92 were handled by No. 98, the *Knickerbocker East*. This run tied up at Gambrinus but connected with 192/2nd 92 — the 11-hour overnight Cleveland-Pittsburgh manifest. *Overland East*, the Cleveland highball, left Toledo about 9 p.m. and filled out with livestock and perishable

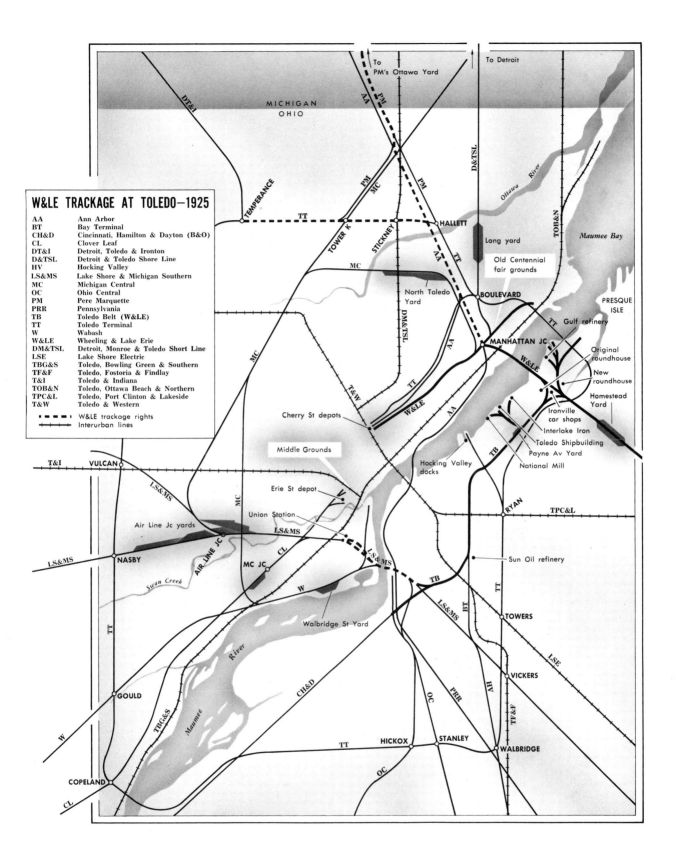

freight from the Nickel Plate at Bellevue. The day's sixth and final fast freight out of Toledo was No. 78, the Erie run, operating on a 10 p.m.-10:30 a.m. schedule to Youngstown. Through 14-hour service between Toledo and Zanesville was provided by the combination of time freights 82 and 184, while

trains 192 and 188 gave overnight delivery from Cleveland to Zanesville.

After the 1914-1915 strike, coal tonnage hauled by the W&LE increased rapidly, reaching a new high of more than 6 million tons in 1918. Until 1932 the road's coal traffic normally ran between 5 and

With bell tolling, an H-6b horses iron ore through Yorkville on the way to Martin's Ferry. The 4300's were rebuilt WPT Consols. After 1918, W&LE numbers indicated an engine's rated tractive effort. Classification was based on cylinder diameter. — *John J. Young Jr.*

7 million tons annually. Increased production in the No. 8 district was promoted by the growing use of electricity and the introduction of a cheap method of mining. Beginning in 1915 non-union operators began using steam shovels to strip away soil and rock in order to expose and mine the No. 8 seam. Huge trenches were cut along hillsides as the shovels followed the seam across Harrison and Jefferson counties. By 1917 the W&LE served

four large stripping operations west of Adena and that year built a 3-mile branch to a pair of new strip mines north of Hurford. Also in 1917, the road opened the Adena, Cadiz & New Athens Railway organized in 1914 to tap promising coal lands west of Adena in Harrison County. Within five years there were six major mines on the 5.72-mile AC&NA, largest of which was operated by the Goodyear Tire & Rubber Company. Coal from this mine moved

Georgia Tramps were built by Baldwin for Atlanta, Birmingham & Atlantic. D-5 2308 worked Cleveland Division passenger trains from 1920 to 1929. — *Collection of Everett L. DeGolyer Jr.*

344

Logrollers were first superheated W&LE engines. They were bought by Receiver Duncan from Alco in 1913. No. 2409 takes a ride on Brewster turntable in 1915.—*W&LE photo.*

Mallet compounds 8401-8420 were Brooks built in 1917 for drags between Brewster and Huron. They had Street stokers, outside ashpan hoppers, and Lackawanna-style pilots. — *Wheeling & Lake Erie photo.*

Green-painted Decapods built for Russia by Alco were rented to railroads for $45 per day by U. S. Government. U. S. 1081 (shown as DT&I 308) was one of 15 such 25 x 28's on W&LE during 1918-1919. — *Collection of Robert V. Hubbard.*

En route to Steubenville, train 102 rattles across Indian Cross Creek at Mingo Junction. Gas-electric M-101, which had MCB-3 trucks with Timken roller bearings, was less than a year out of Brill's Philadelphia plant. — *Wheeling & Lake Erie photo.*

over the W&LE to Mogadore where it was transferred to the Akron, Canton & Youngstown for Akron delivery. From its 1912 opening to about 1919, the AC&Y was operated for all practical purposes as part of the W&LE.

The mines between Rexford and Warrenton, as well as those on the Adena Railroad and AC&NA, were always serviced by mine runs operated out of Pine Valley. Empties for the tipples and outbound loads were concentrated at Adena and at Herrick, a small yard between Adena and Long Run. Increased mining activity west of Adena brought the 1920-1921 construction of new facilities at Jewett. Included were yards holding 600 cars and a five-stall roundhouse. Westbound coal drags could now be dispatched directly from Jewett with maximum tonnage, and the helpers formerly required between Adena and Rexford were eliminated. Jewett's new facilities were also used by P&WV local freight and passenger trains.

LOGROLLERS, MALLETS, AND MIKES

During the 1908-1916 receivership the only new locomotives added to the W&LE roster were 20 super-Consolidations built by Alco's Schenectady works in 1913. Numbered 2401-2420 (later 6051-6070) and classed H-10, these hogs had the 57-inch drivers of the 1905 H-6, coupled with 26 x 30-inch cylinders and Walschaerts valve gear. The H-10's, known to W&LE enginemen as Logrollers, were the first superheated engines on the road and weighed 133 tons. Their 66.6-square-foot grate must have been a challenge for any fireman, and their rated tractive effort of 56,000 pounds represented as much as a one-third increase over earlier 2-8-0's in per-unit hauling power.

Announcements of the appointment of George Durham as W&LE superintendent of motive power and of A. R. Ayers to a similar Nickel Plate post appeared on the same page of the September 29, 1916, *Railway Age Gazette.* The careers of the two men had many parallels in the years that followed. Each altered the motive power personality of his road and each was charged with the management of his railroad through the decisive eras of prosperity, depression, and war. Durham, 41, came to the Wheeling from the Lackawanna, where he was master mechanic at Scranton. Prior to that assignment he had held a variety of mechanical jobs on the Louisville & Nashville. As soon as the end of the long receivership was assured, the new S.M.P. began to upgrade the Wheeling's freight power. During the winter of 1916-1917 ten of the H-6 2-8-0's were rebuilt at Alco's Pittsburgh Works with new 22½ x 28-inch cylinders, Baker valve gear, and firetube superheaters. Ten more were similarly modified at Brewster during the last half of 1917. The rebuilds were classed H-6b and ultimately renumbered 4301-4320. They were used for many years on fast freights between Brewster and Rook.

During 1913-1914 the W&LE tried out a pair of Mallet articulated compound locomotives belonging to the West Side Belt. Mallets proved particularly valuable to hill-country tonnage haulers such as the Wheeling because they afforded greatly increased tractive effort without any appreciable

Wheeling-bound No. 32 pauses at Canton in 1926 after bringing three carloads of W&LE veterans from Cleveland for second annual reunion. Flag-draped depot built by narrow-gauge Connotton Valley in 1881 was torn down in 1938. — *Wheeling & Lake Erie photo.*

increase in axle loading or rigid wheelbase. In addition, the compound use of steam worked for increased efficiency by making a pound of coal do more work. Multiple expansion of steam proved a more practical matter with the Mallet than it had with early two-cylinder machines.

The Mallet had a very large boiler and furnace supported by two independent engines each with its own frame, cylinders, drivers, and machinery. The rear engine was carried in a frame rigidly attached to the boiler in the usual manner, whereas the forward engine was secured only to the rear frame by a hinged connection and could move radially beneath the boiler. Although not actually connected to the boiler, the forward engine helped support it with sliding bearings. Thus, while traversing curves, the lead engine could move out of alignment with the rear engine. Both high-pressure cylinders of the Mallet were mounted on the rear engine; the low-pressure cylinders drove the forward machine. Steam exhausted from the rear cylinders passed into a receiver pipe with flexible joints which supplied the forward cylinders when working compound. Like the cross-compound and Vauclain, the Mallet had an intercepting valve which permitted single-expansion operation when required.

George Durham's enthusiasm for the Mallet was based on the certainty that it would eliminate doubleheading on the Wheeling's worst tonnage grades. Before the end of 1916 the road had ordered 20 2-6-6-2's from Brooks to replace Logrollers working ore and coal drags between Brewster and Huron. I-2's 800-819 (later 8401-8420) were delivered in the spring of 1917. They had huge 90-inch-diameter straight-top inverted slope boilers with 99.2-square-foot grate fired by a Street Type C stoker. All cylinders had piston valves and both engines had Baker valve gear. Cylinder diameter was 25½ inches for the HP and 39 inches for the LP, and the length of stroke of both engines was 32 inches. Drivers were 63-inches and each driving axle carried 30 tons, as in the case of the H-10. Total engine weight in working order was 435,000 pounds. The new W&LE Mallets came from Dunkirk with outside-hopper-type ashpans, Cole trailing truck, and Lackawanna-style pilots.

Originally the I-2's had working steam pressure of 200 pounds and rated tractive effort of 80,484 pounds. Ultimately, steam pressure was raised to

347

Only bread hampers, milk cans, and the agent await morning arrival of Zanesville-Toledo mail at Dundee in 1927. Last passenger train stopped here in 1932. — *W&LE photo*.

Toledo businessmen watch No. 4 leave Homestead for the last time on May 31, 1932. They had ridden motor cars from Cherry Street depot, needed autos to get back to town. — *Collection of Robert V. Hubbard.*

220 pounds producing a tractive rating of 88,382 pounds. Regularly assigned to coal and ore duty on the 80-mile Brewster-Huron territory, the Mallets could take 61 loads of ore (4300 tons) unassisted up Hartland Hill and average 17 mph between terminals. With an H-6 pusher from Milan to Hartland, the displaced Logrollers had a maximum rating of 3065 tons on this run.

During World War I increased traffic and the USRA brought many foreign locomotives to W&LE rails. Four Nickel Plate P class 4-6-0's went into service on the road the day the Government took over, and by July 1918 there were 31 leased engines on the property. Included were a batch of U.S.-owned Alco 2-10-0's built for Russia but confiscated because of international complications. All told, 15 green Decapods worked the Iron Cross between March 23, 1918, and October 7, 1919.

Mikado-type engines first appeared on the Wheeling on May 5, 1918, in the form of Great Northern 3103, 3104, and 3105 — fresh from Baldwin's Eddystone works. These were later joined by GN 3106 and 3110 and AT&SF 3188-3192, also Baldwin-built in April 1918 and diverted to the W&LE on their way west. The 10 2-8-2's labored on the road throughout the summer of 1918 and were released when the W&LE received the first USRA heavy Mikados in October. Built at Dunkirk, 6001-6020 had 27 x 32-inch cylinders and 63-inch drivers. They weighed 321,678 pounds and developed 59,850 pounds tractive effort. The M-1's were outstanding locomotives and did a highly creditable job handling the Cleveland, Youngstown, and Canton highballs. In later years M-1's replaced H-6b's on Brewster-Rook time freights.

Other locomotives permanently assigned by the USRA to the W&LE included five eight-coupled class C-1 switchers built at Pittsburgh in 1918 and 10 2-6-6-2's outshopped by Baldwin in 1919. Numbered 5101-5105, the 0-8-0's were standard 25 x 28 USRA's. I-3 Mallets 8001-8010 had essentially the same adhesive weight as the 1917 engines but smaller cylinders (23-inch HP and 35-inch LP), 57-inch drivers, and tractive rating of 80,300 pounds. Original I-3 equipment included electric headlight, illuminated number boards ahead of the stack, Duplex stoker, and air pumps mounted on the smokebox door.

Decline of Passenger Service

More than anything else, good roads and the serviceable low-priced automobile were responsible for the Wheeling's post-World War I freight traffic boom. Their advent, of course, had the opposite effect on the road's passenger business which was almost entirely local and therefore particularly vulnerable. Passenger revenues hit an all-time peak in 1921, after which there was a sharp and persistent decline. During the decade ending in 1931 receipts from passengers, mail, express, and milk plummeted from $1,126,867 to $171,582. By 1926 the Adena and Huron branches had joined the L&WV and AC&NA as freight-only operations, and service to Chagrin Falls and Zanesville had been reduced to a single round trip. About 1927 Nos. 30 and 31 were discontinued south of Canton and travelers to Carrollton had to ride a combine at the end of the local freight.

After 1926 trains 33 and 34 ran to Wheeling instead of Zanesville and were met at Harmon by Nos. 3 and 4, now operated from Toledo to Zanesville. Routed by way of Massillon, the 3 and 4 required 9 hours to cover their new 205½-mile runs. The Parlor Car Route's only steel passenger stock — and the only new passenger equipment bought after 1904 — were three 60-foot gas-electric combines delivered by Brill early in 1927. These had a six-cylinder 250 h.p. gasoline engine and a pair of Westinghouse motors driving the axles of the lead MCB-3 truck. M-101 originally had a baggage compartment and seated 46. M-102 and M-103 were 44-passenger units with R.P.O. compartments. They were bought to replace steam-powered varnish on Nos. 3 and 4 between Toledo and Zanesville. M-101's original assignment was trains 5 and 6 between Jewett and Steubenville. Five open-platform baggage-smokers were rebuilt in 1927 with roller bearings, storage batteries, and hot water heaters and were used as gas-electric trailers. They proved too much for M-102 and M-103 to pull south of Harmon, and during 1930-1931 Nos. 3 and 4 were terminated at Brewster. During that period the W&LE restored steam-powered parlor-car trains between Cleveland and Zanesville. After being rebuilt in 1931, the noisy motor cars were once again operated through from Toledo to Zanesville and the Cleveland trains were withdrawn.

During 1931-1932 the Wheeling discontinued all parlor-car service and withdrew all passenger accommodations except for a single run each way between Cleveland and Wheeling and the doodlebug between Massillon and Brewster. Casualties included mixed service to Chagrin Falls and Carrollton and the Steubenville connections. The graveyard run between Toledo and Zanesville came on May 31, 1932. Train No. 3, composed of motor cars M-101 and M-102 and a baggage car, left Cherry Street at 2:15 p.m. with Toledo's vice-mayor and more than 100 businessmen who had paid 28 cents for the privilege of riding the last run as far as Homestead Yard. Aboard too was J. F. Sullivan who had fired the first run out of Toledo a half century before.

From 1932 to 1938 the Wheeling continued to

operate trains 32 and 35 between Cleveland, Canton and Wheeling. No. 32 left Commercial Road* at 8 a.m. and made a 5-hour 10-minute run to Wheeling. On the return run No. 35 cleared Wheeling station at 1:45 p.m. and arrived at Cleveland 5 hours later. Although engines were sometimes changed at Harmon, the same cars were used for both trains. Standard consist was an E-1 Atlantic, baggage car, combination R.P.O.-smoker, and either the *Kent* or *Canton* — former parlor cars rebuilt as observation coaches in 1931. Spare equipment included a pair of 1904 coaches, two baggage cars, and two R.P.O. cars. By the end of 1935 two Atlantics had been retired and two motor cars had been sold to the Tonopah & Goldfield. Stripped of its motors, M-101 was running in the hoodlebug.

Revenues produced by the Wheeling's passenger trains in 1933 totaled only $41,006, about $112 for each 304-mile round trip. Only four years before the W&LE had proposed to run its trains into Cleveland Union Terminal for 100 years at an annual rental of $20,000. Even in 1937, a reasonably good year, receipts per train averaged only $65. Without prospect of earning expenses, the W&LE ran its last passenger trains on July 17, 1938. Atlantic 2303 powered both. Some 300 persons wanted to ride the last train from Wheeling to Martin's Ferry, and two coaches were added to No. 35's regular three-car consist. Engineer Frank Eberly and Conductor John Frye drew the last varnish assignments.

The Tranquil Years

When the great contest between O. P. Van Sweringen and Frank Taplin commenced in January 1927, the W&LE was some 8 million dollars behind in payment of the 7 per cent dividend on John D.

*Beginning on January 25, 1929, the W&LE used the Erie's Superior Avenue station with the cost absorbed by the CUT. After about 1932 W&LE trains tied up at Commercial Road, site of the first Connotton Valley station.

Rockefeller's prior-lien stock. Since 1922 the suddenly strategic Iron Cross had been enjoying record earnings — more than double those of 1916. Owing to the huge prior-lien dividend arrearage, the common and preferred stocks had very low market values. Thus the road was both a moneymaker and an attractive speculation. However, Van Sweringen's interest in the W&LE was stimulated primarily by Taplin's reincarnation of the Gould plan to link the Western Maryland and Pittsburgh & West Virginia and complete the extension of the Wabash to tidewater. Largely to frustrate this plan, the Triple Alliance (B&O-NKP-NYC) paid Rockefeller 30 million dollars for his prior-lien stock in February 1927.

After the Van Sweringen coup, Duncan remained as firmly entrenched at the head of the W&LE as ever. Somehow he managed to keep management of the road's affairs aloof from the Van Sweringen-Taplin-Wabash dogfight that dragged into the 1930's. Although the Nickel Plate ended up with Rockefeller's stock, it could not exercise the control over the W&LE that went with it. Taplin was finally allowed to extend his P&WV to the Western Maryland, a development that strengthened the Wheeling's role as a bridge route. Ties with Van Sweringen railroads gave the road technical progress it probably would not have made otherwise and also brought much new traffic. For his part, Duncan began paying the overdue dividends in 1928 and by 1936 not only had satisfied the W&LE's obligation in this respect but was giving the common and preferred holders a return on their investment.

The Wheeling never failed to turn a profit after 1920. Even in the bleak years of 1933, 1934, and 1938 the road cleared more than a million dollars. From 1939 through 1946 profits ranged from 2.7 to 4.1 million and in 1947 the road had 6.5 million left over after paying all charges. Unquestionably the

Racing alongside Nimishillen Creek on the way to Wheeling, classic consist of No. 32 graces verdant Stark County countryside. Last run was only a month away. — *C. W. Burns from collection of Richard J. Cook.*

Gleaming in Ripolin, first of W&LE homemade switchers debuts at Brewster shop in May 1928. General Manager George Durham poses with proud shophands and the new C-1a.

May 1929 finds erection of B-5 3952 well advanced. Thirty such 0-6-0's were outshopped at Brewster between 1929 and 1940. — *Wheeling & Lake Erie photo.*

USRA Mallet works southbound freight 170 through Canton. No. 8002 has just crossed PRR main line at Wandle Tower. — *C. W. Burns from collection of Richard J. Cook.*

Some displaced Mallets found work on mine runs out of Pine Valley. I-3 8009 shoves a long cut of empties up to a tipple on the Adena Railroad. — *Nickel Plate photo.*

De luxe W&LE Berkshires had roller bearings, and Boxpok drivers but dimensions were patterned after those of NKP 700's. No. 6413 pauses between runs at Ironville on September 25, 1949. — *Robert J. Foster.*

Wheeling's earning power was instrumental in keeping the Nickel Plate out of receivership during the depression. In 1936 alone, the Iron Cross paid its desperate parent more than 5 million dollars in accrued dividends.

After 1925 George Durham's influence brought increased W&LE preoccupation with motive power efficiency and performance, an important factor in the road's latter-day success. Until 1928 most W&LE yard and helper assignments were held down by saturated 2-8-0's and 0-6-0's. There were, in fact, only five modern switch engines on the roster — the USRA 0-8-0's of 1918. Pleased with the performance of these engines, the Wheeling built 20 similar machines at Brewster between 1928 and 1930. C-1a's 5106-5125 were dimensional duplicates of the earlier 0-8-0's but had syphons and Chambers front-end throttle. Between 1929 and 1940 Brewster also turned out six-coupled switchers 3951-3980 to replace all remaining saturated yard power. These B-5's had 51-inch drivers like the C-1a's and 21 x 28-inch cylinders. They developed 41,160 pounds tractive effort compared with 52,500 for the 0-8-0's but were 27 tons lighter. All had syphons and roller-bearing drivers, and 15 received tenders equipped with Timken inboard-bearing trucks.

To cope with increasing puller tonnage at Toledo combined with axle-load limitations of the Maumee bridge, the W&LE went to Electric-Motive in 1940-1941 for four standard 1000 h.p. NW2 diesel-electric switchers. Always confined to Toledo, the diesels were identified as D-1, D-2, D-3, and D-4, suggesting that the Wheeling didn't really consider them full-fledged locomotives. Coal-oriented as it was, the road bought six more roller-bearing 0-6-0's from Alco in 1944 in lieu of a second diesel order.

Possibly influenced by the Nickel Plate, Advisory Mechanical Committee, and favorable experience with Erie 2-8-4's on the Youngstown-Toledo time freights, the Wheeling turned to the Berkshire freight engine in 1937. That year Alco delivered 10 class K-1 2-8-4's which were put to work on Brewster-Adena turns. After the new engines demonstrated that they could handle two or three such heavy-tonnage assignments daily, the W&LE bought five duplicates in 1938. During 1941-1942 17 more Alco K-1's were added to the roster. Not only did the 32 Berkshires absorb an increasing volume of freight traffic but between 1939 and 1943 they permitted the W&LE to retire 24 Mallets, a dozen Logrollers, and a number of saturated H-6a 2-8-0's. A handful of 2-6-6-2's were kept to handle mine run assignments.

K-1's 6401-6432 were ultimately used on all lines of the W&LE except the light-rail Carrollton, Chagrin Falls, and Massillon branches. Five of the 1937 engines developed boiler defects and were returned to Schenectady where they received new welded boilers in 1939. With these they had 250 pounds working steam pressure instead of the original 245 and were rated at 65,444 pounds tractive effort. Patterned after the Nickel Plate 700's, the W&LE 2-8-4's had 25 x 34-inch cylinders, 69-inch drivers, 33-ton axle loading, and 22,000-gallon Buckeye tenders. They differed from the S engines in that they came with roller bearings on all axles, inboard-bearing engine truck, Boxpok drivers, Hanna stokers, and foot-board-style pilots. In place of the Worthington feedwater heater of other Van Sweringen Berkshires, the 6400's had the Elesco SL-306 exhaust steam injector mounted on the right side.

Like most railroads, the Wheeling did little during the depression to upgrade its physical plant. However, as part of the Muskingum Watershed flood-control project, high-water-vulnerable portions of the two main lines were relocated during the 1930's. Construction of Dover Dam on the Tuscarawas required a new 14.6-mile high-ground alignment for the Toledo Division between Bolivar and Sherrods-

Trio of Mallets draw westbound coal drag through floodwaters at Valley Junction in 1936. New Bolivar-Sherrodsville high line is at extreme right. Old alignment and depot were abandoned in 1938. — *Wheeling & Lake Erie photo.*

Berkshire 6421 with empty gondolas en route from Brewster to South Lorain crosses Lorain & West Virginia's 760-foot Black River viaduct at Sheffield. — *Richard J. Cook.*

ville. The Cleveland Division also got a new line 9 miles long south of Beach City when a dam was built on Sugar Creek. Both lines were opened to traffic on May 20, 1938. Creation of Atwood Lake by damming Indian Fork brought about the abandonment of the Sherrodsville branch south of Carrollton in 1936.

The year 1943 was but 4 hours 35 minutes old when two detouring Pennsylvania freight trains collided head-on near Valley Junction. Fifteen PRR and W&LE employees were killed or injured and PRR Consolidations 7088, 9448, and 9911 were ruined in this accident which led to the first installation of automatic block signals on the Wheeling. Between 1946 and 1948 automatic signals were installed over 144 miles of the W&LE — from Bellevue to Adena and from Gambrinus to Harmon. Full centralized traffic control operation was initiated

The late John S. Foster at the throttle of the 4312, his regular engine for more than a decade. Best-known latter-day W&LE engineman and his 2-8-0 made their last runs December 10, 1949. — *Richard J. Cook.*

over nearly all of this territory at the same time. On the 139-mile Adena-Bellevue section there was the 6.37-mile stretch of double track at Brewster (non-C.T.C.) and 16 controlled sidings ranging in length from 221-car New Cumberland to 57-car Kenwood.

Starting in 1944 the W&LE began replacing many of its old yard offices, car department buildings, and crew facilities with modern brick structures. This program was intensified after John Davin became the W&LE board chairman in 1947. The only major latter-day terminal improvement was the completion in 1947 of a new seven-stall roundhouse and companion engine facilities at Campbell Road yard in Cleveland. Two years later a fine crew dormi-

tory was erected near this new engine terminal.

The Nickel Plate and Wheeling differed substantially in personality, but in their careers were many parallels. Both had gained lasting, in-depth prosperity late in life and both were admirably successful business enterprises. Like the Clover Leaf and LE&W, the Iron Cross naturally complemented the Nickel Plate, and it was inevitable that they would eventually be operated under the same banner. With the Nickel Plate now fully independent, the Interstate Commerce Commission finally gave its blessing to the long-deferred union. At 12:01 a.m. on December 1, 1949, the Wheeling & Lake Erie became an integral part of the thoroughly revitalized New York, Chicago & St. Louis system.

Wagon train CN-8 heads east through Cedar Glen as east side Cleveland goes to work. The fast moving piggyback train, only 8 hours out of Calumet, will be in Buffalo before noon. Four center tracks belonged to NKP. — *Willis A. McCaleb.*

Dividends, diesels and demise

AFTER leasing Wheeling & Lake Erie, the Nickel Plate stood at the threshold of the most profitable year in its history. Its comparative financial strength, competitive vitality, and earning power were never better. At the end of 1949 the road represented a 418-million-dollar investment and embraced 2266 miles of lines, including 491 under centralized traffic control. Nickel Plate's 16,112 employees constituted one of the most closely knit and productive labor forces in American railroading. Mechanically, this railroad was in a class by itself despite the fact that there were still 414 steam locomotives on a roster of 486 units. The 294-engine freight pool boasted an average of 57,378 pounds tractive effort per unit and was built around 112 Berkshires with an average age of only six and a half years. Of the 29,000 freight cars, more than 18,000 were less than 10 years old or had been completely rebuilt since 1945. Pullman-Standard was about to deliver

a fleet of streamlined sleepers and coaches to complete the modernization of the Nickel Plate's long-haul passenger trains.

The Molding of a Blue Chip

John Davin had recognized that the Nickel Plate's lack of a seaboard outlet was a potentially serious disadvantage. Lack of proper handling by eastern connections, especially those controlled by competitors, could nullify the best service rendered by the Nickel Plate. The Lackawanna was the last independent connection at Buffalo, and together with the Nickel Plate it formed a 919-mile New York-Chicago route, the second shortest between those cities. The two roads had worked closely for more than a half century and their marriage was a natural. In 1947 Davin indicated that he favored a union with the DL&W, which responded by buying 60,000 shares of Nickel Plate common — about 18 per cent of those outstanding. The other potential connection with tidewater was the Alphabet Route (Pittsburgh & West Virginia and Western Maryland) to Baltimore. However, Pennroad Corporation now owned the Taplins' P&WV stock and B&O still held a 42 per cent block of WM stock in trust. Neither B&O nor PRR was likely to accommodate a Nickel Plate bid to reach the sea. The prospect of further expansion was also clouded by the attitude of certain minority stockholders. They had demonstrated little desire to have their equity watered down through mergers and had forced the management to lease W&LE rather than absorb it.

Nickel Plate replaced its fleet of Berkshires and Mikes with 272 general purpose road-switchers after 1950. Electro-Motive GP30 units 900-909 were bought in 1962. They delivered 2250 horsepower, cost $207,000 each, and were used mainly as lead units in combination with older Geeps. — *John A. Rehor.*

Throughout its history the Nickel Plate had been ruled by executives imported from other railroads, notably those which controlled it. The DL&W was not to be given this privilege; nor were any of its men among the six new directors elected to the 15-man board during 1947-1949. Aside from Davin, the directors were an unimpressive collection of Eastern and Midwestern bankers, brokers, and industrialists without practical railroad experience. In the organization itself there had been no dominant personality after Gus Ayers retired in 1948. The man who inherited the revitalized Nickel Plate in 1949 had spent 45 of his 59 years in the industry and had joined the company as executive vice-president a few months before Davin's death. Iowa-born Lynne L. White was probably induced to leave the Chicago & North Western, where he was vice-president of operations, by a coalition of directors who opposed even a casual liaison with the Lackawanna. Elected president and given a seat on the board in January 1949, this forceful and conservative personality soon possessed virtually proprietary control over the Nickel Plate's affairs. Within a year White was also named chairman of the board. For an operating man, he seemed inordinately shrewd in financial matters and he ran a "taut ship." His management was not aggressive, especially in later years when it should have been, but he was wise enough to leave a good operation alone. Perhaps the man was too familiar with economic reality to be bold. At any rate, White never forgot his obligation to the directors. He successfully frustrated the DL&W, and he made Nickel Plate common the best investment in railroading.

The market price of Nickel Plate common rose spectacularly from a 1947 low of 18⅞ to a high of 236½ in 1951. Lackawanna activity in the stock and the small number of outstanding shares (337,434) were partly responsible for the sharp inflation in value. Wall Street, however, was impressed with the growth of earning power stemming from the combination of swollen revenues, improved efficiency, and reduced fixed charges. After payment of the 6 per cent preferred dividend, 1949 earnings amounted to $30.55 per share of common — a showing surpassed only by that of the Cotton Belt. Net income for 1950 was $21,019,542, up 12.5 million dollars from 1949, and earnings soared to $51.35 per share. Under the terms of the W&LE lease, the Nickel Plate was required only to cover the Wheeling's light fixed charges and guarantee a nominal dividend to minority stockholders. Since the Nickel Plate held 80 per cent of W&LE stocks, the dividend obligation came to a mere $538,000 in 1950.

In January 1951 the Nickel Plate offered its common holders 1 new share for each 10 held at a price

At first Calumet's new engine terminal was used by both Nickel Plate and C&O power. Brick and glass-block roundhouse had five stalls for steam road power and three for diesel servicing. With razing of Stony Island terminal, only Buffalo Junction of the six original NKP roundhouses still served its intended function.

of $150, an offering that was immediately subscribed and that added more than 5 million to working capital. The following March 5 the road paid out $16,225,515 to retire the last of the back preferred dividends. This erased the preferred holders' voting rights, but three weeks later the non-voting feature of the stock was eliminated by amendment to the charter. In return for the concession, the preferred holders assented to a 5-for-1 split of the common, which was effected in September 1951. Subsequently the board declared the first common dividend in more than 20 years — 50 cents payable January 2, 1952. The annual dividend was maintained at 2 dollars until the end of 1953, when it was raised to 3 dollars. In August 1953 the road had declared a 10 per cent stock dividend, which meant that 1954 brought a $16.50 return on one share held prior to September 1951. Preferred shareholders continued to receive their 6 dollar dividend until April 1, 1955, when the Nickel Plate sold 36 million dollars' worth of income debentures to cover the cost of calling the 334,166 preferred shares outstanding. This astute move replaced a taxable

2-million-dollar drain on earning power ahead of the common with a 1.6-million-dollar obligation that was deductible from Federal income taxes. It also paved the way for another stock split.

After a 2-for-1 split in 1956 the Nickel Plate had 4,116,780 shares of common outstanding, including 726,000 held by the DL&W. The dividend was restored to 2 dollars in 1957, and this was maintained until the 1964 merger with the Norfolk & Western. A buyer of 100 shares of Nickel Plate common at the 1947 low who was perceptive enough to hold the stock saw his equity swell from $1887 to $63,800 and he received more than $25,000 in cash dividends. Beginning in 1956 the annual return on his investment was considerably more than 100 per cent. This sort of blue chip performance was sensational in an industry notorious for its poor return to security holders. It was, of course, what long-term investors needed as a hedge against inflation during the postwar years. Chairman White participated handsomely through a 1954 stock option plan, buying common at a fraction of market value. Known to have held 26,990 shares, he re-

1918 roundhouse at Indianapolis was converted to diesel maintenance and repair facility in 1951. Machine shop, drop table, concrete floors were added to old LE&W structure.

ceived at least $53,980 as his slice of the annual dividend melon.

IMPROVEMENTS DURING THE WHITE REGIME

Davin's death did not bring an immediate end to the program of physical upgrading started in 1942. The early 1950's brought completion of many improvements programed prior to 1949, including the long-deferred engine terminals at Chicago and Fort Wayne. On July 30, 1951, the Nickel Plate moved from the old 18-stall West Wayne roundhouse to an entirely new set of facilities at East Wayne Yard. A large brick enginehouse with five stalls, 110-foot turntable, yard office, 500-ton coal dock, and enough added tracks to boost yard capacity to 1500 cars were built at a cost of 2.3 million dollars. The new Chicago terminal cost 2.8 million dollars and was situated on a 400-acre tract of reclaimed marshland adjacent to Calumet Yard. Included were a modern eight-stall roundhouse, powerhouse, turntable, and concrete coal dock. The Nickel Plate also built a new two-story yard office and a crew dormitory nearby. Calumet terminal was opened on October 1, 1951, after which the soot-blackened Stony Island roundhouse was razed. In 1952 Calumet also got a passenger-car repair shop and coach yard.

Centralized traffic control was extended over two long stretches of previously unsignaled Nickel Plate lines in 1950. These were the 46.2 miles of W&LE between Bellevue and Homestead Yard and the 59 miles of the LE&W between Muncie and St. Marys. In 1952 automatic block signals were installed on the Nickel Plate-owned westward main track between Silver Creek and Dunkirk. The next year the 3.7 miles of double track between Arcadia and FS Tower became reverse-signal C.T.C. territory controlled from the board at Fort Wayne. Between 1952 and 1954 the road installed C.T.C. on the 85.4 miles of Chicago Division main line connecting Claypool and Vanloon, Ind. This gave the Nickel Plate a total of 692 miles under C.T.C plus 255 miles with conventional automatic block signals. The percentage of C.T.C to total signaled trackage was the highest of that of any major U. S. carrier.

In compliance with the I.C.C.'s general signal order of 1947, the Nickel Plate reduced maximum authorized speeds on the unsignaled portions of the St. Louis Division from 65 to 59 mph for passenger traffic and from 55 to 49 mph for freight. Since only 56 of the 240 miles between Frankfort and Madison had automatic blocks, this promised to slow down the St. Louis manifests at a time when competition was becoming keener than ever. C.T.C. was ruled out and there was no extension of A.B.S. territory on the Clover Leaf. However, between 1951 and 1957 the Nickel Plate extended 20 existing passing tracks and installed three new sidings at critical points on the St. Louis Division. These 23 tracks held 117 to 144 cars and were spaced no more than 10 miles apart. Previously, passing-track capacity had varied from 55 to 95 cars. As part of the St. Louis Division program, the last mainline crossing gate was replaced with an automatic interlocker at Lerna in 1952.

The Nickel Plate installed "ribbon" rail on a 2-mile stretch of the Fort Wayne Division at Millers City in 1951. In this experiment, 39-foot 132-pound rails were welded to form continuous quarter-mile lengths. Nonetheless, the road never adopted welded rail on a massive scale as did many of its contemporaries. Nickel Plate also went to radio communication at an early date. During 1946 Berkshire 728 and a road caboose were equipped with two-way radios, and tests were also conducted that year with yard diesels. Base stations were established at Cleveland and Buffalo in 1947 and at Calumet and Madison in 1949. A total of 52 diesel switchers, including the two Baldwins bought for Toledo, were

S-4 rolls into Rook with a Monessen-bound ore train in August 1954, more than a year after P&WV and joint Brewster-Rook pool trains were dieselized. P&WV switcher crew watches the rare steam appearance. — *John J. Young Jr.*

fitted with radio equipment. A fifth base station was installed about 1950 at the W&LE Campbell Road yard in Cleveland. This was on a different frequency than that used by the Nickel Plate side, but all 24 radio units at Cleveland could use either. The terminal superintendent had a radio-equipped auto and could keep in touch with both base stations as well as with units on the move. Between 1953 and 1957 44 2-8-4's and 65 cabooses got Bendix and Westinghouse three-way sets. By 1954 base stations using a common road frequency were in

service at Buffalo, Bellevue, and 10 intermediate points on the east end. Plans to extend radio operation west of Bellevue never were fulfilled.

During the early 1950's the Nickel Plate enjoyed considerable success in attracting new industries to its lines. The road promoted industrial parks on branches and at terminals where existing yard jobs could provide optimum service and where interference with fast freight operations was best avoided. Outstanding among these was the 700-acre Solon development on the Chagrin Falls Branch.

AJ-12 charges across the Big Four at Wellington behind a pair of Baldwin AS-16 road-switchers. These 1600 h.p. units bought in 1954 were repowered by Electro-Motive five years later. — *Willis A. McCaleb.*

Alco 1600 h.p. RS-3's 541, 557, and 550 take the starch out of West Lafayette Hill with Peoria Division manifest No. 65 on March 20, 1955. Berkshires surrendered this division to diesels in 1954. — *William Swartz.*

It was opened in 1951 and attracted six large industries in as many years. By 1957 two "sub" runs served the branch daily whereas formerly there had been barely enough traffic to support one. Developments on a lesser scale were located on the Shinrock connection, a 2.65-mile line built in 1952 between South Huron Yard and the Cleveland Division; at Fort Wayne's Baer Field on the New Castle Division; adjacent to the new Calumet and East Wayne terminals; and on the State Hospital Branch between Massillon and Navarre.

The Last Generation of Motive Power

After V-J Day the diesel-electric locomotive took the American railroads by storm, providing a life-saving antidote against the ravages of inflation and subsidized competition for many. By the end of 1950 some 14,147 diesel units were accounting for 45 per cent of freight ton-miles and more than half of the passenger train-miles. The high cost of coal and shrinking traffic had already banished steam power from much of New England. Steam was becoming equally rare in the western mountains and deserts. Diesels were even muscling their way into the rosters of eastern coal roads. In 1950 the Pennsylvania gave the builders orders for 337 units and C&O had begun replacing what was probably the finest stable of reciprocating machines ever assembled. Although the Nickel Plate was still confident that a half million Berkshire horsepower had no equal when it came to moving freight, one of its divisions would be devoid of steam by the end of 1951. General Motors' development of a general-purpose version of the F7 freighter, coupled with chronic labor unrest in the coal industry and NKP's desire to end joint terminal operations with C&O, had turned the trick.

On March 2, 1950, during one of the recurrent coal strikes, two 1000 h.p. Lima-Hamilton switchers newly assigned to Kokomo were used to haul manifest SD-2 from Peru to Michigan City. This was the first instance of a Nickel Plate freight being powered by the road's own diesels. The next July Electro-Motive GP7 demonstrator No. 200 made a series of test runs over the Indianapolis Division with the dynamometer car and succeeded where the builder's F3 and F7 models had failed. Thirteen 1500 h.p. duplicates of the demonstrator numbered 400-412 were turned out by the on-line EMD Cleveland plant early in 1951. The new road-switchers, painted black with yellow stripes, displaced 600's between Indianapolis and Michigan City by the end of February 1951.

Unlike the F7, EMD's GP7 proved suitable for both yard and local freight work. This B-B had the F7's model 567B 2-cycle V-16 engine, weighed

A pair of ex-W&LE 4-8-2's at Adena prepare to go to Rexford and Jewett with westbound coal. NKP later renumbered these "water buffaloes" in 840 series, but all of them were out of service by the end of 1953. — *Nickel Plate photo*.

Hauling raw coal to Georgetown, Mallet 940 struggles on the 1.2 per cent westbound grade of the Adena, Cadiz & New Athens branch on June 2, 1953. Last of USRA 2-6-6-2's was laid up in February 1955. — *Willis A. McCaleb*.

Eleven Berkshires and 2-8-2's fill the morning air with steam before leaving Pine Valley for the mines and mills of southeastern Ohio. Diesels did not invade the No. 8 district until the spring of 1957. — *Willis A. McCaleb.*

118 tons, and had a starting tractive effort rating of 59,100 pounds. Four D27B traction motors with 62:15 gear ratio drove axles fitted with 40-inch wheels and Hyatt roller bearings. Not only did the GP7's master the hills at Peru and eliminate the helpers but they had a maximum speed of 65 mph and could do a creditable job on fast freight. Only 56 feet long, the Geeps could use any Nickel Plate turntable, and their 30-ton axle loading allowed them to run over any line on the system. For the first time, use of the most modern and efficient power on branches and secondary lines was possible without massive upgrading of rail, bridges, and terminal facilities.

During 1951 the Nickel Plate remodeled the seven-stall 22nd Street roundhouse at Indianapolis as a maintenance facility for the GP7's and diesel switchers assigned to Indianapolis, Tipton, and Kokomo. In January 1952 the road quit the C&O's Peru facilities and moved into a new terminal of its own on the Circus City's north side. Newly built were a small classification yard, car repair track, diesel facilities, and an office building. From the start GP7's handled all yard chores at Peru and Michigan City.

By 1953 diesels were accounting for 90 per cent of Nickel Plate yard engine miles, and steam switchers were restricted to terminals where steam freight power was serviced. Of the 72 diesel yard goats bought since 1950, Alco had furnished 38, including 16 equipped for multiple-unit service. The first Alco M.U.'s were assigned to W&LE transfer runs at Cleveland during 1950-1951. Six others replaced steam on Gambrinus-Brewster pullers in 1953, while standard 1000 h.p. Alcos took over Canton and Gambrinus yards and the Carrollton branch. Between 1950 and 1953 EMD's Cleveland works built 25 Nickel Plate switchers, including 800 h.p. SW8's for Frankfort and 1200 h.p. SW7's and SW9's for Fort Wayne. Lima-Hamilton's second and last Nickel Plate diesel order was filled in 1950 and covered four 1200 h.p. switchers for Lima. In 1953 Fairbanks-Morse shipped five 1200 h.p. units which joined earlier FM machines at South Lorain, Fostoria, and Bellevue. By the end of 1954 only 37 steam switchers remained on the active roster. All of Bernet's B-11's and U-2's were gone and only nine roller-bearing W&LE B-5's were left.

The Nickel Plate bought 35 more GP7's in 1953 and used them to replace steam power in the Brewster-Rook pool, on the Clover Leaf east of Frankfort, on the New Castle Division, and on most

freights between Cleveland and Brewster. The years 1953-1954 brought to the W&LE a quartet of 1600 h.p. Baldwin road-switchers numbered 320-323. These were big 125-ton B-B's with eight-cylinder in-line engines, 42-inch wheels, and Westinghouse apparatus. The 700's lost their first ground to diesel power when Alco delivered 1600 h.p. road-switchers 535-557 in 1954. The RS-3 B-B's which bumped Berkshires from Peoria Division posts had Alco's series 244 V-12 engine, 1400-gallon fuel capacity (600 more than the GP7), Timken bearings, and General Electric motors with 74:18 gear ratio. In three-unit teams the Alcos proved effective in moving tonnage over Peoria Division hills that had restricted 2-8-4's to 2800 tons. Next came 32 souped-up 1750 h.p. versions of Electro-Motive's GP7 road-switcher which dieselized the St. Louis Division in July 1955. With a 1600-gallon tank, the new GP9 had twice the fuel capacity of its predecessor and was 4 tons heavier. A trio of the new ERS-17 units was the equal of a 700 with the 3500-ton manifests and 49 mph speed limit of the Clover Leaf west of Frankfort.

Inflation and Other Post-Davin Problems

Nickel Plate carloadings rose appreciably after the outbreak of war in Korea in the summer of 1950, and traffic remained at a high level until the recession of 1954. During 1951 the road handled 55.8 million tons of freight good for 11.5 billion ton-miles and 160.7 million dollars in revenue. But while receipts were up 13.8 million over 1950, net income was down 2.5 million. A 15 per cent across-the-board rate hike in 1952 offset higher wages and delivered a 10 per cent boost in net income before taxes, but this gain was nullified by an increase in the corporate income tax rate. The next year Nickel Plate net income dipped to $17,866,796 despite a 6.5-million-dollar rise in revenues. Inflated material and manpower costs were offsetting the fruits of a decade of improvements and frustrating a management that was still pumping millions into C.T.C, diesels, and other betterments in the name of efficiency and improved performance.

Inflation undermined the Nickel Plate's prosperity in many ways. It brought constant labor unrest to industry, particularly to steel and coal mining which were hit by strikes with monotonous regularity after the war. As was painfully demonstrated in later years, the Nickel Plate's fortunes were irrevocably married to those of coal and steel. Not quite so obvious was inflation's vise-like effect on small concerns in highly competitive manufacturing fields. Some simply went out of business; others moved south seeking cheap labor and tax relief. Many that hung on turned to contract truckers or in some cases cut costs by doing their own hauling. The

Nickel Plate lost many shippers — both on and off line — as even large firms joined the exodus south. Fort Wayne's knitting mills closed their doors and the "million-dollar" silk trains the road had once hauled were just a memory. General Electric's transfer of appliance production from Erie to Louisville cost the Nickel Plate a source of traffic that had run as high as 50 carloads a day.

For a decade after World War II the railroads tried to shore up sagging earnings by repeatedly raising freight rates. This only compounded the miseries of many shippers and drove a great deal of lucrative traffic into the hands of nonrail competitors. To railroading's old guard, higher rates seemed the only answer to confiscatory taxation, rigid regulation, and mounting costs. The rails were prevented from reducing much of their operational overhead by ironclad working agreements, state commissions, and obsolete laws. On the other hand, there appears to have been little enthusiasm for the idea of boosting earning power through technological advancement. The pioneer users of C.T.C. in the East had yet to expand their original installations. The diesel locomotive that was saving many railroads evolved largely in spite of rather than because of the industry's attitude. The concept of piggyback — hauling highway trailers on flat cars — was more than 20 years old but many rail executives were still apathetic to it. If a shipment couldn't be handled in a 40-foot box car, open-top hopper, or 50-ton gondola it wasn't worth hauling. Whether the railways could break with Victorian dogma in time to avoid becoming the "vestigial tail of transportation" remained to be seen.

Ignoring the pleas of steelmakers, the Eastern railroads had sought and won rate increases in the depression. This signal blunder had created the long-haul trucking industry in Ohio and western Pennsylvania, and by 1954 the railroads were hauling only 14 per cent of the finished steel moving to Detroit's auto plants. Steel-laden semis clogged Ohio's route 18 and US 224 and rolled through Bellevue in an endless stream on US 20. The truckers could make a round trip to and from Detroit in a day, and they covered the blocked and chained coils of steel to protect them from rust and damage. As did the W&LE, the Nickel Plate ran the expedited steel trains to Toledo, but NKP's iron and steel traffic dropped from 5.9 to 3.7 million tons within three years. In 1954 rates were cut and the Nickel Plate patented a new damage-free car for coil shipments in an attempt to recapture some of the lost business. Gondola cars were fitted with movable skids and buffers to absorb shock and prevent shifting of the coils in transit. Four 35,000-pound coils were handled in a car and were shielded by two removable corrugated steel covers. The design, and variations of it, were eventually used by many other railroads. Another 1954 Nickel Plate innovation was the "basket" car, a flat equipped with end bulkheads and racks for holding metal baskets filled with small forgings. The basket cars, easily loaded by fork-lift trucks, were operated between Ford Motor Company plants at Canton and Detroit.

CRISIS IN COAL

Until 1956 the Nickel Plate normally received from connections 10 to 11 million tons of bituminous coal, mostly consigned to steel centers on the main line. After acquiring the W&LE, the road originated about 7 million tons of coal annually until 1958. About 10 per cent of this was produced by small stripping operations in the Connotton Valley and on the Zanesville line. The rest was loaded within a 20-mile radius of Adena in the small No. 8 field. In 1949 26 mines in the No. 8 district loaded some 80,000 cars with 5.7 million tons of coal for shipment over the W&LE and dispatched another million tons over the PRR and B&O.

The Pennsylvania's disdain for No. 8 coal had ended shortly after World War I, but the big system did not begin to make serious inroads on the Wheeling's coal traffic until 1935. Fourteen years before, the PRR and W&LE had built a 3.7-mile branch to a mine on Little Short Creek along part of the original 1871 W&LE survey. This ran south from Connor, 2½ miles west of Warrenton, to the

Dorothy Mine and was operated by the W&LE during odd-numbered years. The PRR used the W&LE to Connor and served the branch during even years. Then in 1935 PRR's trackage rights were extended 7 miles west to Dunglen where the Hanna Coal Company was establishing a cleaning plant and a large drift mine following the 4½-foot No. 8 seam under the plateau between Big Short Creek and Wheeling Creek. Until 1939 PRR engines and crews ran to Dunglen but thereafter the W&LE provided the service for PRR on a contract basis.

Hanna ultimately became the principal operator in the No. 8 district. About 1933 the firm acquired a big slope mine near the south end of the Adena Railroad which it renamed Willow Grove No. 10; this shipped upwards of 10,000 loads over the W&LE annually. Later Hanna established its Georgetown No. 12 mine on the AC&NA and in 1948 began heavy stripping operations 2 miles west at Tipple E. Most of the 1.5 million tons shipped from Tipple E annually went to washing plants at Dunglen and Piney Fork, a Hanna mine on the NYC north of Dillonvale. Hanna and its successor, Pittsburgh Consolidation Coal, acquired large tracts of land for strip mining around Cadiz in Harrison County. Reserves in this 48-square-mile sector of the No. 8 district were estimated at 100 million tons. In May 1951 Consolidation opened its huge Georgetown Preparation Plant a short distance southeast of Cadiz, 3.3 miles north of the end of the AC&NA at

First mine run on Adena Railroad normally needed two 2-8-4's leaving St. Clairsville with outbound coal. S-4 830 doubles the hill while mate 825 gathers up more tonnage at Saginaw Mine. On a hot, dry day such as this one in September 1956, two Berkshires could get to Harrisville summit with 4000 tons. — *John A. Rehor.*

Circus trains and private cars once were common on LE&W but became rarities in later years. In 1947 Goodman's Wonder Show climbs out of the Illinois River valley at East Peoria between a 2-8-2 and caboose 66 (above). In another Peoria Division scene some years later (below), private car 5 holds down the end of manifest KB-2 as it whips through Paxton, Ill. Superintendent Bob Gleason soaks up sun while looking over his railroad. — *Upper photo, Paul Stringham; lower photo, Willis A. McCaleb.*

Tipple E and 9.8 miles west of Adena. To serve the plant, Nickel Plate extended the AC&NA 2.2 miles north and the PRR built a 3.9-mile spur southeast from its Cadiz branch. The preparation plant was located about midway on a 2.3-mile stretch of joint track connecting the Nickel Plate and PRR branches. All told, the new line was 8.4 miles long and had four jointly owned yards with a total capacity of 1140 cars. The Nickel Plate also had an agent, telegraph office, and car repair forces at Georgetown.

Nickel Plate's 1953 carloadings in the No. 8 district topped 156,000 — nearly twice the 1949 figure — and represented some 8.6 million tons of coal. More than 5.5 million tons moved over the AC&NA and this traffic was about evenly split between westbound "raw" coal and eastbound washed coal headed for consumers. Raw coal was mined at Dunglen and other Hanna mines and hauled under contract to Georgetown for cleaning. When the No. 11 mine at Dunglen was closed in 1955, Consolidation continued working the deep seam from the new Glen Castle drift mine on the Adena Railroad. Solid trains of raw coal moved from Glen Castle to Georgetown on a contract basis.

Willow Grove No. 10, the slope mine extending under the Adena Railroad between Neffs and St. Clairsville, was closed in 1954. Near the north portal of this mine at St. Clairsville, the Saginaw Dock & Terminal Company opened a big deep mine in 1949 which shipped 10,000 carloads or more annually. The other major independent No. 8 operation served by the Nickel Plate was Nelms No. 1, a vertical shaft mine working the seam 475 feet below ground level 5 miles west of Adena. Nelms has produced as much as 1 million tons of high-grade coal annually for rail shipment.

Until the spring of 1957 steam power was used exclusively in the No. 8 district and the 12-stall roundhouse at Pine Valley was host to a wide assortment of steamers, including ex-W&LE 2-8-2's, 4-8-2's, and 2-6-6-2's. In 1950 the first of a dozen H-6 Mikes with boosters appeared and some labored in the coal fields until 1955. Now and then H-5 2-8-2's and G-9 2-8-0's could also be found at Dillonvale. The last Pacific, K-1b 169, ran out her final miles in the same unfamiliar surroundings. After the last Mallet was laid up in 1955, the mine jobs and Yorkville swing runs were given to 2-8-4's. Ex-W&LE 6400's renumbered in the 800 series teamed with older 700's to move coal out of Georgetown and St. Clairsville and even held down the Pine Valley roustabout job. Eight to 10 mine runs were operated daily, including double-headed pullers hauling outbound loads from Georgetown to Jewett where they were classified. On the Adena Railroad two 2-8-4's had a nominal 4000-ton rating, and going west with Jewett-bound pullers such a pair was good for 5000

tons on the rugged 9-mile climb to Rexford Summit.

By 1954 the diesel engine and natural gas had eliminated much of the steam coal market and had sharpened the competition for what was left. The biggest users of No. 8 coal were now the power and light companies, but even here the future looked grim. Ohio's largest producers of electricity had closed many small and inefficient generating plants in favor of high-voltage transmission and modern stations in the Ohio valley where cheap coal was close at hand. Exceptions in this trend were Toledo Edison and Cleveland Electric Illuminating Company. In 1954 Nickel Plate had built a 3-mile line from Homestead Yard north to a new TE generating station on Lake Erie. The road also served one of the four CEI plants and hauled much coal that was consigned to the others into Cleveland. Other big No. 8 customers were located in eastern Michigan. Some of their coal moved by rail through Toledo, but the bulk was dumped into lake freighters at Huron and Presque Isle (Toledo).

For its part, Pittsburgh Consolidation fought rising costs and sharpened competition by expanding stripping operations around Cadiz. In the fall of 1954 workmen began assembling a huge Marion power shovel on the AC&NA near Tipple E. The job took almost eight months and when it was completed Consolidation had the world's largest land vehicle ready to strip overburden in 90-ton bites. Called "The Mountaineer," this electrically operated self-propelled machine was 16 stories high and weighed 2750 tons. The stir that The Mountaineer caused in coal mining circles was nothing to the effect created by Consolidation's 1954 announcement that it planned to build a coal-slurry pipeline from Georgetown to a CEI power station east of Cleveland. Not that anyone was surprised. Eastern Ohio had become something of a proving ground for unique and often impractical schemes for moving raw material. Today there are those who would build a costly toll-free canal between Lake Erie and the Ohio River through this region. After the war, persons identified with the Akron, Canton & Youngstown proposed the Riverlake Belt Conveyor to haul coal, ore, and limestone over much the same route. A bid to give Riverlake the right of eminent domain died in the Ohio General Assembly in 1949. Two years later the belt conveyor promoters had another bill in the hopper at Columbus and not until 1955 was the scheme killed off once and for all.

Consolidation's pipeline was the unanticipated aftermath of the railroads' 1952 effort to win a 12 per cent hike in Ohio intrastate coal rates. In a 1954 address to stockholders Lynne White accurately assessed the pipeline as "a serious threat to the Nickel Plate." His promise to give "a good deal of sober thought to the subject" resulted in a joint Nickel

Pacific 167 is set to leave Peoria with the last run of No. 22 on July 1, 1951. After arriving at Frankfort the K-1b was laid up, never again to run under her own power. Peoria & Pekin Union station, shown here, was destroyed by fire on August 5, 1961. Nickel Plate's last Pacific was retired in 1953. — *Paul Stringham*.

Plate-CEI fight to preserve the low intrastate rate. After a two-and-a-half-year battle they were beaten by Ohio's other coal-hauling railroads in 1957, the year the pipeline went into service. The 108-mile coal conduit from Georgetown to Eastlake cost 13 million dollars and transported about 1.3 million tons of No. 8 annually. This was finely ground, mixed about equally with water, and pumped in slurry form to the power plant at the rate of 150 tons per hour. The 10-inch pipeline had some early operating bugs but was judged a highly successful venture. CEI contracted with Consolidation for delivery of 18 million tons of coal over a 15-year period and turned to trucks for much of its remaining requirements. These developments, following the loss of much of the Toledo Edison coal traffic to a competing rail-water combination, had an unhappy effect on Nickel Plate coal revenues.

Between 1956 and the recession year of 1958 the Nickel Plate's total coal tonnage dropped from 18.3 to 11.1 million tons. By 1962 volume was down to 9.7 million tons, less than the road had received from connections prior to absorbing the W&LE. The Nickel Plate managed to hold its originated coal tonnage after 1958 but the decline in shipments received from other roads persisted until 1964. A steel industry fighting foreign competition had sharply improved production efficiency and had reduced the use of coke in furnace operations by 70 per cent in less than a decade. United States Steel found that it saved money by producing coke at Pittsburgh and

shipping it in trainload lots to Lorain and Gary. This dried up two lucrative sources of Nickel Plate coal traffic. The road got only a portion of the coke movement — this from the Bessemer & Lake Erie at Wallace Junction, Pa.

PASSENGER SERVICE AFTER 1949

Beginning on July 21, 1949, the combination of DL&W No. 3, the *Phoebe Snow*, and NKP No. 5, the *Nickel Plate Limited*, carried a roomette-bedroom car between New York and Chicago. Nickel Plate 6 and DL&W 10, the *New York Mail*, handled a companion sleeper eastbound. The new maroon and gray 10-6 sleepers were Lackawanna owned and bore such interesting names as *Tobyhanna*, *Tunkhannock*, and *Kittatinny*. Early in 1950 they were joined by 25 new Nickel Plate cars built by Pullman-Standard — 10 coaches, 13 roomette-bedroom cars, and a pair of bedroom-diner-lounge cars. These 83-foot lightweights were Advisory Mechanical Committee-designed and were similar to cars built for the C&O. They had stainless-steel sides, picture windows, electromechanical air conditioning, and four-wheel cast-alloy steel trucks with Hyatt roller bearings and Timken hotbox alarms. Coaches 100-109 had two compartments with a total of 52 reclining seats and lounges for men and women. Sleepers 200-212 were named after cities on the Nickel Plate and had six double bedrooms and 10 roomettes. Roomette compartments were of an advanced AMC design featuring a wide and comfortable cutaway

Toward the end, No. 10 trundles across Rocky River viaduct behind a Bluebird. Diner-lounge has been withdrawn and reclining-seat coach replaced by an old 90-series car. October 1959 demise of 9 and 10 marked end of Clover Leaf and LE&W passenger service, commuter patronage west of Cleveland. — *Willis A. McCaleb.*

bed which could be raised or lowered without opening the compartment door. Bedrooms were spacious and had enclosed toilets. Bedroom-diner-lounge cars *City of Cleveland* and *City of Chicago* weighed 68 tons and had five double bedrooms, a crew room and kitchen, dining space for 18, and four lounge chairs.

The bedroom-diner cars went into service on trains 5 and 6 between Cleveland and Chicago early in 1950, and the other new sleepers replaced older Pullmans on all Chicago and St. Louis runs. The *Phoebe Snow-Nickel Plate Limited* combination offered a 10 a.m. New York departure with the usual overnight service from Cleveland to Chicago and 7:40 a.m. La Salle Street arrival. No. 5's standard consist out of Cleveland included three 10-6 cars and bedroom-diner, plus the 12-section Fort Wayne sleeper restored to the night trains in 1946. Trains 5 and 6 were renamed *City of Chicago* and *City of Cleveland* in 1954. No. 8 was called the *New Yorker* after 1956 out of deference to its DL&W connection. After 1949 No. 8 ran on a 20½-hour Chicago-New York schedule with 9:25 a.m. Chicago departure, 5:30 p.m. Cleveland arrival, and overnight Cleveland-New York service. This was the fastest Nickel Plate varnish run, averaging 47 mph between Chicago and Buffalo.

Advent of the new streamlined cars reversed the

decline in Nickel Plate passenger revenues that had persisted since 1944. The year 1952 produced an all-time high of $3.15 revenue per passenger train-mile and passenger revenues 50 per cent above those of 1949. This was quite a showing considering that four of the 10 remaining trains had been withdrawn in the interim. Accommodation trains 21 and 22 were cut back from Lima to Portland, Ind., on March 12, 1950, and on June 4 made their final runs east of Frankfort. They were discontinued east of Cheneyville, Ill., on March 20, 1951. No. 22 left Peoria for the last time on July 1, 1951, the day after the westbound's graveyard run. Next to come off were the mixed trains operated between Charleston and East St. Louis. Usually powered by a Clover Leaf 2-8-0, trains 11 and 12 consumed over 13 hours making their 264-mile daily-except-Sunday ramble through south-central Illinois. The Nickel Plate took them off on April 28, 1952.

After the war, the schedule of No. 6 had again been arranged so that its Cleveland departure followed the arrival of No. 10 from St. Louis. Since through travelers had a 4- to 5-hour layover at Buffalo, an added 10- to 15-minute delay at Cleveland was of little consequence to them. The connecting service was dropped about 1949, after which No. 6 often left the CUT as little as 10 minutes before No. 10 arrived there. Trains 9 and 10, called the

Destined for Fostoria, 4-6-4 170 lifts 11 carloads of Cinerama fans up Cleveland Division ruling grade at Bay Village on February 9, 1957. L-1a went to Museum of Transport eight months later. — *John A. Rehor.*

Hudsons were employed in utility holes to the end of steam. On a Sunday evening in 1955 a pair of L-1's and their crews wait inside CUT for return of excursionists from a Cleveland Indians doubleheader long delayed by rain. CUT's 3000-volt catenary has been gone for some time. — *Herbert H. Harwood Jr.*

With throttle against the peg, Hudson 171 helps a 2-8-4 hurry a westbound freight out of the hole at Continental. April 1956 episode was filmed in the soft light of sunup. — *Willis A. McCaleb.*

Blue Arrow and *Blue Dart* after 1956, were never heavily patronized; but that they were ever a serious drain on Nickel Plate earnings is doubtful. After 1950 their consists included an R.P.O. car, coach, diner-lounge, 10-6 Pullman, and sometimes a C&O private car east of Fostoria. During the general downgrading of passenger service in 1958 the diner came off and Nickel Plate sought to remove the St. Louis trains altogether. Illinois relented first, and the last No. 10 left St. Louis on March 14, 1959. For a week the trains, sans sleeper, ran as far west as Cayuga, after which they were terminated at Coldwater, O. Opposition to the withdrawal was brisk in Ohio and that state forced the operation of trains 9 and 10 through October 17, 1959.

Nickel Plate's use of steam on passenger runs diminished sharply after 1952. Berkshires and Hudsons were called for occasional troop movements during the Korean conflict and once in a while a 4-6-4 would show up on the head end of a regular train. Baseball specials on summer Sundays might bring one or two L-1's to Cleveland, but by the end of 1953 steam accounted for only 30,000 passenger train-miles annually and all the Pacifics had been retired. Although Hudsons still protected mainline passenger runs, the purchase of nine GP9 diesels with steam generators reduced even this modest employment to a minimum. When the 173 was outshopped at Frankfort in June 1957 an announcement was made that this was the last time a 4-6-4 would be overhauled.

Passenger revenues hit a post-1952 high of 3.4 million dollars in 1959 despite the withdrawal of Nos. 9 and 10, curtailed diner and sleeper service on the Chicago trains, and a complete lack of publicity. Convenient service and modern equipment had held a hard core of regular patrons, just as they had in the 1930's. In contrast with trains 5 and 6, the day runs did their heaviest business east of Cleveland, since their schedules allowed shoppers from Erie and Ashtabula a full day in the Forest City. After Ohio and Pennsylvania opened toll-free extensions of the New York Thruway parallel to the Nickel Plate, less than two hours was required to motor from Erie to downtown Cleveland. Along with the Ohio and Indiana turnpikes, I-90 sounded the death knell of Nickel Plate passenger service. The last

On November 23, 1956, No. 5 failed to show at Chicago in time for her Bluebirds to take No. 8 out of the city. In their place, the 173 moves the *New Yorker* out of La Salle Street on Rock Island trackage. — *Frank Barry.*

New Yorker left Chicago on June 2, 1963, and the final *Westerner* was dispatched from the Erie-Lackawanna's Babcock Street station in Buffalo the next day.

In 1956 the Nickel Plate had once again withdrawn the Fort Wayne sleepers from trains 5 and 6, and two years later the through New York sleepers had come off. Also in 1958 the diner-lounge cars handled by the night trains east of Cleveland had been dropped, leaving only the Pullman-operated buffet service between Cleveland and Chicago. Geeps replaced the Bluebird engines in 1962, and finally a lone road–switcher handled a bedroom-diner-lounge car, 10-6 sleeper, and a pair of coaches west of Cleveland on 5 and 6. East of that city, service was provided by a solitary coach. By October 16, 1964, the modernized 80-series coaches were in Mexico, and surplus 10-6 cars were seen on the Chicago & Eastern Illinois, PRR, and other roads.

PIGGYBACK AND FASTER SCHEDULES

A smart pickup in the economy in 1955 gave Eastern railroads three years of relative prosperity before a severe recession and the cumulative effect of many problems drove them to their knees. For the Nickel Plate, 1955, 1956, and 1957 were banner years with sustained high profits. The year 1956 produced 11.9 billion ton-miles of freight and revenues of $174,578,288 — both all-time highs. The next year the road rang up peak merchandise revenues of 136 million. An apprehensive management nevertheless was unable to check a steady rise in the operating ratio during those years.

Piggyback or trailer-on-flatcar service and improved manifest schedules were important factors in the 1955-1957 showing and helped to soften the impact of the economic relapse that followed. With the PRR, Wabash, DL&W, Erie, and B&O, the Nickel Plate pioneered piggyback on July 12, 1954. Initially, service was offered between Cleveland and Chicago with 25 trailers bought from the on-line Fruehauf firm at Avon Lake. Before the end of 1954 service was extended to Buffalo and New York. Ramps were in service at Toledo and Madison and through service was being offered to Philadelphia and Baltimore by 1956. Ultimately, the Nickel Plate had 15 TOFC terminals and 1600 trailers, including flatbeds, open-tops, and mechanically refrigerated vans. Piggyback traffic increased steadily and by 1964 amounted to nearly 65,000 loaded trailers annually. Albeit some in the industry still put forth strong arguments against TOFC, its benefits to a railroad such as the Nickel Plate were manifold. For one, piggyback reduced industrial switching costs — a major source of overhead on a railroad tallying 5 million yard locomotive miles a year. It

also offset the lack of captive accounts, permitting access to any industry in Nickel Plate territory. In an increasingly mobile society new industries no longer needed to locate on a railroad, and piggyback was the one way to reach them. Then, too, TOFC meant lessened dependence on connections and terminal roads. An example of this was the Nickel Plate's heavy TOFC traffic in coiled steel consigned to Detroit auto plants. Trailers were handled by rail to Toledo and by highway the rest of the way. Common-carrier truckers had the flatbeds on the Detroit-Toledo Expressway in minutes and at the Rouge inside of 2 hours.

The keystone of post-depression Nickel Plate policy was the premise that shippers wanted reliable service above all else. The railroad that ran "by the customer's clock" could bank on a regular volume of lucrative long-haul traffic. For this reason few alterations were made to advertised manifest schedules between 1940 and 1955, although hours were slashed from actual running time. This strategy protected traffic delayed en route to the Nickel Plate by permitting departures from initial terminals hours after advertised time. Shippers were so sold on Nickel Plate service by 1953 that the road was getting a line haul on 85 per cent of the 30,000 carloads of meat and perishable traffic delivered annually to the food terminals at Cleveland and Buffalo. The road once hauled the piggyback shipment of a weekly magazine supplement to a Cleveland newspaper without a single delay over a span of 33 months. Frustrated competitors were having a harder time than ever keeping the hustling Nickel Plate from winning the line haul on traffic they originated and, in some instances, also terminated.

Until 1955 the CB-12/PB-12/ST-96 combination was operated to provide second-morning delivery at New York and second-night service to Boston. Even before 1949 CB-12 and PB-12 connected with a W&LE "Alpha-Jet" to offer second-morning service to Baltimore and second-night delivery at Philadelphia in conjunction with the P&WV, Western Maryland, and Reading. Wheeling's No. 98 was originated at Toledo and picked up from the Nickel Plate hotshots at Bellevue en route to Rook. This train got the symbol CSP-12 after 1949 and about 1955 became the AJ-12 in deference to the Alpha-Jet service. In 1955 the Nickel Plate and its eastern connections trimmed advertised schedules to provide second-morning service to Boston and Philadelphia as well as New York and Baltimore. Buffalo arrivals of CB-12 and PB-12 were moved up from 4 a.m. to 2:45 a.m. to allow connections with new DL&W NE-2 and Lehigh Valley SF-2 which left Buffalo before 6 a.m. and offered 4 a.m. delivery at Boston the next day. Alpha-Jet AJ-4 ran off CB-2 and KC-44 and now gave shippers second-morning

Philadelphia deliveries via the Reading. A third Toledo-Rook hotshot, AJ-2, was the Alphabet Route connection for trains OB-2 and MB-98.

Nickel Plate ran four other scheduled freights out of Homestead Yard daily in addition to the three eastbound Alpha-Jets. Included were TC-2, the overnight run to Cleveland via Wellington; and through freight No. 84 to Terminal Junction. AJ-12 set out cars at Brewster for a time freight to Mingo Junction, a Zanesville fast freight, and a Canton puller. Westbound there were three regular Rook-Toledo trains, including the *Michigan Steeler* (MS-1), the latter-day version of W&LE 95. In addition, manifests AJ-1 and AJ-3 ran daily from Rook to Bellevue, where they connected with hot westbounds for St. Louis and Chicago.

THE END OF STEAM

At the end of 1956 Chairman White told Nickel Plate stockholders that "unless a more efficient type of power is developed . . . operations will be completely dieselized by 1962." The announcement followed the demonstration that general purpose diesels could consistently maintain fast freight schedules in 60 mph territory. Early in the summer of 1956 the Nickel Plate received its first Alco road-switchers since 1954. ARS-18a's 558-562 were rated at 1800 h.p., weighed 124 tons, and had turbosupercharged series 251 V-12 engines. These RS-11 or DL-701 models proved popular with enginemen and put Alco back into a Nickel Plate picture that EMD had threatened to dominate entirely. After delivery the DL-701's teamed up with GP9's on the tough 226-mile Frankfort-Bellevue run and performed meritoriously with 4000-ton LE&W manifests. When Electro-Motive shipped 30 additional GP9's in August 1956 the regular use of steam on the LE&W ceased altogether. The new diesels had written the death warrant of the 700's.

The last steam locomotive overhauled at Brewster was outshopped in June 1955; thereafter the big backshop.was devoted to heavy repair and advanced maintenance work on the Nickel Plate's growing diesel fleet. This was the first real revelation of management's conclusion that internal combustion power could do the job. In August 1955 Berkshire 730 was laid up for heavy repairs at Frankfort and was destined never to carry another fire or turn a wheel again under her own power. Up to this time all the 2-8-4's had been in active service. Before the end of 1955 the Lima shop was closed, and a similar fate befell the Frankfort facility in July 1957. This left only Conneaut still doing classified repair work on steam power.

By January 1, 1957, Nickel Plate's 152 diesel road-switchers were in charge of all freight operations on the LE&W and Clover Leaf as well as part of those on the W&LE. Steam could still be found in abundance on the Wheeling, especially east and south of Brewster. All mainline freights were steam powered and, on the whole, steam was still accounting for 52 per cent of gross ton-miles. Between Buffalo and Chicago, 56 Berkshires plied their trade supported by 17 Mikados and five Hudsons. On the W&LE there were 51 active steamers, including 13 700's lately on the LE&W and 24 ex-W&LE 800-series 2-8-4's. Berkshires held sway in the coal fields and were regularly seen moving freight out of Brewster to Toledo, Huron, Zanesville, and Terminal Junction. Now and then a 2-8-4 ventured as far north as Kent.

In the spring of 1957 the Nickel Plate added 36 more diesels to its roster, including 29 heavy-duty C-C versions of standard EMD and Alco road-switchers. Alco DL-702's 325-333 had the model 251 engine and six traction motors, 185 tons working weight, and 92,540 pounds starting tractive rating. EMD SD9's 340-359 weighed about a ton less than the Alcos but had 2400-gallon fuel tanks. With only 30-ton axle loading, the big diesels could work any mine run and even were used safely on the Carrollton branch's 80-pound rail. On the Adena Railroad the 300's were rated at 2400 tons compared with 2000 for a 2-8-4 and 2250 for an I-3 Mallet. The C-C units finished off steam in the coal fields overnight, and each week the line of dead steamers at Brewster grew longer. By July only 11 Berkshires and four Mikados plus a handful of yard goats were active on the W&LE. In November B-5 384 ran into Brewster from Zanesville and the last fires were dumped on the Wheeling.

At the close of 1957 2-8-4's were still forwarding the freezer trains from Calumet Yard to Buffalo and the only diesels seen on the main line were those working LE&W freights between Bellevue and Arcadia. Four dozen 700's held down the million-dollar manifests and were making the 513-mile mainline runs in 12 to 13 hours. Five S-4's from the W&LE worked CS-7 and CC-2 on the Cleveland Division. Mikados 662 and 665 were charged with FS-2 and the local west of Cleveland, while a half-dozen H-5's were employed on short hauls such as the Narlo stone run and Painesville backout. Hudsons 171, 173, and 175 showed up on supply trains, work extras, and other odd jobs. Eight-coupled goats toiled in the yards at Conneaut and Buffalo. Machinists in Conneaut shop were still busy making class repairs to 700's and putting roller-bearing trucks from 800's under the S's tenders. Railfans came from all over America to see and record the Berkshires and to charter steam-powered excursions over the main line. This was one of the last strongholds of reciprocating motive power in the U. S. and train-watchers knew it would fall to the conquering

With her safety valves popping, S-2 754 departs Bellevue for Chicago with No. 55 on a bitter winter day in 1957. Enginemen considered Lima's war-born S-2's the best of NKP's Berkshires. Train-stop equipped, they reigned on the west end until June 1958. — *Willis A. McCaleb.*

diesel long before Mr. White's 1962 target date.

The advent of a severe recession during the winter of 1957-1958 coupled with delivery of 40 new diesels sharply curtailed the use of steam power east of Fort Wayne in March 1958. In the face of declining traffic the Nickel Plate could no longer afford to maintain two separate freight power pools, two sets of shops, and dual facilities at engine terminals. Maintaining the 700's properly was becoming very difficult even though the road had bought out the parts inventories of manufacturers and other railroads. Some components no longer were made and had to be machined to order, an extremely costly business. By May 1958 a Class 3 overhaul cost more than $57,000.

The new diesels — 20 GP9's, 10 DL-701's, and 10 more FM switchers — cut the number of active steamers to 24 by June 1, 1958. Most of these were train-stop-equipped S-2's working the Chicago Division. Of the 212 road diesels, only the Bluebirds and five GP9's were equipped for automatic train stop, but the road rented 25 C&O GP7's with the apparatus. The first of these arrived June 13, 1958, and five days later engine 740 powered the last westbound steam run out of Bellevue. On June 20 Engineer Earl Hiatt and the 740 were called for train 32 at Calumet and arrived at East Wayne a few minutes before midnight. Early the next morning, Jim McConnell took the 740 east with a time freight for Bellevue and wrapped up 77 years of steam operation on the west end. Engineer Ed Curtiss made the last Buffalo Division steam run, bringing the 719 into Conneaut on July 1. The next day Bill Beard ran the 746 with a manifest from Bellevue to Conneaut and, as it developed, brought down the curtain on the Berkshires. Engines 746, 747, 752, and 763 remained in steam at Conneaut until July 22, when their fires were finally dumped. The roundhouse was already filled with dead 700's, including three gleaming in fresh paint. Outshopped in May, they had yet to be broken in.

The Nickel Plate was not officially dieselized until August 1960, and until that time 27 Berkshires were carried on the active roster. Early in 1959 the C&O units were replaced with 30 new train-stop-equipped GP9's and DL-701's. A rapid rise in carloadings in the spring of 1959 forced the Nickel Plate to return five 0-8-0's to service at Conneaut for a two-month period. The return of a number of 700's to east end duty for the normally heavy fall traffic was antici-

To balance power, Nickel Plate often doubleheaded NC-3 on weekends. The westbound manifest shatters the Sunday morning calm of east side Cleveland during the last winter of steam operation. By 1958 such sights were rare indeed. — *Herbert H. Harwood Jr.*

Detouring NYC eastbound waits on No. 3 track at Silver Creek for passage of fast-moving S-3 and her charge. NKP double track between Silver Creek and Dunkirk was once part of LS&MS main line. — *Jim Shaughnessy.*

Labor Day 1957 found a 14-year-old S-1 hard at work on Kimball Hill with a westbound train of pipe out of South Lorain. Kimball, junction with B&O Sandusky Branch, was originally called Higbee. — *Don Wood.*

Berkshire 706 was bumped from Clover Leaf and LE&W assignments, ended her days on W&LE. Last of the 1934 Alcos, she worked on nine divisions and tallied 2 million miles in a 23-year career. On March 18, 1957, the veteran S barrels through a cut near Jewett en route to Mingo Junction with time freight 86. — *John A. Rehor.*

pated. These were readied at Conneaut, but a 116-day steel strike lasted beyond the end of the Great Lakes navigation season and the road managed to get by without firing up one of the 2-8-4's.

After the Nickel Plate added 15 more road-switchers to its fleet in 1960, the coal docks and water tanks were retired along with the remaining serviceable steamers. Later engine purchases included 10 snub-nosed EMD GP30 road-switchers rated at 2250 h.p., a lone 2500 h.p. GP35, and a 2000 h.p. Alco Century 420 unit. The latter two were bought in 1964 to replace power destroyed in an accident. As for the celebrated Berkshires, only three were left on the property on October 16, 1964. Four others had been spared scrapping to join Hudson 170 and six other Nickel Plate locomotives permanently displayed in city parks and museums.

HANGING ON

The recession that began during the latter part of 1957 had an immediate and catastrophic effect on the railroads, especially those in the East. By February 1958 carloadings were 20 per cent under those of the year before, 45 of the 114 Class 1 roads were operating in the red, and railroad employment was at the lowest level since 1900. The railroads' decline would seem for a long time to be utterly irreversible and gloom pervaded the entire industry. For the Nickel Plate, 1958 brought a 25 per cent drop in tonnage, a 31.3-million-dollar dip in receipts, and the highest operating ratio in years despite total dieselization and wholesale layoffs. A partial recovery was made in 1959, but 1961 brought another reversal and revenues tumbled to 130.7 million. Net income for 1961 was only 8.7 million, the lowest figure since 1947. Even this did not accurately indicate Nickel Plate earning power, for management was now liquidating capital investment whereas in 1947 management had been pouring millions into plant and equipment. Earnings per share amounted to $2.10, barely enough to pay the common dividend. During the next two years revenues did not increase

Trainmasters Bill Burr and Ralph Kieser keep track of railfans inspecting East Wayne engine terminal on June 30, 1957. Berkshire 764 (left) powered Illini Railroad Club excursion from Chicago and return. — *Jesse Bennett Jr.*

appreciably, although the net rose to 10.5 million in 1963.

Many factors other than those common to the industry as a whole intensified the Nickel Plate's sudden decline. The coal-slurry pipeline was one of these, but the Nickel Plate managed to head off further inroads into its originated coal tonnage after 1958. By 1963 the road was actually loading more coal on line than it was receiving from connections. Instrumental in this showing was the unit train — 6000 tons or more of coal loaded, weighed, billed, and dispatched as an integral unit from origin to destination. Low unit-train overhead permitted sharply reduced rates which stopped traffic losses and regained some traffic previously lost. NKP operated its first unit train — 7000 tons of coal moved from Georgetown to Buffalo — on January 28, 1961.

Cleveland Electric Illuminating Company announced on May 6, 1963, that the Georgetown-Eastlake pipeline would be shut down as soon as a 10-year contract was executed with the Nickel Plate, NYC, and PRR. This covered the movement of 45 million tons of No. 8 district coal, and in order to meet the tonnage commitment CEI would also divert virtually all coal moving by truck to the three railroads. For their part, the roads offered a unit train rate of $1.88 per ton compared with the old $2.49 pipeline rate. After the pipeline was mothballed, Nickel Plate began running daily unit trains from Georgetown to Avon Lake in August 1963 and also delivered a large volume of coal for CEI's other plants to the NYC at Wellington. By this time

nine weekly unit trains were also being operated into Toledo. Four were dumped at Presque Isle for transshipment to a Detroit utility; four ran to a powerhouse on the Shore Line north of Toledo; and one was operated by rail to a chemical plant at Midland, Mich.

The volume of iron ore handled by the Nickel Plate fell off drastically from the 5-million-ton high

First passenger train south of Harmon in 18 years took 500 riders from Cleveland to Zanesville on August 13, 1950. National Railway Historical Society special was powered by Hudson 176. Scene is at Linden Avenue depot in Zanesville. — *Nickel Plate photo.*

Buffalo Chapter of NRHS chartered May 18, 1958, fan trip to Cleveland and got a last look at a Hudson in action. L-1b approaches Euclid Avenue near end of 184-mile run from Buffalo. During this memorable weekend Cleveland fans rode B&O's last steam-powered varnish run. — *Herbert H. Harwood Jr.*

of 1951 to a 1959 low of 1.2 million tons. Steel mills in the Ohio valley, Pittsburgh-Monessen, and Canton-Massillon districts were the road's biggest ore customers. Closure of the Edgar Thomson works at Braddock, Pa., Republic's Massillon plant, and a number of furnaces around Wheeling were partly responsible for the decline. With the tailing off of high-grade production in the Mesabi Range, the Pennsylvania began hauling imported Labrador ore into the Pittsburgh and Steubenville districts in 1954. This, too, had an adverse effect on ore shipments through Huron. However, the pelletizing of low-grade Lake Superior ore (taconite) and the 1959 opening of the St. Lawrence Seaway underwrote a Nickel Plate comeback in iron ore in the early 1960's.

Not the least of the Nickel Plate's post-1957 problems was the progress made by its rail competitors,

Zanesville branch was last W&LE steam stronghold. M-1 2-8-2 678 rolls southbound way freight past indifferent Amish cows near Sugar Creek (above). Renumbered H-5b 958 drifts past Baltic depot en route to Brewster in 1956 (right). Last Clover Leaf steamer, stoker-fired G-9 915, wheels a northbound work train up Baltic Hill's 2 per cent on May 24, 1957 (far right). — *All photos, John A. Rehor.*

Four radio-equipped GP9's sweep through Avon Lake with NS-1 on a winter morning. Where 700's only lately had ruled, 7000 EMD horsepower appears to have tonnage and 60 mph limit well in hand. — *Willis A. McCaleb.*

particularly the New York Central. In 1954 Robert R. Young finally succeeded in gaining control of the debt-ridden giant and installed Alfred E. Perlman as its president. Perlman did a remarkable overhaul job on his new charge, cutting overhead and speeding up operation with total dieselization, push-button hump-retarder yards, and reverse-signal double-track C.T.C. NYC made certain inroads into Nickel Plate perishable and merchandise traffic and even stole some of its New England piggyback business. Perhaps even more devastating than the NYC revival was the merger of the Erie and the Lackawanna. A good indication of the Nickel Plate's long-haul losses was the rising percentage of originated business. By 1963 overhead traffic accounted for only 26 per cent of carloadings.

Nickel Plate fought back with two new eastbound piggyback trains operated on passenger-train sched-

After more than a year of storage, 0-8-0's were put back to work in Conneaut Yard in 1959. C-17 304 leaves a roundhouse full of dead 700's and shuffles off to a second-trick assignment on May 29, 1959. — *John A. Rehor*.

ules. New CN-8's advertised 10:30 p.m. Calumet departure was 1 hour before No. 6 was due to leave Chicago, and the "wagon train" ran ahead of the *City of Cleveland* all the way to Buffalo on a 12-hour 20-minute schedule. SN-8 left Madison at 5:30 p.m. and was due into Bellevue about 8 a.m., 2 hours behind CN-8. Cars from both "8" trains were added to AJ-12, which was now primarily a fast New York and New England train operated in conjunction with the Reading and Central Railroad of New Jersey. An advance section of AJ-12 was operated to protect traffic from CB-12 and PB-12. Hot westbound Reading and Western Maryland cars for Chicago were now handled in first AJ-1 to Bellevue and then in Advance NC-5 to Calumet. Second AJ-1 ran in connection with new westbounds NC-9 and NS-9 and was built around Jersey Central traffic.

In the fall of 1961 the Nickel Plate reached an agreement with the Erie-Lackawanna covering the joint ownership and operation of an ultramodern electronic hump yard at East Buffalo, N. Y. Bison Yard, built on the site of the old DL&W yards at a cost of 13 million dollars, was designed to handle about 3000 cars a day on some 67 tracks. Bison had such modern appointments as Videograph train scanners, ultrasonic presence detectors, automatic retardation control system, electric snow melters,

and radio and yard intercom systems. A car repair shop and an auto rack unloading terminal were ultimately built at Bison, and Nickel Plate erected a fine crew dormitory nearby. Early in 1963 EL, C&O, and Wabash began using Bison Yard and Nickel Plate was expected to join them in July. Nickel Plate men supervised operations but the road never did run its trains into Bison because of EL labor opposition. Ironically, the Nickel Plate's 7.5-million-dollar investment in Bison and a double-track access route to the yard* served only to provide substantial aid to three of its toughest competitors.

In order to counter the effect of the Erie-Lackawanna merger and eliminate delays at Buffalo, Nickel Plate and Lehigh Valley inaugurated through interline service on February 13, 1964. Trains bypassing Buffalo were operated with pooled motive power from Sayre, Pa., to Bellevue, 425 miles. New LV-1 ran off Lehigh manifest FFW-1 and was due into Bellevue at 4:30 p.m. where it was consolidated with NS-5 and NC-5. Eastbound LV-2 ran off trains OB-2, MB-98, CN-8, and SN-8. The new interline service was so successful that two more runs were added in the summer of 1964. LV-3 brought Lehigh cars into Bellevue in time to make NC-3 and NS-1 departures, and LV-4 ran off CB-12 and PB-12. As much as possible, cars for the LV trains were blocked west of Bellevue in order to reduce delays and congestion at that point.

THE NOBLEST ACHIEVEMENT

Not the least of the Nickel Plate's latter-day accomplishments was a remarkable improvement in safety performance. Compared with many other systems, the road was late in establishing a programed effort to reduce employee casualties. The introduction of safety committees, rules, awards, and full-time safety agents had come in 1938. Even at that late date railroading was considered one of the more hazardous occupations, and any life insurance actuary could produce overwhelming evidence to support this contention. The notion that a major railroad could eventually eliminate fatal and permanently disabling injuries to employees was viewed as a fantasy. There was seldom much enthusiasm for safety at the top of the organization, and this attitude was betrayed by escape clauses built into many early rules. Constantly hounded to deliver both maximum performance and economy, line supervisors often looked upon safety men as anarchists. To this day the belief persists in some railroad circles that full compliance with rules would bring operations to a standstill.

Between 1941 and 1945 some 60 men lost their lives in Nickel Plate service, but after the war the

*In 1963 the Nickel Plate bought 5.44 miles of PRR main track from Blasdell to Buffalo as part of its Bison access route.

NKP's first unit train — 7000 tons of coal moving from Georgetown, O., to Buffalo — rolls east behind an Alco DL-701 and two GP9's on January 28, 1961. The place: Lakewood, O. — *Willis A. McCaleb*.

Canadian canaler docks with Huron's first load of Labrador ore on October 11, 1956. Electric Huletts installed in 1950 needed only 2½ hours to unload 2324-ton cargo. Shallow-draft vessels such as *Meaford* used St. Lawrence canals prior to opening of Seaway.

road made significant progress in reducing both its fatality and over-all casualty ratios. Roy C. Sabens, superintendent of safety from 1949 to 1961, authored a greatly improved safety rule-book and built a systematic approach to accident prevention. Through grass-roots tours conducted on a departmental basis and family safety rallies, Sabens sought to take his program to every employee at least once a year. Despite this intensified effort, fatalities once again began to mount after the W&LE was leased. Management effected an amazing reversal of this trend in 1956 by placing maximum emphasis on supervisor responsibility and strict rule compliance while stepping up the personal contact program. In 1957 the road slashed its casualty ratio by 48 per cent and won its first Edward H. Harriman Memorial Gold Medal for "outstanding safety performance" in competition with other railroads posting 15 million or more locomotive-miles annually. Bestowed by the American Museum of Safety, the coveted Group A medal has been railroading's premier safety award for more than 50 years. After 1956 the Nickel Plate and Union Pacific dominated the Harriman Award competition for larger roads, with UP taking the gold medal in 1958, 1960, and 1962 and Nickel Plate scoring in 1957, 1961, and 1963. Until 1961 the Museum also awarded commendation certificates for best performance on a regional basis. The Nickel Plate won these for Group A Eastern roads in 1958 and 1960. Although the road received no recognition in 1962 (gold medals cannot be won on successive years), this was the first fatality-free year in Nickel Plate history. In fact, no employee fatalities occurred from the spring of 1961 to the fall of 1963.

The Merger

After holding its 18 per cent block of common for four years, the Lackawanna went before the I.C.C. in 1952 and asked for authority to seat two men on the Nickel Plate board. The DL&W also sought to exercise control over its western connection and outlined plans for combining certain departments and operations. Included was the joint use of DL&W's Buffalo facilities, a move that was bound to benefit the Nickel Plate. But Lynne White countered by asking the I.C.C. to order the Lackawanna to divest itself of its Nickel Plate investment, asserting that his road's "progress and well being" depended "on its independence from control by any other railroad." What White really meant was that Nickel Plate was too well off to be won by a suitor offering little more than an aristocratic name. The once-rich DL&W had fallen on bad times owing to the depressed anthracite coal market and increasingly unprofitable terminal and commuter operations. Then, too, as long as Lackawanna held the

stock, the Nickel Plate could not make a better match when and if the opportunity presented itself.

The I.C.C. was obviously not indisposed to the idea of a Lackawanna-Nickel Plate alliance, but DL&W's William White was taking no chances. In an apparent effort to appease the Nickel Plate and forestall a showdown, the DL&W asserted in 1954 that it was not seeking a merger. Nickel Plate refused to take the cue and counter with a merger plan of its own, choosing instead to continue pressing the demand for divestiture. In 1956 the DL&W distributed 97,000 shares of Nickel Plate common to its shareholders and asked for authority to place the rest in trust. This was granted in April 1958 over strenuous Nickel Plate objections. A few months later, though, the DL&W began merger negotiations with the Erie and on March 2, 1959, disposed of its remaining 628,722 shares of Nickel Plate common. For the first time in more than 35 years the Nickel Plate had no apparent ties with another railroad. Ironically, this development precluded all possibility of the future existence of the road as an independent entity.

It became evident in 1957 that the I.C.C. was becoming less and less concerned with the preservation of "intramodal competition" in a national transport picture in which railroads were handling less than half of the intercity freight traffic. The change in attitude was well demonstrated after James M. Symes of the PRR and A. E. Perlman of NYC announced in November 1957 that their roads planned to merge. Although this union of traditional rivals may have been conceived in despair as an effort to dramatize the plight of the railroads, it may also have been a shrewd effort to gauge the public temper on the subject of railway consolidation. No serious opposition to the plan developed. Next, the Norfolk & Western and Virginian railways asked the I.C.C. for permission to marry. This consolidation between parallel and competing roads was allowed in 1959, and before long practically every Eastern road was talking merger.

Less than a year after the DL&W decided to throw in with the Erie, the Nickel Plate was negotiating merger terms with the Norfolk & Western. On May 17, 1960, NKP President F. S. Hales confirmed that talks had been under way for some time, and less than a month later he and N&W President Stuart T. Saunders announced that a tentative plan had been worked out. Stockholders were to receive .45 share of N&W common for each Nickel Plate share held and N&W was to be the surviving corporation. After merger with the Virginian, the N&W embraced some 2700 miles of lines extending mainly from Norfolk to Columbus and Cincinnati. No connection existed with the Nickel Plate but the N&W proposed to buy the 111-mile Pennsylvania branch extending north from Columbus to Bellevue and Sandusky. Before the end of 1960 Saunders also announced that the merger proposal had been expanded to include the Wabash, forming a strong 7400-mile system with promising opportunities to eliminate "wasteful duplication." The plan was magnificent and one that was not formulated overnight. Wabash was to be leased for 50 years, and its stock (99.5 per cent held by PRR) ultimately was to be exchanged for that of N&W. While the Nickel Plate merger would reduce PRR's holdings from 33.7 to 27.8 per cent of N&W's stock, the Wabash stock exchange would restore Pennsy's interest to 32.1 per cent. N&W was also to pay PRR 27 million dollars for the Sandusky Branch, giving the former owner trackage rights over most of the line. The plan was put before the I.C.C. on March 17, 1961, and approved by N&W and Nickel Plate stockholders two months later. Anticipated opposition from the Erie-Lackawanna was disposed of by agreement to negotiate EL's eventual inclusion in the expanded N&W and by Nickel Plate's participation in Bison Yard. Later N&W would agree to lease the P&WV and to buy stock of the Akron, Canton & Youngstown to avoid their intervention in the case. Other interveners included the Department of Justice and four cities on the Clover Leaf.

A favorable recommendation was rendered by I.C.C. examiner Lester R. Conley on April 17, 1963, and the Commission voted 10-1 for approval on June 24, 1964. By this time the PRR-NYC merger had been revived and B&O and C&O appeared destined to unite. The decision had been delayed by the Government's pleas that the N&W-NKP and PRR-NYC mergers be considered in a single proceeding. The I.C.C. decided against this but made approval conditional upon PRR's formulation of an acceptable plan for complete divestiture of its N&W stock. On September 14 the PRR told the I.C.C. that it would accept the requirement of divestiture within 10 years. With the last roadblock removed, the N&W-NKP union was consummated at 12:01 a.m. on October 16. Of all the companies involved (including the W&LE), only the Nickel Plate passed totally out of existence.

Assessment of the events following the Norfolk & Western-Nickel Plate merger remains for some future historian. As matters stood on October 16, 1964, the new N&W possessed 7800 miles of railways, assets of 1.9 billion dollars, working capital of 130 million, and certainly the greatest profit potential of any American railroad. The public will expect the new railway to be all that it promised and more. This must be nothing less than a competitive pacesetter in every sense of the word, a versatile fount of technological progress, a foundation stone of a revitalized Eastern transport system. To cope with the challenges that will surely come with the materialization of the three-system plan, Norfolk & Western will need every measure of individual energy, dedicated enthusiasm, and alert aggressiveness it can muster. Together with the unblemished reputation, the good will, and the tradition of excellence, these were among the Nickel Plate road's most estimable assets. In this day and age few railroads offer a richer legacy.

Herbert H. Harwood Jr.

Locomotives of the Nickel Plate

ROCKY RIVER RAIL ROAD (1868-1886)

Name	Type	Builder	Builder number	Date	Cylinder	Drivers	Engine weight
Rockport	4-2-0T	Baldwin	1727	6-1868	17" x 24"	42"	14,000
Brooklyn	4-2-0T	Baldwin	1728	6-1868	17" x 24"	42"	14,000
Elias Sims	4-2-0T	Baldwin	3662	11-1874	17" x 24"	42"	14,000

Note: The Rockport and Brooklyn were later renamed Hannah and Rhodes. After July 1882 these engines were stored at Cleveland at least until the end of 1885. Ultimate disposition unknown.

LAKE VIEW & COLLAMER RAILROAD (1875-1879)
CLEVELAND, PAINESVILLE & ASHTABULA RAILROAD (1879-1886)

Number	Type	Builder	Builder number	Year built	Cylinders	Drivers
1-3		Globe Iron Works		1875		
4	2-4-2	Baldwin	4670	6-1879	10" x 16"	42"
5	0-4-2T	Baldwin	4761	8-1879		

Note: Nos. 1-3 were steam dummies. They were disposed of about 1877, 1879, and 1883. Engine 5 became NYC&StL 199 and was still in use at Cleveland on December 24, 1885.

NYC&STL — LOCOMOTIVES ACQUIRED 1881-1886

Number	Class	Type	Builder	Builder number	Date
1-5	A	4-4-0	Brooks	537-541	5-1881
6-7	A	4-4-0	Brooks	543-544	6-1881
8-12	A	4-4-0	Brooks	573-577	8-1881
13-19	A	4-4-0	Brooks	598-604	10-1881
20	A	4-4-0	Brooks	606	11-1881
21	A	4-4-0	Brooks	635	1-1882
22	A	4-4-0	Brooks	642	1-1882
23-27	A	4-4-0	Brooks	685-689	4-1882
28-32	A	4-4-0	Brooks	708-712	5-1882
33-39	F	4-6-0	Brooks	784-790	10-1882
40-43	A	4-4-0	Hinkley	1453-1456	11-1881
44-49	A	4-4-0	Hinkley	1457-1462	12-1881
50-53	F	4-6-0	Brooks	796-799	10-1882
54-57	F	4-6-0	Brooks	802-805	11-1882
58-68	F	4-6-0	Brooks	814-824	11-1882
150-151	B	4-4-0	Brooks	643-644	1-1882
152-155	B	4-4-0	Brooks	646-649	1-1882
156-159	B	4-4-0	Brooks	651-654	2-1882
160-164	B	4-4-0	Brooks	660-664	2-1882
165-167	B	4-4-0	Brooks	701-703	4-1882
168	C	4-4-0	Brooks	767	8-1882
169-175	C	4-4-0	Brooks	768-774	9-1882
199		0-4-2T	Baldwin	4761	8-1879
200-204	D	0-4-0	Brooks	667-671	3-1882
205-209	D	0-4-0	Brooks	674-678	3-1882
210-213	E	0-6-0	Brooks	692-695	4-1882

Engine No. 1, one of the 42 class A dual-service 4-4-0's, before leaving the Brooks Works. This 17 x 24, turned out in May 1881, headed the motive power seniority list and had 17 months of construction service when Nickel Plate opened. — TRAINS *collection.*

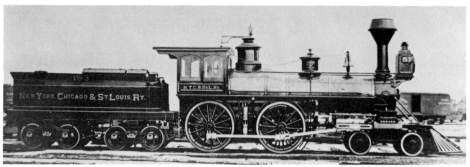

Eighteen class B 4-4-0's had 66½-inch drivers and were purchased for passenger service. Otherwise they were identical to class A machines with an overall length of 53 feet 3 inches and an engine wheelbase of 22 feet 10 inches. Both had 2400-gallon tanks. — *Collection of Gerald M. Best.*

DIMENSIONS OF LOCOMOTIVES (1908)

Class	Cylinders	Drivers	Weight on drivers	Total weight	Boiler pressure	Tractive effort	Grate area
A	17" x 24"	60½"	46,500	70,000	120	11,490	15.42
A-1	17" x 24"	61"	54,000	86,000	140	13,398	18.33 (A)
A-2	17" x 24"	61"	53,000	88,000	125	12,095	16.77 (B)
B	17" x 24"	66½"	46,500	70,000	120	10,390	15.42
B-1	17" x 24"	67"	54,000	86,000	160	14,080	18.33 (A)
B-2	17" x 24"	67"	53,000	88,000	125	10,869	16.77 (B)
C	18" x 24"	66½"	55,000	88,000			16.77
C	18" x 24"	67"	67,000	100,000	150	14,800	18.33 (C)
C-1	18" x 24"	67"	58,000	91,000	160	15,790	18.33 (D)
D	16" x 22"	48"	65,000	65,000			
E	17" x 24"	48"	70,000	70,000			
F	19" x 24"	55¾"	73,500	96,000	130	16,937	16.77
F-1	18" x 24"	55¾"	73,500	96,000	130	16,937	16.77(C)

(A) As rebuilt with new boiler and firebox.
(B) As rebuilt with class C boiler and firebox.
(C) As rebuilt.
(D) As rebuilt with new boiler and firebox; in June 1909 boiler pressure reduced to 150 lbs. and tractive effort to 14,800 lbs.

Wagon-top boilers of class E switchers were interchangeable with those of class A and B 4-4-0's. The 212, at Bellevue roundhouse in the early 1890's, had a backup light on the cab roof and a footboard under the cab—both added after Brooks delivered her in 1882. — *Collection of Frank W. Hager.*

No. 1 — Retired circa 1907

  2 — Rebuilt with new boiler by Brooks January 1892 and reclassed A-1. Later received class B frame and machinery from 162 or 165 and reclassed B-1. Renumbered 2nd 103 in 1910. Last used in helper service at Cleveland. Dismantled June 17, 1916.

3, 5, 7,
and 10 — Retired between 1901 and 1905.

  4 — Sold to Fort Smith & Western October 1902. Apparently FS&W 1st 6, retired about 1918.

  6 — Dismantled October 1903.

  8 — Dismantled March 1904.

  9 — Dismantled October 1905.

  11 — Rebuilt by Brooks with new boiler December 1891 and reclassed A-1. Later received class B frame and machinery from 162 or 165 and reclassed B-1. Renumbered 2nd 5 in 1906 and 2nd 106 in 1910. Employed in yard and helper service in Cleveland after 1913. Retired in 1917.

  12 — Rebuilt by Brooks with new boiler September 1888 and reclassed A-1. Renumbered 2nd 7 in 1906 and 2nd 100 in 1910. Laid up May 1911; dismantled September 24, 1914.

13, 14 — Dismantled October 1904 and October 1903.

  15 — Rebuilt with boiler from class C engine 171 April 1897 and reclassed A-2. Renumbered 3rd 10 in 1908 and 2nd 101 in 1910. Dismantled April 22, 1913.

  16 — Sold December 1902, possibly to Fort Smith & Western.

  17 — Dismantled June 1904.

  18 — Retired circa 1908.

  19 — Sold to Fort Smith & Western September 1902, apparently FS&W 1st 5. To Blue Ridge Coal Company, McCurtain, Okla., circa 1926.

  20 — Retired about 1905.

  21 — Rebuilt with boiler from class C 172 December 1896 and reclassed A-2. Renumbered 3rd 11 in 1908 and 2nd 102 in 1910. Laid up May 1911 and dismantled September 24, 1914.

22-25, 28,
29, and 32 — All retired between 1905 and 1908.

  26 — Sold to Fort Smith & Western August 1907, apparently FS&W 1st 17. Retired circa 1916.

  27 — Dismantled June 1904.

  30 — Dismantled May 1904.

  31 — Sold August 1902, probably to Fort Smith & Western, their 1st 4. To Stewards & Beautelcheis Coal Company, Bokoshe, Okla., about 1924.

  33 — Renumbered 2nd 15 in 1908 and 253 in 1910. Retired 1910.

  34 — Renumbered 2nd 16 in 1908 and 254 in 1910. Dismantled June 16, 1913.

  35 — Renumbered 2nd 17 in 1908 and 255 in 1910. Dismantled January 1914.

  36 — Retired about 1907.

  37 — Received 18 x 24-inch cylinders about 1906 and reclassed F-1. Renumbered 2nd 19 in 1908 and 264 in 1910. Dismantled September 24, 1914.

  38 — Received 18 x 24-inch cylinders about 1906 and reclassed F-1. Renumbered 2nd 20 in 1908 and 265 in 1910. Retired 1910.

  39 — Renumbered 2nd 21 in 1908 and 257 in 1910. Retired 1910.

40, 45,
and 48 — One each of these retired in 1901, 1902, and 1903.

41, 42,
and 44 — Dismantled November 1901.

  43 — Retired about 1904.

  46 — Dismantled September 1901.

47, 49 — Dismantled October 1902.

  50 — Renumbered 2nd 10 in 1906 and retired 1908.

  51 — Renumbered 2nd 11 in 1906, 2nd 29 in 1908, and 262 in 1910. Dismantled September 24, 1914.

  52 — Renumbered 2nd 12 in 1906 and retired 1910.

  53 — Renumbered 2nd 13 in 1906 and 251 in 1910. Dismantled July 18, 1913.

  54 — Renumbered 2nd 14 in 1906 and 252 in 1910. Dismantled April 29, 1913.

55, 56 — Retired in 1907.

  57 — Renumbered 2nd 22 in 1908 and 258 in 1910. Retired 1910.

  58 — Received 18 x 24-inch cylinders about 1906 and reclassed F-1. Renumbered 2nd 23 in 1908 and 266 in 1910. Dismantled September 24, 1914.

  59 — Renumbered 2nd 24 in 1908 and 259 in 1910. Retired 1911.

  60 — Renumbered 2nd 25 in 1908 and retired 1910.

  61 — Renumbered 2nd 26 in 1908 and 261 in 1910. Dismantled February 1914.

  62 — Cylinders to 18 x 24 inches about 1907 and reclassed F-1. Renumbered 2nd 27 in 1908 and 267 in 1910. Dismantled September 24, 1914.

  63 — Cylinders to 18 x 24 inches about 1907 and reclassed F-1. Renumbered 2nd 28 in 1908 and 268 in 1910. Dismantled April 29, 1913.

  64 — Renumbered 2nd 18 in 1908 and 256 in 1910. Dismantled February 1914.

  65 — Retired in 1909.

  66 — Renumbered 263 in 1910 and dismantled June 16, 1913.

67, 68 — Retired in 1909.

150, 152 — One of these retired about 1904 and the other became 2nd 1 in 1906, retired about 1908.

  151 — Dismantled May 1904.

  153 — Dismantled October 1902.

  154 — Rebuilt by Brooks with new boiler March 1893 and reclassed B-1. Renumbered 2nd 3 in 1906 and 2nd 104 in 1910. This engine pulled first regular passenger train from Cleveland to Bellevue October 23, 1882. Dismantled September 24, 1914.

  155 — Renumbered 2nd 4 in 1906 and retired 1907.

  156 — Renumbered 2nd 6 in 1906 and retired 1908.

  157 — Dismantled December 1902.

  158 — Renumbered 2nd 8 in 1906 and retired 1907.

  159 — Wrecked in head-on collision at Silver Creek, N. Y., September 14, 1886. Rebuilt with boiler from class C 168 October 1893 and reclassed B-2. Renumbered 3rd 1 in 1907 and 2nd 107 in 1910. Retired 1910.

  160 — Rebuilt with boiler from class C 170 June 1895 and reclassed B-2. Renumbered 3rd 6 in 1907 and 2nd 108 1910. Retired 1911.

  161 — Retired about 1907.

  162 — Received class A frame and machinery from 2 or 11 and reclassed A. Renumbered 3rd 8 in 1908 and retired 1909.

  163 — Rebuilt by Brooks with new boiler May 1893 and reclassed B-1. Renumbered 3rd 4 in 1908 and 2nd 105 in 1910. Dismantled September 1914.

  164 — Retired about 1907.

  165 — Rebuilt with class A machinery and so classed. Sold to Fort Smith & Western November 1903.

  166 — Rebuilt with class C boiler from 173 May 1895 and reclassed B-2. Renumbered 2nd 9 in 1908 and 2nd 109 in 1910. Retired 1911.

  167 — Retired 1909.

  168 — Rebuilt with new boiler August 1893 and reclassed C-1. Renumbered 2nd 114 in 1910; dismantled June 1916.

  169 — Rebuilt with new boiler June 1897. Renumbered 2nd 110 in 1910. Dismantled April 22, 1913.

  170 — Rebuilt by Brooks with new boiler December 1894 and reclassed C-1. Renumbered 2nd 115 in 1910 and dismantled June 17, 1916.

  171 — Rebuilt with new boiler March 1896. Renumbered 2nd 111 in 1910. Used in helper and yard service at Cleveland after 1913. Dismantled December 1920.

  172 — Rebuilt with new boiler February 1896. Renumbered 2nd 112 in 1910. Dismantled September 1914.

  173 — Rebuilt by Brooks with new boiler August 1894 and reclassed C-1. Renumbered 2nd 116 in 1910. Dismantled September 30, 1916.

  174 — Rebuilt with new boiler by Brooks December 1893 and reclassed C-1. After 1913 used at Cleveland in helper

service. Renumbered 2nd 117 in 1910. Dismantled December 6, 1920.
175 — Rebuilt by Brooks May 1897 with new boiler. Renumbered 2nd 113 in 1910. Dismantled September 30, 1916.
199 — Ex-CP&A 5. Retired not long after December 1885.
200, 208, and 209 — All dismantled June 1899.
201 — Dismantled May 1904.
202 — Dismantled April 1901.

203 — Dismantled May 1900.
204 — Dismantled December 1900.
205 — Dismantled October 1904.
206 — Dismantled June 1903.
207 — Dismantled October 1904.
210-213 — These leased to Cleveland, Columbus, Cincinnati & Indianapolis, 1882-1883. No. 212 leased to Lorain & West Virginia in 1907 and used in construction of that road. All retired prior to 1908.

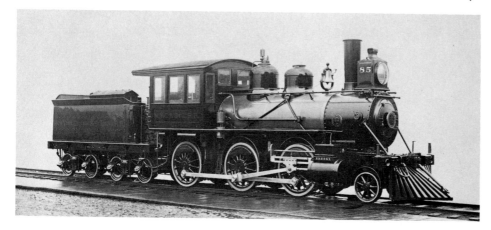

Reputedly the first engines equipped with forward sloping firebox grate, the 1890 Moguls came with straight-top boilers, 56-inch drivers, and 18 x 24-inch cylinders. Like earlier Nickel Plate locomotives, Brooks-built H's were painted green with red trim and lettering. —Schenectady History Center.

Darius Caldwell's class I 4-6-0 freight hauler of 1891 weighed 50 tons and developed 18,220 pounds of tractive effort. Steam dome was located on sloping course of this Brooks wagon-top boiler. Later class J's and class K's were similar. — Schenectady History Center.

NYC&STL — LOCOMOTIVES ACQUIRED 1887-1909

Number	Class	Type	Builder	Builder number	Date
2nd 30-39	P-1	4-6-0	Brooks	46187-46196	5-1909
2nd 40-49	P	4-6-0	Brooks	38827-38836	12-1905
2nd 50-54	P	4-6-0	Brooks	40786-40790	10-1906
2nd 55-64	P-1	4-6-0	Brooks	45226-45235	3-1908
69-73	G	2-6-0	Brooks	1320-1324	1-1888
74-76	G	2-6-0	Brooks	1346-1348	3-1888
77-83	G	2-6-0	Brooks	1414-1420	8-1888
84-88	H	2-6-0	Brooks	1629-1633	3-1890
89-93	I	4-6-0	Brooks	1834-1838	3-1891
94-98	I	4-6-0	Brooks	1880-1884	5-1891
99, 101	J	4-6-0	Baldwin	12905-12906	9-1892
100	J	4-6-0	Baldwin	12933	10-1892
102-104	J	4-6-0	Baldwin	12908-12910	9-1892
105-107	J	4-6-0	Baldwin	12915, 12919, 12921	9-1892
108	J	4-6-0	Baldwin	12932	10-1892
109-113	K	4-6-0	Brooks	2627-2631	1-1896
114-118	K	4-6-0	Schenectady	4396-4400	1-1896
119-128	N	2-8-0	Brooks	4105-4114	2-1902
129-143	N-1	2-8-0	Brooks	28205-28219	10-1903
144-148	N-1	2-8-0	Brooks	29575-29579	3-1904
149	N-2	2-8-0	Brooks	40791	10-1906
2nd 150-158	N-2	2-8-0	Brooks	40792-40800	10-1906
2nd 159-161	N-3	2-8-0	Baldwin	31339, 31355, 31473	8-1907
2nd 162-166	N-4	2-8-0	Brooks	45221-45225	3-1908
176-181	O	4-4-0	Brooks	29730-29735	6-1904

Number	Class	Type	Builder	Builder number	Date
182-185	R	4-6-0	Baldwin	30939, 30988-30990	6-1907
186-187	R	4-6-0	Baldwin	31013, 31062	6-1907
2nd 200, 208	M	0-6-0	Brooks	3461-3462	3-1900
2nd 209	M	0-6-0	Brooks	3470	3-1900
3rd 209	M	0-6-0	Brooks	46197	5-1909
2nd 210-213	M	0-6-0	Brooks	46198-46201	5-1909
214-216	L	0-6-0	Brooks	2637-2639	2-1896
217, 218	M	0-6-0	Brooks	3477, 3486	3/4-1900
219, 220	M	0-6-0	Brooks	3723-3724	1-1901
221-223	M	0-6-0	Brooks	3763-3765	2-1901
224-228	M	0-6-0	Manchester	25966-25970	5-1902
229-233	M	0-6-0	Schenectady	29570-29574	3-1904
234-238	M	0-6-0	Manchester	38822-38826	12-1905
239, 240	M	0-6-0	Baldwin	31352, 31363	8-1907
241-244	M	0-6-0	Baldwin	31408-31410, 31526	8-1907
245-249	M	0-6-0	Brooks	45216-45220	3-1908

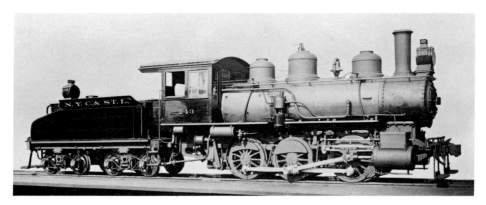

Baldwin's share of the 46 class M engines were built in 1907. Never super-heated, these ponies rode on 50-inch drivers and had a slope-backed 3000-gallon tender. Coal-bunker capacity was 4.4 tons. — *Collection of H. L. Broadbelt.*

DIMENSIONS OF LOCOMOTIVES (1908)

Class	Cylinders*	Drivers	Weight on drivers	Total weight	Boiler pressure	Tractive effort	Grate area
P	19" x 24" s	62"	105,600	136,500	180	21,400	28.54 (A)
P-1	19" x 24" s	62"	106,300	140,500	180	21,400	28.54 (A, W)
G	19" x 24" s	56"	85,500	101,800	145	19,010	16.77 (B)
H	18" x 24" s	56"	83,500	99,000	150	17,558	26 (C)
I, J	18" x 24" s	56"	77,500	100,000	155	18,220	22.41 (D)
K	18" x 24" s	56"	87,000	110,000	160	18,880	22.41
N	19" x 28" p	62"	138,600	157,100	200	27,710	46.25
N	19" x 28" p	63"	146,500	166,350	190	25,800	46.25 (E, F)
N-1	19" x 28" p	62"	142,000	160,000	200	27,710	40.9
N-1	19" x 28" p	63"	142,800	166,100	190	25,800	40.9 (E, F)
N-2, N-3	19" x 28" s	62"	142,000	160,000	200	27,710	40.9 (W)
N-2, N-3	19" x 28" p	63"	142,800	166,100	190	25,800	40.9 (G, W)
N-4	19" x 28" s	62"	150,600	169,000	200	27,710	40.9 (W)
N-4	19" x 28" p	63"	150,600	169,000	190	25,800	40.0 (G, W)
O	18" x 24" p	68"	80,600	123,700	190	18,465	27.6 (H)
R	20" x 26" p	72"	113,700	156,350	200	24,600	40.9 (W)
R	20" x 26" p	73"	117,900	171,500	200	24,220	40 (I, W)
L	18" x 24" s	50"	101,950	101,950	170	22,440	21.34 (J)
M	18" x 24" s	50"	103,450	103,450	170	22,440	21.34 (J)

*s — slide valve; p — piston valve.

(A) Later changed to 63-inch drivers and tractive effort rating of 21,040 lbs.

(B) Boiler pressure reduced to 135 lbs. and tractive effort rating reduced to 17,800 lbs. in June 1909.

(C) Originally 175 lbs. boiler pressure, 20,650 lbs. rated tractive effort.

(D) Engine 92 later received 62-inch drivers. Tractive effort reduced to 16,508 lbs. Engine 100 originally a Vauclain compound with 12 and 20 x 24-inch cylinders. Simpled in September 1907.

(E) With 22-unit Schmidt superheater applied. Rebuilt to 0-6-0, 1920-25 with 19½ x 28-inch cylinders, 57-inch drivers, 30,166 lbs. tractive effort. Class N became B-9a, total weight 155,300 lbs. Class N-1 became B-9b, total weight 160,230 lbs.

(F) Engines 126 and 140 rebuilt by Alco in May 1908 with 20 x 28-inch cylinders. With 63-inch drivers and 180-lb. boiler pressure, these engines had tractive effort rating of 27,180 lbs.

(G) As rebuilt with 24-unit superheater and Universal piston valves.

(H) When 21-unit superheaters installed, boiler pressure and rated tractive effort reduced to 180 lbs. and 17,500 lbs., respectively. Engines 176-178 rebuilt with slide valve cylinders 1906-1907.

(I) As rebuilt with new piston valve cylinders and 22-unit superheater.

(J) Driver diameter later increased to 52 inches and tractive effort reduced to 21,590 lbs.

(W) Walschaerts valve gear.

Second 51 was built by Brooks in 1906 and was renumbered 311 in 1910. This 4-6-0, bought for fast freight duty, had 62-inch drivers, Richardson balanced steam chest valves, and Stephenson link motion. Standard tender held 5500 gallons of water and 14 tons of coal.— TRAINS *collection.*

2nd 30 — Renumbered 325, 1910; laid up December 1923; dismantled May 1925.

2nd 31 — Renumbered 326, 1910; rebuilt March 1923 with superheater, Universal piston valves. Laid up at Frankfort January 1932; retired June 1933.

2nd 32 — Renumbered 327, 1910. Withdrawn June 1924 and used as stationary boiler at Broadway coach yard until May 1926. Dismantled July 1927.

2nd 33 — Renumbered 328, 1910. Retired October 1925 and subsequently dismantled.

2nd 34 — Renumbered 329, 1910. Leased to W&LE January-March 1918. Retired October 1925.

2nd 35 — Renumbered 330, 1910. Leased to W&LE December 1917 through May 1918. Rebuilt with superheater and Universal piston valves August 1923. Equipped with automatic train stop 1929 to 1931. Laid up at Frankfort January 1932; retired June 1933.

2nd 36 — Renumbered 331, 1910. Leased to W&LE December 1917 through May 1918. Rebuilt May 1925 with superheater, Universal piston valves. Dismantled March 31, 1936.

2nd 37 — Renumbered 332, 1910. Rebuilt December 1922 with superheater, Universal piston valves. Laid up October 1933 and subsequently dismantled.

2nd 38 — Renumbered 333, 1910. Laid up April 1923; dismantled November 1923.

2nd 39 — Renumbered 334, 1910. Rebuilt May 1925 with superheater, Universal piston valves. Laid up July 1933; retired October 1933.

2nd 40 — Renumbered 300, 1910. Sold for $10,250 to Akron, Canton & Youngstown, their 300, May 9, 1920. To Missouri & Arkansas 18, September 30, 1936.

2nd 41 — Renumbered 301, 1910. To AC&Y 301, May 9, 1920. To Carey Company June 8, 1929.

2nd 42 — Renumbered 302, 1910. Baker-Pilliod valve gear applied June 1909. Dismantled June 9, 1922.

2nd 43 — Renumbered 303, 1910. To AC&Y 303, May 9, 1920. To Midland Continental 303, June 13, 1930. Retired December 1946 and sold for scrap.

2nd 44 — Renumbered 304, 1910. To AC&Y 304, May 9, 1920. To Dansville & Mount Morris 304, July 6, 1929. Sold June 25, 1957, to Myers Steel & Supply Company but held at Dansville, N. Y., until 1964 when sold to F. Nelson Blount, North Walpole, N. H.

2nd 45 — Renumbered 305, 1910. To AC&Y 305, May 9, 1920. To Peckham Engineering Company July 3, 1929.

2nd 46 — Renumbered 306, 1910. Dismantled June 9, 1922.

2nd 47 — Renumbered 307, 1910. To AC&Y 307, May 9, 1920. Scrapped October 25, 1929.

2nd 48 — Renumbered 308, 1910. To AC&Y 308, May 6, 1920. To Peckham Engineering Company November 14, 1929.

2nd 49 — Renumbered 309, 1910. To AC&Y 309, August 1920. To Midland Continental 309, November 15, 1929. Retired August 1934.

2nd 50 — Renumbered 310, 1910. To AC&Y 310, August 1920. To Peckham Engineering Company July 3, 1929.

2nd 51 — Renumbered 311, 1910. Retired May 1922; dismantled June 9, 1922.

2nd 52 — Renumbered 312, 1910. To AC&Y 312, June 1920. Scrapped October 3, 1934.

2nd 53 — Renumbered 313, 1910. To AC&Y 313, August 1920. To Peckham Engineering Company October 10, 1930.

2nd 54 — Renumbered 314, 1910. To AC&Y 314, June 1920. Scrapped October 3, 1930.

2nd 55 — Renumbered 315, 1910. Last run April 1926. To stationary duty Broadway coach yard May 1926. Retired December 1930; dismantled 1931.

2nd 56-57 — Renumbered 316-317, 1910. Withdrawn 1922. Sold October 31, 1923.

2nd 58-59 — Renumbered 318-319, 1910. Rebuilt at Stony Island with superheaters, Universal piston valves applied May 1923 and June 1925, respectively. Last runs April 1932 on I&MC Division passenger. Both retired June 1933 and subsequently dismantled at Lima.

2nd 60 — Renumbered 320, 1910. Rebuilt February 1923 with superheater and Universal piston valves. Laid up September 1932 at South Lima; retired March 1933 and subsequently dismantled.

2nd 61-63 — Renumbered 321-323. Sold October 31, 1923.

2nd 64 — Renumbered 324, 1910. Rebuilt July 1925 with superheater and Universal piston valves. Laid up at South Lima June 1932; retired June 1933.

69 — Renumbered 4th 200, 1910; 2nd 250 in 1918. Dismantled October 9, 1920.

70 — Renumbered 3rd 201 in 1910, and 2nd 251 in 1918. Dismantled November 5, 1920.

71-72 — Renumbered 3rd 202 and 2nd 203 in 1910. Retired September 1914.

73 — Renumbered 2nd 204 in 1910, and 2nd 252 in 1918. Dismantled November 5, 1920.

74-76 — Renumbered 2nd 205-207 in 1910. All retired September 1914.

77 — Renumbered 3rd 208 in 1910, and 2nd 253 in 1918. To stationary duty at Fort Wayne October 10, 1918. Dismantled 1920.

78 — Renumbered 4th 209, 1910. Dismantled September 1914.

79 — Renumbered 3rd 210 in 1910 and 2nd 254 in 1918. To stationary duty at Broadway 1918. Dismantled November 5, 1920.

80-81 — Renumbered 3rd 211-212, 1910. Dismantled September 1916.

82-83 — Renumbered 3rd 213-214, 1910. Dismantled September 1914 and June 17, 1916.

84 — Renumbered 3rd 215, 1910. Dismantled May 21, 1913.

85-86 — Renumbered 3rd 216, 2nd 217 in 1910. Retired September 1914.

87 — Renumbered 2nd 218, 1910. Dismantled July 7, 1913.

88 — Renumbered 2nd 219, 1910. Dismantled June 17, 1916.

89 — Renumbered 270, 1910. Dismantled 1916.

90 — Renumbered 271, 1910. Dismantled September 13, 1916.

91 — Renumbered 272, 1910. Dismantled December 6, 1920.

92 — Renumbered 273, 1910. Dismantled October 23, 1914.

93-96 — Renumbered 274-277, 1910. All retired December 6, 1920.

97 — Renumbered 278, 1910. Sold June 20, 1917.

98 — Renumbered 279, 1910. Dismantled 1916.

99 — Renumbered 280, 1910. Dismantled October 23, 1914.

100 — Renumbered 281, 1910. Dismantled December 6, 1920.

101 — Renumbered 282, 1910. Sold October 21, 1917.

102 — Renumbered 283, 1910. Dismantled August 2, 1920.

103, 107, and 108 — Renumbered 284, 288, 289 in 1910. Dismantled 1916.

104-105 — Renumbered 285-286, 1910. Dismantled August 10, 1916, and June 17, 1916.

106 — Renumbered 287, 1910. Dismantled May 23, 1913.

109-111 — Renumbered 290-292, 1910. Retired December 6, 1920.

112 — Renumbered 293, 1910. Sold latter part of 1918.

113 — Renumbered 294, 1910. Sold January 30, 1918.

114-118 — Renumbered 295-299, 1910. Retired December 6, 1920.

119 — Renumbered 400, 1910. Superheater applied December 1914. Converted to 0-6-0 and renumbered 3rd 100 November 1922. Laid up at Conneaut March 1931 and retired June 1933.

120 — Renumbered 401, 1910. Superheater applied September 1915. Converted to 0-6-0 and renumbered 3rd 101 February 1921. Laid up at Conneaut November 1931; dismantled there May 1934.

121 — Renumbered 402, 1910. Superheater applied June 1915. Converted to 0-6-0 and renumbered 3rd 102 April 1921. Laid up at Lima July 1933; retired October 1933.

122 — Renumbered 403, 1910. Superheater applied September 1914. Converted to 0-6-0 and renumbered 3rd 103 in November 1920. Laid up at Frankfort May 1946; dismantled there August 9, 1946.

123 — Renumbered 404, 1910. Superheater applied September 1915. Converted to 0-6-0 and renumbered 3rd 104 October 1920. Laid up at Conneaut January 1930; dismantled there January 12, 1931.

124 — Renumbered 405, 1910. Superheater applied October 1911. Converted to 0-6-0 and renumbered 3rd 105 February 1921. Laid up at Conneaut July 1932; retired June 1933.

125 — Renumbered 406, 1910. Superheater applied January 1915. Converted to 0-6-0 and renumbered 3rd 106 December 1920. Laid up at Conneaut October 1932; dismantled there December 1933.

126 — Renumbered 407, 1910. Superheater applied May 1915. Converted to 0-6-0 and renumbered 3rd 107 August 1920. Laid up at Frankfort 1944; dismantled May 31, 1945.

127 — Renumbered 408, 1910. Superheater applied August 1916. Converted to 0-6-0 and renumbered 3rd 108 June 1920. Laid up at Conneaut April 1932; retired June 1933.

128 — Renumbered 409, 1910. Superheater applied March 1915. Converted to 0-6-0 and renumbered 3rd 109 May 1921. Laid up at Conneaut March 1932; retired June 1933.

129 — Renumbered 410, 1910. Superheater applied March 1916. Converted to 0-6-0 and renumbered 3rd 110 December 1923. Laid up at Conneaut March 1931; dismantled there April 18, 1933.

130 — Renumbered 411, 1910. Superheater applied May 1915. Converted to 0-6-0 and renumbered 3rd 111 May 1922. Laid up January 1932; retired March 1933.

131 — Renumbered 412, 1910. Superheater applied May 1916. Converted to 0-6-0 and renumbered 3rd 112 December 1920. Laid up at Lima December 1933; dismantled there February 1934.

132 — Renumbered 413, 1910. Superheater applied June 1917. Converted to 0-6-0 and renumbered 3rd 113

October 1924. Laid up at Lima 1931; retired June 1933.

133 — Renumbered 414, 1910. Superheater applied March 1919. Converted to 0-6-0 and renumbered 3rd 114 July 1923. New boiler GO-19366, No. 2 applied January 1927. Laid up August 1946. Sold to Rubber City Sand & Gravel Company, their 114, on March 10, 1947. Sold for scrap September 1953.

134 — Renumbered 415, 1910. Superheater applied June 1916. Converted to 0-6-0 and renumbered 3rd 115 December 1923. New boiler GO-19366, No. 1, applied October 1926. Laid up July 1946; dismantled November 30, 1946.

135 — Renumbered 416, 1910. Superheater applied June 1919. Converted to 0-6-0 and renumbered 3rd 116 September 1923. Laid up at Conneaut June 1933; dismantled there May 1934.

136 — Renumbered 417, 1910. Superheater applied October 1916. Converted to 0-6-0 and renumbered 3rd 117 April 1922. Laid up at Lima 1931; retired June 1933.

137 — Renumbered 418, 1910. Superheater applied February 1915. Converted to 0-6-0 and renumbered 2nd 118 September 1923. Laid up at Conneaut August 1931; dismantled there May 1934.

138 — Renumbered 419, 1910. Superheater applied October 1914. Converted to 0-6-0 and renumbered 2nd 119 May 1922. Laid up at Lima May 1932; retired June 1933.

139 — Renumbered 420, 1910. Superheater applied October 1914. Converted to 0-6-0 and renumbered 3rd 120 September 1923. Laid up at Lima June 1933; retired October 1933.

140 — Renumbered 421, 1910. Superheater applied August 1915. Wrecked in collision with 70 at Dunkirk December 10, 1905. Converted to 0-6-0 and renumbered 3rd 121 October 1923. Stored November 1931 through July 1933. Laid up at Toledo January 1948 and used in stationary service at Bellevue until November 24, 1948, when sold to Erman-Howell Division, Luria Steel & Trading Corporation.

141 — Renumbered 422, 1910. Superheater applied September 1919. Converted to 0-6-0 and renumbered 3rd 122 October 1923. Reboilered October 1926. Laid up from October 1930 through December 1934. Last miles September 1946. Sold to Republic Steel Corporation, Cleveland, O., March 14, 1947.

142 — Renumbered 423, 1910. Superheater applied April 1915. Converted to 0-6-0 and renumbered 3rd 123 August 1922. Retired October 1933.

143 — Renumbered 424, 1910. Superheater applied May 1920. Converted to 0-6-0 and renumbered 3rd 124 December 1923. Laid up February 1932; dismantled May 1934.

144 — Renumbered 425, 1910. Superheater applied June 1915. Converted to 0-6-0 and renumbered 3rd 125 December 1923. Laid up February 1932; dismantled April 12, 1933.

145 — Renumbered 426, 1910. Superheater applied April 1916. Converted to 0-6-0 and renumbered 2nd 126 October 1923. Retired March 1933.

146 — Renumbered 427, 1910. Superheater applied July 1915. Converted to 0-6-0 and renumbered 2nd 127 July 1923. Laid up at Conneaut August 1930; retired December 1930.

147 — Renumbered 428, 1910. Superheater applied May 1916. Converted to 0-6-0 and renumbered 2nd 128 October 1923. Laid up at Conneaut October 1931; retired June 1933.

148 — Renumbered 429, 1910. Superheater applied July 1916. Converted to 0-6-0 and renumbered 2nd 129 February 1925. Laid up at Conneaut April 1931; dismantled there May 1934.

149 — Renumbered 430, 1910. Superheater and Universal piston valves applied February 1918. Laid up at Lima May 1933; dismantled there July 1933.

2nd 150 — Renumbered 431, 1910. Superheater and Universal piston valves applied December 1917. Laid up at Lima June 1934; dismantled there November 1934.

2nd 151-152 — Renumbered 432-433, 1910. Superheater and Universal valves applied October 1917. Retired June 1933.

2nd 153-155 — Renumbered 434-436, 1910. Superheater and Universal piston valves applied 1917-1918. All laid up at Lima 1931; retired March 1933.

2nd 156 — Renumbered 437, 1910. Superheater and Universal valves applied May 1918. Laid up at Lima April 1932; retired June 1933.

2nd 157 — Renumbered 438, 1910. Superheater and Universal valves applied May 1917. Laid up at Frankfort 1931; retired June 1933.

2nd 158 — Renumbered 439, 1910. Superheater and Universal valves applied August 1917. Retired August 1929.

2nd 159 — Renumbered 440, 1910. Superheater and Universal valves applied June 1917. Leased to E. B. Badger & Sons January 1943 and used in construction of Plum Brook Ordnance Works, Sandusky, O. Laid up at Lima April 1945; dismantled there August 1945.

2nd 160 — Renumbered 441, 1910. Superheater and Universal valves applied May 1917. Laid up at Conneaut June 1930; dismantled March 31, 1936.

2nd 161 — Renumbered 442, 1910. Superheater and Universal valves applied June 1917. Laid up at Conneaut 1930; dismantled there April 3, 1933.

2nd 162 — Renumbered 443, 1910. Superheater and Universal valves applied March 1918. Laid up at Frankfort November 1933; dismantled February 1934.

2nd 163 — Renumbered 444, 1910. Superheater and Universal valves applied November 1917. Dismantled March 31, 1936.

2nd 164 — Renumbered 445, 1910. Superheater and Universal valves applied September 1917. Laid up at Frankfort 1931; dismantled there June 1933.

2nd 165 — Renumbered 446, 1910. Superheater and Universal valves applied September 1917. Laid up and assigned to stationary duty at Stony Island October 1937. Returned to road service November 1942. Laid up at Conneaut January 1945; dismantled there June 20, 1945.

2nd 166 — Renumbered 447, 1910. Superheater and Universal valves applied May 1918. Laid up March 1933; retired October 1933.

176 — Renumbered 2nd 120, 1910, and 2nd 140, June 1922. Slide valve cylinders circa 1907. Superheater and Universal valves December 1913. Dismantled September 1923.

177 — Renumbered 2nd 121, 1910, and 2nd 141, June 1922. Slide valve cylinders circa 1907. Superheater and Universal valves applied July 1912. Dismantled November 1923.

178 — Renumbered 2nd 122, 1910, and 2nd 142, June 1922. Slide valve cylinders circa 1907. Superheater and Universal piston valves applied June 1913. Dismantled October 1923.

179 — Renumbered 2nd 123, 1910, and 2nd 143, June 1922. Superheater applied November 1912. Retired January 1924.

180 — Renumbered 2nd 124, 1910. Superheater applied September 1911. Retired December 6, 1920.

181 — Renumbered 2nd 125, 1910. Superheater applied June 1912. Wrecked at Millers City (rear-end collision) October 1912. Retired December 6, 1920.

182 — Renumbered 3rd 150, 1910. Rebuilt at Conneaut May 1913 with superheater and piston valve cylinders. Walschaerts valve gear modified June 1921. Laid up at Conneaut May 1932; dismantled there December 1933.

183 — Renumbered 3rd 151, 1910. Rebuilt at Conneaut September 1913 with superheater and piston valve cylinders. Walschaerts modified January 1922. Derailed by open switch and wrecked while pulling No. 6 at Hamburg, N. Y., March 23, 1926. Last run made Oc-

tober 1932. Dismantled at Conneaut December 1933.

184 — Renumbered 3rd 152, 1910. Rebuilt at Conneaut December 1912 with superheater and piston valve cylinders. Walschaerts modified March 1921. Rebuilt January 1939 with steel cab and pilot; Precision reverse applied. Laid up at Lima April 1948. Sold to Hyman-Michaels July 31, 1948.

185 — Renumbered 3rd 153, 1910. Rebuilt at Stony Island February 1913 with superheater and piston valve cylinders. Walschaerts modified April 1921. Laid up at Frankfort 1931; retired June 1933.

186 — Renumbered 3rd 154, 1910. Rebuilt at Conneaut November 1913 with superheater and new piston valve cylinders. Walschaerts modified June 1922. Equipped with A.T.S. June 1926 to June 1934. Rebuilt August 1938 with steel cab and pilot, Precision reverse. Laid up at Lima August 1948 and sold November 24, 1948, to Erman-Howell Division of Luria Steel & Trading Corporation.

187 — Renumbered 3rd 155, 1910. Rebuilt at Conneaut August 1913 with superheater and piston valve cylinders. Walschaerts modified March 1921. Steel cab and pilot, Precision reverse applied July 1938. Last run June 1948. Sold to Purdy & Company, Burnham, Ill., November 20, 1948.

2nd 200 — Renumbered 2nd 214, 1906; 4th 4, 1910; 5th 1, March 29, 1924. Laid up February 1924; retired December 1924; dismantled May 1925.

2nd 208 — Renumbered 2nd 215, 1906; 3rd 5, 1910. Retired June 1922.

2nd 209 — Renumbered 2nd 216, 1906; 4th 6, 1910; 3rd 2, March 28, 1924. Laid up February 1928; dismantled March 1929.

3rd 209 — Renumbered 3rd 40, 1910, and 4th 21, April 3, 1924. Laid up February 1926. Sold to Southern Iron & Equipment Company, their 2099, May 1926.

2nd 210 — Renumbered 3rd 41, 1910, and 4th 22, March 18, 1924. Laid up July 1930; dismantled January 17, 1931.

2nd 211 — Renumbered 3rd 42, 1910. Laid up at Conneaut December 1923. Shipped to Birmingham Rail & Locomotive Company February 19, 1924.

2nd 212 — Renumbered 3rd 43, 1910. To Stange Construction Company 4, June 1922.

2nd 213 — Renumbered 3rd 44, 1910, and 4th 24, March 21, 1924. Laid up September 1924. Sold to Birmingham Rail & Locomotive Company January 15, 1925.

214 — Renumbered 3rd 200, 1906, and 4th 1, 1910. Retired December 1920.

215 — Renumbered 2nd 201, 1906, and 2nd 2, 1910. Retired December 1920.

216 — Renumbered 2nd 202, 1906, and 3rd 3, 1910. Retired December 1920.

217 — Renumbered 3rd 7, 1910. Sold October 31, 1923.

218 — Renumbered 4th 8, 1910, and 4th 3, March 20, 1924. Laid up 1927; dismantled March 1929.

219 — Renumbered 3rd 9, 1910. Dismantled September 1923.

220 — Renumbered 4th 10, 1910. Dismantled June 9, 1922.

221 — Renumbered 4th 11, 1910, and 5th 4 March 29, 1924. Laid up 1927; dismantled March 1929.

222 — Renumbered 3rd 12, 1910, and 4th 5, March 29, 1924. Sold to Hamilton Car Company December 1925.

223 — Renumbered 3rd 13, 1910, and 5th 6, March 28, 1924. Laid up October 1929; dismantled January 21, 1931.

224 — Renumbered 3rd 14, 1910. Dismantled at Stony Island June 19, 1922.

225 — Renumbered 3rd 17, 1910. Laid up 1922; dismantled November 1923.

226 — Renumbered 3rd 16, 1910. Sold to Detroit, Bay City & Western June 1920.

227 — Renumbered 3rd 15, 1910, and 4th 7 March 29, 1924. Laid up March 1924; dismantled May 1925.

228 — Renumbered 3rd 18, 1910. Sold October 31, 1923.

229 — Renumbered 3rd 19, 1910. Sold June 20, 1917.

230 — Renumbered 3rd 20, 1910, and 5th 8 March 30, 1924. Dismantled July 1929.

231 — Renumbered 3rd 21, 1910, and 4th 9 March 29, 1924. Laid up March 1928 and used in stationary service until retirement in December 1930. Dismantled January 30, 1931.

232 — Renumbered 3rd 22, 1910, and 5th 10, 1924. Dismantled July 1929.

233 — Renumbered 3rd 23, 1910. Sold to P. T. Clifford & Son, Valparaiso, Ind., February 1924.

234 — Renumbered 3rd 24, 1910, and 4th 12 March 29, 1924. Laid up 1924; dismantled January 1926.

235 — Renumbered 3rd 25, 1910. Laid up 1922; dismantled November 1923.

236 — Renumbered 3rd 26, 1910, and 4th 13 March 26, 1924. Laid up January 1930; dismantled on February 28, 1931.

237 — Renumbered 3rd 27, 1910. Dismantled October 1923.

238 — Renumbered 3rd 28, 1910, and 4th 14 March 31, 1924. Laid up November 1929; dismantled February 20, 1931.

239 — Renumbered 3rd 29, 1910, and 4th 15 March 25, 1924. Sold to Birmingham Rail & Locomotive Company January 1925.

240 — Renumbered 3rd 30, 1910, and 4th 16 March 14, 1924. Sold to Birmingham Rail & Locomotive Company October 1925.

241 — Renumbered 3rd 31, 1910, and 4th 17 March 16, 1924. Laid up January 1925; dismantled January 1926.

242 — Renumbered 3rd 32, 1910, and 4th 18 March 24, 1924. Laid up March 3, 1926. Sold to Southern Iron & Equipment Company in May 1926. To Mississippi Central 107.

243 — Renumbered 3rd 33, 1910, and 4th 19 March 28, 1924. Laid up June 1927; dismantled July 1929.

244 — Renumbered 3rd 34, 1910. Dismantled at Conneaut June 17, 1922.

245 — Renumbered 3rd 35, 1910. Dismantled January 1924.

246 — Renumbered 3rd 36, 1910, and 4th 20 March 24, 1924. Retired March 1933.

247 — Renumbered 3rd 37, 1910. To Southern Iron & Equipment 1884, September 1923. To Brookhaven (Miss.) Gravel Company 6, November 1923.

248 — Renumbered 3rd 38, 1910. Laid up May 1923. To Southern Iron & Equipment 1885, September 1923. To G. L. Mays (Augusta, Ga.) 10, November 20, 1923.

249 — Renumbered 3rd 39, 1910. Dismantled June 19, 1922.

Pre-Bernet P-3's were superheated and equipped for passenger duty. Last of the 1913 clan — No. 366 — held down LE&W passenger assignments until 1936. Here she heads No. 22 on July 20, 1935. — *Clyde E. Helms.*

NYC&STL — LOCOMOTIVES ACQUIRED 1910-1923

Number		Class	Type	Builder	Builder number	Date
3rd	45-49	M	0-6-0	Brooks	47920-47924	4-1910
3rd	50-59	B-11a	0-6-0	Brooks	56303-56312	10-1916
3rd	60-64	B-11b	0-6-0	Lima	5564-5568	5-1917
2nd	65-69	B-11b	0-6-0	Lima	5569-5573	5-1917
2nd	70-74	B-11c	0-6-0	Lima	5676-5680	3-1918
2nd	75-80	S (A)	0-6-0	Brooks	53833-53838	8-1913
3rd	75-79	B-11c	0-6-0	Lima	5681-5685	3-1918
3rd	156-158	R	4-6-0	Brooks	53830-53832	8-1913
3rd	160-163	K-1a	4-6-2	Lima	6317-6320	12-1922
3rd	164-166	K-1b	4-6-2	Brooks	64631-64633	8-1923
2nd	167-169	K-1b	4-6-2	Brooks	64634-64636	8-1923
5th	200	U-2	0-8-0	Lima	5686	5-1918
4th	201-202	U-2	0-8-0	Lima	5687-5688	5-1918
3rd	203-204	U-2	0-8-0	Lima	5689-5690	5-1918
	335-349	P-2	4-6-0	Brooks	47905-47919	4-1910
	350-358	P-2	4-6-0	Brooks	50020-50028	6-1911
	359-366	P-3	4-6-0	Brooks	53822-53829	9-1913
	448-453	N-5	2-8-0	Brooks	50029-50034	5-1911
	454-459	N-6	2-8-0	Brooks	53839-53844	8-1913
	460-469	T	2-8-0	Brooks	28808-28817	1903 (B)
	470-474	T	2-8-0	Brooks	28867-28871	1903 (B)
	500-504	H-5a	2-8-2	Lima	5428-5432	3-1917
	505-507	H-5a	2-8-2	Lima	5433-5435	4-1917
	508-509	H-5a	2-8-2	Lima	5436-5437	5-1917

Number	Class	Type	Builder	Builder number	Date
510-534	H-5b	2-8-2	Brooks	57492-57516	8-1917
601-610	H-6a	2-8-2	Schenectady	59578-59587	10-1918 (C)
611-615	H-6b	2-8-2	Lima	6182-6186	12-1920
616	H-6c	2-8-2	Lima	6187	1-1921
617-626	H-6d	2-8-2	Lima	6307-6316	10-1922
627-631	H-6d	2-8-2	Lima	6432-6436	10-1922
632-646	H-6e	2-8-2	Lima	6635-6649	12-1923

(A) Classification changed to B-10 in March 1934.
(B) Ex-New York Central 5855-5869; originally LS&MS 855-869.
(C) USRA.

Piston-valved 103 was one of 30 Consolidations converted to 0-6-0's between 1920 and 1925. Remaining drivers were changed from 63- to 57-inch diameter and original 5500-gallon tenders were rebuilt with recessed collar for maximum switching visibility. January 17, 1936, found the B-9a at St. Marys. — *Clyde E. Helms.*

Bumped from Cleveland yard assignments by 1000 h.p. Alco diesels, B-11 switchers ran out their last miles at remote secondary terminals. The 77, a Lima B-11c of 1918, found employment at Delphos, where this photo was made on October 5, 1947. — *Clyde E. Helms.*

DIMENSIONS OF LOCOMOTIVES

Class	Cylinders	Valve motion*	Drivers	Weight on drivers	Total weight	Boiler pressure	Tractive effort	Grate area
M	18″ x 24″	s S	50″	107,500	107,500	170	22,440	21.34 (A)
B-11	21″ x 28″	p W	57″	173,000	173,000	180	33,150	32.7
S (B-10)	20″ x 26″	p W	51″	153,100	153,100	160	27,700	23.7 (B)
R (156-158)	20″ x 26″	p W	73″	126,175	173,900	200	24,220	40.9
K-1a	22½″ x 26″	p W	73″	148,500	245,000	200	30,700	50.23 (C)
	22½″ x 26″	p W	74″	159,300	265,100	200	30,200	50.23 (D)
K-1b	22½″ x 26″	p W	73″	155,000	252,000	200	30,700	50.23 (C)
	22½″ x 26″	p W	74″	157,250	255,320	200	30,200	50.23 (D)
U-2	23½″ x 30″	p W	57″	216,500	216,500	185	45,700	50.2
P-2 (335-349)	19″ x 24″	s B	62″	105,000	143,500	180	21,380	28.5 (E)
P-2 (350-358)	19″ x 24″	s B	63″	108,000	143,000	180	21,040	28.5
P-3	19″ x 24″	p B	63″	112,000	150,000	180	21,040	28.5
N-5	19″ x 28″	s B	63″	155,500	175,000	200	27,300	40.9 (F)
	19″ x 28″	p B	63″	159,050	181,900	190	25,800	40.9 (G)
N-6	20″ x 28″	p W	63″	159,100	184,900	180	27,200	40.9 (H)
T	21″ x 30″	p B	63″	161,829	183,700	190	33,900	43
H-5	25″ x 32″	p B	63″	216,500	287,000	180	48,600	56.5 (I)
	25″ x 32″	p B	63″	220,980	290,560	185	49,900	56.5 (J)
	24″ x 32″	p B	63″	224,950	291,750	200	49,750	56.5 (K)
H-6a	26″ x 30″	p W	63″	220,000	292,000	200	54,700	66.7 (L)
	26″ x 30″	p W	63″	228,450	307,420	200	54,700	66.7 (M)

Class	Cylinders	Valve motion*	Drivers	Weight on drivers	Total weight	Boiler pressure	Tractive effort	Grate area	
H-6b	{26″ x 30″	p W	63″	225,000	305,000	200	54,700†	66.7	(N)
	{26″ x 30″	p W	63″	233,000	316,200	200	54,700†	66.7	(O)
H-6c	{26″ x 30″	p W	63″	226,500	307,000	200	54,700†	66.7	(P)
	{26″ x 30″	p W	63″	239,060	320,000	200	54,700†	66.7	(Q)
H-6d	{26″ x 30″	p W	63″	227,000	308,000	200	54,700†	66.7	(R)
	{26″ x 30″	p W	63″	234,000	316,800	200	54,700†	66.7	(S)
H-6e	26″ x 30″	p B	63″	237,050	319,400	200	54,700†	66.7	(T)

*s — slide valve; p — piston valve; B — Baker; S — Stephenson; W — Walschaerts.

†64,100 lbs. rated tractive effort with trailer booster.

(A) Drivers to 52-inch, boiler pressure to 180 lbs., and tractive effort to 23,790 lbs. in 1918. Boiler pressure and tractive effort to 170 and 21,590 lbs., respectively, in 1924.

(B) Later, drivers to 52-inch, tractive effort to 27,200 lbs.; grate area changed to 28.52 square feet.

(C) As originally furnished.

(D) With syphons applied and as otherwise modified.

(E) Saturated; drivers to 63-inch and tractive effort to 21,040 lbs.

(F) Saturated; as originally furnished.

(G) With superheater and Universal piston valves applied.

(H) Superheated; weights shown per Lima Locomotive Works 1927.

(I) As furnished, with superheater but without stoker.

(J) With Duplex stoker. Applied 1923-1925.

(K) With cylinders bushed and as otherwise modified, all engines but 515, 526, and 531.

(L) As furnished, with single pump, Duplex stoker, superheater.

(M) As modified, with 2 cross-compound pumps on pilot deck and Worthington BL feedwater heater applied.

(N) As furnished, with single pump, etc. See notes for modified weights for engines 611 and 614.

(O) Engines 612, 613, and 615 with C-1 booster and BL feedwater heater applied; 2 pumps mounted on pilot deck.

(P) As furnished, with single pump, trailer booster, Duplex stoker.

(Q) With syphons and BL feedwater heater, 2 pumps on pilot deck.

(R) As furnished, with single pump, trailer booster.

(S) As modified, with BL feedwater heater and 2 pumps on pilot deck.

(T) As furnished. Weight of engines 639 and 645, later equipped with syphons, was 320,810 lbs.

Lima K-1a's of 1922 originally had 73-inch drivers and developed a rated tractive effort of 30,700 pounds. These manually fired Pacifics were delivered with Franklin Type D reverse, Woodard outside-connected dome throttle, and single 8½-inch air pump. Nos. 160-163 were received from B&O at Leipsic Junction. — *Allen County Historical Society.*

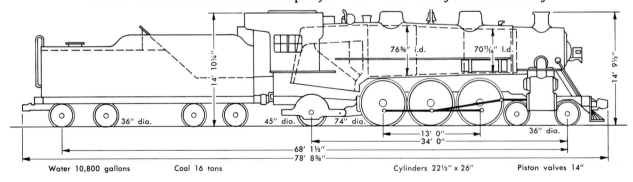

3rd 45 — Renumbered 4th 25 March 24, 1924. Sold to Birmingham Rail & Locomotive Company April 1925.

3rd 46 — To Southern Iron & Equipment Company 1899, November 26, 1923.

3rd 47 — Renumbered 4th 26 March 1924. Sold to Birmingham Rail & Locomotive Company April 1925.

3rd 48 — Sold to Southern Iron & Equipment Company, their 1900, November 1923. To Morgan & Bird Gravel Company (Shreveport, La.) May 1924.

3rd 49 — Sold to Detroit, Bay City & Western August 1920.

3rd 50 — Renumbered 2nd 387 December 1950. Sold to Luntz Iron & Steel Company August 29, 1951.

3rd 51 — Renumbered 2nd 388 December 1950. Laid up April 1951. Sold to United States Steel Corporation, c/o

Dietch Company (Sharpsburg, Pa.), September 25, 1951.

3rd 52-53 — Laid up March 1949. Sold to Purdy & Company May 26, 1949.

3rd 54 — Laid up at Conneaut February 1949. Sold to Purdy & Company June 14, 1949.

3rd 55 — Leased to W&LE August 1922 to February 1923. Renumbered 2nd 389 December 1950. Laid up at Conneaut February 1951. Sold to U. S. Steel, c/o Dietch Company, September 25, 1951.

3rd 56 — Laid up March 1949. Sold to Purdy & Company June 1, 1949.

3rd 57 — Laid up May 1950. Sold to Luntz Iron & Steel (Canton, O.) August 30, 1950.

3rd 58 — Laid up March 1949. Sold to Purdy & Company June 1, 1949.

3rd 59 — Laid up September 1948. Sold to Purdy & Company November 20, 1948.

3rd 60 — Renumbered 2nd 390 December 1950. Laid up December 1952. Sold to Luntz Iron & Steel March 20, 1953.

3rd 61 — Laid up March 1948. Sold to Erman-Howell Division, Luria Steel & Trading Corporation, December 1, 1948.

3rd 62 — Renumbered 2nd 391 December 1950. Sold to Luntz Iron & Steel August 29, 1951.

3rd 63 — Renumbered 2nd 392 December 1950. Laid up November 1952. Sold to Luntz March 20, 1953.

3rd 64 — Renumbered 2nd 393 December 1950. Laid up June 1953. Sold to Luntz August 20, 1953.

2nd 65 — Laid up July 1949. Sold to Purdy & Company December 15, 1949.

2nd 66 — Laid up May 1950. Sold to Luntz Iron & Steel September 1, 1950.

2nd 67 — Laid up June 1949. Sold to Purdy & Company December 20, 1949.

2nd 68 — Renumbered 2nd 394 December 1950. Laid up April 1952. Sold to Luntz Iron & Steel August 23, 1952.

2nd 69 — Laid up November 1948. Sold to Purdy & Company June 22, 1949.

2nd 70 — Laid up March 1948. Sold to Summer & Company (Farrell, Pa.) May 26, 1949.

2nd 71 — Renumbered 2nd 395 December 1950. Laid up March 1951. Sold to Luntz Iron & Steel August 29, 1951.

2nd 72 — Laid up July 1949. Sold to Purdy & Company December 21, 1949.

2nd 73 — Renumbered 2nd 396 December 1950. Laid up April 1952. Sold to Luntz Iron & Steel February 9, 1953.

2nd 74 — Renumbered 2nd 397 December 1950. Laid up September 1953. Sold to Luntz Iron & Steel July 21, 1955.

3rd 75 — Laid up December 1949. Sold to Luntz Iron & Steel September 8, 1950.

3rd 76 — Laid up August 1948. Sold to Erman-Howell Division, Luria Steel & Trading (Chicago, Ill.), November, 1948.

3rd 77 — Laid up December 1949. Sold to Luntz September 8, 1950.

3rd 78 — Laid up March 1949. Sold to Purdy & Company May 29, 1949.

3rd 79 — Renumbered 2nd 398 December 1950. Laid up July 1950. Sold to U. S. Steel Corporation, Northern Indiana Dock (East Chicago, Ind.), September 14, 1951.

2nd 75 — Renumbered 2nd 94, 1918. Laid up December 1948. Sold to Purdy & Company (Burnham, Ill.), March 25, 1949.

2nd 76 — Renumbered 2nd 95, 1918. Laid up April 1948. Sold to Purdy & Company November 23, 1948.

2nd 77 — Renumbered 2nd 96, 1918. Laid up August 1948. Sold to Erman-Howell Division, Luria Steel & Trading, December 1, 1948.

2nd 78 — Renumbered 2nd 97 1918. Laid up December 1948. Sold to Purdy & Company March 25, 1949.

2nd 79 — Renumbered 2nd 98, 1918. Laid up August 1948. Sold to Erman-Howell Division, Luria Steel & Trading, December 1, 1948.

2nd 80 — Renumbered 2nd 99, 1918. Laid up August 1948. Sold to Purdy & Company November 23, 1948.

3rd 156 — To Clover Leaf District 1930. Laid up at Lima August 1948. Sold to Purdy & Company November 20, 1948.

3rd 157 — Equipped with A.T.S. April 1927. Laid up at Lima July 1948. Sold to Purdy & Company (Burnham, Ill.) November 20, 1948.

3rd 158 — Wrecked by open switch at Vermilion, O., pulling No. 1 on May 27, 1922. Laid up at Lima May 1948. Sold to Purdy November 20, 1948.

3rd 160 — Equipped with Nicholson syphons October 1924; A.T.S. June 1926; Elesco exhaust steam injector October 1926. Elesco steam injector and A.T.S. removed January 1948. Last run September 1952. Sold to Luntz Iron & Steel May 29, 1953.

3rd 161 — Syphons applied June 1925. Equipped with Worthington BL-3 feedwater heater November 1924 to January 1948. Equipped with A.T.S. May 1926 to January 1948. Last run on LE&W District May 1951. Sold to Luntz Iron & Steel August 23, 1952.

3rd 162 — Syphons applied June 1925. Equipped with A.T.S. June 1926 to May 1948. Last run May 1951. Sold to Luntz March 20, 1953.

3rd 163 — Syphons applied June 1925; A.T.S. applied June 1926. Last run W&LE District March 1951. Sold to Luntz February 21, 1953.

3rd 164 — Modifications: Syphons 1925; A.T.S. 1926; Elesco exhaust steam injector 1926-1951; Type E header 1929; BK stoker 1947. Derailed and wrecked at Painesville December 22, 1925, and wrecked in a rear-end collision at Moorhead, Pa., July 20, 1929. Last run November 1952. To Luntz February 14, 1953.

3rd 165 — Syphons August 1925; A.T.S. 1926-1948; BK stoker August 1948. Wrecked in rear-end collision at Ashtabula August 20, 1924. Last run August 1953. Sold to Luria Steel & Trading Corporation (East Chicago) August 26, 1953.

3rd 166 — Syphons 1925; A.T.S. 1926; BK stoker 1947. Derailed and badly wrecked at Stony Island June 29, 1927, and again at Panama, Ill., November 14, 1940. Last run August 1951. Sold to Luntz Iron & Steel August 23, 1952.

2nd 167 — Syphons 1925; A.T.S. 1926; BK stoker June 1947. Last run July 1951. Sold to Luntz August 23, 1952.

2nd 168 — Syphons 1925; A.T.S. 1926; Type E header 1929; BK stoker and illuminated boards 1947. Last run November 1951. Sold to Luntz Iron & Steel August 23, 1952.

2nd 169 — Syphons 1925; A.T.S. 1926; Type E header 1929; illuminated boards 1945; BK stoker 1947. Laid up at Brewster December 1953. Sold to Luntz Iron & Steel June 24, 1954.

5th 200 — Laid up August 1954. Sold to Luria Steel & Trading (East Chicago) August 31, 1955.

4th 201-202 — Both sold to Purdy & Company August 23, 1955.

3rd 203 — Laid up January 1954. Sold to Purdy & Company August 23, 1955.

3rd 204 — Laid up March 1953. Sold to Luntz May 29, 1953.

335 — Dismantled October 1923.

336 — Retired December 1924. Dismantled 1925.

337 — Sold to Lima & Defiance Railroad March 1927 for $2000.

338 — Leased to Chicago, Attica & Southern January-March 1926. Laid up at Fort Wayne March 1926; retired August 1929.

339 — Leased to W&LE December 1917-April 1918. Retired 1924.

340 — Sold to Detroit, Bay City & Western, their 14, December 6, 1920. Later Detroit, Caro & Sandusky 14.

341 — Retired August 1929.

342-343 — Retired December 1923; dismantled January 1924.

344 — Retired August 1929.

345 — Dismantled January 1924.

346 — Sold to Detroit, Bay City & Western, their 11, May 10, 1920. Later, Detroit, Caro & Sandusky 11.

347 — Laid up 1930; retired March 1933.

348 — Leased to W&LE December 1917-May 1918. Dismantled June 1928; boiler installed in Indianapolis roundhouse.

349 — Became Detroit, Bay City & Western 12 May 10, 1920. Later DC&S 12.

350 — Leased to Newhall Construction Company March-October 1926. Retired August 1929.

351 — Leased to W&LE December 1917-April 1918. Retired August 1929.

352 — Retired December 1924; dismantled in 1925.

353 — Retired August 1929.

354 — Laid up at Conneaut May 1923; dismantled May 1925.

355 — Leased to Chicago, Attica & Southern January-March 1926. Retired August 1929.

356 — Leased to W&LE January-April 1918. Retired December 1924; dismantled 1925.

357 — Leased to W&LE January-May 1918. Retired August 1929.

358 — Retired August 1929.

359 — Laid up at Frankfort December 1932; retired March 1933.

360 — Laid up at Lima March 1932; retired June 1933.

361 — Last run June 1933; dismantled December 1933.

362 — Last run April 1932; retired March 1933.

363 — Laid up at Lima May 1933; retired June 1933.

364 — Laid up at Frankfort July 1933; retired October 1933.

365 — Laid up 1931; retired June 1933.

366 — Dismantled March 31, 1936.

448 — Superheater and Universal piston valves applied July 1917. Laid up 1931; retired June 1933.

449 — Superheater and Universal piston valves applied May 1917. Laid up November 1947. Sold to Purdy & Company November 18, 1947.

450 — Superheater and Universal piston valves applied June 1917. Last run November 1932. Dismantled at Frankfort February 1934.

451 — Superheater and Universal piston valves applied August 1916. Last run August 1948. Sold to Erman-Howell Division, Luria Steel & Trading, December 1, 1948.

452 — Superheater and Universal piston valves applied November 1917. Last run October 1947. Sold to Purdy & Company November 1947.

453 — Superheater and Universal piston valves applied June 1916. Laid up 1928; retired March 1933.

454 — Last run September 1949. Sold to Hyman-Michaels (Hegewisch, Ill.) December 15, 1949.

455 — Regular yard engine at Bloomington in later years. Last run March 1949. Sold to Purdy & Company June 8, 1949.

456 — Wrecked in head-on collision with 457 at Old Fort June 3, 1923. Last run March 1949. Sold to Purdy & Company June 9, 1949.

457 — Wrecked in head-on collision with 456 at Old Fort. Last run July 1948. Equipped with A.T.S. 1926-1934. Sold to Summer & Company (Buffalo) November 24, 1948.

458 — Equipped with A.T.S. 1926-1934. Wrecked in head-on collision with 55 at Cleveland, September 5, 1929. Last run September 1949. Sold to Hyman-Michaels December 15, 1949.

459 — Last run February 1934. Dismantled at South Lima April 1934.

460 — Laid up 1928; dismantled February 7, 1931.

461 — Laid up at Conneaut November 1930; retired March 1933.

462 — Retired August 1929.

463 — Laid up at Conneaut July 1930; dismantled there April 24, 1933.

464 — Laid up at Conneaut October 1931; dismantled there May 2, 1933.

465-471 — All retired March 1933.

472 — Wrecked at Fostoria June 2, 1926, in head-on with 225. Last run 1931. Retired June 1933.

473 — Last run March 1934. Dismantled at South Lima April 1934.

474 — A.T.S. applied 1926. Laid up February 1933; retired March 1933.

500 — Wrecked December 1925; repaired and returned to service February 1926. Wrecked in rear-end collision at Trilla, Ill., October 19, 1943. Renumbered 950 January 1956. Laid up at Conneaut December 1957. Sold to Luria (Cleveland) February 7, 1962.

501 — Wrecked in head-on at Bellevue August 17, 1955; never repaired. Dismantled at Bellevue November 27, 1955.

502 — Renumbered 951 December 1955. Laid up at Brewster June 1956. Sold to Luntz Iron & Steel (Canton) September 1956.

503 — Wrecked in head-on collision with 627 at Cleveland October 18, 1941. Renumbered 952 January 1956. Laid up at Conneaut February 1958. Sold to Canton Iron & Steel April 1963.

504 — Renumbered 953 December 1955. Laid up at Bellevue September 1956. To Luntz Iron & Steel (Canton) December 20, 1956.

505 — Equipped with A.T.S. May 1926 to August 1930. Laid up July 1954. Sold to Luntz Iron & Steel on July 21, 1955.

506 — Equipped with A.T.S. May 1926 and used in Chicago area thereafter. Laid up at Calumet December 1954. Sold to Purdy & Company December 30, 1955.

507 — Equipped with A.T.S. May 1926. Renumbered 954 December 1955. Laid up at Bellevue May 8, 1958, and stricken from roster August 1960. To Luntz Iron & Steel October 1963.

508 — Renumbered 955, January 1956. Laid up at Bellevue March 1957. To Luntz Iron & Steel (Canton) December 21, 1961.

509 — Equipped with A.T.S. June 1926 to June 1934. Renumbered 956 December 1955. Laid up at Bellevue May 5, 1958. To Luntz Iron & Steel November 1963.

510 — Retired December 1954. To Luntz Iron & Steel (Canton) April 19, 1955.

511 — Renumbered 957 December 1955. Laid up at Brewster April 1957. To Luntz Iron & Steel (Canton) August 20, 1961.

512 — Renumbered 958 December 1955. Laid up at Brewster October 1956. To Luntz Iron & Steel (Canton) December 20, 1956.

513 — Laid up at Brewster April 1955. To Luntz Iron & Steel September 30, 1955.

514 — Laid up at Brewster July 1954. To Luntz Iron & Steel April 19, 1955.

515 — Leased to W&LE August 1922 to June 1923. Demolished by boiler explosion at Valparaiso, Ind., 1924. Rebuilt June 1924 at Dunkirk with new boiler B-18477. Renumbered 959 December 1955. Laid up at Brewster October 1957. To Luntz Iron & Steel February 19, 1958.

516 — Renumbered 960 December 1955. Laid up at Brewster November 1957. To Luntz Iron & Steel (Canton) June 4, 1961.

517 — Laid up at Brewster May 1952. To Luntz Iron & Steel November 22, 1953.

518 — Renumbered 961 December 1955. Laid up at Lima 1956. Sold to Luria Brothers September 1957.

519 — Laid up June 1955. To Luntz Iron & Steel December 28, 1955.

520 — Renumbered 962 December 1955. Laid up at Brewster March 1957. To Luntz Iron & Steel August 13, 1961.

521 — Wrecked in rear-end collision at Jonestown, O., March 23, 1944. Repaired and again wrecked in head-on collision with 636 at Fair Grange, Ill., April 27, 1944. Renumbered 963 December 1955. Laid up at Brewster June 13, 1956. To Luntz Iron & Steel December 20, 1956.

522 — Renumbered 964 December 1955. Last run May 1, 1958, into Conneaut. Stricken from roster August 1960. To Canton Iron & Steel April 1963.

523 — Laid up at Conneaut May 1954. To Marquette Steel Division, Luntz Iron & Steel (Cleveland), June 1961.

524 — Equipped with A.T.S. June 1926 to 1944 and May 1947 to December 1952. Renumbered 965 December

1955. Laid up at Fort Wayne September 1957. Sold to M. S. Kaplan January 31, 1962.

525 — Renumbered 966 December 1955. Laid up at Bellevue April 1958. Sold to Canton Iron & Steel April 1963.

526 — Laid up August 1954. To Luntz Iron & Steel July 21, 1955.

527 — Wrecked in head-on with 6428 at Middlebranch, O., August 11, 1951. Laid up at Brewster March 1954. Sold to Luntz Iron & Steel June 24, 1954.

528 — Renumbered 967 December 1955. Laid up at Bellevue January 1958. To Luntz Iron & Steel December 16, 1961.

529 — Worthington Type 3-B feedwater heater applied March 1922; removed 1942. Used for many years on Leipsic turns out of Fort Wayne. Laid up November 1954. To Luntz Iron & Steel July 21, 1955. Total engine weight with feedwater heater 298,750 pounds.

530 — Renumbered 968 December 1955. Laid up at Conneaut January 1957. Sold to Luntz Iron & Steel August 1957.

531 — Laid up at Brewster July 1955. To Luntz Iron & Steel September 30, 1955.

532 — Renumbered 969 December 1955. Laid up at Brewster November 1957. To Luntz Iron & Steel (Canton) August 19, 1963.

533 — Renumbered 970 December 1955. Laid up at Conneaut November 1956. Sold to Hyman-Michaels December 17, 1956.

534 — Laid up at Brewster December 1954. To Luntz Iron & Steel July 21, 1955.

601 — Worthington BL feedwater heater applied December 1928 (pumps moved to pilot deck same date). Nicholson syphons applied February 1945. Laid up at Frankfort September 1946. Sold to AC&Y, their 409, November 13, 1946. To I. A. Barnett Company, Barberton, O., January 28, 1949.

602 — BL feedwater heater applied June 1927 (pumps moved to pilot deck same date). Leased to AC&Y December 1944 to May 1945. Laid up at Bellevue November 1954. Sold to Luntz Iron & Steel December 20, 1956.

603 — BL feedwater heater applied December 1927 (pumps moved to pilot deck same date). Laid up December 1945 and sold January 1946 to National Railways of Mexico, their 2214.

604 — BL feedwater heater applied November 1928 (pumps moved to pilot deck same date). Laid up August 1946. To AC&Y, their 410, January 3, 1947. To Wilkoff Company for scrap February 2, 1949.

605 — BL feedwater heater applied August 1929 (pumps moved to pilot deck same date). Laid up June 1945. To NdeM, their 2207, October 1, 1945.

606 — BL feedwater heater applied September 1929 (pumps moved to pilot deck same date). Laid up at Frankfort March 1945. To National Railways of Mexico, their 2208, October 1, 1945.

607 — BL feedwater heater applied December 1927 (pumps moved to pilot deck same date). To AC&Y, their 407, December 1945. To Holub Iron & Steel Company June 3, 1948.

608 — BL feedwater heater applied December 1928 (pumps moved to pilot deck same date). Wrecked in rear-end collision at Painesville, O., February 2, 1944. Towed to Conneaut and dismantled there October 1944.

609 — BL feedwater heater applied December 1927 (pumps moved to pilot deck same date). Laid up at Frankfort December 1945; dismantled there June 30, 1946.

610 — BL feedwater heater applied August 1929. Equipped with A.T.S. June 1929 to January 1945. Laid up at Conneaut 1944; dismantled there in December 1945.

611 — C-1 booster applied April 1922. Syphons applied January 1926 (pumps moved to pilot deck same date). Improved superheated booster applied January 1943; removed 1950. Last run August 1953. Sold to Purdy & Company August 30, 1955.

612 — C-1 booster applied May 1922; removed 1950. BL feedwater heater applied October 1926 (pumps moved

to pilot deck same date). Laid up January 1954. Sold to Luntz Iron & Steel August 2, 1954.

613 — C-1 booster applied June 1922; removed 1953. BL feedwater heater applied December 1926 (pumps moved to pilot deck same date). Laid up at Frankfort November 1953. Sold to Purdy & Company August 23, 1955.

614 — C-1 booster applied September 1923; removed circa 1945. BL feedwater heater applied October 1926 (pumps moved to pilot deck same date). Downflow syphons applied March 1940. Laid up at Bellevue May 1957; taken to Frankfort and party dismantled for overhaul. Work suspended June 1957 when shop was closed. Dismantled at Frankfort April 1960.

615 — C-1 booster applied September 1923; removed March 1950. BL feedwater heater applied November 1926 (pumps moved to pilot deck same date). Wrecked in rear-end collision at Oxford, Ind., April 4, 1942. Again wrecked on February 9, 1948, when derailed at Lafayette and went into Wabash River. Laid up at Frankfort June 1953. To Luntz August 20, 1953.

616 — BL feedwater heater applied September 1925 (pumps moved to pilot deck same date). Syphons applied April 1930. Booster removed October 1944. To AC&Y, their 408, October 1946. To I. A. Barnett Company as scrap October 23, 1950.

617 — BL feedwater heater applied September 1925 (pumps moved to pilot deck same date). Booster and feedwater heater removed December 1950. Laid up at Frankfort August 1954. Sold to Robinson Brothers as scrap August 30, 1955.

618 — Feedwater heater applied December 1925 (pumps moved to pilot deck same date). Booster and feedwater heater removed March 1951. Laid up at Frankfort February 1953. Sold to Luntz March 18, 1953.

619 — BL feedwater heater applied November 1925 (pumps moved to pilot deck same date). A.T.S. applied 1926. Booster and feedwater heater removed 1950. Laid up at Fort Wayne October 1956. Sold to Purdy & Company December 17, 1956.

620 — BL feedwater heater applied December 1925 (pumps moved to pilot deck same date). Equipped with A.T.S. June 1926 to January 1945. Feedwater heater removed February 1952. Laid up at Frankfort July 1955. To Purdy & Company January 23, 1956.

621 — BL feedwater heater applied December 1925 (pumps moved to pilot deck same date). Booster and feedwater heater removed February 1953. Laid up June 1954. To Luntz Iron & Steel July 21, 1955.

622 — BL feedwater heater applied October 1925 (pumps moved to pilot deck same date). Equipped with A.T.S. June 1926 to June 1934. Booster and feedwater heater removed December 1952. Laid up at Conneaut July 1954. To Luntz Iron & Steel July 21, 1955.

623 — BL feedwater heater applied September 1926 (pumps moved to pilot deck same date). Multiple-bearing crossheads applied December 1945. Booster and feedwater heater removed 1951. Laid up at Conneaut August 1954. To Luntz Iron & Steel July 21, 1955.

624 — BL feedwater heater applied June 1926 (pumps moved to pilot deck same date). Syphons applied November 1929. Booster removed 1950; feedwater heater 1952. Laid up December 1954; donated to Hammond, Ind., for display September 13, 1955.

625 — BL feedwater heater applied October 1925 (pumps moved to pilot deck same date). Syphons applied August 1929. Booster and feedwater heater removed December 1950. Laid up October 1953. Sold to Luria Brothers August 31, 1955.

626 — BL feedwater heater applied October 1926 (pumps moved to pilot deck same date). Booster and feedwater heater removed August 1950. Laid up at Brewster July 1955. To Luntz Iron & Steel (Canton) September 30, 1955.

627 — BL feedwater heater applied October 1926 (pumps

moved to pilot deck same date). Equipped with A.T.S. 1926-1943. Syphons applied October 1929. Wrecked in head-on with 503 at Cleveland on October 18, 1941. Wrecked in head-on with 655 at FY Tower, Buffalo, January 10, 1942. Booster and feedwater heater removed 1951. Laid up at Frankfort October 1953. Sold to Purdy & Company August 30, 1955.

628 — BL feedwater heater applied July 1926 (pumps moved to pilot deck same date). Syphons applied October 1929. Wrecked by derailment at Cleveland May 11, 1942. Laid up at Brewster October 1953. To Luntz Iron & Steel (Canton) January 28, 1954.

629 — BL feedwater heater applied November 1925 (pumps moved to pilot deck same date). Syphons applied July 1929. Wrecked in side-collision at Conneaut August 13, 1941. Laid up at Frankfort December 1952. To Luntz Iron & Steel March 18, 1953.

630 — BL feedwater heater applied October 1925 (pumps moved to pilot deck same date). Wrecked in rear-end collision at Findlay December 5, 1943. Wrecked again April 1946; not repaired; dismantled November 15, 1946.

631 — Elesco exhaust steam injector applied September 1927; removed February 1948. Booster removed November 1952. Laid up at Bellevue May 1957. To Luntz Iron & Steel (Canton) March 9, 1962.

632 — Wrecked by an open switch at Ashtabula February 28, 1940. Wrecked in head-on with 590 at Brocton, N. Y., September 12, 1943. Repaired October 1943 with new frame, cylinders, and smokebox. Laid up August 1946. To National Railways of Mexico, their 2215, on October 24, 1946.

633 — Booster removed August 1947; feedwater heater removed 1950. Wrecked by a landslide at Ellis, O., July 1952. Taken to Lima; dismantled there December 1955.

634 — Laid up at Frankfort April 1946. To National Railways of Mexico, their 2216, October 24, 1946. Condemned May 2, 1951.

635 — Laid up at Frankfort January 1949. Sold to Erman-Howell Division, Luria Steel & Trading, August 12, 1949.

636 — Wrecked by high-speed derailment at Edwardsville, Ill., February 21, 1942. Wrecked by head-on collision with 521 at Fair Grange, Ill., April 27, 1944. Wrecked by high-speed derailment at Cayuga, Ind., November 23, 1944. Not repaired; dismantled July 11, 1945.

637 — Pumps to front deck August 1930. Laid up at Frankfort May 1949. Sold to Purdy & Company October 3, 1949.

638 — Pumps to front deck November 1929. To National Railways of Mexico, their 2217, October 24, 1946. Condemned March 28, 1957.

639 — Pumps to front deck November 1929. Syphons applied July 1944. New cylinders applied May 1947. Booster, feedwater heater removed December 1952. Last run August 1957 into Bellevue. Donated to Bloomington, Ill., for display on September 3, 1959.

640 — Pumps to front deck 1930. Wrecked by derailment at Neoga, Ill., July 22, 1944. Previously wrecked at Ridge Farm, Ill., by derailment February 27, 1941. Booster and feedwater heater removed 1950. Laid up at Frankfort December 1953. To Luria August 26, 1955.

641 — Pumps to front deck November 1930. Booster removed October 1948. Laid up August 1953. Sold to Luntz Iron & Steel August 2, 1954.

642 — Pumps to front deck November 1929. Laid up at Brewster April 1954. Sold to Luntz Iron & Steel September 30, 1954.

643 — MB crossheads and new firebox applied February 1941. Laid up at Bellevue May 1957. To Luntz Iron & Steel (Canton) November 11, 1961.

644 — Pumps to front deck September 1930. Feedwater heater removed 1951. Laid up at Bellevue June 1956. Sold to Luntz Iron & Steel August 31, 1956.

645 — Pumps to front deck November 1928. MB crossheads, syphons, and new firebox applied October 1944. Feedwater heater removed 1951. Booster removed 1953. Laid up at Bellevue May 1957 and sent to Frankfort for shopping. Sold to M. S. Kaplan April 20, 1961.

646 — Wrecked in rear-end collision at Bluffton, O., May 22, 1940. Wrecked in head-on collision with Jordan spreader and 916 at Cayuga, Ind., May 22, 1945. Booster removed and numberboards applied November 1947. Feedwater heater removed 1950. Laid up October 1956. To Luntz December 20, 1956.

At Peoria & Pekin Union's Peoria engine terminal in November 1947, H-6d 627 sported feedwater heater and booster. Most H-6 engines got illuminated numberboards after the war. Some, such as the 627, got Mars oscillating headlights in 1950's. — *Paul Stringham.*

During postwar traffic lull, Nickel Plate sold 29 surplus Mikes to other roads. Former H-6a 607 became Akron, Canton & Youngstown 407 in December 1945. Unchanged in appearance, the USRA Alco awaits a call at AC&Y's Delphos yard. — *Clyde E. Helms.*

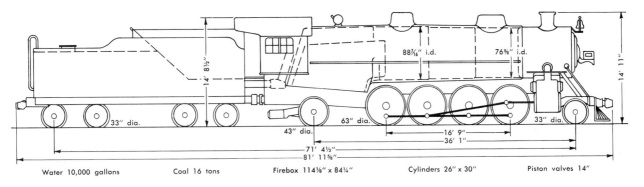

Water 10,000 gallons   Coal 16 tons   Firebox 114⅛" x 84¼"   Cylinders 26" x 30"   Piston valves 14"

NYC&STL — LOCOMOTIVES ACQUIRED WITH THE LE&W
Renumbered to Nickel Plate series March-May 1924

Number	Class	Type	Builder	Builder number	Date	Ex-LE&W number
4th 27-28	B-40	0-6-0	Brooks	3183, 3187	4-1899	4260-4261
4th 29-31	B-40	0-6-0	Brooks	3184-3186	4-1899	4262-4264
4th 32-33	B-54	0-6-0	Pittsburgh	2396-2397	5-1902	4365-4366
4th 34-41	B-54	0-6-0	Pittsburgh	2398-2405	6-1902	4367-4374
4th 42-43	B-55	0-6-0	Brooks	25526, 25533	4-1902	4377, 4384
4th 44	B-55	0-6-0	Brooks	25539	4-1902	4390
4th 45-46	B-55	0-6-0	Brooks	25541-25542	4-1902	4392-4393
3rd 80	B-11d	0-6-0	Schenectady	54064	12-1913	4275
2nd 81-82	B-11d	0-6-0	Schenectady	54066, 54082	12-1913	4276-4277
3rd 205-207	U-3a	0-8-0	Lima	5903-5905	1-1920	4250-4252
2nd 300	C-49	4-4-0	Baldwin	20503	5-1902	4246
2nd 301	C-49	4-4-0	Baldwin	20684	7-1902	4248
2nd 302-303	C-75	4-4-0	Schenectady	4174-4175	1893	4150-4151
2nd 304-305	C-75a	4-4-0	Schenectady	4297-4298	1895	4155-4156
2nd 306-308	C-76	4-4-0	Schenectady	3955-3957	1892	4163-4165
2nd 309	C-76	4-4-0	Schenectady	3958	1892	4168
2nd 310-311	E-40	2-6-0	Brooks	1518, 1520	3-1889	5330, 5332
2nd 312-313	E-40	2-6-0	Brooks	1551, 1549	7-1889	5336-5337
375-378	G-44	2-8-0	Brooks	29677-29680	6-1904	5515-5518
379-383	G-44	2-8-0	Brooks	29682-29686	6-1904	5520-5524
384-398	G-44	2-8-0	Brooks	29662-29676	6-1904	5525-5539
2nd 400-402	G-41	2-8-0	Brooks	3124, 3128, 3125	1-1899	5501-5503
2nd 403-404	G-41	2-8-0	Brooks	3130, 3126	1-1899	5505-5506
2nd 405-407	G-41	2-8-0	Brooks	3131-3133	2-1899	5509-5511
2nd 408-409	G-41	2-8-0	Brooks	3134, 3138	2-1899	5513-5514

Number	Class	Type	Builder	Builder number	Date	Ex-LE&W number
475-484	G-6v	2-8-0	Brooks	49516-49525	4-1911	5605-5614
484-494	G-16v	2-8-0	Brooks	49501-49510	4-1911	5385-5394
495-499	G-16w	2-8-0	Schenectady	51204-51208	6-1912	5395-5399
586-588	H-6o	2-8-2	Baldwin	49682-49684	9-1918	5540-5542
589-600	H-6o	2-8-2	Baldwin	49718-49729	9-1918	5543-5554

Last of the "long barrels," Second 408 pauses at St. Marys on December 5, 1934. She was the only G-41 to survive the depression and received a roomy steel cab before being retired in 1947. — *Clyde E. Helms.*

DIMENSIONS OF LOCOMOTIVES

Class	Cylinders	Valve motion*		Drivers	Weight on drivers†	Total weight†	Boiler pressure	Tractive effort	Grate area
B-40	18" x 24"	s	S	52"	112,300	112,300	160	20,300	18.6 (A)
B-54	19" x 26"	p	S	52"	136,660	136,660	170	26,000	23 (B)
B-55	20" x 26"	p	S	52"	142,540	142,540	180	30,600	28.2 (B)
B-11d	21" x 28"	p	W	57"	172,360	172,360	180	33,150	32.7 (C)
U-3a	25" x 28"	p	B	51"	218,775	218,775	175	51,000	47 (C)
C-49	18" x 24"	s	S	69"	68,375	112,000	180	17,200	17.6
C-75	19" x 24"	p	S	69"	79,700	119,600	170	18,100	28 (C)
C-75a	19" x 24"	p	S	69"	82,500	130,900	170	18,100	28 (C)
C-76	19" x 24"	p	S	69"	94,000	134,600	165	17,600	31.3 (C)
E-40	18" x 24"	s	S	57"	84,000	98,000	160	18,600	15.7
G-44	21" x 30"	p	B	57"	182,640	206,000	185	36,600	46.7 (C)
G-41	20½" x 28"	p	B	57"	161,700	174,980	170	29,800	32.5 (C)
G-6v	23" x 32"	p	W	63"	210,550	236,730	200	45,700	56.5 (C)
G-16v	25" x 32"	p	W	63"	215,730	240,570	180	48,600	56.5 (C)
G-16w	25" x 32"	p	W	63"	208,830	235,140	180	48,600	56.5 (C)
H-6o	26" x 30"	p	W	63"	220,000	292,000	200	54,700	66.7 (D)

*s — slide valves; p — piston valves; B — Baker; S — Stephenson; W — Walschaerts.

†As weighed at Lima Locomotive Works in 1927.

(A) Engine 27, converted to 0-6-0T, had 51-inch drivers, 20,700 lbs. rated tractive effort, weighed approximately 120,000 lbs. in working order. Engine 30 had 24.4-square-foot grate area.

(B) Engines 34 and 46 equipped with Type A superheater.

(C) Equipped with Type A superheater.

(D) As originally furnished, with Duplex stoker and single pump. Engines 586 and 598 with 2 pumps mounted on pilot deck and Worthington Type S feedwater heater weighed 223,650 lbs. on drivers and 300,930 lbs. total in working order.

G-6v's came to LE&W from NYC in 1917. No. 478 was built in 1911. — *Paul Stringham.*

USRA 586 was one of two ex-LE&W Baldwins equipped with Worthington Type S feed-water heaters in 1930. Dual air pumps were moved to the pilot deck at the same time. The Mikado went to Mexico in 1945. — *Robert J. Foster.*

4th 27 — Rebuilt as 0-6-0T in September 1925 and used as shop engine at South Lima. Dismantled August 1927.

4th 28 — Laid up December 1933; dismantled February 1934.

4th 29-30 — Retired October 1925 and December 1930.

4th 31-32 — Retired October 1924 and March 1933.

4th 33 — Retired August 1929.

4th 34 — Laid up August 1933; dismantled October 1934.

4th 35 — Laid up February 1934; dismantled April 1934.

4th 36 — Dismantled at Lima August 1933.

4th 37-38 — Dismantled November 1925 and August 1929.

4th 39 — Laid up March 1933; dismantled January 1934.

4th 40 — Laid up January 1933; retired March 1933.

4th 41-44 — Laid up 1932; retired March 1933.

4th 45 — Laid up October 1933; dismantled January 1934.

4th 46 — Superheater applied November 1923. Laid up January 1933 at South Lima; retired March 1933.

3rd 80 — Renumbered 399 December 1950. Laid up January 1951; sold to Luntz Iron & Steel August 29, 1951.

2nd 81 — Laid up November 1949 and sold to Luntz February 8, 1950.

2nd 82 — Laid up March 1949 and sold to Purdy & Company June 22, 1949.

3rd 205 — Laid up at Madison February 1955. Sold to Robinson Brothers, East Chicago, Ind., August 30, 1955.

3rd 206 — Laid up April 1954 and sold to Luntz August 2, 1954.

3rd 207 — Laid up October 1952 and sold to Luria Brothers February 2, 1953.

2nd 300 — Dismantled October 28, 1925.

2nd 301 — Dismantled March 1929.

2nd 302-303 — Retired October 1925 and October 1924.

2nd 304 — Leased to Lima & Defiance Railroad 1927-1928. Retired August 1929.

2nd 305 — Retired October 1924; dismantled in 1925.

2nd 306 — Retired October 1925.

2nd 307-308 — Retired October 1924; dismantled 1925.

2nd 309-310 — Retired October 1925; dismantled November 1925.

2nd 311-313 — All retired October 1924.

375 — Laid up May 1933; retired June 1933.

376 — Rebuilt at South Lima June 1925 with new cylinders and Baker valve gear. Laid up October 1933 and dismantled January 1934.

377 — Rebuilt at South Lima March 1926 with new boiler GO-8115, No. 2, new cylinders, and Baker valve gear. Laid up at Lima November 1949; sold to Luntz Iron & Steel May 1, 1950.

378 — Laid up October 1933; dismantled January 1934.

379 — Renumbered 930 December 1950. To Luntz March 20, 1953.

380 — Equipped for passenger duty. Rebuilt February 1925 with new Baldwin boiler XO-11558-24, No. 1, new cylinders, and Baker valve gear. Renumbered 931 December 1950. To Luntz March 20, 1953.

381 — Laid up June 1947. To Summer & Company, Buffalo, November 6, 1947.

382 — Demolished in head-on collision with 717 at Albany, Ind., on August 3, 1943. Towed to Lima and dismantled there November 1943.

383 — Laid up February 1933; retired June 1933.

384 — Rebuilt at South Lima April 1926 with new boiler GO-8115, No. 1, new cylinders, and Baker valve gear. Renumbered 932 December 1950. Laid up November 1953 and sold to Luntz August 2, 1954.

385 — Rebuilt at South Lima September 1925 with new Baldwin boiler XO-7754-25, No. 1, new cylinders, and Baker valve gear. Laid up September 1948 and sold to Summer & Company December 1, 1948.

386 — Laid up January 1933; retired June 1933.

387 — Laid up September 1933; retired October 1933.

388 — Rebuilt at South Lima June 1924 with Baker valve gear applied. Laid up at Frankfort October 1933; retired June 1933.

389 — Laid up June 1947. Sold to General Electric Company, Bellevue, O., November 6, 1947.

390 — Laid up January 1932; retired June 1933.

391 — Laid up December 1933; dismantled February 1934.

392 — Rebuilt at South Lima February 1925 with new Baldwin boiler XO-11558-24, No. 2, new cylinders, and Baker valve gear. Laid up August 1947. To Summer & Company, Buffalo, November 6, 1947.

393 — Retired October 1924.

394 — Rebuilt at South Lima April 1924 with new cylinders and Baker valve gear. Retired June 1933.

395 — Laid up January 1934; dismantled May 1934.

396 — Rebuilt at South Lima August 1925 with new Baldwin boiler XO-7754-25, No. 2, new cylinders, and Baker valve gear. Laid up July 1947. To Summer & Company November 6, 1947.

397 — Equipped for passenger duty. Rebuilt at South Lima December 1925 with new boiler GO-6040, new cylinders, and Baker valve gear. Laid up March 1949; sold to Purdy & Company, June 22, 1949.

398 — Laid up at Conneaut August 1945; dismantled there May 1946.

2nd 400-406 — Laid up 1932-1933. All retired March 1933.

2nd 407 — Laid up at Lima December 1933; dismantled there March 1934.

2nd 408 — Laid up at Lima September 1947. To Summer & Company November 6, 1947.

2nd 409 — Laid up at Lima January 1934; dismantled there December 1934.

475 — Sold to Gary Steel Supply Company November 15, 1947.

476 — Laid up at Lima April 1934; dismantled there December 1934.

477 — Laid up at Lima September 1947. To Summer & Company October 25, 1947.

478 — Laid up December 1947. To Gary Steel Supply Company May 1948.

479 — Laid up March 1933; retired June 1933.

480 — Nicholson syphons applied July 1923. Laid up at Lima July 1934; dismantled there December 1934.

481 — Laid up May 1932; used briefly during March 1934; dismantled December 1934.

482 — Laid up at Lima November 1947. To Winifrede Railroad, their 7, November 26, 1947. Scrapped 1955.

483 — Laid up August 1934; dismantled December 1934.

484 — In stationary boiler service April 1932 to October 1942 when shopped at Conneaut and returned to service. Laid up July 1948 and sold to Erman-Howell Division of Luria November 20, 1948.

485 — Laid up August 1947. To Summer & Company October 31, 1947.

486 — Laid up January 1951. To U. S. Steel Corporation, Mifflin Junction, Pa., May 29, 1951.

487 — Laid up June 1931; dismantled November 1934.

488 — Laid up September 1950. To U. S. Steel Corporation May 29, 1951.

489 — Laid up February 1932; dismantled April 1934.

490 — Laid up August 1947. To Summer & Company October 13, 1947.

491 — Laid up November 1948. To Purdy & Company March 25, 1949.

492 — Laid up September 1947. To Gary Steel Supply November 16, 1947.

493 — Equipped with A.T.S. March 1928 to June 1934. Laid up November 1950. To U. S. Steel Corporation, Mifflin Junction, Pa., May 29, 1951.

494 — Laid up December 1933; dismantled November 1934.

495 — Laid up February 1933; dismantled at South Lima December 1934.

496 — Laid up February 1931; dismantled November 1934.

497 — Laid up February 1950. To Luntz April 29, 1950.

498 — Laid up May 1933; dismantled at South Lima November 1934.

499 — Laid up August 1948. To Erman-Howell Division of Luria November 20, 1948.

586 — Equipped with A.T.S. February 1927 to June 1934.

Worthington Type S feedwater heater applied and pumps moved to pilot deck December 1930. Wrecked by a high-speed derailment near Charleston, Ill., March 10, 1940. To National Railways of Mexico, their 2200, October 1, 1945. Condemned 1957.

587 — Equipped with A.T.S. June 1927 to June 1929. Laid up March 1955. Donated to City of Indianapolis on September 7, 1955, and displayed in Broad Ripple Park.

588 — Laid up January 1946 and sent to National Railways of Mexico, their 2209.

589 — To National Railways of Mexico, their 2201, October 1, 1945. Retired November 22, 1956.

590 — Wrecked in head-on collision with 632 at Brocton, N. Y., September 12, 1943. Towed to Conneaut; dismantled there February 29, 1944.

591 — Equipped with A.T.S. February 1936 to September 1945. To National Railways of Mexico, their 2202, October 1, 1945. Condemned March 28, 1957.

592 — Equipped with A.T.S. September 1927 to June 1934. Worthington Type BL-3 feedwater heater applied and pumps moved to front deck December 1929. To National Railways of Mexico, their 2203, October 1, 1945.

593 — Laid up at Bellevue January 1946 and sent to National Railways of Mexico, their 2210.

594 — Pumps moved to pilot deck November 1940. To National Railways of Mexico, their 2211, January 1946.

595 — Equipped with A.T.S. February 1927 to April 1929. Wrecked in head-on collision with 651 near Celina, O., circa 1936. Laid up July 1945, and sold to National Railways of Mexico, their 2204, October 1, 1945.

596 — To National Railways of Mexico, their 2212, January 1946. Retired July 18, 1958.

597 — To National Railways of Mexico, their 2213, January 1946.

598 — Equipped with A.T.S. January 1927 to June 1934. Worthington Type S feedwater heater applied and pumps moved to pilot deck October 1930. Laid up March 1945 and sold to National Railways of Mexico, their 2205, October 1, 1945. Condemned July 4, 1957.

599 — Equipped with A.T.S. December 1926 to June 1934. Laid up July 1953. Sold to Luntz Iron & Steel August 21, 1953.

600 — Laid up August 1945; sold to National Railways of Mexico, their 2206, October 1, 1945.

Rebuilt G-44 382 held down Minster Branch job on March 16, 1936. The chunky Consol was built by Brooks in 1904 as LE&W 408. — *Clyde E. Helms.*

NYC&STL — LOCOMOTIVES ACQUIRED WITH THE CLOVER LEAF
Renumbered to Nickel Plate series in 1924

Number	Class*	Type	Builder	Builder number	Date	Ex-Clover Leaf No.
704	B-5	0-6-0	Rhode Island	2841	1-1893	4
705-706	B-6	0-6-0	Dickson	26027-26028	7-1902	5-6
707-712	B-7	0-6-0	Brooks	44428-44433	8-1907	7-12
714-715	B-8	0-6-0	Baldwin	23657, 23626	1-1904	14, 15
716-717	B-12	0-6-0	Baldwin	54460-54461	1-1921	16-17
731, 733		4-4-0	Rhode Island	1808, 1810	6-1887	31, 33
740-741	P-4	4-6-0	Baldwin	18765-18766	3-1901	40-41
742-743	P-4	4-6-0	Baldwin	18773, 18978	3-1901	42-43
744-745	E-3	4-4-2	Brooks	29270-29271	3-1904	44-45
809-811	P-5	4-6-0	Richmond	3101-3103	8-1900	109-111
820-821	F-6	2-6-0	Baldwin	19028-19029	5-1901	120-121
822-825	F-6	2-6-0	Baldwin	19035-19038	5-1901	122-125
830-831	G-1	2-8-0	Baldwin	20093-20094	2-1902	130-131
832-833	G-2	2-8-0	Schenectady	28614-28615	1-1904	132-133
834-835	G-3	2-8-0	Pittsburgh	2053, 2057	2-1900	134-135
836	G-4	2-8-0	Rogers	45087	2-1908	136
850-859	P-6	4-6-0	Brooks	30338-30347	11-1904	150-159
860-874	G-10	2-8-0	Brooks	30901-30915	2-1905	160-174
875-889	G-10	2-8-0	Brooks	38956-38970	12-1905	175-189
890-894	G-7	2-8-0	Baldwin	40866-40870	11-1913	190-194
901-905	G-8	2-8-0	Lima	5221-5225	12-1916	201-205
906-910	G-9	2-8-0	Lima	6127-6131	12-1921	206-210
911-912	G-9	2-8-0	Lima	6243-6244	5-1922	211-212
914-916	G-9	2-8-0	Lima	6245-6247	5-1922	214-216

*Nickel Plate classifications applied in 1927.

Class B-8 switchers 714-715 were built by Baldwin in 1904 as Toledo Railway & Terminal 10 and 8 respectively. These saturated 18 x 24's came to the Nickel Plate by way of the Clover Leaf. Both were retired in 1928.—*Collection of H. L. Broadbelt.*

DIMENSIONS OF LOCOMOTIVES

Number	Cylinders	Valve motion*	Drivers	Weight on drivers†	Total weight†	Boiler pressure	Tractive effort	Grate area	
704	18" x 24"	s S	51"	92,000	92,000	140	18,144	16.7	
705-706	19" x 26"	s S	51"	121,000	121,000	165	25,740	23	
707-712	19" x 26"	p S	57"	140,000	140,000	180	25,200	29	
714-715	18" x 24"	s S	51"	109,700	109,700	175	22,750	19.2	
716-717	22" x 26"	s W	51"	160,000	160,000	180	37,800	26	
731, 733	17" x 24"	s S	69"	64,000	99,000	180	15,480	17.8	(A)
740	19¼" x 24"	s S	63"	97,000	130,400	180	23,200	27.6	(B)
741	18½" x 24"	s B	69"	103,500	138,500	180	17,500	27.6	(B)
742	18¼" x 24"	s B	69"	103,500	139,500	180	17,200	27.6	(B)
743	18" x 24"	s B	63"	99,000	132,400	180	18,900	27.6	(B)
744-745	19" x 26"	p S	73"	89,000	152,000	200	21,800	42.5	
809, 811	19" x 24"	s B	63"	106,000	137,000	180	21,420	23	(C)
810	19" x 24"	s S	63"	100,000	129,025	180	21,420	23	
820-825	19½" x 26"	s S	63"	118,000	135,380	180	24,075	29.9	
830-831	20" x 26"	s S	57"	127,000	144,500	180	27,900	28.09	
832-833	20" x 26"	s S	57"	128,000	145,000	185	28,675	41.7	
834-835	20" x 28"	s S	57"	132,200	148,500	165	27,550	30.3	

Number	Cylinders	Valve motion*	Drivers	Weight on drivers†	Total weight†	Boiler pressure	Tractive effort	Grate area
836	20″ x 26″	p W	50″	145,000	165,000	180	31,860	33
850-859	19½″ x 30″	s S	63″	130,000	165,000	200	30,800	30.75 (D)
860-889	21″ x 28″	s S	57″	171,000	192,000	200	36,800	47.25
	22″ x 28″	p B	57″	172,000	197,000	185	37,500	47.25 (E)
890-894	22″ x 28″	p B	57″	170,900	196,700	185	37,500	47.25 (F)
901-905	22″ x 28″	p B	57″	177,000	204,000	185	37,500	46.2 (F, G)
906-916	22″ x 28″	p B	57″	180,500	205,900	185	37,500	46.2 (F, G)

*s — slide valve; p — piston valve; B — Baker; S — Stephenson; W — Walschaerts.
†As weighed at Lima Locomotive Works in 1927.
(A) As rebuilt 1905.
(B) As rebuilt 1919. Nickel Plate rated all of these engines at 21,060 lbs. tractive effort.
(C) As rebuilt 1922.
(D) Engines 854 and 857 equipped with Baker valve gear.
(E) Engines 860, 861, 863, 867, and 871 (class G-10a) as rebuilt with new cylinders, syphons, Type A superheaters, and Baker valve gear.
(F) As rebuilt, with Type A superheater.
(G) Later equipped with BK stokers. Weight on drivers 184,900 lbs., total engine weight 209,150 lbs.

Upgraded G-9 is serviced at MC Junction after bringing FT-98 from Delphos on March 16, 1954. The Consol, built as Clover Leaf 216 by Lima in 1922, sports a Nathan low-water alarm, Nicholson syphons, and a BK stoker. — *Willis A. McCaleb.*

704 — Retired July 1927.
705 — Laid up December 1933. Sold to Continental Steel Company February 1934.
706 — Laid up March 1933; retired June 1933.
707 — Laid up February 1934; dismantled at Frankfort May 1934.
708 — Renumbered 6th 8 July 1934. Retired July 1938.
709 — Renumbered 5th 9 July 1934, and 4th 49 April 1942. Laid up June 1946; dismantled October 31, 1946.
710 — Laid up at Frankfort December 1932; retired June 1933.
711 — Laid up at Frankfort September 1932; retired March 1933.
712 — Renumbered 5th 12 July 1934. Laid up September 1934; dismantled November 1934.
714-715 — Retired September 1928.
716 — Renumbered 5th 16 May 1942, and 2nd 316 February 1947. Laid up September 1947 and sold to Summer & Company November 6, 1947.
717 — Renumbered 5th 17 May 1942, and 2nd 317 February 1947. Laid up at Frankfort September 1947. To Summer & Company October 13, 1947.
731, 733 — Both dismantled July 1927 at Frankfort.
740 — Dismantled September 1927.
741-742 — Dismantled September 1928.
743 — Received Vanderbilt tender from 830-series engine in 1927. Retired February 1929.
744 — Laid up at Frankfort in 1931; retired March 1933.
745 — Laid up at Frankfort October 1932. Retired March 1933.
809 — Dismantled August 1927.
810, 811 — Retired in February and July of 1929.
820 — Retired February 1929.
821-823 — All retired January 1929.
824, 825 — Retired in February and January of 1929.
830-831 — Equipped with Vanderbilt tenders. Retired March 1929.
832-833 — Retired in December 1930 and March 1931.
834-835 — Both retired March 1931.
836 — Laid up in 1931 and retired March 1933.
850-851 — Both retired March 1933 after being laid up in 1931.
852 — Retired December 1930.
853 — Dismantled April 1931.
854 — Retired December 1930.

855 — Laid up at Frankfort in 1931; retired March 1933.
856-857 — Retired December 1930.
858 — Dismantled April 1931.
859 — Retired December 1930.
860 — Rebuilt at Frankfort December 1926 with new cylinders, syphons, superheater, cast-steel pilot, and Baker valve gear. Laid up January 1953; sold to Luntz Iron & Steel March 18, 1953.
861 — Rebuilt at Frankfort November 1925 with new cylinders, superheater, cast-steel pilot, and Baker valve gear. Laid up at Frankfort February 1953; sold to Luntz March 18, 1953.
862 — Laid up at Frankfort March 1933; retired June 1933.
863 — Rebuilt at Frankfort July 1926 with superheater, new cylinders, syphons, Baker valve gear, and cast-steel pilot. Laid up at Frankfort October 1954. To Granite City Steel Company, September 8, 1955.
864 — Laid up at Frankfort 1931; retired March 1933.
865 — Last used as a yard engine at Tipton. Laid up at Frankfort June 1934; dismantled there November 1934.
866 — Laid up January 1934; dismantled at Frankfort May 1934.
867 — Rebuilt at Frankfort July 1926, with new cylinders, superheater, syphons, cast-steel pilot, and Baker valve gear. Sold to Republic Steel Company May 7, 1947.
868 — Laid up 1931; retired March 1933.
869-870 — Laid up 1932; both retired June 1933.
871 — Rebuilt at Frankfort June 1927 with new cylinders, syphons, superheater, Baker valve gear, cast-steel pilot. Laid up June 1952; sold to Luntz Iron & Steel Company March 20, 1953.
872-873 — Laid up in 1931 and April 1933; both retired June 1933.
874-875 — Laid up in 1931; retired March 1933 and June 1933.
876 — Laid up at Frankfort February 1932; retired June 1933.
877 — Syphons applied February 1926. Laid up February 1932; retired in June 1933.
878 — Laid up at Frankfort 1931; retired June 1933.
879 — Last used October 1934 at Marion. Dismantled at Frankfort in November 1934.
880-881 — Laid up at Frankfort 1931 and 1932; retired June 1933.
882 — Laid up at Frankfort January 1934; dismantled 1934.

883 — Laid up November 1933; dismantled at Frankfort January 1934.

884-885 — Retired March 1933 and June 1933.

886 — Laid up January 1932; dismantled at Frankfort in 1933.

887 — Laid up January 1934; dismantled at Frankfort in May 1934.

888 — Laid up at Frankfort February 1932; retired June 1933.

889 — Laid up January 1934; dismantled at Frankfort in February 1934.

890 — Laid up at Frankfort March 1952. To Luntz (Kokomo) December 12, 1952.

891 — Laid up at Conneaut August 1952. To Luntz (Canton) March 20, 1953.

892 — Laid up April 1954. To Luntz December 28, 1955.

893 — Laid up October 1952. To Luntz March 18, 1953.

894 — Syphons applied November 1926. Laid up at Frankfort May 1952. To Luntz March 18, 1953.

901 — BK stoker and Precision model 10E reverse applied February 1942. Laid up March 1954; sold to Robinson Brothers April 18, 1956.

902 — BK stoker and 10E reverse applied December 1940. Laid up March 1954; sold to Purdy & Company September 9, 1955.

903 — BK stoker and 10E reverse applied January 1940. Laid up February 1954; sold to Luria Brothers August 26, 1955.

904 — BK stoker and 10E reverse applied September 1941. Laid up September 1953; sold to Purdy & Company August 30, 1955.

905 — BK stoker and 10E reverse applied February 1941. Laid up August 1953; sold to Purdy & Company August 1955.

906 — BK stoker, 10E reverse, and new firebox applied March 1942. Laid up at Brewster March 1954. To Luntz Iron & Steel June 24, 1954.

907 — BK stoker and 10E reverse applied January 1941. Laid up August 1953. To Luntz Iron & Steel August 21, 1953.

908 — BK stoker and 10E reverse applied January 1941. Pulled last run of the Commercial Traveler on March 8, 1941. Laid up March 1954; to Purdy & Company April 20, 1956.

909 — BK stoker applied July 1943. Laid up at Frankfort May 1953. Sold to Luntz Iron & Steel August 2, 1954.

910 — Ragonnet reverse and new firebox applied November 1939. BK stoker applied June 1943. Laid up August 1953; sold to Robinson Brothers August 30, 1955.

911 — BK stoker, 10E reverse, and new firebox applied March 1941. Laid up at Brewster May 1957. To Luntz (Canton) April 17, 1962.

912 — BK stoker, 10E reverse, and new firebox applied April 1941. Laid up March 1954; sold to Purdy & Company August 31, 1956.

914 — BK stoker, 10E reverse, and new firebox applied September 1940. Laid up at Conneaut November 1956; sold to M. S. Kaplan December 17, 1956.

915 — BK stoker and 10E reverse applied February 1940. Laid up at Brewster June 1957. To Luntz (Canton) August 19, 1963.

916 — Syphons applied November 1926. Equipped with Bethlehem tender booster (11,500 lbs. tractive effort) from May 1926 to March 1930. BK stoker applied May 1942. Laid up March 1954. To Purdy & Company September 9, 1955.

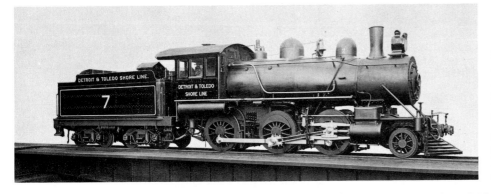

Shore Line bought four 20 x 26 Baldwin Moguls in 1907 and turned them over to the line's owners in January 1924. Grand Trunk Western got Nos. 9 and 10; 7 and 8 wound up as Nickel Plate 826-827. Both were retired in 1933. —Collection of Jack Lozier.

NYC&STL — LOCOMOTIVES ACQUIRED 1924-1949

Number	Class	Type	Builder	Builder number	Date
2nd 170-173	L-1a	4-6-4	Brooks	67211-67214	3-1927
2nd 174-177	L-1b	4-6-4	Lima	7399-7402	11-1929
4th 210-216	U-3b	0-8-0	Lima	6863-6869	5-1924
3rd 217-219	U-3b	0-8-0	Lima	6870-6872	5-1924
2nd 220-229	U-3c	0-8-0	Lima	6938-6947	6-1925
3rd 300-304	C-17	0-8-0	Lima	7617-7621	7-1934
647-661	H-6e	2-8-2	Lima	6650-6664	1-1924
662-671	H-6f	2-8-2	Lima	6853-6862	6-1924
700-703	S	2-8-4	Schenectady	68646-68649	9-1934
2nd 704-707	S	2-8-4	Schenectady	68650-68653	9-1934
2nd 708-712	S	2-8-4	Schenectady	68654-68658	10-1934
713, 2nd 714	S	2-8-4	Schenectady	68659-68660	11-1934
718	G-10s	2-8-0	Frankfort shop		12-1923
2nd 715-718	S-1	2-8-4	Lima	7860-7863	6-1942
719-722	S-1	2-8-4	Lima	7864-7867	6-1942
723-729	S-1	2-8-4	Lima	7868-7874	7-1942
730, 2nd 731	S-1	2-8-4	Lima	8003-8004	3-1943
732, 2nd 733	S-1	2-8-4	Lima	8005-8006	3-1943
734	S-1	2-8-4	Lima	8007	3-1943
735-736	S-1	2-8-4	Lima	8008-8009	4-1943
737-739	S-1	2-8-4	Lima	8010-8012	5-1943
2nd 740-745	S-2	2-8-4	Lima	8414-8419	1-1944
746-751	S-2	2-8-4	Lima	8420-8425	2-1944
752-754	S-2	2-8-4	Lima	8426-8428	3-1944

Number	Class	Type	Builder	Builder number	Date
755-762	S-2	2-8-4	Lima	8663-8670	8-1944
763-769	S-2	2-8-4	Lima	8671-8677	9-1944
770-772	S-3	2-8-4	Lima	9371-9373	3-1949
773-775	S-3	2-8-4	Lima	9374-9376	4-1949
776-779	S-3	2-8-4	Lima	9377-9380	5-1949
826-827	F-7	2-6-0	Baldwin	31954-31955	10-1907

Smooth boiler jacket, lack of auxiliaries on right side gave Lima L-1b's sleek look. One of earliest locomotives delivered with Commonwealth cast integral bed, 1929 speedster cost almost $8000 more than its Brooks counterpart of 1927. Automatic train stop inductor was mounted on rear journal of lead tender truck. — *Collection of Herbert Harnish.*

DIMENSIONS OF LOCOMOTIVES

Class	Cylinders	Valve motion*	Drivers	Weight on drivers	Total weight	Boiler pressure	Tractive effort	Grate area
L-1a	25″ x 26″ 25″ x 26″	p W p W	73″ 74″	175,500 175,800	316,500 318,400	215 225	40,680 42,000	66.7 66.7 (A)
L-1b	25″ x 26″ 25″ x 26″	p W p W	73″ 74″	176,000 176,000	314,000 315,900	215 215	40,680 40,150	66.7 66.7 (B)
U-3b	25″ x 28″	p B	51″	216,500	216,500	175	51,000	47 (C)
U-3c	25″ x 28″	p B	51″	221,000	221,000	175	51,000	47 (C)
C-17	25″ x 28″	p B	51″	239,000	239,000	200	58,350	46.9 (D)
H-6e	26″ x 30″ 26″ x 30″	p B p B	63″ 63″	237,050 239,180	319,400 320,810	200 200	54,700† 54,700†	66.7 66.7 (E)
H-6f	26″ x 30″	p B	63″	236,600	318,900	200	54,700†	66.7 (F)
S	25″ x 34″	p B	69″	261,100	428,900	245	64,100	90.3
S-1	25″ x 34″	p B	69″	261,800	429,500	245	64,100	90.3
S-2	25″ x 34″	p B	69″	264,300	440,800	245	64,100	90.3
S-3	25″ x 34″	p B	69″	266,030	444,290	245	64,100	90.3
F-7	20″ x 26″	s S	63″	138,176	161,976	200	28,200	33.4
G-10s	21″ x 28″	s S	51″	169,000	190,000	185	38,073	47.25

† 64,100 lbs. rated tractive effort with trailer booster.
*p — piston valve; s — slide valve; B — Baker; S — Stephenson; W — Walschaerts.
(A) With second pump added to front deck 1935-1936. Boiler pressure raised circa 1937. With smoke deflectors and cast integral beds, total weight was 323,900 lbs. Illuminated numberboards and valve pilot speed recorders applied 1944-1945.
(B) With second pump added to front deck 1934-1935.
(C) Boiler pressure and rated tractive effort raised to 185 lbs. and 53,950 lbs. 1946-1947.
(D) Original equipment included Type E superheater and syphons.
(E) Engines 649, 651, and 660 with syphons and second air pump added.
(F) Engine 665 with syphons added weighed 320,300 lbs., 238,700 lbs. of which was on the drivers.

C-17 switchers developed 58,350 pounds rated tractive effort, had firebox syphons, and Type E superheater. They were built by Lima in 1934. — *Collection of John A. Rehor.*

Second group of Lima 2-8-4's — the S-1's of 1943 — were rough-riding machines. The 730 was one of 23 Berkshires equipped for passenger service during 1944-1946 and the first of the Nickel Plate's 112 2-8-4's to be permanently deactivated.

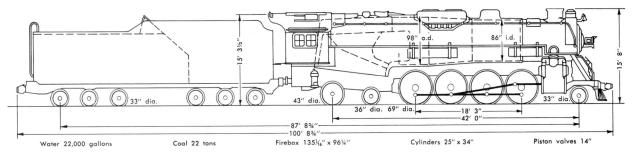

2nd 170 — Rebuilt July-August 1946 with Commonwealth bed, smoke deflectors, and roller-bearing engine truck added. Laid up September 1957. To Museum of Transport, St. Louis, October 1957.

2nd 171 — Smoke deflectors and roller-bearing engine truck applied January 1946. Cast integral bed-cylinders applied August 1946. Laid up at Bellevue February 1957. To Luntz March 6, 1962.

2nd 172 — Roller-bearing engine truck applied March 1946; smoke deflectors August 1946; Commonwealth bed-cylinders January 1947. Exhaust steam injector removed December 1952. Laid up at Bellevue February 1956. To Lederer Iron & Steel September 1956.

2nd 173 — Smoke deflectors added May 1946; roller-bearing engine truck July 1946; Commonwealth bed-cylinders January 1947. Last run June 1, 1958 (Calumet to Fort Wayne). Sold to Louisiana Eastern Railroad March 31, 1961.

2nd 174 — Smoke deflectors and roller-bearing engine truck added July 1946. Laid up January 1958. To Spence Engineering Company, Walden, N. Y., October 28, 1958. To Louisiana Eastern December 4, 1959.

2nd 175 — Smoke deflectors added January 1946; roller-bearing engine truck September 1946. Laid up at Buffalo June 1958. To Louisiana Eastern Railroad December 4, 1959.

2nd 176 — Smoke deflectors and roller-bearing engine truck added January 1946. Wrecked by high-speed derailment while pulling No. 6 at East Cleveland August 19, 1932. Laid up at Conneaut October 1954. Sold to Luria Brothers (Cleveland) August 28, 1956.

2nd 177 — Smoke deflectors and roller-bearing engine truck added January 1946. Laid up at Bellevue June 1953. To Luntz Iron & Steel August 21, 1953.

4th 210 — Laid up at Frankfort June 1952. To Luntz (Kokomo) December 12, 1952.

4th 211 — Laid up July 1953. To Luntz August 21, 1953.

4th 212 — Laid up July 18, 1959 (last steam locomotive in revenue service). To Luntz Iron & Steel (Canton) March 26, 1962.

4th 213 — Laid up March 1954. To Luntz August 2, 1954.

4th 214 — Laid up at Bellevue December 1957. To Luntz April 16, 1962.

4th 215 — Laid up June 1952. To Luntz January 21, 1953.

4th 216 — Laid up November 1954. To Luntz July 21, 1955.

3rd 217 — Laid up July 1951. To Luntz July 24, 1952.

3rd 218 — Laid up April 1952. To Luntz September 9, 1952.

3rd 219 — Laid up at Conneaut July 1959. To Luntz April 3, 1962.

2nd 220 — Initial service at Stony Island. Laid up at Bellevue No-

vember 1957. To Luntz Iron & Steel (Canton) April 9, 1962.

2nd 221 — Initial service at Stony Island. Laid up September 1952. To Luntz March 26, 1953.

2nd 222 — Initial service at Stony Island. Laid up April 1952. To Luntz August 20, 1952.

2nd 223 — Initial service at West Wayne. Laid up September 1952. To Luntz March 26, 1953.

2nd 224 — Initial service at Fostoria. Laid up at Bellevue May 1957. To Luntz (Canton) November 8, 1961.

2nd 225 — Initial service at Bellevue and laid up at that point December 1957. To Luntz (Canton) April 12, 1962.

2nd 226 — Initial service at Bellevue. Laid up March 1952. To Luntz September 18, 1952.

2nd 227 — Initial service at South Lorain. Laid up at Bellevue November 1957. To Luntz Iron & Steel April 11, 1962.

2nd 228 — Initial service at Cleveland. Laid up November 1952. To Luria Brothers February 11, 1953.

2nd 229 — Initial service at Conneaut; laid up there July 1959. To Luntz (Canton) April 5, 1962.

3rd 300 — Laid up at Bellevue November 1957. To Luntz January 17, 1962.

3rd 301 — Laid up at Bellevue November 1957. To Luntz February 23, 1962.

3rd 302 — Laid up at Conneaut July 1959. To Luntz April 4, 1962.

3rd 303 — Laid up at Buffalo April 8, 1958; dismantled there April 1964.

3rd 304 — Laid up at Conneaut July 1959. To Luntz Iron & Steel March 28, 1962.

647 — A.T.S. applied June 1926. New cylinders and firebox applied and booster removed November 1947. Laid up at Bellevue May 1957. To Luntz (Canton) December 7, 1961.

648 — Equipped with A.T.S. February 1926 to December 1948. Booster and feedwater heater removed 1950. Laid up 1954. To Luntz Iron & Steel August 2, 1954.

649 — Equipped with A.T.S. June 1926 to January 1945. Syphons applied October 1929 (pumps moved to pilot deck at this time). Leased to Alton & Southern December 15, 1944 to June 3, 1945. To National Railways of Mexico, their 2218, October 24, 1946. Condemned March 28, 1957.

650 — Equipped with A.T.S. June 1926 to January 1945. Feedwater heater and booster removed October 1950. Laid up May 1953. To Luntz Iron & Steel August 2, 1954.

651 — Equipped with A.T.S. June 1926 to July 1943 and after May 1952. Syphons applied December 1929 (pumps moved to pilot deck at this time). Wrecked in head-on collision near Celina circa 1936. Feedwater heater and booster removed January 1952. Laid up at Bellevue August 1956. To Luntz December 20, 1956.

652 — Equipped with A.T.S. June 1926 to November 1943. Pumps moved to pilot deck December 1928. New cylinders August 1948. New firebox applied and booster and feedwater heater removed October 1952. Wrecked in side collision with B&O passenger train at Broadway April 8, 1954. Towed to Conneaut but not repaired. To Luntz August 2, 1954.

653 — Equipped with A.T.S. June 1926 to October 1945. Pumps to pilot deck October 1928. Booster removed 1947; feedwater heater removed 1950. Laid up at Conneaut December 1955. Sold to M. S. Kaplan December 17, 1956.

654 — Equipped with A.T.S. June 1926 to April 1946. Pumps to pilot deck October 1930. Equipped for passenger service May 1934. Wrecked by high-speed derailment at Maple Grove, O., March 17, 1944. Booster and feedwater heater removed April 1952. Laid up at Bellevue November 1956. To Luntz (Canton) December 12, 1961.

655 — Equipped with A.T.S. June 1926 to January 1945. Pumps to pilot deck June 1929. Wrecked in head-on collision with 627 at Buffalo January 10, 1942. Leased to Alton & Southern December 7, 1944 to June 1, 1945. Feedwater heater removed February 1953. Laid up January 1951. To Luntz Iron & Steel August 20, 1953.

656 — Equipped with A.T.S. June 1926 to April 1943. Pumps to pilot deck June 1929. Feedwater heater removed November 1952. Laid up January 1956. To Luntz Iron & Steel April 23, 1956.

657 — Equipped with A.T.S. June 1926 to December 1948. Feedwater heater removed October 1951. Laid up August 1952. To Luntz February 5, 1953.

658 — Equipped with A.T.S. June 1926 to 1944. Pumps to pilot deck November 1928. To National Railways of Mexico, their 2219, October 24, 1946. Condemned October 31, 1953.

659 — Equipped with A.T.S. May 1926 to January 1945. Feedwater heater and booster removed August 1948. Equipped with Elesco exhaust steam injector from May 1950 to October 1951. Laid up June 1953. To Luntz Iron & Steel August 20, 1953.

660 — Equipped with A.T.S. June 1926 to April 1943. Syphons applied July 1929 (pumps moved to pilot deck at this time). To National Railways of Mexico, their 2220, October 24, 1946.

661 — Equipped with A.T.S. June 1926 to January 1945. Pumps to pilot deck September 1930. Equipped for passenger service May 1934. Wrecked in derailment at Argos, Ind., December 31, 1938. Booster and feedwater heater removed March 1952. Laid up October 1953. To Purdy & Company September 9, 1955.

662 — Pumps moved to pilot deck December 1929. Firebar grates applied January 12, 1930 (first NKP installation). Booster removed and new firebox applied February 1949. Feedwater heater removed July 1951. Last run Cleveland to Bellevue April 30, 1958. To Luntz March 13, 1962.

663 — New firebox applied and booster removed December 1951. Feedwater heater removed November 1952. Laid up June 1955. Sold to Hyman-Michaels December 1956.

664 — Laid up August 1946. To National Railways of Mexico, their 2221, October 24, 1946.

665 — Syphons applied March 1926. New firebox applied; feedwater heater and booster removed January 1953. Laid up at Bellevue January 1958. To Luntz (Canton) December 1, 1961.

666 — Pumps to pilot deck October 1928. Wrecked by derailment at Cleveland September 27, 1941. To National Railways of Mexico, their 2222, October 24, 1946. Condemned March 28, 1957.

667 — Booster and feedwater heater removed circa 1951. Laid up at Brewster December 1954. To Luntz (Canton) July 21, 1955.

668 — Pumps to pilot deck July 1929. Laid up June 1946; dismantled at Lima December 18, 1946.

669 — Laid up May 1949. Sold to Purdy & Company October 4, 1949.

670 — Wrecked by derailment following collision with motor car at Westfield, N. Y., April 29, 1928. Laid up June 1946. To National Railways of Mexico, their 2223, October 24, 1946. Condemned October 31, 1953.

671 — Roller bearings applied to tender truck February 1930. Laid up July 1946. To National Railways of Mexico, their 2224, October 24, 1946.

700 — Laid up at Conneaut October 1957. To Lederer Iron & Steel (Cleveland) April 24, 1961.

701 — Laid up at Brewster August 1956. Sold to Purdy & Company June 1957.

702 — Laid up at Brewster May 1957. To Luntz (Canton) June 28, 1961.

703 — Wrecked in rear-end collision at Coldwater, O., March 28, 1942. Laid up September 1956. To Luntz Iron & Steel May 13, 1957.

2nd 704 — Laid up August 1956. To Luntz May 13, 1957.

2nd 705 — A.T.S. removed May 1943. Equipped with Bendix radio May 1950 to October 1953. Laid up June 1956. To Luntz Iron & Steel August 1957.

2nd 706 — Laid up at Brewster November 1957. To Luntz August 7, 1963.

2nd 707 — Laid up at Conneaut September 1957. Sold April 14, 1961, to Luria Brothers; later dismantled by Great Lakes Scrap Company, Erie, Pa.

2nd 708 — Derailed and wrecked at Bellevue September 28, 1941. Laid up at Brewster November 1957. To Luntz (Canton) April 22, 1961.

2nd 709 — Laid up at Conneaut August 1957. Sold to Luria Brothers April 18, 1961, dismantled by Lederer· Iron & Steel at Cleveland November 1961.

2nd 710 — Laid up August 1956; sold to M. S. Kaplan June 1957.

2nd 711 — Laid up April 1957 at Brewster. Taken to Frankfort for overhaul. To M. S. Kaplan November 6, 1961.

2nd 712 — Laid up at Brewster October 1957. To Luntz (Canton) April 26, 1961.

713 — Laid up at Bellevue May 1957. To Luntz (Canton) November 2, 1961.

2nd 714 — Laid up at Frankfort July 1956. To Luria Brothers June 1957.

2nd 715 — Laid up at Conneaut October 1957. To Luria Brothers April 17, 1961. Dismantled by Great Lakes Scrap Company, Erie, Pa.

2nd 716 — Laid up at Brewster September 1957. To Luntz February 19, 1958.

2nd 717 — Wrecked in head-on collision with 382 at Albany, Ind., August 3, 1943. Laid up at Brewster September 1957. To Luntz February 19, 1958.

718 — Built at Frankfort shop using spare Brooks boiler and machinery bought in February 1905 with Clover Leaf H-6 class engines. Used mainly in yard service at Marion and Frankfort. Laid up at Frankfort March 1934; dismantled there May 1934.

2nd 718 — Laid up at Conneaut January 10, 1958. Subsequently overhauled with roller bearings applied to tender. Stored after shopping and retired August 1960. To Luntz December 1963.

719 — Roller-bearing trucks to tender November 1957. Last run July 1, 1958, Buffalo to Conneaut. To Luntz Iron & Steel January 1964.

720 — Wrecked by derailment at Leipsic Junction July 8, 1943. Wrecked in collision with highway truck at Mount Cory, O., June 13, 1952. Roller-bearing trucks to tender November 1957. Laid up at Conneaut May 20, 1958. To Luntz Iron & Steel October 1963.

721 — Laid up at Frankfort August 1956. To Luria Steel & Trading Corporation June 1957.

722 — Laid up at Lima June 1956. To Luntz Iron & Steel August 1957.

723 — Laid up at Conneaut July 1956. To Luntz August 1957.

724 — Wrecked in side collision with W&LE 6421 at Bellevue April 3, 1943. Laid up at Conneaut December 1957. Sold to Columbia Iron & Metal January 31, 1962.

725 — Roller-bearing trucks to tender August 1957. Laid up at Brewster October 9, 1957. To Luntz (Canton) August 7, 1963.

726 — Wrecked in rear-end collision with troop train at Yellow Creek, O., March 27, 1944. Equipped with Bendix radio September 1950 to July 1956. Laid up at Conneaut December 1957. To Luntz February 16, 1962.

727 — Laid up at Bellevue June 23, 1958. To Luntz November 28, 1961.

728 — Laid up at Brewster September 1957. To Luntz April 23, 1961.

729 — Laid up at Brewster October 1957. To Luntz April 28, 1961.

730 — Laid up at Frankfort August 1955. To M. S. Kaplan November 6, 1961.

2nd 731 — Laid up at Conneaut November 1957. To Luntz February 14, 1962.

732 — Laid up August 1956. To Luntz (Canton) March 2, 1962.

2nd 733 — Laid up at Conneaut May 1957. To Luntz February 2, 1962.

734 — Laid up at Conneaut January 1958. To Luntz January 29, 1962.

735 — Laid up at Conneaut March 16, 1958. To Luntz February 27, 1962.

736 — Laid up at Conneaut August 1957. To Luntz February 20, 1962.

737-738 — Laid up at Conneaut March 26-28, 1958. To Luria (Cleveland) February 7, 1962.

739 — Laid up at East Wayne February 1958. To Purdy & Company May 1961.

2nd 740 — Laid up at Bellevue June 22, 1958 (last active steam engine west of Bellevue). Sold to Luntz August 1963.

2nd 741 — Laid up at Conneaut April 16, 1958, and subsequently overhauled. Stored after overhaul. Sold to Luria (Cleveland) February 7, 1962, for scrap.

2nd 742 — Laid up at Bellevue June 18, 1958. To Luntz (Canton) August 1963.

2nd 743 — Wrecked in rear-end collision at Madison, O., February 12, 1944. Roller-bearing trucks to tender December 1957. Laid up at Conneaut March 28, 1958. Sold to Luria Brothers (Cleveland) February 7, 1962.

2nd 744 — Last run June 8, 1958, East Wayne to Bellevue. To Luntz October 19, 1961.

2nd 745 — Laid up at East Wayne June 24, 1958. To Purdy & Company October 30, 1961.

746 — Last run July 2, 1958, Bellevue to Conneaut (last run for steam road power on NKP). Sold to Luntz Iron & Steel November 1963.

747 — Laid up at Conneaut July 22, 1958. To Luntz (Canton) December 1963.

748 — Last run June 17, 1958, Calumet to East Wayne. To Purdy & Company October 30, 1961.

749 — Last run June 20, 1958, East Wayne to Bellevue. To Luntz December 1963.

750 — Laid up at Bellevue March 28, 1958. Sold to Luntz January 1964.

751 — Laid up at Conneaut March 1958 and partly overhauled at Conneaut shop; dismantled there October 1960.

752 — Laid up at Conneaut July 22, 1958. To Luntz November 1963.

753 — Laid up at Bellevue June 1958. Sold to Purdy & Company April 13, 1961.

754 — Laid up at Conneaut January 1958. Was in the process of being overhauled at Conneaut shop when it closed June 1958; dismantled there October 1960.

755 — Laid up at Conneaut December 1957. Overhauled March-April 1958 and stored thereafter. Donated to city of Conneaut (O.) Historical Railroad Museum, October 1964.

756 — Last run June 15, 1958, East Wayne to Bellevue. To Luntz October 1963.

757 — Last run June 15, 1958, East Wayne to Bellevue. To Pennsylvania State Railroad Museum, Strasburg, Pa., 1966.

758 — Laid up at Conneaut February 1958. Sold April 14, 1961, to Luria Brothers; dismantled by Lederer Iron & Steel at Cleveland.

759 — Laid up January 1958 at Conneaut and subsequently shopped there. Stored after shopping and sold to F. Nelson Blount (Monadnock, Steamtown & Northern) on October 16, 1962.

760 — Laid up January 1958 at Conneaut. Sold April 14, 1961, to Luria Brothers; dismantled by Lederer Iron & Steel at Cleveland.

761 — Laid up March 28, 1958 at Bellevue. To Luntz October 1963.

762 — Laid up at Bellevue June 27, 1958. To Luntz November 1963.

763 — Roller-bearing trucks to tender August 1957. Laid up at Conneaut July 21, 1958. To Roanoke (Va.) Transportation Museum July 28, 1966.

764 — Last run June 17, 1958, Calumet to East Wayne. To Purdy & Company October 30, 1961.

765 — Last run June 14, 1958, Calumet to East Wayne. Renumbered 2nd 767 February 1963. Donated to city of Fort Wayne and installed in Lawton Park on May 4, 1963.

766 — Laid up at East Wayne May 1958. To Purdy & Company October 1963.

767 — Wrecked in high-speed side collision with Wabash passenger train at New Haven, Ind., July 16, 1951. Rebuilt at Conneaut. Laid up at East Wayne April 1958. Renumbered 2nd 765 February 1963. To Purdy & Company October 1963.

768 — Last run June 2, 1958, Calumet to East Wayne. To Purdy & Company January 29, 1962.

769 — Bendix radio applied June 1952, removed September 1955, re-applied April 1957. Laid up at East Wayne June 1958. To Purdy & Company January 29, 1962.

770 — Wrecked in head-on collision with 776 at Plate, N. Y., December 28, 1954. Roller-bearing trucks to tender September 1957. Laid up at Conneaut June 1958. Sold to Columbia Iron & Metal (Cleveland) January 31, 1962.

771 — Roller-bearing trucks to tender August 1957. Laid up at Conneaut April 1958. Sold to Columbia Iron & Metal January 31, 1962.

772 — Roller-bearing trucks to tender August 1957. Laid up at Conneaut April 1958. Sold to Canton Iron & Steel April 1963.

773 — Roller-bearing trucks to tender September 1957. Laid up at Conneaut April 1958. Sold to Canton Iron & Steel April 1963.

774 — Roller-bearing trucks to tender January 1958. Laid up at Conneaut March 1958. To Canton Iron & Steel April 1963.

775 — Roller-bearing trucks to tender January 1958. Laid up at Conneaut March 1958. To Luntz December 1963.

776 — Wrecked in head-on collision with 770 at Plate, N. Y., December 28, 1954. Roller-bearing trucks to tender October 1957. Laid up at Conneaut April 1958. To Luntz Iron & Steel November 1963.

777 — Laid up at Conneaut June 1958. Sold to Luria Brothers April 14, 1961. Dismantled by Great Lakes Scrap Company, Erie, Pa.

778 — Laid up at Conneaut March 1958. Sold to Canton Iron & Metal February 9, 1962. Dismantled by Marquette Steel Company (Cleveland).

779 — Last steam locomotive built by Lima Locomotive Works. Exhibited and run at Chicago Railroad Fair 1949. Laid up at Conneaut March 1958. Donated to city of Lima 1963 for display in Lincoln Park.

ADDITIONAL MODIFICATIONS TO H-6 LOCOMOTIVES

Illuminated Numberboards Applied:
1945 — 618, 633, 635, 640, 641, 642, 644, 647, 656, 658, 660, 666
1946 — 601, 602, 615, 616, 617, 624, 625, 626, 629, 631, 637, 643, 652, 653, 662, 663, 665, 667, 669
1947 — 587, 613, 614, 621, 623, 627, 645, 646, 647, 649, 651, 654, 657, 661
1948 — 599, 611, 612, 619, 620, 622, 628, 639, 655, 659
Multiple-Bearing-Type Crossheads and Guides Applied:
1941 — 599, 603, 604, 605, 607, 637, 643, 644

1942 — 602, 606, 608, 611, 618, 625, 626, 633, 636, 640, 641
1943 — 586, 646
1944 — 645
1945 — 596, 623
1946 — 601, 651
1947 — 639, 647, 653, 654, 656
1948 — 613, 629, 631
1949 — 642, 662

Mars Oscillating Headlight and 1000-Watt Turbogenerator:
1952 — 599, 602, 611, 619, 622, 624, 625, 627, 631, 639, 643, 646, 648, 652
1953 — 587, 614, 617, 621, 623, 640, 641, 642, 645, 647, 651, 654, 656, 662, 663, 665, 667
1954 — 644, 653

ADDITIONAL MODIFICATIONS TO S LOCOMOTIVES

Illuminated Numberboards:
1945 — 700, 702, 703, 706-709, 711, 714-724, 726, 730-735, 739-742, 744, 745
1946 — 701, 705, 712, 713, 725, 728, 729, 737, 746-748, 751, 752
1947 — 704, 727, 736, 738, 743, 749, 750, 753, 754
(Original equipment on 755-779.)

Passenger Service Appliances:
1944 — 719, 722, 731, 734, 735, 743, 744, 766-769
1945 — 715-718, 729, 762-765
1946 — 730, 733, 739

Train Radio and Additional Turbogenerator:
1952 — 743, 769
1953 — 735-738, 740, 741,* 742, 744-746, 748, 763, 771-773, 775, 776, 777-779*
1954 — 733, 734, 761, 762, 770, 774
1955 — 749, 750, 755-760, 767, 768
1956 — 715, 731
1957 — 747, 764-766
*Westinghouse apparatus; all others Bendix.

Mars Oscillating Headlight and Additional Turbogenerator:
1950-1951 — 700-779 inclusive

Valve Pilot Speed Recorder:
1945 — 736, 766
1946 — 709, 713, 716-718, 720, 726-728, 730, 737-740, 743, 745-749, 752, 760, 762-765, 767-769
1947 — 700, 702, 705, 723, 724, 731, 733-735, 750, 755, 757
1948 — 701, 703, 704, 706-708, 710-712, 714, 715, 719, 721, 722, 725, 729, 732, 741, 742, 744, 753, 754, 758, 759, 761
1949 — 751
(Original equipment on 770-779.)

Automatic Train Stop Removed:
1943 — 705-719 inclusive
1949 — 720-727 inclusive
1950 — 728-738 inclusive
(Engines 700-704, 770-779 were never equipped with A.T.S.)

G-2 assigned to the "sub run" shunts cars at Chagrin Falls on May 27, 1952. The 2-8-0 was built by Brooks in 1905 as Wabash Pittsburgh Terminal 2120, rebuilt at Alco's Pittsburgh Works in 1916, and reboilered at Brewster in 1929. It was sold as scrap in 1955. — *Willis A. McCaleb.*

NYC&STL — LOCOMOTIVES ACQUIRED WITH THE W&LE
December 1, 1949

Number	Class	Type	Builder	Builder number	Date
3951	B-5	0-6-0	W&LE	14	4-1929
3952-3954	B-5	0-6-0	W&LE	15-17	5-1929
3955	B-5	0-6-0	W&LE	18	6-1929
3956-3957	B-5	0-6-0	W&LE	19-20	1-1930
3958	B-5	0-6-0	W&LE	21	2-1930
3959	B-5	0-6-0	W&LE	32	5-1935
3960-3962	B-5	0-6-0	W&LE	33-35	6-1935
3963-3964	B-5	0-6-0	W&LE	36-37	7-1935
3965	B-5	0-6-0	W&LE	38	9-1935
3966	B-5	0-6-0	W&LE	39	10-1935
3967	B-5	0-6-0	W&LE	40	9-1937
3968-3969	B-5	0-6-0	W&LE	41-42	10-1937
3970-3971	B-5	0-6-0	W&LE	43-44	11-1937
3972-3975	B-5	0-6-0	W&LE	45-48	12-1937
3976	B-5	0-6-0	W&LE	49	1-1938
3977	B-5	0-6-0	W&LE	50	3-1940
3978-3979	B-5	0-6-0	W&LE	51-52	4-1940
3980	B-5	0-6-0	W&LE	53	5-1940
3981-3986	B-5	0-6-0	Schenectady	71967-71972	6-1944
4156	G-1	2-8-0	Brooks	30863	4-1905
4301	G-2	2-8-0	Brooks	30854	3-1905
4302-4303	G-2	2-8-0	Brooks	30868, 30883	4-1905
4308, 4310	G-2	2-8-0	Brooks	30867, 30882	4-1905
4314, 4320	G-2	2-8-0	Brooks	30852, 30851	3-1905
5101-5105	C-1	0-8-0	Pittsburgh	60153-60157	11-1918
5106	C-1a	0-8-0	W&LE	4	5-1928
5107-5108	C-1a	0-8-0	W&LE	5-6	6-1928
5109	C-1a	0-8-0	W&LE	7	7-1928
5110	C-1a	0-8-0	W&LE	8	8-1928

Number	Class	Type	Builder	Builder number	Date
5111-5112	C-1a	0-8-0	W&LE	9-10	3-1929
5113-5114	C-1a	0-8-0	W&LE	11-12	7-1929
5115	C-1a	0-8-0	W&LE	13	8-1929
5116-5118	C-1a	0-8-0	W&LE	22-24	3-1930
5119-5120	C-1a	0-8-0	W&LE	25-26	4-1930
5121	C-1a	0-8-0	W&LE	27	5-1930
5122-5123	C-1a	0-8-0	W&LE	28-29	6-1930
5124	C-1a	0-8-0	W&LE	30	7-1930
5125	C-1a	0-8-0	W&LE	31	9-1930
6001-6010	M-1	2-8-2	Brooks	59720-59729	8-1918
6011-6020	M-1	2-8-2	Brooks	60375-60384	10-1918
6053, 6056	G-3	2-8-0	Schenectady	53724, 53727	7-1913
6061, 6067	G-3	2-8-0	Schenectady	53732, 53738	7-1913
6401-6410	S-4	2-8-4	Schenectady	68829-68838	4-1937
6411-6412	S-4	2-8-4	Schenectady	69121-69122	12-1938
6413-6415	S-4	2-8-4	Schenectady	69123-69125	1-1939
6416	S-4	2-8-4	Schenectady	69429	2-1941
6417-6422	S-4	2-8-4	Schenectady	69430-69435	3-1941
6423-6431	S-4	2-8-4	Schenectady	70021-70029	8-1942
6432	S-4	2-8-4	Schenectady	70030	9-1942
6803-6806	J-1	4-8-2	Roanoke	237-240	8/9-1926
6808-6809	J-1	4-8-2	Roanoke	242-243	9/10-1926
8001, 8002	I-3	2-6-6-2	Baldwin	52178, 52265	9-1919
8003	I-3	2-6-6-2	Baldwin	52287	9-1919
8009	I-3	2-6-6-2	Baldwin	52350	10-1919

During 1928-1930 Brewster shop turned out 20 class C-1a 0-8-0's which were similar to the Wheeling's Pittsburgh-built USRA machines. All had a Chambers front-end throttle located ahead of the stack. The former 5122 was photographed at Norwalk, O., on October 8, 1956. — *John A. Rehor.*

DIMENSIONS OF LOCOMOTIVES

Number	Cylinders	Valve motion*		Drivers	Weight on drivers	Total weight	Boiler pressure	Tractive effort	Grate area
3951-3964	21" x 28"	p	B	51"	164,900	164,900	200	41,200	33
3965-3980	21" x 28"	p	B	51"	167,850	167,850	200	41,200	33
3981-3986	21" x 28"	p	B	51"	168,000	168,000	200	41,200	33.1
4156	21½" x 30"	p	S	57"	188,112	209,612	200	41,400	50.5
4301-4320	22½" x 30"	p	B	57"	193,700	216,800	200	45,300	50.5
5101-5105	25" x 28"	p	B	51"	214,000	214,000	175	51,200	46.6 (A)
5106-5125	25" x 28"	p	B	51"	219,130	219,130	180	52,500	46.6 (B)
6001-6020	27" x 32"	p	W	63"	239,839	321,678	200	62,900	70.8 (C)
6053, 6056, 6067	26" x 30"	p	W	57"	242,770	273,270	200	60,500	66.6 (D)
6061	26" x 30"	p	W	57"	244,420	274,920	200	60,500	66.6 (E)
6401-6403, 6405, 6407	25" x 34"	p	B	69"	263,045	413,170	250	65,400	90.3
6404, 6406, 6408-6415	25" x 34"	p	B	69"	263,045	413,170	245	64,100	90.3
6416-6432	25" x 34"	p	B	69"	265,500	415,000	245	64,100	90.3
6803-6809	28" x 30"	p	B	63"	273,418	399,150	225	68,900	84.1 (F)
8001-8009	23" and 35" x 32"	p	B	57"	360,000	452,000	225	79,400	76.3

*p — piston valve; B — Baker; S — Stephenson; W — Walschaerts.
(A) USRA with superheater.

(B) Equipped with superheater and syphons.
(C) USRA heavy Mikado with Type HA superheater, syphons; 16,000-gallon tenders. 6003, 6005, 6011, 6013, 6016 had Timken roller-bearing trailer trucks; 6005, 6011, 6013, 6016 had Chicago Type R exhaust steam injectors.
(D) Equipped with superheater and Type MB stoker.
(E) Equipped with superheater, Type MB stoker, and syphons.
(F) 6804, 6806, and 6808 had HT stokers; others had Duplex stokers.

Baldwin USRA 2-6-6-2 8003 and three other class I-3 compounds were working mine runs out of Pine Valley when Nickel Plate leased W&LE in 1949. At 226 tons each, these outweighed all other NKP locomotives. — *John J. Young Jr.*

3951 — Renumbered 2nd 351 April 1951. Last run November 28, 1953. To Luntz Iron & Steel (Canton) April 1, 1954.

3952 — Renumbered 2nd 352 July 1951. Last run September 21, 1951. To Luntz July 29, 1952.

3953 — Renumbered 2nd 353 April 1951. Laid up July 18, 1952. Sold to National Iron & Metals Company January 22, 1953.

3954 — Renumbered 2nd 354 February 1951. Last run February 28, 1953. To Luntz (Canton) June 3, 1953.

3955 — Renumbered 2nd 355 February 1951. Last run March 11, 1953. To Luntz June 3, 1953.

3956 — Renumbered 2nd 356 April 1951. Last run March 31, 1951. To Luntz (Canton) July 29, 1952.

3957 — Renumbered 2nd 357 June 1951. Last run November 20, 1954. To Luntz August 4, 1955.

3958 — Renumbered 2nd 358 February 1951. Last run December 22, 1952. To Luntz March 27, 1953.

3959 — Renumbered 2nd 359 February 1951. Last run November 23, 1953. To Luntz April 1, 1954.

3960 — Renumbered 2nd 360 January 1952. Last run October 1957, Zanesville to Brewster. Donated June 1958 to city of Canton for display at Deuber Park.

3961 — Renumbered 2nd 361 June 1951. Last run September 27, 1951. To Luntz March 26, 1952.

3962 — Renumbered 2nd 362 March 1951. Last run January 15, 1954. To Luntz July 27, 1955.

3963 — Renumbered 2nd 363 June 1951. Last miles September 15, 1956, Brewster yard. To Luntz Iron & Steel (Canton) January 4, 1957.

3964 — Renumbered 2nd 364 March 1951. Last miles December 6, 1956, Brewster yard. To Luntz (Canton) January 6, 1957.

3965 — Renumbered 2nd 365 January 1951. Last miles April 13, 1956, Brewster yard. To Luntz January 4, 1957.

3966 — Renumbered 2nd 366 January 1951. Last miles June 4, 1952, Cleveland yard. To River Terminal Railway, their 366, June 28, 1952. Dismantled May 1956.

3967 — Renumbered 367 May 1951. Last run September 11, 1952. To Luntz February 14, 1953.

3968 — Renumbered 368 June 1951. Last run September 5, 1951. To Luntz March 26, 1952.

3969 — Renumbered 369 June 1951. Last run October 24, 1952. To Luntz February 21, 1953.

3970 — Renumbered 370 June 1951. Last run October 24, 1952. To Luria Steel & Trading March 10, 1953.

3971 — Renumbered 371 January 1951. Last run November 18, 1952. To Luria Steel & Trading March 10, 1953.

3972 — Renumbered 372 August 1951. Last run December 9, 1952. To Luntz March 27, 1953.

3973 — Renumbered 373 March 1951. Last run January 31, 1953. To Luntz March 27, 1953.

3974 — Renumbered 374 April 1951. Last run June 6, 1952. To Luntz January 22, 1953.

3975 — Renumbered 2nd 375 March 1951. Last run February 20, 1953. To Luntz April 4, 1953.

3976 — Renumbered 2nd 376 April 1951. Last run April 17, 1952. To National Iron & Metals (Canton) January 24, 1953.

3977 — Renumbered 2nd 377 April 1951. Last miles June 15, 1952, Brewster to Cleveland. To River Terminal Railway, their 377, June 28, 1952. Dismantled May 1956.

3978 — Renumbered 2nd 378 January 1951. Laid up at Lima April 1956. To Purdy & Company December 17, 1956.

3979 — Renumbered 2nd 379 June 1951. Last miles June 1, 1956, Brewster yard. To Luntz (Canton) January 6, 1957.

3980 — Renumbered 2nd 380 April 1951. Last run May 14, 1952, Cleveland yard. To River Terminal Railway, their 380, June 28, 1952. Dismantled April 1956.

3981 — Renumbered 2nd 381 April 1951. Laid up July 1955. To Luria Steel & Trading December 27, 1956.

3982 — Renumbered 2nd 382 April 1951. Laid up March 30, 1954. To Luntz June 27, 1954.

3983 — Renumbered 2nd 383 January 1951. Wrecked at Wheeling Steel, Mingo Junction works, May 3, 1953; not repaired. To Luntz (Canton) August 28, 1953.

3984 — Renumbered 2nd 384 January 1951. Last run November 1957, Zanesville to Brewster. Donated to city of Lorain June 16, 1960, for display.

3985 — Renumbered 2nd 385 January 1951. Last miles January 2, 1956, Brewster yard. To Luntz Iron & Steel (Canton) January 9, 1957.

3986 — Renumbered 2nd 386 January 1951. Last miles August 4, 1956, Brewster yard. To Luntz January 9, 1957.

4156 — Renumbered 920 January 6, 1951. Last run September 11, 1952, Chagrin Falls to Cleveland. To Luntz March 20, 1953.

4301 — Renumbered 921 January 18, 1951. Last run March 12, 1954, Chagrin Falls to Cleveland. To Luntz (Canton) June 24, 1954.

4302 — Renumbered 922 December 6, 1950. Laid up at Cleveland June 1953. To Luntz September 30, 1955.

4303 — Last run August 5, 1950. Assigned No. 923 in December 1950 but not renumbered. To U. S. Steel Corporation, Mifflin Junction, Pa., May 29, 1951.

4308 — Last run September 1, 1950. Assigned No. 924 but not renumbered. To U. S. Steel Corporation May 29, 1951.

4310 — Renumbered 925 February 21, 1951. Last run June 26, 1954. To Luntz Iron & Steel (Canton) October 8, 1954.

4314 — Assigned No. 926 in December 1950 but not renumbered. Last run February 15, 1951. To U. S. Steel Corporation, Mifflin Junction, Pa., May 29, 1951.

4320 — Renumbered 927 April 20, 1951. Last run September 19, 1955. To Luntz (Canton) February 7, 1956.

5101 — Renumbered 2nd 271 January 1951. Laid up November 28, 1953. To Luntz April 19, 1955.

5102 — Renumbered 2nd 272 June 1951. Laid up at Bellevue October 1957. To Luntz January 19, 1962.

5103 — Renumbered 2nd 273 July 1951. Laid up September 27, 1951. To Luntz July 29, 1952.

5104 — Renumbered 2nd 274 April 1951. Laid up April 12, 1953. To Luntz August 28, 1953.

5105 — Renumbered 2nd 275 August 1951. Last run November 7, 1952. To Luntz February 21, 1953.

5106 — Renumbered 2nd 276 June 1951. Last run March 13, 1954. To Luntz (Canton) June 27, 1954.

5107 — Renumbered 2nd 277 January 1951. Laid up at Conneaut December 1957. Sold to Columbia Iron & Metal (Cleveland) January 31, 1962.

5108 — Renumbered 2nd 278 March 1951. Laid up at Buffalo April 1958. Dismantled there April 1964.

5109 — Renumbered 2nd 279 May 1951. Laid up April 29, 1952. To National Iron & Metals January 22, 1953.

5110 — Renumbered 2nd 280 May 1951. Laid up January 27, 1952. To National Iron & Metals (Canton) January 24, 1953.

5111 — Renumbered 2nd 281 February 1951. Laid up at Brewster July 1957. To Luntz November 13, 1958.

5112 — Renumbered 2nd 282 February 1951. Laid up at Brewster July 1957. To Luntz (Canton) November 13, 1958.

5113 — Renumbered 2nd 283 February 1951. Laid up January 22, 1951. To Luntz July 29, 1952.

5114 — Renumbered 2nd 284 April 1951. Last run November 28, 1952. To Luntz March 31, 1953.

5115 — Renumbered 2nd 285 January 1951. Last run May 1957, Brewster to Buffalo. Dismantled at Buffalo April 1964.

5116 — Renumbered 2nd 286 December 1950. Laid up at Brewster June 1957. To Luntz (Canton) July 29, 1961.

5117 — Renumbered 2nd 287 February 1951. Last run October 7, 1952. To Luntz February 14, 1953.

5118 — Renumbered 2nd 288 March 1951. Laid up at Buffalo December 1957; dismantled there April 1964.

5119 — Renumbered 2nd 289 March 1951. Last miles September 2, 1956, Brewster yard. Cab removed and installed on 285 November 1956. To Luntz September 1, 1957.

5120 — Renumbered 2nd 290 April 1951. Laid up at Brewster July 1957. To Luntz August 1, 1961.

5121 — Renumbered 2nd 291 July 1951. Laid up at Buffalo March 1958; dismantled there April 1964.

5122 — Renumbered 2nd 292 March 1951. Laid up at Norwalk October 1957. To Luntz February 8, 1962.

5123 — Renumbered 2nd 293 January 1951. Laid up at Buffalo January 1957. To Luntz September 1, 1957.

5124 — Renumbered 2nd 294 February 1951. Laid up at Brewster February 25, 1957. To Luntz (Canton) February 19, 1958.

5125 — Renumbered 2nd 295 May 1951. Last run November 22, 1956, Brewster yard. To Luntz (Canton) September 4, 1957.

6001 — Renumbered 2nd 671 January 23, 1951. Last run November 29, 1954. To Luntz October 22, 1955.

6002 — Renumbered 672 December 11, 1950. Last run May 3, 1955. To Luntz October 22, 1955.

6003 — Renumbered 673 January 12, 1951. Last run October 28, 1954. To Luntz July 26, 1955.

6004 — Renumbered 674 December 9, 1950. Last run August 16, 1955. To Luntz (Canton) May 1, 1956.

6005 — Renumbered 675 March 23, 1951. Last run March 31, 1955. To Luntz May 1, 1956.

6006 — Renumbered 676 February 6, 1951. Last run October 10, 1954. To Luntz August 9, 1955.

6007 — Renumbered 677 January 16, 1951. Last run June 23, 1955. To Luntz October 19, 1955.

6008 — Renumbered 678 January 17, 1951. Last run December 12, 1956, Zanesville to Brewster. To Luntz (Canton) February 22, 1958.

6009 — Renumbered 679 January 20, 1951. Last run August 15, 1953. To Luntz April 1, 1954.

6010 — Renumbered 680 April 2, 1951. Last run May 28, 1955. To Luntz October 20, 1955.

6011 — Renumbered 681 January 15, 1951. Last run March 15, 1955. To Luntz (Canton) July 26, 1955.

6012 — Renumbered 682 February 5, 1951. Last run February 6, 1955. To Luntz October 20, 1955.

6013 — Renumbered 683 December 29, 1950. Last run May 22, 1954. To Luntz October 8, 1954.

6014 — Renumbered 684 January 4, 1951. Derailed and wrecked at Dundee, O., March 6, 1954; never repaired. To Luntz July 2, 1954.

6015 — Renumbered 685 February 3, 1951. Last run October 28, 1955. To Luntz (Canton) May 10, 1956.

6016 — Renumbered 686 January 11, 1951. Last run October 4, 1953. To Luntz April 1, 1954.

6017 — Renumbered 687 January 26, 1951. Last run September 28, 1954. To Luntz May 3, 1955.

6018 — Renumbered 688 January 10, 1951. Last run September 5, 1954. To Luntz April 23, 1955.

6019 — Renumbered 689 December 29, 1950. Last run December 28, 1954. To Luntz July 28, 1955.

6020 — Renumbered 690 January 9, 1951. Last run August 26, 1955. To Luntz May 3, 1956.

6053 — Renumbered 928 February 26, 1951. Laid up at Brewster July 1951. To Luntz March 16, 1952.

6056 — Laid up at Brewster January 1950. To Luntz (Warren) August 3, 1950.

6061 — Laid up at Brewster January 1950. To Luntz (Warren) August 7, 1950.

6067 — Laid up at Brewster January 1950. To Luntz (Warren) August 1950.

6401 — Renumbered 801 March 1952. Laid up at Brewster February 1957. To Canton Iron & Metal April 18, 1962.

6402 — Renumbered 802 March 1952. Laid up at Bellevue March 1958. Sold to McLouth Steel Company, Trenton, Mich., for stationary duty November 24, 1959.

6403 — Renumbered 803 April 1952. Laid up at Brewster December 1956. To Luntz (Canton) May 7, 1961.

6404 — Renumbered 804 March 1952. Last steam locomotive repaired in Brewster shop June 1955. Laid up at Conneaut October 1957. To Luntz March 30, 1962.

6405 — Renumbered 805 March 1952. Last run May 6, 1958, Bellevue to Conneaut. To Columbia Iron & Metal Company October 17, 1961.

6406 — Renumbered 806 March 1952. Laid up at Brewster November 1956. To Luntz February 9, 1962.

6407 — Renumbered 807 April 1952. Laid up at Brewster November 1956. Boiler dismantled June 1961; machinery dismantled April 22, 1964.

6408 — Renumbered 808 February 1952. Laid up at Brewster February 1957. To Luntz February 19, 1963.

6409 — Renumbered 2nd 809 April 1952. Laid up at Conneaut March 1958. To Columbia Iron & Metal October 27, 1961.

6410 — Renumbered 2nd 810 February 1952. Last run May 8, 1958, Cleveland to Bellevue. To McLouth Steel Company, Trenton, Mich., November 24, 1959.

6411 — Renumbered 2nd 811 April 1952. Laid up at Brewster June 1957. To Canton Iron & Metal March 30, 1963.

6412 — Renumbered 812 March 1952. Laid up at Brewster October 1957. To Luntz (Canton) May 23, 1961.

6413 — Renumbered 813 April 1952. Laid up at Brewster August 1956. To Canton Iron & Metal April 17, 1962.

6414 — Renumbered 814 February 1952. Last run April 28, 1958, Bellevue to Conneaut. To Luntz December 1963.

6415 — Renumbered 815 April 1952. Laid up at Brewster June 1957. To Canton Iron & Metal March 12, 1963.

6416 — Renumbered 816 April 1952. Laid up at Brewster February 1957. To Luntz March 4, 1963.

6417 — Renumbered 817 March 1952. Laid up at Brewster August 1957. To Luntz (Canton) September 30, 1961.

6418 — Renumbered 818 April 1952. Laid up at Brewster May 1957. To Luntz June 13, 1961.

6419 — Renumbered 819 March 1952. Laid up at Brewster February 1957. To Luntz Iron & Steel May 28, 1961.

6420 — Renumbered 2nd 820 March 1952. Laid up at Brewster May 1957; dismantled there November 30, 1964.

6421 — Renumbered 2nd 821 March 1952. Laid up at Brewster September 1956. To Luntz May 16, 1961.

6422 — Renumbered 2nd 822 May 1952. Laid up at Brewster September 1956. To Canton Iron & Metal March 21, 1963.

6423 — Renumbered 2nd 823 February 1952. Laid up at Brewster April 1957. To Luntz September 16, 1961.

6424 — Renumbered 2nd 824 February 1952. Laid up at Brewster

April 1957. To Luntz Iron & Steel sans tender October 17, 1961.

6425 — Renumbered 2nd 825 March 1952. Laid up at Brewster September 1957. To Luntz December 28, 1961.

6426 — Renumbered 2nd 826 March 1952. Laid up at Brewster October 1956. To Canton Iron & Metal February 24, 1963.

6427 — Renumbered 2nd 827 September 1952. Laid up at Brewster April 1957. To Luntz September 23, 1961.

6428 — Renumbered 828 February 1952. Wrecked in head-on collision with 527 at Middlebranch, O., August 11, 1951. Laid up at Brewster March 1957. To Luntz January 4, 1962.

6429 — Renumbered 829 February 1952. Laid up at Brewster December 1956; dismantled there September 1964.

6430 — Renumbered 2nd 830 February 1952. Laid up at Brewster April 1957. To Luntz September 2, 1961.

6431 — Renumbered 2nd 831 April 1952. Laid up at Brewster June 1957. To Luntz October 9, 1961.

6432 — Renumbered 2nd 832 February 1952. Laid up at Brewster February 1957. To Luntz January 23, 1962.

6803 — Last run December 29, 1949. Dismantled at Brewster May 29, 1952.

6804 — Renumbered 844 January 24, 1951. Last run May 19, 1953. To Luntz (Canton) August 28, 1953.

6805 — Renumbered 845 December 30, 1950. Last run July 24, 1952. To Luntz January 22, 1953.

6806 — Renumbered 846 January 16, 1951. Last run November 6, 1953. To Luntz February 3, 1954.

6808 — Renumbered 848 January 16, 1951. Last run June 7, 1951. To Luria Steel & Trading January 24, 1953.

6809 — Assigned number 849 in December 1950 but never renumbered. Made last run on January 18, 1950. To Luntz Iron & Steel (Canton) October 18, 1952.

8001 — Renumbered 940 January 9, 1951. Withdrawn October 31, 1953, for overhaul at Brewster. Partly dismantled when work suspended; dismantling completed November 11, 1955.

8002 — Renumbered 941 January 1, 1951. Last run February 22, 1955. To Luntz August 9, 1955.

8003 — Renumbered 942 January 19, 1951. Last run March 21, 1953. To Luntz July 21, 1955.

8009 — Renumbered 943 January 29, 1951. Last run March 11, 1954. To Luntz August 12, 1955.

Electro-Motive NW2 switchers 7-10 went into service at Stony Island in 1942; their 1000 h.p. Alco counterparts were assigned to Buffalo. Both groups served for 20 years at those locations, which were the yards closest to the plants of their respective builders. — *Electro-Motive Division.*

NYC&STL DIESEL-ELECTRIC LOCOMOTIVES

Number	Original class	1951 class	Type	Builder*	Builder number	Year	Horse-power	Builder type
1-6	DE-3	AS-10a	B-B	Alco	69924-69929	1942	1000	S-2
7-8	DE-2	ES-10b	B-B	EMC	1750, 1698	1942	1000	NW2
9-10	DE-2	ES-10b	B-B	EMC	1759, 1756	1942	1000	NW2
11-14	DS-5	ES-10c	B-B	EMD	4985-4988	1948	1000	NW2
15-16	DS-5	ES-10c	B-B	EMD	4989-4990	1948	1000	NW2 (A)
17-22	DS-5	ES-10c	B-B	EMD	6088-6093	1948	1000	NW2
25-26	DS-4	AS-10b	B-B	Alco	73931-73932	1947	1000	S-2
27-28	DS-4	AS-10b	B-B	Alco	74972, 74982	1947	1000	S-2
29-30	DS-4	AS-10b	B-B	Alco	75237-75238	1947	1000	S-2
31-33	DS-4	AS-10b	B-B	Alco	75243-75245	1947	1000	S-2
34-35	DS-4	AS-10b	B-B	Alco	75250-75251	1947	1000	S-2
36-42	DS-4	AS-10b	B-B	Alco	75364-75370	1947	1000	S-2
43	DS-4	AS-10b	B-B	Alco	75388	1947	1000	S-2
44-45	DS-12	ASM-10a	B-B	Alco	78015-78016	1950	1000	S-2 (B)
46-53	DS-16	AS-10c	B-B	Alco	78697-78704	1951	1000	S-4
54-60	DS-16	ASM-10b	B-B	Alco	78705-78711	1951	1000	S-4 (B)
61		ASM-10c	B-B	Alco	79520	1952	1000	S-4 (B)
65-73		AS-10d	B-B	Alco	79521-79529	1952	1000	S-4
74-77		AS-10e	B-B	Alco	80468-80471	1953	1000	S-4
78-83		ASM-10d	B-B	Alco	80447-80452	1953	1000	S-4 (B)
85	DS-13	AS-6a	B-B	Alco	78139	1950	660	S-1
90	DS-9	GS-4a	B-B	GE	30249	1949	380	
95-96	DS-10	ES-10a	B-B	EMC	998, 1089	1940	1000	NW2
97-98	DS-10	ES-10a	B-B	EMC	1422-1423	1941	1000	NW2
100-101	DS-6	BS-10a	B-B	B	72849-72850	1947	1000	VO-1000
105-106	DS-15	ES-6a	B-B	EMD	13705-13706	1950	600	SW1
107-114		ES-8a	B-B	EMD	16352-16359	1952	800	SW8
125-133	DS-7	FS-10a	B-B	FM	10L103-10L111	1949	1000	
134-138		FS-12a	B-B	FM	12L721-12L725	1953	1200	
139-145		FS-12b	B-B	FM	12L1082-12L1088	1957	1200	
146-155		FS-12c	B-B	FM	12L1101-12L1110	1958	1200	

Number	Original class	1951 class	Type	Builder*	Builder number	Year	Horse-power	Builder type
180-186	DP-1	AP-20a	A1A-A1A	Alco	75330-75336	1947	2000	PA-1 (B, E)
187-190	DP-1	AP-20a	A1A-A1A	Alco	75454-75457	1948	2000	PA-1 (B, E)
230-232	DS-14	ES-12a	B-B	EMD	12307-12309	1950	1200	SW7
233-237		ES-12b	B-B	EMD	13955-13959	1951	1200	SW9
238-244		ES-12c	B-B	EMD	16360-16366	1952	1200	SW9
305-308	DS-8	LS-10a	B-B	L-H	9324-9327	1949	1000	
309-312	DS-11	LS-12a	B-B	L-H	9413-9416	1950	1200	

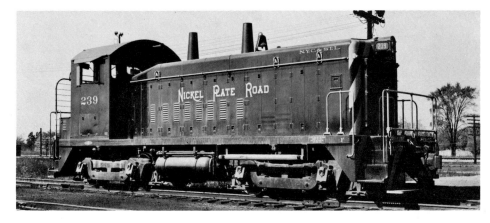

Dieselization of Fort Wayne and Frankfort yards was completed by the purchase of 15 EMD SW7 and SW9 1200 h.p. switchers during 1950-1952. ES-12c 239 awaits second-trick crew at East Wayne on October 18, 1953. — *William Swartz.*

MULTIPLE-UNIT ROAD-SWITCHERS

Number	Class	Type	Builder*	Builder number	Year	Horse-power	Builder type
320-321	BRS-16a	B-B	B-L-H	75943-75944	1953	1600	
	BARS-18a					1800	(C)
322-323	BRS-16b	B-B	B-L-H	76028-76029	1954	1600	
	BERS-17a					1750	(D)
325-332	ARX-18a	C-C	Alco	81955-81962	1957	1800	DL-702
333	ARX-18a	C-C	Alco	82378	1957	1800	DL-702
340-359	ERX-17a	C-C	EMD	23155-23174	1957	1750	SD9
400-412	ERS-15a	B-B	EMD	13692-13704	1951	1500	GP7
413-422	ERS-15b	B-B	EMD	17088-17097	1953	1500	GP7
423-447	ERS-15c	B-B	EMD	18591-18615	1953	1500	GP7
448	ERS-17a	B-B	EMD	20453	1955	1750	GP9
2nd 448	ERS-17a	B-B	EMD	23756	1957	1750	GP9
449-476	ERS-17a	B-B	EMD	20454-20481	1955	1750	GP9
477-479	ERS-17b	B-B	EMD	20482-20484	1955	1750	GP9 (E)
480-482	ERS-17c	B-B	EMD	21908-21910	1956	1750	GP9 (E)
2nd 482	ERS-17c	B-B	EMD	23760	1957	1750	GP9 (F)
483	ERS-17c	B-B	EMD	21911	1956	1750	GP9 (G)
484-485	ERS-17c	B-B	EMD	21906-21907	1956	1750	GP9 (F)
486-497	ERS-17d	B-B	EMD	21912-21923	1956	1750	GP9
2nd 496-497	ERS-17d	B-B	EMD	23757-23758	1957	1750	GP9
498-503	ERS-17d	B-B	EMD	21924-21929	1956	1750	GP9
2nd 503	ERS-17d	B-B	EMD	23759	1957	1750	GP9
504-509	ERS-17d	B-B	EMD	21930-21935	1956	1750	GP9
510-529	ERS-17e	B-B	EMD	24501-24520	1958	1750	GP9
530-534	ERS-17f	B-B	EMD	25073-25077	1959	1750	GP9
535-557	ARS-16a	B-B	Alco	80707-80729	1954	1600	RS-3
558-562	ARS-18a	B-B	Alco	81459-81463	1956	1800	DL-701
563-567	ARS-18b	B-B	Alco	82832-82836	1958	1800	DL-701
568-572	ARS-18b	B-B	Alco	82863-82867	1958	1800	DL-701
573-575	ARS-18d	B-B	Alco	83541-83543	1960	1800	DL-701
576-577	ARS-18d	B-B	Alco	83580-83581	1960	1800	DL-701
578	ARS-20a	B-B	Alco	84792	1964	2000	C-420
700-709	ERS-18a	B-B	EMD	26023-26032	1960	1800	GP18
800-814	ERS-17g	B-B	EMD	25078-25092	1959	1750	GP9 (H)
850-863	ARS-18c	B-B	Alco	83014-83027	1959	1800	DL-701 (H)
864	ARS-18c	B-B	Alco	83394	1959	1800	DL-701 (H)
865-868	ARS-18e	B-B	Alco	83697-83700	1962	1800	DL-701-XAP (H)
869-870	ARS-18e	B-B	Alco	84100-84101	1962	1800	DL-701-XAP (H)

Number	Class	Type	Builder*	Builder number	Year	Horse-power	Builder type
871-872	ARS-18e	B-B	Alco	84105-84106	1962	1800	DL-701-XAP (H)
873	ARS-18e	B-B	Alco	84104	1962	1800	DL-701-XAP (H)
874-875	ARS-18f	B-B	Alco	84102-84103	1962	1800	DL-701-XAP (E)
900-909	ERS-22a	B-B	EMD	27894-27903	1962	2250	GP30 (H)
910	ERS-25a	B-B	EMD	29167	1964	2500	GP35

*Alco — American Locomotive; B — Baldwin Locomotive; B-L-H — Baldwin-Lima-Hamilton; EMC — Electro-Motive Corporation; EMD — Electro-Motive Division, General Motors; FM — Fairbanks-Morse; GE — General Electric; L-H — Lima-Hamilton.

(A) Equipped with dual control.
(B) Equipped for multiple-unit operation.
(C) Repowered by Alco 1959.
(D) Repowered by Electro-Motive 1959.
(E) Equipped with steam generator and train stop.
(F) Equipped with steam generator and dual control.
(G) Equipped with dual control.
(H) Equipped with automatic train stop.

First diesel-electric freight engines on NKP were 13 Electro-Motive GP7's purchased in 1951. These were built at EMD's Cleveland plant (served by the Nickel Plate) and powered by a 1500 h.p. 16-cylinder 567B engine. — *Electro-Motive Division.*

Baldwin-Lima-Hamilton 1600 h.p. road-switchers 322-323 of 1954 were repowered by Electro-Motive in 1959. Hybrid hood units came back from La Grange with 16-cylinder 1750 h.p. 567C engine, the standard GP9 prime mover. — *Electro-Motive Division.*

1 — Sold to Akron, Canton & Youngstown March 5, 1963.
2 — Sold to Kentucky & Tennessee Railway April 4, 1964.
3 — Laid up October 1962. Carbody to Striegel Supply & Equipment Corporation May 5, 1964.
4 — Laid up December 5, 1962. To Medusa Portland Cement Company (Dixon, Ill.), their 10, May 1, 1964.
5 — Laid up October 1962. Sold to Wabash May 1964.
6 — Laid up October 1962. Sold to Akron, Canton & Youngstown May 1964.
7-10 — Removed from service December 1962 and leased to Detroit, Toledo & Ironton. To Wheeling Steel 1964.
95-97 — Ex-Wheeling & Lake Erie D-1 through D-3. To Wabash 347-349 October 13, 1961.

98 — Ex-Wheeling & Lake Erie D-4. To Des Moines Union Railway 5, October 13, 1961.
100-101 — Rebuilt at Brewster April 1960 and December 1959 with parts from Baldwin road-switchers 322 and 323.
180-190 — Sold to Alco in 1961 and leased back. Returned to owner in lots of three during 1961-1962. Main and auxiliary generators, traction motors, train stop apparatus, batteries, and other parts used in units 866-875.
448, 482 — Destroyed in a head-on collision at New Douglas, Ill., December 6, 1956.
498 — Demolished in a head-on collision at New Douglas, Ill., December 6, 1956. Returned to EMD at La Grange, Ill., where it was rebuilt and restored to service in May 1957.

496, 497,
and 503 — Destroyed in a head-on collision at New Douglas, Ill., December 6, 1956.

507 — Destroyed in a high-speed derailment at Mount Cory, O., September 10, 1963.

541-542 — Damaged in a high-speed derailment at Gibson City, Ill., October 14, 1954. 541 rebuilt at Schenectady; 542 rebuilt at Frankfort shop.

551 — Damaged in a high-speed derailment at Gibson City, Ill., October 14, 1954. Subsequently rebuilt at Schenectady and returned to service.

559 — Destroyed in a high-speed derailment at Mount Cory, O., September 10, 1963.

867 — Damaged in a high-speed derailment at Mount Cory, O., September 10, 1963. Repaired at Brewster shop 1964 and returned to duty.

GP18's were delivered in 1960 with new-style black and yellow paint job. These units, numbered 700-709, generally were used between Bellevue and Sayre, Pa., on through LV trains. — *Electro-Motive Division.*

Locomotives of the Lake Erie & Western

FREMONT & INDIANA AND LAKE ERIE & LOUISVILLE LOCOMOTIVES ACQUIRED PRIOR TO 1879

Number	Type	Builder	Builder number	Date	Cylinders	Drivers
1	4-4-0	R. Norris & Son		1861	15" x 22"	60"
2	4-4-0					
3	4-4-0	Schenectady	743	12-1871	15" x 24"	60"
4	4-4-0	Danforth & Cooke	883	10-1872	15" x 24"	60"
5	4-4-0	Danforth & Cooke	901	1-1873	15" x 24"	60"
6	4-4-0	Schenectady	884	6-1873	16" x 24"	60"

1 — Named L. Q. Rawson. Received at Fremont April 5, 1861.
3-4 — LE&W 1898 roster shows these received March 5, 1873, and July 20, 1874. However, annual reports indicate both were on the LE&L at the end of 1872.

6 — Owned by L. Q. Rawson, D. J. Cory, and C. W. Foster and rented to LE&L. 1898 roster shows this engine received September 19, 1874, but annual reports indicate it was on the LE&L at the end of 1873.

La Fayette, Bloomington & Mississippi train No. 4 at Templeton, Ind., on May 12, 1879. Former No. 7 of the LM&B had already been renumbered 13, a number she bore until retirement in 1902. Swap of ominous number had no effect on career of this Brooks alumnus of '76 or that of her engineer, J. W. Gore. Shown at the throttle in this photo, Gore survived perils and rigid discipline of old-time railroading to enjoy a long association with the Peoria Division. — *Collection of John A. Rehor.*

LA FAYETTE, MUNCIE & BLOOMINGTON RAIL ROAD 1876-1879
LA FAYETTE, BLOOMINGTON & MUNCIE RAILWAY 1879

Number	Name	Type	Builder	Builder number	Date
1	La Fayette	4-4-0	Brooks	270	5-1876
2	Muncie	4-4-0	Brooks	271	5-1876
3	Frankfort	4-4-0	Brooks	273	5-1876
4-5		4-4-0	Brooks	274-275	6-1876
6-7		4-4-0	Brooks	277-278	6-1876
8		4-4-0	Brooks	281	7-1876
9	Hoopston	4-4-0	Brooks	286	10-1876
10		4-4-0	Brooks	291	11-1876
17	Leviathan	0-6-0	Baldwin	4720	7-1879

Note: These engines became La Fayette, Bloomington & Muncie 7-17 in April 1879.

LA FAYETTE, BLOOMINGTON & MISSISSIPPI RAIL ROAD 1878-1879

Number	Name	Type	Builder	Builder number	Date
20	W. A. Rankin	4-4-0	Baldwin	4446	10-1878
21	C. Bogardus	4-4-0	Baldwin	4448	10-1878
22	J. H. Cheney	4-4-0	Baldwin	4457	10-1878
23	E. H. R. Lyman	4-4-0	Baldwin	4459	10-1878
24	Gen. Gridley	4-4-0	Baldwin	4460	10-1878
25	Geo. I. Seney Jr.	4-4-0	Baldwin	4461	10-1878

LAKE ERIE & LOUISVILLE RAILROAD 1879
LAKE ERIE & WESTERN RAILWAY 1880-1887

Number	Class*	Type	Builder	Builder number	Date
1		4-4-0	R. Norris & Son		1861
2		4-4-0			
3		4-4-0	Schenectady	743	12-1871
4		4-4-0	Danforth & Cooke	883	10-1872
5		4-4-0	Danforth & Cooke	901	1-1873
6		4-4-0	Schenectady	884	6-1873
7-9	P-7	4-4-0	Brooks	270, 271, 273	5-1876
10-13	P-7	4-4-0	Brooks	274, 275, 277, 278	6-1876
14	P-7	4-4-0	Brooks	281	7-1876
15	P-7	4-4-0	Brooks	286	10-1876
16	P-7	4-4-0	Brooks	291	11-1876
17	T-8	0-6-0	Baldwin	4720	7-1879
18	P-7	4-4-0	Brooks	355	6-1879
19	P-7	4-4-0	Brooks	364	7-1879
2nd 18-19	P-8	4-4-0	Baldwin	4460-4461	10-1878
20-21	P-7	4-4-0	Brooks	369-370	9-1879
2nd 20-21	P-8	4-4-0	Baldwin	4446, 4448	10-1878
22-23	P-7	4-4-0	Brooks	377-378	10-1879
2nd 22-23	P-8	4-4-0	Baldwin	4457, 4459	10-1878
30-31		4-4-0	Brooks	394-395	1-1880
32-34	Q-7	4-4-0	Brooks	441, 443, 444	8-1880
35	Q-7	4-4-0	Brooks	459	10-1880
36-41	Q-7	4-4-0	Brooks	471-476	11-1880
42-43	Z-3	0-4-0	Brooks	480-481	12-1880
44-48	Q-7	4-4-0	Brooks	837-841	1-1883
49-53	Q-7	4-4-0	Brooks	912-916	5-1883

*LS&MS classification of 1902.

DIMENSIONS OF LOCOMOTIVES

Number	Cylinders	Drivers	Weight on drivers	Total weight	Boiler pressure*	Tractive effort*	Grate area
1	15" x 22"	60"		48,000			(A)
2	no data						
3-5	15" x 24"	60"	40,000	60,000			(B)
6	16" x 24"	60"	42,000	64,000			
7-16	16" x 24"	60"	44,000	66,000	125		14.2
17	18" x 22"	48"	70,000	70,000	120	14,800	16.4

Number	Cylinders	Drivers					
18-23 } 30-31 }	16" x 24"	61"	44,000	66,000	125		14.2
2nd 18-23	16" x 24"	60¼"	44,000	66,000	125		14.8
32-41 } 44-53 }	17" x 24"	61"	46,000	70,000	135	10,800	15.1
42-43	15" x 24"	46"	60,000	60,000	120	12,000	10.8 (C)

* Per LS&MS specifications, 1902-1905.
(A) Later rebuilt with total engine weight of 56,000 lbs.
(B) Engines 4-5 had 52-inch drivers by 1898.
(C) LS&MS specifications of 1902 show 52,000 lbs. total weight and 48-inch drivers.

1 — Dismantled at South Lima in June 1895.
2 — Retired 1887.
3 — Sold to Joseph, Joseph & Brother November 14, 1895.
4, 5 — Retired 1899, 1890.
6 — Retired 1899.
7-16 — Ex-La Fayette, Bloomington & Muncie; retired 1902-1903.
17 — Ex-La Fayette, Bloomington & Muncie 17. Renumbered 2nd 7 in 1901; 4265, May 14, 1906. To class B-41, 1906. Dismantled June 14, 1909.
18-23 — Renumbered 24-29 December 1879; retired 1900-1902.
2nd 18-22 — Ex-La Fayette, Bloomington & Muncie 24, 25, 20-22. No. 19 was retired in 1905, the rest in 1902-1903.
2nd 23 — Ex-LM&B 23, renumbered 2nd 11 in 1901, retired 1902.
30-31 — Retired 1901-1902.
32-34 — Renumbered 4200-4202 and classed C-45 in 1905. 4201 retired 1908, others 1907.

35 — Scrapped May 26, 1905.
36-37 — Renumbered 4204-4205, classed C-45 1905; retired 1907.
38-39 — Retired 1903 and 1902.
40-41 — Renumbered 4206-4207 and classed C-45 in 1905. Both sold November 23, 1907.
42-43 — Renumbered 4080-4081 and classed A-40 in 1905. Sold February 19, 1906.
44 — Scrapped May 26, 1905.
45-46 — Renumbered 4209-4210 and classed C-45 in 1905. 4209 sold November 23, 1907. 4210 sold July 1907.
47 — Scrapped June 24, 1902.
48-49 — Renumbered 4211-4212 and classed C-45 in 1905. 4211 sold November 23, 1907. 4212 sold July 1907.
50, 53 — Retired 1903, 1902.
51-52 — Renumbered 4213-4214 and classed C-45 in 1905. 4213 sold November 23, 1907. 4214 sold May 1907.

Four-coupled LE&W 43 closely resembled Nickel Plate's class D switchers of 1882. This 1880 Brooks had 15 x 24-inch cylinders and weighed 26 tons. Before being scrapped in 1906 she was renumbered 4081.—*Collection of John H. Keller.*

CINCINNATI, PERU & CHICAGO RAILWAY 1855-1867
CHICAGO, CINCINNATI & LOUISVILLE RAILROAD 1867-1871

Name	Type	Builder	Builder number	Date	Cylinders	Drivers
G. W. Rogers	4-4-0	Mason	284	7-1868	15" x 22"	60"
Charles Courter	4-4-0	Mason	300	1-1869	15" x 22"	60"

Note: There were also five locomotives turned over to the CC&L with the CP&C in 1867. Their origin and description are unknown. Rogers and Courter went to the Indianapolis, Peru & Chicago in 1871 along with two of the old CP&C engines.

PERU & INDIANAPOLIS RAIL ROAD 1853-1864
INDIANAPOLIS, PERU & CHICAGO RAILWAY 1864-1881

Number	Name	Type	Builder	Builder number	Date	Cylinders	Drivers
1-3		no data					
2nd 1		4-4-0	Grant		1873	16" x 24"	60"
2nd 2		4-4-0	Pittsburgh	319	6-1875	16" x 24"	61"
4	David Macy	4-4-0	Rogers	1023	6-1862	13" x 22"	60"
5	C. B. Robinson	4-4-0	Rogers	1060	3-1863	15" x 22"	54"
6	Indianapolis	4-4-0	Rogers	1091	7-1863	15" x 22"	54"
7	F. Gilman	4-4-0	Rogers	1279	7-1865	15" x 22"	54"
8-10		no data					
11		0-4-0	Danforth & Cooke		1869	14" x 22"	44"
12		4-4-0	Danforth & Cooke		1869	15" x 22"	55"
13		vacant					
14-15		0-4-0	Danforth & Cooke		1870	14" x 22"	44"

Number	Name	Type	Builder	Builder number	Date	Cylinders	Drivers
16		4-4-0	Pittsburgh	114	12-1870	15" x 22"	55"
17		4-4-0	Pittsburgh	115	1-1871	15" x 22"	55"
18		no data					
19		4-4-0	Mason	284	7-1868	15" x 22"	60"
20		no data					
21		4-4-0	Mason	300	1-1869	15" x 22"	60"
22-23		4-4-0	Pittsburgh	138-139	1-1871	15" x 22"	55"
24-25		4-4-0	Pittsburgh	189-190	5-1872	16" x 24"	55"
26-27		4-4-0	Grant		1872	16" x 24"	60"
28		4-4-0	Pittsburgh	318	6-1875	16" x 24"	61"
29		4-4-0	Pittsburgh	361	10-1877	16" x 24"	61"

1-3 — One of these may have been Mason's 4-4-0 No. 50, T. C. Cotting or Cutting, outshopped in September 1856. No. 3 became Wabash, St. Louis & Pacific 503 in 1881.

2nd 1-2 — To WStL&P 501-502, 1881.

4-7 — To WStL&P 504-507, 1881. No. 5 was rebuilt at Peru in 1872.

8-10 — Probably built by Danforth & Cooke. To WStL&P 508-510, 1881. Retired between 1883 and 1885.

11-12 — To WStL&P 511-512, 1881. No. 11 rebuilt at Peru in 1877.

14-17 — To WStL&P 514-517, 1881. No. 14 rebuilt at Peru in 1881.

18-21 — Ex-CC&L acquired 1871. To WStL&P 518-521, 1881.

22-29 — To WStL&P 522-529, 1881. No. 27 rebuilt at Peru in 1880.

FORT WAYNE, MUNCIE & CINCINNATI RAILWAY 1870-1881
FORT WAYNE, CINCINNATI & LOUISVILLE RAILROAD 1881-1890

Number	Type	Builder	Builder number	Date	Cylinders	Drivers
1-2	4-4-0	Grant		8-1870	15" x 22"	56"
3-4	4-4-0	Grant		5-1871	16" x 24"	50"
5-6	4-4-0	Grant		1871	16" x 24"	50"
7	4-4-0	Manchester	629	12-1873	16" x 24"	60"
8	4-4-0	Manchester	628	12-1873	15" x 22"	66"
9	4-4-0	Rhode Island		1874	16" x 24"	60"
10	4-4-0	Manchester	1089	10-1882	16" x 24"	57"
11-12	4-4-0	Baldwin	10163-10164	8-1889	17" x 24"	62"

Note: Engines 1-9 acquired by FWM&C and bore same numbers on FWC&L roster. All of the above locomotives went to the Lake Erie & Western in 1890.

LE&W LOCOMOTIVES ACQUIRED 1887-1900

Number	Class 1902	Class 1905	Type	Builder	Builder number	Date
2nd 1	T-7	B-40	0-6-0	Brooks	3183	4-1899
2nd 2	N-6	E-40	2-6-0	Brooks	1549	7-1889
2nd 3-4	T-7	B-40	0-6-0	Brooks	3184-3185	4-1899
2nd 5	U-4	B-42	0-6-0	Brooks	2132	8-1892
2nd 6	T-7	B-40	0-6-0	Brooks	3186	4-1899
54-58	N-6	E-40	2-6-0	Brooks	1518-1522	3-1889
59-60	N-6	E-40	2-6-0	Brooks	1550-1551	7-1889
61-62			0-4-0	Danforth & Cooke		1870, 1869
63	Z-4	A-41	0-4-0	Danforth & Cooke		1870
64			4-4-0	Rogers	1060	3-1863
2nd 64	T-7	B-40	0-6-0	Brooks	3187	4-1899
65			4-4-0	Mason	24	7-1855
66			4-4-0	Mason	39	4-1856
67			4-4-0	Mason	25	8-1855
68			4-4-0	Mason	284	7-1868
69			4-4-0	Mason	40	5-1856
70			4-4-0	Mason	300	1-1869
71			4-4-0	Mason	55	11-1856
72			4-4-0	Danforth & Cooke		1869
73			4-4-0	Pittsburgh	115	1-1871
74			4-4-0	Rogers	580	5-1855
75			4-4-0	Rogers	1091	7-1863
76			4-4-0	Rogers	1279	7-1865
77-78			4-4-0	Pittsburgh	138-139	1-1871
79	P-9		4-4-0	Pittsburgh	319	6-1875
80-81			4-4-0	Pittsburgh	189-190	5-1872
82			4-4-0	Pittsburgh	318	6-1875
83			4-4-0	Pittsburgh	361	10-1877
84			4-4-0	Grant		1873

Number	Class 1902	Class 1905	Type	Builder	Builder number	Date
85-86	P-9		4-4-0	Grant		1872
87-88			4-4-0	Schenectady		1871
89-90	P-9		4-4-0	Grant		1873
91-92			4-4-0	Grant		8-1870
93-94	P-9		4-4-0	Grant		5-1871
95-96	P-9		4-4-0	Grant		1871
97	P-9		4-4-0	Manchester	629	12-1873
98			4-4-0	Manchester	628	12-1873
99			4-4-0	Rhode Island		1874
100	P-9		4-4-0	Manchester	1089	10-1882
101-102	Q-6	C-47	4-4-0	Baldwin	10163-10164	8-1889
103-105	N-7	E-41	2-6-0	Brooks	2018-2020	12-1891
106-108	N-7	E-41	2-6-0	Brooks	2021-2023	1-1892
109-114	N-7	E-41	2-6-0	Brooks	2035-2040	2-1892
115-124	N-8	E-42	2-6-0	Brooks	2324-2333	6-1893

Wagon-top switcher 5 had a single sandbox and an air compressor. The little Brooks joined the LE&W roster in 1892 and ultimately became B-42 4266. — *Schenectady History Center*.

DIMENSIONS OF LOCOMOTIVES

Number	Cylinders	Drivers	Weight on drivers	Total weight	Boiler pressure	Tractive effort	Grate area
2nd 1, 3, 4, 6	18" x 24"	52"	110,600	110,600	160	20,400	18.6 (A)
2nd 2, 54-60	18" x 24"	56"	84,000	98,000	160	19,200	15.7
2nd 5	17" x 24"	50"	86,000	86,000	145	17,100	14.5
61-62	14" x 22"	44"	50,000	50,000			
63	14" x 22"	50"	55,000	55,000	120	10,100	(B)
64-66	15" x 22"	60"		60,000			
2nd 64	18" x 24"	52"	110,600	110,600	160	20,400	18.6 (A)
67	15" x 22"	66"	41,000	64,000			
68	15" x 22"	60"		60,000			
69	15" x 22"	60"	37,000	57,000			
70	15" x 22"	60"		59,000			
71	15" x 22"	60"	40,000	60,000			
72	15" x 22"	60"		62,000			
73	15" x 22"	54"	37,000	58,000			
74-75	15" x 22"	60"		60,000			
76	15" x 22"	54"		60,000			
77-78	16" x 24"	54"	30,000	60,000			
79	16" x 24"	60/62"	45,000	70,000	120		
80-81	16" x 24"	54"	43,000	67,000			
82	16" x 24"	60"	45,000	70,000			
83-84	16" x 24"	60"	44,000	69,000			
85	16" x 24"	60/61"	44,000	64,000	120		13.9
86	16" x 24"	60"	44,000	68,000			
87-88	16" x 24"	54"	40,000	62,000			
89-90	16" x 24"	60/62"	44,000	68,000	120		13.9
91	15" x 22"	57"	40,000	60,000			
92	15" x 22"	56"	42,000	65,000			

Number	Cylinders	Drivers	Weight on drivers	Total weight	Boiler pressure	Tractive effort	Grate area
93	16″ x 24″	56″	44,000	66,000	120		13.9
94	16″ x 24″	62″	44,000	66,000	120		13.9
95-96	16″ x 24″	50″	44,000	66,000			
97	T6″ x 24″	57/63″	44,000	66,000			
98	15″ x 22″	69″	41,000	63,000			
99	16″ x 24″	60″	42,000	65,000			
100	16″ x 24″	63″	44,000	68,000	120		
101-102	17″ x 24″	62″	56,000	84,000	145	13,200	17.6
103-114	18″ x 24″	56″	92,000	106,000	160	19,200	15.7
115-124	18″ x 24″	56″	94,000	108,000	160	19,200	15.7

(A) Originally had 50-inch drivers, 165 lbs. boiler pressure, 21,780 lbs. tractive effort.

(B) LS&MS rosters 1902-1905 show 15 x 22-inch cylinders.

2nd 1 — Renumbered 4260 July 13, 1905, NKP 4th 27 April 1924.

2nd 2 — Renumbered 2nd 61 November 1900; 5337, May 5, 1905. Rebuilt with new Lima boiler and reclassed E-40a November 21, 1908. To NKP 2nd 313.

2nd 3-4 — Renumbered 4262-4263 June-August 1905. To NKP 4th 29-30, 1924.

2nd 5 — Renumbered 4266 October 17, 1905. Withdrawn for scrapping May 1916.

2nd 6 — Renumbered 4264 April 14, 1905. To NKP 4th 31 April 1924.

54 — Renumbered 5330 October 25, 1905. New boiler applied at South Lima and reclassed E-40 November 3, 1908. To NKP 2nd 310, 1924.

55 — Renumbered 5331 March 6, 1905. Rebuilt with new boiler at South Lima and reclassed E-40a March 22, 1909. Dismantled August 31, 1923.

56 — Renumbered 5332 June 23, 1905. Rebuilt with new boiler at South Lima and reclassed E-40a October 8, 1908. To NKP 2nd 311, 1924.

57 — Renumbered 5333 March 5, 1905. Rebuilt with new Rhode Island boiler at South Lima and reclassed E-40a January 1908. Retired August 1923.

58 — Renumbered 5334 September 28, 1905. Rebuilt with new Rhode Island boiler and reclassed E-40a February 1908. Dismantled August 31, 1923.

59 — Renumbered 5335 August 12, 1905. Rebuilt with new Rhode Island boiler and reclassed E-40a February 1908. Dismantled at Lima August 1923.

60 — Renumbered 5336 May 26, 1905. Rebuilt with new Rhode Island boiler and reclassed E-40a January 14, 1908. To NKP 2nd 312 April 1924.

61 — Ex-Wabash, St. Louis & Pacific 515 acquired April 1887 with former Indianapolis, Peru & Chicago; retired 1899.

62 — Ex-WStL&P 511, retired 1901.

63 — Ex-WStL&P 514; renumbered 4082, 1905; sold 1906.

64 — Ex-WStL&P 505. Sold to Joseph, Joseph & Brother November 14, 1895.

2nd 64 — Renumbered 3rd 2 November 1900; 4261 March 4, 1905; NKP 4th 28, 1924.

65 — Ex-WStL&P 2nd 508. Originally Toledo & Illinois 16, Zephyr. Sold for exhibition purposes June 1897.

66 — Ex-WStL&P 2nd 509. Originally T&I 24, Amazon. Sold for exhibition purposes June 1897.

67 — Ex-WStL&P 2nd 516. Originally T&I Atalanta. Retired 1900.

68 — Ex-WStL&P 519. Sold to Joseph, Joseph & Brother November 14, 1895.

69 — Ex-WStL&P 2nd 520. Originally T&I 25, Nymph. Retired 1900.

70 — Ex-WStL&P 521, dismantled at South Lima March 1892.

71 — Ex-WStL&P 530; originally T&I 26, Boreas. Retired 1899.

72 — Ex-WStL&P 512, dismantled at Lima August 1892.

73 — Ex-WStL&P 517, retired 1901 or 1902.

74 — Ex-WStL&P 2nd 518; originally Lake Erie, Wabash & St. Louis 5. Sold to Joseph, Joseph & Brother November 14, 1895.

75 — Ex-WStL&P 506. Sold to Joseph, Joseph & Brother November 14, 1895.

76 — Ex-WStL&P 507, dismantled at Peru November 1895.

77-78 — Ex-WStL&P 522-523, scrapped 1902, 1901.

79 — Ex-WStL&P 502, sold 1903.

80-84 — Ex-WStL&P 524, 525, 528, 529, 501; retired 1901.

85-86 — Ex-WStL&P 526, 527; retired 1902-1903.

87 — Ex-WStL&P 531, originally a Wabash 171-180 series engine. Destroyed August 1891 in collision with Big Four train at Indianapolis.

88 — Ex-WStL&P 532, originally Wabash 171-180 series. Dismantled at Peru 1891.

89-90 — Ex-WStL&P 499-500, originally Wabash engines. Retired 1902, 1903.

91-92 — Ex-FWC&L 1-2, retired 1900.

93-94 — Ex-FWC&L 3-4, sold 1903.

95-97 — Ex-FWC&L 5-7, scrapped 1902.

98 — Ex-FWC&L 8. Sold to Joseph, Joseph & Brother November 14, 1895.

99-100 — Ex-FWC&L 9-10; retired 1899, 1903.

101 — Ex-FWC&L 11; renumbered 4220 June 19, 1905. Rebuilt January 1909 at South Lima with boiler from engine 5332. Dismantled December 1910.

102 — Ex-FWC&L 12, renumbered 4221 July 1905. Rebuilt at South Lima with boiler and firebox from E-40 class engine April 5, 1909. Withdrawn for scrapping December 31, 1913.

103 — Renumbered 5338 April 21, 1905; dismantled at Lima November 11, 1922.

104 — Renumbered 5339 September 1, 1905; dismantled at Lima June 30, 1922.

105 — Renumbered 5340 March 31, 1905; dismantled October 26, 1922.

106 — Renumbered 5341 November 21, 1905; dismantled December 31, 1914.

107 — Renumbered 5342 September 6, 1905; dismantled at Lima October 18, 1919.

108 — Renumbered 5343 March 11, 1905; dismantled October 26, 1922.

109 — Renumbered 5344 February 17, 1906; dismantled June 30, 1922.

110 — Renumbered 5345 April 5, 1905; dismantled at Tipton November 27, 1919.

111 — Renumbered 5346 November 28, 1905; dismantled October 20, 1920.

112 — Renumbered 5347 July 22, 1905; dismantled at Lima June 30, 1922.

113 — Renumbered 5348 June 17, 1905; dismantled June 30, 1922.

114 — Renumbered 5349 September 18, 1905; retired August 31, 1923.

115 — Renumbered 5350 October 14, 1905; laid up for scrapping June 30, 1922.

116 — Renumbered 5351 February 20, 1905; dismantled August 14, 1920.

117 — Renumbered 5352 August 10, 1905; laid up for scrapping June 30, 1922.

118 — Renumbered 5353 May 25, 1905; laid up for scrapping June 30, 1922.

119 — Renumbered 5354 April 19, 1905; retired April 30, 1916.

120 — Renumbered 5355 August 19, 1905; scrapped 1922.

121 — Renumbered 5356 September 25, 1905; laid up for scrapping June 30, 1922.

122 — Renumbered 5357 July 25, 1905; laid up for scrapping
    April 30, 1916.
123 — Renumbered 5358 February 13, 1905; laid up at South

Lima June 30, 1922, and subsequently dismantled there.
124 — Renumbered 5359 June 6, 1905; dismantled at Lima
    March 19, 1914.

CLEVELAND, DELPHOS & ST. LOUIS RAILROAD
EASTERN & WESTERN AIR LINE RAILWAY
CLEVELAND & WESTERN RAILROAD
Narrow Gauge

Number	Type	Builder	Builder number	Date	Cylinders	Drivers	Total weight
1	4-4-0	Pittsburgh	454	11-1880	12" x 18"	42½"	40,000
2	4-4-0	Pittsburgh	579	5-1882	12" x 18"	42½"	40,000

Note: There was a third engine, details of which are lacking. Pittsburgh 579 may have been No. 3 rather than No. 2. C&W 3 was stored at Delphos until about 1893 when it was taken to Van Wert and rebuilt by a boiler works there. Later, this engine was shipped to Mississippi.

Pittsburgh, Akron & Western Moguls 26-29 were duplicates of those built by Brooks for the Lake Erie & Western. These 1895 machines were renumbered 5360-5363 in 1905. After 1920 they served briefly on the Akron, Canton & Youngstown. — *Schenectady History Center.*

PITTSBURGH, AKRON & WESTERN RAILROAD 1890-1895
NORTHERN OHIO RAILWAY 1895-1901

Number	Type	Builder	Builder number	Date	Cylinders	Drivers	Total weight
21	4-4-0	Pittsburgh	921	3-1890	17" x 24"	62"	71,400
22	4-4-0	Pittsburgh	1060	6-1889	17" x 24"	62"	71,400
23	4-4-0	Pittsburgh	1031	7-1890	17" x 24"	62"	71,400
24	4-4-0	Pittsburgh	1191	12-1890	17" x 24"	62"	71,400
25	4-4-0	Pittsburgh	1059	4-1889	17" x 24"	62"	71,400
26-29	2-6-0	Brooks	2554-2557	8-1895	18" x 24"	56"	108,000
30-35	2-6-0	Brooks	2657-2662	4-1896	18" x 24"	56"	108,000

Note: In addition to above, the PA&W acquired two Brooks engines in June 1891 and two Pittsburgh engines in January 1892. Details of these are lacking.

21 — Received April 23, 1890. To LE&W 2nd 26, 1901.
22 — Received June 1890. To LE&W 2nd 27, 1901.
23 — Received July 10, 1890. To LE&W 3rd 23, 1901.
24 — Received December 1890. To LE&W 2nd 24, 1901.

25 — Received in the spring of 1891. To LE&W 2nd 25, 1901.
26-29 — Originally lettered Pittsburgh, Akron & Western. To LE&W 126-129, 1901.
30-35 — Originally lettered Northern Ohio. To LE&W 130-135, 1901.

Brooks built B-3 Consolidations for LE&W and Lake Erie, Alliance & Wheeling in 1904. Lake Erie's own 400-409 were renumbered 5515-5524 in 1905, reclassed G-44; the 15 LEA&W engines became 5525-5539 in 1906. — *Schenectady History Center.*

LE&W LOCOMOTIVES ACQUIRED 1900-1922

Number	Class	Class	Type	Builder	Builder number	Date
3rd 23	Q-8	C-46	4-4-0	Pittsburgh	1031	7-1890
2nd 24	Q-8	C-46	4-4-0	Pittsburgh	1191	12-1890
2nd 25	Q-8	C-46	4-4-0	Pittsburgh	1059	4-1889
2nd 26	Q-8	C-46	4-4-0	Pittsburgh	921	3-1890
2nd 27	Q-8	C-46	4-4-0	Pittsburgh	1060	6-1889
2nd 28	Q-4c	C-57c	4-4-0	Grant		1881
2nd 29	Q-4b		4-4-0	Schenectady	1483	12-1881
2nd 30	Q-4b	C-57b	4-4-0	Schenectady	1477	12-1881
2nd 39, 47	Q-4a	C-57a	4-4-0	LS&MS		1877-1878
2nd 50, 53	Q-4b	C-57b	4-4-0	Schenectady	1459, 1367	1881
2nd 75-76	R-7	C-49a	4-4-0	Baldwin	20409-20410	7-1902
2nd 77-78	R-7	C-49a	4-4-0	Baldwin	20503-20504	7-1902
2nd 79-80	R-8	C-49b/a	4-4-0	Baldwin	20684-20685	7-1902
2nd 87-88 2nd 91-92 3rd 87, 91	Q-4c	C-57c	4-4-0	Grant		1881
2nd 97	E-1	F-47	4-6-0	Brooks	2223	1-1893
2nd 98-99	Q-4c		4-4-0	Grant		1881
126-129	N-8	E-42	2-6-0	Brooks	2554-2557	8-1895
130-135	N-8	E-42	2-6-0	Brooks	2657-2662	4-1896
136	E-2c	F-48b	4-6-0	Schenectady	4255	1895
151, 178	U-1	B-43	0-6-0	Schenectady	2810, 2814	9-1889
191, 196	U-1	B-43	0-6-0	Schenectady	2813, 2812	9-1889
192	E-1	F-47	4-6-0	Brooks	2225	1-1893
238	E-1	F-47	4-6-0	Brooks	2219	12-1892
239	E-1	F-47	4-6-0	Brooks	2226	2-1893
241	U-1	B-43	0-6-0	Schenectady	2811	9-1889
290	E-2b	F-48c	4-6-0	Brooks	2585	10-1895
300-302	A	G-41	2-8-0	Brooks	3127, 3124, 3128	1-1899
303-305	A	G-41	2-8-0	Brooks	3125, 3129, 3130	1-1899
306, 309	A	G-41	2-8-0	Brooks	3126, 3131	1-1899
307-308	A	G-41	2-8-0	Brooks	3135, 3136	2-1899
310-311	A	G-41	2-8-0	Brooks	3132, 3133	2-1899
312-314	A	G-41	2-8-0	Brooks	3137, 3134, 3138	2-1899
321	E-2a	F-48a	4-6-0	Pittsburgh	1577	11-1895
323-324	E-2b	F-48c	4-6-0	Brooks	2588, 2589	10-1895
331	E-2a	F-48a	4-6-0	Pittsburgh	1582	12-1895
332, 334	E-2b	F-48c	4-6-0	Brooks	2592-2594	10-1895
400-409	B-3	G-44	2-8-0	Brooks	29677-29686	6-1904
4150-4154		C-75	4-4-0	Schenectady	4174-4178	1893
4155-4159		C-75a	4-4-0	Schenectady	4297-4301	1895
4160-4162		C-76	4-4-0	Schenectady	3952, 3953, 3961	1892
4163-4165		C-76	4-4-0	Schenectady	3955-3957	1892
4166-4167		C-76	4-4-0	Schenectady	3959-3960	1892
4168-4169		C-76a	4-4-0	Schenectady	3958, 3954	1892
4250-4252		U-3a	0-8-0	Lima	5903-5905	1-1920
4275-4276		B-11k	0-6-0	Schenectady	54064, 54066	12-1913
4277		B-11k	0-6-0	Schenectady	54082	12-1913
4365-4366	W-3	B-54	0-6-0	Pittsburgh	2396-2397	5-1902
4367-4374	W-3	B-54	0-6-0	Pittsburgh	2398-2405	6-1902
4377, 4384	U	B-55a	0-6-0	Brooks	25526, 25533	4-1902
4390, 4392, 4393	U	B-55a	0-6-0	Brooks	25539, 25541, 25542	4-1902
5002, 5010	I	F-51	4-6-0	Brooks	3333, 3341	10-1899
5385-5394		G-16v	2-8-0	Brooks	49501-49510	4-1911
5395-5399		G-16w	2-8-0	Schenectady	51204-51208	6-1912
5525-5539		G-44	2-8-0	Brooks	29662-29676	6-1904
5540-5542		H-6a	2-8-2	Baldwin	49682-49684	9-1918
5543-5554		H-6a	2-8-2	Baldwin	49718-49729	9-1918
5605-5614		G-6v	2-8-0	Brooks	49516-49525	4-1911

DIMENSIONS OF LOCOMOTIVES

Number	Cylinders	Valve motion*	Drivers	Weight on drivers	Total weight	Boiler pressure	Tractive effort	Grate area
2nd 24-27	17" x 24"	s	62"	46,400	71,400	135	12,800	15.9

Number	Cylinders	Valve motion*		Drivers	Weight on drivers	Total weight	Boiler pressure	Tractive effort	Grate area
2nd 28-53 2nd 91-99 3rd 87, 91	18″ x 24″	s		62″	48,000	75,000	135	11,300	15.1
2nd 75-78	18″ x 24″	s	R	68″	65,000	106,000	180	17,550	17.6 (A)
2nd 79-80	18″ x 24″	s	R	62″	65,000	106,000	180	19,170	17.6 (A)
2nd 97, 192 238, 239	17″ x 24″	s		63″	85,000	110,000	180	17,400	22
126-135	18″ x 24″	s		57″	94,000	108,000	160	18,880	15.7
151, 178, 191 196, 241	17″ x 24″	s		57″	113,000	113,000	160	16,800	23 (C)
290, 321-324 331, 332, 334	17″ x 24″	s		56″	83,000	108,000	160	17,200	22
300-314	20½″ x 28″	s		56″	138,500	156,500	180	32,700	32.4
	20½″ x 28″	p	B	57″	145,600	165,700	180	31,700	32.4 (D)
400-409	21″ x 30″	p	S	57″	181,100	202,900	200	40,900	46.7
	21″ x 30″	p	B	57″	185,000	205,100	180	35,550	46.7 (E)
4365-4374	19″ x 26″	p	S	52″	124,000	124,000	170	26,100	23
4150-4154	18½″ x 24″	s	R	69″	79,700	119,600	190	18,800	28
	19″ x 24″	p	R	69″	81,300	122,000	170	18,190	28 (F)
4155-4159	18″ x 24″	s	R	69″	79,700	119,600	190	18,335	28
	19″ x 24″	p	R	69″	81,300	122,000	170	18,190	28 (F)
4160-4169	19″ x 24″	s	R	69″	92,450	133,000	175	19,200	31.3
	19″ x 24″	p	R	69″	94,000	134,600	165	17,655	31.3 (G)
4250-4252	25″ x 28″	p	B	51″	214,000	214,000	175	51,200	47
4275-4277	21″ x 28″	p	W	57″	170,000	170,000	180	33,200	32.6
5002, 5010	20″ x 28″	s	S	81″	133,000	171,600	200	24,100	33.6
5385-5394	25″ x 32″	p	W	63″	214,400	240,500	180	48,600	56.5
5395-5399	25″ x 32″	p	W	63″	220,000	246,000	180	48,600	56.5
5540-5554	26″ x 30″	p	W	63″	220,000	292,000	200	54,700	66.7
5605-5614	23″ x 32″	p	W	63″	211,500	236,500	200	45,700	56.5

* s — slide valve; p — piston valve; B — Baker; S — Stephenson; R — Allen-Richardson balanced slide valves; W — Walschaerts.

(A) In later years had 69-inch drivers and 17,200 lbs. tractive effort.

(C) Rebuilt from 2-6-0's by LS&MS. About 1905 drivers increased to 58 inches and boiler pressure raised to 165 lbs.

(D) With superheater.

(E) With 30-element Type A superheater.

(F) Engines 4150, 4151, 4153, 4155, 4156, 4158 with superheater, new cylinders applied.

(G) Engines 4163-4165 and 4168 with superheater and new cylinders.

Rebuilt at South Lima in 1919, C-76 4164 had a lengthened tender and electric headlight mounted on smokebox door. Upgrading included application of 19 x 24-inch piston-valve cylinders and superheater. — *Collection of Roy W. Carlson.*

Big Four 100 was bought from Schenectady in 1892 for express passenger service. Features included cap stack, Belpaire firebox and clerestory on cab roof. The engine's 69-inch drivers were stroked by 19 x 24-inch cylinders. In 1906 this C-76 became LE&W 4160. — *Collection of John H. Keller.*

F-48C 5215, built by Brooks for the LS&MS in 1895, toiled on the Lake Erie from 1902 to 1916, when she was retired. The Ten-Wheeler normally was used in freight service but was assigned to a passenger run when this photo was made at Muncie.— *Collection of John H. Keller.*

3rd 23 — Ex-Northern Ohio 23; relettered August 1901. To 4215 May 16, 1905. Dismantled at South Lima October 17, 1910.

2nd 24 — Ex-NO 24; relettered August 1901. To 4216 July 10, 1905. Dismantled at South Lima December 31, 1910.

2nd 25 — Ex-NO 25; relettered August 1901. To 4217 March 23, 1905. Dismantled at South Lima October 28, 1910.

2nd 26 — Ex-NO 21; renumbered August 1901. To 4218 1905. Dismantled at South Lima March 22, 1909.

2nd 27 — Ex-NO 22; renumbered August 14, 1901. To 4219 June 5, 1905. Dismantled November 22, 1910.

2nd 28 — Ex-LS&MS 25, acquired 1901; renumbered 4234, 1905; sold July 1907.

2nd 29 — Ex-LS&MS 198, acquired 1901; scrapped April 1905.

2nd 30, 39 — Ex-LS&MS 234, 264 acquired 1902; renumbered 4231, 4228 in 1905; retired 1907.

2nd 47 — Ex-LS&MS acquired 1901; renumbered 4229, 1905; retired 1907.

2nd 50, 53 — Ex-LS&MS 184, 502 acquired 1902; renumbered 4232-4233, 1905; retired 1907.

2nd 75 — Ex-Lake Erie, Alliance & Wheeling 5 acquired 1902. Renumbered 4244 March 27, 1905; dismantled at South Lima June 30, 1922.

2nd 76 — Ex-LEA&W 6 acquired 1902. Renumbered 4245 February 20, 1905; withdrawn for scrapping August 31, 1923.

2nd 77 — Ex-LEA&W 7 acquired 1902. Renumbered 4246 April 8, 1905; to NKP 2nd 300 April 1924.

2nd 78 — Ex-LEA&W 8 acquired 1902. Renumbered 4247 March 13, 1905; withdrawn for scrapping August 31, 1923.

2nd 79 — Ex-LEA&W 9 acquired 1902. Renumbered 4248 April 29, 1905; to NKP 2nd 301, 1924.

2nd 80 — Ex-LEA&W 10 acquired 1902. Renumbered 4249 May

20, 1905; dismantled at South Lima on June 30, 1922.

2nd 87 — Ex-LS&MS 38 acquired 1901. Scrapped 1902.

3rd 87 — Ex-LS&MS 522, bought 1902. Renumbered 4235, 1905.

2nd 88 — Ex-LS&MS 41 acquired 1901, retired 1905.

2nd 91-92 — Ex-LS&MS 44, 130. 92 renumbered 4238, 1905.

3rd 91 — Ex-LS&MS 532, bought 1902. Renumbered 4237, 1905.

2nd 97 — Ex-LS&MS 97 acquired 1902. Renumbered 5200, 1905; dismantled at South Lima June 8, 1920.

2nd 98-99 — Ex-LS&MS 523, 530 acquired 1901; retired 1904.

126 — Ex-NO 26; renumbered 5360, 1905. To Akron, Canton & Youngstown 5360, 1920; scrapped September 1921.

127 — Ex-NO 27; renumbered 5361, 1905. To AC&Y 5361, 1920; scrapped 1922.

128 — Ex-NO 28; renumbered 5362, 1905. To AC&Y 5362, 1920; scrapped September 1922.

129 — Ex-NO 29; renumbered 5363, 1905. To AC&Y 5363, 1920. Sold to Rubber City Sand & Gravel Company, September 1922; sold for junk March 1947.

130 — Ex-NO 30; renumbered 5364, 1905. To AC&Y 5364, 1920; scrapped September 1922.

131 — Ex-NO 31; renumbered 5365, 1905. To AC&Y 5365, 1920; scrapped September 1921.

132 — Ex-NO 32; renumbered 5366, 1905. To AC&Y 5366, 1920; scrapped September 1922.

133 — Ex-NO 33; renumbered 5367, 1905. To AC&Y 5367, 1920. Sold to Cambridge (O.) Block Coal Company January 1923.

134 — Ex-NO 34; renumbered 5368, 1905. To AC&Y 5368, 1920; scrapped September 1921.

135 — Ex-NO 35; renumbered 5369, 1905. To AC&Y 5369, 1920; scrapped March 1922.

136 — Ex-LS&MS 136 acquired 1902. Renumbered 5212, 1905;

withdrawn for scrapping at South Lima November 30, 1916.

151 — Ex-LS&MS 151 acquired 1903. Renumbered 4270 May 26, 1905; dismantled at South Lima June 30, 1922.

178 — Ex-LS&MS 178 acquired 1903. Renumbered 4271 November 29, 1905; dismantled at Peru July 31, 1920.

191 — Ex-LS&MS 191 acquired 1903. Renumbered 4272 September 1905; withdrawn for scrapping May 31, 1916.

192 — Ex-LS&MS 192 acquired 1902. Renumbered 5201, 1905. Demolished by boiler explosion while pulling passenger train 3 miles west of South Bend, Ind., August 4, 1916.

196 — Ex-LS&MS 196 acquired 1903. Renumbered 4273 January 12, 1906. Withdrawn for scrapping December 30, 1916.

238 — Ex-LS&MS 56 acquired 1902. Renumbered 5202, 1905; dismantled November 30, 1916.

239 — Ex-LS&MS 239 acquired 1902. Renumbered 5203, 1905; dismantled at South Lima August 14, 1920.

241 — Ex-LS&MS 241 acquired 1903. Renumbered 4274 February 11, 1905; withdrawn for scrapping at South Lima December 1917.

290 — Ex-LS&MS 290 acquired 1902. Renumbered 5213, 1905; withdrawn for scrapping April 30, 1916.

300 — Ex-LS&MS 300 acquired 1903. Renumbered 5500 June 30, 1905. Dismantled at South Lima September 1, 1921.

301 — Ex-LS&MS 301 (originally numbered 296) acquired 1903. Renumbered 5501 September 5, 1905. Rebuilt at South Lima October 1919; to NKP 2nd 400 April 1924.

302 — Ex-LS&MS 302 acquired 1903. Renumbered 5502 April 12, 1905. Rebuilt October 1920; to NKP 2nd 401 April 1924.

303 — Ex-LS&MS 303 (originally 297) acquired 1903. Renumbered 5503 November 1905. Rebuilt at Beech Grove September 1918; to NKP 2nd 402.

304 — Ex-LS&MS 304 acquired 1903. Renumbered 5504 July 14, 1905; dismantled June 30, 1922.

305 — Ex-LS&MS 305 acquired 1903. Renumbered 5505 April 20, 1905. Rebuilt at Beech Grove January 1919; to NKP 2nd 403 April 1924.

306 — Ex-LS&MS 306 (originally 299) acquired 1903. Renumbered 5506 August 5, 1905. Rebuilt at Beech Grove November 1920; to NKP 2nd 404.

307 — Ex-LS&MS 307 (originally 316) acquired 1903. Renumbered 5507 September 16, 1905; dismantled June 30, 1922.

308 — Ex-LS&MS 308 (originally 318) acquired 1903. Renumbered 5508 April 12, 1905; dismantled September 1, 1921, with boiler subsequently placed in stationary service at Tipton roundhouse.

309 — Ex-LS&MS 309 acquired 1903. Renumbered 5509 September 13, 1905. Rebuilt at Beech Grove September 1918; to NKP 2nd 405 April 1924.

310 — Ex-LS&MS 310 acquired 1903. Renumbered 5510 September 25, 1905. Rebuilt at Elkhart October 1918. To NKP 2nd 406 April 1924.

311 — Ex-LS&MS 311 acquired 1903. Renumbered 5511, 1905. Rebuilt at Beech Grove November 1918; to NKP 2nd 407, 1924.

312 — Ex-LS&MS 312 (originally 321) acquired 1903. Renumbered 5512 February 8, 1906; dismantled June 30, 1922.

313 — Ex-LS&MS 313 acquired 1903. Renumbered 5513, 1905; rebuilt at Beech Grove May 1918; to NKP 2nd 408 April 1924.

314 — Ex-LS&MS 314 (originally 322) acquired 1903. Renumbered 5514 March 8, 1905. Rebuilt at Beech Grove May 1919; to NKP 2nd 409 April 1924.

321 — Ex-LS&MS 321 (originally 91) acquired 1902. Renumbered 5210, 1905; withdrawn for scrapping November 30, 1916.

323 — Ex-LS&MS 323 acquired 1902. Renumbered 5214, 1905; withdrawn for scrapping November 30, 1916.

324, 332, 334 — Ex-LS&MS 324, 332, 334 acquired 1902. Renumbered 5215-5217, 1905; withdrawn for scrapping December 30, 1916.

331 — Ex-LS&MS 331 (originally 124) acquired 1902. Renumbered 5211, 1905; withdrawn for scrapping November 30, 1916.

400 — Renumbered 5515 March 6, 1906. Superheater applied at Beech Grove July 1912; Baker valve gear applied April 1923. To NKP 375, 1924.

401 — Renumbered 5516 November 27, 1905. Superheater applied at South Lima May 1913. To NKP 376 April 1924.

402 — Renumbered 5517 August 9, 1905. Superheater applied at South Lima December 1913. To NKP 377, April 1924.

403 — Renumbered 5518 August 19, 1905. Superheater applied at South Lima June 1913; rebuilt at South Lima July 1923. To NKP 378, 1924.

404 — Renumbered 5519 September 28, 1905. Superheater applied at South Lima July 1912. Dismantled at Collinwood August 1921; believed to have been wrecked previously in head-on collision at Denver, Ind.

405 — Renumbered 5520 October 11, 1905. Superheater applied at South Lima October 1912; Baker valve gear applied May 1923. To NKP 379, 1924.

406 — Renumbered 5521 March 16, 1905. Superheater applied at South Lima August 1913. To NKP 380 April 1924.

407 — Renumbered 5522 March 16, 1905. Superheater applied at South Lima November 1911; Baker valve gear applied July 1923. To NKP 381, 1924.

408 — Renumbered 5523 March 11, 1905. Superheater applied at South Lima February 1913; rebuilt at South Lima December 1923. To NKP 382, 1924.

409 — Renumbered 5524 April 22, 1905. Superheater applied at South Lima July 1913; rebuilt at South Lima March 1923. To NKP 383 April 1924.

4150 — Ex-Big Four 7119 (originally 195) acquired 1906. Rebuilt at South Lima June 1920. To NKP 2nd 302, 1924.

4151 — Ex-Big Four 7120 (originally 196) acquired 1906. Rebuilt at Collinwood October 1918. To NKP 2nd 303, 1924.

4152 — Ex-Big Four 7121 (originally 197) acquired 1906, dismantled June 1922.

4153 — Ex-Big Four 7122 (originally 198) acquired 1907. Rebuilt at Collinwood September 1918; withdrawn for scrapping August 31, 1923.

4154 — Ex-Big Four 7123 (originally 199) acquired April 26, 1907. Withdrawn at South Lima for scrapping June 30, 1922.

4155 — Ex-Big Four 7125 (originally 189) acquired 1907. Rebuilt at South Lima February 1920. To NKP 2nd 304, 1924.

4156 — Ex-Big Four 7126 (originally 190) acquired April 23, 1907. Rebuilt at Collinwood May 1918. To NKP 305, 1924.

4157 — Ex-Big Four 7127 (originally 191) acquired 1907; dismantled at South Lima December 2, 1922.

4158 — Ex-Big Four 7128 (originally 192) acquired 1907. Rebuilt at Collinwood March 1918; withdrawn for scrapping August 31, 1923.

4159 — Ex-Big Four 7129 (originally 193) acquired 1907; retired June 30, 1922.

4160 — Ex-Big Four 7130 (originally 100) acquired 1907; retired June 30, 1922.

4161 — Ex-Big Four 7131 (originally 105) acquired 1907; withdrawn for scrapping at South Lima June 30, 1922.

4162 — Ex-Big Four 7132 (originally 205 and then 113) acquired 1907; withdrawn for scrapping at South Lima June 30, 1922.

4163 — Ex-Big Four 7133 (originally 148) acquired June 29, 1907. Rebuilt at South Lima April 1919. To NKP 2nd 306 April 1924.

4164 — Ex-Big Four 7134 (originally 149) acquired 1906. Rebuilt at South Lima March 1919. To NKP 2nd 307, 1924.

4165 — Ex-Big Four 7135 (originally 160) acquired 1906. Rebuilt at South Lima September 1919. To NKP 2nd 308, 1924.

4166 — Ex-Big Four 7136 (originally 195, then 169) acquired 1907. Withdrawn for scrapping June 30, 1922.

4167 — Ex-Big Four 7137 (originally 201, then 222) acquired 1906. Withdrawn for scrapping June 30, 1922.

4168 — Ex-Big Four 7138 (originally 193, then 159) acquired July 8, 1907. Rebuilt at Beech Grove April 1919. To NKP 2nd 309, 1924.

4169 — Ex-Big Four 7139 (originally 134, then 168) acquired 1907. Dismantled 1922.

4250-4252 — To NKP 3rd 205-207, 1924.

4275 — Ex-New York Central 610 acquired 1917. Renumbered October 31, 1918. To NKP 3rd 80 April 1924.

4276 — Ex-NYC 612 acquired 1917. Renumbered May 22, 1919. To NKP 2nd 81.

4277 — Ex-NYC 628 acquired 1917. Renumbered October 10, 1918. To NKP 2nd 82, 1924.

4365 — Ex-LS&MS 4365 (originally 365) acquired September 1906. To NKP 4th 32.

4366 — Ex-LS&MS 4366 (originally 366) acquired April 1907. To NKP 4th 33.

4367 — Ex-LS&MS 4367 (originally 367) acquired January 1907. Superheater applied at South Lima August 1923. To NKP 4th 34, 1924.

4368 — Ex-LS&MS 4368 (originally 368) acquired March 1907. To NKP 4th 35.

4369 — Ex-LS&MS 4369 (originally 369) acquired January 1907. To NKP 4th 36.

4370 — Ex-LS&MS 4370 (originally 370) acquired September 1906. To NKP 4th 37.

4371 — Ex-LS&MS 4371 (originally 371) acquired September 1906. To NKP 4th 38.

4372 — Ex-LS&MS 4372 (originally 372) acquired December 1906. To NKP 4th 39.

4373-4374 — Ex-LS&MS 4373-4374 (originally 373-374) acquired September 1906. To NKP 4th 40-41, 1924.

4377,4384 — Ex-LS&MS 4377, 4384 (originally 377, 384). Relettered LE&W January 1914. To NKP 4th 42-43, 1924.

4390 — Ex-LS&MS 4390 (originally 390). Relettered LE&W January 1914. Acquired by LE&W and placed in service at Tipton December 10, 1912. To NKP 4th 44 April 1924.

4392 — Ex-LS&MS 4392 (originally 392). Relettered LE&W January 1914. To NKP 4th 45, 1924.

4393 — Ex-LS&MS 4393 (originally 393) acquired December 10, 1912. Lettered LE&W January 17, 1914. Superheater applied November 1923. To NKP 4th 46.

5002 — Ex-LS&MS 5002 (originally 602). Lettered LE&W January 17, 1914. Dismantled at Elkhart July 19, 1918.

5010 — Ex-LS&MS 5010 (originally 610). Lettered LE&W January 17, 1914. Dismantled at South Lima November 1919.

5385-5394 — Ex-NYC&HR 5300-5309. Renumbered and lettered LE&W July 1915. To NKP 485-494, 1924.

5395-5399 — To NKP 495-499, 1924.

5525 — Ex-Lake Erie, Alliance & Wheeling 5550 (originally 50), renumbered February 25, 1907. Superheater applied April 1913. To NKP 384, 1924.

5526 — Ex-LEA&W 5551 (originally 51), renumbered August 4, 1906. Superheater applied at Collinwood December 1912. To NKP 385, 1924.

5527 — Ex-LEA&W 5552 (originally 52), renumbered January 28, 1907. Superheater applied at South Lima July 1913. Rebuilt at South Lima March 1924. To NKP 386, 1924.

5528 — Ex-LEA&W 5553 (originally 53), renumbered August 22, 1906. Superheater applied at Beech Grove October 1912. Rebuilt at South Lima April 1923. To NKP 387, April 1924.

5529 — Ex-LEA&W 5554 (originally 54), renumbered February 25, 1907. Superheater applied at South Lima December 1912. To NKP 388, 1924.

5530 — Ex-LEA&W 5555 (originally 55), renumbered January 30, 1907. Superheater applied at Beech Grove July 1912. Rebuilt at South Lima January 1923. To NKP 389, 1924.

5531 — Ex-LEA&W 5556 (originally 56), renumbered August 17, 1906. Superheater applied at Elkhart February 1913. Rebuilt at South Lima March 1923. To NKP 390, April 1924.

5532 — Ex-LEA&W 5557 (originally 57), renumbered August 16, 1906. Superheater applied at South Lima September 1913. Rebuilt at South Lima November 1923. To NKP 391, 1924.

5533 — Ex-LEA&W 5558 (originally 58), renumbered December 14, 1906. Superheater applied at Beech Grove February 1913. To NKP 392, 1924.

5534 — Ex-LEA&W 5559 (originally 59), renumbered August 20, 1906. Superheater applied at Beech Grove October 1912. To NKP 393, 1924.

5535 — Ex-LEA&W 5560 (originally 60), renumbered July 28, 1906. Superheater applied at South Lima May 1912. To NKP 394, 1924.

5536 — Ex-LEA&W 5561 (originally 61), renumbered January 10, 1907. Superheater applied at South Lima January 1912. Rebuilt at South Lima March 1923. To NKP 395, 1924.

5537 — Ex-LEA&W 5562 (originally 62), renumbered January 30, 1907. Superheater applied at South Lima November 1912. To NKP 396, 1924.

5538 — Ex-LEA&W 5563 (originally 63), renumbered September 10, 1906. Superheater applied at Beech Grove February 1913. To NKP 397, 1924.

5539 — Ex-LEA&W 5565 (originally 64), renumbered June 3, 1907. Superheater applied at Elkhart December 1911. Rebuilt at South Lima January 1923. To NKP 398, 1924.

5540-5547 — Received September-October 1918 with tenders lettered U. S. To NKP 586-593, 1924.

5548-5552 — Received January 1919, tenders lettered U. S. To NKP 594-598, 1924.

5553-5554 — Received October 18, 1918, lettered U. S. To NKP 599-600, 1924.

5605-5609 — Ex-NYC&HR 5605-5609 acquired 1917. To NKP 475-479, 1924.

5610 — Ex-NYC 5610 acquired 1917. Nicholson syphons applied July 1923. To NKP 480, 1924.

5611-5614 — Ex-NYC 5611-5614 acquired 1917. To NKP 481-484, 1924.

Locomotives of the Clover Leaf

LE&W's first new locomotives after 1904 were the five G-16w "two-door sedans" of 1912. Schenectady-built 5395-5399 were superheated, had Walschaerts valve gear and 25 x 32-inch piston-valve cylinders. In working order these 2-8-0's weighed 123 tons and developed 48,600 pounds tractive effort.

PREDECESSORS OF THE TOLEDO, CINCINNATI & ST. LOUIS
Narrow Gauge
TOLEDO & MAUMEE NARROW GAUGE RAILROAD 1874-1879

Number	Name	Type	Builder	Builder number	Date	Cylinders	Total weight
1	Gen. Hunt	0-4-0	Porter, Bell	184	6-1874	8″ x 16″	16,500
2		0-4-0	Porter, Bell	203	10-1874	8″ x 16″	16,500

Note: To Toledo, Delphos & Burlington 1-2 August 1879.

DELPHOS & KOKOMO RAILWAY 1878-1879

Number	Name	Type	Builder	Builder number	Date	Cylinders	Drivers
1	Hugh McKee	0-4-0	Baldwin	4297	3-1878	9″ x 16″	36″

Note: Received at Delphos November 3, 1878. To TD&B 4 August 1879.

TOLEDO, DELPHOS & INDIANAPOLIS RAILWAY 1877-1879

Number	Name	Type	Builder	Builder number	Date	Cylinders	Drivers	Total weight
1	Dupont	0-4-2T*	Porter, Bell	273	5-1877	9″ x 16″		24,000
2	J. W. Hunt	0-4-2T*	Porter, Bell	304	6-1878	9″ x 16″		36,000
3	Delphos	4-4-0	Pittsburgh	388	11-1878	9″ x 16″	43″	30,000

* Wheel arrangements uncertain.

1 — To TD&B 6 August 1879.
2 — Ordered by J. W. Hunt and owned by Clark, Post & Martin. To TD&B 7 August 1879.
3 — Received at Delphos November 3, 1878. To TD&B 8 August 1879.

DELPHOS, BLUFFTON & FRANKFORT RAILROAD 1878-1879

Number	Name	Type	Builder	Builder number	Date	Cylinders	Drivers	Total weight
1	Bluffton	4-4-0	Pittsburgh	351	8-1878	9″ x 16″	42½″	28,000

Note: Owned by Clark, Post & Martin. To TD&B 9 August 1879.

DAYTON, COVINGTON & TOLEDO RAILROAD 1878-1880

Number	Name	Type	Builder	Builder number	Date	Cylinders	Drivers	Total weight
1	Stillwater	4-4-0	Baldwin	4380	7-1878	12″ x 16″	43″	40,000
2		0-6-0	Porter, Bell	349	12-1879	12″ x 16″		36,000

Note: Owned by Clark, Post & Martin. To TD&B 10-11 June 1880.

DAYTON & SOUTHEASTERN RAILROAD 1876-1881

Number	Name	Type	Builder	Builder number	Date	Cylinders	Drivers	Total weight
1	Washington	4-4-0	Baldwin	3978	8-1876	11″ x 16″	42″	36,000
2	Xenia	4-4-0	Baldwin	3990	9-1876	11″ x 16″	42″	36,000
3	Jamestown	4-4-0	Baldwin	4115	7-1877	11″ x 16″	42″	36,000
4	Frankfort	2-4-0	National		1877			24,000
5		2-6-0	Brooks	358	7-1879	12″ x 18″	36″	36,000
6		2-6-0	Brooks	335	9-1878	12″ x 18″	36″	36,000
7		2-6-0	Brooks	330	11-1878	11″ x 16″	36″	36,000
8		2-8-0	Baldwin	5358	11-1880	15″ x 18″	37″	56,000
9		2-8-0	Baldwin	5434	1-1881	15″ x 18″	37″	56,000

1-5 — To Toledo, Delphos & Burlington 28-32 July 1881.
6-7 — Ex-Springfield, Jackson & Pomeroy 8 and 10 acquired September 1879. Owned by J. E. Gimperling. To TD&B 34-35 1881.
8 — Owned by J. E. Gimperling. To TD&B 36 July 1881.
9 — To TD&B 33 July 1881.

TOLEDO, DELPHOS & BURLINGTON RAILROAD 1879-1882

Number	Name	Type	Builder	Builder number	Date
1		0-4-0	Porter, Bell	184	6-1874
2		0-4-0	Porter, Bell	203	10-1874
3		4-4-0	Baldwin	4221	12-1877
4		0-4-0	Baldwin	4297	3-1878
5		4-4-0	Baldwin	4288	3-1878
6	Dupont	0-4-2T*	Porter, Bell	273	5-1877
7		0-4-2T*	Porter, Bell	304	6-1878
8	Delphos	4-4-0	Pittsburgh	388	11-1878

Number	Name	Type	Builder	Builder number	Date
9	Bluffton	4-4-0	Pittsburgh	351	8-1878
10	Stillwater	4-4-0	Baldwin	4380	7-1878
11		0-6-0	Porter, Bell	349	12-1879
12	Geo. W. Kneisley	0-6-6T	Mason	627	8-1880
13	L. Downing Jr.	0-6-6T	Mason	629	8-1880
14	Geo. Wm. Ballou	0-6-6T	Mason	630	9-1880
15	Calvin S. Brice	0-6-6T	Mason	631	9-1880
16	James Irvine	0-6-6T	Mason	635	10-1880
17	G. W. T. Riley	0-6-6T	Mason	636	10-1880
18	Toledo	0-6-4T	Hinkley	1362	2-1881
19-23		0-6-4T	Hinkley	1363-1367	1881
24		0-4-4T	H. K. Porter	428	5-1881
25		0-4-4T	H. K. Porter	429	6-1881
26-27		0-4-4T	H. K. Porter	440-441	7-1881
28	Washington	4-4-0	Baldwin	3978	8-1876
29	Xenia	4-4-0	Baldwin	3990	9-1876
30	Jamestown	4-4-0	Baldwin	4115	7-1877
31	Frankfort	2-4-0	National		1877
32		2-6-0	Brooks	358	7-1879
33		2-8-0	Baldwin	5434	1-1881
34		2-6-0	Brooks	335	9-1878
35		2-6-0	Brooks	330	11-1878
36		2-8-0	Baldwin	5358	11-1880
37-38		2-8-0	Baldwin	5764-5765	8-1881
39-40		4-4-0	Mount Savage		1-1882
41-42		0-6-4T	Hinkley	1483-1484	1-1882
43-44		0-6-4T	Hinkley	1485-1486	2-1882
45-46		0-6-4T	Hinkley	1487-1488	4-1882
47		4-4-0	Paul & Son		3-1882

*Wheel arrangements uncertain.

1 — Ex-Toledo & Maumee 1. Retired 1880 or 1881.
2 — Ex-Toledo & Maumee 2. Retired 1882.
3 — Ex-Springfield, Jackson & Pomeroy 3, Springfield, purchased by Clark, Post & Martin on August 18, 1879, for $2750 and leased to TD&B. To TC&StL 3, 1882.
4 — Ex-Delphos & Kokomo 1. To TC&StL 4, 1882.
5 — Ex-Springfield, Jackson & Pomeroy 5, Washington, purchased by Clark, Post & Martin on August 18, 1879, and leased to

TD&B. To Toledo, Cincinnati & St. Louis Railroad 5, 1882.
6-8 — Ex-Toledo, Delphos & Indianapolis 1-3. To TC&StL 6-8, 1882.
9 — Ex-Delphos, Bluffton & Frankfort 1. To TC&StL 9, 1882.
10-11 — Ex-Dayton, Covington & Toledo 1-2. To TC&StL 10-11, 1882.
12-27 — Owned by George Ballou and F. W. Holmes. To TC&StL 12-27, 1882.
28-36 — Ex-Dayton & Southeastern 1-5, 9, 6-8. To TC&StL 28-36, 1882.
37-47 — To TC&StL 37-47, 1882.

FRANKFORT & STATE LINE RAILROAD 1879-1881

Number	Type	Builder	Builder number	Date	Cylinders	Total weight
1	2-4-0	Porter, Bell	316	7-1879	10" x 16"	36,000

Note: To Toledo, Cincinnati & St. Louis 1, 1882.

MIAMI VALLEY RAILWAY 1876-1880
CINCINNATI NORTHERN RAILWAY 1880-1885

Number	Name	Type	Builder	Builder number	Date	Cylinders	Drivers
1	Warren County	4-4-0	Baldwin	4207	12-1877	12" x 18"	42"
2	Leila	4-4-0	Baldwin	4292	3-1878	12" x 18"	42"
3		2-4-0*	H. K. Porter	401	11-1880	10" x 16"	
4		*	Mason	645	3-1881	13" x 16"	36"
5		0-4-4T*	Mason			12" x 16"	42"
6		2-6-0	Brooks	610	11-1881	14" x 18"	41"
7		2-6-0	Brooks	659	2-1882	14" x 18"	41"
8-11		2-6-0	Rome	21-24	4-1883	16" x 20"	48"

*Wheel arrangements uncertain.

1 — To TC&StL 2, June 1883.
2 — To TC&StL 2nd 4, June 1883.
3 — To TC&StL 2nd 96, June 1883.
4 — Bogie, wheel arrangement unknown. Wrecked in head-on collision with Cincinnati & Eastern 2 at Idlewild Junction Feb-

ruary 15, 1883. Taken to Delphos but never repaired. Assigned No. 54 by TC&StL but never renumbered.
5 — A secondhand Bogie acquired in 1881, believed to have been Mason's 581 of April 1877. Originally the Admiral Almy of New York & Manhattan Beach. To TC&StL 55, June 1883.

6 — Built as Cincinnati & Eastern 6. To TC&StL 56, June 1883.
7 — To TC&StL 77, June 1883.

8-11 — Lettered C.N. Ry. — Avondale Branch. To TC&StL 48-50, 90 in 1883.

FRANKFORT & KOKOMO RAILROAD 1874-1881

Number	Name	Type	Builder	Builder number	Date	Cylinders
1	Coe Adams	4-4-0	Danforth & Cooke	838	3-1874	14" x 22"
2	E. Y. Comstock	4-4-0	Pittsburgh	337	8-1874	15" x 22"

Note: Used until 1881. Disposition unknown.

Former *Admiral Almy* of New York & Manhattan Beach is believed to have been one of the two Bogies purchased by the Cincinnati Northern from Mason in 1881. Walschaerts-geared 0-4-4T of 1877 was probably returned to the builder as part payment for some new engines for the Long Island narrow gauge. Bogies were used on CN suburban short hauls. — *Collection of Thomas Norrell.*

IRON RAILROAD 1852-1881; IRON RAILWAY 1884-1902

Number	Name	Type	Builder	Builder number	Date	Cylinders	Drivers	Total weight
	Essex	4-2-0	Seth Boyden		1837			
	Elk		A. Harkness & Son		1851			38,000
5	Mount Vernon	0-6-0	Baldwin	1138	5-1863	13½" x 18"	44"	35,000
6	Olive	0-6-0	Baldwin	1671	10-1867	15" x 18"	43"	50,000
7		0-4-0	Pittsburgh	71	4-1870	14" x 22"	48"	50,000
8	John Ellison	4-4-0	Pittsburgh	277	4-1873	15" x 22"	55"	60,000
9	Thomas W. Meany	4-4-0	Pittsburgh	403	12-1879	15" x 22"	55"	64,000
10	John Campbell	4-6-0	Baldwin	14206	1-1895	18" x 24"	50"	100,000
11	Charles R. Batt	2-6-0	Baldwin	16642	4-1899	17" x 24"	50"	92,000
12		2-6-0	Baldwin	19720	11-1901	19" x 26"	54"	121,000

Essex acquired in 1852 from Morris & Essex Railroad. Retired about 1870.

Elk had four drivers, was acquired circa 1857 from the Columbus & Xenia. Retired prior to 1880.

5-9 — On the Iron Railroad when it was absorbed by the TC&StL, but these locomotives were not renumbered or relettered. To Iron Railway July 1884.

9-12 — Became Detroit Southern (DT&I) 62, 64, 63, and 65.

TOLEDO, CINCINNATI & ST. LOUIS RAILROAD 1881-1886
Narrow Gauge

Number	Type	Builder	Builder number	Date	Cylinders	Drivers	Total weight
1	2-4-0	Porter, Bell	316	7-1879	10" x 16"		36,000
2	4-4-0	Baldwin	4207	12-1877	12" x 18"		40,000
3	4-4-0	Baldwin	4221	12-1877	11" x 16"	42"	36,000
4	0-4-0	Baldwin	4297	3-1878	9" x 16"	36"	
2nd 4	4-4-0	Baldwin	4292	3-1878	12" x 18"	42"	40,000
5	4-4-0	Baldwin	4288	3-1878	11" x 16"	42"	36,000
6	0-4-2T*	Porter, Bell	273	5-1877	9" x 16"		24,000
7	0-4-2T*	Porter, Bell	304	6-1878	9" x 16"		48,000
8	4-4-0	Pittsburgh	388	11-1878	9" x 16"	43"	30,000
9	4-4-0	Pittsburgh	351	8-1878	9" x 16"	42½"	28,000
10	4-4-0	Baldwin	4380	7-1878	12" x 16"	43"	40,000
11	0-6-0	Porter, Bell	349	12-1879	12" x 16"		36,000
12-13	0-6-6T	Mason	627, 629	8-1880	13" x 16"	36"	72,000
14-15	0-6-6T	Mason	630-631	9-1880	13" x 16"	36"	72,000
16-17	0-6-6T	Mason	635-636	10-1880	13" x 16"	36"	72,000

Number	Type	Builder	Builder number	Date	Cylinders	Drivers	Total weight
18	0-6-4T	Hinkley	1362	2-1881	13" x 16"		66,000
19-23	0-6-4T	Hinkley	1363-1367	1881	13" x 16"		66,000
24	0-4-4T	H. K. Porter	428	5-1881	12" x 16"		48,000
25	0-4-4T	H. K. Porter	429	6-1881	12" x 16"		48,000
26-27	0-4-4T	H. K. Porter	440-441	7-1881	12" x 16"		48,000
28	4-4-0	Baldwin	3978	8-1876	11" x 16"	42"	36,000
29	4-4-0	Baldwin	3990	9-1876	11" x 16"	42"	36,000
30	4-4-0	Baldwin	4115	7-1877	11" x 16"	42"	36,000
31	2-4-0	National		1877			24,000
32	2-6-0	Brooks	358	7-1879	12" x 18"	36"	36,000
33	2-8-0	Baldwin	5434	1-1881	15" x 18"	37"	56,000
34	2-6-0	Brooks	335	9-1878	12" x 18"	36"	36,000
35	2-6-0	Brooks	330	11-1878	11" x 16"	36"	36,000
36	2-8-0	Baldwin	5358	11-1880	15" x 18"	37"	56,000
37-38	2-8-0	Baldwin	5764-5765	8-1881	15" x 18"	37"	56,000
39-40	4-4-0	Mount Savage		1-1882			44,000
41-42	0-6-4T	Hinkley	1483-1484	1-1882	13" x 16"		70,000
43-44	0-6-4T	Hinkley	1485-1486	2-1882	13" x 16"		70,000
45-46	0-6-4T	Hinkley	1487-1488	4-1882	13" x 16"		70,000
47	4-4-0	Paul & Son		3-1882			44,000
48-50	2-6-0	Rome	21-23	4-1883	16" x 20"	48"	64,000
51	2-6-0	Baldwin	5978	12-1881	14" x 20"	45"	56,000
52-53	2-4-4T*	Mason		1874	12" x 16"	42"	40,000
54	vacant						
55	0-4-4T*	Mason		1877	12" x 16"	42"	40,000
56	2-6-0	Brooks	610	11-1881	14" x 18"	41"	44,000
57-66	2-8-0	Grant		6-1882	15" x 20"		60,000
67-71	4-4-0	Grant		8-1882	14" x 20"	46"	48,000
72-76	4-4-0	Grant		1-1883	14" x 20"	46"	48,000
77	2-6-0	Brooks	659	2-1882	14" x 18"	41"	44,000
78-82	2-6-0	Hinkley	1595-1599	3-1883			52,000
83-84	2-4-6T	Mason	648-649	5-1881	14" x 18"	48"	74,000
85-86	2-4-6T	Mason	650-651	6-1881	14" x 18"	48"	74,000
87	2-6-0	Brooks	834	12-1882	15" x 18"	37"	47,500
88-89	2-6-0	Brooks	901-902	4-1883	15" x 18"	37"	47,500
90	2-6-0	Brooks	905	5-1883	15" x 18"	37"	47,500
2nd 90	2-6-0	Rome	24	4-1883	16" x 20"	48"	64,000
91	2-6-0	Brooks	906	5-1883	15" x 18"	37"	47,500
92-93	2-6-0	Brooks	918-919	5-1883	15" x 18"	37"	47,500
94-96	2-6-0	Brooks	930, 929, 937	6-1883	15" x 18"	37"	47,500
2nd 96	2-4-0*	Porter, Bell	401	11-1880	10" x 16"		36,000
97-98	2-6-0	Brooks	941-942	7-1883	15" x 18"	37"	47,500
99	2-6-0	Brooks	951	8-1883	15" x 18"	37"	47,500
100	2-6-0	Brooks	964	8-1883	15" x 18"	37"	47,500
101-102	2-6-0	Brooks	965-966	10-1883	15" x 18"	37"	47,500

*Wheel arrangements uncertain.

1 — Ex-Frankfort & State Line 1, relettered in 1884. To Toledo, St. Louis & Kansas City 1, 1886.

2 — Ex-Cincinnati Northern 1. Wrecked by derailment near Lebanon, O., November 15, 1883. Wrecked by trestle collapse at Highland, O., January 22, 1884. Returned to CN July 1884.

3, 5 — Ex-TD&B 3, 5. To TStL&KC 3, 5 in 1886.

4 — Ex-TD&B 4. Wrecked June 8, 1882, when run into Miami & Erie Canal at Delphos. Dismantled with boiler installed in new Dayton roundhouse 1884; machinery kept at Delphos for several years afterward.

2nd 4 — Ex-CN 2. Returned to that road in July 1884.

6 — Ex-TD&B 6. Laid up in 1882 and retired about 1886.

7 — Ex-TD&B 7. Laid up December 1883.

8 — Ex-TD&B 8. Wrecked in a head-on collision with No. 27 August 5, 1883.

9 — Ex-TD&B 9. To TStL&KC 9, 1886.

10 — Ex-TD&B 10. To Dayton & Ironton June 1884. Later to Nash City Lumber Company; Norfolk, Albemarle & Atlantic; Lancaster & Chester.

11 — Ex-TD&B 11. Used as a switcher at Ironton. To D&I in June 1884.

12 — Ex-TD&B 12. Returned to owners Ballou and Holmes in January 1885. Probably sent to Americus, Preston & Lumpkin, a Georgia narrow gauge, in April 1885.

13-14 — Ex-TD&B 13-14. Used on Southeastern Division. Both destroyed by Dayton roundhouse fire of January 1884.

15-17 — Ex-TD&B 15-17. Worked out of Wellston on mine runs. To Ballou and Holmes January 1885. Believed sold to Americus, Preston & Lumpkin in April 1885.

18 — Ex-TD&B 18. Destroyed by collapse of Salt Creek trestle, near Richmond Dale, O., on October 15, 1884.

19-23 — Ex-TD&B 19-23. Used on Southeastern Division. To Ballou and Holmes, January 1885. Four of these became Manistee & Luther 1-4.

24-26 — Ex-TD&B 24-26. Used on Zoo Line at Cincinnati. To Ballou and Holmes, January 1885. May have gone to Americus, Preston & Lumpkin.

27 — Ex-TD&B 27. Destroyed in a collision with No. 8 August 5, 1883.

28 — Ex-TD&B 28. To Dayton & Ironton 28, June 1884. To Cincinnati, New Richmond & Ohio River circa 1887.

29-33 — Ex-TD&B 29-33. To D&I 29-33, June 1884.

34 — Ex-TD&B 34. To D&I 34, June 1884. To Cartagena & Magdalena, April 1893.

35 — Ex-TD&B 35. To D&I 35, June 1884. To Kingwood Railway, 1887; Tunnelton, Kingwood & Fairchance, 1888; West Virginia Northern, 1895.

36 — Ex-TD&B 36. To D&I 36 June 1884.

37-38 — Ex-TD&B 37-38. To TStL&KC 1886.

39-40 — Ex-TD&B 39-40. Believed repossessed by owner, American Loan & Trust Company, in December 1885.

41-46 — Ex-TD&B 41-46. To TStL&KC, 1886.

47 — Ex-TD&B 47. Repaired January 1885 and returned to builder.

48 — Ex-CN 8. Returned to Rome and sold in 1886 to Portland & Willamette Valley, their 2. To South Pacific Coast 24, April 1897. Scrapped January 1902.

49 — Ex-CN 9. Returned to Rome and sold in 1886 to Portland & Willamette Valley, their 3. To South Pacific Coast 25, April 1897; Mitchell Mining Company, August 1, 1907; Nevada County Narrow Gauge, their 6, in 1910. Scrapped 1935.

50 — Ex-CN 10. Returned to Rome and rebuilt. To Marietta & North Georgia 1, 1885.

51 — Named Chillicothe. Apparently returned to owner, American Loan & Trust Company, in 1886.

52-53 — Acquired about January 1882 after being repaired by Mason. Believed to have been the former 7-8 of the New Brunswick Railway, Mason 531-532, June 1874, 42-inch gauge. To TStL&KC in 1886.

55-56 — Ex-CN 5-6, returned to that road in July 1884.

57-59 — To Dayton & Ironton 57-59, July 1884. Returned to Grant in 1887.

60-61 — To D&I 60-61, July 1884. Sold by Grant to Post, Martin & Company June 3, 1887.

62, 64-66 — To D&I 62, 64-66, July 1884. Returned to Grant in April 1887.

63 — To D&I 63 in July 1884. Laid up at Dayton April 1887. Sold by Grant to Oregon Improvement Company September 30, 1887. Became Columbia & Puget Sound 9 shortly afterward. Barged to Alaska in 1898 to become White Pass & Yukon 3, later 53. Scrapped in 1918.

67 — Repossessed by Grant and turned over to Cleveland, Delphos & St. Louis for repairs October 12, 1885. Sent to Florida March 1886.

68 — Received by TC&StL September 7, 1882. To CD&StL for repairs October 1885. Sold by Grant to Jacksonville, St. Augustine & Halifax River in December 1885.

69 — Received September 5, 1882. To HR&E 5 circa 1887.

70-71 — Received September 7 and 10, 1882. Repaired by CD&StL October-November 1885 and sent to Florida by Grant.

72 — Received February 1, 1883. Repossessed October 1885; repaired by CD&StL; sold December 15, 1885, to Florida Commercial Company. Became Florida Southern 24.

73 — Received February 3, 1883. Returned to Grant in 1886 and sold by them to Havana, Rantoul & Eastern on September 20, 1887. Became HR&E 6.

74-76 — Received February 1883 and returned to Grant 1886. No. 74 became Havana, Rantoul & Eastern 7 thereafter. Nos. 75-76 apparently became Baltimore & Lehigh 8-9 circa 1892.

77 — Ex-CN 7. Returned to that road and renumbered 7 in July 1884. Sold to Britzer & Company.

78-79, 80,

81-82 — Received April 4, March 29, April 6 and 8, 1883, respectively. Owned by E. B. Phillips. To TStL&KC, 1886.

83-86 — Received February 28, 1883 after being repaired by Mason. Originally New York & Manhattan Beach Manhattan, Wm. Kieft, East New York, and Gravesend. Owned by E. B. Phillips. To TStL&KC in 1886.

87 — Received January 23, 1883. Laid up 1884. Returned to owner E. B. Phillips in 1885.

88-89 — Received April 30, 1883. Owned by E. B. Phillips. To Florida Southern 22-23, December 1885.

90 — Sent by Brooks to Chicago in June 1883 for display at the National Exposition of Railway Appliances. Ultimately became Cincinnati & Eastern 7.

2nd 90 — Ex-CN 11. Returned to Rome in 1885. Rebuilt as a standard-gauge engine March 1889 and became Monterey & Mexican Gulf 2nd 4.

91-95 — Leased by Receiver Dwight of TC&StL in August 1883. Purchased by Toledo, St. Louis & Kansas City in 1886.

96 — Probably not delivered by builder. To Cincinnati Northern 2nd 8 January 1885. Ran away on Walnut Hills trestle February 5, 1885, and wrecked. To Cincinnati, Lebanon & Northern 8, August 1885; Browning Manufacturing Company, October 1895; Wellington & Powellsville, August 1903.

2nd 96 — Ex-CN 3, returned to that road July 1884.

97 — Probably not delivered by builder. To CN 2nd 9, January 1885; CL&N 9, August 1885; Potts Valley Iron Company, about 1893; Allegheny Ore & Iron Company, April 1902; Southern Iron & Equipment Company 274; W. T. Smith Lumber Company 3, May 23, 1904. Scrapped 1948.

98, 101 — Not delivered by builder. To St. Joseph & Desloge; to Mississippi River & Bonne Terre 5, 4.

99, 100 — Not delivered by builder. To Pittsburgh & Western 20, 19.

102 — Not delivered by builder. To Cincinnati, Georgetown & Portsmouth 4.

TOLEDO, ST. LOUIS & KANSAS CITY RAILROAD 1886-1889
Narrow Gauge

Number	Type	Builder	Builder number	Date
1	2-4-0	Porter, Bell	316	7-1879
3	4-4-0	Baldwin	4221	12-1877
5	4-4-0	Baldwin	4288	3-1878
7	0-4-2T	Porter, Bell	304	6-1878
9	4-4-0	Pittsburgh	351	8-1878
10-11	4-4-0			
12-16	2-6-0	Hinkley	1595-1599	3-1883
17-18	0-6-4T	Hinkley	1483-1484	1-1882
19-20	0-6-4T	Hinkley	1485-1486	2-1882
21-22	0-6-4T	Hinkley	1487-1488	4-1882
23-24	2-8-0	Baldwin	5764-5765	8-1881
25-26	2-4-6T	Mason	648-649	5-1881
27-28	2-4-6T	Mason	650-651	6-1881
91	2-6-0	Brooks	906	5-1883
92-93	2-6-0	Brooks	918-919	5-1883
94-95	2-6-0	Brooks	930, 929	6-1883
	2-4-4T	Mason*		1874

* Mason Bogie 52 or 53 probably renumbered. Details lacking.

1 — Ex-TC&StL 1. Disposition unknown.

3-9 — Ex-TC&StL, same numbers. Returned to owners Clark, Post & Martin April 18, 1889.

10-11 — Details lacking. These may have been TC&StL 39-40, Mount Savage 4-4-0's. Off the roster by the end of 1887.

12-16 — Ex-TC&StL 78-82. Renumbered 100-104 circa 1887. Converted to standard-gauge 0-6-0's 1889-1890.

17-22 — Ex-TC&StL 41-46. Renumbered 105-110 circa 1887. Converted to standard-gauge yard engines 1889-1890.

23-24 — Ex-TC&StL 37-38. No. 23 off the roster by 1887. No. 24 collapsed bridge at Bluffton on July 30, 1886, and was badly

damaged. Later used as a yard engine at Delphos. Renumbered 4 in 1887. Converted to standard gauge August-September 1888.

25-26 — Ex-TC&StL 83-84. Renumbered 6, 10 circa 1887. Converted to standard gauge and used in passenger service 1888-1889.

27-28 — Ex-TC&StL 85-86. Renumbered 3, 5 circa 1888. Converted to standard gauge August-September 1888.

91-95 — Ex-TC&StL, same numbers. No. 94 wrecked in bridge collapse near Frankfort December 27, 1886. Repaired and returned to service. All were converted to standard-gauge 0-6-0's at Delphos — 92 in October 1888, the rest in 1889.

TOLEDO, ST. LOUIS & KANSAS CITY RAILROAD 1887-1900
Standard Gauge

Number	Type	Builder	Builder number	Date
1	0-6-0			
2	0-6-0	Baldwin		
3	2-4-6T	Mason		1881
4	2-8-0	Baldwin	5765	8-1881
2nd 3-4	0-6-0	Rhode Island	2840-2841	1-1893
5-6	2-4-6T	Mason		1881
9	no data			
10	2-4-6T	Mason		1881
11-23	4-4-0	Rhode Island	1802-1814	6-1887
24-26	2-6-0	Rhode Island	1840-1842	9-1887
27-29	4-6-0	Rhode Island	2053-2055	10-1888
30-31	2-6-0	Rhode Island	1936, 1935	12-1888
32	2-6-0	Rhode Island	1938	12-1888
33-34	2-6-0	Rhode Island	1950-1951	12-1888
35-39	4-6-0	Rhode Island	2146-2150	1-1889
40-44	4-6-0	Rhode Island	2141-2145	2-1889
45-46	4-6-0	Rhode Island	2194-2195	12-1889
47-49	4-6-0	Rhode Island	2196-2198	2-1890
50	4-6-0	Rhode Island	2319	2-1890
51-54	4-6-0	Rhode Island	2540-2543	6-1891
55-58	4-6-0	Rhode Island	2566-2569	6-1891
59-60	4-6-0	Rhode Island	2574-2575	6-1891
61	4-6-0	Rhode Island	2806	8-1892
62-65	4-6-0	Rhode Island	2824-2827	8-1892
66-68	4-6-0	Rhode Island	2802-2804	9-1892
69-70	4-6-0	Rhode Island	2718-2719	9-1892
71-75	4-6-0	Rhode Island	2846-2850	1-1893
91-93	0-6-0	Brooks	906, 918, 919	5-1883
94-95	0-6-0	Brooks	930, 929	6-1883
100-104	0-6-0	Hinkley	1595-1599	3-1883
105-110	0-6-4T	Hinkley	1483-1488	1882

Lima accepted six Rhode Island 4-6-0's as the Clover Leaf's down payment on five new H-9 Consolidations in 1922. Two of the 1892-1893 19 x 24's, 103 and 108, are known to have ended up on the Chicago, Attica & Southern. — *Collection of Roy W. Carlson.*

DIMENSIONS OF LOCOMOTIVES

Number	Cylinders	Drivers	Weight on drivers	Total weight	Boiler pressure	Tractive effort	Grate area
1	no data						
2	18" x 24"	48"	66,000	66,000	130	17,940	17.42
3, 5, 6, 10	14" x 18"	48"		76,000			
2nd 3-4	18" x 24"	50"	89,700	89,700	140	18,480	16.38
11-12	17" x 24"	68"	60,350	94,950	150	12,975	17.32

Number	Cylinders	Drivers	Weight on drivers	Total weight	Boiler pressure	Tractive effort	Grate area
13-23	17″ x 24″	62″	57,600	93,000	150	14,250	17.32
24-26 30-34	18″ x 24″	54″	66,900	86,200	140	17,150	17.5
27-29 35-50 56-60	18″ x 24″	55″	80,650	107,910	160	19,200	18.54
51-55 61, 66-70	18″ x 24″	54″	80,650	107,910	160	19,600	18.54
62-65 71-75	19″ x 24″	56″	83,450	109,950	160	21,120	18.96
91-95	15″ x 18″	37″		43,000			
100-104				52,000			
105-110	13″ x 16″			70,000			

1-2 — Purchased in used condition from South Chicago Dock Company June 1891. Subsequently rebuilt at Delphos. No. 1 retired about 1898.

3, 5 — Converted narrow-gauge engines, outshopped at Delphos in August-September 1888. Both retired by 1898.

4 — Converted to standard gauge at Delphos August-September 1888.

6, 10 — Converted to standard gauge at Delphos 1889 and used in passenger service. No. 10 wrecked in head-on collision with No. 17 on September 5, 1892.

11-18 — Placed in service June 25, 1887.

19-20 — Placed in service June 29, 1887.

21-23 — Placed in service July 1, 1887.

24-26 — Placed in service October 10, 1887.

27-29 — Placed in service October 23, 1887.

30-34 — Placed in service January 10, 1889.

35-39 — Placed in service January 25, 1889.

40-44 — Placed in service March 7, 1889.

45-46 — Placed in service January 14, 1890.

47-50 — Placed in service March 4, 1890.

51-60 — Placed in service June 15-23, 1891.

61-62 — Placed in service September 4, 1892.

63-65 — Placed in service September 1, 1892.

66-70 — Placed in service September 21-28, 1892.

71-75 — Placed in service January 17-21, 1893.

91-95 — Converted from narrow-gauge 2-6-0 at Delphos 1888-1889. No. 95 destroyed by boiler explosion at East St. Louis September 13, 1890. Others retired by 1898.

100-110 — Converted from narrow-gauge engines at Delphos 1889-1890. All retired by 1898.

Fast freights on east end of Clover Leaf received Brooks Ten-Wheelers 150-159 in 1904. E-4's had 63-inch drivers and Fox tender trucks. These 4-6-0's had a Cole boiler horsepower rating of 1132 at 200 pounds steam pressure. — *Schenectady History Center.*

TOLEDO, ST. LOUIS & WESTERN RAILROAD 1901-1923

Number	Class 1904	1909	Type	Builder	Builder number	Date
2			0-6-0	Baldwin		
3-4	A	B-5	0-6-0	Rhode Island	2840-2841	1-1893
5-6	A-1	B-6	0-6-0	Dickson	26027-26028	7-1902
7-12	A-2	B-7	0-6-0	Brooks	44428-44433	8-1907
14-15		B-8	0-6-0	Baldwin	23657, 23626	1-1904
16		B-9	0-6-0	Baldwin	54460	1-1921
17-19	D	F-5	2-6-0	Rhode Island	1951, 1950, 1938	12-1888
2nd 17		B-9	0-6-0	Baldwin	54461	1-1921
20-21	D	F-5	2-6-0	Rhode Island	1936, 1935	12-1888
22-24	D	F-5	2-6-0	Rhode Island	1842, 1841, 1840	9-1887
25-26	B	D-8	4-4-0	Rhode Island	1802-1803	6-1887
27-30	B-1	D-8a	4-4-0	Rhode Island	1804-1807	6-1887
31, 33	B-2	D-9	4-4-0	Rhode Island	1808, 1810	6-1887
32, 34-37	B-1	D-8a	4-4-0	Rhode Island	1809, 1811-1814	6-1887
40-42	E-3	G-7	4-6-0	Baldwin	18765, 18766, 18773	3-1901
43	E-3	G-7	4-6-0	Baldwin	18978	5-1901
44-45	C	E-3	4-4-2	Brooks	29270-29271	3-1904
50	E	G-4	4-6-0	Rhode Island	2319	2-1890
51-55	Ea	G-4a	4-6-0	Rhode Island	2540-2543, 2566	6-1891
56-58	E	G-4	4-6-0	Rhode Island	2567-2569	6-1891
59-60	E	G-4	4-6-0	Rhode Island	2574-2575	6-1891

Number	Class 1904	Class 1909	Type	Builder	Builder number	Date
61	Ea	G-4a	4-6-0	Rhode Island	2806	8-1892
62-64	E	G-4	4-6-0	Rhode Island	2053-2055	10-1888
65	E	G-4	4-6-0	Rhode Island	2146	1-1889
66-68	Ea	G-4a	4-6-0	Rhode Island	2802-2804	9-1892
69-70	Ea	G-4a	4-6-0	Rhode Island	2718-2719	9-1892
71-74	E	G-4	4-6-0	Rhode Island	2147-2150	1-1889
75-79	E	G-4	4-6-0	Rhode Island	2141-2145	2-1889
80-81	E	G-4	4-6-0	Rhode Island	2194-2195	12-1889
82-84	E	G-4	4-6-0	Rhode Island	2196-2198	2-1890
100-103	E-1	G-5	4-6-0	Rhode Island	2824-2827	8-1892
104-108	E-1	G-5	4-6-0	Rhode Island	2846-2850	1-1893
109-111	E-2	G-6	4-6-0	Richmond	3101-3103	8-1900
120-121	D-1	F-6	2-6-0	Baldwin	19028-19029	5-1901
122-125	D-1	F-6	2-6-0	Baldwin	19035-19038	5-1901
130-131	F	H-4	2-8-0	Baldwin	20093-20094	2-1902
132-133	F-1	H-5	2-8-0	Schenectady	28614-28615	1-1904
134-135		H-3	2-8-0	Pittsburgh	2053, 2057	2-1900
136		H-2	2-8-0	Rogers	45087	2-1908
150-159	E-4	G-8	4-6-0	Brooks	30338-30347	11-1904
160-174	F-2	H-6	2-8-0	Brooks	30901-30915	2-1905
175-189	F-2	H-6	2-8-0	Brooks	38956-38970	12-1905
190-194		H-7	2-8-0	Baldwin	40866-40870	1-1913
201-205		H-8	2-8-0	Lima	5221-5225	12-1916
206-210		H-9	2-8-0	Lima	6127-6131	12-1921
211-212		H-9	2-8-0	Lima	6243-6244	5-1922
214-216		H-9	2-8-0	Lima	6245-6247	5-1922

Yard duty at Charleston was the long-time lot of the Nine-Spot, one of six Brooks 0-6-0's bought by the Clover Leaf in 1907. Saturated goat became NKP 709 in 1924 but was reassigned her original number shortly before this June 26, 1934, photo was made at Delphos. This last of the B-7's survived until 1946. — *Clyde E. Helms.*

DIMENSIONS OF LOCOMOTIVES

Number	Cylinders	Valve motion*		Drivers	Weight on drivers	Total weight	Boiler pressure	Tractive effort	Grate area	
2	18″ x 24″	s	S	48″	66,000	66,000	130	17,940	17.42	
3-4	18″ x 24″	s	S	51″	90,000	90,000	140	18,144	16.7	
5-6	19″ x 26″	s	S	50″	121,000	121,000	180	28,721	23	(A)
7-12	19″ x 26″	p	S	57″	138,000	138,000	180	25,200	29	
14-15	18″ x 24″	s	S	51″	109,700	109,700	180	23,310	19.2	(B)
16, 2nd 17	22″ x 26″	s	W	51″	160,000	160,000	180	37,750	26	
17-24	18″ x 24″	s	S	55″	66,900	86,200	140	16,806	17.5	
25-26	17″ x 24″	s	S	68″	60,350	94,950	150	12,975	17.32	
27-30, 32, 34-37	17″ x 24″	s	S	63″	57,600	93,000	150	14,037	17.32	
31, 33	17″ x 24″	s	S	69″	64,000	99,000	180	15,380	17.8	(C)
40	19¼″ x 24″	s	S	63″	97,000	130,400	180	23,200	27.6	(D)
41	18½″ x 24″	s	B	69″	103,500	138,500	180	17,500	27.6	(D)
42	18¼″ x 24″	s	B	69″	103,500	139,500	180	17,200	27.6	(D)
43	18″ x 24″	s	S	63″	99,000	132,400	180	18,900	27.6	(D)
44-45	19″ x 26″	p	S	73″	88,000	150,000	200	21,900	42.5	
50, 56-60, 62-65, 71-84	18″ x 24″	s	S	56″	80,650	107,910	160	18,880	18.54	(E)
51-55, 61, 66-70	18″ x 24″	s	S	54″	80,650	107,910	160	19,600	18.54	

Number	Cylinders	Valve motion*		Drivers	Weight on drivers	Total weight	Boiler pressure	Tractive effort	Grate area
100-108	19" x 24"	s	S	57"	83,450	109,950	160	20,720	18.96 (F)
109-111	19" x 24"	s	S	62"	99,125	127,200	180	21,041	23
	19" x 24"	s	B	62"	106,000	137,000	180	21,041	23 (G)
120-125	19½" x 26"	s	S	63"	116,300	133,380	180	24,075	29.9
130-131	20" x 26"	s	S	57"	125,500	142,500	180	27,915	28.1
132-133	20" x 26"	s	S	56"	128,000	145,000	200	31,017	41.7 (H)
134-135	20" x 28"	s	S	57"	132,200	148,500	180	30,000	30.3 (J)
136	20" x 26"	p	W	50"	145,000	165,000	180	31,820	33
150-159	19½" x 30"	s	S	63"	129,000	164,000	200	30,780	30.75
160-189	21" x 28"	s	S	57"	171,000	192,000	200	36,800	47.25
190-194	21" x 28"	s	S	57"	168,500	191,350	200	36,800	46.2
	22" x 28"	p	B	57"	172,000	197,000	185	37,500	47.25 (K)
201-216	22" x 28"	p	B	57"	173,500	200,400	185	37,500	46.2

*s — slide valve; p — piston valve; S — Stephenson; B — Baker; W — Walschaerts.

(A) Driver diameter later increased to 51 inches, boiler pressure reduced to 165 lbs. and rated tractive effort to 25,905 lbs.

(B) Boiler pressure and rated tractive effort later reduced to 175 and 22,663 lbs.

(C) As rebuilt in 1905.

(D) Shown as rebuilt in 1919. Originally had 19 x 24-inch cylinders, 63-inch drivers, and total engine weight of 122,000 lbs.

(E) Boiler pressure and rated tractive effort later reduced to 150 and 17,700 lbs.

(F) Boiler pressure and rated tractive effort later reduced to 150 and 19,428 lbs.

(G) These dimensions are for engines 109 and 111 as rebuilt in 1922.

(H) Boiler pressure and rated tractive effort later reduced to 185 and 28,691 lbs. Drivers to 57-inch about 1907.

(J) Boiler pressure and rated tractive effort reduced to 170 and 28,320 lbs. in January 1921. Reduced to 165 and 27,550 lbs. in March 1923.

(K) These dimensions are as rebuilt 1922-1923.

Consolidations 130-133 were the general purpose engines of the Third and Fourth subdivisions. F-1 133 came from Schenectady in 1904. — *Schenectady History Center.*

2 — Retired 1902. Dismantled at Delphos with boiler installed in Delphos shop.

3 — Retired September 22, 1923. Sold March 1924 to Kokomo Rod Mill.

4-12 — To NKP 704-712, 1924.

14-15 — Ex-Toledo Railway & Terminal 10 and 8 acquired 1915. To NKP 714-715.

16,

2nd 17 — Received December 1922. To NKP 716-717, 1924.

17-18 — Ex-TStL&KC 34, 33. Used in yard service after 1898. Sold 1908.

19 — Ex-TStL&KC 32. Yard engine after 1898. Dismantled 1909.

20 — Ex-TStL&KC 31. Yard engine after 1898. Sold 1908.

21 — Ex-TStL&KC 30. Yard engine after 1898. Dismantled November 7, 1909.

22-23 — Ex-TStL&KC 26, 25. Yard service after 1898. Sold about 1915.

24 — Ex-TStL&KC 24. Yard engine after 1898. Dismantled August 30, 1918.

25, 27 — Ex-TStL&KC 11, 13. Retired 1915.

26, 28 — Ex-TStL&KC 12, 14. Retired 1902-1905.

29 — Ex-TStL&KC 15. Retired February 9, 1917.

30 — Ex-TStL&KC 16. Retired 1910.

31, 33 — Ex-TStL&KC 17, 19. Rebuilt with new Belpaire boilers in 1905. To NKP 731, 733 in 1924.

32, 34 — Ex-TStL&KC 18, 20. Retired 1906.

35 — Ex-TStL&KC 21. Retired 1916.

36 — Wrecked in head-on collision with 162 at Warren, Ind., August 17, 1913. Dismantled December 19, 1917. Originally TStL&KC 22.

37 — Ex-TStL&KC 23. Dismantled October 11, 1922.

40-41 — Rebuilt March 1919 with new frames. 41 got Baker valve gear at that time. To NKP 740-741, 1924.

42 — Equipped with Baker-Pilliod valve gear in 1908, first locomotive so equipped. Rebuilt with new frame March 1919. To NKP 742.

43 — Rebuilt 1919. To NKP 743, 1924.

44-45 — To NKP 744-745, 1924.

50 — Ex-TStL&KC 50. Retired about 1910.

51-55 — Ex-TStL&KC 51-55. Retired and sold 1906-1907.

56 — Ex-TStL&KC 56. Yard engine at Frankfort after 1907. Retired 1915.

57, 59 — Ex-TStL&KC 57, 59. Sold 1906-1907.

58 — Ex-TStL&KC 58. Destroyed by boiler explosion at Continental, O., July 17, 1902.

60, 66,

68-70 — Ex-TStL&KC, same numbers. Sold in 1907.

61 — Ex-TStL&KC 61. Yard engine at Frankfort, Madison after 1907. Dismantled February 9, 1917.

62-64 — Ex-TStL&KC 27-29. 64 to Kanawha & West Virginia 1. Others retired about 1905.

65 — Ex-TStL&KC 35. Sold in 1905.

67 — Ex-TStL&KC 67. Retired about 1910.

71 — Ex-TStL&KC 36. To yard duty in 1907. Retired about 1915.

72-74,
76, 78 — Ex-TStL&KC 37-39, 41, 43. Retired and sold in 1905.
75 — Ex-TStL&KC 40. To yard duty in 1907. Dismantled December 5, 1919.
77 — Ex-TStL&KC 42. Sold about 1905 to Hutchinson & Southern, their 20. Later became AT&SF 2nd 148. Scrapped April 1915.
79 — Ex-TStL&KC 44. To yard duty in 1907. Retired about 1915.
80-84 — Ex-TStL&KC 45-49. Sold 1906-1907. 82 to Cincinnati, Bluffton & Chicago.
100 — Ex-TStL&KC 62. To Lima Locomotive Works March 12, 1922.
101 — Dismantled July 15, 1920. Originally TStL&KC 63.
102 — Dismantled December 5, 1919. Originally TStL&KC 64.
103 — Ex-TStL&KC 65. To Lima Locomotive Works March 12, 1922. Later became Chicago, Attica & Southern 103.
104 — Ex-TStL&KC 71. Dismantled December 5, 1919.
105-108 — Ex-TStL&KC 72-75. To Lima Locomotive Works March 12, 1922. 108 later became Chicago, Attica & Southern 108.
109-111 — Originally built as Baltimore & Lehigh 1-3; acquired from builder on February 13, 1901. 109, 111 rebuilt at Frankfort in 1922 with new frames, Baker valve gear. To NKP 809-811, 1924.
120-125 — To NKP 820-825, 1924.
130-133 — To NKP 830-833, 1924.

134-135 — Purchased from General Equipment Company November 1917. Formerly Wheeling & Lake Erie 671 and 675. Received at Toledo December 3, 1917. Overhauled and placed in service January 7, 1918. To NKP 834-835.
136 — Purchased from General Equipment Company December 1917 and placed in service January 1918. Formerly Morristown & Erie 1.
150-159 — Used in freight service. 154 and 157 rebuilt at Frankfort with Baker valve gear October-November 1923. To NKP 850-859, 1924.
160-189 — To NKP 860-889, 1924.
190-191 — Rebuilt at Frankfort May 1923 with new piston valve cylinders, superheater, Baker valve gear, and cast-steel pilot. To NKP 890-891, 1924.
192 — Rebuilt at Frankfort September 1922 with new piston valve cylinders, superheater, Baker valve gear, and cast-steel pilot. To NKP 892, 1924.
193 — Rebuilt at Frankfort June 1923 with new piston valve cylinders, superheater, Baker valve gear, and cast-steel pilot. To NKP 893, 1924.
194 — Rebuilt at Frankfort July 1923 with new 22 x 28-inch piston valve cylinders, superheater, Baker valve gear, cast-steel pilot. To NKP 894, 1924.
201-216 — To NKP 901-916, 1924.

The Clover Leaf was an early user of electric headlights and the first road to try Baker-Pilliod valve gear. Physical restrictions forced the TStL&W to stay with basic design of its 1905 2-8-0's. — *Collection of George M. Sittig.*

Locomotives of the Wheeling & Lake Erie

WHEELING & LAKE ERIE RAILROAD 1876-1880
Narrow Gauge

Number	Name	Type	Builder	Builder number	Date	Cylinders	Drivers	Total weight
1	Milan	4-4-0	National		4-1877	9" x 16"	36"	22,000
2	Norwalk	4-4-0	National		1877			
		0-4-4T	Mason*	582	5-1877	12" x 16"	42"	40,000
		0-4-4T	Mason*	585	6-1877	12" x 16"	42"	40,000

*The Mason Bogies were formerly the Manhattan and New York of the New York & Manhattan Beach. They were acquired in 1879. In the summer of 1881 the Mason Machine Works rebuilt these engines as standard-gauge 2-4-4T's, W&LE 6-7.

1 — Cost $4400. Received at Norwalk on May 5, 1877. Laid up in 1879. Reportedly went to a lumber road at Lawton, Mich.

2 — Received about July 1, 1877. Disposition of the 4-4-0 is unknown.

According to veteran enginemen, the sweetest machines on the old W&LE were Mason 0-6-6T's of 1882. No. 3, the yard goat at Norwalk, was first locomotive in Midwest with Walschaerts valve gear. W&LE boarded up rear window and replaced wood pilot with footboards. — *Collection of Everett L. DeGolyer Jr.*

Master Mechanic O. P. Dunbar transformed a wrecked 2-4-6T Bogie into this 4-4-0 at Norwalk in 1886. As rebuilt, the engine had a slab frame and 4-foot drivers. New 16 x 24-inch cylinders and machinery were supplied by Rome. — *Collection of Everett L. DeGolyer Jr.*

W&LE RAILROAD 1881-1886
W&LE RAILWAY 1886-1899
Standard Gauge

Number	Type	Class	Builder	Builder number	Date
2nd 1-2	2-4-6T		Mason	646-647	5-1881
3rd 1-2	0-6-0	B-3	Cooke	2337-2338	4-1896
3-4	0-6-6T		Mason	653-654	7-1881
5	0-6-6T		Mason	659	10-1881
6	2-4-4T		Mason	582	5-1877
7	2-4-4T		Mason	585	6-1877
2nd 5-7	0-6-0	B-1	Pittsburgh	1346-1348	7-1892
8-9	2-4-6T		Mason	668-669	1-1882
10-11	2-4-6T		Mason	671-672	2-1882
12-15	2-4-6T		Mason	675-678	3-1882
16	2-4-6T		Mason	679	4-1882
2nd 16	4-4-0		Grant	1319	10-1880
17	2-4-6T		Mason	680	4-1882
2nd 17	4-4-0		Grant		9-1881
18	2-4-6T		Mason	686	7-1882
19-22	4-4-0	D-2	Mason	687-690	8-1882
23-25	4-4-0	D-2	Rome	47-49	10-1883
26	4-4-0	D-2	Rome	56	11-1883
27-28	4-4-0	D-3	Rome	67-68	2-1884
29-30	4-4-0	D-3	Rome	82-83	7-1884
31-32	4-6-0	G-1	Rome	202-203	11-1886
33-35	4-6-0	G-1	Cooke	1872-1874*	12-1887
36-38	4-6-0	G-1	Rome	357-359	6-1888
39-41	4-6-0	G-1	Pittsburgh	1104-1106	1-1890
42-44	4-6-0	G-1	Cooke	2042-2044	9-1890
45	0-6-0	B-1	Cooke	2045	10-1890
46-53	4-6-0	G-1	Rome	676-679, 686-689	2-1891
54-63	4-6-0	G-1	Pittsburgh	1258-1267	8-1891
64	0-6-0	B-1	Pittsburgh	1349	7-1892
65-69	4-6-0	G-2	Pittsburgh	1421-1425	4-1893
70	4-6-0	G-2	Pittsburgh	1426	5-1893
71-72	4-6-0	G-2	Cooke	2092, 2091	9-1891
91-96	4-6-0	G-4	Cooke	2327-2332	3-1896
97-100	4-6-0	G-4	Cooke	2333-2336	4-1896

*Per Cooke records, verified by photographs.

DIMENSIONS OF LOCOMOTIVES

Number	Cylinders	Drivers	Weight on drivers	Total weight	Boiler pressure	Tractive effort	Grate area	
2nd 1	⎰15″ x 22″	42″						
	⎱16″ x 24″	56″		60,000				(A)
2nd 2⎱ 8, 9, 18⎰	15″ x 22″	42″						
3-5⎱ 10-17⎰	17″ x 24″	49″	66,000	77,700			22.17	(B)
3rd 1-2	19″ x 26″	56″	112,200	112,200	150	21,370	23	
2nd 5-7	17″ x 24″	50″	83,200	83,200	150	17,684	21.3	
6-7	12″ x 16″	42″						
2nd 16	16″ x 24″	63″						
2nd 17	17″ x 24″	63″						
19-22	16″ x 24″	68½″	47,000	77,300	150	11,436		
23-26	16″ x 24″	62″	56,800	88,100	150	12,635	14.6	
27-28	17″ x 24″	62″	57,200	89,200	150	14,267	17	
29-30	17″ x 24″	62″	53,000	84,000	150	14,267	15.6	
31-32	17″ x 24″	56″	72,100	98,500	155	16,323	16.8	
33-35	⎰17″ x 24″	50″	73,500	100,200	150	17,684		(C)
	⎱17″ x 24″	50″	69,700	94,200	150	17,684	16	(D)
36-38	17″ x 24″	56″	72,100	98,500	155	16,323	17	
39-41⎱ 54-63⎰	17″ x 24″	50″	71,300	98,200	155	18,273	17.1	
42-44	17″ x 24″	50″	69,700	94,200	150	17,684	16	
45	17″ x 24″	50″	80,700	80,700	150	17,684	15.3	
46-53	17″ x 24″	56″	73,500	100,200	155	16,323	16.8	
64	17″ x 24″	50″	83,200	83,200	150	17,684	21.3	
65-70	18″ x 24″	50″	79,800	104,900	155	20,487	22.7	(E)
71-72	18″ x 24″	56″	85,000	111,600	155	18,294	16.8	
91-100	19″ x 26″	56″	94,200	120,800	150	21,370	25.3	

(A) As rebuilt to 4-4-0 type.
(B) Engine 14 rebuilt as 4-4-0 with 16 x 24-inch cylinders, 48-inch drivers, and slab frame.
(C) As delivered — double-cab slack burners with Wootten firebox.
(D) Rebuilt with conventional cabs and Belpaire fireboxes.
(E) Boiler pressure and rated tractive effort reduced to 150 and 19,828 lbs. in 1912.

2nd 1 — Received at Creston May 10, 1881. Wrecked in head-on collision near Creston November 20, 1882. Rebuilt at Rome July 1883 as 4-4-0 with slab frame, 16 x 24-inch cylinders. Leased to Cleveland & Marietta March-May 1884. Renumbered 2nd 27, April 1896. Retired 1898.

3rd 1 — Renumbered 3rd 22 November 26, 1899; 3rd 100 March 21, 1905; 2nd 2107 May 12, 1919. Last run June 28, 1929. Dismantled at Brewster September 25, 1929.

2nd 2 — Received at Creston May 10, 1881. Retired 1893.

3rd 2 — Renumbered 2nd 23 December 10, 1899; 2nd 101 December 31, 1904; 2nd 2108 August 22, 1919. Last run February 28, 1930. Dismantled at Brewster September 18, 1930.

3 — Received at Creston August 3, 1881; was the switcher at Norwalk. Retired 1895.

4 — Received at Creston August 3, 1881. Used as a switcher at Toledo. Leased to Detroit, Lansing & Northern 1882-1883. Retired 1897.

5 — Received at Creston September 15, 1881. Badly damaged in the fire which leveled Creston roundhouse December 7, 1882. Dismantled with boiler installed in Norwalk shop September 1883.

2nd 5 — Renumbered 4th 16 March 31, 1903; 3rd 30 July 14, 1905. Retired November 23, 1917, and sold.

6 — Rebuilt by Mason, received October 13, 1881. Used in passenger service between Norwalk and Toledo. Retired 1890.

2nd 6 — Renumbered 4th 31 June 3, 1905; 1752 June 4, 1920. Dismantled July 1923.

7 — Rebuilt by Mason, received October 13, 1881. Used as a switch engine at Huron. Renumbered 1st 99, 1892. Retired 1893. Boiler installed in Ironville carshop November 28, 1893.

8 — Leased to Cleveland & Marietta October 16, 1883, to February 6, 1885. Retired 1894.

9 — Leased to Cleveland & Marietta September 24, 1882, to July 21, 1883. Retired 1894.

10 — Received February 8, 1882. Retired 1894.

11 — Received February 8, 1882. First engine over the Steubenville branch in the fall of 1890. Retired 1894.

12 — Received March 21, 1882. Leased to Cleveland & Marietta November 17, 1884, to February 1, 1885. Rebuilt 1886 with frame and drivers from No. 14. Retired 1896.

13 — Wrecked in head-on collision at Creston with 14 June 18, 1884. Rebuilt at Norwalk with frame from No. 12 and restored to service July 10, 1886. Retired 1897.

14 — Received March 31, 1882. Leased to Cleveland & Marietta January-June 1884. Wrecked in head-on with 13 near Creston June 18, 1884. Rebuilt at Norwalk by O. P. Dunbar with cylinders, slab frame, and machinery bought from Rome. Outshopped as a 4-4-0 December 14, 1886. Renumbered 2nd 22, April 1896. Retired 1899.

15 — Received March 31, 1882. Leased to Cleveland & Marietta October 9, 1882, to June 21, 1883. Rebuilt with drivers from No. 12 in 1886. At one time was named Calamity Jane. Retired 1896.

16 — Received April 24, 1882. Sold to Cleveland & Marietta, their 10, July 14, 1883.

2nd 16 — Originally Fontaine Engine Company 1, a 4-2-2 friction-drive type, E. Fontaine's patent. Purchased by O. P. Dunbar and rebuilt to conventional 4-4-0 at Rome in March 1885. Received on W&LE March 29, 1896. Renumbered 2nd 25 April 1896. Retired 1898.

17 — Received April 24, 1882. Sold to C&M, their 11, January 13, 1883.

2nd 17 — Originally Fontaine Engine Company 2, 4-2-2 friction-drive type. Purchased by M. D. Woodford and rebuilt to conventional 4-4-0 at Rome in March 1885. Initial run on W&LE April 6, 1885. Renumbered 2nd 35, April 1896. Retired 1899.

18 — Retired 1895.

19 — Named Sidney Dillon. Wrecked at Homestead Yard 1894 —

cornered standing cars and tore off right-hand cylinder. Subsequently retired.

20 — Named G. J. Forrest. Wrecked at Norwalk about 1894. Renumbered 2nd 28, April 1896; 2nd 57, 1900. Retired 1901 and apparently sold to J. C. Carland Company of Toledo.

21 — Named C. K. Garrison. Renumbered 2nd 53 February 9, 1900; 310 November 17, 1905. Made last run on May 29, 1909. Dismantled at Norwalk on September 11, 1909.

22 — Retired in 1895.

23 — Renumbered 2nd 54 December 10, 1899; 318 November 20, 1906; 1254 January 13, 1919. Boiler pressure and tractive effort to 130 and 10,950 lbs. November 1921. Last run November 19, 1925. Dismantled April 12, 1926.

24 — Renumbered 2nd 55 April 12, 1900; 319 October 7, 1905. Sold to J. C. Carland Company December 1, 1906.

25 — Wrecked in head-on collision at Garrigan's on New Year's Day 1893. Never repaired and subsequently scrapped.

26 — Renumbered 2nd 56 May 18, 1900; 320 May 11, 1905. Sold to J. C. Carland Company, their 8, December 1, 1906. Later used in building of the Ohio Electric Railway between Bellefontaine, Lima, and Toledo.

27 — Renumbered 2nd 33 April 1896; 2nd 60 January 30, 1900; 323 December 3, 1904; 1403 October 26, 1919. Dismantled at Brewster October 10, 1927.

28 — Renumbered 2nd 34 April 1896; 2nd 61 December 11, 1899; 324 November 30, 1904. Dismantled September 30, 1911.

29 — Rented by Rome to Lackawanna & Pittsburgh, their 205, until October 1884. Repaired at Rome and sold to W&LE January 1885. Renumbered 2nd 31, April 1896; 2nd 58 February 28, 1900; 321 April 25, 1905; 1401 December 8, 1918. Dismantled at Brewster October 7, 1926.

30 — Rented by Rome to L&P, their 206, until October 1884. To W&LE January 1885 after being repaired by Rome. Renumbered 2nd 32 April 1896; 2nd 59 November 9, 1899; 322 May 20, 1905; 1402 December 12, 1919. Dismantled at Brewster December 1924.

31 — Renumbered 2nd 41, April 1896; 2nd 81 October 3, 1899; 550 March 10, 1905. Leased to Wabash Pittsburgh Terminal December 14, 1912, to April 11, 1913. Last run December 4, 1913. Condemned December 1915. Sold to I. Gerson & Sons January 20, 1917.

32 — Renumbered 2nd 42, April 1896; 2nd 82 September 19, 1899; 551 August 9, 1905. Condemned July 26, 1918. Was assigned new number 1502 in 1918 but was not renumbered. Dismantled at Brewster June 15, 1923.

33 — Rebuilt with Belpaire firebox and conventional cab circa 1891. Renumbered 2nd 70 April 1896; 3rd 17 August 9, 1900; 110 February 11, 1903; 579 December 8, 1904. Last run July 30, 1908. Dismantled at Norwalk June 23, 1909.

34 — Rebuilt circa 1891. Renumbered 2nd 71 April 1896; 2nd 18 September 21, 1899; 111 October 25, 1902; 580 September 15, 1905. Last run February 5, 1911. Dismantled at Brewster November 20, 1911.

35 — Rebuilt circa 1891. Renumbered 2nd 72, April 1896; 2nd 19 July 6, 1900; 112 February 7, 1903; 581 May 9, 1905. Last run December 2, 1910. Dismantled at Brewster November 7, 1911.

36 — Renumbered 2nd 43, April 1896; 2nd 83 December 11, 1899; 552 January 25, 1906. Overturned at Somerdale in 1889. Wrecked in head-on with 141 at Newburgh in April 1901. Leased to WPT April 18 to November 20, 1913. Assigned 1601 in 1918 but not renumbered. Condemned October 15, 1918. Dismantled at Brewster June 15, 1923.

37 — Renumbered 2nd 44, April 1896; 2nd 84 October 16, 1899; 553 September 23, 1905. Dismantled at Brewster August 9, 1913.

38 — Renumbered 2nd 45, April 1896; 2nd 85 September 10, 1899; 554 April 24, 1905. Blew up while double-heading ahead of 196 April 19, 1902. Made last run April 24, 1914. Condemned December 22, 1915. Sold to I. Gerson & Sons January 20, 1917.

39 — Renumbered 2nd 65, April 1896; 105 September 21, 1899; 573 May 18, 1907. Leased to Pittsburgh, Lisbon & Western June 8, 1904 to 1907; to AC&Y November 1911 to January

1912. Last run December 2, 1913. Condemned December 22, 1915. Sold to I. Gerson & Sons January 20, 1917.

40 — Renumbered 2nd 66, April 1896; 106 September 7, 1899; 574 January 11, 1905. Last run January 16, 1914. To I. Gerson & Sons January 20, 1917.

41 — Renumbered 2nd 64, April 1896; 104 November 1, 1899; 575 January 31, 1905. Last run January 27, 1915. To I. Gerson & Sons January 20, 1917.

42 — Renumbered 2nd 67, April 1896; 2nd 14 November 29, 1899; 107 January 2, 1902; 576 December 16, 1904. Wrecked by derailment at Jewett in 1894. Last run March 18, 1914. Dismantled at Brewster November 6, 1915.

43 — Renumbered 2nd 68, April 1896; 2nd 15 September 9, 1899; 108 October 31, 1902; 577 July 31, 1905. Last run January 9, 1916. To I. Gerson & Sons January 20, 1917.

44 — Renumbered 2nd 69, April 1896; 3rd 16 April 7, 1900; 109 January 24, 1903; 578 January 25, 1905. Went through open draw of Maumee River bridge June 26, 1903. Condemned December 23, 1915. To I. Gerson & Sons January 20, 1917.

45 — Renumbered 2nd 8, April 1896; 4th 25 November 27, 1904. Sold to General Equipment Company March 31, 1920.

46 — Renumbered 2nd 86 September 25, 1899; 555 December 31, 1904. Last run June 4, 1914. To I. Gerson & Sons January 20, 1917.

47 — Renumbered 2nd 87 September 10, 1899; 556 November 16, 1904. Condemned December 22, 1915. Repaired February 1916 and returned to service. Again condemned July 16, 1918. To General Equipment Company April 25, 1919.

48 — Renumbered 2nd 88 November 25, 1899; 557 September 8, 1905. Condemned July 26, 1918. Dismantled at Brewster June 15, 1923.

49 — Renumbered 2nd 89 October 31, 1899; 558 June 9, 1905. Last run January 26, 1914. To I. Gerson & Sons January 20, 1917.

50 — Renumbered 90, September 15, 1899. Assigned number 559 in 1905 but not actually renumbered. Last run October 9, 1906. Dismantled at Norwalk June 30, 1909.

51 — Renumbered 2nd 91 November 5, 1899; 560 June 17, 1905. Retired and sold November 30, 1917.

52 — Renumbered 2nd 92 October 28, 1899; 561 March 9, 1905. Leased to PL&W December 25, 1915. Sold to PL&W January 12, 1916.

53 — Renumbered 2nd 93 October 25, 1899; 562 February 28, 1906. Condemned October 15, 1918. To General Equipment April 15, 1919.

54 — Renumbered 2nd 94 September 23, 1899; 563 November 20, 1905. Condemned December 22, 1915. To I. Gerson & Sons January 20, 1917.

55 — Renumbered 2nd 95 November 4, 1899; 564 June 19, 1906; 1807 January 22, 1919. Dismantled at Brewster June 15, 1923.

56 — Renumbered 2nd 96 November 9, 1899; 565 October 30, 1908. Last run on December 25, 1905. Dismantled at Norwalk March 16, 1910.

57 — Renumbered 2nd 97 December 3, 1899; 566 November 5, 1904; 1808 March 21, 1919. Leased to AC&Y April-October 1912. Dismantled at Brewster June 15, 1923.

58 — Renumbered 2nd 98 October 31, 1899; 567 March 6, 1906. Last run November 20, 1915. To I. Gerson & Sons January 20, 1917.

59 — Renumbered 3rd 99 November 4, 1899; 568 July 29, 1905. Last run January 17, 1916. To I. Gerson & Sons January 20, 1917.

60 — Renumbered 2nd 100 September 28, 1899; 569 December 29, 1904. Last run June 16, 1914. To I. Gerson & Sons January 20, 1917.

61 — Renumbered 101 October 5, 1899; 570 December 31, 1904. Last run July 11, 1913. Condemned December 22, 1915. To I. Gerson & Sons January 20, 1917.

62 — Renumbered 102 November 4, 1899; 571 December 31, 1904. Last run December 12, 1913. Dismantled at Brewster November 8, 1916.

63 — Renumbered 103 October 14, 1899; 572 May 15, 1905. Last

run November 30, 1914. Dismantled at Brewster November 20, 1915.

64 — Renumbered 2nd 3 April 1896; 3rd 14 May 29, 1903; 3rd 33 March 1, 1905. Retired and sold November 30, 1917.

65 — Renumbered 81, April 1896; 121 October 1, 1899; 583 November 20, 1904; 1952 September 2, 1920. Last run June 30, 1927. Dismantled October 21, 1927.

66 — Renumbered 82, April 1896; 122 October 24, 1899; 584 December 10, 1904; 1953 February 13, 1919. Last run October 29, 1925. Dismantled at Brewster April 15, 1926.

67 — Renumbered 83, April 1896; 123 October 25, 1899; 585 May 25, 1905. Retired and sold November 30, 1917.

68 — Renumbered 84, April 1896; 124 September 10, 1899; 586 December 31, 1904. Retired and sold November 30, 1917.

69 — Renumbered 86, April 1896; 126 September 5, 1899; 587 August 12, 1905; 1954 November 25, 1918. Last run December 7, 1925. Dismantled at Brewster October 8, 1926.

70 — Renumbered 85, April 1896; 125 September 6, 1899; 588 January 1, 1905. Last run September 24, 1913. To I. Gerson & Sons January 20, 1917.

71 — Ex-Toledo, Ann Arbor & North Michigan 47. Rebuilt by Cooke May 1893. To W&LE September 1894. Renumbered 87, April 1896; 127 September 6, 1899; 590 February 4, 1905; 1810 December 13, 1920. Retired January 2, 1926. Dismantled at Brewster April 23, 1926.

72 — Ex-TAA&NM 48. Rebuilt by Cooke May 1893. To W&LE September 1894. Renumbered 88, April 1896; 128 November 25, 1899; 589 April 29, 1905; 1809 February 9, 1921. Dismantled at Brewster December 1924.

91 — Renumbered 161 September 7, 1899; 630 June 12, 1905;

2nd 2114 September 2, 1919. Received boiler from engine 636 and renumbered 2nd 636 December 15, 1917. Last run November 30, 1924. Dismantled April 28, 1926.

92 — Renumbered 162 September 7, 1899; 631 January 2, 1905; 2nd 2110 January 13, 1920. Last run January 13, 1928. Dismantled May 11, 1928.

93 — Renumbered 163 September 29, 1899; 632 December 16, 1909; 2nd 2111, 1920. Dismantled at Brewster June 15, 1923.

94 — Renumbered 164 September 12, 1899; 633 April 29, 1905. Wrecked at Brilliant about 1904. Retired and sold November 30, 1917.

95 — Renumbered 165 September 14, 1899; 634 March 12, 1905; 2nd 2112, 1919. Dismantled at Brewster June 15, 1923.

96 — Renumbered 166 October 13, 1899; 635 August 22, 1905; 2nd 2113 1920. Dismantled at Brewster June 15, 1923.

97 — Renumbered 167 September 12, 1899; 636 November 13, 1904. Dismantled at Brewster December 1917; boiler applied to engine 630.

98 — Renumbered 168 September 20, 1899; 637 March 23, 1905; 2nd 2115 January 29, 1919. Leased to Wabash Pittsburgh Terminal January 1910 to July 1911. Last run July 23, 1926. Dismantled at Brewster September 11, 1926.

2nd 99 — Renumbered 169 September 21, 1899; 638 December 8, 1905; 2nd 2116 November 16, 1920. Last run April 7, 1928. Dismantled May 16, 1928.

100 — Renumbered 170 September 5, 1899; 639 November 9, 1904; 2nd 2117 March 27, 1919. Received new boiler No. 1 at Brewster November 1913. Last run April 7, 1928. Dismantled at Brewster May 24, 1928.

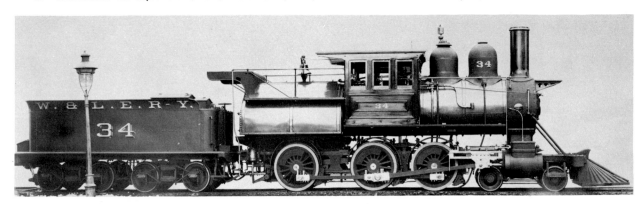

Spanking-new W&LE Camelback No. 34 posed for this portrait at the Cooke Locomotive & Machine Works at Paterson, N. J., in 1887. — *Collection of John H. Keller.*

PREDECESSORS OF THE CLEVELAND, CANTON & SOUTHERN
CARROLL COUNTY RAIL ROAD 1852-1859
58-inch Gauge

Name	Type	Builder	Builder number	Date	Cylinders	Drivers
McNeill	4-2-0	Stephenson & Company	103	2-1835	10" x 15"	54"

Note: Assembled by Thomas Rogers at Paterson, N. J., for the Paterson & Hudson River Railroad. Acquired by Isaac Atkinson from that road's successor, New York & Erie Railroad, for $550 in 1855. To Carroll County the same year. Had a four-wheel tender, wood cab, and copper firebox and flues. Laid up at Carrollton in 1859 and was still stored there as late as September 1867. In his "Pioneer Locomotives of North America," Railway & Locomotive Historical Society bulletin 101, the late Robert R. Brown identified McNeill as an 0-4-0 built in 1833 by Braithwaite, Milner & Company of London. The Stephenson identification advanced in W. A. Lucas' "From the Hills to the Hudson" is well supported by P&HR records and Sinclair's "Development of the Locomotive Engine."

CARROLLTON & ONEIDA RAILROAD 1860-1873
58-inch Gauge

Name	Type	Builder	Date	Tractive effort
Carroll	0-4-0T	Novelty Iron Works	1867	14,000

Note: Placed in service September 4, 1867, and used until July 1874. It is possible that it was then taken to the Bowling Green Rail Road.

Pride of the Connotton Valley were two 23-ton passenger engines turned out by Brooks in 1883. Engines 18 and 19 came from Dunkirk with fancy cap stacks, Westinghouse air brakes, and 4-foot drivers. — *Collection of Sylvan R. Wood.*

OHIO & TOLEDO RAILROAD 1874-1878
YOUNGSTOWN & CONNOTTON VALLEY RAILROAD 1878-1879
CONNOTTON VALLEY RAILROAD 1879-1880
CONNOTTON VALLEY RAILWAY 1880-1885
CLEVELAND & CANTON RAILROAD 1885-1888

Narrow Gauge

Number	Name	Type	Builder	Builder number	Date	Cylinders	Drivers	Total weight
1	E. R. Eckley	2-4-0	National		1874			24,000
2	Connotton	4-4-0	National		1875			33,000
3	C. G. Patterson	4-4-0	Porter, Bell	335	7-1879	12" x 18"	44"	36,000
4	Canton	4-4-0	Porter, Bell	355	1-1880	12" x 18"	44"	36,000
5	Dell Roy	2-8-0	Baldwin	5141	6-1880	15" x 18"	36"	57,000
6	Kent	2-8-0	Baldwin	5258	9-1880	15" x 18"	36"	57,000
7	Bowerstown	2-8-0	Baldwin	5259	9-1880	15" x 18"	36"	57,000
8	C. G. Patterson	4-4-0	Porter, Bell	385	8-1880	13" x 18"	44"	37,000
9	Mogadore	4-4-0	Porter, Bell	396	12-1880	13" x 18"	48"	43,000
10	Newburgh	4-4-0	Porter, Bell	397	12-1880	13" x 18"	48"	43,000
11	A. B. Proal	4-4-0	H. K. Porter	465	12-1881	13" x 18"	48"	43,000
12	Bedford	2-8-0	Baldwin	5932	11-1881	15" x 18"	36"	57,000
13	Carrollton	2-8-0	Baldwin	5930	11-1881	15" x 18"	36"	57,000
14	Cleveland	4-4-0	H. K. Porter	468	12-1881	13" x 18"	48"	43,000
15	Connotton	4-4-0	H. K. Porter	473	1-1882	13" x 18"	48"	43,000
16	Wharf Rat	0-6-0T	Baldwin	5989	1-1882	14" x 18"	31"	50,700
17	Mapleton	2-8-0	Baldwin	5992	1-1882	15" x 18"	36"	57,000
2nd 17	Oscar Wilde	4-4-0	Brooks	345	2-1879	12" x 16"	42"	
18		4-4-0	Brooks	883	3-1883	14" x 18"	48"	46,410
19	W. J. Rotch	4-4-0	Brooks	884	3-1883	14" x 18"	48"	46,410
20		2-6-0	Brooks	854	2-1883	15" x 18"	37"	46,800
21	Mohammed	2-6-0	Brooks	855	2-1883	15" x 18"	37"	46,800
22		2-6-0	Brooks	863	2-1883	15" x 18"	37"	46,800
24	Howadji	2-6-0	Brooks	864	2-1883	15" x 18"	37"	46,800
25-26		2-6-0	Brooks	870-871	3-1883	15" x 18"	37"	46,800

1 — Probably renamed. Said to have been converted to 0-4-0T and named Fido.

2 — Probably renamed. To New York Equipment Company 1889. Later to Fremont, Elkhorn & Missouri Valley.

3 — Probably renamed. Opened the Canton extension May 15, 1880, and pulled the last narrow-gauge train on November 18, 1888. To New York Equipment Company.

4 — Wrecked in head-on collision with 22 near Canton in 1883. Never repaired. Scrapped at Canton in 1885.

5 — Wrecked by a washout at Brimfield February 4, 1883. Repaired and returned to service. To New York Equipment Company 1889. Became Manistee & Luther 5 or 6.

6 — Originally named Leesburg. To New York Equipment Company 1889. May have ended up on the Sumpter Valley.

7 — Renamed. To New York Equipment Company 1889. To Farmville & Powhatan 1889.

8 — To New York Equipment Company. Later to Salt Lake & Eastern 8, 1889.

9 — To Salt Lake & Eastern 9, 1889.

10 — To New York Equipment Company. To Au Sable & Northwestern circa 1889.

11 — To New York Equipment Company, 1889.

12 — To New York Equipment Company, 1889. To Farmville & Powhatan (later known as Tidewater & Western). Scrapped 1917.

13 — To Salt Lake & Eastern 13, 1889. Later Utah Central, Rio Grande Western 02, and Sumpter Valley 7.

14 — To New York Equipment Company, 1889. Later to Pine Bluff & Eastern.

15 — To SL&E 15, 1889. Later Salt Lake & Ogden 15.

16 — To Salt Lake Valley & Ft. Douglas 16, 1889.

17 — John Forbes, engineer. Renumbered 23 in 1883. To New York Equipment Company, 1889. Ended up on Vaccaro Brothers Railroad in Honduras in July 1910. May have previously seen service on the Sumpter Valley.

2nd 17 — Originally Texas & St. Louis 5, J. W. Paramore. Acquired 1882 by Connotton Valley & Straitsville. G. Kingsbury, engineer. To SLV&FD 17, 1889.

18 — John Sexton, engineer. To New York Equipment Company and in 1889 became Rochester & Glen Haven 8.

19 — Ed Pedlar, engineer. To New York Equipment Company and in 1889 became Rochester & Glen Haven 9.

20 — To New York Equipment Company, 1889.

21 — To New York Equipment Company and to Galveston & Western in 1889. To Shreveport & Houston; to Houston, East & West Texas 15, June 1891; to J. J. White, 1895.

22 — Wrecked in head-on with No. 4 near Canton in 1883. Never repaired; scrapped about 1887.

23 — See 1st 17.

24 — To New York Equipment Company, 1889. To Galveston & Western December 1889; to Houston, East & West Texas 17, 1891; to Cameron Lumber Company, 1897.

25 — To New York Equipment Company, 1889; to Galveston & Western April 1890; to Houston, East & West Texas 16, 1891.

26 — M. Jackson, engineer. To New York Equipment Company 1889. Later the same year became Au Sable & Northwestern 6.

CANTON & WAYNESBURG RAILROAD 1885-1888
56¾-inch Gauge

Number	Name	Type	Builder	Builder number	Date	Cylinders	Drivers	Total weight
1	John Hadley	0-4-0	Pittsburgh	786	7-1885	14" x 22"	43"	56,000

Note: To Cleveland & Canton 1, 1888.

PAINESVILLE, CANTON & BRIDGEPORT NARROW GAUGE RAIL ROAD 1877-1880
CHAGRIN FALLS & SOUTHERN RAILROAD 1880-1890
Narrow Gauge

Number	Name	Type	Builder	Builder number	Date	Cylinders	Total weight
1		2-4-0	National		11-1877		27,000
2	Wm. Hutchings	2-4-0	H. K. Porter	638	4-1884	9" x 14"	33,000

Note: Both engines were on CF&S roster in 1890 when the road was converted to standard gauge. Disposition unknown.

Tip-Top Route's biggest 4-4-0 was the 51, turned out by Brooks in 1889. With 62-inch drivers, she was better suited to the narrow-gauge alignment and profile of the CC&S than the Brooks eight-wheelers of 1888. — *Collection of Jack Lozier.*

CLEVELAND & CANTON RAILROAD 1888-1892
CLEVELAND, CANTON & SOUTHERN RAILROAD 1892-1899
Standard Gauge

Number	Type	Builder	Builder number	Date	Cylinders	Drivers	Total weight
2nd 1	0-4-0	Pittsburgh	786	7-1885	14" x 22"	43"	56,000
2nd 2-3	0-6-0	Brooks	1377-1378	11-1888	17" x 24"	48"	81,000
4	0-6-0	Brooks	1379	11-1888	17" x 24"	48"	81,000
2nd 5	0-4-0	Brooks	1898	6-1891	16" x 24"	48"	73,600
2nd 6	0-6-0	Brooks	1897	6-1891	18" x 24"	50"	102,300
2nd 7	0-6-0	Brooks	1792	1-1891	17" x 24"	48"	83,000
2nd 8-9	0-6-0	Brooks	2310-2311	6-1893	17" x 24"	48"	86,000
2nd 10	0-4-0	Brooks	2308	6-1893	17" x 24"	48"	81,000
2nd 16-17	2-6-0	Brooks	1523-1524	4-1889	19" x 24"	56"	101,600
2nd 18-23	2-6-0	Brooks	1403-1408	11-1888	19" x 24"	56"	101,600
2nd 24-26	4-6-0	Brooks	1892-1894	6-1891	19" x 24"	56"	116,500
27-28	4-6-0	Brooks	2313-2314	6-1893	19" x 24"	56"	116,500

Number	Type	Builder	Builder number	Date	Cylinders	Drivers	Total weight
29	4-6-0	Brooks	2312	6-1893	18" x 24"	56"	117,500
40	4-4-0	Taunton	398	12-1866	15" x 22"	60"	57,900
41	4-4-0	Taunton	413	8-1867	16" x 22"	60"	68,600
42	4-4-0	Taunton	484	12-1869	16" x 22"	60"	61,300
43	4-4-0	Taunton	519	12-1870	16" x 22"	60"	63,000
2nd 42-43	4-4-0	Brooks	1895-1896	6-1891	16" x 24"	62"	80,000
44-46	4-4-0	Brooks	1399-1401	11-1888	16" x 24"	68"	86,000
47	4-4-0	Brooks	1192	2-1887	16" x 24"	62"	80,300
48-49	4-4-0	Brooks	2306-2307	6-1893	16" x 24"	62"	80,000
50	4-4-0				16" x 24"		
51	4-4-0	Brooks	1528	4-1889	17" x 24"	62"	95,700
52	4-4-0	Taunton	389	6-1866	15" x 22"	60"	58,000
		Brooks	1616	1-1890	15" x 22"	56"	66,000*
53	4-4-0	Taunton	421	12-1867	16" x 22"	60"	58,000

*As rebuilt.

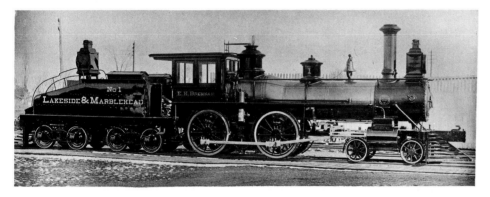

Few 4-4-0's left the builder's plant intended for switching duty. An 0-6-0 soon replaced this ark on the Ohio quarry road. The *E. H. Brennan* joined the Cleveland & Canton's roster in 1889. As No. 47 of the CC&S and W&LE, she worked on the Kent accommodation.—*Schenectady History Center.*

2nd 1 — Ex-C&W 1. Scrapped 1893.

2nd 2-4 — To W&LE 2nd 10, 2nd 11, 2nd 4, August 1899.

2nd 5-6 — To W&LE 4th 1, 2nd 21, August 1899.

2nd 7 — Ordered by CC&S as Cleveland Belt Line 100. To W&LE 2nd 12.

2nd 8-9 — To W&LE 2nd 13, 2nd 9, August 1899.

2nd 10 — To W&LE 4th 2 August 1899.

16-28 — To W&LE 141-153 August 1899.

29 — To W&LE 129 August 1899.

40 — Ex-Old Colony 88 acquired 1888. Originally Taunton Branch Railroad, then Boston, Clinton & Fitchburg 34, E. Baylies. Renumbered 54, July 1891. To W&LE 3rd 42, August 1899.

41 — Ex-Old Colony 90, Fitchburg. Originally BC&F 8. New boiler 1884. To CC&S in 1888. Renumbered 55 July 1891. To W&LE 3rd 43.

42 — Ex-Old Colony 92, N. Thayer, acquired 1888. Originally BC&F 11. Demolished by boiler explosion leaving Newburgh with train 13 for Chagrin Falls February 3, 1891.

43 — Ex-Old Colony 94, H. A. Blood, acquired 1888. Originally BC&F 14. Renumbered 56 July 1891. Scrapped about 1894.

2nd 42-43 — To W&LE 2nd 51-52 August 1899.

44-46 — To W&LE 3rd 44, 3rd 45, 2nd 46 August 1899.

47 — Ex-Lakeside & Marblehead 1, E. H. Brennan, acquired 1889 for $7600. It is possible that this was yet another Old Colony Taunton reboilered by Brooks. To W&LE 2nd 47 August 1899.

48 — To W&LE 2nd 48 August 1899.

49 — Derailed and rolled down embankment south of Carrollton on August 19, 1896; so badly damaged that it was never repaired. Scrapped 1899 by W&LE.

50 — Named Prosperity. Acquired 1888 in used condition. Some claim this was a former Cleveland & Pittsburgh engine; others say she came from the PFW&C. Intended to be deliberately wrecked in head-on with 52 on C&W branch in 1889, but when the stunt was dropped this engine was rebuilt by Master Mechanic John Bean about 1891. Scrapped by the W&LE in 1899.

51 — Renumbered 2nd 40 July 1891. To W&LE 2nd 62 August 1899.

52 — Ex-Old Colony 32, Dighton, acquired in 1889. After staged wreck was dropped, this engine was sent to Brooks and rebuilt with new boiler. Outshopped in January 1890. Prior to being rebuilt, was named Free Trade. Renumbered 2nd 41 July 1891. To W&LE 3rd 41.

53 — Ex-Old Colony 35, St. James, acquired in 1889. Retired about 1894.

W&LE 618 — shown resting at Canton in 1906 — was built by Brooks in 1893 as Cleveland, Canton & Southern 27. CC&S Ten-Wheelers had far greater steaming capacity than the over-cylindered Moguls which were first employed on the road's standard-gauge coal drags. — *Collection of John A. Rehor.*

CLEVELAND BELT & TERMINAL RAILROAD 1892-1899

Number	Type	Builder	Builder number	Date	Cylinders	Drivers	Total weight
100	4-6-0	Brooks	2130	8-1892	17″ x 24″	50″	102,000

Note: To W&LE 2nd 20 August 1899.

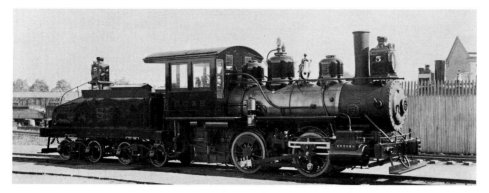

CC&S paid Brooks $7575 for 0-4-0 No. 5 in 1891. Tiny-appearing, the pony was heavier and more powerful than any of the narrow-gauge engines that formerly worked the Tip-Top Route. The W&LE assigned her class A-1 and the number 1 in 1899. — *Collection of Jack Lozier.*

CC&S subsidiary Cleveland Belt & Terminal owned a wagon-top 4-6-0 with 50-inch drivers. It was built by Brooks in 1892 and became W&LE 20 in 1899. — *Schenectady History Center.*

W&LE — LOCOMOTIVES ACQUIRED 1899-1916

Number	Type	Class	Builder	Builder number	Date
4th 1	0-4-0	A-1	Brooks	1898	6-1891
4th 2	0-4-0	A-2	Brooks	2308	6-1893
2nd 4, 10, 11	0-6-0	B-1	Brooks	1379, 1377, 1378	11-1888
3rd 3-4	0-4-0	A-3	Baldwin	22184-22185	5-1903
3rd 5	0-4-0	A-3	Baldwin	22199	6-1903
2nd 9, 13	0-6-0	B-1	Brooks	2311, 2310	6-1893
2nd 12	0-6-0	B-1	Brooks	1792	1-1891
2nd 20	4-6-0	G-1	Brooks	2130	8-1892
2nd 21	0-6-0	B-2	Brooks	1897	6-1891
2nd 24	0-6-0	B-2	Pittsburgh	2269	2-1901
3rd 25, 2nd 26	0-6-0	B-2	Pittsburgh	2270-2271	3-1901
3rd 27-28, 2nd 29	0-6-0	B-2	Pittsburgh	2364-2366	1-1902
2nd 30, 3rd 31-32	0-6-0	B-2	Baldwin	22181, 22224, 22225	6-1903
3rd 41	4-4-0	D-1	Brooks	1616	1-1890
3rd 42	4-4-0		Taunton	398	12-1866
3rd 43	4-4-0		Taunton	413	8-1867
3rd 44-45, 2nd 46	4-4-0	D-2	Brooks	1399-1401	11-1888
2nd 47	4-4-0	D-2	Brooks	1192	2-1887
2nd 48	4-4-0	D-2	Brooks	2306	6-1893
2nd 51-52	4-4-0	D-2	Brooks	1895-1896	6-1891
2nd 62	4-4-0	D-3	Brooks	1528	4-1889
2nd 63, 3rd 64-65	4-4-0	D-4	Baldwin	22229-22231	6-1903
3rd 66-68	4-4-0	D-4	Baldwin	22259, 22308, 22329	6-1903
129	4-6-0	G-2	Brooks	2312	6-1893
141-142	2-6-0	F-1	Brooks	1523-1524	4-1889
143-148	2-6-0	F-1	Brooks	1403-1408	11-1888

Number	Type	Class	Builder	Builder number	Date
149-151	4-6-0	G-3	Brooks	1892-1894	6-1891
152-153	4-6-0	G-3	Brooks	2313-2314	6-1893
191-200	2-8-0	H-3	Pittsburgh	2052-2061	2-1900
201-202	2-8-0	H-3	Pittsburgh	2367-2368	1-1902
203-204	2-8-0	H-4	Pittsburgh	2369-2370	2-1902
250-251	2-8-0	H-5	Baldwin	21997, 22003	5-1903
252-253	2-8-0	H-5	Baldwin	22036-22037	5-1903
254-256	2-8-0	H-5	Baldwin	22051-22053	5-1903
257-259	2-8-0	H-5	Baldwin	22105-22106, 22114	5-1903
260-262	2-8-0	H-5	Baldwin	22140, 22149, 22150	5-1903
263-264	2-8-0	H-5	Baldwin	22189, 22270	5-1903
270	4-6-0	G-5	Brooks	3140	2-1899
349	4-4-0		Baldwin	11034	7-1890
2001-2006	4-4-2	E-1	Brooks	30916-30921	4-1905
2101-2110	2-8-0	H-6	Brooks	30845-30854	3-1905
2111-2150	2-8-0	H-6	Brooks	30855-30894	4-1905
2201-2206	0-6-0	B-4	Rogers	37537-37542	4-1905
2207-2208	0-6-0	B-5	Rhode Island	41177-41178	9-1906
2209-2214	0-6-0	B-5	Rhode Island	41179-41184	10-1906
2302, 2306-2308	2-8-0	H-7	Baldwin	29130, 29182-29184	10-1906
2309-2310	2-8-0	H-7	Baldwin	29196, 29230	11-1906
2311-2314	2-8-0	H-7	Baldwin	29246-29248, 29257	11-1906
2315-2318	2-8-0	H-7	Baldwin	29270-29272, 29287	11-1906
2319-2321	2-8-0	H-7	Baldwin	29296, 29304-29305	11-1906
2322-2325	2-8-0	H-7	Baldwin	29338-29341	11-1906
2326-2327	2-8-0	H-7	Baldwin	29389, 29406	11-1906
2328-2330	2-8-0	H-7	Baldwin	29429, 29495, 29511	12-1906
2401-2420	2-8-0	H-10	Schenectady	53722-53741	7-1913

Cross-compounds 203-204 had 33-inch low-pressure cylinder on left side, 22-inch high-pressure cylinder on right. When working compound these engines had only two exhausts per driver revolution. Intercepting valve permitted single-expansion operation. These 1902 Pittsburghs were simpled in 1909. — *Schenectady History Center.*

Fat-boilered D-4's came from Baldwin in 1903 for new W&LE express trains. They had 72-inch drivers, weighed more than 70 tons, and boasted a whopping 44 square feet of grate. The D-4's were renumbered into the 350 series in 1905, ultimately became the 2201-2206 and worked varnish as late as 1932. — *Collection of H. L. Broadbelt.*

DIMENSIONS OF LOCOMOTIVES

Number	Cylinders	Valve motion*		Drivers	Weight on drivers	Total weight	Boiler pressure	Tractive effort	Grate area
4th 1	16" x 24"	s		48"	73,600	73,600	150	16,320	15.3
4th 2 2nd 4th, 10, 11	17" x 24"	s		48"	81,000	81,000	150	18,423	15.4
3rd 3-5	17" x 24"	s		50"	92,600	92,600	160	18,842	15.4
2nd 9, 13	17" x 24"	s		48"	86,000	86,000	150	18,423	15.4
2nd 12	17" x 24"	s		48"	83,000	83,000	150	18,423	15.4
2nd 20	17" x 24"	s		50"	78,000	102,000	150	17,784	22.6
2nd 21	18" x 24"	s		50"	102,300	102,300	150	19,828	19
2nd 24-26	18" x 24"	s		51"	99,500	99,500	165	21,388	15.2
3rd 27-29	18" x 24"	s		51"	107,500	107,500	165	21,388	15.2
2nd 30-32	18" x 24"	s		51"	109,000	109,000	160	20,736	15.4
3rd 41	15" x 22"	s		56"	44,000	66,000	150	11,271	
3rd 42	15" x 22"	s		60"		58,000			
3rd 43	16" x 22"	s		60"		68,600			
3rd 44-46	16" x 24"	s		68"	58,000	86,000	150	11,520	15.1
2nd 47	16" x 24"	s		62"	51,600	80,300	150	12,842	15.3
2nd 48, 51, 52	16" x 24"	s		62"	52,000	80,000	150	12,635	15.1
2nd 62	17" x 24"	s		62"	61,200	95,700	150	14,267	16.2
2nd 63-68	19½" x 26"	s		72"	94,740	140,240	190	22,175	44.1
129	18" x 24"	s		56"	91,000	117,500	155	18,294	22.6
141-148	19" x 24"	s		56"	85,400	101,600	160	21,040	16.6
149-153	19" x 24"	s		56"	93,600	116,500	160	21,040	21.7
191-200	20" x 28"	s		57"	132,200	148,500	180	30,064	30.3 (A)
201-202	20" x 28"	s		57"	135,600	151,200	180	30,064	30.2
203-204	22" and 33" x 28"	s		57"	142,000	161,000	200	31,700	30.2 (B)
	20" x 28"	s		57"	135,600	151,200	180	30,064	30.2 (C)
250-264	15½" and 26" x 30"	p		57"	169,040	190,940	180	35,512	47 (D)
	21" x 30"	s		57"	163,160	186,460	200	34,650	47 (C)
270	19½" x 30"	s	S	63"	118,000	158,000	180	27,704	32.5
349	no data								
2001-2006	21" x 26"	p	S	79"	100,400	190,500	200	24,670	46.7 (E)
	21" x 26"	p	S	79"	101,430	191,530	190	23,440	46.7 (F)
2101-2150	21" x 30"	p	S	57"	187,360	208,860	200	39,110	50.5 (E)
	21½" x 30"	p	S	57"	187,360	208,860	200	41,360	50.5 (G)
	21½" x 30"	p	S	57"	188,112	209,612	200	41,360	50.5 (H)
	22½" x 30"	p	B	57"	193,700	216,800	190	43,031	50.5 (J)
2201-2206	19" x 28"	s	S	57"	142,780	142,780	180	27,132	32.5
2207-2214	21" x 26"	p	S	52"	159,240	159,240	180	33,840	
2302-2330	22" x 30"			58"	198,600	224,000	200	42,558	
2401-2420	26" x 30"	p	W	57"	236,000	266,500	185	55,948	66.6 (K)
	26" x 30"	p	W	57"	244,420	274,920	200	60,484	66.6 (L)

* s — slide valve; p — piston valve; S — Stephenson; B — Baker; W — Walschaerts.

(A) Boiler pressure and tractive effort reduced to 165 and 27,577 lbs. in 1921.
(B) Cross-compound.
(C) After being simpled.
(D) Vauclain compound.
(E) As originally furnished.
(F) With arch tubes. These engines not superheated.
(G) With cylinders bored to 21½-inch diameter. Class H-6a.
(H) With superheater applied. Class H-6c.
(J) As rebuilt with new cylinders, superheater. Class H-6b. Boiler pressure and tractive effort increased to 200 and 45,296 lbs. in 1920.
(K) As originally furnished with superheater, Walschaerts. Known as "Logrollers."
(L) Boiler pressure increased to 200 lbs. 1916-1919. Weights shown are for engines with syphons and stokers added. Engines with syphons only weighed a total of 269,550 lbs. Those with stoker only weighed 273,270 lbs.

4th 1 — Ex-CC&S 5 renumbered September 19, 1899. To 1501, 1920. Dismantled at Brewster June 15, 1923.

4th 2 — Ex-CC&S 10 renumbered October 10, 1899. Laid up November 20, 1915. To I. Gerson & Sons January 20, 1917.

3rd 3 — Renumbered 1851 May 10, 1919. Last run July 3, 1931. Dismantled December 10, 1931.

2nd 4 — Ex-CC&S 4, relettered September 1899. Renumbered 3rd 15 November 9, 1902; 4th 28 May 16, 1905. Sold to General Equipment Company April 25, 1919.

3rd 4 — Renumbered 1852 January 12, 1921. Dismantled at Brewster July 1923.

3rd 5 — Renumbered 1853, 1920. Dismantled at Brewster July 1923.

2nd 9 — Ex-CC&S 9, relettered September 1899. Renumbered 3rd 35 August 19, 1905; 1806, 1920. Dismantled at Brewster July 1923.

2nd 10 — Ex-CC&S 2 renumbered September 27, 1899. To 3rd 26 January 19, 1905; 1801 March 13, 1919. Dismantled at Brewster July 1923.

Rhode Island B-5's 2207-2214 built in 1906 were owned by Lee, Higginson & Co. They were the biggest switchers on the Wheeling and had a tractive effort rating of 33,840 pounds. No. 2210 is shown at Columbia not long before she was sent to the Wabash on July 29, 1910. — *Collection of John A. Rehor.*

2nd 11 — Ex-CC&S 3, renumbered September 6, 1899; to 4th 27 February 6, 1905; 1802 September 10, 1920. Dismantled at Brewster September 12, 1921.

2nd 12 — Ex-CC&S 7 renumbered September 24, 1899; to 3rd 29 July 17, 1905; 1804, 1920. Leased to Cuyahoga Valley Railway December 5, 1918, to April 18, 1919. Dismantled at Brewster July 1923.

2nd 13 — Ex-CC&S 8 renumbered September 24, 1899; to 3rd 34 November 10, 1905; 1805 September 12, 1919. Dismantled at Brewster July 1923.

2nd 20 — Ex-CB&T 100 renumbered September 24, 1899; to 113 November 2, 1902; 582 November 14, 1904. Derailed and rolled down embankment near Carrollton October 14, 1908. Last run May 5, 1914. To I. Gerson & Sons January 20, 1917.

2nd 21 — Ex-CC&S 6 renumbered September 10, 1899; to 2nd 36 December 29, 1904; 1951 September 24, 1918. Dismantled at Brewster July 1923.

2nd 24 — Renumbered 2nd 37 February 25, 1905; 2nd 2101 April 10, 1919. Last run June 1, 1928. Dismantled at Brewster December 7, 1928.

3rd 25 — Renumbered 2nd 38 November 17, 1904; 2nd 2102 December 17, 1918. Laid up November 25, 1929. Dismantled at Brewster June 6 1930.

2nd 26 — Renumbered 2nd 39 January 8, 1905; 2nd 2103 April 3, 1920. Leased to United Furnace Company November 25, 1918, to June 11, 1919. Laid up November 22, 1929. Dismantled June 4, 1930.

3rd 27 — Renumbered 2nd 40 February 8, 1905; 2nd 2104 November 14, 1918. Last run November 24, 1929. Dismantled at Brewster May 28, 1930.

3rd 28 — Renumbered 4th 41 March 23, 1905; 2nd 2105 December 14, 1918; laid up May 12, 1928. Dismantled at Brewster July 5, 1929.

2nd 29 — Renumbered 4th 42 January 19, 1905; 2nd 2106 February 6, 1920; laid up November 25, 1929. Dismantled at Brewster June 1, 1930.

2nd 30 — Renumbered 4th 43 November 27, 1904; 2051 May 8, 1920. Last run April 22, 1929. Dismantled July 16, 1929.

3rd 31 — Renumbered 4th 44 November 27, 1904; 2052 March 22, 1919. Laid up February 9, 1929. Dismantled at Brewster September 20, 1929.

3rd 32 — Renumbered 4th 45 April 15, 1905; 2053 May 20, 1923. Last run February 1, 1928. Dismantled at Brewster December 7, 1928.

3rd 41 — Lettered W&LE September 1899. Renumbered 300 December 28, 1904. Last run March 28, 1907. Dismantled at Norwalk May 15, 1909.

3rd 42 — Ex-CC&S 54 renumbered October 18, 1899. Dismantled at Canton July 14, 1900.

3rd 43 — Ex-CC&S 55 renumbered September 15, 1899. Dismantled at Canton July 14, 1900.

3rd 44 — Ex-CC&S 44 relettered September 1899. Renumbered 311 December 26, 1904. Leased to PL&W October 14, 1907, to January 2, 1908. Last run December 15, 1908. Dismantled at Norwalk May 15, 1909.

3rd 45 — Ex-CC&S 45 relettered September 1899. Wrecked by an open switch at Cassingham Mine November 4, 1902; Engineer J. C. Reinhold killed. Renumbered 312 January 13, 1905. Last run December 31, 1915. To I. Gerson & Sons January 20, 1917.

2nd 46 — Ex-CC&S 46 relettered September 1899. Renumbered 313 January 25, 1905; 1151, 1920. Dismantled at Brewster June 15, 1923.

2nd 47 — Ex-CC&S 47 relettered September 1899. Renumbered 314 April 15, 1905. Dismantled at Brewster December 2, 1911.

2nd 48 — Ex-CC&S 48 relettered September 1899. Renumbered 315 January 10, 1905; 1251 November 18, 1919. Dismantled December 14, 1925.

2nd 51 — Ex-CC&S 2nd 42 renumbered September 3, 1899; to 316 December 24, 1904; 1252 June 24, 1919. Last run January 6, 1927. Dismantled at Brewster April 12, 1927.

2nd 52 — Ex-CC&S 2nd 43 renumbered September 17, 1899; to 317 January 10, 1905; 1253 April 27, 1919. Dismantled at Brewster June 1923.

2nd 62 — Ex-CC&S 2nd 40 renumbered October 18, 1899; to 325 June 7, 1905; 1404 November 29, 1918. Dismantled at Brewster December 14, 1925.

2nd 63 — Renumbered 350 February 14, 1905; 2nd 2201 February 5, 1920. Wrecked when ran into rear of freight train at Twinsburg August 2, 1911. Last run September 5, 1931 (into Canton). Dismantled December 22, 1931.

2nd 64 — Renumbered 351 March 25, 1905; 2nd 2202 February 15, 1920. Last run February 25, 1932 (No. 3, Harmon-Toledo). Dismantled July 11, 1933.

3rd 65 — Renumbered 352 July 9, 1905; 2nd 2203 December 8, 1919. Wrecked in head-on collision with 354 near Zoar in 1915. Wrecked by derailment at Cowans August 14, 1918. Last run March 16, 1932 (No. 34 into Brewster). Dismantled at Brewster August 4, 1932.

3rd 66 — Renumbered 353 November 30, 1906; 2nd 2204 November 25, 1918. Last run April 19, 1927. Dismantled at Brewster June 6, 1927.

3rd 67 — Renumbered 354 November 25, 1904; 2nd 2205 April 25, 1919. Wrecked by derailment at Barrs Mills 1904. Wrecked in head-on with 352 near Zoar in 1915. Leased to WPT November 20, 1913, to June 20, 1914. Last run May 24, 1931 (into Pine Valley). Dismantled December 19, 1931.

3rd 68 — Renumbered 355 December 22. 1904; 2nd 2206 September 6, 1919. Last run August 2, 1932 (into Brewster). Dismantled November 24, 1932.

129 — Ex-CC&S 29 renumbered September 6, 1899; to 591 January 6, 1906; 1811 September 12, 1919. Dismantled at Brewster July 1923.

141 — Ex-CC&S 16 renumbered September 18, 1899; to 606 December 14, 1904. Last run February 19, 1916. To I. Gerson & Sons January 20, 1917.

142 — Ex-CC&S 17 renumbered September 6, 1899; to 607 December 29, 1904. Dismantled at Brewster August 31, 1911.

143 — Ex-CC&S 18 renumbered September 10, 1899; to 600 December 27, 1904. Assigned 2109 in 1918 but not renumbered. Condemned July 26, 1918. Dismantled at Brewster June 15, 1923.

144 — Ex-CC&S 19 renumbered September 23, 1899; to 601 June 23, 1905. Last run June 24, 1914. To I. Gerson & Sons January 20, 1917.

145 — Ex-CC&S 20 renumbered September 19, 1899; to 602 February 15, 1906. Last run May 5, 1915. To I. Gerson & Sons January 20, 1917.

146 — Ex-CC&S 21 renumbered September 3, 1899; to 603 February 24, 1906. Condemned and sold November 30, 1917.

147 — Ex-CC&S 22 renumbered September 29, 1899; to 604 September 15, 1908. Dismantled at Brewster March 3, 1913.

148 — Ex-CC&S 23 renumbered September 11, 1899; to 605 March 26, 1905. Wrecked in head-on collision with Morgan Run Railway 1 near Coshocton November 25, 1899. Dismantled at Brewster March 22, 1913.

149 — Ex-CC&S 24 renumbered September 5, 1899; to 615 February 25, 1905. Wrecked by a washout near Morgan Run about 1900. Dismantled at Norwalk February 4, 1910.

150 — Ex-CC&S 25 renumbered September 4, 1899; to 616 May 23, 1905. Last run July 6, 1916. Retired and sold November 30, 1917.

151 — Ex-CC&S 26 renumbered September 27, 1899; to 617 November 23, 1904. Dismantled at Norwalk May 13, 1910.

152 — Ex-CC&S 27 renumbered September 30, 1899; to 618 January 10, 1906; assigned No. 1812 in 1918 but not renumbered. Last run August 8, 1918. Dismantled July 1923.

153 — Ex-CC&S 28 renumbered September 15, 1899; to 619 July 25, 1905. Dismantled at Brewster June 21, 1913.

191 — Renumbered 670 December 10, 1904; 3001 September 30, 1920. Last run August 15, 1926. Dismantled at Brewster September 10, 1926.

192 — Renumbered 671 February 3, 1905. Leased to PL&W March 16-May 28, 1915. Sold to General Equipment Company November 30, 1917. To Clover Leaf 134 and Nickel Plate 834.

193 — Renumbered 672 February 3, 1905; 3002 November 26, 1920. Last run February 1, 1927. Dismantled at Brewster April 12, 1927.

194 — Renumbered 673 March 13, 1905; 3003 August 11, 1923. Last run November 22, 1928. Dismantled at Brewster July 19, 1929.

195 — Renumbered 674 November 17, 1904; 3004 July 3, 1919. Wrecked when overturned at high speed near West Lafayette about 1910. Wrecked in head-on collision with 2107 at Norwalk November 9, 1914. Last run September 4, 1929. Dismantled at Brewster September 30, 1929.

196 — Renumbered 675 January 28, 1905. Sold to General Equipment Company November 30, 1917. To Clover Leaf 135 and Nickel Plate 835.

197 — Renumbered 676 November 5, 1904; 3005 October 3, 1919. Leased to Wabash Pittsburgh Terminal July 14, 1909, to January 27, 1910. Last run September 9, 1930. Dismantled at Brewster May 26, 1931.

198 — Renumbered 677 January 26, 1905; 3006 August 4, 1920. Leased to WPT June 29, 1909, to January 5, 1910. Last run February 2, 1929. Dismantled at Brewster July 23, 1929.

199 — Renumbered 678 January 6, 1905; 3007 December 30, 1919. Leased to PL&W November 19, 1907, to June 6, 1908. Last run November 13, 1927. Dismantled December 8, 1927.

200 — Renumbered 679 May 2, 1905; 3008 December 10, 1920. Last run May 31, 1928. Dismantled at Brewster July 12, 1928.

201 — Renumbered 680 December 10, 1904; 3009 January 25, 1921. Last run July 5, 1933. Dismantled at Brewster August 4, 1933.

202 — Renumbered 681 May 26, 1905; 3010 February 3, 1919. Last run October 29, 1927. Dismantled at Brewster December 8, 1927.

203 — Renumbered 682 July 7, 1905. Simpled at P&LE's McKees Rocks (Pa.) shops April 9, 1909, and reclassed H-3. Last run June 13, 1914. Retired December 31, 1916.

204 — Renumbered 683 December 23, 1904; 3011 December 6, 1920. Simpled at McKees Rocks March 29, 1909, and reclassed H-3. Last run May 25, 1926. Dismantled at Brewster June 21, 1926.

250 — Renumbered 700 November 29, 1905; 3551 July 7, 1919. Simpled at McKees Rocks October 7, 1907. Last run April 1, 1931. Dismantled May 28, 1931.

251 — Renumbered 701 October 30, 1905; 3552 August 22, 1923.

Simpled at McKees Rocks October 19, 1907. Last run May 10, 1932. Dismantled August 5, 1932.

252 — Renumbered 702 January 11, 1906; 3553 October 8, 1918. Simpled at Lima Locomotive & Machine Works June 8, 1909. Last run December 5, 1930. Dismantled at Brewster May 29, 1931.

253 — Renumbered 703 July 6, 1905; 3554 July 23, 1920. Simpled at Norwalk January 31, 1907. Last run April 1, 1931. Dismantled May 31, 1931.

254 — Renumbered 704 November 29, 1904; 3555 August 13, 1920. Simpled at Lima May 15, 1909. Last run July 1928. Dismantled October 12, 1928.

255 — Renumbered 705 November 5, 1904; 3556 December 4, 1919. Simpled at Norwalk November 28, 1906. Last run January 18, 1932 (Brewster to Zanesville). Dismantled at Brewster August 3, 1932.

256 — Renumbered 706 November 21, 1905; 3557 November 13, 1919. Simpled at McKees Rocks September 12, 1907. Last run September 20, 1932 (Zanesville to Brewster). Dismantled November 2, 1932.

257 — Renumbered 707 May 27, 1905; 3558 November 20, 1919. Simpled at Norwalk June 12, 1907. Last run August 31, 1928. Dismantled December 14, 1928.

258 — Renumbered 708 October 6, 1905; 3559 March 13, 1919. Simpled at Norwalk February 28, 1907. Last run March 22, 1930. Dismantled May 16, 1930.

259 — Renumbered 709 March 30, 1905; 3560 September 27, 1919. Simpled at Norwalk March 29, 1907. Last run March 15, 1928. Dismantled July 13, 1928.

260 — Renumbered 710 February 11, 1905; 3561 June 29, 1919. Simpled at Norwalk December 31, 1906. Last run September 26, 1931. Dismantled at Brewster December 12, 1931.

261 — Renumbered 711 January 20, 1905; 3562 July 23, 1919. Simpled at Norwalk February 28, 1906. Last run September 9, 1931. Dismantled December 21, 1931.

262 — Renumbered 712 April 15, 1905; 3563 January 19, 1919. Simpled at Norwalk September 29, 1906. Last run August 23, 1933. Dismantled October 6, 1933.

263 — Renumbered 713 January 22, 1905; 3564 January 19, 1919. Simpled at Norwalk July 16, 1908. Last run January 22, 1931. Dismantled May 31, 1931.

264 — Renumbered 714 September 23, 1905; 3565 November 10, 1918. Simpled at Norwalk August 14, 1906. Last run March 26, 1929. Dismantled July 2, 1929.

270 — Ex-Coshocton, Otsego & Eastern 3 renumbered January 1, 1917; renumbered 2751 February 20, 1919. Last run August 17, 1931. Dismantled December 17, 1931.

349 — Ex-Pittsburgh, Lisbon & Western 4, received at Norwalk July 12, 1904. Lettered W&LE and renumbered January 3, 1905. Demolished in a wreck at Bridgeville, Pa. (WPT) April 29, 1907. Taken to Norwalk and dismantled there May 1908.

2001 — Ex-Wabash Pittsburgh Terminal 2001 relettered October 31, 1905. Renumbered 2301 May 17, 1919. Leased to Wabash December 29, 1907, to March 4, 1909. Last run July 16, 1938 (No. 35, Harmon to Cleveland). Dismantled at Brewster October 12, 1938.

2002 — Ex-WPT 2002 relettered October 12, 1905; renumbered 2nd 2302 December 5, 1918. Last run April 29, 1938 (No. 35, Wheeling to Harmon). Dismantled at Brewster October 6, 1938.

2003 — Ex-WPT 2003 relettered December 14, 1905. Renumbered 2303 July 9, 1919. Last run July 17, 1938 (No. 35, Wheeling to Cleveland). Dismantled at Brewster October 4, 1938.

2004 — Ex-WPT 2004 relettered October 12, 1905. Renumbered 2304 November 17, 1918. Last run November 20, 1932 (No. 35, Harmon-Cleveland). Dismantled at Brewster June 22, 1934.

2005 — Ex-WPT 2005 relettered September 6, 1905; renumbered 2305 October 14, 1918. Last run October 19, 1935 (No. 32, Cleveland to Harmon). Dismantled at Brewster May 5, 1937.

2006 — Ex-WPT 2006 relettered September 22, 1905. Renumbered 2nd 2306 June 25, 1920. Leased to Wabash December 29, 1907, to March 4, 1909. Collapsed a burning trestle near Beach City July 27, 1924, while pulling No. 7 out of Zanesville. Engineer Harry Johnson killed. Wrecked by collision with an oil truck at Tiltonsville April 11, 1928, while pulling No. 35. Repaired with Timken type C roller bearings applied to tender journals. Last run June 20, 1938 (No. 35, Wheeling to Harmon). Dismantled at Brewster September 28, 1938.

2101 — Ex-WPT 2101 relettered September 12, 1905; to H-6a June 4, 1912; renumbered 4101 January 11, 1919. Last run December 1, 1937. Dismantled October 2, 1939.

2102 — Ex-WPT 2102 relettered October 16, 1905; to H-6a October 21, 1911; renumbered 4102 November 19, 1918. Last run October 17, 1939. Dismantled November 8, 1941.

2103 — Ex-WPT 2103 relettered October 30, 1905; to H-6a May 31, 1910; renumbered 4103 July 30, 1920. Received boiler 30892 from 4120 April 1927. Last run November 3, 1945. Dismantled December 19, 1945.

2104 — Ex-WPT 2104 relettered October 18, 1905; to H-6a October 8, 1911; renumbered 4104 September 23, 1918. Last run June 19, 1939. Dismantled October 13, 1939.

2105 — Ex-WPT 2105 relettered September 1905; to H-6a November 5, 1911; to H-6b at Brewster and renumbered 444 September 1917; renumbered 4315 January 31, 1920. Last run May 6, 1949. To Luntz Iron & Steel August 14, 1950.

2106 — Ex-WPT 2106 relettered September 27, 1905; to H-6a May 1, 1911; renumbered 4105 February 10, 1919. Received boiler 30889 from 4310 November 1924. Last run July 13, 1944. Dismantled August 1, 1944.

2107 — Ex-WPT 2107 relettered October 10, 1905; to H-6a June 19, 1911. Wrecked in head-on collision with 674 at Norwalk November 9, 1914. Received boiler 30856 from 2112; rebuilt as H-6c, and renumbered 4153 June 12, 1919. Last run October 21, 1948. To Luntz Iron & Steel November 25, 1949.

2108 — Ex-WPT 2108 relettered December 1905; to H-6a March 3, 1912; to H-6b and renumbered 443 September 1, 1917; renumbered 4314 May 21, 1919. To NKP 4314 December 1, 1949.

2109 — Ex-WPT 2109 relettered October 17, 1905; to H-6a November 19, 1910; renumbered 4107 February 20, 1920. Roof canted to clear Robertsville tunnel April 1932. Laid up at Mingo Junction July 23, 1944. Dismantled at Brewster August 11, 1944.

2110 — Ex-WPT 2110 relettered October 11, 1905; to H-6a July 15, 1911; to H-6b at Alco's Pittsburgh Works January 1917; renumbered 430 April 14, 1917; 4301 June 17, 1919. To NKP 4301.

2111 — Ex-WPT 2111 relettered September 1905; to H-6a November 5, 1911; To H-6b at Brewster and renumbered 445 October 18, 1917; 4316 September 24, 1918. Last run May 6, 1949. To Luntz (Warren, O.) August 14, 1950.

2112 — Ex-WPT 2112 relettered September 7, 1905; to H-6a August 22, 1911; rebuilt at Brewster with new boiler No. 2, classed H-6c, and renumbered 4152 April 14, 1919. Last run January 31, 1946. To Luntz Iron & Steel (Canton, O.) November 25, 1949.

2113 — Ex-WPT 2113 relettered September 23, 1905; to H-6a October 8, 1911; renumbered 4109 December 6, 1918. Last run August 22, 1941. Dismantled November 11, 1941.

2114 — Ex-WPT 2114 relettered September 19, 1905; to H-6a July 18, 1911; renumbered 4110 December 6, 1918. Last run July 3, 1944. Dismantled August 3, 1944.

2115 — Ex-WPT 2115 relettered October 12, 1905; to H-6a May 2, 1911; to H-6b at Brewster and renumbered 440 June 19, 1917; renumbered 4311 May 19, 1919. Last run February 23, 1949. To Luntz (Warren, O.) August 22, 1950.

2116 — Ex-WPT 2116 relettered October 5, 1905; to H-6a October 10, 1911; Renumbered 4111 November 27, 1918. Laid up at Ironville December 3, 1937. Dismantled at Brewster November 7, 1938.

2117 — Ex-WPT 2117 relettered October 26, 1905; to H-6a August 9, 1912. Wrecked by head-on with 2416 at Long Run tunnel November 14, 1914. To H-6b at Brewster November 13, 1917; renumbered 4317 November 19, 1918. Last run August 8, 1948. To Summer & Company (East Buffalo) September 5, 1950.

2118 — Ex-WPT 2118 relettered September 16, 1905; to H-6a February 13, 1911; renumbered 4112 July 20, 1920. Last run November 16, 1940. Dismantled November 6, 1941.

2119 — Ex-WPT 2119 relettered November 13, 1905; to H-6a February 8, 1912. Wrecked by boiler explosion near Navarre (O.) August 12, 1906; rebuilt. To H-6b 448 at Brewster December 1917; renumbered 4319 December 23, 1918. Wrecked in 1919 and rebuilt at Brewster in January 1920 with Stephenson valve gear. Reclassed H-6c and renumbered 4156 at that time. To NKP 4156.

2120 — Ex-WPT 2120, relettered October 21, 1905; to H-6a August 7, 1911; to H-6b 431 at Pittsburgh December 1916; renumbered 4302 December 22, 1918. Received boiler 30868 from 4318 in May 1929. To NKP 4302.

2121 — Ex-WPT 2121 relettered November 15, 1905; to H-6a February 11, 1912; renumbered 4113 June 28, 1919. Last run December 12, 1939. Dismantled December 30, 1929.

2122 — Ex-WPT 2122, relettered October 21, 1905; to H-6a April 17, 1911; to H-6b 432 at Pittsburgh March 1917; to 4303 March 21, 1919. Received boiler 30864 from 4302 August 1930. Laid up October 3, 1940, and returned to service June 20, 1941, with boiler 30883 from 4123. To NKP 4303.

2123 — Ex-WPT 2123, relettered October 18, 1905; to H-6a June 1, 1911; to H-6c 4151 January 13, 1919. Boiler to 4308 July 2, 1946. Machinery dismantled October 8, 1946.

2124 — Ex-WPT 2124, relettered December 8, 1905; to H-6a March 17, 1912; to H-6b 447 at Brewster November 17, 1917; to 4318 October 27, 1918. Received boiler 30894 from 4312 September 1928. Last run October 25, 1948. To Luntz Iron & Steel (Warren, O.) July 27, 1950.

2125 — Ex-WPT 2125, relettered October 4, 1905; to H-6a March 9, 1912. Leased to WPT May 2, 1913, to January 9, 1914. Renumbered 4115 July 29, 1919. Last run July 31, 1944. Dismantled at Brewster August 7, 1944.

2126 — Ex-WPT 2126, relettered September 25, 1905. Leased to Wabash August 9, 1905, to July 29, 1910. To H-6a in 1911; to H-6b 433 at Pittsburgh December 1916 (not renumbered until April 11, 1917); to 4304 September 9, 1919. Last run November 23, 1949. To Luntz Iron & Steel July 31, 1950.

2127 — Ex-WPT 2127, relettered September 30, 1905. Wrecked by collapse of a bridge at Connor February 10, 1910. To H-6b at Pittsburgh February 1917 and renumbered 434 March 31, 1917; to 4305 June 5, 1920. Last run June 18, 1949. To Luntz September 6, 1950.

2128 — Ex-WPT 2128, relettered October 12, 1905; to H-6a July 10, 1911; renumbered 4116 November 1, 1918. Last run July 6, 1944. Dismantled July 11, 1944.

2129 — Ex-WPT 2129, relettered September 1905; to H-6a March 18, 1911. Rebuilt at Brewster with boiler 30851 from 4153, classed H-6c, and renumbered 4154 August 1919. Dismantled November 20, 1946 with boiler applied to 4320.

2130 — Ex-WPT 2130, relettered September 11, 1905; to H-6a December 4, 1911; to H-6b 449 at Brewster December 29, 1917; to 4320 November 30, 1918. Received boiler 30851 from 4154 October 1946. To NKP 4320.

2131 — Ex-WPT 2131, relettered September 21, 1905; to H-6a January 26, 1911; to H-6b at Pittsburgh January 1917. Renumbered 435 April 12, 1917; 4306 October 16, 1918. Last run September 20, 1949. To Luntz July 20, 1950.

2132 — Ex-WPT 2132, relettered September 25, 1905. Leased to Wabash August 10, 1905, to July 29, 1910. To H-6a December 26, 1910; renumbered 4118 December 31, 1918. Last run July 10, 1944. Dismantled July 21, 1944.

2133 — Ex-WPT 2133, relettered October 28, 1905; to H-6a March 27, 1912; renumbered 4119 October 10, 1919. Last run July 20, 1944. Dismantled July 28, 1944.

2134 — Ex-WPT 2134, relettered November 13, 1905; to H-6a May 2, 1911; to H-6b at Pittsburgh December 1916; renumbered 436 March 30, 1917; 4307 December 9, 1918. Last run May 1, 1949. To Luntz (Warren, O.) August 25, 1950.

2135 — Ex-WPT 2135, relettered November 1905. To H-6a August 3, 1911. Rebuilt at Brewster with boiler 30873 from 2129, classed H-6c, and renumbered 4155 October 28, 1919. Last run January 17, 1946. To Luntz November 25, 1949.

2136 — Ex-WPT 2136, relettered September 6, 1905; to H-6a July

29, 1911; renumbered 4121 December 15, 1918. Demolished by boiler explosion while double-heading behind 4306 at Lonas August 3, 1924; rebuilt. Made last run November 30, 1938. Dismantled at Brewster December 30, 1938.

2137 — Ex-WPT 2137, relettered October 4, 1905; to H-6a May 27, 1911; to H-6b at Pittsburgh February 1917. Renumbered 437 March 27, 1917; 4308 December 30, 1918. Received boiler 30867 from 4151 September 1946. To NKP 4308.

2138 — Ex-WPT 2138, relettered October 16, 1905; to H-6a December 13, 1911; renumbered 4122 November 15, 1918. Received boiler 30890 from 4108 February 1924. Last run April 19, 1938 (Zanesville to Brewster). Dismantled October 27, 1938.

2139 — Ex-WPT 2139, relettered September 25, 1905. Leased to Wabash August 10, 1905 to July 29, 1910. To H-6a December 23, 1910; renumbered 4123 March 19, 1920. Last run November 24, 1939. Dismantled with boiler applied to 4303 November 4, 1941.

2140 — Ex-WPT 2140, relettered November 7, 1905. Wrecked by a washout near Rockdale, W. Va., on WPT July 1910. To H-6a September 7, 1911. Collapsed Black River trestle near Wellington, O., March 25, 1913; three men killed. Salvaged and rebuilt. Renumbered 4124 September 13, 1920. Last run October 2, 1945. Dismantled at Brewster November 24, 1945.

2141 — Ex-WPT 2141, relettered November 29, 1905; to H-6a February 13, 1911; renumbered 4106 June 29, 1919. Received boiler 30850 from 4105 March 1925. Last run January 25, 1939. Dismantled October 6, 1939.

2142 — Ex-WPT 2142, relettered October 14, 1905; to H-6a October 18, 1911; to H-6b 442 at Brewster August 4, 1917; renumbered 4313 September 20, 1918. Last run March 1, 1949. To Luntz Iron & Steel July 18, 1950.

2143 — Ex-WPT 2143, relettered October 20, 1905; to H-6a September 30, 1911. Pulled first highball freight from Cleveland to Toledo February 15, 1914. To H-6b at Pittsburgh March 1917; renumbered 438 April 6, 1917; 4309 April 7, 1919. Last run November 3, 1949. To Luntz July 20, 1950.

2144 — Ex-WPT 2144, relettered November 7, 1905; to H-6a 1911; renumbered 4114 November 21, 1919. Received boiler 30879 from 4155 September 1921. Last run December 6, 1937 (Zanesville to Brewster). Dismantled November 2, 1938.

2145 — Ex-WPT 2145, relettered November 11, 1905; to H-6a December 17, 1911; to H-6b at Pittsburgh January 1917; renumbered 439 April 2, 1917; 4310 February 12, 1919. Blew up at Halls (on Adena Railroad) May 9, 1924. Rebuilt with boiler 30882 from 4122 August 1924. To NKP 4310.

2146 — Ex-WPT 2146, relettered September 25, 1905. Leased to Wabash July 24, 1905, to January 20, 1911. To H-6a September 28, 1911; renumbered 4108 August 18, 1919. Received boiler 30888 from 4114 May 1923. Last run May 15, 1940. Sold to Otis Steel Company July 22, 1941.

2147 — Ex-WPT 2147, relettered October 14, 1905; to H-6a March 18, 1912; renumbered 4117 April 3, 1920. Last run March 20, 1937. Dismantled November 7, 1938.

2148 — Ex-WPT 2148, relettered September 21, 1905; to H-6a March 26, 1912; renumbered 4120 January 14, 1920. Received boiler 30893 from 4125 January 1926. Last run October 21, 1945. Dismantled December 10, 1945.

2149 — Ex-WPT 2149, relettered November 9, 1905; to H-6a September 1, 1912; renumbered 4125 April 11, 1920. Received boiler 30885 from 4106 October 1925. Last run September 26, 1938. Dismantled October 4, 1938.

2150 — Ex-WPT 2150, relettered October 5, 1905; to H-6a February 26, 1911; to H-6b 441 at Brewster July 15, 1917; renumbered 4312 October 20, 1918. Received boiler 30847 from 4103 in 1928. Last run December 11, 1949. To Luntz Iron & Steel (Warren, O.) July 27, 1950.

2201 — Ex-WPT 2201, relettered October 1905; renumbered 2701 January 23, 1919. Laid up at Mingo Junction July 29, 1937. To Luntz December 11, 1937.

2202 — Ex-WPT 2202, relettered October 1905; renumbered 2702 April 21, 1919. Laid up at Ironville November 7, 1935. Dismantled March 19, 1937.

2203 — Ex-WPT 2203, relettered December 5, 1905; renumbered 2703 November 30, 1918. Laid up at Mingo Junction September 28, 1936. Dismantled at Brewster March 30, 1927.

2204 — Ex-WPT 2204, relettered October 14, 1905; renumbered 2704 December 1, 1918. Last run July 25, 1935 (No. 163, Brewster to Gambrinus). Dismantled March 27, 1937.

2205 — Ex-WPT 2205, relettered October 18, 1905; renumbered 2705 December 11, 1918. Laid up at Zanesville August 16, 1935. Dismantled March 22, 1937.

2206 — Ex-WPT 2206, relettered September 23, 1905; renumbered 2706 December 3, 1918. Laid up July 15, 1936 (at Mingo). Dismantled March 24, 1937.

2207-
2214 — To Wabash 525-532 1909-1910.

2302-
2330 — To Wabash, same numbers, 1909-1910.

2401 — Renumbered 6051 March 12, 1920. Syphons applied July 1929. Last run August 5, 1933. Dismantled at Brewster November 1, 1941.

2402 — Renumbered 6052 May 18, 1919. Syphons applied December 1929. Last run May 26, 1935. Dismantled at Brewster October 21, 1941.

2403 — Renumbered 6053 October 25, 1918. Modified type B stoker applied December 1928. To NKP 6053.

2404 — Renumbered 6054 July 6, 1920. Duplex stoker applied November 1927. Last run January 3, 1933. Dismantled at Brewster October 1, 1941.

2405 — Renumbered 6055 September 29, 1918. Leased to PRR February 5 to May 2, 1918. Modified type B stoker applied April 1929. Leased to P&WV January 23, 1943, and was demolished in a wreck on that road March 11, 1943.

2406 — Renumbered 6056 June 13, 1919. Modified type B stoker applied May 31, 1928. To NKP 6056.

2407 — Renumbered 6057 February 3, 1919. Last run July 10, 1935. Dismantled October 14, 1941.

2408 — Renumbered 6058 November 10, 1919. Syphons applied November 1929. Last run May 23, 1930. Dismantled at Brewster October 28, 1941.

2409 — Renumbered 6059 October 5, 1918. Last run September 18, 1935. Dismantled October 30, 1941.

2410 — Renumbered 6060 June 4, 1919. Leased to AC&Y November 18, 1919, to February 29, 1920. Syphons applied September 1929. Last run November 8, 1944. To Luntz Iron & Steel November 25, 1949.

2411 — Renumbered 6061 October 23, 1919. Modified type B stoker applied 1928. Syphons applied March 1932. To NKP 6061.

2412 — Renumbered 6062 July 23, 1919. Type B stoker and syphons applied April 1930. Last run December 23, 1942. To P&WV under own steam December 31, 1942. P&WV 950 thereafter.

2413 — Renumbered 6063 December 25, 1919. Modified type B stoker applied July 1928. Syphons applied March 1931. Last run January 21, 1947. To Luntz Iron & Steel (Canton) November 25, 1949.

2414 — Renumbered 6064 September 19, 1919. Leased to Hocking Valley 1913. Wrecked at Hopedale, O., (P&WV) on December 25, 1917. Duplex stoker applied November 1927; syphons applied June 1930. Last run July 21, 1946. To Luntz Iron & Steel November 25, 1949.

2415 — Renumbered 6065 March 26, 1920. Damaged by fire at at Cleveland roundhouse May 29, 1924. Syphons applied October 1929. Last run May 28, 1935. Dismantled at Brewster October 16, 1941.

2416 — Renumbered 6066 November 4, 1919. Wrecked in head-on collision with 2117 at Long Run tunnel November 14, 1914. Modified type B stoker applied October 1928. Last run, to P&WV under own steam December 31, 1942. Became P&WV 951.

2417 — Renumbered 6067 May 5, 1919. Modified type B stoker applied February 1929. To NKP 6067.

2418 — Renumbered 6068 October 19, 1919. Syphons applied November 1929. Last run May 20, 1935. Dismantled 1941.

2419 — Renumbered 6069 September 11, 1919. Last run June 11, 1930. Dismantled at Brewster October 9, 1941.

2420 — Renumbered 6070 October 29, 1918. Last run June 11, 1930. Dismantled October 24, 1941.

"Logrollers" were just about the ultimate in Consolidations. Built by Schenectady in 1913, 2401-2420 (6051-6070) had a 66.6-square-foot grate, developed 60,484 pounds tractive effort, and weighed almost as much as a USRA light Mikado. — *Robert J. Foster.*

LOCOMOTIVES OF AFFILIATED COMPANIES
COSHOCTON, OTSEGO & EASTERN RAILROAD 1909-1917

Number	Type	Builder	Builder number	Date	Cylinders	Drivers	Total weight
1	no data						
2	0-4-0	Pittsburgh	1146	7-1890	17″ x 24″	50″	
3	4-6-0	Brooks	3140	2-1899	19½″ x 30″	63″	158,000

2 — Ex-Pittsburgh & Lake Erie 45 acquired about 1910.
3 — Ex-Lake Shore & Michigan Southern 5050 (originally numbered 355) acquired about 1911. To Wheeling & Lake Erie 270 in 1917.

Acquisition of Coshocton, Otsego & Eastern in 1917 added this Brooks 4-6-0 to W&LE roster. Prior to becoming CO&E 3 about 1911, the engine had been the 5050 of the LS&MS. As W&LE 2751, the 63-inch-drivered G-5 takes on coal at Cleveland on June 22, 1927. — *Rev. James H. Dean.*

ZANESVILLE BELT & TERMINAL RAILWAY

Number	Type	Builder	Date	Cylinders	Drivers	Total weight
1	0-6-0	Pittsburgh	1882	17″ x 24″	49″	72,000

Note: Assigned class B-1 by W&LE. Boiler pressure 120 lbs., rated tractive effort 14,430 lbs., grate area 20.3 square feet. Dismantled at Brewster October 25, 1911.

LORAIN & WEST VIRGINIA RAILWAY

Number	Class	Type	Builder	Builder number	Date	Cylinders	Valve motion*	Drivers	Total weight
1	H-9	2-8-0	Brooks	47767	12-1910	21″ x 28″	S	51″	191,000

*S — Stephenson, with piston valves.
Note: Originally built as Buffalo & Susquehanna 172 but never delivered to that road. To L&WV February 1912, cost $16,550. Boiler pressure 185 lbs., rated tractive effort 38,073 lbs., grate area 54.5 square feet. No superheater. Dismantled at Brewster October 1, 1946.

Zanesville Belt & Terminal's lone engine was an old Pittsburgh wagon-top with 17 x 24-inch cylinders. W&LE records indicate that it was acquired by the ZB&T in 1901 and probably came from the B&O. The 0-6-0 was dismantled at Brewster in 1911.

WEST SIDE BELT RAILROAD 1908-1916

Number	Class	Type	Builder	Builder number	Date	Cylinders	Drivers	Total weight
1-2	H-2	2-8-0	Pittsburgh	27190-27191	6-1903	22" x 28"	54"	176,400
3	G-2	4-6-0	Pittsburgh	1591	1-1896	18" x 24"	50"	104,380
4	B	0-6-0	Pittsburgh	722	3-1884	14" x 22"	43"	44,000
5	A-3	0-4-0	Pittsburgh	970	2-1888	17" x 24"	50"	74,100
340	D-5a	4-4-0	Brooks		1893	18" x 26"	62"	99,000
1000-1001	I-1	0-6-6-0	Schenectady	47113-47114	5-1910	20½" and 33" x 32"	54"	324,500

1-2 — Renumbered 750-751 January 1908. To PW&V 1-2 1917.
3 — Originally Pittsburgh & Lake Erie 81. To P&WV 3 1917.
4 — Originally Little Saw Mill Run 4. To Hunkin Brothers Contracting Company January 31, 1907, for $1600, F.O.B. Huron. Used in building of new docks at Huron, Ohio.
5 — Originally P&LE 39; renumbered 6 January 6, 1908. Retired 1915.

340 — Originally Union Pacific (W&LE records show it was UP 795). Acquired 1911 and retired 1916.
1000-1001 — Developed 93,500 lbs. tractive effort working simple; 73,900 lbs. working compound. 72.2-square-foot grate area. Converted to 2-6-6-0. Both leased to W&LE April 30, 1913. 1001 returned December 13, 1913; 1000 returned February 25, 1914. To P&WV 20-21, 1917. Later to Delaware & Hudson 1500-1501.

WABASH-PITTSBURGH TERMINAL RAILWAY 1904-1916

Number	Class	Type	Builder	Builder number	Date
1	G-1	4-6-0	Schenectady		
2	H-1	2-8-0	Altoona Shop		1882
3	H-1	2-8-0	Altoona Shop	609	1881
4	B-2	0-6-0	Baldwin	9536	10-1888
5	G-2	4-6-0	Pittsburgh	1153	8-1890
6	G-2	4-6-0	Pittsburgh	1155	8-1890
330-331	D-5	4-4-0	McKees Rocks		9-1896
900-901	H-7a	2-8-0	Brooks	45990-45991	4-1909
910-919	H-8	2-8-0	Brooks	45980-45989	4-1909
2001-2006	E-1	4-4-2	Brooks	30916-30921	4-1905
2101-2110	H-6	2-8-0	Brooks	30845-30854	3-1905
2111-2150	H-6	2-8-0	Brooks	30855-30894	4-1905
2201-2206	B-4	0-6-0	Rogers	37537-37542	4-1905

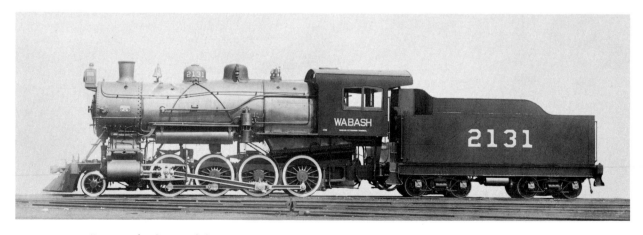

Piston-valved Consolidations 2101-2150 were outshopped at Dunkirk for Wabash-Pittsburgh Terminal in 1905. No. 2131 was rebuilt 12 years later and as the 4306 made her last run in 1949. — *Schenectady History Center.*

DIMENSIONS OF LOCOMOTIVES

Number	Cylinders	Drivers	Weight on drivers	Total weight	Boiler pressure	Tractive effort	Grate area
1	17" x 24"	55½"			120	12,740	
2-3	20" x 24"	50"	85,500	98,500	140	22,848	22.8
4	18" x 24"	50"	76,000	76,000	145	19,168	24.7
5-6	18" x 24"	50"	72,400	99,000	140	18,507	22.5
330-331	18" x 24"	68"	65,200	104,700	160	15,552	18.1
900-901	22" x 30"	55"	197,800	225,300	200	44,880	50.5
	25" x 30"	55"	197,800	225,300	160	46,393	50.5
910-919	22" x 32"	58"	200,500	228,400	200	45,395	50.5
	25" x 32"	58"	200,500	228,400	160	46,896	50.5
2001-2206	(See page 449, W&LE roster, for dimensions.)						

1 — Sold to Northwestern Car & Equipment Company July 21, 1906.

2 — Acquired 1904 by Pittsburgh, Carnegie & Western for construction work. Ex-PRR 1686; renumbered 820 March 1, 1905. Retired 1911.

3 — Acquired 1904 by PC&W. Ex-Pennsylvania 800. Sold to Northwestern Car & Equipment Company July 21, 1906.

4 — Originally Cornwall & Lebanon 4. Renumbered 175 November 5, 1904. Retired February 3, 1914.

5 — Ex-Pittsburgh & Lake Erie 64. Renumbered 805 November 5, 1904. To P&WV 805 1917.

6 — Ex-P&LE 66. Renumbered 806 May 8, 1905. To P&WV 806 1917.

330-331 — Ex-P&LE 9297-9298 acquired 1909. To P&WV 330-331 1917.

900-901 — Rebuilt 1912, class H-7b. To PW&V 1917. Scrapped 1937.

910-919 — Rebuilt 1910-1912 and classed H-8a. To P&WV, same numbers, 1917.

2001-2206 — To W&LE, same numbers, 1905.

"Georgia Tramps" 2307-2310 came from the Atlanta, Birmingham & Atlantic. These 1910 saturated Baldwins had 67-inch drivers and 19 x 26-inch cylinders. AB&A 34 became W&LE 2310 in 1921 and was scrapped in 1930. — *Collection of Roy W. Carlson.*

W&LE — LOCOMOTIVES ACQUIRED 1917-1949

Number	Class	Type	Builder	Builder number	Date
800-809	I-2	2-6-6-2	Brooks	57043-57052	4-1917
810-819	I-2	2-6-6-2	Brooks	57704-57713	5-1917
2nd 2307, 2310	D-5	4-4-0	Baldwin	34420, 34419	3-1910
2nd 2308-2309	D-5	4-4-0	Baldwin	34271, 34301	2-1910
3571-3572	H-7	2-8-0	Brooks	3882, 3892	6-1901
3573, 3574, 3578	H-7	2-8-0	Brooks	4065, 4069, 4066	12-1901
3575, 3579, 3580	H-7	2-8-0	Brooks	4089, 4090, 4073	1-1902
3576, 3577	H-7	2-8-0	Brooks	25939, 25942	10-1902
3951-3955	B-5	0-6-0	W&LE	1418	1929
3956-3958	B-5	0-6-0	W&LE	19-21	1930
3959-3966	B-5	0-6-0	W&LE	32-39	1935
3967-3975	B-5	0-6-0	W&LE	40-48	1937
3976	B-5	0-6-0	W&LE	49	1-1938
3977-3980	B-5	0-6-0	W&LE	50-53	1940
3981-3986	B-5	0-6-0	Schenectady	71967-71972	6-1944
5101-5105	C-1	0-8-0	Pittsburgh	60153-60157	11-1918
5106-5110	C-1a	0-8-0	W&LE	4-8	1928
5111-5115	C-1a	0-8-0	W&LE	9-13	1929
5116-5125	C-1a	0-8-0	W&LE	22-31	1930
6001-6010	M-1	2-8-2	Brooks	59720-59729	8-1918
6011-6020	M-1	2-8-2	Brooks	60375-60384	10-1918
6401-6410	K-1	2-8-4	Schenectady	68829-68838	4-1937
6411-6412	K-1	2-8-4	Schenectady	69121-69122	12-1938
6413-6415	K-1	2-8-4	Schenectady	69123-69125	1-1939
6416	K-1	2-8-4	Schenectady	69429	2-1941
6417-6422	K-1	2-8-4	Schenectady	69430-69435	3-1941
6423-6431	K-1	2-8-4	Schenectady	70021-70029	8-1942
6432	K-1	2-8-4	Schenectady	70030	9-1942
6801-6810	K-3	4-8-2	Roanoke shop	235-244	6/10-1926
8001-8002	I-3	2-6-6-2	Baldwin	52178, 52265	9-1919

Number	Class	Type	Builder	Builder number	Date
8003-8006	I-3	2-6-6-2	Baldwin	52287-52290	9-1919
8007	I-3	2-6-6-2	Baldwin	52313	9-1919
8008-8010	I-3	2-6-6-2	Baldwin	52330, 52350, 52424	10-1919

Mallet compounds 800-819 (later 8401-8420), bought from Brooks in 1917, were designed to haul heavy tonnage at low speeds with maximum fuel economy. After 1925-1926, these engines were rated at 88,382 pounds tractive effort when worked as two simple machines. — *Schenectady History Center*.

USRA articulateds 8001-8010 were Baldwin built and weighed 452,000 pounds in working order. Berks had replaced the Mallets on mainline freights by 1942. — *W&LE photo*.

DIMENSIONS OF LOCOMOTIVES

Number	Cylinders	Valve motion*		Drivers	Weight on drivers	Total weight	Boiler pressure	Tractive effort	Grate area
800-819	25½" and 39" x 32"	p	B	63"	362,500	435,000	200	80,484	99 (A)
2nd 2307-2310	19" x 26"	s	W	67"	97,350	144,950	190	22,624	33.2 (B)
3571-3580	21" x 30"	p	S	63"	158,000	180,000	200	35,700	43
3951-3955	21" x 28"	p	B	51"	164,900	164,900	190	39,102	33 (C, D)
3956-3964	21" x 28"	p	B	51"	164,900	164,900	200	41,160	33 (D)
3965-3980	21" x 28"	p	B	51"	167,850	167,850	200	41,160	33 (D, E)
3981-3986	21" x 28"	p	B	51"	168,000	168,000	200	41,160	33.1 (D)
5101-5105	25" x 28"	p	B	51"	214,000	214,000	175	51,200	46.6 (F)
5106-5125	25" x 28"	p	B	51"	219,130	219,130	180	52,500	46.6 (G)
6001-6020	27" x 32"	p	W	63"	239,839	321,678	190	59,850	70.8 (H)
6401-6415	25" x 34"	p	B	69"	263,045	413,170	245	64,135	90.3 (J, K)
6416-6422	25" x 34"	p	B	69"	265,500	415,000	245	64,135	90.3 (K)
6423-6432	25" x 34"	p	B	69"	265,500	414,500	245	64,135	90.3 (K, L)
6801-6810	28" x 30"	p	B	63"	273,418	399,150	225	68,880	84.1 (M)
8001-8010	23" and 35" x 32"	p	B	57"	360,000	452,000	225	80,300	76.3 (N)

* s — slide valve; p — piston valve; B — Baker; S — Stephenson; W — Walschaerts.

(A) Boiler pressure and tractive effort raised to 210 and 84,365 lbs. November 1917; to 220 and 88,382 lbs., 1925-1926. Delivered with Street Type C stoker, Type A superheater, DL&W type pilot. Cost, $53,427.65 each.

(B) "Georgia Tramps." Engine 2308 had 98,060 lbs. on drivers, 145,660 lbs. total engine weight.

(C) Boiler pressure and tractive effort later increased to 200 and 41,160 lbs.

(D) Equipped with Type A superheater, syphons, Timken roller bearings.

(E) Equipped with Timken inboard-bearing tender trucks; later replaced with conventional friction-bearing trucks.

(F) Equipped with Type A superheater.

(G) Equipped with superheater and syphons.

(H) Boiler pressure and tractive effort increased to 200 and 62,949 lbs. 1926. Delivered with Duplex stoker, Type A superheater.

(J) Engines 6401-6403, 6405, 6407 had 250 lbs. boiler pressure and 65,444 lbs. rated tractive effort.

(K) Delivered with Type E superheater, syphons, Elesco exhaust steam injector, Timken roller bearings, Hanna Type SF stoker, 22,000-gallon Buckeye tender with Timken roller bearings.

(L) Equipped with Type HT stoker.

(M) Equipped with Duplex stoker, Type A superheater, Baker long-lap valve gear. BL feedwater heaters removed by W&LE.

(N) Equipped with Duplex stoker and Type A superheater. Cost, $71,967 each.

Inefficient collection of ancient 0-6-0's and saturated Consolidations yielded yard jobs to 50 homemade switchers between 1928 and 1940. B-5's 3951-3980 had superheaters, syphons, and roller bearings. — *Wheeling & Lake Erie photo.*

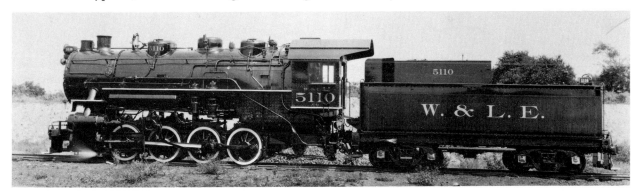

C-la's 5106-5125 were improved homemade versions of USRA 0-8-0's built for the Wheeling in 1918. August 1928 photo of 5110 was made shortly after the engine was fired up for the first time. — *Wheeling & Lake Erie photo.*

800 — Renumbered 8401 September 19, 1919. Modified type B stoker applied July 1930. Last run May 5, 1937. Dismantled June 28, 1939.

801 — Renumbered 8402 July 22, 1919. Last run June 21, 1937. Dismantled at Brewster July 24, 1939.

802 — Renumbered 8403 October 23, 1918. Last run January 24, 1939. Dismantled August 24, 1939.

803 — Renumbered 8404 November 21, 1918. Modified type B stoker applied October 1929. Last run February 3, 1937. Dismantled July 11, 1939.

804 — Renumbered 8405 October 2, 1919. Last run November 7, 1937. Dismantled August 31, 1939.

805 — Renumbered 8406 January 20, 1920. Modified type B stoker applied May 1927. Last run November 9, 1937. Dismantled September 6, 1939.

806 — Renumbered 8407 March 24, 1920. Syphons and modified type B stoker applied January 1929. Last run January 23, 1939. Dismantled August 16, 1939.

807 — Renumbered 8408 October 14, 1918. Last run October 25, 1935. Dismantled July 18, 1939.

808 — Renumbered 8409 July 16, 1919. Syphons and modified type B stoker applied November 1933. Last run January 12, 1936. Dismantled July 28, 1939.

809 — Renumbered 8410 February 8, 1920. Last run July 3, 1937. Dismantled August 7, 1939.

810 — Renumbered 8411 October 7, 1918. Last run July 11, 1935. Dismantled August 29, 1939.

811 — Renumbered 8412 July 26, 1920. Duplex stoker applied February 1924. Last run December 24, 1936. Dismantled September 11, 1939.

812 — Renumbered 8413 July 1, 1920. Timken bearings to tender trucks May 1926. Modified type B stoker applied May 1929. Last run October 26, 1937. Dismantled July 5, 1939.

813 — Renumbered 8414 May 13, 1920. Last run August 31, 1937. Dismantled August 2, 1939.

814 — Renumbered 8415 November 1, 1918. Last run July 14, 1935. Dismantled September 20, 1939.

815 — Renumbered 8416 April 30, 1920. Last run May 17, 1935. Dismantled at Brewster August 3, 1939.

816 — Renumbered 8417 October 13, 1919. Last run November 22, 1937. Dismantled September 13, 1939.

817 — Renumbered 8418, July 12, 1920. Last run October 10, 1930. Dismantled August 10, 1939.

818 — Renumbered 8419 July 24, 1919. Last run January 22, 1939. Dismantled at Brewster July 22, 1939.

819 — Renumbered 8420 October 31, 1918. Last run December 25, 1936. Dismantled at Brewster September 18, 1939.

2nd 2307 — Ex-Atlanta, Birmingham & Atlantic 35 received August 19, 1920. Initial run August 24, 1920. Last run August 23, 1929. Dismantled September 27, 1929.

2nd 2308 — Ex-AB&A 30 initial run on W&LE September 3, 1920. Last run April 22, 1929. Dismantled at Brewster July 12, 1929.

2nd 2309 — Ex-AB&A 31 initial run on W&LE February 9, 1921. Last run March 27, 1928. Dismantled at Brewster December 14, 1928.

2nd 2310 — Ex-AB&A 34 initial run on W&LE February 9, 1921. Dismantled at Brewster April 17, 1930.

3571 — Ex-NYC 5755 (originally LS&MS 755) leased May 5, 1923, and purchased August 15, 1923. Renumbered November 22, 1923. Last run March 30, 1931. Dismantled May 31, 1931.

3572 — Ex-NYC 5765 (originally LS&MS 765) purchased August 15, 1923. Renumbered October 26, 1923. Last run September 15, 1931. Dismantled at Brewster December 15, 1931.

3573 — Ex-NYC 5783 (originally LS&MS 783) leased May 6, purchased August 15, renumbered September 6, 1923. Last run August 29, 1930. Dismantled May 31, 1931.

3574 — Ex-NYC 5787 (originally LS&MS 787) leased July 11, purchased August 15, renumbered November 19, 1923. Last run October 15, 1931. Dismantled November 16, 1933.

3575 — Ex-NYC 5807 (originally LS&MS 807) leased May 8, purchased August 15, renumbered August 19, 1923. Last run October 16, 1931. Dismantled November 17, 1933.

3576 — Ex-NYC 5818 (originally LS&MS 818) purchased August 15, 1923. Renumbered November 25, 1923. Last run October 19, 1929. Dismantled December 12, 1929.

3577 — Ex-NYC 5821 (originally LS&MS 821) leased May 6, 1923. Purchased August 16, 1923. Last run July 16, 1930. Dismantled May 31, 1931.

3578 — Ex-NYC 5784 (originally LS&MS 784) leased, purchased, and renumbered August 1923. Last run February 11, 1929. Dismantled July 8, 1929.

3579 — Ex-NYC 5808 (originally LS&MS 808) leased and purchased August 1923. Renumbered January 30, 1924. Last run April 4, 1929. Dismantled July 2, 1929.

3580 — Ex-NYC 5791 (originally LS&MS 791) leased July 19, 1923; purchased August 15, 1923; renumbered November 12, 1923. Last run May 9, 1931. Dismantled at Brewster December 10, 1931.

3951-3986 — To NKP 3951-3986.

5101-5125 — To NKP 5101-5125.

6001 — Syphons applied May 1926. To NKP 6001.

6002 — Syphons applied September 1926. HT stoker applied 1930. To NKP 6002.

6003 — Sellers exhaust steam injector, syphons, and modified type B stoker applied October 1929. Wrecked at Pryor May 14, 1936,while double-heading with 6011. Wrecked by rockslide at Unionvale July 25, 1940. To NKP 6003.

6004 — Modified type B stoker applied March 1925. Syphons applied March 1928. To NKP 6004.

6005 — Sellers exhaust steam injector applied July 1925; replaced with Chicago type R in 1944. Syphons applied December 1927. Timken bearings to trailer June 1942. Boiler exploded because of low water August 24, 1944. To NKP 6005.

6006 — Syphons applied March 1929. To NKP 6006.

6007 — Syphons applied April 1926. To NKP 6007.

6008 — Syphons applied November 1926. Modified type B stoker applied 1931. To NKP 6008.

6009 — Syphons and type HT stoker applied November 1927. Wrecked in collision on P&WV at Avella, Pa., September 12, 1945. To NKP 6009.

6010 — Syphons applied November 1927. To NKP 6010.

6011 — Syphons and Timken bearings to trailer applied May 1925. Sellers exhaust steam injector applied August 1929; replaced with Chicago type R April 1944. To NKP 6011.

6012 — Syphons applied August 1926. To NKP 6012.

6013 — Syphons applied May 1928. Sellers exhaust steam injector applied 1929; replaced by Chicago type R in February 1944. Wrecked at Sherrodsville August 21, 1941. Wrecked at Connotton May 31, 1945. Timken bearings to trailer August 1942. To NKP 6013.

6014 — Syphons applied June 1926. HT stoker applied 1931. To NKP 6014.

6015 — Syphons applied September 1926. HT stoker applied 1930. To NKP 6015.

6016 — Syphons applied October 1927. Sellers exhaust steam injector applied 1929; replaced with Chicago type R in 1944. Wrecked at Jewett in head-on collision with P&WV 1000 July 16, 1937. To NKP 6016.

6017 — Syphons applied October 1926. Modified type B stoker applied 1929. To NKP 6017.

6018 — Syphons applied May 1926. HT stoker applied 1931. Wrecked by rockslide at Rockdale, W. Va., on P&WV June 10, 1947. To NKP 6018.

6019 — Syphons applied March 1926. To NKP 6019.

6020 — Syphons applied August 1926. HT stoker applied 1931. Wrecked at Bridgeville, Pa., on P&WV April 25, 1945. To NKP 6020.

6401-6403 — To NKP 6401-6403.

6404 — Wrecked in rear-end collision at Spencer, O., June 17, 1944. To NKP 6404.

6405-6408 — To NKP 6405-6408.

6409 — Wrecked in collision at Herrick April 14, 1945. To NKP 6409.

6410 — To NKP 6410.

6411 — Derailed and rolled into swamp at Snively December 17, 1941. Was dismantled at scene of accident and reassembled in Brewster shop January 1942. To NKP 6411.

6412-6420 — To NKP 6412-6420.

6421 — Hit broadside by NKP 724 at Bellevue April 3, 1943. To NKP 6421.

6422-6432 — To NKP 6422-6432.

6801 — Ex-Richmond, Fredericksburg & Potomac 515 (originally Norfolk & Western 200) initial run March 15, 1948. Last run October 24, 1949. To Luntz Iron & Steel October 18, 1952.

6802 — Ex-RF&P 516 (originally N&W 201) initial W&LE run April 9, 1948. Last run November 13, 1949. To Luntz Iron & Steel October 18, 1952.

6803 — Ex-RF&P 517 (originally N&W 202) initial W&LE run April 27, 1948. To NKP 6803.

6804 — Ex-RF&P 518 (originally N&W 203) initial W&LE run May 19, 1948. HT stoker applied April 20, 1949. To NKP 6804.

6805 — Ex-RF&P 519 (originally N&W 204) initial W&LE run June 7, 1948. To NKP 6805.

6806 — Ex-RF&P 520 (originally N&W 205) initial W&LE run June 17, 1948. To NKP 6806.

6807 — Ex-Denver & Rio Grande Western 1550 (originally N&W 206) initial run October 9, 1948. Last run October 4, 1949. To Luntz October 18, 1952.

6808 — Ex-D&RGW 1551 (originally N&W 207) initial W&LE run August 14, 1948. HT stoker applied June 1949. To NKP 6808.

6809 — Ex-D&RGW 1552 (originally N&W 208) initial run September 4, 1948. To NKP 6809.

6810 — Ex-D&RGW 1553 (originally N&W 209) initial run July 17, 1948. Damaged by fire at Norwalk March 12, 1949. Last run June 23, 1949, and sent to Brewster for overhaul. Work partly completed but suspended in 1950. Dismantled August 25, 1952,at Brewster.

8001 — Modified type B stoker applied July 1933. Derailed and overturned on Adena Railroad October 20, 1948, after colliding with truck. To NKP 8001.

8002-8003 — Modified type B stoker applied 1930 and 1933. To NKP 8002-8003.

8004 — Last run September 10, 1945. Dismantled at Brewster June 15, 1946.

8005 — Modified type B stoker applied 1931. Last run March 4, 1946. Dismantled at Brewster April 20, 1946.

8006 — Last run February 1, 1937. Dismantled December 31, 1941.

8007 — Last run June 1, 1943. Dismantled at Brewster October 28, 1943.

8008 — Last run February 10, 1935. Dismantled December 30, 1941.

8009 — To NKP 8009.

8010 — Last run March 5, 1943. Dismantled October 24, 1943.

"Water Buffaloes" 6801-6810 were built as Norfolk & Western 200-209 at Roanoke in 1926. W&LE brought about the 1948 reunion of K-3 clan after they had gone to Rio Grande and RF&P to ease wartime power shortages. — *Norfolk & Western Railway.*

Wheeling's Alco Berks featured Boxpok drivers, Timken roller bearings on all axles, Elesco exhaust steam injectors, and footboards. Nos. 6416-6422 were outshopped at Schenectady in 1941.

1000 h.p. DIESEL-ELECTRIC SWITCHING UNITS

Class	Type	Builder	Builder number	Date	Total weight	Tractive effort
D-1	B-B	Electro-Motive	998	4-1940	248,830	61,325
D-2	B-B	Electro-Motive	1089	8-1940	247,580	61,325
D-3	B-B	Electro-Motive	1422	6-1941	248,740	61,325
D-4	B-B	Electro-Motive	1423	8-1941	249,020	61,325

Note: To NKP 95-98, 1950-1951.

Diesel-electrics D-1 through D-4 were bought in 1940-1941 when volume of transfer traffic at Toledo outstripped capacity of steamers permitted to cross weak Maumee River bridge. These NW2's had Timken roller bearings. — *Electro-Motive Division.*

NICKEL PLATE ROAD
BUSINESS CARS

Number before and after 1930		Builder	Year	Over-all length	Capacity*	Light weight (tons)	Number of wheels	Body	Under-frame
1	1	Pullman	1929	83' 11"	9	91.3/107.3	12	steel	steel
2nd 27	2	Pullman	1925				12	steel	steel
	2nd 2	Pullman	1929	84'	7	95.7/98.1	12	steel	steel
22	3	Pullman	1916	81' 10"	8	91.4/94.5	12	steel	steel
2nd 25	4	Barney & Smith	1911	78' 9"	9	76.2	12	wood	steel
30	2nd 4	Pullman	1925	85' 9"	7	99.9	12	steel	steel
24	5	Pullman	1883	76' 4"	8	81.8	12	wood	steel
26	6	Pullman	1881	58' 5"	8	48/67.5	8/12	wood	wood
				67' 2"					steel
	2nd 6	Pullman	1923	82'		94	12	steel	steel
23	7						12	wood	steel
	2nd 7	Pullman	1923	82'		94	12	steel	steel
21	8	Jackson & Sharp	1887	59' 8"			12	wood	wood
27		Pullman	1883	58' 5"	3	43.9	8	wood	wood

*Plus accommodations for two porters.

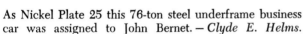

As Nickel Plate 25 this 76-ton steel underframe business car was assigned to John Bernet. — *Clyde E. Helms.*

Through the efforts of John H. Keller, car 5 has been preserved and renovated. — *Clyde E. Helms.*

From 1881 to 1920 car 26 was the rolling home of NKP's paymaster. The Pullman carried a copious inventory of indispensables, including one American Beauty flat iron, eight nickel-plated cuspidors, 10 brass finger bowls, 10 nut picks, and a dozen oyster forks. In later years the car carried number 6 and was assigned to the LE&W District superintendent. — *Clyde E. Helms.*

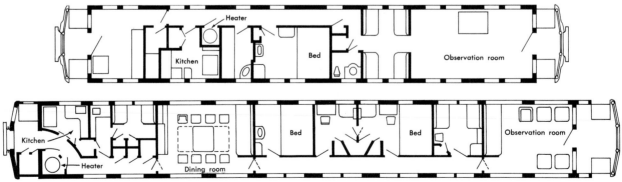

Cars 6 (upper) and 3, Pullman built in 1881 and 1916 respectively, accommodated eight.

Heaviest of all NKP business cars, the One-Spot was also the best riding. — *Clyde E. Helms.*

Car 2, built by Pullman as the *Friendship* in 1929, joined the Nickel Plate roster in 1941. — *Richard J. Cook.*

1 — Equipped with electromechanical air conditioning in 1934; modernized and equipped with Hyatt roller bearings 1948-1949. To N&W 1, 1965.

1st 2 — Sold 1933 or 1934.

2nd 2 — Purchased 1941 from Thomas F. Carey Company. Originally built for Paul Block and named Friendship. Equipped with Timken roller bearings. Total weight with air-conditioning equipment 98.1 tons.

3 — Originally Clover Leaf 400. Mechanical air conditioning added 1937. Total weight 94.5 tons.

4 — Built as NYC&StL 25. USRA 138 from 1918 to 1921; became camp car X-58524, 1952.

2nd 4 — Originally C&O diner 967; rebuilt as business car 30, 1934. Leased from C&O in 1943; purchased 1944. Renumbered from 30 to 4, 1951. Equipped with Timken roller bearings and mechanical air conditioning. To N&W 4, 1965.

5 — Lake Erie & Western 100 prior to 1923. Rebuilt with steel underframe at Stony Island 1924. Donated to city of Lima.

6 — Originally used as a pay car. Lengthened and rebuilt with steel underframe, new six-wheel trucks in 1921. To camp car X-58522 in 1951.

2nd 6 — Originally 8-section buffet-lounge, Carleton Club. Rebuilt as a business car at Calumet in 1951. Now used as dormitory car at Brewster, O.

7 — Prior to 1923 was LE&W business car 69. To camp car X-53083 in 1942.

2nd 7 — Originally 8-section buffet-lounge Pullman, Kitchi Gammi Club. Rebuilt as business car at Calumet in 1953.

8 — Prior to 1923 was Clover Leaf business car 60. Off the roster about 1934.

1st 27 — Prior to 1911 carried the number 25; sometimes used as the pay car. Damaged in 1918 and retired in 1920.

COACH AND CHAIR CARS

Number	Builder	Year	Over-all length	Capac-ity	Light weight	Wheels	Underframe	Body
1-24	Pullman	1882	60' 3"	60	24.4	8	wood	wood
27-32	Ohio Falls	1893	60'	62	30.6	8	wood	wood
33-42	Barney & Smith	1901	59' 10"	62	32/34.1	8	wood	wood
43-48	AC&F	1907	68' 6"	72	46.2/50.9	8	wood/steel	wood
49-58	AC&F	1910	68' 6"	72	46.2/50.9	8	wood/steel	wood
60-66	Pullman	1934	83' 3"	78	79.4/85	12	steel	steel
75-78	AC&F	1913	70'	72	56.5	8	steel	steel
80-89	Pullman	1923-1924	74' 9"	80	63.5	8	steel	steel
			74' 3"	52	73	8		
90-97	Pullman	1930	79'	80	62.5/72.5	8	steel	steel
100-109	Pullman-Standard	1950	82' 10"	52	63.5	8	steel	stainless steel/aluminum
250-259	Pullman	1882	60' 3"	64	24.4	8	wood	wood
842, 843, 853	Barney & Smith	1892	60'	57	28.2	8	wood	wood
855-871	Pullman	1906	78' 10"	84	52.5/58.5	12	wood/steel	wood
880-887	Pullman	1906	67' 8"		45.2	8	wood	wood
935	Jackson & Sharp	1887	59' 8"	62		8	wood	wood
951, 952, 956, 957	Jackson & Sharp	1888	59' 8"	62		8	wood	wood
960	Jackson & Sharp	1888	59' 8"	64		8	wood	wood
962, 963	AC&F	1900	67' 4"	72		8	wood	wood

Number	Builder	Year	Over-all length	Capacity	Light weight	Wheels	Underframe	Body
964-966	Barney & Smith	1904	78'	86		8	wood	wood
975	St. Charles	1894	59' 4"	54		8	wood	wood
976-977	St. Charles	1891	62' 4"	56		8	wood	wood
978-979	AC&F	1900	78'	46		12	wood	wood
980	Barney & Smith	1904	78' 2"	56		12	wood	wood

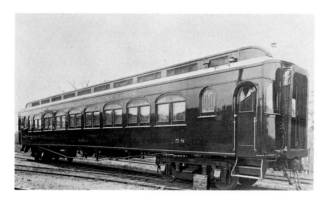

AC&F turned out 16 vestibuled coaches for *Nickel Plate Express* and sister trains. — *Collection of Arthur D. Dubin.*

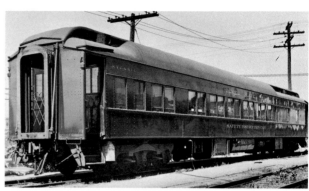

Pullman 12-1 sleeper *East Berkshire* was converted to safety instruction car 11 in 1953. — *Willis A. McCaleb.*

First all-steel passenger cars on NKP were four 70-foot coaches from AC&F. — *Collection of Arthur D. Dubin.*

Open-platform coach 843 was built by Barney & Smith in 1892 for the Lake Erie & Western. — *Clyde E. Helms.*

1-24 — Steam heat and automatic couplers applied 1894; Pintsch gas lights 1896; Gould steel platforms 1909-1913.
1 — To camp car X-53014, 1926.
2 — Retired 1929.
3, 4, 12, 16, 17, 24, 13, 19 became camp cars X-53000-X-53006, X-53008 in 1923.
5 — Retired 1926.
6, 8 — To camp cars X-53013, X-53009, 1925 and 1924.
9, 11,
15, 23 — Sold to Railway & Manufacturers' Agents 1921.
10 — Retired 1934.
14 — Destroyed in a wreck February 1911.
18 — Destroyed in a collision at Dover June 1891.
20 — Sold to South Buffalo Railway 1920.
21 — Retired 1918.
22 — Destroyed on NYC&HR December 1906.
27-32 — Equipped with steam heat and gas lights.
27 — Renumbered 2nd 22, 1911. To X-53007, 1923.
28-30, 33 — To camp cars X-53011, X-53012, X-58066, X-53010, 1924.
31 — To South Buffalo Railway 1920.
33-42 — Equipped with steam heat and gas lights. Nos. 39-42 rebuilt 1910 with vestibules. Total weight 34.1 tons.
33-36, 38 — To camp cars X-53019, X-53015 through X-53018, 1926.
37 — To camp car X-50987, 1925.
39-40 — To camp cars X-53028, X-53029, 1931-1932.
42 — To camp car X-53031 in 1931.
41 — Retired 1931.
43-58 — Equipped with vestibules, Gould platforms, steam heat. Rebuilt with steel underframes 1923-1925. Total weight 50.9 tons.
43-48 — To camp cars X-53078, X-53072, 2nd X-53006,

2nd X-53010, X-53077, and X-53073 circa 1939-1942.
49 — Destroyed by fire at Indianapolis May 1930.
50, 52, 56 — Retired 1946, 1951, 1944.
51, 53 — To camp cars 2nd X-58526 and 2nd X-53011 in 1952 and 1950.
54, 55,
57, 58 — To camp cars X-53079-X-53082, 1939-1942.
60-66 — 65-66 delivered with mechanical air conditioning; rest so equipped 1936-1937. Maximum weight 85 tons. All retired 1960.
75-78 — 75, 78 sold for scrap 1964; 76, 77 to camp cars X-58531, X-58532, 1952.
80-89 — Rebuilt and modernized 1946-1947 with 52 reclining seats, Frigidaire mechanical air conditioning, flat ceiling, radiant heat, large windows, aluminum sash. To Mexico 1964.
90-97 — Pullman mechanical air conditioning installed 1937. 97 to portable depot at Terminal Junction, O., 1959; 92-96 retired 1960 and sold for scrap 1964.
100-109 — Equipped with Hyatt roller bearings, Timken hotbox alarms, two compartments, two lounges, individual reclining seats, Frigidaire mechanical air conditioning, air-operated sliding doors.
250-259 — 250 demolished 1886 at Silver Creek; rebuilt as a combine in 1887. 251-254 retired 1918. 255-259 steam heat and automatic couplers 1894, Pintsch gas lights 1896, leather seats in place of rattan 1907, Gould platforms 1912. 255, 258, and 259 sold to South Buffalo Railway 1920. 256 and 257 retired 1931, 1925.
842, 843 — Ex-LE&W 142, 143. To camp cars X-55039, X-55040, 1925.
853 — Ex-LE&W 153. Retired 1926.
855-871 — Ex-LE&W 155-171. Most were rebuilt with steel underframes after 1924. Total weight 58.5 tons.
861, 865 — Destroyed by fire, Indianapolis, May 1930.

856, 857, 860 — To camp cars X-53045, X-53046, X-53063, 1934.

867, 870, 864 — To camp cars X-53074 through X-53076, 1939.

855, 858 — To camp cars 2nd X-53071, 1944; X-53085, 1953.

859, 862, 863 — Retired 1945-1946.

868 — Retired 1951.

866 — To camp car 2nd X-53012, 1949.

869 — To camp car 2nd X-53003, 1947.

871 — To camp car X-53084, 1942.

880-887 — Ex-LE&W 80-87 vestibuled. 880, 882-885, 887 rebuilt as combination mail-and-smoker cars 1923-1925; 881, 886 converted to camp cars X-53064, X-53066 during 1934.

935 — Ex-Clover Leaf 135. To camp car X-58068, 1926.

951-960 — Ex-Clover Leaf 151-160 with open platforms. 956, 957, 951 to camp cars X-58523 through X-58525, 1930; 952's body used as depot at Ossian, Ind., since 1932; 960 sold to D&TSL, their bunk car 152, 1929, and retired 1950.

962-966 — Ex-Clover Leaf 162-166. Vestibuled; some steel-sheathed. To camp cars X-53052 through X-53056, 1934.

975-977 — Ex-Clover Leaf 175-177 vestibuled chair cars. To camp cars X-58520, X-58521, 1st X-58526, 1927-1930.

978-979 — Ex-Clover Leaf 178-179 vestibuled cafe-chair cars. To X-53067, X-53057, 1934.

980 — Ex-Clover Leaf 180 cafe-chair car. Retired 1933.

DINING CARS, PARLOR CARS, SLEEPERS

Number	Builder	Year	Over-all length	Capacity	Light weight	Wheels	Under-frame	Body	Type
100-101	Wagner	1893	70'	30d	56.2	12	w	w	diner
102-103	Barney & Smith	1901, 1904	70'	30d	60.9	12	w/s	w	diner
104-105	Pullman	1927	81' 1"	30d	84/94	12	s	s	diner
106-108	Pullman	1930	81' 1"	30d	84/94	12	s	s	diner
120-121	Barney & Smith	1907	72'	18d	53.7/79.4	12	w/s	w	cafe-parlor
125-126	Pullman	1930	84' 6"	18d-20L	83.9/95.9	12	s	s	cafe-lounge
132-133	Pullman	1927	82' 11"	16d-7L	89.2	12	s	s	diner-lounge
150-151	Pullman-Standard	1950	82' 10"	18d-4L-5 dbr	67.8	8	s	a/ss	bedroom-diner-lounge
200-212	Pullman-Standard	1950	82' 10"	6 dbr-10 room.	68.5	8	s	a/ss	bedroom-roomette
215-216	Pullman-Standard	1939, 1937	84' 6"	18 room.	61	8	s	a/s	roomette

Ranked among the finest passenger cars ever built in America, *City of Cleveland* and *City of Chicago* were purchased for use in trains 5 and 6 between their namesake cities. The 1950 lightweights have five double bedrooms, an 18-seat dining room. — *Pullman-Standard.*

Pullman delivered 13 new blue and silver 10-6 sleepers to the Nickel Plate in 1950. — *Clyde E. Helms.*

Coaches 100-109 have two compartments with 52 reclining seats and two lounges. — *Pullman-Standard.*

100-101 — Cost, $14,147.71 each. Pintsch gas lights and steam heat added 1911. Electric lights and fans 1913-1914. 100 retired 1926. 101 became work diner X-53022 in 1928.

102-103 — Cost $12,770.65 each. Delivered with steel platforms, wide vestibules, gas lights, and steam heat. Electric lights and fans applied 1914. Both rebuilt with steel underframes about 1926. 102 to work diner X-53009, 1936; 103 to work diner X-53025 in 1936, now assigned to Frankfort relief train.

104 — Delivered with Timken roller bearings. Mechanical air conditioning added and revamped as diner-lounge, 1937. Dining compartment seats 18, lounge 10. Renumbered 127 in 1949.

105-108 — All delivered with roller bearings. Mechanical air conditioning added 1937. All revamped as diner-lounge cars and modernized. Renumbered 128-131, 1947-1948.

120-121 — Delivered with gas lights, steam heat, vestibules, and steel platforms. Rebuilt with steel underframes about 1926. To work diners X-53032 and X-53068 in 1936. X-53032 now assigned to Bellevue relief train.

465

125-126 — Equipped to seat 18 in dining area. There are 12 lounge chairs and 4 settees. Equipped 1940 with lounge and air conditioning. Modernized 1947, 1946.

132-133 — Converted from Pullman 6-bedroom buffet-lounges Commander and Captain in 1951, 1953. Both retired 1958.

150-151 — Equipped with Hyatt roller bearings, Timken hotbox detectors, air-operated sliding doors, mechanical air conditioning, kitchen, crew room. Named City of Cleveland and City of Chicago.

200-212 — Equipped same as 150-151 with Hyatt roller bearings, etc.

Named City of Buffalo, City of St. Louis, City of Lorain, City of Indianapolis, City of Painesville, City of Erie, City of Toledo, City of Peoria, City of Kokomo, City of Muncie, City of Findlay, City of Lima, City of Fort Wayne.

215, 216 — Equipped with Timken roller bearings, mechanical air conditioning. These are the original Pullman roomette demonstrators, No. II and No. I. Placed in service on trains 5/6 in August 1940. Originally named Robert de La Salle and Moses Cleaveland; renamed City of St. Marys and City of Coldwater in 1950.

COMBINATION CARS

Number	Builder	Year	Over-all length	Capac-ity	Light weight	Wheels	Underframe	Body
250, 252	Pullman	1882	60' 3"	42	24.4	8	wood	wood
821-826	Barney & Smith	1892	56'	28	37.2	8	wood	wood
880, 882, 885, 887	Pullman	1906	67' 8"	56	52.3	8	wood/steel	wood
883, 884	Pullman	1906	67' 8"	36	52.3	8	wood/steel	wood
902	TStL&W	1901	62' 6"	32		8	wood	wood
910	Jackson & Sharp	1887	56' 7"	30		8	wood	wood
912, 913	Jackson & Sharp	1889	56' 7"	26/34		8	wood	wood
914, 915	AC&F	1900	70' 10"	36		8	wood	wood

250 — Retired about 1918.
252 — To camp car X-53020, 1926.
821 — Ex-LE&W 121. Retired 1930.
822 — Ex-LE&W 122. To camp car X-55518, 1925.
823-824 — Ex-LE&W 123-124. Retired 1926.
825-826 — Ex-LE&W 125-126. To camp cars X-55055, X-55519, 1925.
880-887 — Ex-LE&W 80-87. Rebuilt 1923-1925 with steel underframe and converted to combination R.P.O.-smoker cars.
887 — Destroyed by fire at Indianapolis May 1930.
880 — To camp car X-53070, 1938.

882, 883 — To camp cars X-58527, X-50910, 1953 and 1956.
884, 885 — To camp car X-53065, 1934, and baggage car 303, 1942.
902 — Ex-Clover Leaf 102, rebuilt 1922 to R.P.O.-smoker. To X-58528, 1930.
910, 912, 914, 915 — Ex-Clover Leaf 110, 112, 114, 115 R.P.O.-smokers. To X-58522, X-58529, X-58530, X-58531, 1930.
913 — Ex-Clover Leaf 113, R.P.O.-smoker. Retired about 1930.

BAGGAGE, MAIL, AND EXPRESS CARS

Number	Builder	Year	Over-all length	Light weight	Wheels	Under-frame	Body	Type
300-309	Pullman	1882	45'	22.1	8	w/s	w	baggage
2nd 303	Pullman	1906	67' 8"		12	s	w	baggage
310-314	Barney & Smith	1901	56'	31.7	8	w	w	baggage
315-320	AC&F	1907	60' 9" / 64' 1"	39.4 / 44.5	8	w/s	w	baggage
321-325	AC&F	1910	60' 9" / 64' 1"	39.4 / 44.5	8	w/s	w	baggage
326-327	Pullman	1923	64' 7"	53.8	8	s	s	baggage and express
328-332	Pullman	1929	64' 6"	54.5	8	s	s	baggage and express
340-342	Pullman	1924	73' 4"	63.5	12/8	s	s	baggage and auto
343-344	Pullman	1929	73' 4"	59.5	12/8	s	s	baggage and auto
345-349	AC&F	1945	73' 7"	56.3	8	s	s	baggage
350-353	Pullman	1882	56'	39.3	8	w/s	w	R.P.O.-baggage
354-355	Pullman	1887	59' 9"	39.3	8	w	w	R.P.O.-baggage
356-359	Pullman	1924	73' 3"	67	12	s	s	R.P.O.-baggage
360	Pullman	1929	73' 4"	66	12	s	s	R.P.O.-baggage
361	St. Louis	1934	73' 11"	69.5	12	s	s	R.P.O.-baggage
800	Collinwood	1903	63'	35.8/43.5	8	w/s	w	baggage
802-804	Collinwood	1903	63'	35.8/43.5	8	w/s	w	baggage
810-811	Collinwood	1906	63'	37.8/45	8	w/s	w	baggage
812-813	Collinwood	1906	63'	37.8	8	w	w	baggage
814-815	Collinwood	1890	52' 10"	34.4	8	w	w	baggage
827		1890	60' 11"	30.8	8	w	w	R.P.O.-baggage
828-829	Collinwood	1906	70'	45	8	w	w	R.P.O.-baggage
830-832	Standard	1914	73' 5"	68	12	s	s	R.P.O.-baggage
920, 922	TStL&W	1898	52' 9"		8	w	w	baggage
921, 923	Jackson & Sharp	1887	52' 9"		8	w	w	baggage
929	Jackson & Sharp	1889	52' 9"		8	w	w	baggage
930	Jackson & Sharp	1887	51' 6"	28.5	8	w	w	baggage
990-991	Pullman		72' 8"	59	12	w/s	w/s	baggage

W&LE parlor cars *Wheeling, Toledo,* and *Cleveland* were AC&F built in 1900.—*Collection of Arthur D. Dubin.*

W&LE parlor-cafe car *Kent* ended her days as a portable station at Warrenton.—*Glenn Grabill Jr.,* TRAINS *collection.*

1900-model open-platform combines 095-097 were equipped with Timken roller bearings, storage batteries, and hot water heaters in 1927. Thereafter they were used as doodle-bug trailers on Toledo-Zanesville runs until their demise in 1932. — *Collection of John A. Rehor.*

05 — Rebuilt to parlor-obs. 018, Kent, circa 1907. To 37-pass. cafe-coach, 1931. To portable depot at Warrenton, 1945.

06 — Rebuilt to parlor-obs. 017, circa 1907. Sold about 1917.

013 — Originally numbered 048. To 2nd 011 circa 1908. To 42-passenger cafe-coach 1931; to bunk car, 1938; body to South Lorain 1945 for use as bunkhouse.

014-015 — Originally numbered 049, 047.

016 — To 60-passenger coach, 1931; to bunk car 918, 1933; to NKP X-56918, 1951; to Clyde Barber, 1962.

019-028 — Purchased from Pullman in 1913 in used condition. Builder and vintage unknown. 019 became bunk car 807 in 1924. 021 became bunk car 922 in 1934. Had been equipped with Timken roller bearings 1924.

032 — After 1918 was used to shuttle employees between Cherry Street and Homestead Yard at Toledo.

035-036, 038, 040-042, 063-067 — Became bunk cars in 1931.

071, 088 — Destroyed in Beach City wreck 1924.

072-087 — Became bunk cars in 1932, 1934, 1938.

090 — Equipped with Timken roller bearings in 1927 and subsequently used as a trailer with gas-electric motor cars until 1928.

095-097 — Equipped with Timken roller bearings, hot water heaters, and storage batteries June 1927 and used until 1932 as trailers for gas-electric cars. To bunk cars 919-921, 1933.

098-0101 — Converted to combination R.P.O.-smoker cars 0117, 0120, 0118, 0119 1914-1924.

0107-0108 — Purchased from Lackawanna in 1919. 0107 converted to baggage car 0146 in 1926; converted to bunk car 917 in 1932.

0116 — Converted to tool car 1938; to NKP X-56200.

0117 — Converted to tool car 1938; body to Pine Valley as car-shop office 1942.

0120, 0140 — Converted to tool cars 1938.

0144 — Purchased from Lackawanna in 1919.

0145 — Body installed at car repair track, Pine Valley, 1944.

Brill doodlebug M-102 was powered by six-cylinder, 4-cycle 250 h.p. gasoline engine and two Westinghouse WH-557 motors. Combination R.P.O. car is shown at Brewster shortly after its delivery in 1927. Before going to the Tonopah & Goldfield in 1935 M-102's seating capacity was reduced from 44 to 18. — *Collection of John A. Rehor.*

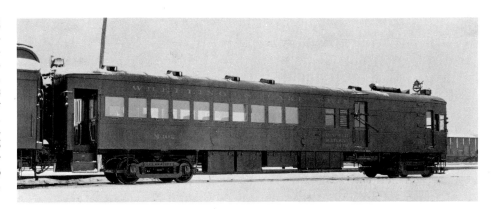

SELF-PROPELLED GAS-ELECTRIC MOTOR CARS

Number	Builder	Year	Over-all length	Seating capacity	Light weight	Wheels
M-101	J. G. Brill	1927	60'	46/54	45.9	8
M-102	J. G. Brill	1927	60'	44/18	47.9	8
M-103	J. G. Brill	1927	60'	44/18	47.8	8

M-101 — Combination passenger-baggage. Initial run, No. 5 out of Steubenville, January 4, 1927. Equipped with Timken roller bearings. Rebuilt at Brewster 1931 with baggage compartment converted to smoker and seating capacity increased to 54. Motors removed 1935 and used in Massillon-Brewster shop train until April 1, 1939. Body installed July 1942 as car repair track office at Huron.

M-102 — Combination passenger-baggage-R.P.O. car. Initial run, No. 4 out of Toledo, January 6, 1927. Rebuilt at Brewster Feb- ruary 1931 with seating capacity reduced to 18. Sold to Tonopah & Goldfield Railroad for $4500 and shipped to that road September 6, 1935.

M-103 — Combination passenger-baggage-R.P.O. car. Equipped with Timken roller bearings. Initial run, No. 3 out of Harmon, January 12, 1927. Rebuilt at Brewster 1931 with seating capacity reduced to 18. Sold to Tonopah & Goldfield Railroad for $5000 and shipped to that road on October 18, 1934.

Exceptionally large for their day, original NKP cabooses were 35 feet long and weighed 19.5 tons. No. 1017, shown holding down the rear of a Chicago Division manifest in 1964, was outshopped by the La Fayette (Ind.) Car Works in 1881 and was rebuilt by AC&F in 1907. — *John A. Rehor.*

NICKEL PLATE CABOOSES

Number	Builder	Year	Length over end sills	Light weight	Super- structure		
46-60, 79-82, 90 93, 99, 100, 117 118, 120, 121, 137			35' 6"		wood	C	(A)
61, 74, 88, 94, 96 104-116, 119, 123 124, 126, 130-136 139-147			31' 6"		wood	C	(A)
206-254	Frankfort	1914-1915	35' 8"		wood	C	(B)
255-292					wood	C	(B)
300	Conneaut	1951	41' 8"		steel	B	
400	Ironville	1952	37' 8"	23.8	steel	B	
401-425	Ironville	1955-1956	37' 8"	24.1	steel	B	
426-450	Conneaut	1960	37' 8"	24.1	steel	B	
451-500	Morrison- International	1962	37' 11"		steel	B	
700-760	Ironville	1948-1949	34' 3"	22.7	steel	C	(C)
761-784	Ironville	1953-1954	34' 3"	23.4	steel	C	
826-839	Ironville	1914-1916	34' 2"	19.4	wood	C	(C)
840-864	Ironville	1917	34' 2"	19.5	wood	C	(C)
865-894	Ironville	1920-1921	34' 2"	19.5	wood	C	(C)
895-905	Ironville	1923-1924	34' 2"	19.5	wood	C	(C)
906	Ironville	1928	35'	20.8	wood	C	(C)
911-918	Ironville	1937	35'	20.8	wood	C	(C)
1000-1080	La Fayette	1881-1882	35'	19.6	wood	C	
1082-1095	Peninsular	1888	35'	19.6	wood	C	
1096-1121	Stony Island	1900-1901	35'	19.6	wood	C	
1122-1155	AC&F	1907-1909	35'	19.6	wood	C	
1156-1185	Stony Island	1916	35'	19.6	wood	C	
1186-1191	Conneaut	1921-1922	35'	19.6	wood	C	
1192-1208	Conneaut	1923-1924	35' 9"	21.2	wood	C	
1343-1362	Conneaut	1943-1944	40' 5"		wood	C	
1363-1374	Conneaut	1942-1943	40' 5"		wood	C	
1375-1399	Conneaut	1942	40' 5"		wood	C	

(A) Ex-LE&W.
(B) Ex-TStL&W.
(C) Ex-W&LE.

206-254 — Rebuilt from box cars. All have been retired.
255-292 — Retired.

300 — Rebuilt from 13000-series 40-foot steel box car.
1343-1399 — Rebuilt from 10000-series box cars.

Offset-cupolated 132, rebuilt by LE&W from a single trucker, measured 31 feet 6 inches. — *Clyde E. Helms.*

Rider cars were assigned to locals and other trains with six-man crews in the days of steam. — *Clyde E. Helms.*

Glistening in a coat of fresh red paint, the former 0846 of the W&LE emerges from Ironville shop in 1952. This was one of 92 double-truck crummies built in the Wheeling's car shop between 1913 and 1937. A few still used in puller service at Toledo and Cleveland. — *Willis A. McCaleb.*

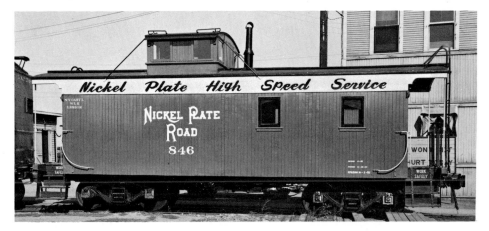

Forty-foot box cars with Bettendorf trucks were rebuilt to ease wartime caboose shortage. — *Paul W. Prescott.*

No. 1258 was one of 25 arch-bar arks purchased from parent C&O during World War II. — *Clyde E. Helms.*

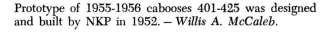

All-steel 761-784 were built to preconsolidation W&LE design at Ironville during 1953-1954.—*Willis A. McCaleb.*

Prototype of 1955-1956 cabooses 401-425 was designed and built by NKP in 1952. — *Willis A. McCaleb.*

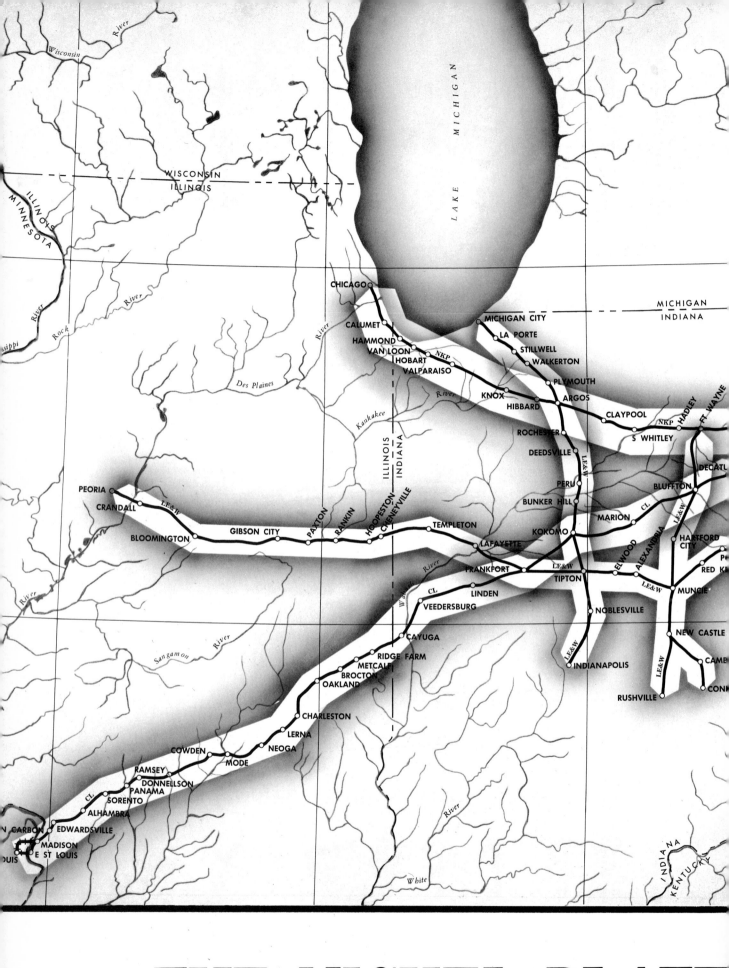

THE NICKEL PLATE

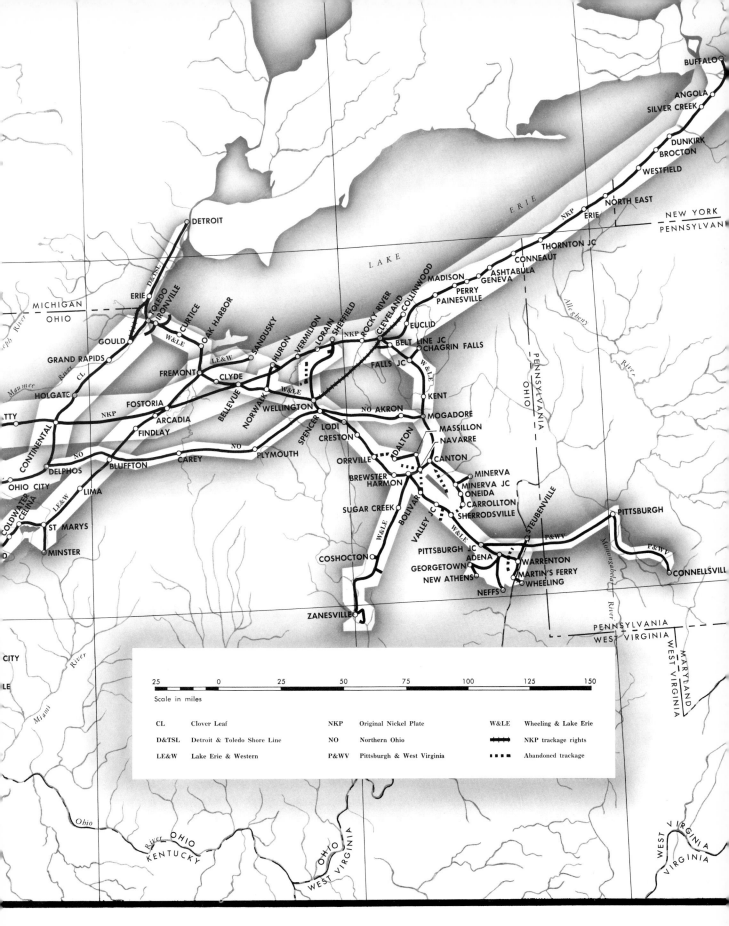

ROAD

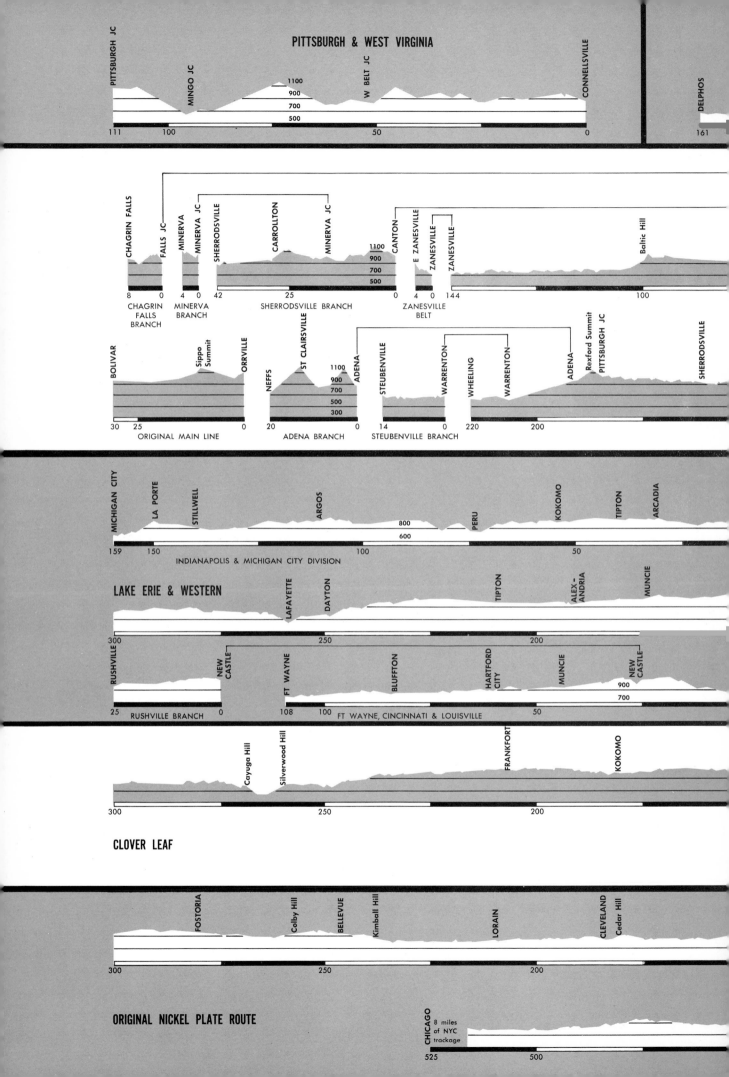

PITTSBURGH & WEST VIRGINIA

PITTSBURGH JC

MINGO JC

W BELT JC

CONNELLSVILLE

DELPHOS

1100
900
700
500

111   100   50   0   161

CHAGRIN FALLS

FALLS JC

MINERVA

MINERVA JC

SHERRODSVILLE

CARROLLTON

MINERVA JC

CANTON

E ZANESVILLE

ZANESVILLE

ZANESVILLE

Baltic Hill

1100
900
700
500

8   0   4   0   42   25   0   4   0   144   100

CHAGRIN FALLS BRANCH

MINERVA BRANCH

SHERRODSVILLE BRANCH

ZANESVILLE BELT

BOLIVAR

Sippo Summit

ORRVILLE

NEFFS

ST CLAIRSVILLE

ADENA

STEUBENVILLE

WARRENTON

WHEELING

WARRENTON

ADENA

Rexford Summit

PITTSBURGH JC

SHERRODSVILLE

1100
900
700
500
300

30   25   0   20   0   14   0   220   200

ORIGINAL MAIN LINE

ADENA BRANCH

STEUBENVILLE BRANCH

MICHIGAN CITY

LA PORTE

STILLWELL

ARGOS

PERU

KOKOMO

TIPTON

ARCADIA

800
600

159   150   100   50

INDIANAPOLIS & MICHIGAN CITY DIVISION

LAKE ERIE & WESTERN

LAFAYETTE

DAYTON

TIPTON

ALEX-ANDRIA

MUNCIE

300   250   200

RUSHVILLE

NEW CASTLE

FT WAYNE

BLUFFTON

HARTFORD CITY

MUNCIE

NEW CASTLE

900
700

25   RUSHVILLE BRANCH   0   108   100   FT WAYNE, CINCINNATI & LOUISVILLE   50

Cayuga Hill

Silverwood Hill

FRANKFORT

KOKOMO

300   250   200

CLOVER LEAF

FOSTORIA

Colby Hill

BELLEVUE

Kimball Hill

LORAIN

CLEVELAND

Cedar Hill

300   250   200

ORIGINAL NICKEL PLATE ROUTE

CHICAGO

8 miles of NYC trackage

525   500

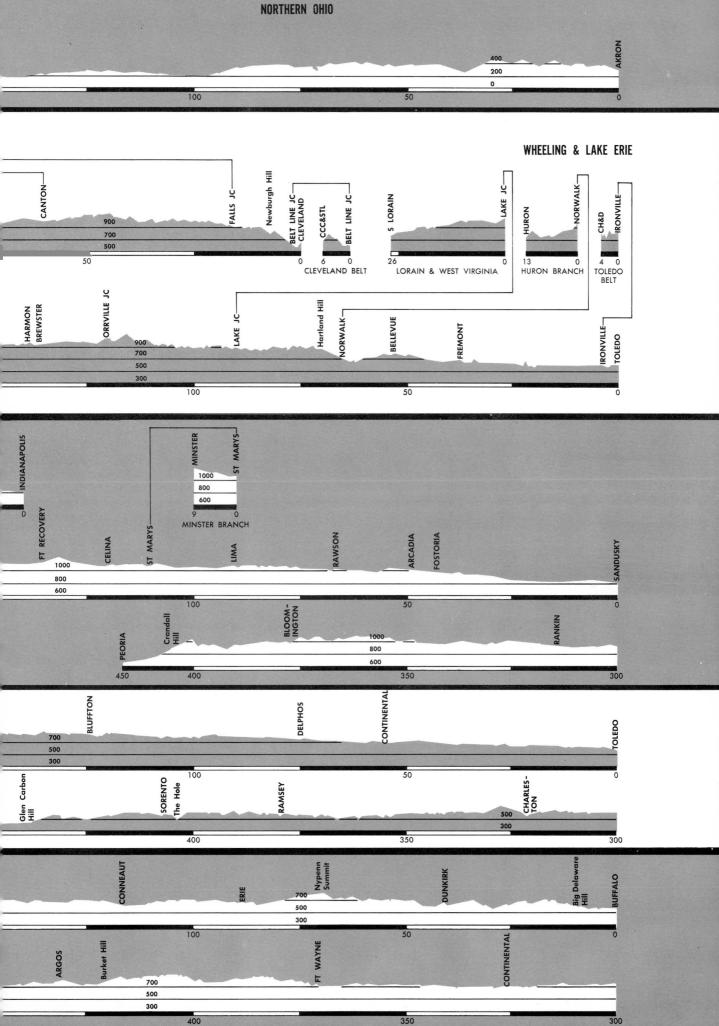

Acknowledgments

IT is my contention that no one individual can hope to produce a comprehensive review of a major railway system's affairs without the aid of a host of kindred spirits. Certainly that was the case with this volume on the Nickel Plate, whose managers were usually too preoccupied with matters of the moment to have much interest in the past. Most of the road's early documents were destroyed in a 1931 housecleaning at West 25th Street Station in Cleveland. About the same time, most LE&W and Clover Leaf records vanished, and what survived was stored in old box cars for years. The W&LE, while more conscious of its history, made no organized effort to chronicle its interesting career. This book, then, had to be a collection of material gleaned from many sources through the indulgence of many persons.

But for the encouragement of George Hilton and David Morgan I would not have dared undertake this long-cherished ambition. My close friend Willis McCaleb not only exhorted me to push on but gave unstintingly of his keen intellect and magnificent collection. Willis also discovered the William L. Bennett negatives and provided the fine camerawork of Corman Moore and Rev. James Dean. I am particularly beholden to John H. Keller for access to his profound collection and to that of the Allen County Historical Society. Included were a virtually complete set of Nickel Plate public timetables, the Lima Locomotive Works negatives, a library rich in Ohioana, and the Mother Lode of LE&W and Clover Leaf artifacts. Richard J. Cook's important contributions included a collection of W&LE glass plate originals and some fine examples of his own photography. Dick was putting his bicycle aboard baggage cars to record events in far-off Frankfort and Charleston when I was still trying to stop 2-8-2's on Greenhouse Curve with a Univex. But for the fact that Clyde Helms spent his depression lunch hours photographing trains at St. Marys, this book would be devoid of illustration of many early locomotive types.

I relied heavily on trade journals such as *Railway & Locomotive Engineering, Railway Mechanical Engineer, Railroad Gazette, Commercial and Financial Chronicle, Railway Age,* and *American Railway Journal*; early issues of the *Official Guide*; annual reports; newspapers; and local histories. Such material has been preserved by a relatively few institutions, and I am indebted to the Chicago Historical Society, University of Michigan Transportation Library, and Cleveland Public Library for the privilege of browsing through their stacks. Miss Agnes Hanson of Cleveland Public's Business Information Division produced the Ohio Railroad Commission's reports from 1867 to 1905, a complete set of Poor's *Manual of the Railroads of the United States,* and answers to a multitude of questions presented on short notice. The Ohio State Museum permitted the examination of George Hayes Coleman's files of W&LE data. Early LE&W history was revealed by material found in the Rutherford B. Hayes Library at Spiegel Grove in Fremont. Included were copies of the *Firelands Pioneer,* Fremont's *Democratic Messenger* and *Journal,* and Isadore Burgoon's bound volume of annual reports of the Fremont & Indiana and successors for the years 1855 to 1877. Discovered in a Mansfield (O.) bookshop in 1963, the latter was a priceless find and the only such book ever in existence.

Particularly vexing was the dearth of material on the Clover Leaf and its narrow-gauge antecedents. Paul Stringham helped mightily by going through early Illinois newspapers and annual reports of the Illinois Railroad and Warehouse Commission. The *Delphos Herald* proved a veritable gold mine, and I am obligated to Publisher Murray Cohen for the opportunity to examine early issues of this newspaper. Discovery of the original profile books enabled me to trace the building of the Little Giant across Illinois; and the Federal Records Center at Chicago yielded a bonanza of depositions and other documents relative to this hapless Clover Leaf ancestor and its locomotives. Retired Trainmaster Clyde Eyrse offered his photo collection and storehouse of memories of the Clover Leaf. G. M. Best, Thomas Norrell, and Roy Carlson also produced needed material. Cornelius Hauck did the research on the Cincinnati Railway Tunnel.

The Wheeling & Lake Erie was an incredibly well-photographed railroad, but nothing of substance was ever written about this fascinating property. I have Ernest Rouhier and Bill Gessaker to thank for preserving the voluminous "diary" of W&LE motive power; the late Dale Smith for saving a huge collection of company negatives; Keith Buchanan for his research on the Carroll County roads and the locomotive *McNeill*; John Wert Helfrich for placing at my disposal a lifetime of work on the Carroll County and successors; the late Uriah G. Reinhold for his photos, memories, and correspondence with CC&S veterans; Sylvan R. Wood for the recollections of F. M. Westcott and some rare photos; D. W. McLaughlin for his Wabash-Pittsburgh Terminal data; and Robert V. Hubbard, Jack Lozier, Harry L. Brown, and J. J. Young Jr. for the use of their W&LE material.

Charles E. Fisher, S. R. Wood, and other members of the Railway & Locomotive Historical Society furnished data from builders' records essential to the locomotive rosters. I am also indebted to Nickel Plate's C. B. Bennett for arranging my inspection of the road's mechanical records and to D. J. Coon and scores of other Nickel Platers for their enthusiastic accommodation. In tracing the Super-Power story I had the help of Robert E. Le Massena. Electro-Motive data and photos were furnished by Al Kamm Jr. Nickel Plate's early affairs and pre-1910 locomotive retirements were disclosed by those letters of General Superintendent A. J. Johnston which survived the 1931 disaster. Other early records saved by Master Mechanic Roy Kieser provided an early Clover Leaf locomotive renumbering and particulars on LE&W motive power during the LS&MS era.

According to legend, photographers filmed the building and early operation of the Nickel Plate, but their negatives supposedly were destroyed at West 25th Street. Thanks to John A. Tyler, Russell Lyon, and the late Harold Ludlow, copies of some of these scenes appear in the early chapters. Paul F. Laning helped on many aspects of early Nickel Plate history and afforded me the fruits of his extensive NYC research. Herbert H. Harwood Jr. unraveled some of the intricacies of the Van Sweringen corporate empire. Finally, it would be remiss of me to overlook the assistance received from Arthur D. Dubin, Preston Calvert of Pullman-Standard, Gustave Erhardt, Albert Schimpke, Leonard W. Siegel, Howard Watson, the Terminal Tower Company, and Paul Prescott. All played a vital role in the makeup of this book, and I can never adequately express my gratitude to them.

Index

An asterisk (*) indicates a photo reference

479